BRITAIN IN THE ROMAN EMPIRE

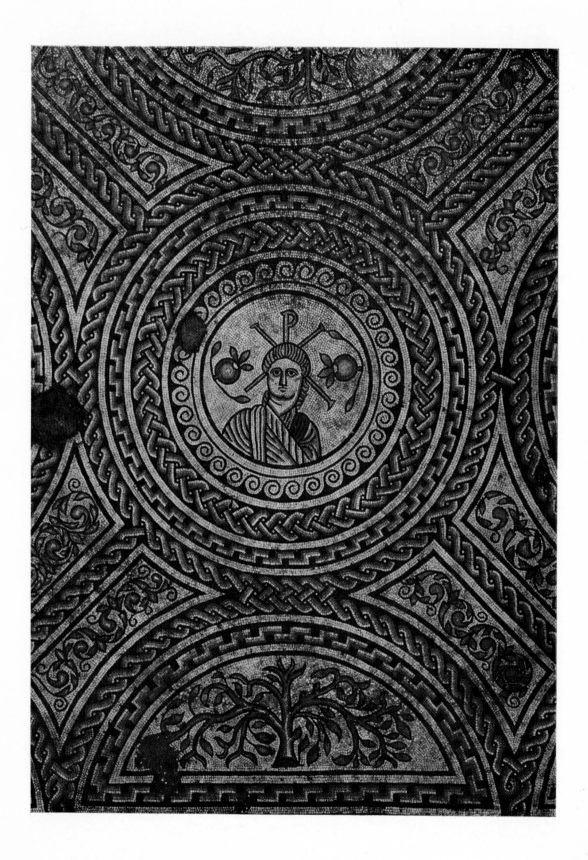

BRITAIN IN THE ROMAN EMPIRE

BY JOAN LIVERSIDGE

FREDERICK A. PRAEGER, *Publishers*
New York · Washington

BOOKS THAT MATTER

*Published in the United States of America in 1968
by Frederick A. Praeger, Inc., Publishers
111 Fourth Avenue, New York, N.Y. 10003*

© 1968 in London, England by Joan Liversidge

*All rights reserved
Library of Congress Catalog Card Number: 68-15432*

Printed in Great Britain

To my Mother

Contents

vi

Figures in the text

List of figures

xvi

xviii

xxi

Maps

xxii

Plates

List of plates

xxiv

c Flavia Augustina and her family. Height 68 inches. *Photograph: Warburg Institute* (*O. Fein*)

All Yorkshire Museum, York

26 Stone tomb reliefs:

a Mother and child, Murrell Hill, Cumberland. Height 51 inches. Carlisle Museum, Tullie House. *Photograph: Warburg Institute* (*O. Fein*)

b Julia Brica and her daughter, York. Height 70½ inches. Yorkshire Museum. *Photograph: Warburg Institute* (*O. Fein*)

c Julia Velva and her family, York. Height 55 inches. Yorkshire Museum, York. *Photograph: Royal Commission on Historical Monuments.* (*England*) *Crown Copyright*

27 *a* Stone tomb relief, Chester. Height 20 inches. Grosvenor Museum. *Photograph: Grosvenor Museum, Chester. Copyright Chester Corporation*

b Stone tomb relief, York. Height 46 inches. Yorkshire Museum, York. *Photograph: Royal Commission on Historical Monuments* (*England*), *Crown Copyright*

c Stone tomb relief of Philus, Cirencester. Height 86½ inches. Gloucester City Museum. *Photograph: Gloucester City Museum*

28 *a* Stone female head. York. Height 11 inches. Yorkshire Museum. *Photograph: H. Hiscoe*

b Stone female head, Bath. Height 22¼ inches. Roman Baths Museum. *Photograph: R. Croydon-Fowler*

c Part of a stone male head, York. Height 5 inches. Yorkshire Museum. *Photograph: Royal Commission on Historical Monuments* (*England*), *Crown Copyright*

29 Altar of Mithras, Carrawburgh, Northumberland. Third century. Height 47 inches. Museum of Antiquities, King's College, Newcastle-upon-Tyne. *Photograph: Warburg Institute* (*O. Fein*)

30 Jewellery:

a Jet pendant, York. Height 1¼ inches. Yorkshire Museum, York

b Jet pendant, York. Height 2¼ inches. Yorkshire Museum, York

c ? Necklet of rectangular gold plates, each 1 inch long, set with carnelians or blue pastes, filigree borders, Nantmel, Rhayader, Radnorshire. British Museum

d Gold two-piece bracelet with applied gold-wire ornament, Nantmel, Rhayader, Radnorshire. Length 7 inches. British Museum

e Gold pendant set with blue-green stones and pearls. Southfleet, Kent. Length *c.* 9 inches. British Museum

f Jet pin, York. Height 3¼ inches. Yorkshire Museum, York

Photographs: a, b, f Royal Commission on Historical Monuments (*England*). *Crown Copyright. c–e British Museum. By courtesy of the Trustees*

31 Scenes of cooking and bread-making from the Igel Column. *Photograph: Rheinisches Landesmuseum, Trier*

32 Wicker chair imitated in stone. From the tomb at Weiden. *Photograph: Römisch-Germanisches Museum, Cologne*

33 Table-leg of Kimmeridge shale, Colliton Park, Dorchester, Dorset. Probably second century. Height 19 inches. *Photograph: Warburg Institute* (*O. Fein*)

34 Glass. Back row from Shefford, Bedfordshire, Hauxton and Litlington, Cambridgeshire. Front row, Hauxton and Gravel Hill Farm, Cambridge. Cambridge University Museum of Archaeology and Ethnology. *Photograph: L. P. Morley*

35 Pewter. Back row from Sutton near Ely, Quaveney and Whittlesea Mere. Front row from Abington Pigotts and between Reach and Upware. All Cambridgeshire. Cambridge University Museum of Archaeology and Ethnology. *Photograph: L. P. Morley*

36 Silver:
a Skillet-handle, Capheaton, Northumberland. Late second or early third century. Height of figure work portion 7¾ inches. British Museum. *Photograph: Warburg Institute (O. Fein)*
b Platters from the Mildenhall Treasure, Suffolk. Fourth century. Diameter 7⅜ and 7¼ inches. British Museum. *Photograph: British Museum. By courtesy of the Trustees.*

37 Floor-mosaics:
a Orpheus and the Beasts. Barton Farm villa near Cirencester, Gloucestershire. Probably fourth century. The square containing the scene measures 14 feet 8 inches. Corinium Museum, Cirencester. *Photograph: Warburg Institute (O. Fein)*
b Dido and Aeneas, one of the Virgilian scenes from the Low Ham villa, Somerset. Taunton Castle Museum, Somerset. *Photograph: Warburg Institute (O. Fein)*

38 Floor-mosaics:
a Detail, 'Spring', from the Bellerophon and Chimaera mosaic, Lullingstone villa, Kent. Fourth century. *In situ. Photograph: Ministry of Public Buildings and Works. Crown Copyright*
b Male bust. Lufton villa, Somerset. *Photograph: H. Tilzey. Courtesy of L. Hayward*
c Female bust. Brantingham villa, Yorkshire. Museum of Archaeology, Kingston-upon-Hull, Yorkshire. *Photograph: I. M. Stead. Courtesy of I. M. Stead and the Ministry of Public Buildings and Works. Crown Copyright*

39 Floor-mosaic. Detail, 'Winter', Chedworth villa, Gloucestershire. Probably fourth century. Height of triangle 29 inches. *In situ. Photograph: Warburg Institute (O. Fein)*

40 Paved Roman road on Blackstone Edge between Rochdale and Halifax, Yorkshire. *Photograph: I. D. Margary*

41 Entry to a Roman iron-mine, Lydney Park, Gloucestershire. Probably mid or late third century. *Courtesy of Sir R. E. Mortimer Wheeler and the Society of Antiquaries*

42 Iron work:
a Sickle or reed-cutter at the top from Worlington, Suffolk, coulter on the right from Abington Pigotts, Cambridgeshire. Otherwise saw-blade, smith's pincers, socketted chisel, mower's anvil, and hammers from a hoard of ironwork found at Great Chesterford, Essex
b Chain, possibly for a cauldron, also from the Great Chesterford hoard. Cambridge University Museum of Archaeology and Ethnology. *Photographs: L. P. Morley*

43 Stone reliefs:
a Large dog. Height 23 inches. Grosvenor Museum, Chester. *Photograph: Grosvenor Museum. Copyright, Chester Corporation*
b Boy-charioteer. Height 7½ inches. 1 Lee Road, Lincoln (Mrs K. Harding). *Photograph: Warburg Institute (O. Fein)*
c A hound chasing a hare, found near Bath, Somerset. Height 21 inches. Roman Baths Museum, Bath. *Photograph: M. Owen*

d Boy holding a pet hare. Height 22 inches. Cathedral Library, Lincoln. *Photograph: City and County Museum: Lincoln*

44 Toys:
a Pottery figurines from a child's grave, Colchester. Second half of first century. Height up to 6¾ inches. Colchester and Essex Museum. *Photograph: Warburg Institute (O. Fein)*
b Bronze dog, Carrawburgh, Northumberland. Second century. Length 1½ inches. Chesters Museum, Northumberland. *Photograph: Warburg Institute (O. Fein)*
c Bronze dog, Kirkby Thore. Westmorland. Second century. Length 2¼ inches. Carlisle Museum, Tullie House. *Photograph: Warburg Institute (O. Fein)*
d Bronze mouse from a burial, York. Length 1¾ inches. Yorkshire Museum. *Photograph: Royal Commission on Historical Monuments (England). Crown Copyright*

45 Stone tomb relief from Arlon, Belgium, depicting a family meal. Above, the master and mistress sit at table. Below, the children gather round a cauldron, one playing double pipes and another restraining a pet dog. Musée de Metz, France. *Photograph: Musée de Metz*

46 Roman lighthouse, Dover Castle. *Photograph: Mustograph Agency*

47 Roman canal, the Car Dyke, at Cottenham, Cambridgeshire, when filled with water during the 1947 floods. *Courtesy of Professor J. G. D. Clark and the Society of Antiquaries*

48 The Roman quay wall, Roodee, Chester. *Photograph: Grosvenor Museum, Chester. Copyright: Chester Corporation*

49 Bronze statuette of Venus, Verulamium. Second century. Height 8 inches. Verulamium Museum, Hertfordshire. *Photograph: Verulamium Museum*

50 Bronze statuette of Mercury from the temple site, Gosbecks Farm near Colchester. Second century. Height 21 inches. Colchester and Essex Museum. *Photograph: Colchester and Essex Museum*

51 Bronze model of ploughman and oxen, Piercebridge, County Durham. Length 2¼ inches. British Museum. *Photograph: British Museum. Courtesy of the Trustees*

52 Bronze fragments which probably belong to a priest's or magistrate's baton, Willingham, Cambridgeshire. The upper part, *c* 4 inches in height, shows the god Taranis, with his wheel and a dolphin on the left side, and a three-horned bull's head in profile on the right. Cambridge University Museum of Archaeology and Ethnology. *Photograph: L. P. Morley*

53 Bronze statuettes:
a Mercury from the temple site, Bruton, Somerset, Height 2¼ inches. Property of Mrs C. M. Bennett. *Photograph: Warburg Institute (O. Fein)*
b Girl with a *tibia*, Silchester, Hampshire. Height 4¼ inches. Reading Museum (on loan from His Grace the Duke of Wellington). *Photograph: Warburg Institute (O. Fein)*
c Priest, from Barham, Kent. Height 3¼ inches. Royal Museum, Canterbury. *Photograph: Warburg Institute (O. Fein)*
d Lar from Lakenheath, Suffolk. Height 4 inches. British Museum. *Photograph: British Museum. Courtesy of the Trustees*
e River God from Great Chesterford, Essex. Height 5 inches. Cambridge University of Archaeology and Ethnology. *Photograph: L. P. Morley*

54 Bronze bust, probably representing a deity, from Worlington, Suffolk. Height 4⅛ inches.

Acknowledgements

The author wishes to express her gratitude to all those who directly or indirectly assisted her in writing this book. It was one of several projects begun during her tenure of a research fellowship from Newnham College and grateful acknowledgement is due to the College for its generosity, and also to colleagues and staff at the Cambridge University Museum of Archaeology and Ethnology for their help and encouragement. Imperfections are only too apt to appear in so large a work and while Professor Jocelyn Toynbee, the late Professor Sir Ian Richmond, Mrs N. K. Chadwick, Eric Higgs, Ronald Jessup, Tom Lethbridge and Miss Joyce Reynolds have all most kindly read parts of the manuscript or made valuable suggestions, they must in no way be held responsible for the final result.

Details of the provenance and location of objects, and the sources of all photographs and reproductions will be found in the lists of illustrations. Warmest thanks are tendered to all the individuals, Government Departments, societies, museums and firms who have so generously given permission for their material to be used in this way. Thanks are also especially due to Mr H. J. M. Green, Mr R. Jessup, Mr P. Marsden and Dr David Smith for the drawings of the Godmanchester baths (fig. 14), the Holborough stool (fig. 63), the Blackfriars boat (fig. 155) and the plan of the Shrine of the Nymphs (fig. 170); to Mr John Christiansen for his invaluable collaboration over the planning and drawing of over sixty figures; to Mr A. L. F. Rivet for the opportunity to read a chapter from a forthcoming work before publication; to Mrs Sylvia Christiansen who made the Index; to the Society for the Promotion of Roman Studies for the loan of the block for the Frontispiece and to Mrs N. K. Chadwick and the Cambridge University Press for permission to use the quotation which concludes Chapter V. The author is also indebted to the Loeb Classical Library (Harvard University Press and William Heinemann Ltd.) as the source of the translated quotations from Classical authors, and to Mr R. Wright for translations of the inscriptions cited from R. G. Collingwood and R. P. Wright, *The Roman Inscriptions of Britain I* (Clarendon Press, Oxford, 1965).

JOAN LIVERSIDGE

20.12.66

CHRONOLOGICAL TABLE

B.C.
55–54   Julius Caesar's expeditions to Britain

A.D.
Principal Emperors

Gaius (Caligula)
37–41   Cunobelinus ruling over much of south-eastern Britain

Claudius
41–54   43   Roman invasion with army of four legions led by Aulus Plautius

49–50   Foundation of Colonia Victricensis at Colchester (Camulodunum)

Nero
54–68   60–61   Suetonius Paulinus, governor, attacks Anglesey. Iceni rebel under Boudicca and are suppressed after devastating Colchester, London, and Verulamium (St Albans)

Vespasian ⎫   71–74   Petilius Cerealis, governor, conquers the Brigantes. Legionary fortress at York (Eboracum)
69–79   ⎪
           ⎪   74–78   Sextus Julius Frontinus, governor, subdues and garrisons Wales. Legionary fortresses at Caerleon (Isca) and Chester (Deva)
           ⎪ THE FLAVIANS
Titus   ⎪
79–81   ⎪   78–85   Gnaeus Julius Agricola, governor. Campaigns in northern Britain end with defeat of the Caledonians at Mons Graupius. Roman fleet circumnavigates Britain. Legionary fortress at Inchtuthil. Agricola recalled
Domitian   ⎪
81–96   ⎭   *c.* 90–96   Foundation of Colonia at Lincoln (Lindum). Fortress at Inchtuthil probably abandoned at this time

Nerva
96–98   *c.* 96–98   Foundation of Colonia at Gloucester (Glevum)
Trajan
98–117   Legionary fortresses and many forts rebuilt in stone during this reign

Hadrian
117–138   122   Hadrian visits Britain
           122–133   Construction of northern frontier from Tyne to Solway (Hadrian's Wall)
           c. 125–130   Serious fire in London about this time

XXX

Antoninus 138–161	Pius 139–143	Lollius Urbicus, governor, campaigns in northern Britain. Construction of Antonine Wall from the Firth of Forth to the Firth of Clyde
	c. 155	Serious fire at Verulamium
	155–158	Rebellions in north Britain. Temporary evacuation of Antonine Wall
Marcus Aurelius 161–180	161–165	Rebuilding by governor, Calpurnius Agricola
Commodus 180–192	*c.* 187–196	Antonine Wall abandoned between these dates
Septimius Severus 193–211	196–197	Clodius Albinus, governor, takes troops from Britain to Gaul in an attempt to seize the throne. He is defeated and killed by Severus. Meanwhile Hadrian's Wall is overrun and many forts destroyed by northern tribes, especially the Maetae from the Antonine Wall area
	197–208	Rebuilding of forts and Hadrian's Wall
	208–211	Severus arrives in Britain with his sons Caracalla and Geta. The northern tribes are heavily defeated after several campaigns
	211	Septimius Severus dies at York
Caracalla 211–217	212	Roman citizenship extended to all free provincials. Area between Hadrian's and Antonine Walls settled as a Roman protectorate. Britain probably divided into two provinces about this time
Gallienus 253–268	259–274	Britain becomes part of the Gallic Empire ruled by usurpers including Postumus and his successors such as Victorinus and Tetricus
Aurelian 270–275	275–287	Saxons raiding in the Channel
Diocletian 284–305	287–293	Carausius, commander of the British fleet, seizes control of Britain and Gaul
Maximian, co-emperor, 286–305 307–308		From 292–324 the Empire is ruled by two emperors

(The Antonines — bracketing Antoninus Pius through Commodus)

		(Augusti) assisted by two Caesars. Britain and Gaul are governed by Constantius and, later, by his son Constantine, first as Caesars and then as Augusti
	293–4	Constantius wins most of Gaul back from Carausius. Carausius murdered and his power seized by Allectus
	296	Constantius defeats Allectus and recovers Britain. Barbarian attacks in the north necessitate rebuilding on Hadrian's Wall and at York and Chester. Britain divided into four provinces with military and civil administration separated
Constantius 305–306	306	Constantius and Constantine campaign in Scotland. Constantius dies at York
Galerius, co-emperor, 305–311		
Constantine I Caesar, 306		
emperor, 307–337	313	Edict of Milan grants toleration to the Christian Church
	314	Council of Arles attended by three British bishops
	From 324	Constantine rules as sole emperor. Succeeded by his three sons Constans, Constantius and Constantine
Constans 337–350	343	Constans in Britain
Constantine II 337–340		
Constantius II 337–361	359	British bishops at Council of Rimini
Julian 360–363	360	Lupicinus sent to repel raids of Picts and Scots

Division of Empire into East and West

Valentinian I, emperor of the West, 364–375	364	Serious raids by Picts, Scots, Attacotti and Saxon pirates
Gratian 367–383	367	Disastrous invasion by Picts, Scots and Attacotti. Hadrian's Wall overthrown by treachery. Saxon raids. Franks attack in Gaul
	369	Valentinian sends Count Theodosius to restore order.

Hadrian's Wall defences roughly rebuilt and many of the coastal signal stations constructed

Theodosius
379–395   383   Magnus Maximus, commander in Britain, seizes power in Britain, Gaul and Spain. Hadrian's Wall overrun and this time not re-occupied

388   Magnus Maximus defeated by Theodosius at Aquileia

Honorius
395–423   395   Stilicho carries out some reorganisation in Britain. With Rome in danger from Alaric and the Goths, troops gradually withdrawn and usurpers appear in Britain

406   Usurper Constantine III attempts to hold Gaul and Spain with the aid of troops from Britain. Killed in 411

410   Honorius advises civitates of Britain to look to their own defences

Valentinian III
425–455   429   Traditional date of visit of St Germanus

Abbreviations

The abbreviations used in the footnotes will be found with the corresponding full titles incorporated in the bibliography at the end of the book.

I
Introduction

The idea of adding yet another volume to the extensive literature on Roman Britain was inspired by many discussions of Romano-British problems with students and friends interested in the subject. From these it became apparent that while the tendency to view Roman Britain as a study in itself, isolated from the rest of the Empire, is now less prevalent, there are many aspects of life in Britain as a Roman province which have rarely been considered, and some, indeed, which have been practically ignored. The aim of the present work, therefore, is to present as complete a picture as possible of life as it must have appeared to the Romano-Britons, the British people who encountered, sometimes fought, and eventually mostly accepted, the rule and the ways of Rome.

As direct references to this country are rare in the works of contemporary authors, none of whom were British, most of the facts for such a study must be drawn from archaeology, and nowadays, with so much excavation in progress, new material is often abundantly forthcoming. Meanwhile, nothing brings the past to life more vividly than the reliefs and inscriptions from tombstones, altars or *graffiti*, and the increasing number of specialised reports on such subjects as human skeletons, animal bones, cereals or textiles, all provide fresh and valuable information. To fill the gaps where the British evidence is scanty or even non-existent, comparative material from Italy and the other western provinces has been included to provide a background depicting what was customary elsewhere in the Empire. It is always difficult to decide to what extent such material is admissible, and here it is used particularly in the later chapters when discussing the more unfamiliar topics. Much new knowledge must have come to Britain with the army and the consequent influx of traders and craftsmen. More may well have been brought back by Britons visiting other provinces on official or private business, especially about such subjects as Roman law, education or medicine which leave few traces behind them. However, the discussion of such subjects in the following pages is only intended to be a tentative introduction. My chief object is to arouse interest and curiosity, in the hope of spurring on others, better qualified, to further research into these matters which formed part of the world of Britons in the Roman Empire.

As this study is chiefly concerned with civilian life, no attempt is made to give a chronological account of the Roman invasion of Britain and the military history of the next four hundred years. However, individual soldiers will appear from time to time, and military equipment and customs may be discussed when they seem to shed light on civilian activities. A number of modern authors have already described the Roman occupation,[1] but to provide a convenient framework for events mentioned in the following pages, a chronological summary will be found on p. xxx. Maps of the British tribes and of towns and villas, showing many of the places mentioned in the text, are also included, but for the best complete picture the Ordnance Survey Maps of Roman Britain (1956 ed.) and of Hadrian's Wall (1964 ed.) should be consulted.

The Britain which attracted Julius Caesar's interest in the first century B.C. had been populated by a series of European migrations beginning in the distant days of the early Stone Age when the island still formed part of the European mainland. After the melting of the glaciers and the sinking of the land cut Britain adrift, the people learnt to practise agriculture and domesticate animals, centuries after these skills had been discovered in the Near East. The strange and impressive religious beliefs which inspired the building of the great megalithic stone burial chambers and the construction of Avebury and Stonehenge may have come with some of the invaders, while others may have brought the knowledge of metallurgy which was to revolutionise prehistoric life. The raw materials for bronze and iron, used first for weapons and then for tools and agricultural implements far superior to the old flint scrapers and stone axes, could be mined in this country. The increased wealth brought by their use led to trade in objects of beauty and luxury, many of them originating in Europe and the East. Improvements in weapons and methods of war, however, were

[1] E.g. Richmond (1963); S. S. Frere, *Britannia* (1967).

2

apt to bring in fresh invaders who either killed the inhabitants or else drove them out of the best areas for cultivation into the less attractive highland regions. There they either mingled with the more primitive tribes who had already been dislodged or drove them into even less salubrious surroundings.

It has to be remembered that at this early period forest and woodland were impenetrable enemies to the inhabitants of Britain. The most desirable areas for settlement therefore comprised the open country of the south and east where the soil was fertile and well-drained, although wooded districts such as the Weald had still to be avoided. The rivers and the grass trackways along higher ground such as the Downs provided communications. The less fortunate people were forced to till the stonier soil of the hilly country of the north and west, where the mountain barriers and comparative lack of navigable rivers, while making contacts difficult, also offered a refuge for the weaker, less well-armed tribes. This natural division of the country into prosperous lowland and poorer highland zones remained an important factor during the Roman period.

At the time of Caesar's visits to Britain in 55 and 54 B.C., Kent, where he landed, was occupied by the Cantii. They seem to have flourished as Caesar refers to their numerous farms and large numbers of cattle, and his description is supported by the fact that when storms damaged his fleet on his first expedition, his two legions found sufficient corn supplies in the fields round their camp to keep them from starvation.[1] The Cantii were only one of a group of tribes who came to Britain in the first century B.C. They are collectively referred to as the Belgae and they continued to immigrate from Gaul after Caesar's departure. Excavations have shown that their expansion was sometimes bitterly opposed by the earlier inhabitants, but to no avail. Better armed and organised, the Belgic conquests were only checked by the arrival of the legions of Claudius in A.D. 43. When they in their turn waged a bitter but unsuccessful war against a better equipped and trained foe, they found that some of the tribes they had sought to subjugate, as well as Belgic splinter groups, had become the allies of the Romans.

During the period of Belgic expansion between the campaigns of Caesar and Claudius, there is evidence for considerable trade between Britain and Gaul. Strabo relates in an oft-quoted passage that British exports comprised wheat, cattle, gold, silver, iron, hides, slaves and hunting dogs, and that they imported jewellery and glass. Archaeological excavation has shown that they also imported large quantities of wine, many fine bronze vessels and sometimes pieces of bronze furniture. The Belgic king Cunobelinus, who died a few years before the Claudian invasion, had his capital at Camulodunum on a site on the

[1] *De Bello Gallico* IV. 22; V. 12.

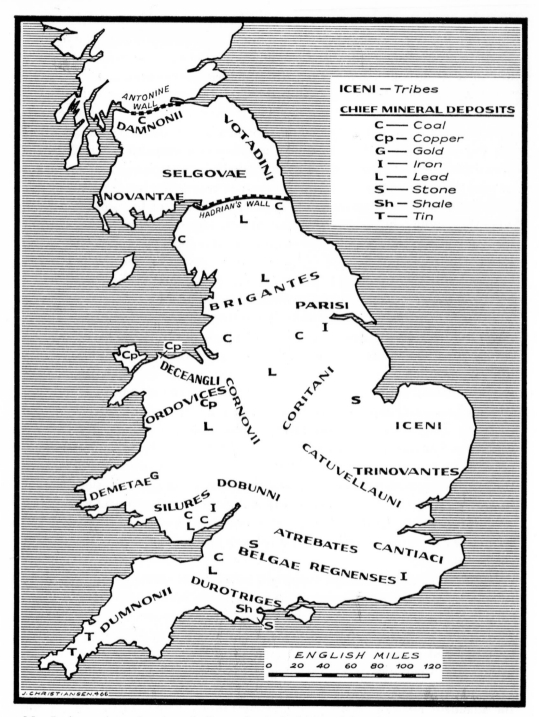

Map I. Approximate location of tribes and principal mineral deposits

outskirts of modern Colchester. It seems to have consisted of groups of huts, flimsily built of timber and wattle and daub. They probably largely resembled the dwellings of earlier date found at Little Woodbury near Salisbury, where the farmer and his family and possibly some of the livestock lived under the same thatched roof, and a wooden palisade enclosed both hut and farmyard. Racks were used for corn-drying and the corn was stored in pits which were later used for rubbish. In Camulodunum the tribesmen may have had less space and fewer livestock, but they were obviously wealthy enough to import much fine pottery from Gaul and also the fine red Arretine ware from Italy, in addition to quantities of the glass mentioned by Strabo.[1] No doubt traders sailed up the river Colne with such cargoes and carried back into slavery the captives obtained in raids on other tribes. Slave-chains like the one found at Lords' Bridge, Cambridgeshire, which could be clamped round the necks of six unfortunate victims, are a grim reminder of this practice.

The miles of banks and ditches which defend the sites at Camulodunum and other Belgic settlements show that someone, presumably the king or chieftain, must have exercised considerable authority as numerous tribesmen or their captives would be needed to build them, and the work must have required a substantial organisation. Excavations at Camulodunum and Verulamium (St Albans, Hertfordshire) have produced evidence for mints, a reminder that the Belgae were the first to introduce currency into Britain. In the beginning they first imported and then copied coinage of various Gallo-Belgic types. These mostly imitated the gold staters of Philip of Macedon, which flooded the Roman market and spread into western Europe during the second century B.C. These coins had a head of Apollo on one side and a two-horse chariot on the other, features which suffered various strange changes as the native currencies developed. The names of the Belgic kings and marks which denoted the mints at Verulamium and Camulodunum are also sometimes found. By the time of the Roman conquest, less sophisticated coin-types were being struck by some non-Belgic tribes.[2]

So the Britain the Romans found in A.D. 43 was a country split up among warring tribes, some of whom could find men and money with which to build extensive defences and engage in foreign trade, even though they lived in flimsy huts in rather sordid conditions. In some areas conquered groups nursed vengeance in their hearts and bided their time, ready to turn on their oppressors, while others lived in fear of imminent attack. Further north among the hills and

[1] D. B. Harden, in Hawkes and Hull (1947), Appendix III p. 287 *et seq.*
[2] R. P. Mack, *The Coinage of Ancient Britain* (1953); D. F. Allen, 'The Belgic Dynasties of Britain and their Coins', *Arch.* XC (1944) 1–46.

moors of the highland zone, more tribes led a still harder life, snatching a scanty living from the poorer soil or leading a pastoral existence with their flocks and herds. No foreign imports found their way to them, even iron tools were a luxury, and some still used the stone axes or flint blades of their forefathers.

2
Roman administration in Britain and the development of town life

To the native inhabitants of Britain the Roman conquest brought great changes. Instead of the political ebb and flow of war and peace, conflict or alliance between the various tribes, the country now formed part of a vast empire ruled from one centre, and to the Britons the arrival of all the complexities of the Imperial administration must have seemed bewildering. The organisation needed to govern a Roman province was to grow increasingly complicated as time went on, so, in order to obtain a background for the archaeological discoveries of our own country, it may be helpful if we first consider how this organisation worked and the classes of society which developed under it.

The Roman Empire was divided into provinces nominally ruled by the Senate in Rome or by the Emperor on the Senate's behalf, and the newly acquired or partially conquered areas such as Britain were always among those in the Imperial charge. They were normally entrusted to a governor, or *legatus Augusti pro praetore*, who was both commander-in-chief of the army and head of the civilian administration. We are fortunate that from the time of Aulus Plautius, who commanded the invading forces in A.D. 43, we have a fairly complete list of the governors of Britain.[1] As military affairs were important during much

[1] Best summarised by Professor E. Birley in G. Askew, *The Coinage of Roman Britain* (1951) Appendix I.

of our Roman period, soldiers who had already served here with distinction tended to re-appear in higher posts. Among them were Petilius Cerealis who, as governor, was responsible for the first settlement on the site of York, and Agricola, while the future Emperor Vespasian himself was among the officers commanding the legions taking part in Aulus Plautius' successful campaigning. As in the case of the Emperors, not all the governors were of Roman or even Italian birth; and, as we shall see, it was possible for provincials to reach the very highest positions.

The governorship of a province such as Britain was one of the most important in the Empire and the men who obtained it were all drawn from the Roman aristocracy, members of the Senate in Rome who had worked their way through a recognised series of posts designed to give them varied experience. Literary sources and the custom of erecting inscribed monuments detailing the careers of the persons commemorated have made it possible for scholars to work out the stages of this *cursus honorum*; and one of the best illustrations of it is provided by the career of an individual who spent many years in Britain, Gnaeus Julius Agricola. Most of our information comes from the biography written by his son-in law, the historian Tacitus, supplemented by archaeological research.

Agricola was born in A.D. 40 at Forum Julii, the modern Fréjus in Provence, then the most Romanised part of Gaul. His father, an important landowner living in retirement after some trouble at court, died while he was still a baby, probably executed by order of the Emperor Gaius (Caligula). After this his mother took him to live at Marseilles (Massilia), a town founded as a Greek colony more than six centuries earlier and now a centre of culture where well-to-do young men gathered to study with eminent teachers. At the age of nineteen or twenty Agricola made his way to Rome where the Emperor Nero was now ruling with his former tutor, the Spaniard Seneca, as his chief minister, and the Gaul, Afranius Burrus, in command of the Praetorian Guard. Both may have been friends of Agricola's father Graecinus and probably used their influence to help his son. Agricola was eventually successful in obtaining an army commission as a staff officer, or military tribune, to the governor Suetonius Paulinus in Britain. So at the age of twenty-one, he visited this country for the first time, and under Paulinus' command he took part in the battles against the tribes of northern Wales, including the attack on the druidic stronghold on Anglesey. He must also have witnessed the harrowing scenes of A.D. 60 when Queen Boudicca triumphantly led the rebellious Iceni against the Roman citizens of Camulodunum (Colchester), and when Paulinus could not move his army in time to save the people of London and Verulamium (St Albans) from

8

massacre in their turn. No doubt Agricola helped to avenge them in the war which ended when the defeated Boudicca committed suicide.

In A.D. 62 Agricola returned to Rome to begin his civil career, and presumably became one of the twenty young senators chosen every year to perform certain administrative duties in that city. These included supervising the mint and various public works, or acting as police-court magistrates. In later times such posts were usually held before a man entered the army. The next stage was the election to a quaestorship. In this capacity the rising young Roman was chiefly concerned with financial administration, and his posting either in Rome or to one of the provinces was decided in theory at least, by lot. Agricola was lucky enough to be sent to Asia Minor, and on the way there he may have visited Athens and other cities already renowned for their learning and antiquity. A year later he was back in Rome and in A.D. 66 he became one of the ten Tribunes of the People. By A.D. 68 he was elected praetor. The holders of this office could gain much useful legal experience by presiding over the law-courts, but there was rarely sufficient work of this kind to go round. For many, including Agricola, it was chiefly significant as a necessary qualification for a number of important posts, mostly abroad. However, under Galba, the emperor who reigned briefly after Nero's death, Agricola was given the task of investigating a series of thefts of artistic and other treasures from the Roman temples. During the famous fire of Nero's reign there had been much looting and he had some success in restoring missing property. Galba was murdered and in the ensuing civil wars Agricola became an adherent of Vespasian who eventually secured the throne. As a result he was put in command of the Twentieth Legion and returned to Britain. Since his legion was one that had supported Vespasian's rivals in the struggle for the Empire, it was still considered unreliable and its new commander had to be carefully chosen. Agricola was successful in restoring its morale and eventually he led it up western England in support of the campaigns of the governor, Petilius Cerealis, against the Brigantes and other northern tribes. In A.D. 73 or 74 he was recalled, and the Emperor made him a member of the Roman nobility by conferring on him patrician status. In A.D. 74 he became governor of Aquitaine, a peaceful province of central and south-western Gaul which needed no army units, apart from the governor's guard of honour. Here his work must have been chiefly judicial. Since no native court could pass a death sentence, he had to review all serious criminal cases, as well as complicated civil suits which often involved problems arising from the conflict of Roman law with native customs. Summoned back to Rome in less than three years, he was then made consul and in A.D. 78 he became Governor of Britain. His term of office lasted for seven years, an unusually long period.

In Britain, as commander-in-chief of the army of four legions, much of his time was spent in the field, beginning, as had his earliest army service in Britain, with a battle against the tribes of North Wales and the re-occupation of Anglesey. After that he gradually worked his way further north, consolidating his gains with forts and roads, until in A.D. 84 he won a great victory over the Caledonian tribes somewhere in north-eastern Scotland. The extent of his campaigning is still not fully known, but every year air-photography reveals traces of Roman forts and camps creeping ever further north, many of which will probably turn out, when excavated, to be of Agricolan date. Between campaigns the governor would carry out many of the duties which still fall to the lot of heads of states today (Pl. 7). He travelled round his province, staying with his retinue at the new towns which were springing up in many places, and his arrival must have caused the local administrators to collect supplies of food and firewood, some of them perhaps not too willingly provided. Each town would receive him with religious ceremonies and speeches of welcome in which any petitions and grievances might be diplomatically raised, and he would inspect new buildings, bridges and roads. His work as Lord Chief Justice of the province would take time. He would have to ensure that criminals were hunted down and that peace and order were maintained. He must also prevent food shortages in bad seasons, and cope with a regular flow of dispatches to and from Rome.

To help him the governor may have had a staff of about thirty to forty individuals, including personal assistants and secretaries, police officials, couriers, accountants and clerks, some of them certainly slaves or freedmen; but even so the burden of all this work may have proved too heavy. It was probably during Agricola's period of office that this was realised, and for the first time a special representative of the Emperor was sent to Britain in the shape of the *legatus iuridicus*, or law-officer, who could go on circuit to attend to some of the legal work and prevent too many cases piling up while the governor was at the front. The names of five of these officials who served here are known.[1]

While it was the duty of the governor to watch over his people and prevent them being unjustly treated by tax-gatherers, Roman moneylenders or anyone else, the financial administration of an imperial province was entirely the responsibility of a high-ranking procurator. These officials were chosen from among the *equites*, or 'knights', the class which ranked socially below the senatorial order and which also had its own *cursus honorum* of military and civilian posts with stages described in the inscriptions on various monuments. Thus, in the second century, Marcus Maenius Agrippa Lucius Tusidius Campester, born at Camorinum

[1] Birley (1961) 51, 54.

in Italy, began his military career as Prefect of the Second Cohort Flavia Brittonum, a cavalry unit.[1] He was selected by the Emperor Hadrian to take part in a campaign in Britain, and then became Tribune of a cavalry cohort of Spaniards, and Prefect of an Ala Cataphractii or heavily armoured detachment of Gauls and Pannonians. After this he became Procurator and Prefect of the British fleet and then Procurator of Britain. He thus spent much of his life as a soldier, ending up with an important civilian post, while his son eventually held senatorial rank. Another interesting career on less characteristic lines was that of one Lucius Julius Vehilius Gratus Julianus in the time of the Emperor Commodus.[2] He was also Prefect and Procurator of detachments of the fleet and army at various times, including one post in time of war in Britain. He then rose to be financial secretary to the Emperor, Prefect of the Grain-Supply and Prefect of the Praetorian Guard and thus attained very high office.

Other important posts held by *equites* included the secretaryships of state in the various departments of the civil service, and posts in charge of the revenue from the mines, imperial estates and provinces. The procurators were always the Emperor's agents and were directly responsible to him and not to the provincial governors, and this arrangement sometimes led to ill-feeling between the two types of official. We know that in Britain the greed of the procurator Decianus Catus was largely responsible for Boudicca's revolt. Unnerved by the storm he had provoked, after the fall of Camulodunum and the defeat of the Ninth Legion, he fled to Gaul. The governor, Suetonius Paulinus, exacted so bitter a vengeance after Boudicca's death that the province, with its fields unsown and its people still rebellious, was in danger of utter ruin. Its condition inspired the new procurator, Julius Classicianus, to appeal to Rome for a new governor, as he felt that Suetonius was now too much inspired by a personal desire for revenge. The Emperor Nero sent over a commission of enquiry under one of his secretaries of state, a Greek freedman called Polyclitus, and this recommended that Suetonius Paulinus, who deserved praise for his speedy action in checking the revolt, should be confirmed in his position for the time being. Nevertheless he was recalled soon after on a rather trifling excuse and his successor, Petronius Turpilianus, was instructed to work for conciliation and peace. Classicianus, whose timely protest on behalf of the British made him most unpopular in military circles—he gets a very 'bad press' from Tacitus—presumably remained as procurator. He was certainly of provincial origin himself, probably coming from northern Gaul, and he seems to have died in Britain before the end of his term of office. This is suggested by a very important discovery. In 1852 part of the bolster-shaped top of an inscribed tombstone in the

[1] Dessau no. 2735. [2] *Ibid.* no. 1327.

form of an altar was found at Trinity Place, Minories. It had originally been built into one of the fourth-century bastions attached to the earlier Roman wall surrounding London. In 1935, further building operations at the same place produced more of the inscription built into the same bastion, upside down. It was dedicated to the spirits of the departed and of Gaius Julius Alpinus Classicianus. The middle section, which must have given particulars of his career, is still missing, but the lower portion continued 'Procurator of the province of Britain; Julia Pacata I(ndiana), daughter of Indus, his wife, had this built'. Julia Pacata was probably also a Gaul, a member of a family living near Trier; and these pieces of the memorial she erected to her husband can now be seen in the British Museum (fig. 1). In an emergency, particularly in the later period, tombstones were often collected and used for building defences, so it might be claimed that even after his death Classicianus was still helping to protect the Romano-Britons.

The system of taxation under which the procurators collected the imperial revenue from a province may be divided into two classes: direct and indirect. Under the first heading comes the *tributum soli*, a tax on land and fixed property based on the theory that, as all provincial soil belonged to the Roman state, the occupiers of it could reasonably be expected to pay rent. Owners of taxable property were required to register it at the local record office. Besides this there may also have been the *tributum capitis*, a poll-tax which was levied on property other than land, really a tax on industry and commerce. The basis for this was a census taken from time to time together with a registration of property. Taxes were mostly paid in coin, but grain, hides and other payments in kind were sometimes demanded. Britain must have had to provide the corn, lard and leather used by armies stationed here, and this would either have been regarded as taxation or paid for at prices fixed by the government. Finding the corn and delivering it to the army must have been a considerable burden in the years following the conquest as the necessary organisation would take time to develop. According to Tacitus, Agricola found that some Britons were obliged to take corn to posts unnecessarily distant from their homes instead of supplying the nearest camps, and this was one of the abuses which he rectified. Agricola also initiated more equitable methods of assessing the tax, and dealt with dishonest officials who were using it to make extortionate demands for their own benefit.[1] In an earlier chapter Tacitus remarks that the Britons were willing to supply men for the army, pay the tribute and carry out official orders without grumbling, so long as the demands were just and not oppressive.[2] This happier

[1] *Agricola* XIX.
[2] *Ibid.* XIII.

1 Tombstone of Julius Classicianus

picture must have been one result of Agricola's reforms for, as the Emperor Tiberius had pointed out, a good shepherd shears his sheep, he does not skin them.[1] The burden of such taxation, whether in cash or in kind, varied over the years according to the number of legions and auxiliary cohorts in the province. Britain was unfortunate in having to meet the upkeep for so many troops. There were also indirect taxes which may have included customs duties on goods crossing the provincial frontiers; a small sales or purchase tax of $\frac{1}{2}$ to 1 per cent; the *Aurum Coronarium* or money paid by the provinces on the accession of a new emperor; a manumission tax payable when a slave was freed; and a 5 per cent duty on legacies which was only due from Roman citizens. In A.D. 301 the taxation system was extensively re-organised by the Emperor Diocletian.

By his Edict of 301 Diocletian also attempted a policy of freezing wages and prices throughout the Empire. Prices were fixed and copies of the Edict widely displayed. Numerous examples of it have survived. However, it proved impossible to enforce in spite of the sentences of death and exile which could be imposed on those failing to obey it. It remains a most valuable document for the social and economic historian, giving a wonderful picture of the variety of things on sale in the fourth century. For example, prices are given for different

[1] Suetonius, *Tiberius* XXXII.

kinds of wine, Gallic, Pannonian or Egyptian beer, or for various kinds of fish. In addition, Diocletian had to devalue a highly inflated coinage and a note has survived from a government official in Egypt who obviously had inside information about the impending change. He orders his agent Apio to make haste to spend all his Italian money, buying with it any goods he can find, before the value of each *sestertius* is reduced by half.[1]

Another of Diocletian's measures was the re-organisation of the Roman Empire into twelve new units called dioceses. Each diocese was supervised by a *vicarius* and was divided into smaller provinces. About the beginning of the third century Britain had already been divided into two provinces, Britannia Superior and Britannia Inferior; and now it became one diocese with four divisions, Britannia Prima, Britannia Secunda, Maxima Caesariensis and Flavia Caesariensis. Maxima Caesariensis was governed by a man of consular rank, the others by lesser dignitaries known as *praesides*. References in the *Notitia Dignitatum* and by Ammianus Marcellinus show that a fifth division, Valentia, appeared a little later.

Little is known of how these provinces were distributed geographically. The evidence of literature and inscriptions shows that as the result of the earlier division, York and Lincoln may have been in Britannia Inferior and Chester and Caerleon in Britannia Superior, while Cirencester is believed to have been the capital of the later Britannia Prima.[2] The *vicarius* of the new diocese was responsible not directly to the Emperor, but to the Praetorian Prefect of Gaul, who governed the seventeen Gallic provinces from Trier; these posts were now purely civilian ones. The army in fourth-century Britain was controlled by three commanders, the *Dux Britanniarum*, in charge of the northern frontier with headquarters at York; the *Comes Litoris Saxonici* or Count of the Saxon Shore, controlling the coast defences which had now been erected against overseas raiders; and the *Comes Britanniarum*, who commanded a standing army ready to go wherever it was needed.

Besides those provincials who attained the ranks of senator or knight in Rome and so could rise to high office, from the first century onwards an increasing number of less-distinguished Britons obtained the Roman citizenship. As we know from the familiar reference relating to St Paul,[3] this was a much coveted status carrying with it social advantages which made its attainment particularly attractive to the ambitious. Only Roman citizens, or those holding the more limited form of the citizenship known as Latin Rights, which may have included

[1] L. and R. II p. 463.
[2] R. Courteault, 'An Inscription recently found at Bordeaux', *J.R.S.* XI (1921) 101 *et seq.*, *R.I.B.* 103, Dio Cassius, *History* lv, 23.   [3] *Acts* XVI. 37; XXII. 25-8.

many Britons, possessed such privileges as *conubium* and *commercium*. *Commercium* was the right to enter into contracts with another Roman according to Roman law (*ius civile*) enforceable in Roman courts, and Latin citizens usually, but not invariably, possessed it. With *conubium*, a Roman citizen marrying a non-citizen, could make a marriage recognised by Roman law, his children would be legitimate and their family property and inheritance rights safeguarded. Here again, not all Latin citizens had this privilege. Auxiliary soldiers, however, usually received it on discharge so that any alliances they might have already made with local women could be legalised. The children became Roman citizens but not the mother. A marriage without *conubium*, was not, of course, forbidden; but it was not legally valid.

There were various ways of obtaining the citizenship. Besides receiving it at the end of their service, auxiliaries who belonged to a regiment which distinguished itself in action, might get it as a reward while still serving soldiers. Lucius Vitellius Tancinus, whose tombstone dating from *c.* A.D. 47, has been found at Bath, was a trooper in such a unit, the Ala Vettones, which bore the proud title, *civium Romanorum*.[1] The emperors also conferred the citizenship on the inhabitants of certain towns for various reasons, and individuals might get it through the influence of a patron. In some cases local government officials obtained it after holding office. Finally, in A.D. 212, the Emperor Caracalla published an Edict granting Roman citizenship to practically all the free peoples of the Empire.

Before A.D. 212 the free people of the Empire who had not attained the rights of Roman or Latin citizenship were known as *peregrini*. They included all those who belonged to provincial communities with any form of local autonomy and they conducted their affairs according to their own laws. Three fragmentary dedication slabs found at Silchester were put up on behalf of a guild of *peregrini*; these may have been business men from some other *civitas*, possibly only temporarily resident in Silchester.[2]

In addition to those individuals who possessed the rights of citizenship, or who were free people hoping to obtain them, there were also the freedmen and slaves. It is difficult for us to envisage a civilisation based on such a social structure and in any case we do not know how high the proportion of slave to free was in Britain. From the early first century the lot of the Roman slave steadily improved as emperor after emperor passed legislation protecting him from ill-treatment, making the killer of a slave liable to prosecution as a murderer, and preventing masters from casting off their slaves when old or ill, or from forcing them to follow immoral ways of life or to fight in the arena.

[1] R.I.B. 159. [2] R.I.B. 69–71.

Slaves working in the fields on big estates or on public works must often have led a very hard life, but in other branches of public service or in the household, they had frequent opportunities to rise to positions of trust or become loved members of the family. They were often specialists at their work; and skilled cooks, hairdressers, readers and scribes were very expensive to buy. A few contracts drawn up at slave sales in other provinces have survived, and they show that in the first and second centuries the price of even an unskilled slave might be between two hundred and a thousand *denarii*, a fact which encouraged masters to feed and clothe them properly. One such contract found in Dacia describes how a boy of Greek origin, warranted to be in good health, guiltless of theft or other crime, and not a vagrant, a runaway, or an epileptic, was bought by Dasius, an Illyrian, for six hundred *denarii*.[1] Another purchase was made by a naval officer, Gaius Fabullius Macer of the trireme 'Tigris', from a member of his crew; and it concerned a seven-year-old boy, named Abbas or Eutyches, bought for two hundred *denarii*.[2] Some of the Oxyrhynchus Papyri provide us with contracts for slave-apprentices who would learn a trade and then go out and make money for their masters, one of these boys being trained as a weaver and another being sent for two years to learn shorthand symbols from a scribe.[3] In the household we may recall Cicero's delicate slave-secretary and later freed-man, to whom he wrote affectionate letters begging him to take as much care of himself as he did of his master. 'Add this to the numberless services you have done and I shall value it more than them all. Take care, take care of yourself, Tiro mine.'[4] Buyers of slaves had to pay sales tax on their purchases and customs duty when they imported or exported them.

As we have already seen, slavery was no new thing in Britain. After the conquest the governors and other high officials and wealthy citizens presumably had the large retinues of attendants customary to their rank; slaves to look after their clothes and their toilet, butlers and ushers, messengers, grooms, cooks and bakers, slaves in charge of inferior slaves and slaves waiting on superior ones. But the status of the artisans, shop assistants, and farm labourers who did not belong to such big establishments is unknown; presumably some were bond and others free. We have a scrap from one business contract found in London ordering the sale of a slave girl and an inscription from Malton (Yorkshire) mentions a slave apparently working for his master as a goldsmith.[5]

---

[1] C.I.L. III p. 940, no. VII.
[2] E. Thompson, 'On a Latin Deed of Sale of a Slave', *Arch.* LIV (1895) 433–8.
[3] L. and R. p. 220; *Oxyrhynchus Papyri* nos. 275, 724.
[4] *Epistulae Ad Familares* XVI. 5, 6.
[5] *R.I.B.* 712. See below p. 190.

Evidence of a rather more intimate nature occurs on a Chester tombstone erected by Pompeius Optatus to his slave boys, Atilianus and Antiatilianus aged 10, who appear to have been twins, and Protus, aged 12.[1]

Other evidence is provided by a small number of funerary inscriptions concerned with freedmen and their former masters. These accord with the large quantity of such texts from all over the Empire, especially from Italy, which bear witness to the numerous slaves who gained their freedom. This was achieved in several different ways and for various reasons. Sometimes slaves would be freed as an economy to save the cost of their upkeep, and they would pay a percentage of their earnings to their old masters. Or masters with large households might leave directions in their wills that after their deaths a certain number of slaves should be freed, either as a reward for faithful service or as a means of drawing attention to the testator's wealth and importance. While the master was still alive it was customary to pay a slave small sums of money and these savings, known as the *peculium*, could be accumulated and used to buy freedom. The freed slave then became a client of his former master, now his patron, and normally took his master's family name as his own, with his own slave name retained as a personal name. The patron was supposed to watch over his freedman's welfare and the freedman in return rendered him certain services and could be prosecuted for failing to do so. Freedmen as a class prospered considerably, most commercial dealings being in their hands; many rose very high in the civil service of the Empire. One order of priesthood which is found in Italy and some Western provinces, that of the *seviri augustales* who were concerned with the cult of the deified emperors, was almost entirely reserved for them. Those freed by Roman citizens usually became citizens in their turn. Normally they had to be over thirty and their patrons at least twenty at the time of their manumission. In theory they were completely excluded from the army, the equestrian or senatorial ranks of the Roman aristocracy, and from the most important priesthoods, but there are exceptions and in any case the descendants of freedmen were not affected by these restrictions.

British evidence for freedmen in this country occurs on altars such as the one erected to Diana by the freedman, Vettius Benignus, 'on his own behalf' at Bath,[2] or the dedication at Colchester to the Deities of the Emperors and to the god Mercury Andescociuoucus, Imilico, freedman of Aesurilinus, from his own resources gave this altar in marble.[3] A tombstone found at High Rochester (Northumberland) was erected to Felicio, a freedman who died when only twenty,[4] and many inscriptions are concerned with the relationship between

[1] *R.I.B.* 560.   [2] *R.I.B.* 138.
[3] *R.I.B.* 193.   [4] *R.I.B.* 1290.

2 Tombstone of Etacontius

freedman and patron in which one affectionately puts up a memorial to the other. At Chester we find the tombstone dedicated to Etacontius, his deserving freedman, put up by his patron, Gaius Asurius Fortis (fig. 2).[1] Meanwhile, one of the finest pieces of relief sculpture found in Roman Britain is the portrait of Marcus Favonius Facilis, centurion of the Twentieth Legion. His tombstone was erected by his freedmen Novicus and Verecundus at Colchester and dates from the first century (Pl. 1). He is shown in uniform armed with sword and dagger and carrying the vinestick which was his badge of office. In London there is a tombstone dedicated to Sempronius Sempronianus, a centurion aged fifty-one, and his brothers Sempronius . . . and Sempronius Secundus; erected by their freedmen for their well-deserving patrons.[2] By way of contrast, another fine relief sculpture found much further north, at South Shields, shows a man reclining on a couch on a mattress with striped cover and fringed pillow. Most of the face has been destroyed but enough remains to suggest it was a careful portrait. The deceased holds a wine-cup in one hand and a small attendant (? slave) offers him another drink filled from a large bowl on the ground at his feet. The inscription tells us that this is the tombstone erected to the freedman Victor, a Moor, by his patron Numerianus 'who most devotedly conducted him to the tomb'.[3]

In the case of women slaves the story may sometimes have had the conventional happy ending. An inscription found at Lincoln was dedicated to her husband Flavius Helius, a Greek, by Flavia Ingenua, his wife.[4] The fact that both have the family name Flavius suggests that the wife had once been her husband's slave, and that he had set her free and married her; since a freed slave

[1] *R.I.B.* 559. [2] *R.I.B.* 15. [3] *R.I.B.* 1064.
[4] *R.I.B.* 251; for another example see *R.I.B.* 155 from Bath.

18

regularly took his or her former master's name. A clearer example of such a marriage is known from the tombstone of Regina, a British slave belonging to the tribe of the Catuvellauni who became the freedwoman and wife of Barates, a Palmyrene (Pl. 2)[1] She died aged 30, and is shown sitting on a basket chair with her work-basket, distaff, and thread on one side of her, and her jewel-box on the other, possessions which suggest that she was an industrious wife whose hard work was appreciated and rewarded with gifts. Like Victor's, her tombstone is also in the South Shields Museum, and another tombstone found at Corbridge 28 miles away, may possibly belong to her husband, Barates.[2] Regina's Latin inscription is repeated in Palmyrene and the attitude in which she is portrayed so much resembles that of other reliefs actually found at Palmyra that it has been suggested that a compatriot of Barates carved it for him. A certain similarity in style suggests that Victor's tombstone may also be the work of the same hand.

After this brief sketch of the imperial administration and the different classes of people affected by it we may now consider local government. In Britain in the Roman period this is closely bound up with a great innovation, the development of town life. Before A.D. 43 the people tended to live chiefly in small settlements or isolated farms with the great hill-forts and other fortified sites as places of refuge in time of war. The chieftains or kings may have habitually dwelt with their families at such fortified sites or in some other form of tribal centre, accompanied by a bodyguard of the leading warriors and waited on by slaves. Besides Cunobelinus' capital at Camulodunum, the chieftain Tasciovanus at an earlier date lived on the Prae Wood site near Verulamium at St Albans, and an important settlement associated with metalworking at Bagendon may have been the forerunner of the later town of Corinium (Cirencester). Belgic levels also underlie the Roman ones at Verulamium showing that the site was occupied before the Roman town was built there, and traces of them have been found at Silchester. The evidence seems to indicate that the huts were built with no suggestion of town-planning and their earthen floors are sometimes thick with rubbish. The chieftain usually lived in a finer hut than his henchmen and the fact that this was easily distinguishable has been proved by the recent excavations on Hod Hill, Dorset. This was a hill-fort successfully attacked soon after the Roman invasion by the legionaries probably led by Vespasian. The excavators found a concentration of missiles from the Roman *ballistae* confined to a remarkably small space. Further investigations showed that this target apparently consisted of a single dwelling. Behind its door, where in most of the other huts a pile of sling-stones seems to have been kept ready for use, was

[1] *R.I.B.* 1065. [2] *R.I.B.* 1171.

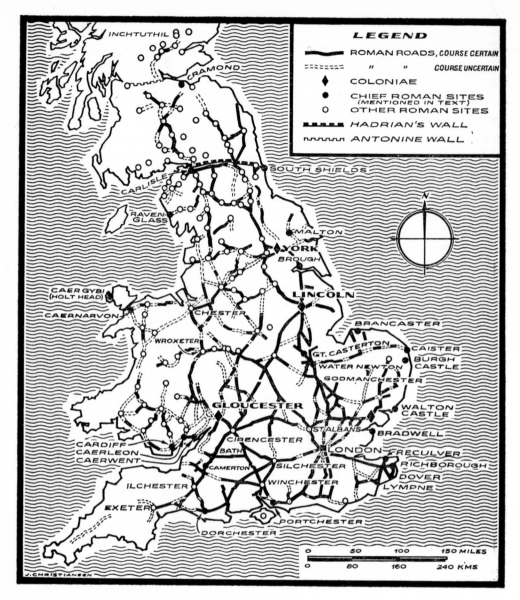

Map II. Roman road system and chief Roman sites

found a much rarer weapon, part of a fine iron spear. Obviously this was the chief's house, easily identified by the invaders, who consequently concentrated all their artillery fire on it. The chief may have been taken by surprise and killed before he could take up his spear; the tribe seem to have surrendered, as there is no evidence for any further fighting or for a massacre.

The first town built in Britain was founded by the Romans near the site of the old Belgic capital at Camulodunum and it was a *colonia* or town of the highest rank, a settlement of Roman citizens, mostly retired legionaries, who received a grant of land instead of money on leaving the army. This was a common practice in a newly conquered province, as it provided a nucleus of townsfolk loyal to Rome who were able to supervise the building of the new town, hold office on its council, spread Roman ideas, and organise the defences if necessary. The name chosen was *colonia Claudia Victricensis*. This includes an allusion to the ruling Emperor Claudius, and may indicate that the settlers came from the Fourteenth and Twentieth Legions which both bore the proud title of the Victorious. In spite of this the town continued to be called Camulodunum. Many Britons cannot have regarded it at this early period with any great enthusiasm. Some of them must have had land taken from them for the new settlers, and Roman tax-gatherers and money-lenders soon had the tribal aristocracy deep in debt.

The new *colonia* was built on top of the hill where apparently no one had lived before, probably near the site of the by then disused legionary fortress which had housed the invading armies. From the beginning it was intended to be the capital of the province, designed to impress the Britons with the civilisation and might of Rome. The people who fled from the Belgic settlement on the slopes of the hill during the fighting of A.D. 43, must have gradually filtered back. Soon the hillside was covered with workshops where tiles, stone and timber were prepared for the builders, lime was burnt ready for mortar, and quantities of iron nails were manufactured. These materials were used for the new Temple of Claudius, a magnificent building erected in honour of the Emperor, where priests chosen from the wealthiest of the citizens probably carried on his worship with elaborate rites and ceremonies (Pl. 6). To the Britons, no doubt, the Emperor was the personification of the might of Rome, which must be more powerful than their own gods since it had overcome them in battle, and so it was something which must be venerated and appeased.

The temple itself was an oblong building, 80 by 105 feet in size, consisting of one large hall or *cella* erected on a great *podium* or platform of masonry. It was approached up a flight of steps and through a portico with a pedimented roof supported in front by eight columns. Colonnades of columns ran on either side and the plan has been compared with that of the Temple of Mars Ultor in Rome. It was unusually large, being only surpassed by the Capitolium at Narbonne, another close parallel. It stood in a large precinct and remains of white stucco mouldings and pieces of alabaster hint at its rich decoration. Nothing survives of the superstructure today, it is known to have been destroyed in the Boudiccan rebellion and all traces of the destruction removed in

21

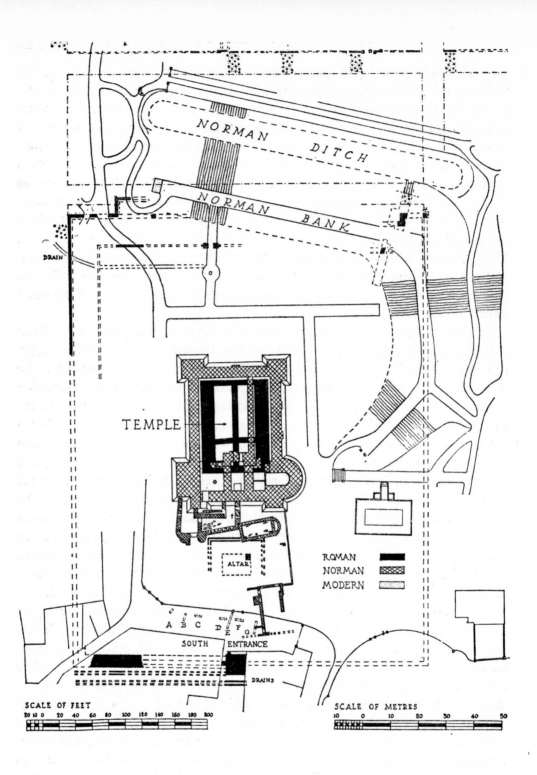

3 Plan of the area including the Temple of Claudius, Colchester

the thorough ritual cleansing which must have taken place before it was rebuilt. The remains of the later temple were used by the Normans for the construction of Colchester Castle between 1076 and 1086. The great platform, however, has survived and can be seen as part of the castle foundation and ground floor. Because of the shortage of local stone, its builders did not erect it as a solid mass, but built it with large hollow vaults under the floor where there was no great weight to support. These hollow spaces were originally left filled with the natural sand of the site. In the seventeenth century this was removed and gaps made in the walls of the vaults so that it is now possible to go down and inspect them, relics of the oldest roofed stone building erected in this country.

Not only the temple was destroyed in the Boudiccan rising. Tacitus, in his account of the omens which forecast this disaster, mentions other features of Claudian Colchester. The statue of victory fell from its base without apparent cause, and lay extended on the ground with its face averted, as if the goddess yielded to the enemies of Rome. In the council chamber of the Romans, hideous noises were heard in a foreign accent, savage howlings filled the theatre, and near the mouth of the Thames the image of a *colonia* in ruins was seen,[1] presumably reflected in the water. Nothing is known of the whereabouts of the statue or of the council-chamber, but solid carved foundations in Insula XIII at Colchester may hint at the position. The plan of the temple area in post-Boudiccan times shows that in front of the temple, 92 feet to the south, a vaulted drain runs for 70 feet, parallel with the south front, with a right-angled turn at each end (fig. 3). This probably lay inside an architectural screen around an open air altar. A rough foundation belonging to the altar was found, with a tile pedestal on either side which must have supported statues. The plan is reminiscent of the altar of Rome and Augustus which lay outside the *colonia* at Lyons and stood between two statues of Victory. The combination of altar and temple at Colchester, however, which may indeed have already existed in the time of Claudius, is an unusual fusion of two architectural schemes for the celebration of the rites of the imperial cult. It recalls the temple of Divus Julius and his commemorative altar in the Forum at Rome. The temple and altar in the Forum at Augst in Switzerland also give some idea of its appearance although in this case we have neither pedestals nor architectural screen.

The Colchester plan shows the temple occupying a great court, somewhat irregularly planned at the back, where it is built up on the northward slope. The temple is not in the centre, either because another monument stood near it or because the court was planned to fit in with some other features. The main street front on the south was cut off by a great ornamental screen wall associated

[1] *Annals* XIV. 32.

with a monumental central entrance with attached angle columns, and consisting of panel-walls linking large ashlar-faced piers projecting to the north and south. The piers seem to have carried arcades with columns on the inside and the whole gate stood on a masonry platform 15 feet wide. The screen walls were faced with marble, some British Purbeck, but there were also at least eight foreign varieties, from Africa, Greece and Italy, including Carrara. At one time it was believed that the temple stood in the Forum but it is now thought that the Forum must be looked for elsewhere, perhaps further south. The street grid was laid down and the area divided into *insulae* in the post-Boudiccan rebuilding, as a coin of Nero was found mixed in with the primary metalling of one street and the burnt layer underlies others. The main east to west street also shows an awkward dog-leg turn to allow for part of the precinct wall of the temple, but the other public buildings still await discovery.[1]

Three other towns in Britain are known to have held the status of *coloniae* but all were founded at a later date than Colchester. The official name of Gloucester, *colonia Nervia Glevensium*, shows that it was founded during the reign of the Emperor Nerva (A.D. 96–98). It is usually called Glevum and seems to have developed from a civilian settlement of camp-followers or squatters which had grown up near the legionary fortress, probably built by the Twentieth Legion about A.D. 49. Later the Second Legion Augusta occupied the fortress until it moved to Caerlon *c*. A.D. 75. Comparatively little is known of the buildings of the new *colonia* although a number of mosaic pavements have been found at various times. It may always have been overshadowed by the town of Corinium (Cirencester) 17 miles away. However, it is interesting to compare Glevum with the *colonia* at Lindum (Lincoln) which dates from about the same period, perhaps a year or so earlier. This had been the home of the Ninth Legion until Petilius Cerealis took it further north to found another fortress at York in A.D. 71. Both *coloniae* in fact lay near the frontier between friendly and unconquered territories where, as at Colchester, a nucleus of army veterans spreading Roman ways of life would be an added safeguard. Unlike the other *coloniae*, Lindum is actually built on the site of the earlier fortress. It occupied about 43 acres compared with Glevum's 46 and the 108 at Camulodunum, and the resemblance between Glevum and Lindum is so close that the same public works contractors might well have built both of them.[2] They resemble such foundations in other parts of the Empire, as Timgad in North Africa. Although the settlers would take land from the neighbouring tribes the country round Lincoln is so marshy that it would be of little value until drained and developed. Unlike Colchester,

[1] Richmond (1947b) 57 *et seq.*; Hull (1958) p. 160 *et seq.* (1963a) p. 25.
[2] Richmond (1963) p. 72.

where territory was confiscated as an act of war, compensation may have been paid and so the loss was probably not resented. Lindum grew in size until by about the end of the second century its buildings covered 97 acres. Not very much is known of them apart from the walls although excavation wherever opportunity offers on such a heavily built-over site is gradually adding fresh discoveries. Evidence has been found for colonnades lining the streets in front of substantial buildings and terracing for structures placed on the steep hillside. But the inscriptions, the fragments of finely carved architectural decoration and of tombstones, and the rich burials give us a picture of a prosperous town where the Roman way of life had established itself very firmly.

Unlike the three sites already mentioned, the fourth *colonia* grew up beside a legionary fortress which still continued in occupation. As in the case of Lincoln and Gloucester, the site of York controls an important river crossing and occupied a ridge of high ground in marshy country. The value of its position was realised by Cerealis in A.D. 71 and the legionary fortress which was built there was the home of the Ninth Legion until its mysterious disappearance early in the second century, presumably the result of a transfer to the continent or even of an unrecorded defeat. It was replaced by the Sixth Legion, the Victorious, and became a base for the legionaries who built the great walls of Hadrian and Antoninus Pius along the northern frontiers. Recruits must have been drilled here as practice camps have been found close by, and no doubt legionaries came back on leave and for fresh training and their families made their homes in the town. In these circumstances it is not surprising that a flourishing civilian settlement grew up on the side of the river Ouse opposite the fortress. When Eboracum, as it was called, became *colonia Eboracensium* is uncertain. This was not a case of a new town being founded to spread romanisation, but rather of the granting of the honour of a charter to a flourishing community. At the beginning of the third century, the governor, Clodius Albinus, took most of the army in Britain with him to the continent in an attempt to seize the Imperial power. He was defeated by Septimius Severus, but meanwhile the unconquered tribes in the north had seized the opportunity to break through the frontier defences and lay the country waste as far south as York. The new emperor hastily sent fresh troops to the province and came himself with his family in A.D. 208 to live in York while a great military campaign was planned against the northern tribes. Severus died there in A.D. 211 while the fighting was still in progress, but his son Antoninus (Caracalla) completed the task victoriously and Britain had peace for over eighty years. As we have already noted, Britain about the beginning of the third century was divided into two provinces, perhaps partly as a precaution against another governor controlling as many resources as Albinus. Eboracum is believed to have been the capital of Britannia Inferior and possibly this was the moment when the town became a *colonia*. This suggestion is supported by the discovery of traces of important buildings including colonnades with massive stone columns and decorated capitals dating from the third century. Large public baths, altered and enlarged on several occasions, have been excavated on the site of the old Railway Station, and evidence for several temples and houses with mosaic pavements in some rooms, as well as a wealth of inscriptions and small objects, has also been found.

The form of local government which controlled the affairs of a Roman *colonia* in Britain must have first made its appearance at Colchester, although, unhappily, we have no records of any of its officials. Modelled on the administration of Rome itself, it consisted of a senate or *ordo* of up to one hundred members usually known as decurions. Normally most of these would be men who had already held office, but in a new province trustworthy members of the tribal aristocracy and other influential people may occasionally have been nominated to serve with the retired army officers or their descendants. It was an expensive honour, as decurions were expected to contribute to the town treasury and help to pay for baths and other public buildings. The *ordo* was responsible to the Procurators for tax collection and could also levy and collect any local taxes authorised by the central government. Every year four magistrates were elected by the townsfolk, a senior pair, the *duoviri iuredicundo*, who were chiefly concerned with the administration of justice in those cases which were not important enough to be sent to the governor, and a junior pair, the *duoviri aediles*, who supervised public works, including roads, and saw that public order was maintained. These magistrates were obliged to consult the *ordo* about any matters of importance, and on retirement they became decurions. Every five years the senior magistrates were responsible for bringing the census up to date, checking the property registers and choosing decurions to fill any gaps in the *ordo*. They were then called *duoviri quinquennales* and the office was one of particular honour and trust.

Voting for the new magistrates in the early years of the Roman Empire could be quite a lively business. Some of the rules for election procedures have survived in the charters of three cities in Spain. These are closely based on Italian town charters and from them we learn that the candidates were nominated before the ruling magistrates and a list of their names prominently displayed. They had to be at least twenty-five years old, and they had to have certain property qualifications. On election day the people were divided into wards corresponding to various parts of the town, each with its own polling stations. The votes were inscribed on tablets and placed in ballot boxes. At each polling station three citizens from a different ward guarded and counted the ballots, and they had to take an oath to do this in good faith. One friend of each candidate was also allowed to watch the voting at the polling station, and he could cast his vote there instead of in his own ward. In case of equal voting a married man was to be elected in preference to a bachelor, and if both candidates were married, the one with the most children was successful. Two children dead in infancy or one child dying in its teens would be counted as one surviving child. If there was still a tie after all these factors had been considered, then the magistrate cast lots. Election notices still visible on the walls of streets in Pompeii appeal to us by the familiarity of the sentiments expressed. They include the dignified appeal to elect Epidius Sabinus *duovir iuredicundo*, because he is a worthy man, upright and public-spirited, who has the *ordo's* support; the equivalent of the rate-payer's candidate, Bruttius Balbus, because he will protect the treasury; and the appeal to an individual voter—'Proculus, make Sabinus *aedile* and he will do as much for you'! Fruit-dealers, goldsmiths, and various fellow workers support particular candidates as do groups of neighbours. One inscription reads: 'His neighbours urge you to elect Lucius Statius Receptus *duovir iuredicundo*; he is worthy. Aemilius Celer, a neighbour, wrote this. May you take sick if you maliciously erase this.' Other notices of a less impressive kind urge the election of one candidate as *aedile* because the late drinkers and petty thieves support him. The *aedile* would be in charge of the police. As a final comment, a *graffito*, scratched on the wall instead of painted remarks, 'I wonder, O Wall, that you have not fallen in ruins from supporting the stupidities of so many scribblers.'[1]

The new magistrates had to swear by Jupiter, the deified Emperors, and by whatever gods were worshipped locally, that they would perform their duties according to the laws of the town and in the public interest, allowing no personal considerations to influence them. These oaths were sworn at a public ceremony, and a Pompeian wall-painting shows it taking place with the four *duoviri* gathered round an altar. Unfortunately from the second century onwards local interest in provincial elections seems to have waned steadily. The expenses of holding office increased, and after the Edict of A.D. 212 it ceased to be of value as one of the ways of obtaining the Roman citizenship. The new magistrates were then simply nominated by the decurions and the people only met together to pass formal votes of thanks to benefactors or retiring magistrates.

Information from inscriptions about local government officials is very scanty. A fragment of a tombstone built into the city wall at Bath reads . . . 'Decurion

[1] The evidence for voting procedures and the Pompeian election notices are included in L. and R. II p. 321 *et seq.*

DEC COL⁰ ✠ NÆGLE V
VIXTAN· LXXXQVI

4 Part of the tombstone of a decurion of Glevum, found at Bath

of the *colonia* of Glevum . . . lived eighty years':[1] unfortunately the name is lost (fig. 4). A larger fragment, originally part of the Roman wall at Lincoln and now in the British Museum, shows the busts of two women in high relief, somewhat damaged. Below them is an inscription saying that the stone was erected by Aurelius Senecio, decurion, to his deserving wife, Volusia Faustina, a citizen of Lindum who died aged 26 (Pl. 4).[2] At York a stone coffin of probable fourth-century date belonged to Flavius Bellator, decurion of the *colonia Eboracensium*, who lived just over twenty-eight years.[3] His skeleton lay inside it; a small man, wearing on one finger a gold ring set with a ruby.

The title of *colonia* was the highest to which a town could aspire. Next to it in rank came the *municipium* with a charter conferred by the Roman government on a pre-existing town not of its foundation. A reference in Tacitus and the discovery of Belgic levels under the Roman ones at Verulamium (St Albans), suggests that this town may have held such a status, especially as it has the site of the earlier Belgic capital of Tasciovanus nearby.[4] Part of an inscription on a bronze military diploma or soldier's discharge certificate issued in A.D. 106 to one Novanticus, a Briton who fought for the Emperor Trajan in Dacia, describes him as *civis Ratis*, a man of Leicester, rather than as *civis Coritanus*, a member of the local tribe of the Coritani. This might mean that Leicester was already important enough to have municipal status.[5] It has also been suggested that York may have had this status at some stage of its development, before it became a *colonia*.[6] Apart from the *colonia* or the *municipium* the status enjoyed by the Romano-British towns is very problematic. It seems probable that the

[1] R.I.B. 161.   [2] R.I.B. 250.   [3] R.I.B. 674.
[4] Frere (1964) 79 *et seq.*
[5] C.I.L. XVI. 160; J. Reynolds, 'Legal and Constitutional Problems', in J. Wacher ed. (1966) p. 73.
[6] *Eburacum* (1962) p. xxxvi.

larger and more prosperous among them also developed the system of local government by magistrates and *ordo*, with the *ordo* consisting of either Roman or 'Latin' citizens, some probably ex-soldiers, so that in time an 'upper-class' of citizens would develop. The Romans normally accepted any elements of tribal organisation they found, so long as it was co-operative and not hostile to them, but in a province as new to town life as Britain, it seems probable that the administration would tend to develop very much according to the Roman pattern.

Many towns in Britain had Latin names which suggest that they were tribal centres or *civitates*, for example, Calleva Atrebatum (Calleva of the Atrebates, or Silchester), Venta Icenorum (Caistor-by-Norwich), or Venta Belgarum (Winchester). The exact significance of this word *civitas*, sometimes translated 'canton' is one of the greatest problems, did it refer to the town itself or to the tribal area and its inhabitants? Evidence from Gaul is sometimes cited in this connection but it is not conclusive, and the complications of this phrase are the subject of recent research.[1] It may have had different meanings in different periods or provinces. Probably the tribal administration was carried on from these centres while for purely urban organisation they had the status of the *vicus*, a term which seems to have been applied to communities of varying size. Several *vici* may have sometimes developed within one tribal territory and there is evidence to suggest that the Durotriges in the Dorset area for example, had *civitates* at Dorchester and Ilchester.[2] The existence of a British *vicus* is shown by the discovery of an inscription at Brough (Yorkshire) dedicated to the Emperor Antoninus Pius by Marcus Ulpius Ianuarius who describes himself as *aedile* of the *vicus* of Petuaria (fig. 5).[3] This, however, does not prove that Petuaria was the centre of the local tribe, the Parisii, although it seems very likely. Recent excavations have shown that the Roman site at Brough was first occupied as a fort for about thirty years from *c*. A.D. 71, after which it was vacated and taken over by the civilian population.[4] Apparently it prospered as the rest of Ianuarius' inscription relates that, filled with civic pride, he gave a new stage to the theatre which must have already existed there. The word *vicus* may also apply to the electoral division or ward of a town as well as to a separate settlement. Evidence for this usage in Britain comes from Lincoln where an inscription found among the ruins of a building in the *colonia* was apparently erected by a guild of the worshippers of Mercury living in a *vicus* of this sort.[5] The *vici* which sprang up outside the forts along Hadrian's Wall also had some form

[1] Frere (1961) 29 *et seq.*; Reynolds, *op. cit.* pp. 70 *et seq.*, 74.
[2] *R.I.B.* 1672, 1673. [3] *R.I.B.* 707
[4] Wacher (1960) 58 *et seq.* [5] *R.I.B.* 270.

5 Inscription from the Roman theatre, Brough, Yorkshire

of local government, but this must have been largely unofficial as such settlements would be controlled by the military administration.[1]

As time went on some British *vici* may have been upgraded into chartered towns, and in such cases the new urban administration and that of the tribal organisation may have been carried on side by side in the same place. It is possible that Verulamium was both a *municipium* and also the *civitas Catuvellaunorum* whose existence is known from an inscription left by a working party probably helping to rebuild Hadrian's Wall in A.D. 369.[2] An illustration of such an arrangement is provided by the tribal centre at Aventicum (Avenches, Switzerland) where monuments were set up by both the *colonia* and also by the *civitas Helvetiorum*. Langres, too, has inscriptions mentioning both *colonia* and *civitas Lingonum*.[3]

For administrative purposes each British *civitas* may have been divided into a number of territorial sub-divisions called *pagi*. No inscriptions or other evidence mentioning a *pagus* have yet been found but this was the usual practice and such administrative units are known in Gaul. All the *civitates* sent representatives to the provincial council (*concilium provinciae*) which met at Colchester every year to elect a high priest and to offer sacrifices at the great temple. These assemblies were intended to foster loyalty to Rome and they included the foremost and best-educated citizens. While they had no power to legislate, they could petition the Emperor about laws which they regarded as unjust, and they could pass a vote of censure on an unpopular governor, instead of offering him the customary vote of thanks or setting up a statue in his honour. These meetings provided an opportunity to ventilate grievances and gave watchful officials some idea of provincial points of view. In Rome a senator was often invited to act as *patronus*, that is to watch the interests of a particular province and further its petitions.

Evidence of a provincial council at work is provided by an inscribed pedestal

[1] P. Salway, *The Frontier People of Roman Britain* (Cambridge, 1965) pp. 10 *et seq.*; 179 *et seq.*
[2] R.I.B. 1962.
[3] J. Reynolds, *op. cit.* p. 7.

6 Inscription from a statue pedestal, Caerwent,
Glamorganshire

found at Vieux in Normandy.[1] It belonged to the statue of Titus Sennius
Sollemnis, and was erected on a site given by his tribe, the Viducasses, because
he had represented them on the *concilium provinciae* of Gaul which met at Lyons,
and had there been elected high priest. In the course of the meeting the retiring
governor of part of Gaul, Tiberius Claudius Paulinus, seems to have been unjustly accused of some misdemeanour during his period of office and letters of
thanks reproduced on the statue's base express gratitude to Sollemnis for successfully defending him. In A.D. 219–20, after holding the consulship, Paulinus
became governor of Britannia Inferior and he is mentioned on an inscription
from High Rochester.[2] This was not his first visit to the province as another
inscription mentioning him at an earlier stage of his career has been found at
Venta Silurum (Caerwent). Again it comes from the pedestal of a statue (fig. 6).
When the abbreviated Latin is translated in full it reads 'To [Tiberius Claudius]
Paulinus, legate of the Second Legion Augusta, proconsul of the province of
Narbonensis, emperor's propraetorian legate of the province of Lugudunensis,
by decree of the council, the Canton of the Silurians (set this up)'.[3] While commanding the Second Legion at Caerleon a few miles away from Caerwent,
Paulinus must have become the patron of the Silures, who presumably erected
this statue while he was still in Gaul. He seems to have got on well with the
local populations in the countries to which he was posted. The wording of the
inscription is interesting with its allusions to a decree of the *ordo* and to the

[1] Abbott and Johnson, *Municipal Administration in the Roman Empire* (1926) p. 493 *et seq.*, no.
140.
[2] *R.I.B.* 1280.
[3] *R.I.B.* 311.

7   Inscription from the entrance to the Forum, Wroxeter, Shropshire

respublica of the *civitas* of the Silures—the whole community or tribe. Another inscription with beautifully cut lettering on a large stone slab, twelve feet long, was dedicated to the Emperor Hadrian by the *civitas* of the Cornovii about A.D. 130 (fig. 7).[1] This was the tribe which had its centre at Uriconium, the modern Wroxeter in Shropshire, where this slab was originally placed above the entrance to the Forum.

[1] *R.I.B.* 288.

3
The development of town life (1)
Public buildings and defences

From local government we must turn to consider more closely the nature of the towns themselves and their buildings. The *coloniae*, cities of a rather special type which often owed their foundation to Rome, have already been briefly discussed; what other conditions led to the springing up of Romano-British towns? In many cases trade followed the flag, and the traders and camp-followers who originally depended on the soldiers' custom for their living were sufficiently well-established to remain where they were when the army advanced, and develop their settlements into market towns. Recent excavations have shown that first-century forts preceded many such towns, among them Cirencester (Corinium) and Brough-on-Humber (Petuaria).[1] In time, civilian settlements also grew up outside the forts which guarded the frontiers. As the network of new Roman roads spread across the country, road junctions attracted settlers; and so did river crossings which had always been well-frequented. In some cases the Iron Age inhabitants had already occupied a site before the Roman period—Silchester, Leicester and Verulamium provide examples of this—and in others the occupation of an important hill-fort was succeeded by a town at a more convenient level. The fact that so many modern English towns are of Roman origin pays tribute to the suitability of the new sites; this list, in addition

[1] G. Webster, 'Fort and town in Roman Britain', in J. Wacher ed. (1966) pp. 31–45.

to some already mentioned, includes London, Chester, Winchester, Worcester, Canterbury, Chichester, the two Dorchesters, Exeter and Bath. Their rate of growth varied very much, Colchester, London and Verulamium being among the earliest sites. Governors after Suetonius Paulinus seem to have encouraged urban development and real enthusiasm for it was aroused in the time of Agricola. Tacitus relates that during his period of office he helped the new towns to build themselves *fora*, temples and houses, probably, as we may suppose, by lending them army surveyors, engineers and craftsmen; and that he also encouraged the education of the chieftains' sons and used to express his conviction of the superiority of the British native intelligence over the studied eloquence of the Gauls. As a result the Britons began to learn Latin and those who were entitled to do so were seen wearing the toga. And so, says Tacitus, they drifted into the demoralising pleasures of porticos and bath-establishments and elegant dinner-parties.[1]

In some cases the townsfolk seem to have been over-ambitious. This was believed to be the case at Wroxeter where the late first-century baths were never finished, but it now seems possible that these baths were begun for a legion which then moved on before the local population were in a position to take them over. The famous inscription (fig. 7) from this town tells us that in A.D. 130 their site was used for the new Forum instead,[2] and this reflects a fresh wave of enthusiasm for town-building caused by the visit of the Emperor Hadrian. Increasing prosperity is apparent in many towns later in the second century in the Antonine period, and while there may have been some stagnation in the third, town-life on certain sites, at least, flourished again in the fourth century. It then gradually faded away in the fifth century as the unsettled conditions caused by the invasions of the Picts, Scots and Saxons from beyond the frontier and across the sea made it almost impossible. A few communities may have held out for some years behind the shelter of their walls.

In Britain the first examples of town-planning date from Roman times. The earlier *coloniae* were probably laid-out by surveyors loaned from the army, and their plans recall those of fortresses with two main streets crossing at right angles and emerging from four gates. At the intersection of these streets, where the fortress would have its headquarters building, the town should have its Forum but in actual fact, while *fora* are usually centrally placed, their position varies. Round them the other buildings—shops, houses, temples or baths—were aligned in rectangular blocks or *insulae*, laid out along the straight lines of numerous side streets. If some buildings were already standing before the town-planners got to work they were either demolished or fitted into the

[1] *Agricola* XXI.   [2] See above p. 32.

new plan somehow, often rather awkwardly, as in the case of the temple at Colchester.[1] Away from the town centre the planning may be less precise, and some ribbon development occurred along the main roads leading out into the country. By the time the town defences were built, any suggestion of a regular four-sided plan had often ceased to exist; and the new walls might have to be constructed in straight stretches of varying length with not a few angles, the whole enclosing a polygonal area. These problems are well illustrated by one of the tribal capitals, Calleva Atrebatum (Silchester), near Reading. This is one of the sites which did not develop into an English town, it fell into decay and is now covered by green fields. Consequently it has been possible to excavate it without having to remove later buildings. Much of the work was done in the late nineteenth and early twentieth centuries before archaeologists had at their disposal many of the techniques they use today but, as we shall see, Silchester has produced much valuable information in spite of this.[2]

The earliest inhabitants of Silchester seem to date from the Belgic Iron Age and the first Roman town is believed to have been founded about A.D. 45, soon after the Claudian invasion. It stands at the junction of seven important Roman main roads which were all probably built within a few decades after A.D. 43 (fig. 149). In the town, the main east–west street was really part of the road from London to Caerleon and apart from this, no other early streets have yet been identified. They may not have been needed at this stage as the gravel surface of Silchester Common is naturally well-drained enough to carry light traffic. The first houses seem to have been sited haphazardly. Also to this period may belong the Public Baths, probably dating from the reign of Nero (A.D. 54–68), in which case they were one of the earliest buildings of this type constructed in Britain, four temples, and the Forum and Basilica built towards the end of the first century. Closer dating is difficult as the earlier excavators did not fully distinguish between different building periods. After Hadrian's visit in A.D. 122, if not earlier, Silchester, like so many other towns, seems to have taken stock of its situation and a proper town-plan was devised, with *insulae* bounded by a grid of new streets. A piece of inspired detective work based on the old excavation reports, a little fresh excavation and air photographs, has shown recently that it is possible to discriminate between the second- and first-century towns. It is clear that the older buildings lie out of alignment with the new street plan, three of the temples fitting in very awkwardly, while five feet of the portico of the first-century baths had to be demolished because it was in the way. In the Antonine period the town was provided with defences consisting

[1] See above p. 24.
[2] Conveniently collected in Boon (1957).

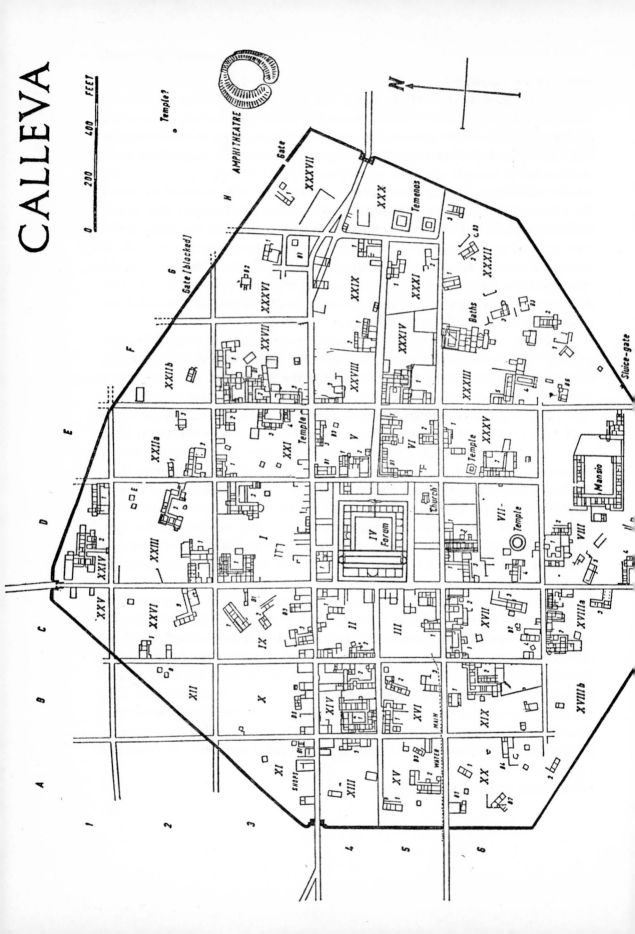

CALLEVA

FEET
0 200 400

Temple?

AMPHITHEATRE

Gate
XXXVII

Gate [blocked]

XXXVI

XXVII

XXIIb

XXIIa

XXIII

XXIV

XXV

XXVI

XII

X

XIV

XVI

XI

XIII

XV

XX

XIX

XVIIIb

XVIIIa

VIII

Mansio

VII
Temple

Church

Temple

XXXV

VI

V

XXI

Temple

I

IV
Forum

II

III

XVII

IX

XXVIII

XXXIII

XXXIV

XXIX

XXXI

Temenos

XXX

XXXII

Baths

Sluice-gate

MAIN
WATER

SHOPS

of a bank about 8 feet wide and a ditch 7 feet deep. These were later replaced in the late second or early third century by the stone wall which remains such an impressive feature of the site. It cuts across some of the streets, showing that the town had not expanded as much as the earlier planners had expected, and it encloses an area of 100 acres. The polygonal *enceinte*, consisting of stretches of wall of varying length meeting at an angle of about 45°, was probably designed to enclose all the built-up areas (fig. 8). Towards the end of the third century some of the town, including the Basilica, was burnt, possibly as the result of the battle between the rebel Allectus and the Emperor Constantius Chlorus.[1] Probably it was soon rebuilt. Alterations to the Public Baths suggest that urban life was still flourishing here in the mid-fourth century, and finds of coins and pottery show that occupation continued at Silchester into the fifth and possibly the sixth century. The town was not burnt down or sacked in the Dark Ages but seems to have fallen into gradual decay.

The Silchester excavations provide further material for the consideration in greater detail of the various public buildings usually erected in a Romano-British town. The largest and most important, of course, was the Forum or town centre, a large square in which public meetings might be held and where the governor might address the people if he visited the town. Public announcements, news items and advertisements were displayed for passers-by to study, business men met their clients there and poor men paid court to rich and influential ones. Grievances were ventilated and gossip exchanged. At Silchester the Forum and its associated buildings covered nearly two acres of ground and measured 275 by 313 feet (fig. 9). On three sides of the square there was a portico with carved Bath stone columns 14 or 15 feet high, supporting a low sloping roof. A similar portico surrounded the whole block of buildings on the outside, and the Forum was reached on the east side through a monumental entrance resembling a triumphal arch supported by more columns. This may have been the site of an important inscription carved on greyish-green Purbeck marble and picked out in red paint.[2] It only survives in small fragments and it was probably a dedication resembling the one from Wroxeter already noted. On one side of the entrance was a small room which may have contained a staircase leading to an upper floor. Eight rooms each about 22 feet square occupied the rest of the eastern range and may have been shops. Similar apartments were found along the north side, with a small subsidiary entrance leading into them. One room was subdivided, and next door to it was a room reduced in size by a semicircular wall in front of which may have stood a statue. On the southern side the rooms are larger and two of them had apsidal ends. In his

[1] See below p. 172. [2] R.I.B. 75.

8 **OPPOSITE** Plan of the Roman town, Silchester

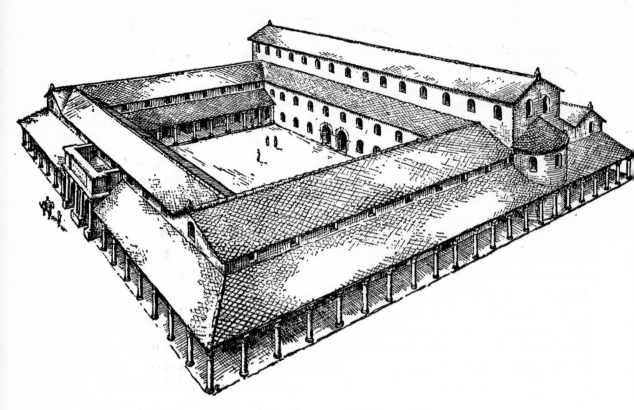

9 Imaginative reconstruction of the Forum and Basilica at Silchester
as seen from the north-east

book, *Roman Silchester*, Mr Boon points out that the excavations showed that
these rooms, and a square one between them, were apparently kept much
cleaner than the others; suggesting that they may have been for official use.
This would have been a convenient site for the offices concerned with taxation
and the checking of weights and measures.

The walls of the Forum were 3 to 4 feet thick and built of coursed flints
strengthened with tiles. The buildings may have stood about 45 feet high and
were roofed with tiles or else with slates of Pennant Grit or Old Red Sandstone.
The whole of the fourth side was occupied by the great Basilica or Town Hall
with a range of local government offices leading out of its west side. These
included the *curia* or council chamber of the *ordo*. Built about A.D. 100, the
Basilica measured $233\frac{1}{2}$ by 58 feet and so was larger than the London Guildhall.
At each end it had an apse with its floor built at a higher level, and in these apses
were probably the courts where the magistrates sat when they were dispensing
justice. The Basilica was entered from the inner portico of the Forum. Inside
the roof was supported on two rows of Bath stone columns, 27 feet high, and the

38

effect was that of a nave lit by clerestory windows with two side aisles with lower sloping roofs. The columns were surmounted by capitals decorated with acanthus foliage and belonging to the Corinthian order. They resemble columns found in the Rhineland, and were probably worked by Rhenish masons who may also have been responsible for some of the work on the great temple of Sulis-Minerva at Bath. The excavators noted numerous pieces of sandstone which had been used for sharpening the chisels and gouges, and also the holes for the timber scaffolding used in constructing the building. After the fire at the end of the third century, the Basilica was rebuilt in a simplified form which followed much the same ground plan. Little was recovered of the interior decoration, but the earlier building seems to have had a floor of red *tesserae* with more elaborate mosaics in the apse. The walls were gaily painted and pieces of white marble wall-veneers were found in the *curia*. Fragments of green glass from the clerestory windows were also noted. Statues probably played a part in the embellishment of the Forum and a fragment of bronze may come from a large figure of a first-century emperor. Three fragments of stone probably belong to a representation of the *tutela* or guardian goddess of the Atrebates, shown twice lifesize and wearing a crown in the shape of a city wall or tower. This may have stood in the *curia*. It was probably smashed when the Basilica was burnt down.

The Forum at another tribal capital, Venta Silurum (Caerwent in Monmouthshire), followed much the same plan as Silchester (fig. 10). It was correctly placed in the centre of the town at the point where the two main streets, the *cardo maximus* and the *decumanus maximus*, intersected, and it occupied a whole *insula*. An external portico was only found on the south, running on either side of the main entrance which had the usual monumental archway. The Forum had an internal colonnade on three sides, its roof supported by dwarf pillars standing on a low wall. Shops occupied the south and east sides and one in the corner close to the Basilica seems to have been an oyster bar or fishmongers' establishment. Pungent odours of fried fish may have emanated from it. On the west stood government offices of some kind, but at a later period a temple was built in the centre of the range, interrupting the colonnade and projecting into the courtyard. The Basilica on the south side was approached up a flight of three steps. It was smaller than the Silchester example but of much the same design, apart from the fact that the semicircular apses at each end were here replaced by rectangular rooms, cut off from the rest of the hall by dwarf walls supporting wooden screens. One of these rooms was heated; apparently the *duoviri iuredicundo* of the Silures felt the cold more keenly than their colleagues at Calleva. Columns with Corinthian capitals, gaily painted walls and concrete

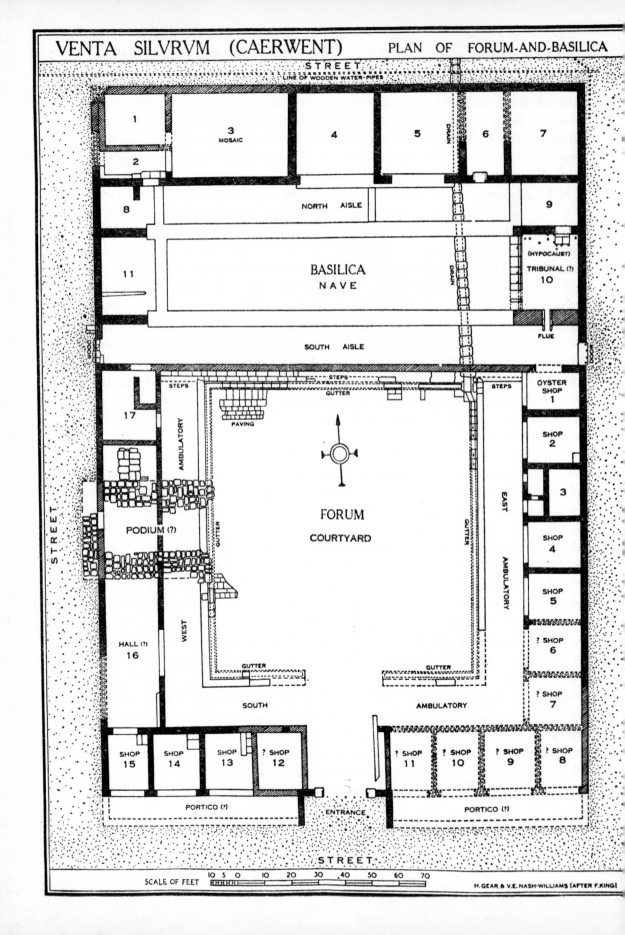

VENTA SILVRVM (CAERWENT)   PLAN OF FORUM·AND·BASILICA

STREET

LINE OF WOODEN WATER·PIPES

1

2

3
MOSAIC

4

5

DRAIN

6

7

8

NORTH   AISLE

9

11

BASILICA
NAVE

DRAIN

(HYPOCAUST)

TRIBUNAL (?)
10

FLUE

SOUTH   AISLE

DOOR

STEPS

STEPS

GUTTER

STEPS

OYSTER
SHOP
1

17

AMBULATORY

PAVING

SHOP
2

3

FORUM

COURTYARD

SHOP
4

EAST

AMBULATORY

PODIUM (?)

GUTTER

GUTTER

SHOP
5

? SHOP
6

WEST

? SHOP
7

HALL (?)
16

GUTTER

GUTTER

AMBULATORY

SOUTH

SHOP
15

SHOP
14

SHOP
13

? SHOP
12

? SHOP
11

? SHOP
10

? SHOP
9

? SHOP
8

PORTICO (?)

ENTRANCE

PORTICO (?)

STREET

STREET

SCALE OF FEET   10 5 0   10   20   30   40   50   60   70

H. GEAR & V.E. NASH·WILLIAMS (AFTER F.KING)

floors completed the interior decoration. The range of rooms behind the Basilica which probably included the *curia*, the registry, and the treasury, produced a mosaic floor, and walls with painted columns and panels above a dado of imitation marbling. On the south wall was scratched a *graffito*, 'Domitilla sends her sweetheart Victor her love', followed by the comment in another hand 'For shame'![1]

Fora have been excavated at other sites, including Wroxeter, Cirencester and Verulamium. Generally speaking, the British Forum and Basilica, as represented by the examples from Caerwent and Silchester, show a much simplified type of plan compared with those known from Italy and the South-European or North African provinces. It has been suggested that these British buildings may owe their design either to military architects influenced by the arrangements of the headquarters buildings in fortresses and forts or to the *fora* which had recently been built in Gaul. When considering the latter alternative we may recall the possibility of Rhenish masons being employed at Silchester. The Gaulish type of plan, however, is larger and more elaborate and usually includes a temple and its precinct placed in the middle of the courtyard. With the exception of Caerwent, where it seems to have been a subsequent addition, nothing of this kind has yet been found in Britain. Possibly the architects of the same government department which had recently designed *fora* specially suited to the needs of Gaul, went on to adjust their plans still further to allow for the resources or convenience of the Romano-Britons.[2]

Next in importance to the Forum and Basilica and one of the outstanding developments of Roman civilisation were the Public Baths. Every town of any importance had at least one set and often there were several, both publicly and privately owned. Their origin seems to lie far back in ancient Greece where, from the fourth century B.C. onwards, *gymnasia*, consisting of a courtyard surrounded by a covered colonnade, were in use for wrestling and other sports. Rooms for undressing and washing were placed close by and these gradually increased in importance. Originally they were heated by braziers, and with the appearance of the hypocaust in the first century B.C. they became a major feature. This form of heating is said by the Elder Pliny to have been the invention of a Roman called C. Sergius Orata; his last name may have been a nickname given on account of his fondness for golden trout (*auratae*). A well-known business

---

[1] V. E. Nash-Williams, 'The Forum and Basilica and Public Baths of the Roman Town of Venta Silurum', *Bull. of the Board of Celtic Studies* XV (1953) 159–63, fig. 2.
[2] For further consideration of Romano-British Fora see D. Atkinson, *Report on Excavations at Wroxeter 1923–7* (Oxford, 1942) p. 55 *et seq.*; R. Goodchild, 'Origins of the Romano-British Forum', *Antiquity* XX (1946) 70–7.

10 OPPOSITE Plan of the Forum and Basilica, Caerwent

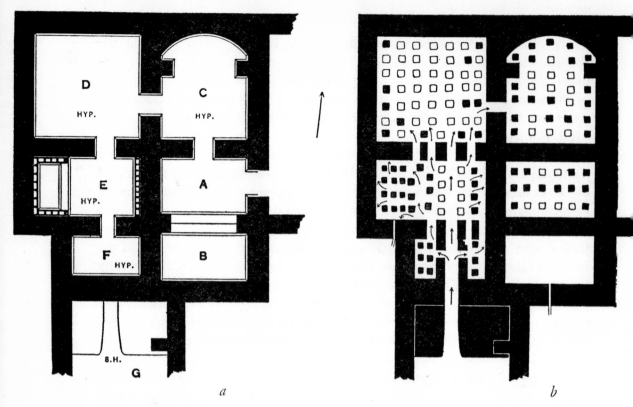

11 Plan of part of the Public Baths at Caerwent showing the arrangement of the hypocaust. *a* is the plan at floor-level, *b* the arrangement of the
pilae beneath the floors. The hot air came from the furnace and stoke-hole
(S.H.) at G.

man, he made much of his money from his oyster beds and he may have used
his new invention to heat stone fish tanks. Later it was adapted for domestic
heating. The rooms with a hypocaust have raised floors supported by small
pillars (*pilae*) of stone or of tiles about 7 to 10 inches square. Into the space
between the floor and ground level flows hot air from a furnace stoked from
outside the building. Sometimes only one room was heated but often several
benefited, the partition walls being carried on archways so that the heat could
continue to circulate under the floors (fig. 11).[1] A later refinement was the addition of flues in the shape of oblong box tiles open at each end, built into the
walls one above another so that heat could travel up them. So far no chimneys
have been certainly identified in Roman buildings nor do they appear on the
houses shown on reliefs or wall-paintings, it is therefore probable that the heat
and smoke from the hypocaust escaped up these channels through small gaps

[1] Forbes, VII (1958) p. 36 *et seq.*

in the flue-tiles and the exterior walls at ceiling height. Recent experiments have shown that a room 17 by 15 feet heated in this way, could easily be kept at an even temperature of 73°.[1] It took a day and a half for the floor to get thoroughly hot, but once this was achieved it was only necessary to stoke the furnace twice a day to maintain it. Charcoal, brushwood, coal occasionally, and all kinds of rubbish could be burnt in the furnaces. In Italy the hypocaust is usually only found in the baths, but in cooler climates such as Britain, its use for heating living rooms was soon appreciated. When a really high temperature was wanted people had to wear shoes with thick soles to protect their feet from the hot floors. The Younger Pliny relates an unpleasant tale of how Larcius Macedo, a cruel master, was attacked by the slaves at his villa and thrown upon the floor of the hot bath to find out whether he were really dead.[2]

For a good example of the Baths in a provincial town in Britain, we turn again to Silchester (fig. 12), where they were among the earliest of the buildings erected, possibly dating back to the reign of Nero. They seem to have had an imposing entrance through a portico supported by columns of Bath stone. Inside, the bather came first to an open courtyard 28 by 45 feet surrounded by colonnades. This was the *palaestra* or sports ground where all kinds of exercise could be taken and games played. Visiting the baths was an enjoyable social relaxation and people could stroll round the colonnades and meet their friends. Then, the bather would go into the *apodyterium* or undressing room, where clothes could be left in niches or lockers in charge of a slave. Next he went into a series of rooms each hotter than the last, the system closely resembling a modern turkish bath. First came the *frigidarium* with a water tank for those desiring a cold plunge and a large basin for others content with a douche (Pl. 11). Next the *tepidarium*, normally the heated room furthest from the furnace and so only slightly warmed, but at Silchester no trace of a hypocaust survives in this room from the early period, although one was added later. Possibly the room was heated with braziers. Thence one passed into the *caldarium* or hot room, with a hot-water bath next to the wall adjacent to the furnace. A basin of cold water to revive the bathers was probably placed in the apse at the other end of the room. Vitruvius in his famous treatise on Architecture directs that the basins for washing should be placed under a window, with plenty of space round them so that the bathers can see what they are doing and not get in each other's way. For those wanting a hotter, drier temperature, a small *sudatorium* was reached through an anteroom also leading out of the *tepidarium*. Having perspired to his satisfaction, the bather scraped the dirt and moisture off his skin with a hook-shaped bronze implement called a strigil (fig. 50a). After a dip in

[1] Boon (1957) p. 106. [2] *Epistulae* III. 14.

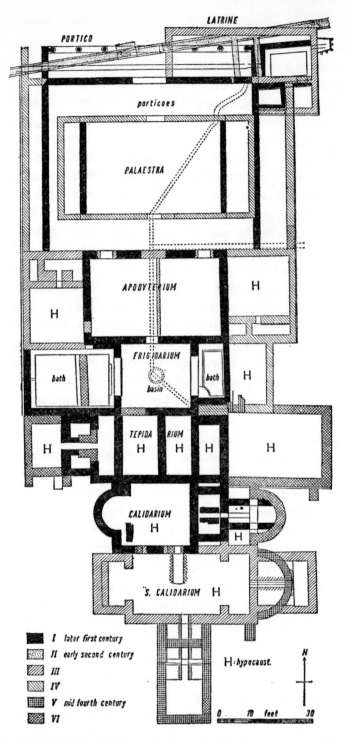

LATRINE

PORTICO

porticoes

PALAESTRA

APODYTERIUM

H

H

FRIGIDARIUM

bath basin bath

H

TEPIDARIUM

H H H H

H

CALIDARIUM

H

H

S. CALIDARIUM H

I later first century
II early second century
III
IV
V mid fourth century
VI

H:hypocaust.

N

0   10 feet   30

12   Plan of the Public Baths at Silchester

the hot bath he finally made his way back to the *frigidarium* for a cold douche before emerging. On the way he might find a slab or bench where he could lie down, and one of the bath attendants would come and massage him with perfumes and olive oil. These were most frequently carried in little spherical glass bottles with narrow necks and metal handles, often suspended together from a ring with the strigil (fig. 50*b*). Numerous fragments of such glass containers were found in the Silchester baths as well as nail cleaners, ear picks and tweezers for depilation (fig. 50*d*). The building continued in use for over 300 years and alterations and refurbishing belonging to six different periods were distinguished by the excavators. Among the additions was a second *caldarium* added in Period III, and until Period VI, dated to the late fourth century, we find a steady increase in size.[1]

The baths at Caerwent seem to have been of similar type and also to have had a long history. From the earliest period, dating from the late first or early second century, only the entrance with its portico and the courtyard with colonnades, probably the *palaestra*, have been found. In Period II (early second to third century), this seems to have been replaced by a large hall. Presumably a bath suite existed behind it but only the *frigidarium*, containing at one end a sunk cold water bath with a combined step and seat, has been identified. Adjoining it was a circular chamber with its floor at a depth of 7 feet, possibly a storage tank or cistern for the water supply. An *apodyterium* of third-century date probably belongs to Period III and it is only in Period IV (? fourth to fifth century) that we find the furnace, *caldarium* and *tepidarium*, appearing. Possibly the earlier versions of these rooms were destroyed when the surviving rooms were built.[2] Other baths of more elaborate type, with some of the rooms duplicated, are known from several sites but not in detail. At Wroxeter, the monumental bath-building underlying the later Forum seems to have been started soon after A.D. 90 and reached roof level, but then it was never completed. About A.D. 150 the townsfolk constructed another elaborate set of baths, partly by adapting and combining two earlier buildings, on the other side of the main street.[3] At Leicester, baths of the first half of the second century also overlie earlier structures. They were discovered when the Jewry Wall site was acquired by the corporation of Leicester for a twentieth-century bath building, fated never to be erected owing to a later decision to preserve the Roman structures *in situ*.

Another elaborate bathing establishment excavated at Lydney (Gloucestershire) was placed near a guest house built for the pilgrims to the Temple of Nodens (fig 13). Dating from the second half of the fourth century, its several

[1] Boon (1957) p. 101.   [2] Nash-Williams, *op. cit.* 163–7.
[3] D. Atkinson, *op. cit.* p. 25 *et seq.*

13 Reconstruction of the temple-settlement, Lydney, Gloucestershire

caldaria and *sudatoria* were heated by three different furnaces and seem to have been reached through an anteroom with a stone bench round the walls. Outside, the whole building was painted deep crimson, some of it covered by a later coating of greenish-yellow. Inside, the walls were plastered and painted, bands or panels of red and yellow being noted in the *frigidarium*. The floors were paved with stone slabs carefully fitted together, and one room, which may also have been a *frigidarium*, started life with a floor of red coloured cement or *opus signinum*. At a later period, a stone bench was constructed round its margins and the remaining space was then used as a basis for a fine geometric mosaic of *pelta* or amazon shield pattern in yellow, red, white and blue. Parts of this became worn and were roughly repaired with stone slabs. A small mosaic for the apse of one of the heated rooms shows a two-handled vase in a border of guilloche or cable pattern.[1] Decorative features such as wall-painting, marble basins and wall-veneers, and mosaics were customary in baths, and it is a pity that they have so rarely survived in Britain.

So far we have considered the larger and more important public baths. By way of contrast, it is interesting to compare with them a much smaller establish-

[1] Wheeler (1932) pp. 52, 66.

ment probably frequented by the visitors to the inn and the other inhabitants of a little Roman town at Godmanchester (Huntingdonshire). It was built in the late first century with the usual sequence of cold, warm and hot rooms. Before it was completed the plan was altered, probably to allow for a double set of baths for men and women respectively. In the late third or early fourth century, the building was burnt down and only a few rooms continued in use. These underwent some alterations and the baths were still being used at the end of the fourth century, if not later. In his study of the construction of this building, the excavator suggests that after the site had been cleared and levelled, foundations were marked out and dug to a depth of some 5 feet and the walls erected. Postholes provided proof that scaffolding was used as their height increased. The foundations for the hypocaust and bathroom floors followed, and then the roof. This may have been vaulted, as the walls of flint rubble and yellow mortar are strong, and both exterior and interior walls seem to be designed to carry a weight. Above ground level they were faced with Upware ragstone sawn into rectangular slabs, and then rendered with two undercoats containing crushed tile, separated by a layer of tiles $\frac{3}{4}$ inch thick. This use of crushed tile to improve the hydraulicity of the plaster agrees with the recommendations of the first-century Roman architect Vitruvius, for the defence of walls against damp. He also advised the use of vertical tiles in walls particularly exposed to moisture. These precautions were only recommended for the first three feet above the ground and sure enough, the remains of the Godmanchester walls, shown by their decoration to come from above the level of the dado, lack the tile layer and contain much less powdered tile in the rendering. On the outside, these walls had a red painted dado showing obvious signs of weathering and above it came cream paint splashed with buff spots, making quite a gay exterior. A reconstruction of the building is shown on fig. 14. Inside, a concrete raft of flints and mortar about 6 inches thick was constructed in the natural gravel, and covered with a hard core of broken tile and stone 4 to 12 inches in depth, as another precaution against damp. Over this came the waterproofed layer of red concrete made of sand, lime and crushed tile (*opus signinum*) used for the base of the floor of the hypocaust and for the plunge baths. This type of Roman construction is well-known for its strength, and here it proved so strong that it broke the point of a pneumatic drill when the site was later cleared. In room 2 a floor of grey and white *tesserae* was found, and the builders had taken care to ensure this against subsidence. First the level had to be raised with a layer of sand a foot thick, covered by a wooden floor of oak boards which acted as a raft. Next, came 6 inches of hard core, and the same depth of *opus signinum* carrying the *tesserae*. A similar floor in another room was covered with a $\frac{1}{2}$-inch

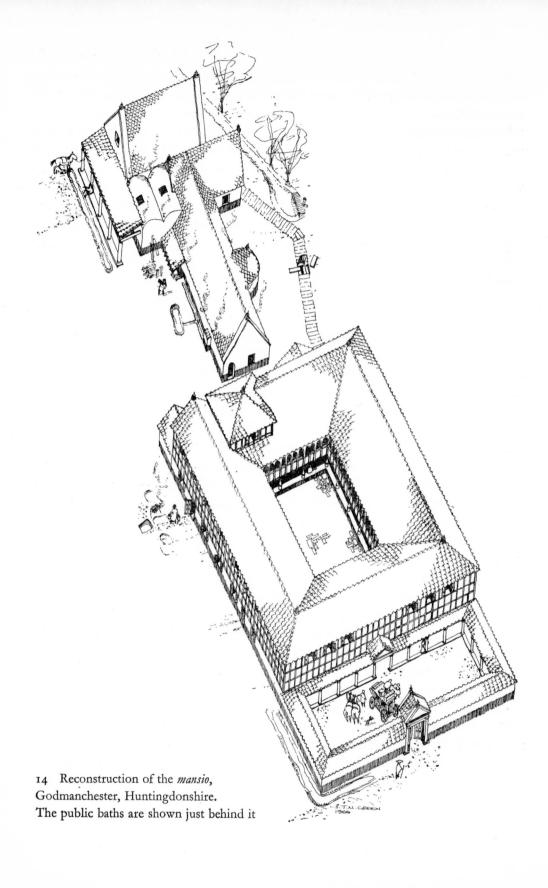

14 Reconstruction of the *mansio*,
Godmanchester, Huntingdonshire.
The public baths are shown just behind it

layer of deposit from the hard water used in the cold bath. In other rooms, the floors of *opus signinum* or hard white plaster had been polished. Much window glass of different periods was found on this site, lying on the ground where it had fallen from the windows. The bath house was roofed with Collyweston slates, graduated and increasing in size from ridge to eaves. One slate with traces of soot on its underside may come from above the point where smoke and hot air emerged from a wall flue.[1]

Just outside this building, the excavators found a small hoard of coins and jewellery buried in a pit, mixed up with rubbish from the rebuilding of the baths after the fire. The finds include a small bronze coin of Claudius pierced for suspension, and another larger one of the later first century, grooved, probably bitten, perhaps by a child. Most of the coins, however, are of third-century date. The jewellery comprises intaglios from rings showing Ganymede feeding an eagle and Mercury with a purse; a silver and four bronze rings; fifteen glass beads strung on wire, presumably part of a necklace or trimming from a garment; six bone pins, and a chain with a pendant. On each side of the pendant appears a crude *repoussé* design, probably a human mask, set in a filigree border. No pot or other container was found, but the collection of objects suggests the contents of a woman's trinket box, hastily buried for some unknown reason.[2]

Baths, as we have noted, were largely financed by public benefactors so that admission to them only cost the bather a very small fee. Children, soldiers, and sometimes slaves, were admitted free. Bathing establishments closed at sunset, their hours of opening varied, and were announced by ringing a bell. Certain hours earlier in the day might be reserved for women. Detailed directions to the lessee of some baths at a mining establishment in Portugal have survived, and from them we learn that a good supply of hot water had to be maintained in the hot rooms, sufficient fuel kept in readiness for the furnaces, and all bronze implements must be cleaned and coated with fresh grease every thirty days. If the baths were not kept running efficiently, the lessee would be fined by the procurator. Lucian, in his satiric dialogue *The Bath*, written in the second century, describes an ideal establishment sumptuously decorated and roomy; and, after enumerating the various hot and cold rooms, etc., he lists among the amenities copious illumination and full indoor lighting, exercising floor and cloak rooms. 'Moreover, it is beautified with all other marks of thoughtfulness

---

[1] H. J. M. Green, 'An architectural survey of the Roman baths at Godmanchester', *Arch. News Letter* VI (1959) 223–9. I am much indebted to Mr Green for unpublished information about this site and for his drawing (fig. 14) of the new reconstruction.
[2] *Ibid.* 'Romano-British hoard from Godmanchester', C.A.S.P. L (1957) 85–8.

with two toilets, many exits, and two devices for telling time, a water clock that makes a bellowing sound, and a sundial.'[1]

By way of contrast to this picture, one turns to the less appreciative one provided by Seneca. He lived and tried to write above a bathing establishment in a provincial town.

Imagine what a variety of noises reverberates about my ears! . . . When your strenuous gentleman, for example, is exercising himself by flourishing leaden weights; when he is working hard, or else pretends to be working hard, I can hear him grunt; and whenever he releases his imprisoned breath, I can hear him panting in wheezy and high-pitched tones. Or perhaps I notice some lazy fellow, content with a cheap rub down, and hear the crack of a pummelling hand on his shoulder, varying in sound according as the hand is laid on flat or hollow. . . . Add to this the arresting of an occasional roisterer or pickpocket, the racket of the man who always likes to hear his own voice in the bathroom, or the enthusiast who plunges into the swimming tank with unconscionable noise and splashing. . . . Then the cake-seller with his varied cries, the sausage man, the confectioner, and all the vendors of food hawking their wares, each with his own distinctive intonation.[2]

The baths were closely connected with another important public amenity, the provision of a water supply. Rivers and springs were used where they occurred conveniently, but the majority of Roman settlements in Britain depended very largely upon wells. These are frequently found and are very helpful to the archaeologist, as a remarkably large number of interesting objects were accidentally dropped into them. One well found in the Walbrook area of Londinium in 1949 contained an almost complete leather boot, metal handles from wooden buckets, bronze and jet bracelets, a lock and animal bones. The bottom was lined with chalk rubble, and on it was lying a coin of the Emperor Postumus (A.D. 259–68) dating these finds to the late third century. In such damp conditions leather, wickerwork and wooden objects may be preserved, and in this case the timber structure of the well itself has survived. Ten feet in depth, this lining was of heavy square-cut timbers carefully mortised together, increasing in size as they neared the bottom. Outside the timber work was a packing of chalk rubble. The actual well-head was constructed of light planks reinforced with struts at the corners. No doubt it was originally covered by a roof, and provided with a windlass for raising and lowering the buckets.[3]

Numerous examples of wells were found by the excavators at Silchester, where a plentiful water supply could be obtained by digging through the gravel subsoil to the underlying beds of sand and clay. Their depth varies with the lie

[1] L. and R. p. 228.   [2] *Epistulae Morales* LVI. Trans. E. P. Barker.
[3] Merrifield (1965) p. 270, no. 264.

of the land to between 8 and 30 feet, and they are believed to have held 5 to 11 feet of water. Usually, the shafts were $2\frac{1}{2}$ to $3\frac{1}{2}$ feet wide, and lined with flint near ground level. Below the flint work came a timber lining of split oak planks with clay rammed in behind them, resting on a wooden curb at the bottom. Sometimes old wooden barrels with the bottoms removed were used for these linings, and several of these survive in the museum at Reading. They probably arrived full of Bordeaux wine and are made of silver fir from the Pyrenees. A number of complete pots were recovered from these wells, together with a bronze jug and bronze bowls, leather shoes, a rope and part of a basket, remains of vegetation and even insects.[1]

In some cases the available supply from wells was insufficient and had to be augmented by means of aqueducts. In Britain, the best example so far found is the one discovered at Lincoln, designed to supply the *colonia* in its early days as the dwellers on the hilltop site could otherwise only obtain water from very deep wells. As far back as 1700, stretches of earthenware pipes had been noted outside the city running underground and extending for over a mile. A section of one of these pipes, now in the Lincoln Museum, is 3 feet long and $7\frac{1}{2}$ inches in diameter, narrowing at one end into a spigot which fitted into the wide end of the next pipe making a water-tight joint. Excavations from 1950 onwards showed that these pipes were sheathed in a very hard pink concrete and ran over a foundation of limestone slabs. Sand-filled post holes beneath this were intended for sighting posts required in setting out the course of the aqueduct, and for determining the gradient of the pipe line, a practice paralleled in modern pipe-laying. Their course was traced to a stream known as Roaring Meg which had been dammed in Roman times to produce a pool. For the first stages of their journey they were carried across difficult ground on stone piers rising to 8 feet in height, probably spanned by timbering rather than by an arch. Then they were supported on a solid bank until they reached the point at which they went underground. A pump placed in some form of pump-house would have to lift the water 10 feet to gain enough pressure to force it through the pipeline to the reservoir at Lincoln. Probably a double-action force pump was used, as the remains of an installation of this type was found at Silchester consisting of two lead cylinders 22 inches long and 3 inches in diameter, mounted on either side of a block of wood hollowed out to contain a bell-shaped reservoir 7 by 5 feet (fig. 15). Two pistons, manipulated by rods and handles from the surface, worked alternately in the cylinders, forcing water into them by opening and shutting leather flap-valves at the lower end. The water then passed through holes in the sides into the central reservoir, and then up the supply pipe known

[1] Boon (1957) p. 159.

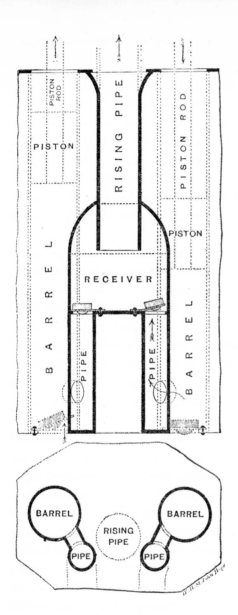

15   Conjectural restoration of the force-pump found at Silchester

as a 'trumpet'. It is suggested that with the Lincoln aqueduct such a pump could lift the water from the pool at the rate of 10 gallons per minute. Some of this may have been lost, but even so, a sixteen-hour day at five gallons a minute would produce 5,000 gallons. A larger pump could have doubled this figure, and the lack of sedimentation in the pipes suggests that some form of settling tank existed, showing that the aqueduct was indeed intended to provide drinking water.[1] The force pump was probably invented by Ctesibus in the second

[1] For the Lincoln aqueduct see F. Thompson, *Roman Lincoln* 1945–54 (Lincoln, 1955); and in *Arch. J.* CXI (1954) 106 *et seq*. The Silchester force pump is discussed in Boon (1957) p. 160.

century B.C., it is well described by Vitruvius,[1] and examples are known from elsewhere in the Empire.[2]

By the beginning of the third century the *colonia* at Lincoln had spread down the hill, and in 1953 excavations in the High Street revealed a large octagonal water tank built of massive limestone blocks and waterproofed with *opus signinum*. It was surrounded by a carefully laid pavement of contrasting orange-coloured Lias slabs and seems to have been a public fountain, possibly supplied by a branch pipeline from the main aqueduct.[3] Details of the tanks or water tower from which the supply of water from the aqueduct was distributed remain undiscovered. In Rome, the water from the great aqueducts was collected in numerous tanks or *castellae* and then distributed to three classes of user: the emperor—whose share also supplied the public baths; private consumers who paid a water rate; and public utilities including barracks and official and public buildings, theatres, cisterns and fountains. The overflow from fountains and baths was used for flushing drains. Pipes for private consumers were limited in size, usually made of lead, and carefully stamped by the inspectors of the water board. Unauthorised tapping of the mains was a serious offence and, in case of water shortage, private supplies could be cut off so that baths and public buildings might have priority. Elaborate systems of pipes supplying water to public baths and private houses have been found at Pompeii and bronze taps for both hot and cold water are known from Bienne (Switzerland) and Rottweil (Germany). Sometimes taps were decorated with model cocks or small animals, and their spouts frequently took the form of lions' heads.[4]

Recognisable *castellae* are so far lacking in Romano–British towns but some interesting tanks at the head of pipelines have been found on military sites including Fendoch, Lyne and High Rochester. One fine example of a *castellum aquae* was found in the fort at Benwell on Hadrian's Wall, supplied by an underground conduit with a gravitational flow of water from a spring on high ground at Denton Hill Head, three miles away. It was constructed in the courtyard of the headquarters building in the position often occupied by a well on sites where water was more readily available. The water flowed into five tanks leading out of each other. The first two acted as filter beds overflowing through channels near the top into no. 3. From here the water passed into nos. 4 and 5 through a series of small masonry ducts cut near the top, in the middle, and at

---

[1] *De Architectura* X. 7.
[2] A force pump made of bronze, found at Bolsena in Etruria, may now be seen in the British Museum.
[3] F. Thompson, *op. cit.*; *J.R.S.* XLVI (1956) 23.
[4] K. Kretzschmer, 'La Robinetterie romaine', *Rev. Arch. de l'Est* XI (1960) 89–113.

the bottom of the cross-walls. The object of these was to aerate the water which had grown flat and dead on its long journey, and so deliver it in sparkling and palatable condition. Platforms built out into tanks 3, 4 and 5 at some period after their construction would enable a number of men to draw water at a time. In this connection it is interesting to remember that Benwell was occupied by the cavalry with horses to water as well as soldiers' thirsts to quench— when offered nothing better.[1]

Another method of bringing water to a town was by means of an open conduit or water course. A good example of this fed Durnovaria (Dorchester, Dorset), one of the tribal centres of the Durotriges. Long stretches of it still exist and are scheduled as an ancient monument; and, as the engineers had to follow a winding course to maintain a slight slope, it is more than eight miles long. In the town itself it ran in a channel 4 feet wide, lined with masonry walls and a tiled floor and was probably covered in. It dates from the end of the first century A.D. and was only in use for about a hundred years. As Dorchester can be easily supplied with water by means of wells, the conduit may have been an ambitious project of the city fathers, allowed to fall into disuse when it proved an unnecessary expense.[2] The army made a much better job of supplying the fort at Greatchesters in this manner. Their aqueduct starts at the Haltwhistle burn just over two miles off, and winds its way for six carefully surveyed and well-engineered miles.[3] Such skilled engineers seem to have been lacking at Leicester where a similar type of aqueduct appears to have been attempted with insufficient slope so that in spite of some raising of the channel, it must have been a failure. Further investigation, however, may show that it was more skilfully designed than at present seems to be the case. A later attempt to supply the baths with water from the river raised by a force-pump or water-wheel to a water-tower also seems to have been unsuccessful, and the enormous number of fragments of large jars found in the Leicester excavations suggest that carrying up water by hand was the only solution.[4] Wall is another site which may have had an aqueduct and possibly a water-tower,[5] and the baths at Lydney seem to have been fed from a tank nearly 20 feet square through a stone-lined conduit, carefully zigzagged to control the flow down a steep slope.[6]

[1] F. G. Simpson and I. A. Richmond, 'The Roman fort on Hadrian's Wall at Benwell', *Arch. Ael.* 4S XIX (1941) 14 *et seq.*
[2] K. Kenyon, 'The Roman Aqueduct', *Ant. J.* XX (1940) 435–9.
[3] Richmond (1957) p. 152.
[4] Kenyon (1948) pp. 34, 40.
[5] G. Webster, 'The bath-house at Wall', B.A.S.T.P. LXXIV (1958) 20; F. W. Robins, *The Story of Water-Supply* (1946) p. 74 *et seq.*
[6] Wheeler (1932) p. 54.

16 Altar to the Nymphs and Fountains, Chester

Another aqueduct must have supplied the townsfolk of Wroxeter where water-mains have been uncovered running along several streets. They date from between A.D. 160–275 and include lead pipes showing signs of repairs in places where they have burst. Another system involved the use of wooden pipes, connected by metal collars consisting of cylinders of iron with sharp edges and a central stop-ridge, hammered into place so that the edges penetrated the wood and made the joint water-tight. Complete wooden pipes of this type are preserved in the London Museum and made of squared oak baulks $7\frac{3}{4}$ inches by $4\frac{1}{2}$ feet, pierced by a central channel with a diameter of $1\frac{3}{4}$ feet, connected by the same type of iron collars. Caerwent also produced iron collars from water mains and lead piping; and lead pipes from Chester bear a stamp showing that they were made at the beginning of the governorship of Agricola in A.D. 79 (fig. 93a). They probably led to a water supply $1\frac{1}{4}$ miles away where an altar has been found dedicated to the spirits of the Nymphs and Fountains (fig. 16).[1]

Some of the Wroxeter water seems to have flowed along Watling Street in an open gutter from which supplies could be drawn off through sluices for household purposes. In one house, a long covered water-channel was found leading from the main, the water being diverted into it by opening and shutting a sluice gate. It ran under a portico and one room, and then along the side of the house to the back. Here there was a latrine constructed by digging out the soil for several feet below ground level. The flooring and a row of wood or stone seats were constructed over this pit and the water channel entered at one end, passed under the seats and out the other side, and then continued as a drain down to the river.[2] Other towns have also produced traces of drains and sewers. A fine vaulted tiled drain can be seen at Colchester running from near the Castle, down the hill and out of the north-east gate. It was probably used to drain off

[1] R.I.B. 460.
[2] Bushe-Fox (1916) p. 12 et seq.

surplus rainwater and may have finished up in the town ditch. Another drain, possibly a water conduit, was found on the south side of the temple, and this had an opening with a stone manhole cover.[1] A main sewer running north to south and built of stone blocks covered with flat slabs was identified at Lincoln, with lateral sewers leading off and house-drains 14 feet square running into it. Manholes for inspection and cleaning by slaves or criminals were also noted.[2] By way of contrast, Silchester seems to have had no drains apart from street gutters or wooden pipes for rainwater; and the inhabitants had to dig cesspits in the gravel.

It is to be hoped that some day we may know more about these drains and water supplies as the subject was of considerable interest to the Romans. In Rome itself, the magistrates were originally responsible for it, until regulations laid down in the time of the Emperor Augustus set up a water board with a chairman of consular rank, the *curator aquarum*, and a staff of high-ranking technicians, architects, clerks and many slaves. Several of Britain's first-century governors, including Didius Gallus and Petronius Turpilianus, had held this important post, and another, Julius Frontinus, is famous for the thesis on Aqueducts which he wrote after being *curator aquarum* in A.D. 97–8. He was very proud of these great public works, remarking 'with such an array of indispensable structures carrying so many waters, compare, if you will, the idle pyramids or the useless, though famous, works of the Greeks!'[3] Indeed, the great Roman aqueducts carrying water across the countryside on arched constructions of masonry where the supplies could not be conveyed underground, are not a feature of Italy alone. In Western Europe they can also be seen in France and Spain, notably at the Pont du Gard and at Segovia.

The taste and purity of water was also considered as well as the best ways of locating it. The Elder Pliny gives some advice on the subject and Vitruvius devotes several chapters of his book on Architecture to it. Water is often to be found, he notes, in misty places and where water-loving vegetation such as alder, willows, and reeds flourish. In such places a hole 5 feet deep should be dug and a bronze basin smeared with oil buried upside down at sunset and covered with reeds and earth. If there are drops of water in the bowl next morning, water will be found thereabouts. Alternatively, an unbaked clay vessel or a fleece might be buried and, if the spot were suitable, the damp could be wrung out of the fleece and the bowl would fall to pieces. Water from springs found in flat country was apt to be flat, tepid or salt; mountain springs, especi-

[1] Hull (1958) pp. 87, 175.
[2] Richmond (1947b) 36.
[3] *De aquis urbis Romae* I. 16. Trans. C. E. Bennett.

ally those facing north, produced the sweetest and coldest water. The effect of certain mineral waters on health was also realised and a list of springs with special properties is included. These include a spring in Arcadia which made the people who drank of it abstemious, and was injurious to vines, and a small spring at Susa whose waters could cause people to lose their teeth. Before deciding to use a spring for an aqueduct or other water-supply the people who live near it should be examined; if they look healthy, the local water should be satisfactory. Green vegetables boiled in such water should cook quickly.[1]

Among the buildings we would expect to find in a town of any size would be restaurants, wine-shops, and one or more inns or hotels. Probably some travellers would receive hospitality from friends, but there must have been numerous strangers travelling on business who arrived in need of refreshment or of a lodging for the night. Some idea of the kind of facilities which might be provided can be obtained by considering examples excavated at Ostia and Pompeii, as they give us a clear picture of the type of establishments which probably existed elsewhere in the Empire. At Ostia the traveller visiting one well-known bar in the Via di Diana would find it had small seats on either side of the doorway, and space for customers to stand there drinking. At the entrance were two masonry counters meeting each other at right angles; these are the structural features which usually survive and help the archaeologist to identify a bar, and they are also found in the shops at the corners of most of the cross roads at Pompeii and Herculaneum. The counter at Ostia was covered with thin marble slabs and two stone basins were placed on it. Inside, tiers of shelves were used to display food and above them is a wall-painting of fruit and vegetables. Beneath the counter three large wine jars still stand and others are stacked nearby. At the back of the shop, three bronze hooks found screwed into a marble slab on the rear wall, may have been used for hanging up clothes. At Pompeii and Herculaneum, jars and basins were often let into the counters and filled with stews and other food, heated in adjacent kitchens or on hearths in the corner of the shop, and hot water would also be available. Strings of sausages and bunches of fruit were hung round the walls and above the counter. One Pompeian wine shop was decorated with pictures of the guests, and among them is a painting showing a party of travellers, still wrapped in their cloaks, seated on stools round a three-legged table, enjoying their wine. A small boy is waiting on them and above their heads sausages, a ham and other eatables hang from nails. Comments painted on the walls in the same house include a request for a little water to mix with the wine, and a complaint that the landlord sells watered wine while drinking it undiluted himself. Larger establishments

[1] *De Architectura* VIII. 1, 5.

provided more elaborate meals, served in dining-rooms with couches where guests could recline.

For the traveller needing a bed for the night, there were inns like the second-century example still to be seen at Ostia. It consists of a rectangular central courtyard, with one long room for a dormitory and a small room for the inn-keeper on one side and on the other, a large room which seems to have been used as a stable because it was provided with a drinking trough. Small rooms on the upper floor, reached by a staircase, may also have been to let. At Pompeii we have proof that inns, as in mediaeval and modern times, were named after animals, as one example has an inscription outside it telling us that Sittius restored the Elephant, with the elephant's picture above it. This repainted sign, however, does not seem to have attracted enough custom as another painted notice nearby begins 'Inn to let—*Triclinium* with three couches . . .' the rest is illegible.[1] Inns were frequently situated near the city gates so that merchants could drive up and unload the heavy wagons which were not allowed on the streets. Also in Pompeii is the small inn of Hermes near the Stabian gate, in what must have been a very busy and noisy quarter. It was an oblong building entered through a wide doorway with a bar on either side. On the right, stairs led to the upper rooms and behind the stairs were a hearth and a water heater. Three dormitories were partitioned off on the ground floor, and the rest of the space was presumably occupied by the parked wagons, with a small stable for the animals at the back complete with the water trough. Hay or other fodder must have been provided for them.

A larger inn nearer the Forum had a big central room which probably served as a dining-room, entered directly from the street. Six bedrooms and a small kitchen opened off it with the usual stable at the rear. The names of several guests were found scratched on the bedroom walls; two friends, Lucifer and Primigenius, sharing one room and four actors, one named Martial, another. This room also contains a *graffito*, telling us that 'Here slept Vibius Restitutus all by himself, his heart filled with longings for his Urbana'. Eupor and nineteen friends seem to have held gay parties at this inn on three occasions. Next door was a bar with a separate dining-room.

As well as these actual buildings found in Italy, some Gaulish tombstones and place-names provide evidence for the existence of inns and innkeepers, and there is one inscription which seems to be an invitation to the traveller to read the menu or wine list displayed outside a restaurant.[2] Certain of these discoveries may refer more to the country inns found along the Roman roads, connected

[1] Mau-Kelsey (1902) p. 400 *et seq.*
[2] T. Kleberg, *Hôtels, restaurants et cabarets dans l'antiquité romaine* (Upsala, 1957).

with the *mansio* or posting station where the messengers of the imperial post changed horses.[1] In some cases, travellers seem to have journeyed with their own tents and other equipment, and some small settlements may have provided little but shelter and cooking facilities. The Antonine Itinerary, a third-century road-book which has come down to us with later additions, includes a number of routes giving the names of the posting stations in various parts of the Roman Empire. Some of these have been identified in Britain, e.g. Venonae (High Cross) at the intersection of Watling Street and the Fosse Way. Along Stane Street, the Roman road from Chichester to London, excavation has shown that these posting stations seem to have been placed about twelve miles apart. They vary in size from $2\frac{1}{2}$ to 4 acres and consist of a bank surrounding a rectangular enclosure, with the road running through the middle of it. Two Sussex sites excavated at Hardham and Alfoldean produced traces of stables, cart sheds and simple living accommodation. Hardham was occupied from about A.D. 50 to 150, when the *mansio* may have been moved to Pulborough. Alfoldean, which stood near a bridge over the river Arun, seems to have continued in use for three hundred years. Posting stations of this kind may perhaps be compared with the small country inns used by later stage coaches; and this analogy can be carried further when we imagine the scenes at the inns in the towns when the travellers were demanding their fresh horses, and the carriages and wagons were being led out and loaded up.

Our best British parallel to the Roman inns already described is a site at Silchester standing just inside the south gate. It is far larger than any of the private houses and is built round three sides of a courtyard. A large entrance flanked with pillars in the centre of the north side admitted the visitor into a spacious vestibule, leading him either into the court or along corridors to apartments which may have been private suites, each comprising two large and two small rooms. At least five of these suites were found in the north and south wings. On the west side of the courtyard were larger rooms, three of them heated. This part of the building seems to have been altered at various times. Kitchens may have been placed at the north end with a staircase to an upper storey. Outside, another building may have been a stable and wagon shed, complete with a fodder store. On the east, the rectangle of the courtyard was completed by a wall with a walled garden or another court beyond it. On the further side of this was a large suite of baths reached by a corridor leading from the south wing of the inn. Two heated apsidal rooms and an anteroom seem to have been the earliest part of the bath building, as they are slightly out of alignment with the rest, larger rooms, both heated and unheated, and a latrine

[1] See below p. 390.

being added at a later date. Water seems to have been supplied from a reservoir 6 feet square, fed by springs.[1]

So far no other towns have produced such a good example of what was probably an inn as Silchester; but another possibility is known from Caerwent. It is a large house with over forty rooms which stood near the South gate on the site of an earlier dwelling. It was approached through an outer yard with an entrance 8 feet 4 inches wide through which traffic could turn in from the narrow street. This yard seems to have been a later feature, added, perhaps, as a wagon park. Room 3 leading off the yard had a hearth and may have been the inn kitchen and more hearths were found in room 35 on the other side of the courtyard.[2] Apart from the recently excavated site at Godmanchester (fig. 14) there is little other evidence, although towns such as London and Verulamium must have possessed establishments of similar size or larger. Smaller inns would be difficult to identify, but a lodging house for seamen is believed to exist among the buildings recently uncovered at the Roman port of Caister-near-Yarmouth (Norfolk).[3] The only other large building of this nature so far discovered in Roman Britain was probably not intended for either the official traveller or the casual wayfarer. It is one of the structures built in the fourth century inside the Iron Age hill fort at Lydney (fig. 13). The other buildings included the baths already mentioned and the temple,[4] and it is believed that this guest house may have sheltered visiting pilgrims. Like the Silchester inn it had a quadrangular plan and was built round a courtyard, and it may have had an upper storey. Entering on the south side the visitor came into a large hall, and we can imagine a party of new arrivals crowding in here, and then being led into the courtyard or along the inner corridors to the suites of small rooms in the west and north wings, some with mosaic floors and painted walls. On the east side there seems to have been a large stable and wagon-shed. A short distance from the guest house is the separate bath building, placed at the end of a long corridor.[5]

The inn at Silchester was situated just inside the south gate, a reminder that many towns in Roman Britain were defended against raiders in times of unrest by earthworks or walls, although the reasons for the erection of these fortifications are still not fully understood. No town could build defences without government permission, and while they may sometimes have formed an outlet for urban pride, such works must have been a heavy burden on local resources. Government subsidies and advice from military architects may well

---

[1] Boon (1957) p. 116 *et seq.*
[2] T. Ashby, 'Excavations at Caerwent', *Arch.* LIX (1905) 299.
[3] *J.R.S.* XLIII (1953) 122. [4] See below p. 462. [5] Wheeler (1932) p. 44 *et seq.*

have been necessary and the problem remains, why, if defences were built as a result of government orders, did some towns have them, and not others?

Little evidence exists for fortifications in the first century. Colchester is known to have been an open city when Boudicca attacked it, and so was London. Verulamium, however, had a defensive bank and ditch, at least by the last quarter of the century, and these may even have been constructed to enclose the new *municipium* in the reign of Claudius, or else been an emergency measure in the time of Boudicca. Early in the second century they were levelled and filled in.[1] Silchester also had first-century earthworks, and there are possibilities at one or two other sites.[2]

The second half of the second century, however, seems to have been the chief period for building defences of this type. Some towns appear to have constructed them earlier than others, but it must be emphasised that the dating of town defences is a difficult task depending upon good fortune in recovering useful chronological material during excavations. Recent work at Cirencester has shown that a rampart and two ditches surrounded the town at this period, crossed by a bridge on the east side, where the river Churn had been diverted outside the main built-up area. The east or Verulamium gate seems to have been built in stone on a monumental scale with two D-shaped towers. Passages for pedestrians and light traffic flanked two wider carriage-ways. Fragments of carved mouldings and of a large column drum are proof of architectural decoration, showing that this structure was not erected in a hurry.[3] It is either contemporary with the earthwork defences or may even be slightly earlier. Was it constructed as a free standing stone monument, does it show a change of plan in the building of defences due to some emergency, or does it, perhaps, indicate financial miscalculations? Earthworks would be comparatively quick and cheap to erect, not so stone buildings.

Some similar situation may have existed at Verulamium. There the stone built London and Chester gates are comparable in plan to the Verulamium gate at Cirencester, and seem to be associated with the rampart known as the Fosse Earthwork which enclosed part of the north-western area of the growing city. This earthwork, however, seems never to have been completed, as extensive searches have been made for it in vain. Did the emergency pass while it was still under construction? Parallels to the gates may exist at Silchester and at Lincoln and their plan echoes early Roman town gates built in France at Autun, Arles and Nîmes. Earthwork defences dated to the second century have also

[1] Frere (1964b) 104.
[2] J. Wacher (1964) p. 106; *ibid.* ed. (1966) p. 62.
[3] J. Wacher (1961) 65.

17 Reconstruction of the Balkerne Gate, Colchester

been found at other sites including Rochester, Dorchester (Dorset) and Kenchester. At present Dorchester (Oxfordshire) dated to *c.* A.D. 185, and Chichester at *c.* A.D. 200 are the latest in the series.[1] Normally these gates were probably timber built.

The crisis, whether due to unrest in Wales or further north, or to the unsuccessful attempt of Clodius Albinus, the governor of Britain, to usurp the Empire in A.D. 196, may have passed. However, events such as the devastation caused in the north by the barbarian inroads which followed Albinus' departure to the continent may have caused the Roman government to give further consideration to the advisability of town defences for Britain. The Roman walls which are still such an imposing sight at Colchester (Pl. 5), London, Verulamium, Silchester and other sites appear at the end of the second or during the third century, probably mostly built between *c.* A.D. 230 and 280, but here again the chronology is uncertain. The walls of the *colonia* at Colchester may come early in the series. They have a circumference of two miles enclosing an area of 108 acres and were built with a concrete core, faced with roughly squared blocks of septaria stone and laced together with tile coursing. They are 8½ feet thick, 11 feet thick at foundation level, and still survive to a height of 10 to 15 feet. At least six gates and two posterns have been identified, as well as small internal towers which may have contained steps leading up to the rampart. Much can still be seen of the West or Balkerne Gate, described as a 'positively theatrical stage-setting for the principal entry to the town'.[2] This has two footways and also two carriage-ways, each 17 feet wide (fig. 17) and the reconstruction accepts the fact that carriage-ways of such unusual width demand lofty arches not less than 25½ feet high. This would make the floor level of the upper storey at least 27 feet above the road. Quadrant-shaped guard-rooms exist

[1] J. Wacher (1964) 104; *ibid.* ed. (1966) p. 62.
[2] Hull (1958) p. xxix.

62

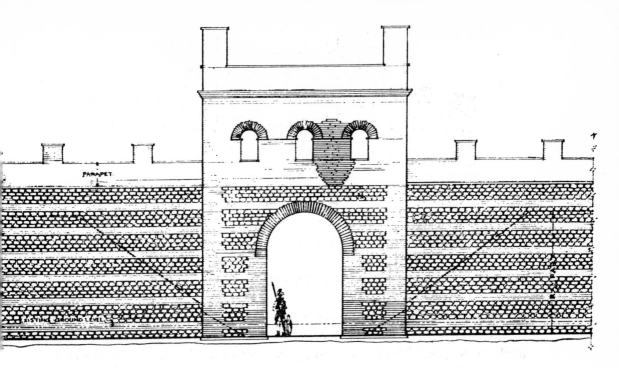

18 Reconstruction of the North-East Gate, Colchester

on either side, and over all was a first-floor gate-house covering the whole gate. Traces of pilasters were found which must have supported some lost architectural decoration. As in the case of the London (Pls. 8, 9) and Chester gates at Verulamium, the Balkerne Gate echoes earlier designs in France and Italy, and further research might even yet prove it to be contemporary with an earlier earthen rampart which still awaits discovery. After all, the *coloniae* at Lincoln and Gloucester seem to have had second-century defences, but these cities, of course, probably reconditioned the ramparts of the legionary fortresses which preceded them. Remains of the small north-east gate on the other side of Colchester show that it consisted of a single-arched passage-way 10 feet 8 inches wide. Much of the tiled outer face of the tower which surmounted it was found lying on the ground nearby, including fragments of two windows. This evidence has been used in an attempted reconstruction (fig. 18). Doors in the tower led out onto the rampart walk.

At Silchester, similar small gates on the north and south admitted travellers who had come along the less-frequented minor roads. The East and West gates, however, on the important roads from London and Wales, had dual carriage-ways each 13 feet wide and guard-rooms on either side with towers above, but no passage-ways (fig. 19). Evidence was found for wooden doors about 4$\frac{1}{2}$ inches thick. Three postern gates, consisting of simple passage-ways,

19   Reconstruction of the West Gate, Silchester

are also known. The walls were originally about 20 feet high, built of flint rubble faced with dressed flints with bonding courses of Bath stone. Outside, a ditch varying in width from 25 to 45 feet was probably crossed by causeways.[1]

At Verulamium, flint walls with tile bonding courses backed by an internal earth-bank were erected probably sometime in the first quarter of the third century, although earlier and later dates have been suggested. Outside, a ditch 30 feet wide and 20 feet deep was dug 15 feet away, as an additional precaution. Unlike the earlier defences which had depended on the river for part of their protection, the new wall completely enclosed the city. The London (Pl. 8) and Chester gates were incorporated and new gates built, including the south-west or Silchester gate, with one wide central roadway and passages for pedestrians on either side. Triumphal arches to commemorate the limits of the original *municipium* were also probably erected within the city at this time.[2]

Walls built of stone are known from sites such as Brough-on-Humber, Lincoln, Cirencester or Exeter.[3] Extensive stretches survive at Caerwent where interior projections or counterforts probably indicate the whereabouts of steps up to the ramparts. Gates consisting of a single archway without guard-rooms, were blocked up at some period.[4] Excavations at Great Casterton (Rutland) uncovered a stone wall dated to *c*. A.D. 195, protected by a deep ditch 21 feet wide cut out of solid rock.[5] During the fourth century *c*. A.D. 350, this ditch was

[1] Boon (1957) p. 84 *et seq.*   [2] Frere (1964a) 71; *ibid.* (1962) 153.
[3] A. Fox, *Roman Exeter* (Manchester, 1952) p. 20.
[4] V. E. Nash-Williams, 'Further Excavations at Caerwent', *Arch.* LXXX (1930) 229–88.
[5] For this and a general discussion of later Romano-British defences see P. Corder, 'The Reorganisation of the Defences of Romano-British Towns in the Fourth Century', *Arch. J.* CXII (1956) 20–42.

filled up with material from a new ditch 60 feet wide, cut through the rock a little distance away. Some of this rock was also used to build rectangular bastions at the vulnerable angles of the town walls. About this time, ditches were re-dug and bastions added on other sites, including London, Aldborough (Yorkshire), Brough-on-Humber, Cirencester, Kenchester and Chichester. At Caerwent, the bastions were semi-octagonal in plan and probably had timber flooring at the level of the rampart walk which was reached by means of a ladder. The ground floor space may have been used as a store.

These additions reflect a change in defensive tactics. At Great Casterton the late second-century wall is presumed to be about 18 feet high and its chief defence is the steep-sided ditch designed to prevent the erection of scaling ladders (fig. 20). It was within easy range of the spears and arrows of the townsfolk, and together the wall and ditch were intended to frustrate surprise attacks, not to withstand a siege. In the fourth century the threat was greater and the waves of raiding Picts, Scots (from Ireland) or Saxons, larger and better organised. The townsfolk may still have rallied to their own defence, but now their efforts were assisted and manpower was saved by the use of artillery. This consisted of the *ballista*, really an enormous bow mounted on a wooden frame which hurled either an iron-headed bolt or a stone ball 6 to 8 lbs in weight. This device had been used by the Roman army for centuries. Now, in the fourth century, it was used in towers or bastions which were provided with floors at rampart level to act as a firing platform. Because it was difficult to aim a *ballista* at an enemy near the foot of a wall, the ditch was moved further away so that the attacking forces would be caught at the most effective range. Several *ballistae*, probably a couple, were mounted on swivels in each tower, firing out of lateral windows so that the whole area near the walls was in the field of fire. Four men were needed to fire them, and the towers had to be roofed as the *ballista* cords must be kept dry.

Whether the towns possessed garrisons at any time is unknown. The discovery that an early fort formed part of Roman London may indicate their presence in a few important centres. Elsewhere, once the army had established itself in Wales and along the northern frontier, a few veterans or low-grade soldiers may possibly have manned the guard-rooms at the gates and generally acted as police, backed up by the able-bodied townsfolk when necessary. Until the large-scale raids began in the fourth century, the need for protection was slight and usually only arose when a governor or other pretender to the imperial purple persuaded the army in Britain to support his claims, and follow him to the continent to give battle to the legitimate ruler. This left the province denuded of troops and vulnerable to the attacks of the tribes north of Hadrian's Wall.

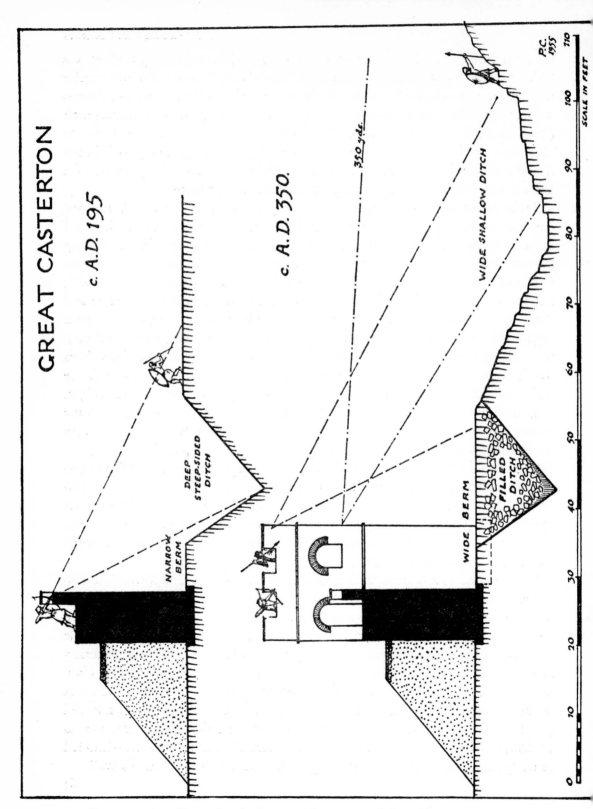

GREAT CASTERTON

c. A.D. 195

c. A.D. 350.

DEEP STEEP-SIDED DITCH

NARROW BERM

WIDE BERM

FILLED DITCH

WIDE SHALLOW DITCH

350 yds.

P.C. 1955

SCALE IN FEET

0 10 20 30 40 50 60 70 80 90 100 110

20 Reconstructions illustrating the late second-century and the mid-fourth-century defences at Great Casterton

The exact date and circumstances of the fourth-century reconstructions are still uncertain. Trouble in the north brought the Emperor Constans to Britain in A.D. 343 in such haste that he even risked crossing the Channel in January, and it is possible that he issued a decree ordering the towns to look to their defences. Certainly when in A.D. 367 the Saxons, Picts and Scots combined together for the first time in attacking Britain, and were successful in defeating the defending armies, the towns survived, none of them producing evidence of destruction at this time. One factor which emerges from all the investigations so far carried out on the subject of town defences is that neither the late second and third, or the fourth-century constructions, show any signs of hasty erection in a time of emergency. All the walls are well built, and individually planned, to suit towns of varying shapes and sizes. The towns held out well into the fifth century, even when all units of the Roman army had been withdrawn.[1]

Occasionally a little evidence is found relating to the methods used by the labour force when building was in progress. The wall at Caerwent can be divided into a series of fourteen lengths, probably built simultaneously by as many gangs of labourers. On the inner face, the places where each stretch joined its neighbour can be discerned, as it was only roughly finished. The builders knew the earthen bank would conceal the join. Outside, however, great care was taken to hide such details. The south gate was built by another party, and three gaps were deliberately left to the end so that temporary roads could emerge from them for the builders' convenience. This is known because excavation has shown that the wall at these points covers a road surface. Verulamium also produced proof of the existence of different working parties. In some places the flint-rubble is most carefully pitched and coursed; in others, hardly any coursing can be found. The lacing-courses of tile also vary in thickness and appear at slightly different levels. A wider variation of skill in craftsmanship existed here than at Caerwent.

[1] S. S. Frere, 'The end of towns in Roman Britain', in J. Wacher ed. (1966) pp. 87–100.

4
The development of town life (2) Shops and houses

Within the limits of the towns, private dwellings are sometimes identifiable. Until recently, comparatively little was known about them, but now excavations at several sites have uncovered a remarkable series, occupied throughout the Roman period. Verulamium has produced some of the earliest discoveries, including a row of timber-framed shops built in the reign of Claudius and fronting on to Watling Street. Each consisted of a room about 16 by 20 feet in size with a slightly smaller room behind, sometimes divided by a partition wall. The shops are arranged in blocks of four, and in front of them was a colonnade with wooden columns supporting a sloping roof which provided the passers-by with a covered walk. The earth here was much trampled, showing heavy pedestrian traffic. The plan seems too comprehensive for individual shopkeepers. A landlord-tenant relationship appears more likely, and possibly the shops represent an investment by the Catuvellaunian aristocracy, assisted by loans from Roman moneylenders. A block of shops along Watling Street would be a profitable speculation.[1] Unfortunately they were all destroyed by Boudicca in A.D. 60. A few walls seem to have escaped burning and were pulled down afterwards, and this may indicate that the fire was started in the street and a west wind blew some of the flames away from them.

[1] S. S. Frere, 'Excavations at Verulamium 1958', *Ant. J.* XXXIX (1959) 3; Frere (1964a) 63, reconstruction fig. 5; Frere (1964b) 105.

68

The site was carefully cleared but it was more than fifteen years before the shops were rebuilt on much the same plan but with an increasing number of rooms behind. These buildings were occupied for about 80 years and inside they show signs of alterations and renewals belonging to at least four periods. Probably the timbers used in their construction rotted away and had to be replaced. The lower half of one external wall, a foot thick and belonging to the latest period, was well-preserved. It consisted of wooden uprights measuring 6 by 3 inches placed 14 inches apart, with a few small vertical slats in between, fixed into the sleeper beam lying flat in the foundation trench. Clay was plastered on to this framework and roughened into a chevron pattern with a trowel or wooden roller, as a keying for the surface covering of wall-plaster. Internal partition walls were only 6 inches thick and the clay and plaster were applied over a hurdle-work of withies. Evidence for wooden floors was also found. An alley 2½ to 3 feet wide was left between each building with a timber drain for the eavesdrip. Gravel paths led up to the back doors. In the colonnade, post-holes of the latest period suggest that counters were built out in front of the shops. One shop may have been a bakery as ovens were discovered in a room behind it, and a nearby building situated on a cross-roads may, from the number of broken wine-jars found there, have been an inn or wine-shop.[1]

About A.D. 155 a disastrous fire destroyed at least 52 acres of the city and after this the shops along Watling Street were not rebuilt for over a hundred years. Elsewhere, however, the builders were soon at work and most of the houses so far excavated belong to this period. Such traces of earlier timber and wattle and daub dwellings as have been found seem surprisingly unostentatious for the Verulamium City Fathers. Nevertheless, evidence for interior decoration begins to appear as their walls were plastered and colour-washed with designs of lines and stripes outlining rectangular panels, or else stippled to imitate wall-veneers of marble or granite.[2] On one site (Insula XXVIII) a sequence of four timber-framed houses preceded the fire of A.D. 155. Little is known of the two earliest buildings (XXVIII, 3c, 3b.) although a coin of Nero was found with one of the walls of the upper one (3b). Above it came a house of oblong plan, with the narrow end parallel with the street (XXVIII, 3a). Along one long side an open fronted verandah may have looked out on to a gravelled yard. The majority of the rooms had floors of *opus signinum*. This house was probably erected in the early second century and shortly before A.D. 155 it was replaced by a larger house with an L-shaped plan (XXVIII, 3) (fig. 21). This building

[1] S. S. Frere, 'Excavations at Verulamium 1957', *Ant. J.* XXXVIII (1958) 6; *ibid.* XXXIX (1959) 4.
[2] Wheeler (1936) p. 93.

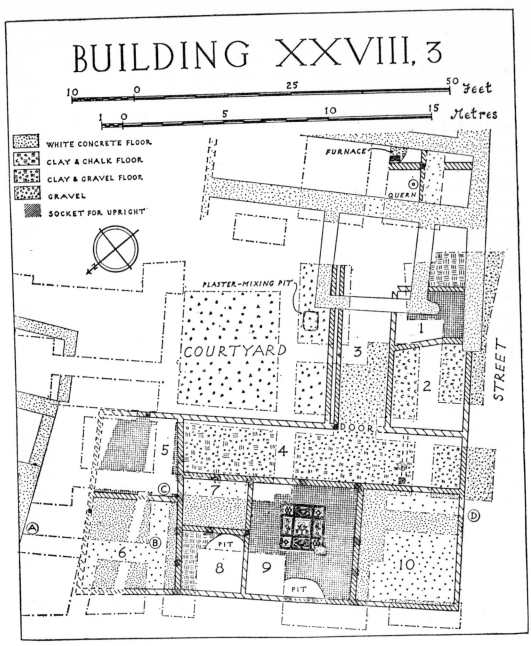

21 Plan of House XXVIII.3 at Verulamium, a timber-framed building destroyed in the fire of *c.* A.D.155

provides substantial evidence for the rising standards of the mid-second century and for the existence of the interior decorators whose work survives in such quantity from Verulamium. In room 9 a mosaic floor was found

70

depicting a geometric pattern with a central panel which shows a fountain consisting of two jets of water springing out of a two-handled vase (Pl. 19). Two dolphins play in the water, their tails twined round the vase-handles. A wide border of plain red tile cubes (*tesserae*) surrounds this mosaic and it probably decorated the dining-room (*triclinium*) with the couches of the diners standing on the undecorated parts of the floor. The walls of this room and of room 3 were covered with wall-paintings.[1]

Before the mosaic floor began to show any signs of wear, the house was burnt down.[2] The site was cleared and sealed by a gravel courtyard belonging to a far more elaborate establishment erected close by (XXVIII, 1) (fig. 22). Like most of the new buildings of this period it was constructed with foundations of flint and mortar, and it was originally intended to be a quadrangular house with shops or rooms surrounding the courtyard on all four sides. However, it was never completed, and the point where building ceased is shown by the impression on an outer wall of one of the wooden pegs which marked out the site for the builders. The resulting plan was L-shaped and included a large house placed far back from the main street and approached by two different entrances, both provided with porter's lodges and reached through long corridors (2, 15). The thickness of some of the walls suggest a two-storey house with a staircase in the narrow room, no. 17. Three living-rooms were provided with heating distributed from no. 22 into nos. 18 and 19 by means of tiled flues running under the floor. Most of the apartments near the street seem to have been shops. At one corner two tiled chutes connect a small latrine with a sewer running along the road and at 4 a drain runs off this sewer through a much larger apartment. This may have been a public convenience accommodating ten or more people. Next door a most unexpected and surprising find was made, a ramp (no. 5), leading down into an underground corridor $8\frac{1}{2}$ feet high with flint walls strengthened at the corners with tiles. A series of niches at regular intervals may have held lamps. After turning two corners this corridor led into an underground room with an apse at the farther end raised 2 feet 3 inches above the floor level and $6\frac{1}{2}$ feet in height—high enough to hold a life-sized statue. Presumably we have here the shrine of some deity, unfortunately no clues survive by which the cult may be identified. No traces of any decoration were found, so, as in the case of the house, the shrine may never have been completed. Possibly the man who was responsible for both died before they were finished and his descendants carried his work no further. In any case the site seems to have been occupied until late in the fourth century, probably by

[1] See below p. 95.
[2] *Ant. J.* XXXIX (1959) 10 *et seq.*

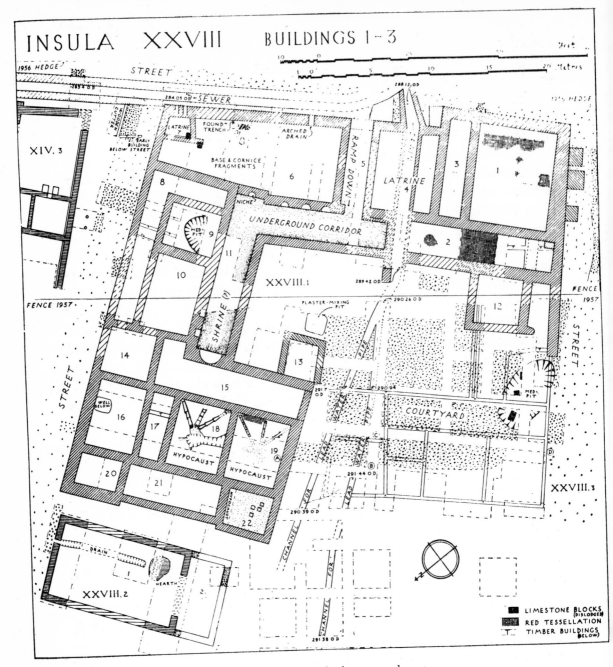

22 Plan of House XXVIII.1 at Verulamium in the late second century

an important citizen whose income included the rents from the shops and the proceeds from the public convenience.

Evidence for other fine second-century houses with mosaics and wall-painting was recovered during the earlier excavations at Verulamium.[1] With improved building methods, frequent replacements and alterations became unnecessary and most of the structures erected after A.D. 155 seem to have continued in use with few changes until the end of the third century. The fourth century was a period of renewed prosperity and fresh building starts soon after A.D. 300. The empty space along Watling Street which may have been planned after 155 for some public building, never to be erected, was once more filled with shops constructed on chalk or flint and mortar foundations. One, perhaps also the home of a prosperous shopkeeper, had had several mosaic floors and also a large cellar, timber lined and with a wood floor, reached down wooden steps. In it were found a fine collection of iron tools including a carpenter's plane, a bronze jug and plate and a bronze statuette of Venus which is one of Verulamium's special treasures (Pl. 49).[2]

Some of the houses built *c.* A.D. 300 continued in use for some years and the builders were still at work in Verulamium until late in the fourth century. A small house a short distance away from Watling Street was built *c.* 370 and in its kitchen was a tiled circular bread-oven. Ten or twenty years later it was reconstructed with new mosaic floors and floral wall decorations.[3] It must have survived well into the fifth century. A much larger house (XXVII, 2), built round a courtyard, had had much the same history with a fine mosaic constructed in a heated room (8) in the later phase (fig. 23). A mosaic inserted into another room in the same house was in use until parts of it became worn and had to be repaired. By about 410–20, unrest due to the progress of Anglo-Saxon and other raiders began to make country life difficult, and people worked behind the shelter of town walls, as far as possible. So the channels for a corn-drying oven[4] were cut through the worn mosaic floor (16). Some time after this the house was demolished and a large building consisting of a single room, constructed with foundations of chalk and re-used fragments of tile, was built over part of it. This was destroyed in its turn, but cutting through it were the remains of the wooden pipes of a water-main, showing that the inhabitants of Verulamium still wanted a good water-supply and had the craftsmen available to provide it. This discovery must belong to the mid-fifth century or even later and it was quite unexpected.[5] Discoveries at other sites such as Cirencester and Catterick, however, show that town life must have continued in Britain far later than was formerly suspected. Such evidence is not easy to find because the fourth- and

[1] Wheeler (1936) Ins. II. 1 (p. 86); III. 2 (p. 94)); IV. 1, 2 (p. 96 *et seq.*); IV 8 (p. 102).
[2] S. S. Frere, 'Excavations at Verulamium 1959', *Ant. J.* XL (1960) 10; *ibid.* XXXIX (1959) 10.
[3] *Ibid.* XXXVIII (1958) 8.
[4] See below p. 221.   [5] *Ant. J.* XL (1960) 19.

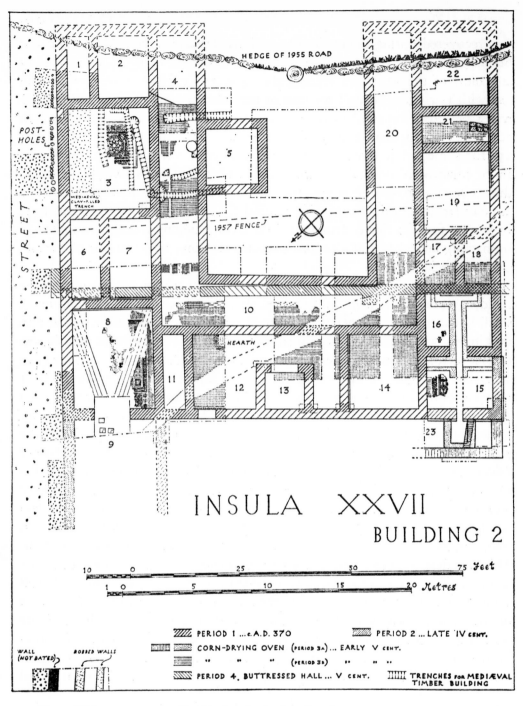

Within the plan image:

HEDGE OF 1955 ROAD

1 2 4 22

POST-HOLES

20 21

STREET

3

MEDIAEVAL CLAY-FILLED TRENCH

5 19

1957 FENCE

6 7 17 18

16

10

HEARTH

8

15

11 12 13 14

9

23

INSULA XXVII

BUILDING 2

10   0   25   50   75 Feet

1 0   5   10   15   20 Metres

PERIOD 1 ... c. A.D. 370   PERIOD 2 ... LATE IV cent.

CORN-DRYING OVEN (PERIOD 3A) ... EARLY V cent.

"   "   "   (PERIOD 3B)   "   "   "

PERIOD 4. BUTTRESSED HALL ... V cent.   TRENCHES FOR MEDIAEVAL TIMBER BUILDING

WALL (NOT DATED)   ROBBED WALLS

23   Plan of House XXVII.2. at Verulamium in the late fourth century

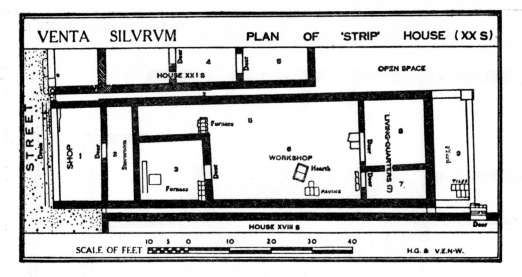

24 Plan of House xx s at Caerwent

fifth-century deposits of Roman sites lie near the modern ground levels and so have often been destroyed.

Houses found in other Romano-British towns include a variety from Caerwent, but there they were excavated in the early years of the twentieth century before archaeological techniques were far enough advanced to enable the excavators to date them satisfactorily. The existence of earlier buildings under later walls, was, however, often noted, and a modern excavation of one of the untouched areas of the town should have very illuminating results. A number of narrow or 'strip' houses were found, mostly situated along the main east-to-west street not far from the Forum. Their doorways are in the narrow end fronting on to the street, and the front room was probably a shop with a store room behind. Behind this came a workshop, with the living quarters at the back of the house looking out on to a small yard reached by an alley-way. The house shown in plan (fig. 24) had white-painted plaster still remaining on its walls, and millstones, a large stone with an iron ring fixed in it, probably a weight, and two uninscribed altars were found in the workshop.[1] The whole row of shops seems to have been roofed with old sandstone slates, purplish in colour, and with ridge stones and decorative finials of freestone probably quarried at Dundry near Bristol.

Rooms in the larger houses were reached from a corridor or verandah in front, and sometimes another corridor was added behind. More rooms could also be added at one or both ends of the building, looking on to a courtyard

[1] T. Ashby, 'Excavations at Caerwent', *Arch.* LXII (ii) (1911) 437.

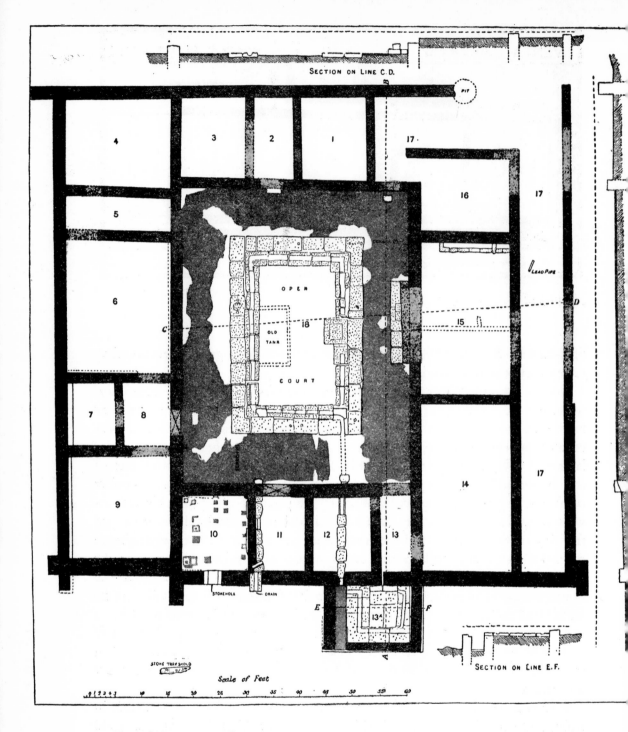

25   Plan of House IIIS at Caerwent

or garden surrounded by a boundary wall. In the south-western corner of the town one house was planned with a colonnade surrounding one of these interior court yards, over 52 by 42 feet in size, with its lean-to roof supported by large stone columns with shafts 17 inches in diameter and at least 5 feet or more in height. These stood on stone bases and had capitals of simple Romano-Doric mouldings. Small holes in the ground between the bases and in one column-shaft suggested that the open spaces between the columns were filled in with a light wooden screen. The central part of the courtyard was left open and probably used as a garden, and a base for an altar or statue was found in it, immediately opposite the steps which lead down into the colonnade from the main entrance of the house (fig. 25). While lacking the *atrium* and other rooms typical of the Pompeian house, this courtyard does recall the classical peristyle and we can imagine it complete with bushes and flower-beds and possibly even statues and a fountain.[1]

Further north, just inside the west gate, was another fine house with an open yard and outbuildings behind it (fig. 26). It possessed two fine reception rooms leading out of each other (nos. 6, 7) connected by an opening 17 feet wide which could be screened off with long curtains when one room was not in use. Room 6 had a mosaic floor of red, yellow, black and white *tesserae* designed round a large central panel set in an octagonal frame. Unluckily this has been destroyed. It may possibly have contained a picture of Orpheus with his dog or a fox, playing to the animals. Four roundels let into the corners of this central design contained winged Cupids, and in each of the outer corners was a bust of the Seasons. Autumn was lost, but Spring with a chaplet of flowers, Summer with a horn of plenty, and Winter, well muffled up in a cloak, were all there. At central points along the outer edges of the floor were small panels containing a lion, a leopard, a bear, and probably a boar; the animals who form Orpheus' audience. In room 7 there was a much simpler pavement which mostly consisted of black and white check. Underneath this was found a more colourful geometric mosaic which belonged with an earlier house. Its discovery is of particular interest because this room also produced wall-paintings of two periods.[2]

The excavations at Verulamium and Caerwent produced several fine houses of courtyard or quadrangular plan, and at Silchester we also find evidence for them. There too, the L-shaped corridor plan, often with the best rooms at the end of the wing, well away from the noise and bustle of the household and the street, was popular.[3] Both Silchester and Caerwent could almost be described as

[1] A. Martin and T. Ashby, 'Excavations at Caerwent' *Arch.* LVII (ii) (1901) 301–10.
[2] T. Ashby, 'Excavations at Caerwent', *Arch.* LVIII (i) (1902) 138–47. For wall-paintings see below p. 88 and fig. 34.
[3] Boon (1957) p. 136 *et seq.*

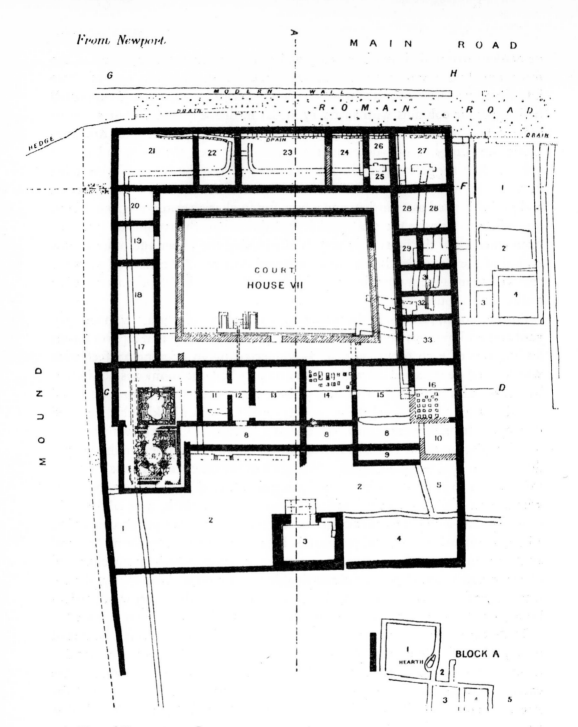

From Newport

MAIN ROAD

G   H

MODERN WALL

R·O·M·A·N R·O·A·D

DRAIN   DRAIN

HEDGE

21   22   23   24   26   27

25

F   1

20   28   28

19   29   2

18   COURT   30

HOUSE VII   31   3   4

17   32

33

16   D

C   11   12   13   14   15

8   8   8   10

9

2   5

2

1   2   3   4

M O U N D

1

HEARTH   2   BLOCK A

3   5

26   Plan of House VIIs at Caerwent

78

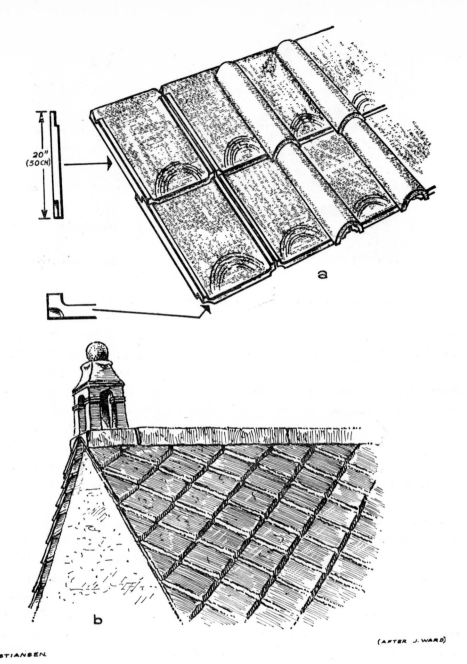

20"
(50CM)

a

b

J. CHRISTIANSEN

(AFTER J. WARD)

27 Reconstructions of *a* a tiled roof, *b* slated roof with cresting and
finial from the Llantwit Major villa, Glamorganshire

garden cities except in the shopping centres near the Forum; there was no
overcrowding and plenty of room for open spaces and houses with large
gardens or orchards (Pl. 12 and fig. 8). As at Verulamium, timber construction

28 Imaginative reconstruction of House 1, Insula XXIII, Silchester

was replaced by an increased use of stone or flint masonry as time went on, the flint walls having bonding courses of tile and quoins of brick or dressed stone.

There is a little more to add about some of the structural features of our Roman houses. Where local supplies of suitable materials existed, as at Caerwent, roofs were usually slated, but at Silchester and Verulamium, where even the stone for such important decorative features as the temple columns had to be brought some distance, roofs had to be thatched or tiled, the flat *tegula* with its upturned edges being used alternately with the semicircular *imbrex* and the roof decorated with baked clay antefixes at eaves level, instead of stone finials (fig. 27).

The main entrance to many large houses seems to have been through a gateway of up to 10 feet wide. One example noted at Caerwent had a threshold made up of three blocks of stone with huge sockets $8\frac{1}{2}$ feet apart. Into these must have fitted the pivots of large double doors of wood. A small column lay nearby, apparently part of an ornamental frame or porch for the doorway, similar to the one shown in fig. 28.[1] Where stone was scarce, jambs and thresholds were often made of timber, and the presence of such wooden door-sills was shown by the nails lying on the mortar foundations in the Silchester houses.[2] Other thresholds were tiled or tessellated. Internal doorways seem to have varied between 2 feet 9 inches and 6 feet in width, wider apertures, perhaps, being shut off by curtains, or by folding wooden doors of the type so familiar from Herculaneum. Pompeii and Herculaneum also furnish examples

[1] T. Ashby, 'Excavations at Caerwent', *Arch*. LXI (ii) (1909) 568.
[2] W. Hope, 'Excavations at Silchester', *Arch*. LVIII (i) (1902) 25.

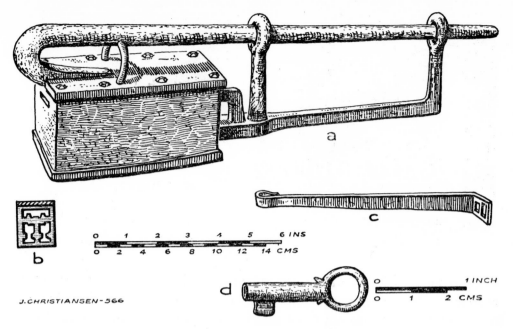

29 *a, b* Large lock and end of a key of the type which would fit it.
c, d Keys. All from Great Chesterford

of the solid wooden front doors studded with iron and bronze nails and other ornaments with which our Romano-British houses were probably provided. A door of this type was actually found at the entrance to the strong room of the fort at Chesters on Hadrian's Wall. Made of oak, studded and bound with iron, it disintegrated shortly after discovery.[1] Strap hinges are sometimes found, and locks of all sizes. They include barrel locks, with a bolt held in position by a spring like the barbs of an arrow. The right key would lift and so release the bolt. The large L-shaped keys are often discovered and occasionally complete locks of the size illustrated. One (fig. 29*a*) comes from Great Chesterford where it must surely have guarded some very substantial front door. The complete key shown (fig. 29*c*) does not fit it, but it can be unlocked with a specially made perspex key, the spring is still in working order. Tumbler locks were also known. These, however, are useless for small containers such as caskets which could be turned upside down, a position in which the tumblers would fall back of their own accord without the need of a key. Simple lever locks with keys which have a more familiar look to us were consequently also used (fig. 29*d*). The Romans, however, never seem to have invented a lock which could be worked from both sides of a door.

Windows remain an intriguing problem as British buildings rarely survive to

[1] J. Ward, *Romano-British Buildings and Earthworks* (1911) p. 268.

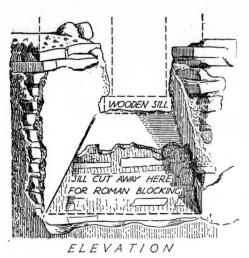

ELEVATION

30   Cellar window, Verulamium

a height sufficient to provide much information about them. The few facts we possess mostly come from cellars. A particularly useful cellar was found under a second-century shop during the earlier excavations at Verulamium (Pl. 10). It was entered through doorways in the west and north walls, both probably approached by ramps. The sill of one doorway still retained the sockets for the pivot and bolt of the door. The walls were covered with white plaster and most of the wall-space was filled by shelves supported by brackets. In the west wall the lower part of a window was excavated *in situ* (fig. 30). The socket for the wooden sill-beam 3 inches square and about 3 feet long, which may have supported vertical iron or wooden bars, gives some idea of the window's size. Inside, it had a splayed sill and jambs, and the jamb on the southern side was more widely splayed than that on the north so that the light would be directed towards the middle of the cellar. The white plastering would also reflect the light.[1]

Another cellar under a house at Caerwent had a splayed window 4 feet square on the inside narrowing to a slit of $1\frac{1}{2}$ feet in the outer wall.[2] Obviously windows with squared or rounded heads, splayed sides and sloping sills were usual and pieces of painted wall-plaster shaped to fit them are found not infrequently. Clerestory windows may also have been small but in the wing rooms larger windows are very probable. These are known to exist at Pompeii where upper windows of $2\frac{1}{2}$ by 4 feet also occur. Sliding wooden shutters were sometimes used but frequent discoveries of window glass show that glazing was quite normal. And large amounts, dating from the mid-first century onwards have been recovered from sites including the baths at Godmanchester, and the villa

[1] Wheeler (1936) p. 80 *et seq.*
[2] T. Ashby, 'Excavations at Caerwent', *Arch.* LXII (ii) (1911) 439.

at Great Casterton (Rutland). It all seems to have been made from a muff, a process of manufacture in which the glass is blown into a cylinder and then cut down its length and opened out.[1] Some fragments from Godmanchester were reconstructed to form a piece about $15\frac{1}{2}$ by $10\frac{1}{4}$ inches and nine panes of this type could have been used for a window about $3\frac{1}{2}$ by 4 feet, according to the size of the glazing bars of the frame. They seem to have been fixed in position with cement. A large piece of fallen masonry found in the apse of the *caldarium* of the Silchester baths belonged to a window of this size which probably had a wooden frame.[2] Remains of such a frame were found in the *tepidarium* of the baths of the House of Diomedes at Pompeii, and into it fitted four panes of glass $10\frac{1}{2}$ inches square.[3] Iron objects made of two small bars fixed together at right angles are sometimes found, and have long been thought to be connected with windows. Recent research has shown that they were not fixed to the glass or its frame but rather to an exterior iron grille, where they acted as an additional means of discouragement to intruders. The best example of such a grille comes from Duston (Northamptonshire) and consists of four bars one inch wide fastened at right angles to each other. Their ends were turned over so as to fit into the wooden frame of an opening 20 inches square and the small objects mentioned above were attached to them at intervals.[4] Again, a variety of grilles, some similarly protected, can be quoted from Pompeii as comparative material.[5] Remains of another large glazed window were noted in one of the apses of the hot room at the military bath-house attached to the fort at Great Chesters on Hadrian's Wall. The splaying of the sill started about one foot above the floor level and the opening seems to have been about 5 feet wide and 4 feet high inside, and at least 3 feet wide on the outside. Broken window glass lay on the floor beneath.[6]

House plans and structural details may seem to be only the bare bones of the homes we are trying to picture, but their variations do in fact give a glimpse of the ideas and preferences of individuals. The different types of plans which flourished side by side in the towns must reflect the means and status, and also the conservative or advanced views of their inmates, regarding the type of house in which they wished to live. In this connection it is a noteworthy fact

[1] D. Harden, 'Domestic Window Glass, Roman, Saxon and Mediaeval', in E. M. Jope ed. *Studies in Building History* (1961) pp. 44–52.
[2] Boon (1957) p. 109. [3] Mau-Kelsey (1902) p. 351.
[4] G. Webster, 'Roman Windows and Grilles', *Antiquity* XXXIII (1959) 10–14. See also J.R.S. LVI (1966) 213 Pl. X.2.
[5] Spinazzola, '*Pompei alla luce degli scavi nuovi di Via dell' Abbondanza* (1910–23) (Rome, 1953) p. 32.
[6] J. P. Gibson, 'Excavations at Great Chesters', *Arch. Ael.* (2) XXIV (1903) 48.

that among the large amount of evidence for wall-painting and mosaic floors that has now been collected, there is little repetition apart from the occasional re-use of geometric motifs. The designs for these wall-paintings and mosaics accord with the contemporary fashions current in the Roman Empire which were largely inspired by those developed in Rome, Pompeii and other Italian sites. These in their turn had used ideas derived from Greece and the Hellenistic world. In this art, figure scenes portraying well-known events in the lives of the gods and heroes of mythology play an important part, depicted in a framework of architectural, floral or geometric motifs. It used to be believed that the Britons, skilled in the abstract curvilinear art of pre-Roman times, had the new, more naturalistic ideas forced upon them, and joyfully discarded them with the coming of the Dark Ages. Fresh discoveries and modern scholarship, however, are gradually proving to us that this belief is mistaken, that interest in the current artistic trends was widespread, and that *Britannia*, far from being a distant and barbarous province, contributed its share of good things to the sum total of the Roman artistic heritage. In many of our towns there probably existed firms of interior decorators founded by one of the artists of Syrian or East Mediterranean origin who seem to have travelled so widely about the Empire doing this work. He may have been assisted by local craftsmen and trainees, the whole establishment being possibly financed by some local business man. The artists seem to have used pattern-books full of favourite scenes and motifs; and the client must have looked through these and chosen whatever appealed to him and would suit the size and shape of his rooms. Occasionally, as we shall see, he did not understand the significance of the designs he chose; or sometimes the decorators lacked the skill and experience required to carry them out, and so got into difficulties.

Although we know that even the small remote farms of this period often made some attempt at simple painted wall decorations (no doubt with father acting on the do-it-yourself principle in many cases) the study of the evidence for Roman wall-painting in this country is still in its early stages. Owing to its fragile nature and the fragmentary conditions in which it comes to light, the material is difficult to excavate and preserve. Fragments and a few drawings and records survive from old excavations; some of them of plaster then still in place on the walls but steadily destroyed by the weather. Modern excavators, however, have been fortunate in finding much fresh material, sometimes in the form of complete walls lying in a broken state on tessellated floors; and when the delicate task of lifting it is accomplished, the sorting and study of the resulting jigsaw needs much storage space and hours of patient study. These considerations, however, are easily put aside in the excitement of seeing a design last

31 Relief probably showing decorators at work, found at Sens, France

visible perhaps in the second century A.D. unfold, and realising that fresh facts are being made available for the study of Romano-British art.

In general, the wall was marked out with a stylus and some of the guide lines made at this stage can still be seen today. The surface had been finished with coats of fine plaster and while still damp the first colours were applied. Colour applied carefully to the plaster surface while it is still damp does not fade, but lasts for ever, remarked Vitruvius, and the evidence of our own eyes demonstrates the truth of this observation. The method of painting known as *buon fresco* (true fresco) was probably used for the background. On it the design was applied in *fresco secco* and for this, small areas were probably damped with lime water, and then the painter used pigments mixed with milk or some other binding agent for his work. A delightful picture of these processes going on is provided for us by a relief on the tombstone of a Roman painter at Sens in France (fig. 31). The work takes place in a corridor where a low scaffolding has been erected, supported by trestles and reached by a short ladder. On the right is the plasterer with his float in his left hand, applying the final coat. On the floor near the ladder is a stool with a trough of plaster on it, and nearby an assistant seems to be frantically mixing either plaster or the colours for the painter. He is following close on the plasterer's heels so that he can apply his paint while the surface is still damp. Behind him is a roll of parchment in a round box, probably the scheme for that part of the decoration. Nearby another figure, probably the master-painter himself, sits on some steps under an

85

archway, calmly regarding an open book. Presumably he is checking up on the designs his client has selected in his pattern-book.

The pigments were made of various materials. Red was a favourite colour and many shades of it occur, used for both designs and backgrounds. It was obtained from red ochre, red lead, vermilion or cinnabar. Red ochre had been known as a pigment since pre-historic times and Pliny mentions it as having several qualities. The best was used for brush painting, another quality for panelling, and the cheaper, darker shade for dadoes. Pinks were obtained by mixing the reds with white prepared from chalk, lime, gypsum, china clay or white lead. For blues, blue frit, and indigo were employed, and traces of blue frit, the most important, were found at the settlement site, possibly a fairground, at Wood Eaton (Oxfordshire).[1] It is a powdered glaze which had to be applied with yolk of egg when used *al secco*. Remains of a frit factory have been found at El Amarna in Egypt and, as in the case of red, Pliny describes several shades and qualities of it in his *Natural History*. For yellow, natural iron oxides (ochres or limonite) sometimes mixed together, and orpiment (natural sulphide of arsenic) were used. Yellow lead oxide or litharge could also provide a variety of shades varying from very pale yellow to deep orange. Green might be made from malachite (basic copper carbonate) which, as Pliny duly notes, often occurs in mines, the best being found with copper. The raw material was ground and sifted several times and then treated with alum and a herb, the yellow dye-wood, to obtain the required shade. Modern experiments have shown that this method is quite feasible. Pliny goes on to describe the best variety resulting from it as resembling in colour the joyous verdure of the blade of corn. Verdigris was also manufactured for pigments and Pliny lists *terre verte* or green celadonite earth as 'one of those new-fangled colours of the cheapest sort called Appian green'. *Terre verte* has been identified from wall-paintings at Pompeii and Dura Europos and, as it is found in Germany, France, and in Cornwall, it may possibly have been used in this country. Certainly both the blues and greens used for Romano-British wall-paintings are apt to be very friable and easily destroyed, requiring very careful handling. There remains black, for which soot, particularly lamp black or bone black, and powdered charcoal were used, mixed with size.[2]

The walls which received elaborate decoration were usually those of the baths, the best living-rooms or the inner wall of the corridor round a courtyard, and they seem to have been about 9 to 12 feet high. The lowest levels to a height of about 3 feet formed a dado; above this would come large stretches of

[1] E. M. Jope and G. Huse, 'Blue pigment from Woodeaton', *Oxoniensia*. V (1940) 167.
[2] For a discussion of ancient pigments see Forbes III p. 202 *et seq.*

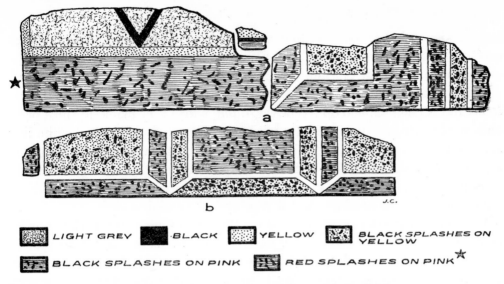

32 Wall-painting imitating marble wall-veneers. Aldborough, Yorkshire

colour set in a framework of stripes and finer lines, outlining panels about $3\frac{1}{2}$ to 4 feet wide but 4 to 5 feet high, the proportions varying. Doors and windows interrupted the scheme and sometimes a wall would have panels of varying size, so that all could be fitted in, or else the panel was continued round the corner on to the adjacent wall. Evidence for the upper parts of the walls very rarely survives, but it is believed that sometimes the area above the panels was simply painted in one of the background colours and otherwise left undecorated. In one or two cases, however, an elaborate painted frieze existed at this level.

Very popular for dado decoration was imitation marbling. For this, paint was flicked off a brush to produce a stippled effect of spots and splodges of varying size, and streaks were painted in at random to give the effect of veining. The intention was to give an impression of the fine marble wall-veneers used in Italy and occasionally also in this country as at Colchester.[1] Sometimes it is possible to hazard a guess as to what stone the artist had in mind. Among the designs from a villa at Box in Wiltshire which produced a large quantity of imitation marbling is a dark greyish green background finely stippled with dark red and white spots—probably intended to be a fine-grained granite or serpentine. A fine-grained red was depicted by a dark red ground with small splashes of white, and a large-grained pink granite by a lighter pinkish-red ground with large splashes of white and smaller spots of red.[2] This last design seems to have been a great favourite as it occurs at several places, sometimes enlivened with

[1] See above p. 24.
[2] H. Brakspear, 'The Roman villa at Box', *W.A.M.* XXXIII (1904) 244 *et seq.*

larger spots of darker red or yellow, or with streaks of white or black. A variation of it forms part of some wall-paintings found in the early nineteenth-century excavations at Isurium Brigantum (Aldborough, Yorkshire, fig. 32). Another design from the same town illustrates sprays of blue leaves with red stems and veining painted on a yellow ground, with a grey diamond and a plain pink border for one design, and a border of the same grey with a white line and yellow leaves for the other (fig. 33*a*, *c*). Below come two geometric motifs: a pink and yellow diamond and a grey circle outlined with pink and white concentric circles, both on a blue ground outlined in white above a grey stripe, with a pink vertical band on the left (fig. 33*b*).

Brief allusions in the excavation reports show that Caerwent was rich in wall-paintings, and here we have a site where important finds may also occur in future. In several cases detailed drawings exist of the early twentieth-century discoveries, among them those already briefly noted in one of the rooms with mosaic floors in House VIIs (fig. 34).[1] This wall shows two periods. From the earlier comes a dado with black or mauve rectangles framed in a border of blue and red stripes outlined in white, separated by yellow and black stripes from a band of black and white stippling on a green ground at floor level. Another band of marbling with red instead of black spots may have existed at the top of the whole design. When the walls were redecorated this colour scheme was replaced by a deeper band of the favourite red and white marbling on a pink ground at ground level. Above it came an architectural design apparently intended to portray part of a room with yellow walls. Leading out of it is a recess or niche with a red wall and a pink horizontal stripe at top and bottom, above a green band which may represent the floor or a rug. Dark brown lines outline the perspective of the whole drawing. It seems to have been contemporary with the simple floor of black and white check, and presumably the other design decorated the room when the geometric mosaic was complete. Sprays of green leaves from the upper part of the later wall-decoration were also found. Interest in this architectural drawing was aroused afresh by the discovery at Leicester in 1958 of another dado showing apsidal recesses repeated at intervals. These may possibly prove to be niches with figures standing in them, as fragments of draped human figures were also recovered by the excavators, as well as the upper part of a winged Cupid standing in a niche or under an archway.[2]

The Museum at Newport (Monmouthshire) contains wall-paintings from several other Caerwent houses. A gay brown hare is depicted on a blue ground beneath a band of honeysuckle pattern; probably he had other four-footed

[1] See above p. 77.
[2] Toynbee (1964) p. 218; (1963) no. 172.

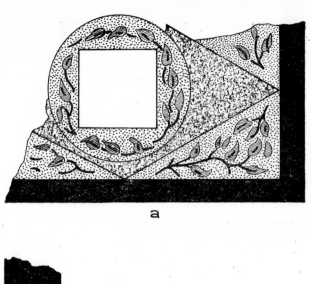

a

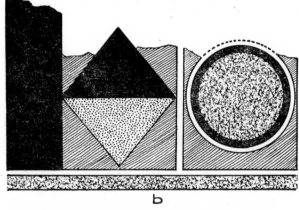

b

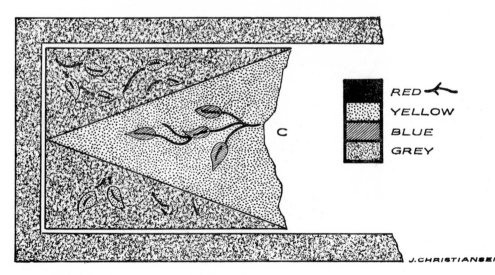

c

RED
YELLOW
BLUE
GREY

J.CHRISTIANSEN

33 Wall-painting showing floral and geometric motifs. Aldborough

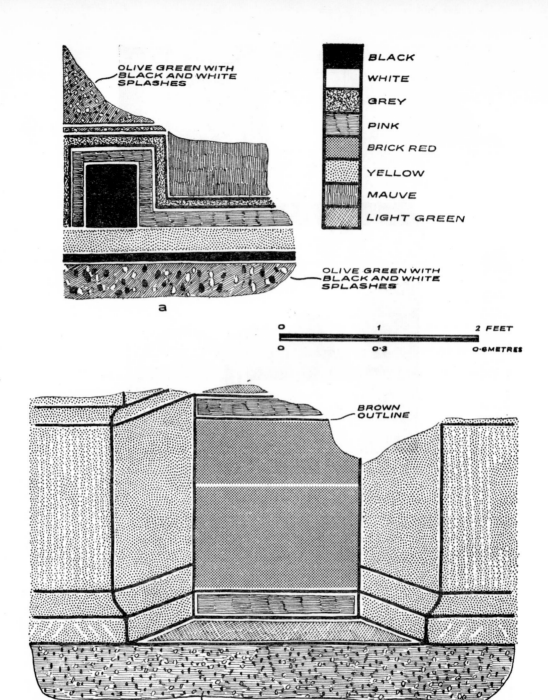

OLIVE GREEN WITH
BLACK AND WHITE
SPLASHES

BLACK
WHITE
GREY
PINK
BRICK RED
YELLOW
MAUVE
LIGHT GREEN

OLIVE GREEN WITH
BLACK AND WHITE
SPLASHES

a

0   1   2 FEET
0   0·3   0·6 METRES

BROWN
OUTLINE

J. CHRISTIANSEN

PINK WITH RED AND WHITE SPLASHES

b

34 Wall-painting from House VIIS at Caerwent showing decoration of
two different periods

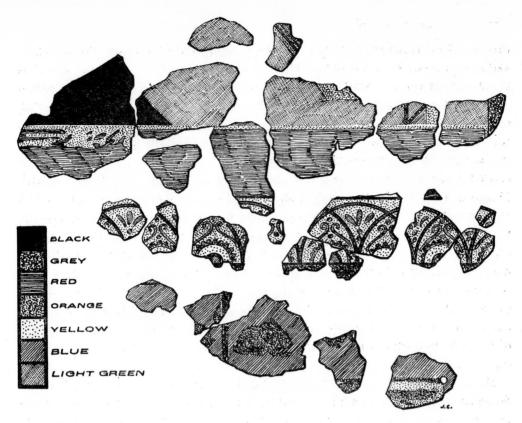

BLACK
GREY
RED
ORANGE
YELLOW
BLUE
LIGHT GREEN

35 Wall-painting from Caerwent

companions (fig. 35).[1] The torso of a human figure appears on another frag-ment, and the draped arm and hand which is all that survives of a girl wearing a blue robe, holds a flower (Pl. 16*b*). A charming face with curly hair might belong to the same girl (Pl. 16*c*). In any case these pieces show that the wall-paintings at Caerwent certainly included figure scenes, and the excavators' reports actually note that various draped figures in panels were painted on the walls. Part of another face with eyes and eyebrows heavily outlined in black and brown, found at the little town of Letocetum (Wall, Staffordshire) must be of later date.

Other Roman towns, notably Cirencester (Pl. 14)[2] and Malton, have produced much wall-painting decorated with geometric and floral designs, and the frag-ments from Venta Icenorum (Caistor-by-Norwich) include the heads of a dog and a horse. Another interesting collection of material comes from London, mostly found many years ago and consisting of the isolated pieces which are all

[1] T. Ashby, 'Excavations at Caerwent', *Arch.* LX (1907) Pl. XLIII.
[2] E.g. J. Wacher, 'Cirencester 1962', *Ant. J.* XLIII (1963) 19.

that survived from several sites. To the student, the nineteenth-century excavation reports make sad reading. They record heaps of fresco painting noted in Fenchurch Street; or paintings *in situ* in 1868 on the walls found under Cannon Street Station with panelling, trellis work and imitation marbling ('a powdering of fancy-coloured spots').[1] Much of our information about these lost treasures we owe to the antiquary Charles Roach Smith and he tells us, writing in 1859, that such finds were exceedingly numerous. 'In some localities I have seen them carried away by the cartloads'.[2] Items in his collection, now in the British Museum, include a trellis-work design in yellow on a red ground with white eight-petalled flowers and small nude male figures in the enclosed squares. A border of white and purple, now lost, appeared above it in the original design (fig. 36*b*). Other pieces show a yellow beaded line which must have outlined a panel, decorated at intervals with sprays of green leaves and painted on a deep rose ground and the lower part of the face and neck of a woman's head rising out of a calyx of blue and brown leaves. One scrap shows a lively white goat and another a striking mask of Mercury wearing his winged cap, the brown cap and dishevelled hair giving the impression that he may actually have been in flight (fig. 36*a*). Unhappily this piece has been lost.

More evidence of Roman wall-painting is preserved in Guildhall Museum. Some of it, including a charming design of birds and honeysuckle, comes from recent excavations; another piece, found years ago, shows sprays of flowers in the centre of small circles of beaded lines and rose petals; they may come from a dado or even from a ceiling. One very interesting fragment, only just over 4 inches long, shows the upper parts of two figures apparently dancing with a garland. One is a girl with her hair in a large heavy bun or chignon, the other is probably a boy. They may form part of a procession of maenads and satyrs, possibly belonging to some Dionysiac scene.[3] And, as a final example of the material from London, the leaf spray from the site of the basilica must be mentioned. Painted on a red ground, it shows leaves delicately portrayed in varying shades of green, with traces of yellow buds or flowers and dark brown leaves and stems.[4] Again only about 4 inches in size, this fragment yet gives the impression of being the work of a master hand—impressionistic painting of a type worthy of the garden scenes at Pompeii or reminiscent of the variety of plant life to be seen on the walls of the garden room from the Empress Livia's villa at Prima Porta, now reconstructed in the Museo Nazionale in Rome.

[1] Royal Commission on Historical Monuments (England), *Roman London* (1928) pp. 113, 118.
[2] C. Roach Smith, *Illustrations of Roman London* (1859) p. 62.
[3] W. R. Lethaby, *Londinium: Architecture and the Crafts* (1923) p. 171, figs. 117, 118.
[4] Merrifield (1965) Pl. LV.

J.C. 866

36 Fragments of wall-painting found in London. *a* Head of Mercury, flesh tints and a purple cap on a red ground. *b* Linear crosses enclose squares in which are white rosettes with yellow centres and miniature nude male figures. White paint on a red ground ruled with incised guide lines at right angles

After considering the tantalisingly fragmentary evidence of London and Caerwent we find a more satisfactory state of affairs when we turn to consider the recent excavations at Verulamium. When these started in 1955, discoveries at the Lullingstone villa[1] had already shown archaeologists that in cellars and at similar depths they might sometimes hope to find quantities of fallen wall-plaster which it would be possible to reconstruct, but obviously these conditions would not often occur. As it happened, one of the 1955 discoveries at Verulamium was a cellar with a simple scheme of decoration *in situ*, white walls with red vertical stripes at the corners, and a dado marbled in purple, black and white below a band of red and narrower yellow lines. Nearby, a thick bed of plaster some inches thick was found, not in the cellar, but on the red tessellated floor of the corridor. It was made up of four layers of painting lying on top of each other, some face down and some face up. At first it was thought that a wall painted on both sides had fallen in, but later it was realised that it was all one surface of a fragile clay wall which had collapsed concertina fashion.[2] Much of it was lifted and disentangled, and the scheme of decoration seems to have included red panels with yellow beaded lines and green and white garlands of leaves and flowers divided by broad yellow stripes with red leaves. Below this came a white band, and a dado of squares marked out with wide red lines and containing smaller yellow and blue rectangles. The same season's excavations covered the site of another house which, while it produced no great stretches of wall-painting, had fragments from at least five different periods.[3] This was a valuable contribution as most of the scattered finds from our other Roman towns are quite undated. Walls were being painted in Roman Britain from towards the end of the first century till about the beginning of the fifth and fashions must have changed in that time as they did elsewhere in the Empire. Here were fragments of the imitation marbling which seems to have been a favourite at all periods, together with various floral designs which tend to grow bolder as time goes on—evidence of the varying artistic tastes in one Romano-British house over several hundred years. Elsewhere at Verulamium some fourth-century wall-decoration was found but otherwise, apart from this house, the wall-paintings date from the second century. So much of it was recovered that it is possible to imagine oneself wandering into house after house at this period, each with its own individual scheme of decoration. In one was found a charming design of yellow trellis work and white roses with red centres, reminiscent of the one from London but without any human figures.

[1] See below p. 276.
[2] S. S. Frere, 'Excavations at Verulamium', *Ant. J.* XXXVI (1936) 2.
[3] *J.R.S.* XLVI (1956) 135.

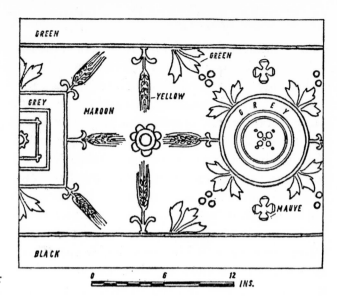

GREEN

GREEN

YELLOW

GREY

GREY

MAROON

BLACK

MAUVE

37   Wall design from Silchester

0   6   12
                              INS.

It also recalls a design of leaves and berries found at Silchester (fig. 37) in a lattice of golden wheat ears painted on a red ground. Green fern leaves came from another Verulamium house, and the inmates of a third had perhaps seen the same pattern-book as people in London and Caerwent, for they too decorated their walls with honeysuckle.

In 1958 House no. 3, Insula XXVIII, already mentioned above on page 71, was excavated at Verulamium. One wall of room 3, probably a corridor, was found lying face down on the floor with the white plaster flecked with red which had belonged to room 2 next door lying on top of it. This was removed and it proved possible to lift and reassemble the room 3 wall-painting in an unusually complete state. The design (Pl. 18) was painted on a purple ground with columns about 4 feet apart and $3\frac{1}{2}$ feet high, of cream colour covered with a dark red network to give an impression of marble, surmounted by small capitals. In the intervening spaces come panels covered with an all over design of either pale green and purple, or yellow and red. These probably represent marble wall-veneers but the red and yellow pattern can be viewed as a full-blown rose, a little reminiscent of a motif found at the Lullingstone villa. The columns stand on a plinth represented by a purple band, below which comes the dado also painted on a purple ground. It consists of small rectangles outlined in cream paint immediately below each column, alternating with oblongs which repeat the panel designs. The effect is one of sombre magnificence which would be shown up by the white concrete floor. Proceeding further into the same house we come to the dining-room with the mosaic floor, and in here large fragments of a design of more classical type were found. It is based on a fanciful interpretation of the *candelabrum*, the tall bronze candlestick or lamp-holder found in quantities at Pompeii and other Italian sites. Pompeian painters had already made this design their own, using it in even more fantastic ways as a framework for panelling; wreathing vegetation round the lamp standards many feet in height, or making it support garlands, strung from *candelabrum* to *candelabrum* all round the wall. At Verulamium the *candelabra* are usually sur-mounted by a wheel or crown from which sprout four or five lights, and in this room sprays of green leaves branch out from the main stem with, at intervals, small subsidiary *candelabra*, slightly suggestive of mushrooms or open parasols, but each with its row of candles of various colours standing on the top. This motif is easily recognisable and fine examples of it also occur at Leicester and several other sites. It is of great importance as a link with Pompeian painting. Examples of *candelabra* are also known from other provinces, including the Roman villa found at Perignat in France[1] and the Romano-Celtic temple at Elst, near Arnhem in Holland;[2] while numerous examples exist among the treasury of Roman wall-painting now preserved in the Landesmuseum at Trier. Further evidence for it is known from other houses at Verulamium, notably from the second-century levels of House 2, Insula XXI.[3] It comes from the inner wall of the corridor no. 3 round a courtyard. On a red ground are painted panels, each containing two *candelabra* complete with their bases, and with delicate stems occasionally embellished with some kind of leaf or spiral decoration. One end of a garland of blue flowers is tied with a ribbon below each crown of candles, the other end being attached to a support depicted hanging from the wide band of colour above the panel. Perhaps we should regard this as a ceiling but the suspension of garlands in space is quite usual in such designs. Small baubles hang from the supports and in the centre of each panel is a dove, also painted blue, on a perch. When the fragments of this wall were raised it was found that it had protected another layer of plaster which consequently was lifted in an unusually complete state. It proved to be painted purple with a lattice work of golden wheat-ears, rather like the one found at Silchester, enclosing blue flowers and birds, probably doves. At first it was thought to be another wall but it is now believed to be the ceiling of this corridor with the red wall and *candelabra* (Pl. 17*b*).

In the courtyard outside the corridor of the same house lay a further sheet of fallen plaster 12 feet in length and 5 feet high. Reconstructed by Dr Norman

[1] E. Chanel, 'Peintures murales de la villa gallo-romaine de Pérignat, *Bull. archeologique du Comité des travaux historiques et scientifiques* (1909) 5–13.
[2] J. Bogaers, *De Gallo-Romeinse Tempels te Elst* (The Hague, 1955), Pl. XXII.
[3] S. S. Frere, *op. cit. Ant. J.* XXXVII (1957) 13.

Davey, it can now be seen in the British Museum, the greatest treasure of this collection of wall-paintings. Painted on a ground of golden yellow is a scroll of green and black acanthus leaves and stalks, with great scarlet buds seen in profile.[1] In its curves pheasants disport themselves, alternating with animal masks—probably intended to be panthers—painted in purple with white stripes or highlights. Like *candelabra*, leaf-scrolls peopled with birds or animals running among the foliage or emerging from flowers, were a favourite Roman decorative motif. But the use of disembodied masks is so far without parallel. The acanthus buds too, just bursting into flower, are unusual but they do occur among British mosaics from Roman towns at Dorchester and Cirencester and there is one example from Verulamium itself. Presumably these ideas come from a pattern-book only in use in this country and not circulating elsewhere. Above the design is a band of red, which curves slightly inwards, showing that here at last we have the top of a wall, with the leaf-scroll decorating a frieze about 4 feet 6 inches deep just below the ceiling. Fragments of a similar leaf-scroll but unpeopled, were found near the wall-painting discoveries in House 3, Insula XXVIII, but it has not been possible to decide whether it belonged above the pillared wall or with the *candelabra* decoration.

Further excavations in House XXVIII, 3, in 1959 showed that a corridor (no. 2) turning at right angles out of corridor no. 3 had a ceiling with a similar design of birds in a lattice work of wheat-ears, but painted on a red instead of on a purple ground. A fragment showing a winged human mask also came from this area. Room 4, partly enclosed within the angle formed by these two corridors, had walls of deep emerald green divided into panels by a framework of red lines above a dark red dado. The plaster from its walls had fallen onto a mosaic floor depicting a lion devouring a stag, so here again it was possible to recover a complete scheme of interior decoration.[2] The subject of the mosaic recurs on a fourth-century mosaic found in Insula XIV in 1958.[3] Such close repetition of a design is unusual especially after such a lapse of time.

One further exciting discovery has been made at Verulamium, not in the town itself but two miles away in a Roman house on the Gorhambury estate. Here excavations carried out between 1955 and 1960 have revealed another site where, with the decay of the building, plaster from an upper room had fallen into the cellar beneath.[4] Possibly this room possessed some form of barrel

---

[1] *Ibid.* 14. Colour Pl. V.
[2] S. S. Frere, 'Excavations at Verulamium 1959', *Ant. J.* XL (1960) 17.
[3] S. S. Frere, 'Excavations at Verulamium 1958', *Ant. J.* XXXIX (1959) 10.
[4] I. Antony, 'The Roman Building at Gorhambury', St.A.A.S.T. 1961, 21–30; *ibid.* forthcoming J. Liversidge, Appendix.

vault because the discoveries from it include traces of a painted cornice and various mouldings in stucco, together with fragments of small human hands and feet, bodies and a small face moulded in high relief, which may have decorated a frieze. Stucco decoration, of course, is well known from sites in Italy but so far it is of very rare occurrence in the western provinces of the Empire. Trier, a very rich and important city, has produced the best examples and now it has come to light in Roman Britain.

When we come to consider the other important factor in interior decoration, namely mosaic floors, some of the best evidence comes from Verulamium, including those already described. Among the finest examples of the art found in Roman Britain is one of the earliest in the series, a semicircular panel from an apse, probably dating between A.D. 130–50 (Pl. 15). The design consists of a beautiful scallop-shell, its fluting indicated by blue shading outlined in black, on a ground of red *tesserae* in a border of black wave pattern on white; the whole set in a plain border of alternate bands of red or yellow. While the niches in which statues of the gods often stood in Roman houses were frequently completed with a semi-circular top modelled in stucco in the shape of a scallop-shell, the design is rarely found on a floor-mosaic. Another, but inferior rendering of it, is known from Leicester. A slightly later pavement of mid-second century date was found in two adjacent rooms of a house, Insula IV, 2. Set in the familiar border of plain red *tesserae* with a yellow band, it resembles a carpet covered all over with designs symmetrically arranged, some geometric and some floral. Under the archway or wide doorway which separated the rooms is a panel of acanthus scroll with flowers resembling those found on the great painted frieze described above.[1] The colours used for the mosaic are chiefly black and white with some yellow, red and blue. Painted red panels outlined in blue, yellow, green, white and purple were noted among the fragments which had fallen from the walls.[2]

An elaborate house nearby (Insula IV, 8) which has been partly preserved, produced two rooms which probably formed part of a bath suite with mosaics dating from later in the second century. In room 7 was another carpet-like design with sixteen square panels each containing a flower and outlined with a two-stranded guilloche or cable pattern. The colours used include red, white, yellow and black. At each end are oblong panels the width of the room, patterned with interlacing circles. This pavement had been repaired and may have continued in use for many years. The next room also had a second-century mosaic; destroyed and replaced in about A.D. 300 by a later floor. Of this an

[1] See above p. 97.
[2] Wheeler (1936) p. 145, Pls. XL, XLVIA.

oblong end panel showing an elaborate acanthus scroll survived, quite different in character from the second-century examples but resembling fourth-century work from elsewhere in the Empire. In room 4 of the same house which adjoined the bath suite, was another second-century floor. It was decorated with a wide border of black key pattern on a white ground with flowers at each corner and two-handled *canthari* in the centre of each side, two of them containing ladles. In the centre is the head of the sea-god Oceanus, bearded and with lobster claws growing out of his hair.[1] He occurs on other Romano-British pavements, including one from Durnovaria (Dorchester) where he is flanked by a dolphin and a tunny fish, but this is much the finest British representation of him. He also appears on mosaics from other parts of the Empire.

Other towns where mosaic pavements have been found include London, Colchester, Canterbury, Winchester, Dorchester, Silchester, Cirencester, Gloucester, Bath, Caerwent, Leicester, Lincoln, York and Aldborough (Yorkshire). Some of the most interesting discoveries have been made at Corinium (Cirencester), the *civitas* of the Dobunni. This seems to have been a very rich and flourishing town, probably one of the centres of the woollen industry, and wall-paintings and interesting sculptural remains have also been recovered from its buildings. The floors include four figured mosaics. One showing Orpheus playing to the animals belongs to a group of pavements devoted to this subject,[2] and as the other examples come from villas, it is better considered later.[3] The second pavement is a magnificent affair found in a hypocausted room.[4] In the centre, in a circular frame of guilloche, are three hunting dogs, one large one wearing a red collar, and two smaller ones. Unluckily the fragment showing their quarry has been destroyed. Two masks of Oceanus appear in the body of the pavement and one corner shows a head of Medusa with some of her snaky locks ending in snakes' heads. Round the edges are geometric motifs and two semicircles, one containing a winged sea-dragon close on the tail of a dismayed-looking dolphin, the other a sea-leopard more playfully chasing a dolphin or fish. Another room in the same house produced a pavement made up of nine circular medallions.[5] In the four corners were busts of women depicting the Seasons. Winter is lost but Autumn is there, wearing a wreath of grapes and holding a pruning knife, and also Summer with ears of corn and a sickle. Spring in the fourth corner seems to be the work of a less practised hand, she has blue,

[1] *Ibid.* p. 146, Pls. XLI, XLII, XLVB, XLVIB, XLVIIIA.
[2] K. J. Beecham, *History of Cirencester and the Roman City of Corinium* (1886) Pl. opp. p. 266.
[3] See p. 278.
[4] Toynbee (1964) p. 269; J. Buckman and C. H. Newmarch, *Illustrations of the Remains of Roman Art in Cirencester* (1850) Pl. VI opp. p. 36.
[5] Toynbee (1964) p. 269; (1963) no. 181.

yellow, white and red flowers (? poppies) in her hair, a bird sits on her shoulder and she carries a flowering branch. One of the other circles is lost and only the fore-legs of a horse (? part of a Centaur) survive from the central medallion. The others show the fragmentary remains of Bacchus holding a *thyrsus;* Silenus, the jovial companion of Bacchus, reclining comfortably on the back of a white ass with a red harness; and Actaeon, the unfortunate hunter who accidentally intruded upon the goddess Diana, was turned into a stag and hunted down by his own hounds. The mosaicist shows him with antlers sprouting from his head, already attacked by two dogs and with blood flowing from one leg. A Medusa mask and a dancing Satyr also survive in small panels between the medallions. The whole pavement is very fine work and the symbolic meaning of its subjects includes Bacchic bliss, prosperity, the warding off of evil (by the Medusa head) and a warning example of the fate of those who offend the gods. A third pavement which has not survived was devoted to Marine scenes.[1] A Nereid and a Cupid rode on dolphins and another Cupid was clutching at a chariot which may have held Neptune. The pavement was completed with sea-beasts, conger eels, crabs, fish and shells, and would not have looked out of place in Rome itself. There is little dating evidence for these four mosaics but they are presumed to belong to the second century. The choice of subjects and the craftmanship they show is outstanding and, as we shall see when we come to consider the discoveries from Gloucestershire villas, it seems very probable that Corinium was an important centre for mosaicists working in this area.

Two mosaics with unusual subjects have been found at Leicester.[2] One has for centrepiece a magnificent peacock exhibiting all the glories of its tail. Only a single octagonal panel survives of the other and this shows a rather touching illustration of the myth in which the youth, Cyparissus, accidentally killed a stag to which he was very attached, and was so overcome with grief that he was changed into a cypress tree.[3] Here the two appear together, the stag affectionately regarding his friend, and a winged Cupid, symbol of their devotion, is about to shoot an arrow from his bow. Possibly the missing portions of the pavement depicted the fateful accident and the appearance of the cypress tree.

Further north we may note in passing a mosaic at York which seems to have come from a dining-room as it is decorated with deer and joints of venison,[4] and a fourth-century floor from Malton.[5] This seems to have depicted the Seasons.

---

[1] Toynbee (1963) no. 182.
[2] Toynbee (1964) p. 279.   [3] *Ibid.* Toynbee (1963) no. 183.
[4] *Eburacum* p. 53, no. 27, Pl. XXIII.
[5] N. Mitchelson, 'Roman Malton: the Civilian Settlement', *Y.A.J.* XLI (1964) Pl. IX opp. p. 216.

One alone survives, the bust of a woman cloaked and hooded and holding a bare branch, the personification of the bleak northern winter. At Aldborough, however, the most northern town in Roman Britain, mosaics are surprisingly abundant, but they also provide us with our best examples of what happened when elaborate figure scenes got into the hands of inexperienced artists; the geometric mosaics reach a higher standard. The most ambitious scene was an attempt to portray the Nine Muses and of these only the figure of Clio (History) holding her scroll has survived and she has lost her head.[1] Her name appears in Greek beside her. Part of another figure may belong to Melpomene or Tragedy. Mosaics with the same subject but better rendered are known from other provinces including examples from Trier, Valencia and Sousse (North Africa). One at Lisbon also incorporates a request to the servants reading, 'Don't hurt the mosaic with a scratchy broom, but be careful of it.'[2] Another Aldborough pavement has a central panel with a lion sitting beneath a tree, presumably awaiting his prey.[3] Stylised trees often appear on mosaics, we shall meet them again separating the animals who accompany Orpheus, and this is a leafier and rather better tree than most. But the animal is not a success, his identification as a lion is open to doubt, he could be a panther or even a bear. The subject of the third figured pavement from Aldborough could hardly be more classical, it shows Romulus and Remus, the founders of Rome, beneath a tree with the wolf who acted as their foster mother (Pl. 13)[4]. Perhaps the craftsman had the scene described to him by his client, he surely did not see it in a pattern-book. The tree, which should by rights be a fig, is indeterminate, and the wolf looking out with a beaming smile, has saw-teeth and ears like a cat. This must be incompetence as wolves still roamed in Roman Britain and could not have been an unfamiliar sight. This wolf is also shirking her duties as instead of suckling the twins she is standing with uplifted paw, apparently urging them on as they dance a merry jig. And yet, in spite of its shortcomings, this pavement, now in the Leeds Museum, has a lively quality which makes it attractive; at least to those seeing it today. What its owner thought of it, history does not relate.

[1] Toynbee (1964) p. 284.   [2] Toynbee (1964) p. 285 n. 6.
[3] Toynbee (1964) p. 284.   [4] Toynbee (1964) p. 284.

5
The development of town life (3)
London and Bath

A survey of the evidence provided by Romano-British towns shows that as they developed they brought to the Britons social and political status and administration; increased security; public amenities such as *fora*, water supplies, shops and inns; and personal comfort in the form of well-built private houses. Verulamium in particular reflects how the official encouragement given to urban life by Agricola and Hadrian was followed by the periods of growth and prosperity in the second half of the second and in the fourth centuries. This was probably the pattern for most of the province although, of course, not all sites began so early or went on so late. Apart from Verulamium, however, little attempt has been made here to describe individual towns so some account of two sites of unusual character which do not fall into any of the categories of known *coloniae*, *municipia*, or *civitates* may be of interest, namely, London and Bath.

Londinium offers more tantalising problems than any other town in Britain. Built on a site which has been lived on intensively for centuries, most of the Roman levels have been disturbed or destroyed, and later buildings overlie the traces of the earlier ones. Some records exist of chance discoveries made during building or dredging operations in the last two or three centuries, and nowadays a careful watch is maintained by the Roman and Medieval London Excavation

Council for any opportunities for further investigations. The damage done by the aerial activities of the 1939–45 war has enabled much new information to be obtained,[1] but for the excavators it has, of course, been a race against time. The foundations of the new buildings now being erected go far deeper than those of their predecessors so that little evidence of earlier structures can survive beneath them. The recent excavations have frequently had to take place amid bomb-rubble in old cellars and basements in a confined space, and these restrictions usually make it impossible to regain the plan of a whole room, much less a complete building. Such conditions, of course, obtained in other bombed towns, notable Canterbury and Exeter, and, in view of these difficulties, it is remarkable how much of value has been recovered from the rescue work done in this way.

So far as we know, London is a Roman foundation as no traces have been found of any form of pre-Roman trading settlement. The Romans seem to have realised the striking possibilities of this site where stretches of hard gravel in otherwise marshy country made possible the building of a bridge over a tidal river deep enough for sea-going ships. It is quite clear that the new settlement grew into the most important town in the province for trade and commerce. The vital main roads built to facilitate the threefold advance of the legions soon after their arrival all radiate out from London; then as now it was the natural meeting point for road and sea traffic. By A.D. 60, Tacitus is describing the new town as a place not dignified with the title of *colonia*, but nevertheless the chief residence of the merchants and a flourishing trade-centre;[2] one may imagine the hum of activity among the simple first-century timber buildings. All this was interrupted by Boudicca's attack and the thick layer of ash which survives from it bears as striking a testimony to those days of terror in Londinium as it does at Camulodunum and Verulamium. Rebuilding soon followed, however. The early occupation centred on a small plateau now known as Cornhill in the heart of the modern city of London and it eventually spread westwards down Ludgate Hill. The area was drained by a stream called the Walbrook which ran into the river at a point not far from Cannon Street Station. The site of the bridge may have been a short distance to the east of the modern one. It was probably timber-built, and like Tower Bridge today, may have had a drawbridge in the middle which could be raised to allow for the masts of large ships (Pl. 20).

One of the most unexpected discoveries made by post-war excavators was

---

[1] For an up-to-date account of Londinium see Merrifield (1965) the basis for much of this and the following pages.

[2] *Annals* XIV. 32.

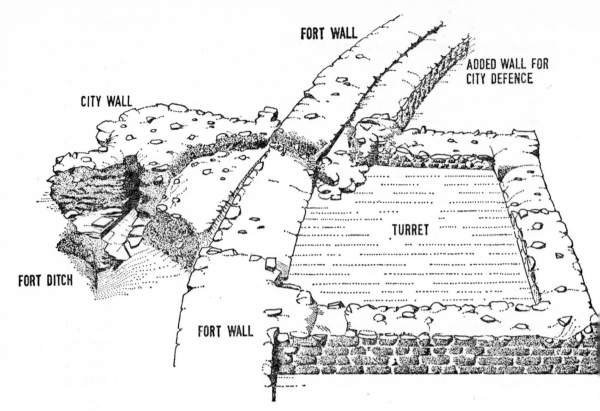

FORT WALL

ADDED WALL FOR
CITY DEFENCE

CITY WALL

TURRET

FORT DITCH

FORT WALL

38 The south-west corner of the Roman fort, London, at its junction
with the city wall

that of the fort at the north-west corner. During an investigation of the city wall
in the Cripplegate and Newgate area, it was realised that one short stretch consisted of not one wall but two, lying side by side and defined by a straight longitudinal joint between them. The inner face showed the normal wall construction but it had been built into an earth bank which had been cut back to accommodate it. Originally this bank was piled against an earlier wall of different
construction which now survived as the outer face. Further investigation followed in whatever cellars were accessible to north and south. Near Aldersgate
the city wall was known to turn west at an angle, and this was the area where
the solution to the mystery was found. The later wall ceased but the outer,
earlier wall curved east and attached to its inner face near the curve was a small
almost rectangular building. This was recognised as the corner turret of a fort
measuring about 250 by 235 yards, large enough for 1,500–2,000 men. The
wall, 4 feet thick, was built of ragstone defended by a slight V-shaped ditch
which may also have served as a drain (fig. 38). The north gate was the forerunner of the mediaeval Cripplegate. Wood Street passes close to the site of the
104

south gate, and the foundations of the west gate were found in Silver Street. This was a double gate with two carriage-ways and turrets containing guard-rooms on either side. An interior road has been identified behind the bank backing the wall, and the stone foundations of the barrack blocks and other buildings have also been found.

The fort is believed to date to soon after A.D. 100 and its purpose is not entirely clear. London, like so many other towns, may well have had a brief military occupation soon after the conquest although the evidence for this is still lacking. However it has recently been pointed out that the Roman road which underlies Lombard Street was almost certainly in existence before A.D. 60. It runs parallel to the river and at right angles to the probable site of the bridge and could very well be the main road of a carefully planned area. It is feasible that this is of military origin and the same may apply to an early stone building, the foundations of which were found on the north side of Lombard Street. On the other hand, town-planning with a rectangular street grid of the Claudian period has been found at Canterbury and Verulamium so it may also be of pre-Boudiccan date in London. If the theory about an early fort is correct and the army left the site within a few years, why was a new fort built elsewhere about fifty years later, at a time when there seems to have been no unrest in southern Britain to make it necessary? The answer to this problem seems to be connected with the even greater problem which arises over the status of London after A.D. 60/61.

Reference has already been made to the discovery of the fragments of the tombstone of Julius Classicianus, Procurator of Britain after the Boudiccan rebellion (fig. 1) and this is usually believed to indicate that the offices of the financial administration of the province were now in London. Much rebuilding was absorbing the local resources of Colchester, the capital and centre of the imperial cult, and little affection was probably felt for procurators in that city. New offices presumably had to be built somewhere. Did Classicianus decide to make a break with the past, and reconstruct the provincial finances afresh in this more conveniently sited town which had already shown such promising commercial possibilities? A wooden writing tablet found in the Walbrook area some years ago has a circular stamp impressed on the back with the words PROC AVG DEDERVNT/BRIT PROV, and this probably means 'Issued by the Imperial Procurators of Britain' (fig. 39). Tiles stamped P.PR.BR. LON, which may have a similar meaning, with the addition of Londinium, have also been found but such finds, of course, are of later date than the time of Classicianus.

Meanwhile, from the late first century onwards, London was rebuilt as a

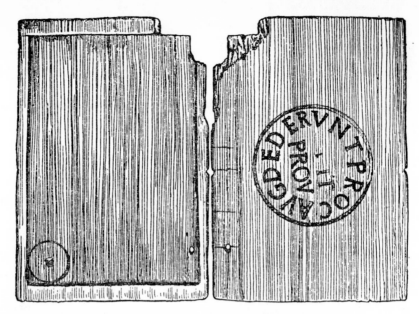

39 Wooden writing tablet branded PROC AVG DEDERVNT/BRIT
PROV (Issued by the Imperial Procurators of the Province of Britain)

Roman town with fine public buildings. Between A.D. 125 and 130 a serious
fire, apparently accidental, destroyed over 65 acres and a rise in the water level
began to cause trouble later in the second century. Sometime, probably fairly
early in the third century, the town walls were built. About A.D. 286 Carausius
declared himself Emperor in Britain and north-west Gaul and established a mint
at Londinium. In the troubles which followed, the Emperor Constantius I
made a successful landing and defeated the rebels and the mint may have continued in use for a short time (fig. 40). In 360 the Emperor Julian sent over
Lupicinus, one of his chief officers, with a force to deal with some serious
attacks by the Picts and Scots and he seems to have visited London. After the
disasters of 367, a very distinguished soldier, Count Theodosius, was sent to the
rescue and he found the city protected by its walls but in a state of seige. Dis-
persing the rebels he seems to have remained there while he reorganised the
government and planned his campaigns. Sometime during this century the city
received the title of Augusta, and the *Notitia Dignitatum* mentions the existence
of a *praepositus thesaurorum* there, an official in charge of the Treasury, possibly
the treasury of one of the five provinces into which Britain was now divided or
even of the whole diocese.

It seems reasonable to surmise that London, as Augusta, was the chief city
of one of these small fourth-century provinces but did it ever hold a more important status? It is sometimes suggested that by the second century it had
106

40   Medallion of Constantius I found at Arras showing the Relief of London by combined operations

already supplanted Colchester as the capital of the whole of the province of Britannia, and that the reason for the new fort at this period is to provide a headquarters for the governor's bodyguard and military staff. A little support to this theory is provided by the tombstone of Celsus erected by three comrades and found in Blackfriars.[1] Both the deceased and his friends are described as *speculatores* of the Second Legion, and *speculatores* are usually military policemen attached to the General Staff. Another tombstone, from Ludgate Hill, was erected to the 19-year-old Claudia Martina by her husband Anencletus, who described himself as the slave of the province.[2] This inscription is probably of late first-century date and might suggest that by now the provincial council had also moved to London. On the other hand these inscriptions may simply indicate that both Celsus and Claudia Martina succumbed when visiting or passing through London and were buried where they happened to die.

Another piece of second-century evidence is a fragment of a fine inscription reading 'To the Deity of the Emperor the province of Britain (set this up)'.[3] This was found built into a later wall near Cannon Street and could suggest that the centre of the imperial cult had been moved from Colchester. No traces of any such temples, however, have ever been found and the one at Colchester was rebuilt after A.D. 60 and continued in use. The imperial cult could, of course, have been practised in more than one place, whichever was the chief. In support of London it is sometimes pointed out that at the council of Arles in 314, Britain was represented by bishops from London, York and a third place which might be some other town such as Lincoln rather than Colchester. This could suggest that London was now of greater religious importance, but again, these may not have been the only bishops in Britain.

It is, of course, quite possible that while London was the financial capital by

[1] *R.I.B.* 19.
[2] *R.I.B.* 21.   [3] *R.I.B.* 5.

the late first or second century, it may not have become then, if ever, the chief political or religious centre. Is there a case, perhaps, for placing its promotion later, when the province was divided into two, making York the northern capital and obviously initiating extensive administrative reorganisation? York may then have received the status of *colonia*, why not London? Only the discovery of more inscriptions can provide the answer to what is one of the most fascinating problems of Roman Britain.

The wall which eventually surrounded Roman London was only built on three sides, the river apparently acting as sufficient defence on the fourth. Two miles in length, it survived into mediaeval times and stretches of it can still be seen today, notably on Tower Hill and in Trinity Place, in the underground car park along London Wall, with the wall of the Cripplegate fort in Noble Street and also with the remains of the later city defences in St Alphage's churchyard. It was of massive construction, built of ragstone and rows of tiles, with a sandstone plinth at the base. The stone was brought from Kent by water and the wall was 6 to 8 feet thick and is known to have been at least $14\frac{1}{2}$ feet high. Its original height may well have been 20 feet. A gateway similar to the fort west gate has been identified at Newgate, and another gate with a double carriage-way, but with projecting towers, has been found at Aldersgate. This may have been inserted after the building of the wall. The usual town ditch, 10 to 16 feet wide and $4\frac{1}{2}$ to $6\frac{1}{2}$ feet deep, was dug outside about 10 to 15 feet away. A series of 21 bastions was added to the wall at some period and these are usually divided into two groups. The eleven so far found east of Moorgate include fragments of tombstones and other re-used stones among their materials, and are generally accepted as belonging to the late Roman period; the western series are believed to be later, possibly post-Roman.

Regrettably little is known of the buildings inside the town. Remains of a Basilica with several different periods which grew to be larger than any other in Britain, comparable in size with those built in Rome itself, were found under Leadenhall Market. It may date from the time of Agricola in which case the Forum planned to accompany it does not seem to have been built until the time of Hadrian. Traces of substantial buildings, however, lay beneath the Forum and may have belonged to an earlier town centre.

In addition to the Basilica there is evidence for a few other London buildings. Most important of them all is the temple of Mithras discovered in 1954,[1] and inscriptions, statuettes and fragments of sculpture bear witness to the worship of various deities. Public baths may have stood in Lower Thames Street where several heated rooms were found in 1848 and 1859, with window glass and

[1] See below p. 449.

fragments of a stone pillar and cornice; and hypocausts were also found in Threadneedle Street and Mincing Lane. Further along Threadneedle Street were remains of buildings which produced elaborate wall-paintings and several geometric mosaics. Fragments of these are preserved in the British Museum. In 1964 baths were also found in Upper Thames Street and a more complete bath suite was discovered opposite the Church of St Mary-le-Bow in 1955. Built in the late first or early second century, it was later reconstructed and enlarged but in the third century the building seems to have been demolished.

Water for the baths and for the population in general seems to have depended upon wells, and a large concentration of wells in Queen Street may have been dug for the public supplies. London was so well provided with springs that aqueducts were unnecessary and some of the water seems to have been directed into wooden water-pipes. Drainage was very necessary if low-lying sites were to escape becoming water-logged and drains of tile or timber have been identified. One of the objects of post-war excavation has been to discover more about the Walbrook. This was believed to have been a tributary of the Thames, running through the midst of the Roman town and deep enough to carry ships. It is now shown to have been a stream no more than 12 to 14 feet wide, its sides revetted with piles and horizontal timbering. While thickly occupied on both banks it can never have been the site of quays, but seems to have been a centre for light industry and shop-keeping. Rubbish was dumped here to raise the ground level or dwellings were erected on piles or timber rafts to counteract the marshy conditions. The temple of Mithras stood on the east bank, and a building with at least two mosaic floors of the late second or third century was found further north, under the Bank of England, in 1933-4.

Elsewhere houses of stone, rubble and tile succeeded the earlier timber buildings, although roof-tiles are surprisingly scarce and many houses must have been roofed with thatch. One building found in 1959 in Lime Street seems to have started life in the late first or early second century. Its history after this is somewhat incomplete, but there does seem to have been considerable rebuilding of the north part of the site in the late third century. This was dated by the discovery of a hoard of copper coins found in a small hole made below a corner of the new walls—possibly a foundation offering. The building was burnt down some time after A.D. 350. Another house, at 11, Ironmonger Lane, was also built or rebuilt in the late third century. Further east, in Fenchurch Street, remains of a large warehouse or granary have been identified. On the whole London, like other Romano-British towns, seems to have had areas of both dense and scattered occupation with space for expansion within the walls. Its growth was gradual and not fully planned.

March 1. 1854

Individual discoveries which bear witness to the wealth and importance of Londinium include the fine bronze head from a colossal statue of the Emperor Hadrian, now in the British Museum. It was found in the Thames, and like the head of Claudius discovered in the River Alde and believed to be loot from Colchester, it must have belonged to a memorial, standing perhaps at the entrance to the bridge or in the Forum. Enormous hands which may possibly belong to the same statue have also been found in Lower Thames and Grace-church Streets. Stone had to be brought from some distance and consequently Roman buildings were intensively robbed and their materials re-used. Much of the sculpture recovered consists of fragments used in strengthening the wall and many of these are tombstones. Bastion 10, for example, in Camomile Street, produced several fragments of fluted column-shafts, a Corinthian capital and the top of a decorative arch or canopy, as well as a lion and a fine figure of a soldier wearing a cloak (fig. 45), both probably coming from tombs. Column-shafts decorated with scale pattern are known from other sites and a fragment found in Blomfield Street shows lattice work enlivened with small flowers and baskets. Some consideration has already been given to London's wall-paintings, but there are a few other examples of mosaics which show that this art also flourished. Early in the nineteenth century a floor was found between Broad Street and Bishopsgate (fig. 41). Its decoration consisted chiefly of geometric motifs, with scallop shells and a lotus flower border, but it also had a central panel showing either a Bacchante riding on a panther or Europa on the bull. Nearby a female head partly constructed of glass *tesserae* is also reported. Another head, possibly a female portrait of late date, was found in Cornhill, and part of an oblong panel showing a peacock and *cantharus* came to light in Fenchurch Street and is now in the British Museum. In 1869 a very fine geo-metric mosaic was found at Bucklersbury, under the line of the present Queen Victoria Street and close to the site of the Mithraeum (fig. 42). It can now be seen in the Guildhall Museum. The design consists of two interlaced squares of guilloche surrounding a medallion with a four-petalled flower. Beyond this at one end is a panel of very naturalistic acanthus scroll and the room ended in an apse, filled in with a scallop-shell design, reminiscent of the one at Verulamium. The room was heated by a hypocaust and wall flues. Another figured mosaic was found in Leadenhall Street and pieces of it too are in the British Museum. Three fragments show *peltae* or guilloche and the circular central medallion illustrates a vine-crowned Bacchus with *thyrsus* and wine cup, riding very com-fortably on the back of a splendidly striped tiger, who turns his head to look round at him.

The British, London and Guildhall Museums are full of the bric-à-brac of

41 OPPOSITE   Mosaic pavement showing a Bacchante

42 Mosaic pavement from Bucklersbury

Roman daily life. Post-war excavation has centred very largely round the Wal-brook and there the damp conditions have preserved tools and leather work with unusual success. From the bed of the stream came a wooden ladder and part of a workman's wicker basket. A nearby rubbish pit produced sixteen cooking pots and two jugs, apparently crushed by a large *amphora* which had been thrown in after them, while finer pottery came from the old ground level. All were covered by the ash of the fire of A.D. 60 which filled up the pit, sealing it completely. Another pit produced fine first-century glassware imported from Gaul, including a beautiful two-handled cup of white glass of rare type and a drinking horn. Lamps and candle-sticks, tools and toilet articles, have been found all over with bronze and pewter jugs, bowls and plates, and fragments of glass of many colours. Occasionally jewellery comes to light, like the gold ring from the site of the General Post Office, inscribed with its owner's initials, Q. D. D. Some of the pieces of red-glazed samian ware also have the names of their owners scratched on them: Audax, Felicula, Paullus or Glycera. Roof-tiles showing the marks of sandalled feet or the paws of dogs and cats where the unwary had stepped on the half-finished articles awaiting baking, are found not infrequently. Memories of ancient grievances are preserved on thin pieces of lead. One reads: 'Titus Egnatius Tyrannus is cursed; and Publius Cicereius Felix is cursed.'[1] A nail-hole in the centre of the plate shows that it was nailed up, and on the back the inscription is repeated less successfully; perhaps this side was used as a trial-piece to work out the spacing for the finished object. Another begins, 'I curse Tretia Maria and her life and mind and memory and liver and lungs mixed up together, and her words thoughts and memory; thus may she be unable to speak what things are concealed. . . .'[2] Obviously these are curses, similar to examples found at Bath and elsewhere. Unfortunately the misdemeanours committed by Tyrannus and Felix are not recorded and no one knows why it was so important for Tretia (or ?Tertia) Maria to keep her mouth shut. But seven nails were driven through the back of her lead plate after it was inscribed.

The other town which remains for consideration is one of the very small class of Romano-British health resorts of which Buxton is another probable example. Bath in Roman times had much the same importance as it has now; it was a spa. The existence and curative powers of its hot springs were already known and appreciated and the baths erected in connection with them remain partially in use till this day. The small town of about 22 acres sprang up towards the end of the first century. It never grew very much and remained a health resort, visited by invalids and visitors in search of rest and recreation. At some period it was walled and remains of various structures have been discovered within its limits. Most important of all were the baths built towards the end of the first century and subsequently altered and extended several times.[3] In their original form they probably included three deep plunge baths or swimming-pools. The one on the east, called the Lucas bath, occupies the greater part of a long oblong hall. It measured about 30 by 15 feet and 5 feet deep, and the bather descended into it by three massive stone steps. It was constructed of small stones set in courses and covered with cement and the floor was also covered with great sheets of lead half an inch thick. The hall itself had a stone

---

[1] *R.I.B.* 6.   [2] *R.I.B.* 7.
[3] A. J. Taylor, *The Roman Baths at Bath* (Bath, 1954); W. H. Knowles, 'The Roman Baths at Bath', *Arch.* LXXV (1926) 1–18.

floor and at each end were small apsidal plunge baths, one only 3 feet deep, the other 5½ feet in depth. The deeper one had a cement covered seat running round it. On the west of the Lucas bath was the Great Bath, also set in the centre of a spacious hall 111 by 68 feet. When first built it was open to the sky as we see it today but the hall surrounding it was covered (Pl. 24). The remains of the great piers which probably supported the roof of this colonnade on transverse arches are still visible. In the middle of the north side of the bath a fountain provided fresh cold water for the bathers. Still further west is a small rectangular room occupied by the circular swimming-bath. Lead lined, it is uncertain if this was filled with hot or cold water. One of its drains flushed the latrine in an adjoining vestibule which may have been the entrance to the whole establishment. Smaller baths, some heated by a furnace, existed further west, and on the north is the great reservoir fed by the hot springs which supplied the Great Bath and the East Bath with the healing waters. Some of the water-channels leading out of it are still in use. One culvert, made of lead with a timber lining, had a dipping place where water for drinking was probably obtained. Several bronze and pewter jugs and bowls were discovered near it. Offerings of coins of all periods were found in the lead-lined reservoir and also a small lead plate inscribed with a curse. It begins, 'May he who carried off Vilbia from me become as liquid as water.'[1] There follows a list of names and it is believed that the writer was in love with Vilbia and wished Sulis Minerva, the goddess of the springs, to get rid of all her rival suitors for him. The dropping of a written petition in a sacred spring was a favourite way of attracting the attention of a deity and, as is often the case with curses, the text is written with each word reversed. Other offerings included jewellery and dice. At later periods Roman baths of the usual type with rooms heated by hypocausts were added at the east and west ends of the great plunge baths, the eastern one covering a large first period water tank of uncertain purpose. The Great Bath was completely roofed in by a masonry vault with a span of 35 feet, the steam from the water escaping through circular openings at each end; pieces of this vaulting can be seen lying beside the bath. Traces of mosaic floors may also belong to this period, but regrettably little survives of the fine decorations, statuary and sculptural ornament which must have made the building a splendid sight in its heyday. We are fortunate, however, in being still able to see the baths, one of the most impressive Roman monuments in Western Europe.

In appreciation of the powers of Sulis Minerva a great temple decorated with fine sculpture was erected in her honour to the north of the baths.[2] A fine head of the goddess in gilt-bronze was found near the baths in 1727 and may have

[1] R.I.B. 154.   [2] See below p. 436.

114

stood at the entrance or near the reservoir (Pl. 23), and there is also a roughly carved relief of her holding a spear and her shield with an owl perched on it. Another relief shows the god Mercury. Large stone blocks depicting figures of Jupiter, Hercules, Bacchus and Apollo may come from an altar placed outside the temple and visible from the baths. Another large public building is known to exist to the east of the temple.[1]

Altars dedicated to various deities have been found in the town. Sulis, very properly, leads the list with eight offerings to date, mostly made on behalf of soldiers. A centurion of the Second Legion fulfilled his vow for himself and his kindred,[2] and the freedmen Aufidius Eutuches and Aufidius Lemnus, probably Bath business men, each erected an altar to their patron, Aufidius Maximus, a centurion of the Sixth.[3] Priscus, son of Toutius, a stonemason from near Chartres, also erected an altar to Sulis.[4] He may have helped to build her temple and so may the sculptor Sulinus who made a dedication to the Suleviae both here and at Cirencester.[5] Mars and Diana are other deities commemorated at Bath,[6] and unfortunately the names of the deity and worshipper are lost from the altar which the 'son of Novantius, set up for himself and his family as the result of a vision'.[7] Apparently, he was not alone in having visions, as far away on Hadrian's Wall, one inspired Flavius Secundus, Prefect of the Hamian Archers, to set up an altar to the Emperor's Fortune in the fort bath-house at Carvoran,[8] and another led to Fortune the Preserver being commemorated by Antonia at Kirkby Thore (Westmorland).[9]

A number of tombstones have been discovered and, of these, one shaped like an altar is probably the most important. It was erected to Gaius Calpurnius Receptus, priest of the goddess Sulis, who lived 75 years. Calpurnia Trifosa, his freedwoman and wife had this set up.[10] Soldiers and civilians alike ended their days in Bath, among them Successa Petronia, dearest daughter of Vettius Romulus and Victoria Sabina, who lived 3 years, 4 months, 9 days.[11] Several graves must have had magnificent memorials. A stone head of a woman, larger than life size and wearing an elaborate hair-style datable to the late first century (Pl. 28*b*) probably belonged to a tomb, and so may another fragment of a dog attacking a stag.[12]

The memories of the past glories of earlier times were sometimes preserved by the writers of later generations who frequently imagined that the ruins of

---

[1] Barry Cunliffe, 'The Temple of Sulis Minerva at Bath', *Antiquity* XL (1966) 199–204.
[2] *R.I.B.* 146. [3] *R.I.B.* 143, 144. [4] *R.I.B.* 149.
[5] *R.I.B.* 151, 105. [6] *R.I.B.* 138, 140. [7] *R.I.B.* 153.
[8] *R.I.B.* 1778. [9] *R.I.B.* 760. [10] *R.I.B.* 155.
[11] *R.I.B.* 164. [12] Toynbee (1964) p. 143.

Roman buildings were the remains of the military strongholds of great princes, destroyed by war or plague. One brief reference of this type concerns Carlisle and it occurs in the Anonymous Life of St Cuthbert. In the seventh century the saint was visiting the city at a time of much warfare and unrest. While awaiting news of a battle one Saturday at the ninth hour, he is described as being shown by Waga the reeve, the city wall and the well, formerly built in a wonderful manner by the Romans. Bede, in his life of St Cuthbert based on the Anonymous Life, replaces the well by a 'marvellous fountain of Roman workmanship',[1] perhaps similar to the fountains existing at Corbridge, Bath and other sites. Another more romantic description is given in an Anglo-Saxon poem of the eighth century called 'The Ruin'; this is usually believed to be a description of Bath and it makes a fitting epilogue to our study of town life.

Wondrous is this masonry, shattered by the Fates. The fortifications have given way, the buildings raised by giants are crumbling. The roofs have collapsed; the towers are in ruins. . . . There is rime on the mortar. The walls are rent and broken away, and have fallen undermined by age. The owners and builders are perished and gone, and have been held fast in the earth's embrace, the ruthless clutch of the grave, while a hundred generations of mankind have passed away. Red of hue and hoary with lichen this wall has outlasted kingdom after kingdom, standing unmoved by storms. The lofty arch has fallen. . . . Resolute in spirit he marvellously clamped the foundations of the walls with ties. There were splendid palaces and many halls with water flowing through them; a wealth of gables towered aloft. . . .

And so these courts lie desolate, and the framework of the dome with its red arches sheds its tiles . . . where of old many a warrior, joyous hearted and radiant with gold, shone resplendent in the harness of battle, proud and flushed with wine. He gazed upon the treasure, the silver, the precious stones, upon wealth, riches and pearls, upon this splendid citadel of a broad domain. There stood courts of stone, and a stream gushed forth in rippling floods of hot water. The wall enfolded within its bright bosom the whole place which contained the hot flood of the baths. . . .[2]

[1] Trans. B. Colgrave, '*Two Lives of St Cuthbert* (Cambridge, 1940) pp. 123, 243.
[2] Trans. N. Kershaw, *Anglo-Saxon and Norse Poems* (Cambridge, 1922) p. 55. I am indebted to Mrs N. Kershaw Chadwick and the Cambridge University Press for permission to use this quotation.

6
Family life

Even if the owners and the builders are perished and gone enough survives of the walls and buildings of Roman Britain to stir the imagination, and arouse our curiosity about the people who lived in them. The first question to be asked therefore is, what did they look like? Unfortunately, the statues of worthy citizens which must once have decorated the Forum in many towns have all vanished, no portraits survive among our wall-paintings, and no accounts of family life are preserved in our sparse literary sources. We should have no idea of the appearance of those early ancestors of ours, were it not for one of those things we still hold in common with them—a loving respect for the dead. The tombstones of Roman Britain provide a gallery of figures, not all very skilfully carved and frequently damaged by the unkind hand of time, but sufficient for our purpose. Sometimes the accompanying inscriptions tell us the names of the persons portrayed, the ages at which they died, and who had the sad task of raising this last memorial to a loved one.

A number of tombstones of this type come from a cemetery on the Mount at York, and among them is one erected by a soldier of the Sixth Legion which was stationed there for many years (Pl. 25c). His name was Gaius Aeresius Augustinus, and in the relief he appears on the right, wearing civilian dress and holding a rolled-up document in his hand. His family accompany him.

Beside him stands his wife, Flavia Augustina, who died aged 39 years 7 months and 11 days, and in front are their two children. The inscription states that the boy died aged a year and the girl at 21 months, but they are depicted looking older than their stated ages. How long, one wonders, did their father survive these losses?

Another tombstone shows Aelia Aeliana lying on a couch with her husband's arm round her and a little girl, who may be her daughter, standing close by (Pl. 25*a*). Her name is all that survives, the rest of the inscription having been destroyed, and we can only hope that her husband did not have to lament the loss of the little girl as well as that of his wife. This seems to have been the sad case with a third York tombstone on which Marcus Aurinius Simnus commemorates Mantinia Maerica and her mother, Candida Barita.[1]

We pass next to a rather more elaborate scene accompanied by a complete inscription (Pl. 26*c*), which tells us that the lady reclining on the couch was Julia Velva, who died at the age of 50. Her son-in-law, Aurelius Mercurialis, stands near her, and her daughter sits in a basket chair at the foot of the couch playing with a bird on her knee. Food and drink for the funeral banquet are placed on a little table, and a small boy who may be a grandson, stands, wine-jug in hand, ready to serve his elders. Aurelius Mercurialis inherited, it seems, a fortune from his mother-in-law, and he erected this memorial to her as a token of gratitude from himself and the rest of the family.

Another tombstone (Pl. 29*b*) depicts a cleanshaven man with his hair combed forward over his brow. He holds a scroll in one hand and a bunch of leaves, possibly symbolising prosperity in the after-life, in the other.[2] Fragments of two heads, both probably from funerary monuments, show more of the Roman inhabitants of York (Pl. 28*c*), and a fine head with the hair and beard styles fashionable in the time of Antoninus Pius survives from Carlisle.[3] Another realistic portrait showing an elderly clean-shaven man appears between the paws of the magnificent sphinx which once guarded a grave at Colchester (Pl. 58). This probably dates from the very end of the first century, and the human hands and the bones depicted must also belong to the owner of the tomb. The sphinx is winged and shown as half woman and half feline, and the serene expression on the man's face suggests that he envisages her as his protectress.[4]

A good portrait of another Romano-British lady survives in the Tullie House Museum, Carlisle (Pl. 26*a*). She sits in a high-backed chair, fanning herself with one hand, while the other arm is placed lovingly round the little

[1] *Eburacum* p. 124 no. 84; R.I.B. 689. The reading varies.
[2] Toynbee (1964) p. 199.   [3] *Ibid.* p. 198.   [4] *Ibid.* p. 113.

boy who plays with the pet bird on her lap. Unfortunately, the inscription has vanished, so we do not know their names. The same is the case with another memorial-stone found at Chester, on which the dead woman surveys us cheerfully as she reclines on a couch with a wine-cup in her hand.[1] Near her stone stands another erected to Curatia Dinysia, aged 40 at the time of her death, by her grateful heir.[2] Comfortably settled on her high-backed couch, with a wine-cup in one hand and a rug over her knees, Curatia wears the air of a lively, alert woman, mistress of her household and, as a widow, accustomed to managing her own affairs. The head of another determined looking lady survives from York (Pl. 28*a*). Carved in a rather intractable stone, the pupils and irises of her eyes were never marked in, so the portrait may be unfinished unless some details were originally added in paint. From certain angles the face seems to be faintly smiling and the subject may have been quite a young woman.[3]

So far as we know, the social position of women in Roman Britain was inferior to that of men. No doubt a daughter led a sheltered life in her father's care until he arranged her marriage, which gave her more freedom as the mistress of her own household. She could not, however, take part in public life, except as a priestess of some religious cults; but even there her activities were very limited. Nevertheless, there must have been many wives who helped and advised their husbands efficiently, especially in the circles of traders and shopkeepers; and no doubt there were some henpecked husbands. Such inscriptions as to 'Grata, daughter of Dagobitus, aged 40; Solinus had this erected to his dearest wife';[4] 'In Memory of Aurelia Aia . . . a very pure wife who lived 33 years without any blemish';[5] or to 'Aurelia Aureliana lived 41 years. Ulpius Apolinaris set this up to his very beloved wife',[6] show the very proper sentiments felt by widowers, and wording of this description is not uncommon. Widows, however, are far more reserved about deceased husbands; and two examples found in London, erected, one to Vivius Marcianus by his most devoted wife, Januaria Martina,[7] the other to Flavius Agricola, described by Albia Faustina as a peerless husband,[8] are noteworthy as being rather exceptional. At Chester, the tombstone of Titinius Felix of the Twentieth Legion, aged 45, was set up by his wife and heiress Julia Similina, and this reminds us that widows were often much better off than wives, since they could inherit some of their husband's property as well as retaining their dowries, and were able to decide either for themselves or with the advice of a guardian, how it

---

[1] R.*I.B.* 568.   [2] R.*I.B.* 562.
[3] Toynbee (1964) p. 63.   [4] R.*I.B.* 22.
[5] R.*I.B.* 1828.   [6] R.*I.B.* 959.
[7] R.*I.B.* 17.   [8] R.*I.B.* 11.

should be invested.[1] This probably accounts for the independent and vivacious appearance of Julia Velva and Curatia Dinysia.

Very touching are the memorials erected in memory of dead children. One tombstone found at Chester and dedicated to Flavius Callimorphus, aged 32, and Serapion, aged 3 years 6 months, was erected by Thesaeus 'to brother and son'.[2] Callimorphus reclines on a couch with the little boy in his lap. The bird on the table in front of the couch was probably the child's pet. At Caerleon, Julia Iberna aged 16 is lovingly remembered by her mother, Flavia Flavina,[3] and at Corbridge in Northumberland Julius Marcellinus raises a tombstone to his dearest daughter, Julia Materna, aged 6.[4] At Chesters in the same county, a mother and father bewail the loss of Fabia Honorata, a sweet daughter.[5] But perhaps the best known and most touching of all the memorials to children is the inscription on the side of a small stone coffin found at York, 'To Simplicia Florentina, a most innocent soul, who lived 10 months'.[6] Pictures of these children include a boy shown sleeping very comfortably on an altar tombstone from Chester. Below his couch a mother bird feeds a vociferously squawling chick (Pl. 3). A small bronze head found at Otterbourne in Hampshire shows the plump face of a young girl with the large almond-shaped eyes, which are the sign of Celtic artistic influences. The eyelashes are indicated by hatching and the pupils are filled in with small black pebbles. The treatment of the face, mouth and simply waved hair, however, are typically Roman.[7]

Foster children are also sometimes mentioned. Mercatilla, freedwoman and foster daugher of Magnius, died at Bath when only a year old.[8] Hyllus, a beloved foster child is commemorated at York,[9] Hermagoras at High Rochester,[10] and Ylas, aged 13, at Old Penrith.[11] In some cases when parents, perhaps, were dead, other relations erect the memorial. At Carvoran, Lucius Senofilus does this for his niece Lifana, and Aurelia Pusinna laments a most devoted and very much missed sister.[12]

Children, too, remembered parents, as in the case of the tombstone at Risingham of Aurelia Lupula, whose son Dionysius Fortunatus erected it to the memory of his most affectionate mother adding, 'May the earth lie lightly on thee'.[13] Again, there are inscriptions at Caerleon dedicated to Tadia Vallaunius, aged 65, and to Tadius Exupertus, aged 37, who died in the German campaign. We read that 'Tadia Exuperata, the devoted daughter, set this up to her mother

---

[1] J. P. V. D. Balsdon, *Roman Women* (1962) pp. 188, 222.
[2] R.I.B. 558.   [3] R.I.B. 377.   [4] R.I.B. 1182.   [5] R.I.B. 1482.   [6] R.I.B. 690.
[7] Toynbee (1964) p. 57, Pl. VIII*b*.
[8] R.I.B. 162.   [9] R.I.B. 681.   [10] R.I.B. 1291.
[11] R.I.B. 937.   [12] R.I.B. 1829, 1830.   [13] R.I.B. 1250.

and brother beside her father's tomb'.[1] We wonder what happened to Tadia
Exuperata. Was she left the sole survivor of a once happy and united family, or
had she husband and children of her own?

All these inscriptions show us how much lower was the expectation of life
in Roman times than it is today, for records of people living to what we now
regard as a normal old age rarely occur. At Lincoln a tombstone was dedicated
to Claudia Crysis, aged 90, by her heirs,[2] and at Caerleon is an inscription in
memory of Julius Valens, a veteran of the Second Legion, who lived to be a
hundred.[3] These are most exceptional, and one feels that the hardy old soldier
certainly deserved, if not the nearest Roman equivalent to a telegram from the
Emperor, at least the congratulations of the governor of Britain. Unluckily no
portrait of him survives. He left a wife and son and we know that the wife,
Julia Secundina, also lived to the ripe old age of 75, since her tombstone, erected
by Julius Martinus to his devoted mother, has also been found at Caerleon.[4]

Information about the more intimate details of family life can be gained from
various sources. In a Romano-British household getting up in the morning
would be a simpler affair than it is today. A visit to the baths—either the public
baths in a town or those belonging to a private house—would probably take
place later in the afternoon or early evening, so that washing first thing was not
considered essential. Breakfast, too, was not a formal meal, a drink of water, and
some bread or fruit, perhaps, being taken as required. Nightclothes were not
used; a man slept in some of his day clothes, and then simply stepped out of
bed, put on his sandals and perhaps one extra garment, presumably combed his
hair, and was prepared to face the day.

Some idea of the clothes worn by Romano-Britons may be obtained from
the tombstones and other sculptures, but, of course, these tell us nothing about
underclothes. The inhabitants of Rome and Italy are known to have sometimes
worn a loincloth of wool or linen knotted round the waist or short drawers;[5]
and it is possible that underclothing of this simple type was also worn by
Romanised provincials. Over the loincloth came a tunic made of two pieces of
narrow-width material sewn together at the sides and on the shoulders. Slits
were left for the head and arms to go through; or there might be sleeves of
varying lengths.[6] A carving found at Housesteads (fig. 43) shows a man wearing
a knee-length tunic with sleeves reaching to just below the elbow; and another
stone found nearby has the sleeves down to the wrist. The man on the York

---

[1] *R.I.B.* 369.   [2] *R.I.B.* 263.
[3] *R.I.B.* 363.   [4] *R.I.B.* 373.
[5] L. M. Wilson, *Clothing of the Ancient Romans* (Baltimore, 1938) p. 72.
[6] Wilson, *op. cit.* p. 55 *et seq.*

43 Tombstone showing a man wearing a tunic and a short fringed cloak fastened with a brooch on the shoulder. Found at Housesteads

tombstone (Pl. 27*b*) and also Aurelius Mercurialis on Julia Velva's tombstone (Pl. 26*c*) wear sleeved tunics of similar type. Two tunics were often worn, one above the other, and possibly more in cold weather. No doubt most individuals would have several tunics made of woollen materials of varying thicknesses folded away in their chests. White was the favourite colour, but other shades were probably obtainable; and poorer men had garments of unbleached wool. The tunic was worn slightly bloused out above a belt or girdle and draped so as to come just below the knees, shorter in front than behind. For manual work and active pursuits such as hunting, short tunics pulled well above the knee were found more practical, and these are worn by the smith at York (Pl. 25*b*) or the hunters on the East Coker mosaic. No Romano-British mosaics or sculptures appear to show civilians wearing any covering for the legs other than boots. Nevertheless, we may guess that the close-fitting trousers or *bracae* reaching to the ankle,[1] which are known to have been worn by the Gauls, found their way to Britain, and formed part of the costume of countryfolk of native stock in the less Romanised districts—the sort of people who appear less frequently in works of art. Indeed, *bracae* are worn by figures personifying the province of Britain on coins of Hadrian and Antoninus Pius. *Bracae* were part of the costume of European horse-riding tribes and were not a Gaulish invention: they were also worn by Germanised Dacians. The Romans regarded them as typical barbarian dress and classical writers frequently refer to them contemptuously. No self respecting Roman would appear in them; but in cold weather, or for riding, some form of knee-breeches—the *feminalia*—were worn and these may also have

[1] Wilson, *op. cit.* p. 73.

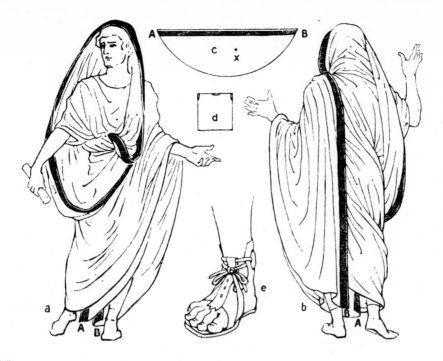

44 The toga

been adopted by provincials who were Roman citizens and who disdained the long *bracae*. Leg wrappings like puttees may have accompanied the *feminalia*.

To what extent the toga—that distinctively Roman garment—was worn in Britain is also an open question. It consisted of a large elliptical piece of material about 18½ feet long and 7 feet deep at its widest point (fig. 44).[1] Usually its colour was that of the natural wool, but youths under 16 and magistrates had a scarlet or purple stripe along the straight edge, candidates for office wore pure white, and mourners black or a dark colour. The toga was a very dignified garment and its correct draping was a matter of some complexity, needing the assistance of a second person, often a slave skilled in toga arrangement. A point about 6 feet from the end A (fig. 44) along the straight edge was placed first on the left shoulder and the rest of A allowed to fall down in front to the ground. The remaining material was draped round the back of the shoulders and under the right arm. Then it was grasped at a point X about a third of its depth from the straight edge, and gathered into a flap or overfold which hung down in front. More folds were gathered and twisted at the right side of the waist and then the fold at X was firmly tucked into the girdle of the tunic beneath. The overfold was arranged to fall to knee-level in a curve. The rest of the toga with end B was thrown over the left shoulder and draped down the back to the feet.

[1] *Ibid.* p. 36 *et seq.*; M. Houston, *Ancient Greek, Roman and Byzantine Costume* (1961) p. 89 *et seq.*

Such a garment had to be worn with circumspection if the folds were not to become upset. Even in Rome the citizens began to think it a nuisance and several of the emperors had to issue edicts giving orders that it must be worn on formal occasions. In the provinces some new citizens may have adopted it with enthusiasm and Tacitus tells us in the *Agricola* that this was the case in Britain. However, it may only have been donned by the leading citizens for important ceremonies and after the second century it seems to have become more in the nature of academic dress. A sarcophagus in Guildhall Museum depicts a man wearing a garment which may be a toga,[1] but for daily use the toga must have been replaced by the more practical and popular cloak.

The relief from Housesteads already mentioned (fig. 43) shows a man wearing a cloak fastened on the shoulder with a circular brooch. These may be examples of the *lacerna*, a wrap said to be popular among all classes in Rome in fine or wet weather.[2] 'A cloudy sunset proclaims a rainy season,' says Pliny, 'and straightway the price of *lacernae* goes up',[3] and there are other references to it in the writings of Martial and Juvenal. Cloaks were made in many different colours, each of a piece of material roughly semicircular in shape. The straight upper edge went round the neck and was pinned on the shoulder, while the curved lower edge reached to the knee. On the other hand, the cloak seen in fig. 43, with its fringed ends, may be the *sagum*.[4] This is usually thought of as part of the dress of the Roman soldier, but the soldier originally acquired it from the Gauls, whose striped *saga* are described by Diodorus and Virgil.[5] The *sagum* was really a thick blanket worn with its upper half folded back and pinned on the shoulder by day, and then used as a covering at night. For really bad weather both soldiers and civilians took refuge in the *paenula*, a hooded cloak of thick wool, felt, or leather. A good representation of this as worn by a soldier in undress uniform occurs on a sculpture found in London (fig. 45). The *paenula* was too thick and heavy to be fastened by a brooch and must have been fitted round the neck and secured by a clasp or tied by strings or thongs. The London example is held together in front by buttons, studs or clasps. A separate hood was stitched to the back of the *paenula*. When folded back this is described as looking like a leaf of bindweed and both soldiers and barbarians are shown wearing it on the Arch of Septimius Severus in Rome.[6] A thick scarf was often worn under the *paenula*.

Another head covering, the *cucullus*, consisted of a hood with a cape of varying length. It could be used with the *lacerna* or other cloaks, and is often mentioned as worn by slaves or others whose activities took them out in bad

[1] R.I.B. 20, Pl. II.   [2] Wilson, *op. cit.* p. 117 *et seq.*   [3] *Ibid.* p. 118.
[4] *Ibid.* p. 104.   [5] *Aeneid* VIII 660.   [6] Wilson, *op. cit.* Chap. VII.

45 The *paenula*. Stone relief from a tomb re-used for a
bastion of the Roman Wall round London

weather. The bronze figure of a ploughman from Piercebridge (Pl. 51) is
probably wearing one,[1] and so is the small figure representing Winter among the
Seasons on the Chedworth mosaic (Pl. 39). This garment is also the distinguish-
ing dress of the minor deities called *Genii Cucullati*,[2] who are known from reliefs
such as the one found at Netherby, Cumberland.[3] Other reliefs of the *cucullati*
show them wearing a longer and more voluminous hooded cloak,[4] and this
may be the *byrrus*, a long heavy cape of wool or skins with a hood attached. It is
known from literary references from the second century onwards and in Diocletian's edict fixing the prices of goods in A.D. 301, several qualities are listed.
The cheapest is the African *byrrus* which could cost up to 1,500 *denarii*, the best
seems to have been the Nervian, presumably made in Gaul, or the Laodicean
variety which imitated the Nervian. This cost 10,000 *denarii*. A *byrrus Britannicus*
is also mentioned for 6,000 *denarii*, one of the better qualities. Some have thought
that the cloth for these cloaks was made at the imperial weaving mill known
from the *Notitia Dignitatum* to have existed in Britain at 'Venta', the Venta
meant in this connection is either Venta Belgarum (Winchester), or Venta
Icenorum (Caistor-by-Norwich), both probably in the centre of sheep-farming
areas.[5] A recent writer, however, has pointed out that while the wool possibly

[1] See below p. 216.
[2] See below p. 432.
[3] Toynbee (1964) p. 177, Pl. XLIVa.
[4] E.g. Toynbee (1963) p. 156 no. 77.
[5] W. Manning, 'Caistor-by-Norwich and *Notitia Dignitatum*', *Antiquity* XL (1966) 49–50.

came from the surrounding area, the state mills would probably be busy working for the army, and it is more likely that the *byrri* were made in weaving shops on the large estates.[1] A good example of a possible *byrrus* appears on a first-century tombstone found near Cirencester (Pl. 27*c*). The inscription identifies the wearer as Philus, a citizen of the Sequani, a tribe found near Besançon.[2] He may have been a merchant so perhaps his is a Nervian *byrrus*.

An amusing reference to a British cloak occurs as part of an inscription on a lead tablet found in the Caerleon Amphitheatre. It reads, 'Lady Vengeance, I give thee this cloak and these boots; let the man who deposited them not withdraw them except at the cost of his life-blood.'[3] Apparently the clothes belonged to a gladiator who left them in the dressing-room while he went to fight in the ring. His enemy came and laid a curse on his belongings hoping that even if the gladiator survived the fight, death would soon overtake him, and he economically offers the clothes to the goddess Nemesis as a thankoffering for her good offices. The word used here for cloak is *pallium*, a light rectangular mantle of Greek origin, also used by the Romans.[4]

Models show that babies were wrapped in swaddling bands, and one infant is depicted lying in its cradle under several blankets kept in place with straps with the pet dog asleep at the foot.[5] Children were dressed in much the same way as their parents. The small boy shown standing beside his mother at Carlisle (Pl. 26*a*), wears one or two tunics and a cloak, and so do the little Augustini (Pl. 25*c*). Girls usually wear longer tunics made of two pieces of cloth stitched together from under the arms to the hem. The unjoined portions are then folded back so that they hang down outside from the neck to below the waist forming a deep apron. The top of the garment is then gathered in folds on the shoulders along the crease, and secured with brooches or by a seam, holes being left for the head and arms. A girdle tied round the waist kept the loose fold in position. A tombstone in Carlisle dedicated to the memory of Vacia aged three (fig. 46) shows this arrangement very clearly: the tunic is worn over an under tunic with elbow-length sleeves; she also wears a plaited girdle and a cloak. The little girls on the York tombstones of Aelia Aeliana (Pl. 25*a*) and Julia Brica (Pl. 26*b*) are dressed in similar tunics.[6]

When we turn to women's dress, we find the same lack of evidence for under-

---

[1] J. P. Wild, 'The Byrrus Britannicus', *Antiquity* XXXVII (1963) 193–202.
[2] *R.I.B.* 110.
[3] V. Nash-Williams, *Catalogue of the Roman Inscribed and Sculptured Stones found at Caerleon* (Cardiff, 1935) no. 99.
[4] Wilson *op. cit.* p. 78 *et seq.*
[5] H. Eydoux, *La France Antique* (Paris, 1962) fig. 200, from Beaune.
[6] *Eburacum* p. 124 no. 80.

46 Tombstone of Vacia, Carlisle

clothes as in the case of men but there is some indication that a band of linen
was worn round the bust and served the same purpose as a modern brassière.
Over this came the under tunic; and in Italy this varied in type according as to
whether the wearer was a matron or an unmarried girl. But it is uncertain how
far these distinctions were observed in the provinces. Above the under tunic a
girl would probably wear an outer tunic of Vacia's type. Married women wore
the longer, more voluminous garment called the *stola*.[1] Women's tunics, like
those of men, were made of wool or linen in varying weights, and when a lady
of means went shopping in Londinium she would probably look for finer

[1] Wilson, *op. cit.* p. 160.

materials than those woven by the women of her household. Silk and cotton were worn by Roman women and may have occasionally found their way to the big provincial towns. In any case wool and probably linen textiles would be available in many designs and colours, including various shades of purple ranging from blue to red, as well as sea-green or saffron yellow. Fair complexioned ladies enhanced their beauty by wearing black, and white was recommended for the dark-skinned. Garments were conservative in shape but fashions in colours came and went. Very bright and gaudy colour-schemes were regarded as critically as they are today, otherwise the matron was free to make her choice, and embroidery and ornamental fringes were used to enliven her dress. The figure on the right of a carving found at Chester shows clearly a woman wearing a plain long-sleeved tunic (Pl. 27a), probably like the one of pale brown wool with traces of blue decoration found in a grave at Martres-de-Veyre.[1] Possibly she is an attendant to the lady on the left who is holding a mirror.[2] The latter's more voluminous *stola* with long pointed sleeves is covered by a wrap with straight-fringed hanging ends. Flavia Augustina is similarly dressed, and so is Regina (Pl. 2). Some of these tunics seem to show a certain bulkiness round the neck. This has also been noted on some of the Gaulish tombstones, and it is believed to be caused by the presence of a scarf or comforter, or by actual padding. In the case of the Chester lady just mentioned, it has been described as a jabot. The Murrell Hill lady seems to be showing the edge of her under tunic beneath her *stola* (Pl. 26a). Like the others she wears a cloak or *palla*. This was a rectangular mantle or shawl of varying size, colour and thickness, usually made of wool. Heads and faces are unfortunately the first features of sculptures to be destroyed; but as far as we can tell from our British carvings, women were mostly depicted with their heads uncovered. But since it was not customary for a lady to appear bareheaded in public, the *palla* must have been draped over the head on going out. Veils and small *pallae* or kerchiefs, were also worn. The *mappa*, a piece of cloth like a napkin or large handkerchief, was sometimes carried in the hand or over the shoulder, and used to wipe away dust and perspiration. Whether it was also used for blowing the nose is uncertain, as it is doubtful to what extent noses were blown before the end of the third century.[3]

We know very little about coverings for the feet such as socks and stockings. In 1850 an ancient burial was found preserved in the peat on Grewelthorpe Moor, 10 miles from Ripon, Yorkshire, and the shoes and the nature of the

---

[1] A. Audollent, 'Les Tombes des Martres-de-Veyre', *Man* XXI (1921) 163, Pl. I fig. 1.
[2] Wright (1955) no. 120.
[3] Carcopino (1956) p. 173.

clothes worn by the body led people to believe that it was of Roman date.[1] This man had a green cloak, a scarlet garment which may have been a tunic, and yellow stockings, the only evidence for stockings of this period discovered so far in this country. They are, however, known elsewhere; a burial found at Martres-de-Veyre in central France produced a pair of stockings, brown this time, with fringed tops, and belonging to a woman. One was marked with the letters PRI in white wool.[2] Another grave revealed a pair of socks with ankle-straps, and several figures on reliefs from Sens, Lillebonne and Neumagen seem to be wearing thick socks under their sandals.[3] Fragments of knitted socks also turned up in the town of Dura Europos in Syria, and there enterprising archaeologists have been able to work out the actual knitting pattern used in making them.[4] In the light of this evidence it seems possible that socks and stockings were worn by Romano-Britons. A long bronze needle, pointed at both ends like a modern sock needle, was found at the Lullingstone villa, and a set of knitting needles at Sutton Scotney.

Leather shoes are less perishable than textiles and numerous examples survive in wells and rubbish pits, preserved by the damp atmosphere. In general they were made of very supple leather, often in small pieces. They have no heels and are rounded to the natural shape of the foot. The characteristic sandal consisted of a leather sole held to the foot by a thong which passed between the first and second toes and was looped round the ankle, but there were also more substantial shoes covering the foot in varying degrees. These often have uppers with cut-out decoration, and some were threaded with thongs which tied round the ankle or were wrapped round the leg. Figure 47*d* shows an elaboration of the sandal with some of these features and *fig.* 47*a* shows an open work shoe found in London. The *calceus*, a more substantial high shoe or bootee, which might have uppers of cloth or leather completely covering the foot, was the correct outdoor wear for the Roman citizen in the towns when he went out wearing the toga. Varying forms of *calcei* were a sign of rank. They tended to be replaced, however, as time went on and dress grew less formal, by the *gallica*, a shoe or sandal of Gallic origin which spread into Italy and other provinces.[5] The boots of the Caerleon curse are *galliculae*, and *gallicae* for runners, single-soled for men and double-soled for farmworkers are all mentioned in Diocletian's edict and cost between 60 and 80 *denarii* a pair.[6] The soles were built up of several layers

[1] G. Home, *Roman York* (1925) p. 176.
[2] Audollent, *op. cit.* p. 163, Pl. I no. 3.
[3] E. IV nos. 2793; 3122; VI no. 5145.
[4] R. Pfister and L. Bellinger, *The Excavations at Dura Europos* IV ii (The Textiles) (New Haven, 1945) pp. 4, 54 *et seq.*
[5] Duval (1952) p. 104.   [6] IX. 12–14.

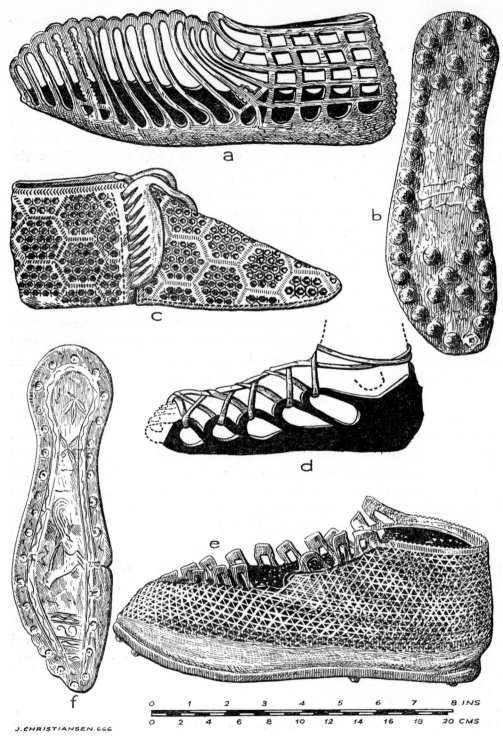

J. CHRISTIANSEN. 666

47 Shoes. *a* London. *b* Sole with hob-nails, London. *c* Found with a
burial, Southfleet, Kent. *d-f* London

of leather tied together by hob-nails. The nails are often arranged in decorative patterns (fig. 47*b*) and cleats and boot protectors are found occasionally. Thick heavily nailed soles come from the *caligae*, the typical military sandal, kept in position with straps across the foot and instep and thongs wound round the ankle up to the calf. According to Diocletian's edict, *caligae* without hobnails were also worn by women and mule drivers.[1] Women's shoes found in graves at Martres-de-Veyre included sandals with uppers, and shoes leaving the sides of the heel entirely bare but with an interior lining of wool, very light slippers made of a single piece of goatskin leaving the instep largely uncovered and kept on by laces wound round the legs, and clogs with wooden soles, kept on with straps. Women's shoes were usually fashioned of softer leather and brighter colours than those of men.

Among the discoveries made in Britain are pieces of more than thirty sandals and boots, from the site of a tannery at the villa at Lullingstone. Some were complete with iron or bronze buckles and a large piece of leather was also found. A burial at Southfleet (Kent) produced a fine slipper of purple leather with traces of gilding (fig. 47*c*). Many shoes have been unearthed in the marshy ground near the Walbrook in the city of London, including heavy nailed soles and slippers with elaborately cut-out uppers. The sole of a woman's shoe decorated on the upper-side with a design of a long-tailed bird, was discovered during the building of the Bank of England (fig. 47*f*). Numerous shoes belonging to soldiers, women and children were found in pits at the fortress of Newstead, including *caligae*, *calcei* and slippers.[2]

Hairdressing was an important feature of the Roman citizen's toilet. Numerous barber's shops existed in the towns; and these were favourite meeting-places and centres for gossip and scandal. Barbers were often able to retire as wealthy men. Customers sat on benches waiting their turn, and when it came they were swathed in a large *mappa* or in a wrap of cambric or muslin. Fashions in hairdressing were much influenced by the tastes of the reigning emperor. In the first century A.D. citizens were mostly clean-shaven, but beards were worn from the second century onwards. The Roman Londoner wearing the *paenula* referred to on p. 124 is clean-shaven, but Aurelius Mercurialis on Julia Velva's tombstone, Aelia Aeliana's husband, and heads found at Housesteads and Carlisle all have beards. For the Romans, shaving had a certain religious significance, and a young man's first shave was a rite of some importance. The hair

[1] IX. 5, 10.
[2] Curle (1911) p. 150 *et seq.* See also A. L. Busch, 'Die römerzeitlichen Schuh und Lederfunde der Kastelle Saalburg, Zugmantel und Kleiner Feldburg', *Saalburg Jahrbuch* XXII (1965) 158–210.

removed by shaving was placed in a glass or metal vessel and offered to the gods, and the occasion was marked by feasting and rejoicing. The only razors available were bronze and iron knives (fig. 48), to which frequent sharpening on the whetstone could never impart a keen edge; and as soap was unknown, and only water was used on the skin before shaving, men suffered a good deal in the cause of beauty. An implement which is believed to be a folding iron razor was discovered in the Park Street villa a few years ago (fig. 48*b*),[1] and another possible razor was found at Silchester (fig. 48*c*).[2] Unpleasant cuts were not uncommon and Pliny prescribes for them a plaster made of spider's webs soaked in oil and vinegar![3] No wonder that when his admiration for things Greek, or his wish to hide an ugly scar, inspired the Emperor Hadrian to wear a beard, he was joyfully imitated by many humbler people. In the first century men's hair was usually cut short with iron shears with blades not joined by a common pivot (fig. 48*d*), so that the trim inevitably had a ragged edge. With beards, curls became fashionable, and these were produced with the comb or with a heated curling iron. Some writers poke fun at the barber's ageing clients whose thin hair is curled and dyed in a feverish attempt to hide the bald patches.[4] Face-cream and rouge, patches, epilation and depilatories were all known to Roman dandies, as well as the perfumed oils which most people used at the baths.

Women's hairdressing was also a long and elaborate business and forms a fascinating subject of study. Ovid finds that it would be easier to number the leaves of an oak, or the bees on Hybla, than to enumerate the various styles in fashion at court in the first century;[5] and the time and money spent on elaborate hairdressing often arouses the disapproval of Christian writers.[6] Plaits, waves, curls and ringlets all played their part, curls reaching the apex of their glory in the gigantic erections fashionable at the end of the first and beginning of the second century during the reign of the Flavian Emperors and of Trajan. A head found at Bath (Pl. 28*b*) shows an arrangement of this kind. No doubt the curls were made mostly of false hair dressed over some kind of wire framework, and the construction of such an edifice must have been a long and arduous task. Portraits of the empresses, easily studied on the coins in daily use (fig. 75*a–d*) show their hair styles clearly, sometimes varying according to the guise in which they were portrayed; and it is interesting to learn that their statues in Rome were made with detachable hair, so that their coiffures could be altered as they grew

[1] A. D. Saunders, 'Excavations at Park Street', *Arch. J.* CXVIII (1963) p. 128 no. 10.
[2] Boon (1957) fig. 15 no. 5.
[3] *N.H.* XXIX. 114.
[4] Carcopino (1956) p. 158 *et seq.*
[5] *Ars Amatoria* III. 149.
[6] E.g. I *Timothy* ii. 9; I *Peter* iii. 3, Tertullian, *De cultu feminarum* 2, 7.

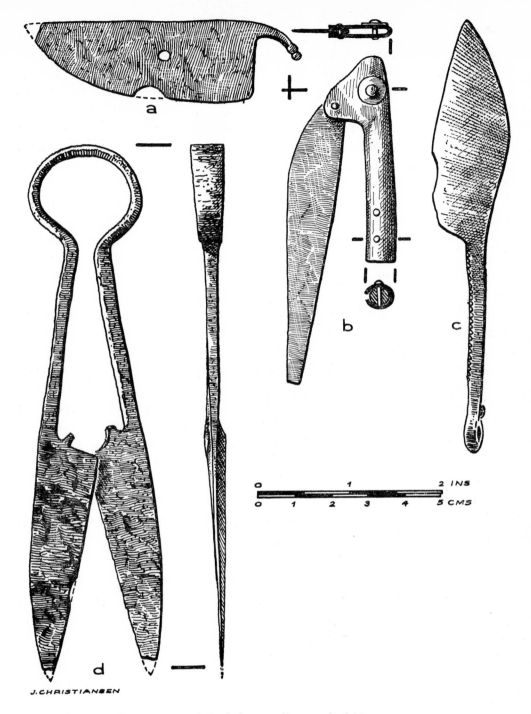

J.CHRISTIANSEN

48 *a-c* Razors. *a* Roman razor. *b* Park Street villa, Hertfordshire.
c Silchester. *d*. Shears. Unprovenanced

older or fashions changed.[1] In the provinces simpler arrangements were customary, but rich townswomen with maids skilled in hairdressing no doubt did their best to keep up to date with whatever extravagant fancy was then the rage in Rome.

By the middle of the second century, less elaborate styles with waves and plaits had been adopted even by empresses, and two of our York ladies, Julia Velva and her daughter (Pl. 26*c*) seem to wear their hair parted in the middle and waved on either side of the face, and then, perhaps, plaited and pinned up in a bun behind, the daughter having thicker hair and deeper waves than her mother. In both cases the ears are covered, but Candida on a tombstone of much the same date has her hair parted on the left and her ears exposed. The details of Aelia Aeliana's hair (Pl. 25*a*) are not so clear; possibly she had a coronet or plaits in the style of the Empress Faustina I, wife of Antoninus Pius. The third-century fashions of heavily waved or plaited hair falling on to the neck and then looped up over a pad or into a bun at the back, are represented by the woman's head from York (Pl. 28*a*), by the statue of a Mother Goddess from Housesteads, or by a relief of a Mother Goddess from Bewcastle now in the Tullie House, Carlisle.[2] A coil of real hair from a woman's skeleton is preserved in the Yorkshire Museum; it is now a rich auburn in colour, set off by polished jet hair-pins. Auburn ringlets were found with another York burial. The burials at Matrres-de-Veyre also produced thick plaits of auburn and fair hair belonging to a middle-aged and a young woman respectively, and a coil of false hair attached to a piece of leather. From a child's grave came a thick tress which speedily perished, and only the box-wood comb which held it on top of her head survives.[3]

False hair, of course, played an important part in this elaborate hairdressing and we may recall Ovid's remark that

'A woman flaunts in yards of purchased curls,
Failing her own she buys another girl's.'[4]

Roman wigs and other artificial aids were made of hair obtained from German slave girls, and black hair was sometimes imported from India. Ovid also notes the lady who was so startled by his sudden arrival that she put her wig on back to front.[5] As in Italy today, blondes were much admired, and some of

[1] Lady Evans, 'Hairdressing of Roman Ladies as illustrated on Coins', *Numismatic Chronicle* VI (1906) 37–65.
[2] Toynbee (1964) pp. 101, 173.
[3] Audollent, *op. cit.* p. 163 fig. 6.
[4] *Ars Amatoria* III. 165.
[5] *Ibid.* 243–6.

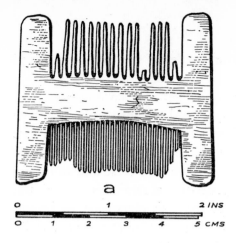

a

b

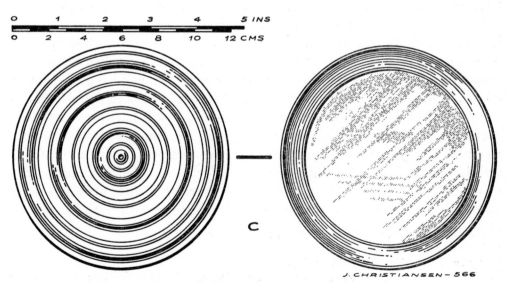

c

J. CHRISTIANSEN - 566

49   Toilet equipment. *a* Bone comb. *b* Parasol, from a relief found at
Avezzano, Italy. *c* Bronze mirror, London

the false hair was bleached with a mixture of goat's fat and beech-ash called *sapo*, mostly manufactured at Mainz.

Besides being experienced in the use of *sapo*, depilatories, curling-irons, and the dressing of hair and wigs, the skilled lady's maid had also to be expert in the application of cosmetics. Chalk and white lead were used to whiten face and arms, red ochre was a favourite for the tinting of lips and cheeks, and powdered antimony or ashes for darkening eyebrows.[1] All these aids to beauty were purchased in little phials and jars of glass or alabaster, spread out and mixed on small oblong stone palettes, and applied with glass rods, or bronze or bone implements with small flat blades. We may picture the maid packing them in the toilet box ready for the afternoon visit to the baths. She would add the strigil and oil flask, dentifrice of powdered horn, unguents and perfumes, comb, mirror and manicure implements (figs. 49, 50), and woe betide her if she forgot anything and her mistress was unable 'to replace by art the eyebrows' wilted tips',[2] after the heat of the bath. This make-up stayed in position until bedtime and Martial says of a lady of his acquaintance, 'Your tresses, Galla, are manufactured far away, you lay aside your teeth at night just as you do your silk dresses, and you lie stored away in a hundred caskets. Your face does not sleep with you yet you wink with that eyebrow which has been brought out for you this morning.'[3]

We leave this rather depressing picture of a Roman lady with the belief that there must have been plenty of young and beautiful girls in Britain who owed their fair skins more to the island climate than to the contents of pots and boxes, and continue with the next category of objects of female adornment, namely jewellery. Rich Roman women possessed numerous bracelets, armlets, rings, necklaces and even anklets, as well as jewelled nets and other hair ornaments, and some fashions in necklaces and ear-rings from Pompeii have been found echoed in Britain. The heavy necklets called torques had been popular in this country before the Roman conquest and they may still have been worn by people of importance. Regina wears one (Pl. 2), a torque of twisted wire with a crescent-shaped pendant appears on a figure carved on a Carlisle tombstone,[4] and the bronze head of a native god from Worlington (Suffolk) wears a fine example round his neck (Pl. 54).[5] Then there were gold chain necklaces made up of double links of gold wire; several of these, dating from the second or

[1] Carcopino (1956) p. 171; Balsdon, *op. cit.* p. 260 *et seq.*
[2] *Ars Amatoria* III, 201.
[3] *Epigrams* IX. 37 (trans. W. Ker, 1961).
[4] F. Haverfield, *Catalogue of the Roman Inscribed and Sculptured Stones in the Tullie House, Carlisle Museum* (1922) no. 132.
[5] Toynbee (1963) no. 2.

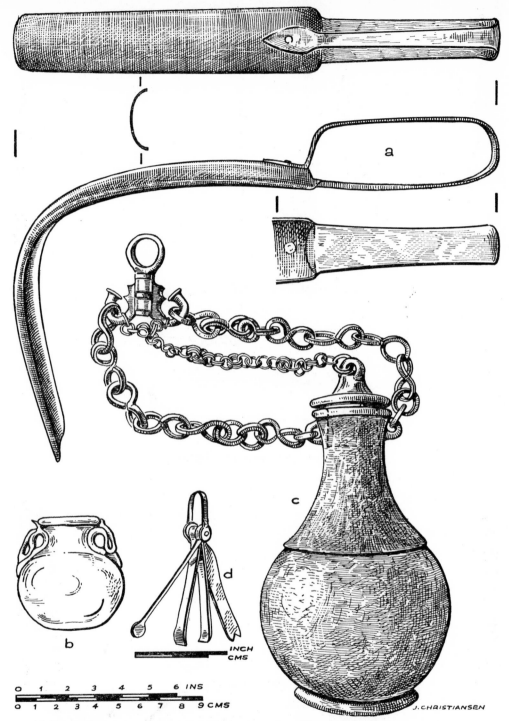

50 Toilet equipment. *a* Bronze strigil, Bartlow, *b, c* Glass and bronze
perfume or oil flasks. Unprovenanced. *d* Tweezers, ear scoop and nail
cleaner, Ashdon, Essex

51 Jewellery. Gold chains. *a* With sapphires, Richborough, Kent.
b Wincle, Cheshire. *c* Backworth, Northumberland. *d* Hadrian's Wall near
Newtown, Carlisle, Cumberland

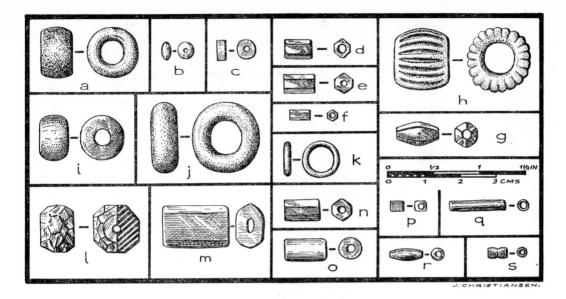

J. CHRISTIANSEN.

52   Beads. *a–g* Icklingham, Suffolk. *a* amber, the rest green glass. *b* melon
bead, Great Chesterford. *i–k* Blue glass, Sea Mills, Somerset. *l* Crystal,
Haslingfield, Cambridgeshire. *m–r* Blue or green glass, Verulamium.
s Silver glass, Verulamium

third century A.D., may be seen in the British Museum. The triple chain illustrated (fig. 51*d*) was found along the line of Hadrian's Wall near Carlisle, and
it has a spacer bar of three rings soldered together placed in the centre to prevent the chains getting tangled up with each other. Gold chains found at Backworth, Northumberland (fig. 51*c*) have an eight-spoked wheel attached to one
end with a loop into which the other end hooked as a fastening. One of them
also had a crescent pendant like the one on the Carlisle tombstone. Both are
ancient charms, the wheel perhaps being a symbol of the sun or of the magic of
love, and the crescent being worn to avert the evil eye. These ornaments were
also found at Pompeii. In fact, Roman women probably thought of a necklace
as a convenient way of wearing charms and amulets as well as a means of adornment. A bracelet from Backworth (fig. 55*d*) also has the wheel, and in this case
a hollow bead is strung in the middle of each link of golden chain made up of
double strands of wire.[1] The gold chain and other objects found in the baths at
Godmanchester has already been described.[2] Another hoard found at Wincle
(Cheshire) included three gold chains, one, 22 inches long with 8 green stone
beads inserted at intervals (fig. 51*b*), two gold rings and a gold brooch of

[1] D. Charlesworth, 'Roman Jewellery in Northumberland', *Arch. Ael.* (4) XXXIX (1961) 1–36.
[2] H. J. M. Green, 'A Romano-British Hoard from Godmanchester', C.A.S.P. L (1957) 85–8,
Pls. VI, VII.

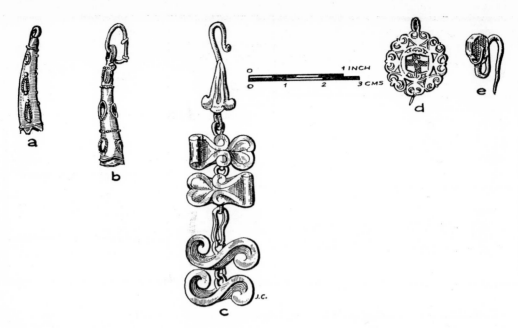

53 Gold ear-rings. *a* Ashtead villa, Surrey. *b* London. *c* Housesteads, Northumberland. *d* With setting for emerald bead, Silchester. *e* With emerald bead, Silchester

crossbow type with knobbed terminals. The brooch dates this little collection to the fourth century.[1] Part of a collar made of squares of gold-backed filigree work enclosing oval settings for flat sards and cabochon blue pastes comes from Nantmel (Radnorshire) (Pl. 30c). The squares are linked underneath by thin gold covering plates embossed with a design of Amazon's shields.

Bead necklaces seem to have been popular and beads of glass, coral, amber, jet, ivory, bone, shell, pottery or stone of many different shapes and colours have been discovered. The typical Roman example is made of glass frit covered with a turquoise glaze and ridged like a cantelupe—hence the name 'melon bead'. Illustrated (fig. 52) are a variety of beads from Verulamium, a melon bead from Great Chesterford, and a necklace from Icklingham (Suffolk). Ear-rings are rarely found, but simple rings of gold wire occasionally turn up with burials, and two hollow cone-shaped examples from the Ashtead (Surrey) Roman villa, and from Walbrook, London, are both in the British Museum (fig. 53a, b). A fine gold ear-drop was discovered just inside one of the gates of the fort at Housesteads (fig. 53c) and two ear-rings decorated with emerald beads were lost in the baths at Silchester, one of them ornamented with filigree (fig. 53d).[2]

[1] F. H. Thompson, *Roman Cheshire* (Chester, 1965) p. 108, Pl. XLVII.
[2] Boon (1957) p. 112. Other ear-rings illustrated by Charlesworth, *op. cit.* 22, 35.

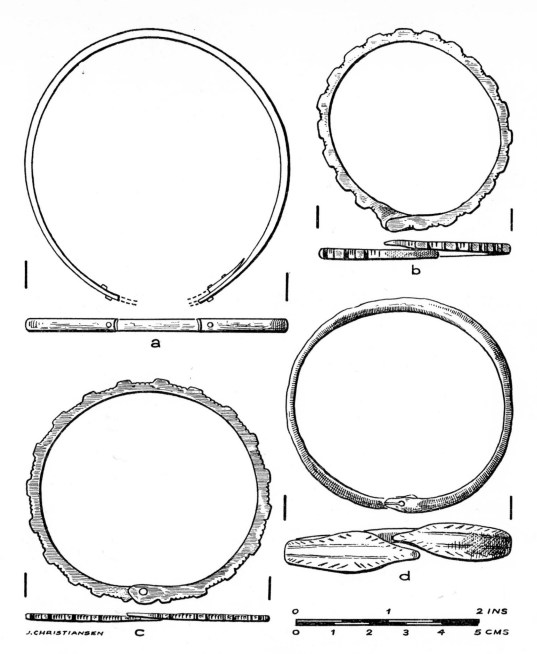

J.CHRISTIANSEN

54 Bracelets. *a* Bone, Guilden Morden, Cambridgeshire. *b, c* Bronze,
Great Chesterford. *d* Bronze, Sandy, Bedfordshire

Bracelets are also frequently found and range from plain armlets of shale, jet,
bone, or ivory to the various bronze types illustrated here (figs. 54, 55). More
spectacular serpent armlets occur occasionally, and two massive gold examples
were discovered with two more chain necklaces at Dolaucothi near Llandovery,

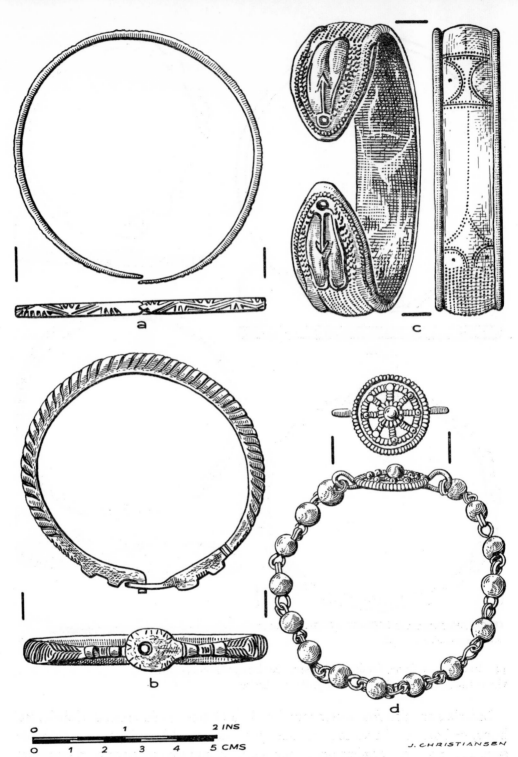

J. CHRISTIANSEN

55   Bracelets. *a* Bronze, Sampford, Essex. *b* Bronze, Hadstock, Essex.
c Silver, Castlethorpe, Buckinghamshire. *d* Gold, Backworth,
Northumberland

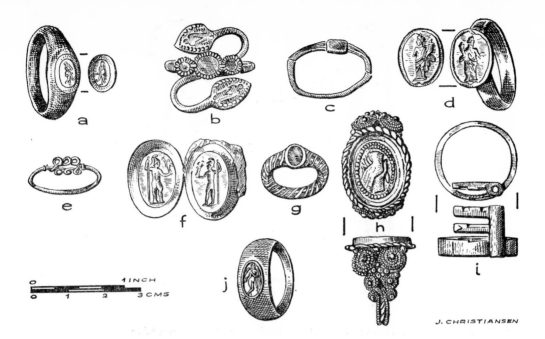

J. CHRISTIANSEN

56 Rings. *a* Gold, Backworth, Northumberland. *b* Silver serpent, Ditton, Cambridgeshire. *c* Gold, London. *d* Bronze with glass intaglio, London. *e* Bronze wire, London. *f* Iron with glass intaglio imitating onyx, London. *g* Glass, London. *h* Gold. Clasped hands in relief on bezel, Richborough. *i* Bronze key, Newnham, Cambridgeshire. *j* Gold with oval bezel showing Cupid, London

South Wales. The serpent's neck is cross-hatched to imitate scales, and in one case an oval box-setting containing a sard is attached to its mouth. Two clip-on silver snake bracelets were found at Castlethorpe (Buckinghamshire) (fig. 55*c*) and other gold examples come from Newport Pagnell[1] and Southfleet. The Southfleet bracelet was accompanied by a gold ring and a gold 'ladder pendant' (Pl. 30*e*) originally set with bluish-green stones and pearls: it was found in a child's grave. A gold bracelet of very different type comes from Nantmel and consists of a curved band with applied gold wire ornament (Pl. 30*d*). Bracelets of twisted wire are also sometimes found.

Roman rings occur in endless variety. Made of gold, of silver or of gilded or plain bronze or bronze wire (fig. 56*e*), iron, jet and glass, and sometimes set with semi-precious stones, they may have been worn more by men than by women. Ostentatious gentlemen wore rings on each finger, and some of the small rings now in museum collections can only have fitted over the top joint. Children wore them too, and a small gold ring was found with bracelets in a child's

[1] F. Marshall, *Catalogue of Jewellery in the British Museum* (1911) no. 2789.

143

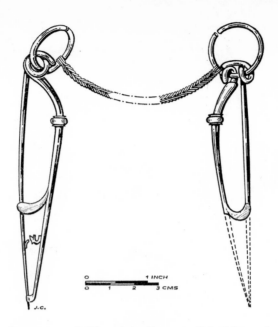

57 Silver brooches, drawn as probably originally worn linked by a silver chain, Great Chesterford

grave at Chalkwell, Kent. A massive gold hoop with an oval sardonyx intaglio engraved with an ant turned up with the other jewellery from Rhayader, and several rings were found with the Backworth treasure. One was of gold with an oval nicolo intaglio showing Cupid leaning on a pickaxe, and another was a serpent ring resembling the one found at Ditton, Cambridgeshire (fig. 56a, b). Silchester has produced an example of gold filigree set with a garnet. Rings of many types have been found in London and they include a gold one with a Cupid engraved on the bezel (fig. 56j), very like the one from Backworth, and a plainer gold circlet of later date (fig. 56c). A bronze third-century ring has a glass intaglio showing a woman holding a horn of plenty, probably the goddess Abundantia (fig. 56d). An iron ring has an intaglio of black and white paste (? imitating onyx) showing a fierce armed figure (? an emperor or the god Mars) (fig. 56f). A small Victory has alighted on his outstretched hand and she holds a laurel wreath with which she intends to crown him. Another London ring is made of yellow and white glass with a green glass bezel (fig. 56g). A bronze ring of the second or third century found at Richborough has a charming intaglio with two chickens, one pecking at the ground and the other holding up a twig, and the list of subjects portrayed on rings in this manner is endless. More elaborate were the gold rings set with a coin showing the emperor's portrait, probably bestowed as military decorations, or the fourth- and fifth-century filigree rings like the one illustrated from Richborough (fig. 56h). This has a

144

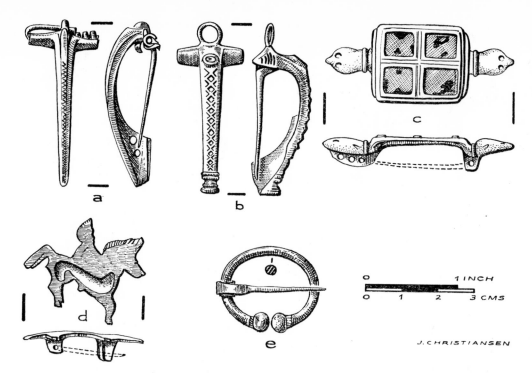

58 Bronze brooches. *a* Barrington, Cambridgeshire. *b* Hauxton,
Cambridgeshire. *c* Tortoise with traces of red enamel, Cambridge.
d Horse and rider with traces of enamel, Undley, Suffolk. *e* Clayhythe,
Cambridgeshire

plate soldered on to the bezel, engraved with two clasped right hands so that it
was probably a betrothal ring. A gold ring from Bradwell (Essex) had the same
design carved on an onyx cameo.[1] Less decorative and more practical were the
bronze key-rings (fig. 56*i*), a convenient way of carrying about the key of the
strong box or jewel-casket.

Brooches were an essential article of dress, used to fasten the clothes of both
men and women and many examples have been found. The simple *fibula* or
safety-pin, made out of a single piece of bronze wire, was known in pre-Roman
Britain and it underwent various developments, one of which is illustrated by
a pair of first-century silver brooches from Great Chesterford (fig. 57). These
may have been used to fasten a cloak, since they were joined by a short silver
chain and must have looked very handsome. Several later first-century developments of the *fibula* are illustrated, and include an unusually pretty bronze fantail
brooch found at Lakenheath (Suffolk) (fig. 146). This bow is decorated with a
rosette with a human head upside down in its centre, and a fight between a man
and an animal is depicted on the 'fantail'. A large handsome gilt bronze example

[1] F. Marshall, *Catalogue of Rings in the British Museum* (1907) no. 561.

145

59   Brooches. *a, b* Bronze, both from Richborough. *c* Silver-gilt,
Backworth, Northumberland. *d* Bronze, with blue, red, and yellow enamel,
Norton, Yorkshire. *e* Bronze, Brough, Westmorland. *f* Silver, London.
g Bronze, with glass boss. No provenance. Scale ⅔

of similar type from Great Chesters (Northumberland), the famous 'Aesica'
brooch, is decorated with Celtic trumpet scroll design in relief.[1]

Late first- and second-century headstud brooches were usually decorated with
enamel and they have rings through which chains could be threaded if they were
used to fasten cloaks or other garments (fig. 58*b*). Contemporary with them
in northern England was the trumpet brooch, and a magnificent specimen of
this made of silver gilt was found with the other jewellery in the Backworth
treasure (fig. 59*c*). A group of bronze disk brooches is decorated in repoussé
with figures of warriors or trumpet scroll designs of Celtic type, and some of
these may have been made at Brough (Yorkshire) in the second century.[2] Disk

[1] Toynbee (1964) p. 341.   [2] *Ibid.* p. 342; Bushe-Fox (1949) p. 139 no. 170.

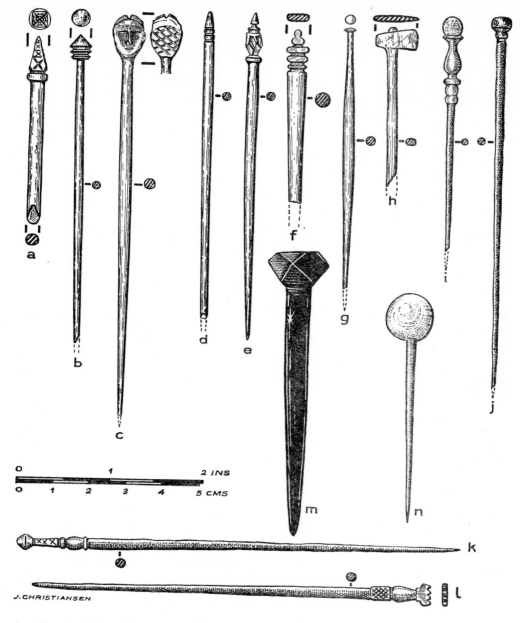

60 Pins. *a–h* Bone. *i–l* Bronze. All from Great Chesterford. *m* Jet, Lincoln. *n* Bone with pearl head, York

brooches with glass bosses, more like some modern costume jewellery, also became popular at this time (fig. 59*g*). Numerous small enamelled brooches of various amusing types are often found. Illustrated are a star-shaped floreate disk and a mother hare with two young from Richborough (fig. 59*a, b*), a tortoise

147

from Cambridge (fig. 58c), and a horse and rider from Undley (Suffolk) (fig. 58d). An example of a fine dragonesque brooch, another north-country speciality (fig. 59d), comes from Norton (Yorkshire). Two small brooches of more un-usual type are the bronze swastika from Brough (Westmorland), and the silver dolphin found in London (fig. 59e, f), and penannular brooches resembling those sometimes worn today were also used (fig. 58e). By the fourth century brooches had grown very much larger and more elaborate, and the favourite type was the cross bow, which was to develop eventually into the enormous square-headed brooch so popular among the Anglo-Saxons.

Pins, too, were a very necessary feature of Roman everyday life and they were used in large quantities. For fastening clothes there were simple bone and bronze pins with round heads, and examples found in graves at York have heads of jet, silver or pearls (fig. 60).[1] More elaborate types also probably func-tioned as hairpins. Some of these have heads decorated with hands holding fruit (fig. 61c) or with busts of goddesses and empresses. A figure of Fortuna holding a horn of plenty surmounts one bone pin (fig. 61a), a silver one is adorned with Venus, and a bronze pin has an openwork head from which hang small bronze pendants that may have jingled as the wearer moved (fig. 61b, d). Jet pins with faceted heads, like the ones in the coil of hair from York, are of fairly frequent occurrence (fig. 60m).

Two other discoveries provide us with unique information about the acces-sories of our Roman lady's toilet. From one of the York burials came the ivory sticks of a fan probably resembling the one in the hand of the figure on the Murrell Hill tombstone (Pl. 26a). The fan itself may have been of leather and a special ivory catch kept the sticks together when it was folded (fig. 62).[2] Fans made of peacocks' feathers may also have been used, but they have left no traces in Britain. The other discovery made in the same cemetery consists of the ribs of a parasol with stains showing that originally the ivory was sheathed in silver.[3] Usually covered in bright green, the fan and parasol were employed as a means of emphasising feminine attractions as well as for the mundane purposes of dispelling heat, dust and flies (fig. 49b). An amusing fourth-century villa mosaic, found at Piazza Armerina in Sicily, shows a bevy of dancing girls or female athletes of whom one is carrying a striped fan, and all wear as their chief garment what we should describe as a bikini, brief drawers laced on each hip.[4] These were also worn in London because a garment of this type made of

[1] *Eburacum* Pl. LXXI.
[2] *Ibid.*; H. Eydoux, *op. cit.* fig. 362 illustrates another fan from a tombstone at Autun.
[3] Richmond (1947) p. 79 fig. 13.
[4] Balsdon, *op. cit.* Pl. XII.

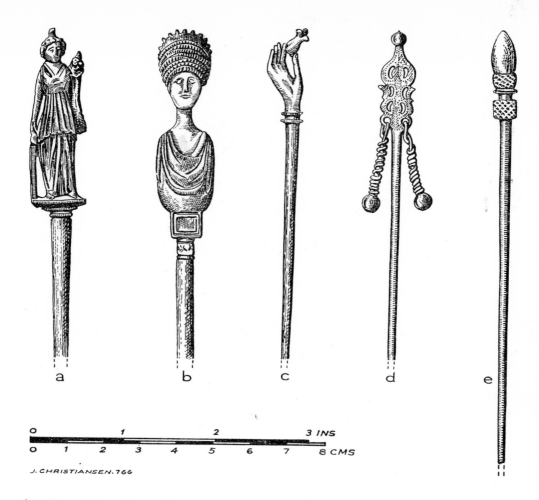

J. CHRISTIANSEN. 766

61 Pins. *a* Bone. Figure of Fortuna, London. *b* Bone. Unprovenanced.
c Silver, London. *d* Bronze, London. *e* Bronze, Richborough

leather was found in a rubbish-pit in Walbrook during recent excavations.[1] One side is still laced up, the other lace has been knotted and broken. To judge by their size, the drawers could only have fitted a boy or a very slim girl.

While the mistress of the house attended to her toilet, her servants were busy sweeping and dusting, polishing the wooden doors and the mosaic floors and scrubbing the tiled ones, and airing and shaking the hangings and cushions. The small bedrooms contained little furniture; and probably only a table, a chair or stool, some chests for clothes or blankets, and a footstool would be found in them, as well as the bed, most important of all. Sometimes this was simply a mattress placed on a chest or oblong masonry support, covered with

[1] Merrifield, Pl. CXVI.

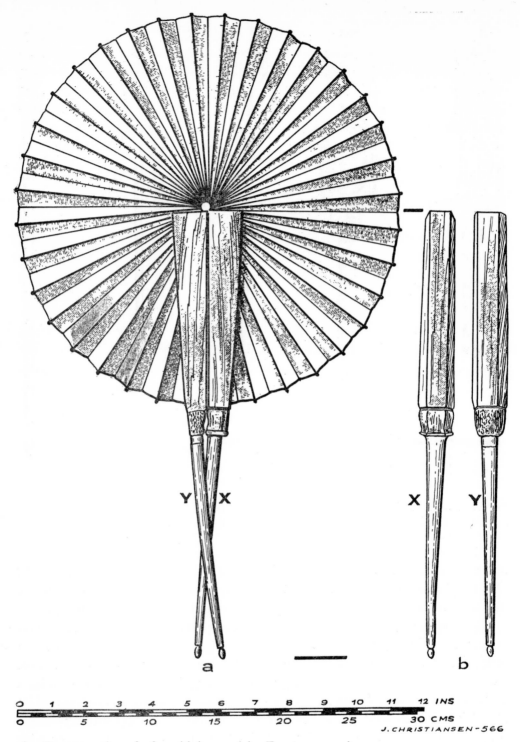

62 Reconstruction of a fan with ivory sticks. From a woman's sarcophagus, York

cushions and bedclothes like a modern divan. An illustration of this is provided by the child's tombstone at Chester (Pl. 3). Couches with head and foot-rests and sometimes with high backs were also used, particularly for the older and more important members of the family. Similar couches were used in the day-time in the other rooms of the house, particularly in the dining-room, where the diners reclined on them round the small table spread with the banquet. A couch with head and foot-rests is visible on Julia Velva's tombstone (Pl. 26*c*), and examples with high backs and legs decorated with mouldings were used by Aelia Aeliana (Pl. 25*a*) and appear on many of the Chester tombstones.[1] Usually they were made of wood, and the head and foot-rests might be decorated in various ways with carving or with bronze ornaments, while the rails along the edge of the seat were inlaid or carved in different patterns. The actual seat was probably not constructed of solid wood but had a latticework of cords or leather thongs stretched across its frame. The timber selected for furniture was seasoned before use and the various parts were held together with wooden dowels and tenons, metal rails and glue. Methods of improving the appearance of the finished article included polishing with cedar, juniper-oil or wax, and the application of decorative veneers of finer woods, maple for example, or box or holly. More expensive materials such as tortoiseshell, bone, ivory, bronze and silver were sometimes employed to decorate the couches of rich Romans. But whether any of these embellishments found their way into Romano-British homes is still uncertain; although the use of applied ornament of bone or bronze seems not unlikely. Some of the high-backed couches may have been upholstered. Other-wise the comfort needed for the human frame was provided by such refine-ments as mattresses and cushions.

Mattresses vary in size and Julia Velva is comfortably settled upon a luxuri-ously thick one. Cushions seem to have been plentiful and they varied in shape and size from square pillows to large, fat bolsters with rounded ends. Usually they were made of wool or linen stuffed with wool, flax, feathers, straw, rushes or other vegetable materials. Sometimes they were decorated with fringe or tassels like the one visible on the tombstone of Victor the Moor at South Shields.[2] No detailed carvings of bedclothes and other draperies survive in this country, but the coverings depicted elsewhere certainly convey an impression of comfort, and we know that textiles with woven designs or heavily em-broidered in many different colours were used in other parts of the Roman Empire. Bands of such decoration can be seen on the cover of Victor's mattress, and probably our Romano-British ancestors tucked themselves up under gaily

[1] J. Liversidge, *Furniture in Roman Britain* (1955) Pls. I, VII, VIII, XI, XII.
[2] *Ibid.* Pl. II.

coloured woollen coverings or skin rugs; and the same materials were used for mattress covers, for the curtains which were often hung in doorways, and for table-cloths. A relief in Florence shows us shoppers inspecting a display of rugs and draperies no doubt intended for these purposes,[1] and fringed table-cloths often appear on the Gaulish reliefs showing funeral banquet scenes.[2]

It is amusing to discover that the favourite individual seat in the provincial Roman household was a rounded low-backed wicker chair very like the light woven bedroom or garden chairs so popular today. Julia Velva's daughter is sitting in one of them (Pl. 26c) and so is Regina (Pl. 2); and they can be examined in detail by looking at a full size stone model from a grave near Cologne (Pl. 32). They seem to have been particular favourites with women when nursing children or making their toilets, and probably we would not be far wrong in visualising one in every lady's bedroom. The Murrell Hill lady is sitting in a chair of the same shape (Pl. 26a) with rounded back and solid base, but here the wickerwork pattern, usually so carefully rendered, is missing from the carving. Such chairs frequently appear on the Gaulish reliefs used by both men and women; they were probably made of wood. Seat-cushions made them more comfortable.

As well as chairs, there must have been numerous wooden stools of various sizes, and burials at Bartlow (Essex) and Holborough (Kent) have produced two folding stools made of iron with bronze decorations. The Holborough find, made as recently as 1954, has benefited by the most modern methods of excavation and preservation. When opened, it was arranged like a modern deck-chair (not like a campstool), one seat-bar being behind the sitter, the other in front, under his thighs. The front bar, however, was split into two small sections each supported by a bracket, a queer arrangement the purpose of which is by no means clear. The reconstruction of the stool illustrated (fig. 63) shows this curious feature. It had a leather seat and the pivot-hinges of the framework were covered with bronze caps. Scientific examination showed that the stool was probably burnt on the funeral pyre with its owner, and thin threads of bronze and traces of vegetable matter suggest that it had a seat-cushion stuffed with chaff and decorated with bronze ribbon. In wealthy homes these stools were often accompanied by bronze tripods with three or four folding legs, decorated in various ways and often supported by claw-feet or hooves. When unfolded a tray or large bowl was placed on top of this frame-work.[3]

Of rather more practical use than the bronze tripods were the small three-

[1] Balsdon, *op. cit.* Pl. XVb.
[2] E.g. E. VI p. 334, no. 5146; p. 362, no. 5166.
[3] Liversidge, *op. cit.* p. 34 *et seq.*

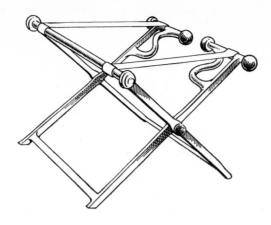

63   Reconstruction of the folding stool found in the Holborough barrow, Kent

legged tables which seem to have been extremely popular all over the Roman Empire. Set with the funeral meal, they appear with fairly straight legs in front of Julia Velva's couch (Pl. 26c), while the more usual bandy-legged variety can be seen on Aelia Aeliana's tombstone (Pl. 25a). Wood, bronze, or marble were the materials used for these tables on the continent and probably in this country, but the Romano-Britons also had the original idea of making them of Kimmeridge shale. This is a black substance intermediate between coal and slate, found on the Dorset coast and extensively used in prehistoric and Roman times for fashioning beads and bracelets. A dense black in colour, it must have looked very fine when waxed and polished, but as the shale splits like slate it cannot have been easy to carve. Nevertheless, skilled and patient craftsmen managed to work it, and a series of fragments of the shale table legs that they made has been discovered, mostly in Dorset. The one illustrated (Pl. 33) was found at Dorchester and resembles in shape the legs of Aelia Aeliana's table (Pl. 25a). But her table is quite undecorated, whereas here we have an animal's head with pointed ears and open mouth appearing on the upper half of the leg, while the foot is carved in the shape of a lion's claw, the first appearance in this country of the claw-foot, still often used for furniture decoration. In Italy recognisable lions' and panthers' heads of great beauty can be seen on Roman tables and these were probably the models for the British craftsmen. But the intractability of his material, aided perhaps by an inborn liking for strange patterns, led him to produce a series of these rather uncanny creatures.[1] The table-tops consisted of a circular piece of shale turned on the

[1] *Ibid.* p. 37 *et seq.*

64 Cupids busy making shoes. From a wall-painting from Herculaneum

lathe, and fragments of them have been found in the Roman towns at Caerwent and Silchester. Presumably the three-legged tables were most at home in
the dining-room, sitting-room, or bedroom, while for more practical purposes
larger wooden tables on four undecorated legs were required. No traces of
them have survived in Britain, but pictures of such tables exist elsewhere and
the example illustrated comes from a wall-painting at Herculaneum (fig. 64). It
shows winged Cupids making shoes. A cupboard with folding doors holds some
of their lasts and others appear on the shelf above their heads. Such shelves and
cupboards must have also found a place in Romano-British homes. Big wooden
chests held clothes, blankets and other belongings, and smaller cupboards or
round boxes contained the cherished books written on rolled-up scrolls. Martial's Epigram on a Bookcase, 'Unless you provide me with choice books
I will let in moths and savage book-worms,'[1] indicated its importance. It also
reminds us that moths are no new addition to a housewife's troubles, and bed
bugs[2] and some kind of furniture beetle may also have been among her worries.
Caskets like the one standing beside Regina's feet (Pl. 2) held jewellery and
other small objects, and the foot-stool was also an item of domestic furnishing.[3]

While the polishing and dusting of the furniture went on, the kitchen staff
was already preparing lunch. Usually this was not an elaborate repast, since the
evening meal was the important event of the day, and *prandium*, as it was called,
might only consist of a cold snack or some light dishes. Occasionally, however,
guests were expected or suddenly invited, as when Ausonius in third-century
Gaul sends a servant to summon neighbouring landowners to a meal of which
his cook can only have had two hours notice. He goes into the kitchen and says
to him, 'Sosias, I must have lunch. . . . Taste and make sure—for they often

[1] XIV. 37. (trans. W. Ker, 1961).
[2] For a Roman bed bug found at Alcester, Warwickshire, see *Daily Telegraph* 15 March 1966.
[3] Liversidge, *op. cit.* p. 57.

154

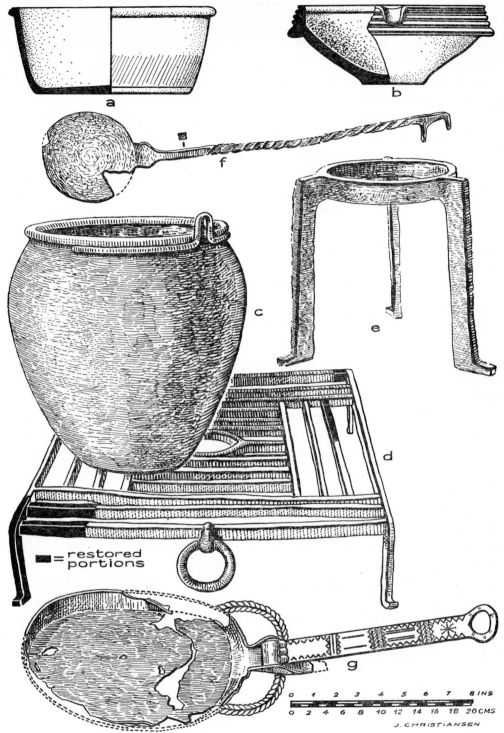

0 1 2 3 4 5 6 7 8 INS
0 2 4 6 8 10 12 14 16 18 20 CMS

J. CHRISTIANSEN

65   Kitchen equipment. *a* Pie-dish, Great Chesterford. *b* Mortarium.
Unprovenanced. *c* Bronze cooking pot, Newstead. *d* Gridiron,
Silchester. *e* Iron Tripod and *f* ladle, Great Chesterford. *g* Iron
frying pan, London, reconstructed after folding pan found in Egypt

play you false—that the seasoned dishes are well soused and taste appetisingly. Turn your bubbling pots in your hands and shake them up; quick, dip your fingers in the hot gravy and let your moist tongue lick them as it darts in and out. . . .'[1] One can imagine the uproar in the kitchen as the red-faced cook stands over his pans stirring and tasting, and his scullions and kitchen-maids hurry about fetching and preparing food (Pl. 31). Most of the cooking was done in earthenware jars or bronze pans on tripods or gridirons over burning charcoal, and a selection of this kitchen equipment is illustrated by fig. 65. Gaulish reliefs show us that sucking pig and similar larger items were cooked in cauldrons hung on chains over log fires.[2] There was an abundance of things to eat; and writers of the period are very fond of discussing food. Fish was popular, and varieties mentioned include salmon, trout, turbot, bream and roach. One writer, Macrobius, describes a banquet at which the Emperor Septimius Severus was present when a sturgeon was brought in by attendants crowned with flowers and moving to the music of flutes,[3] an early instance of the sturgeon as a royal dish. Tunnyfish in oil was a Provençal speciality exported to other parts of Europe, and the pike, considered an inferior fish for eating, was 'fried in cook-shops rank with the fumes of his greasy flavour'.[4] Possibly the Romano-Britons had a higher opinion of the pike, as it is identifiable among the fish depicted on a mosaic floor from the baths of the Lufton villa in Dorset. The Roman partiality for a tasty oyster is well known, and quantities of oyster shells occur on most Romano-British sites. Remains of other small shellfish are also found, and Ausonius tells us that the mussel 'makes up a course for early luncheon—a food delightful to the taste of lords and cheap enough for poor folks' kitchens'.[5]

Poultry and game, such as guinea-fowl, pigeons or hares, were all eaten, as well as small birds.[6] Joints provided for the meat course were similar to those eaten today, and vegetables and salads included artichokes, cabbage, beets, radish, turnips, parsnips, asparagus, endive, cos lettuce and watercress. Parsley and many familiar herbs were used as seasonings with pepper and salt. Dessert comprised such fruits as plums, cherries, quinces, apples, nuts, and cakes and pastries sweetened with honey and sometimes made into elaborate confections. Food was cut up and eaten with the fingers and the iron knives used for this purpose with bronze or bone handles are often found. A favourite design was

---

[1] *Ephermeris VI* (trans. H. Evelyn White, 1951).
[2] E. XI no. 7762. [3] *Satires* III. 16.
[4] Ausonius, *Mosella* 123 (trans. H. Evelyn White, 1951).
[5] *Epistulae* XV, a letter also discussing the delights of oysters.
[6] See below p. 351.

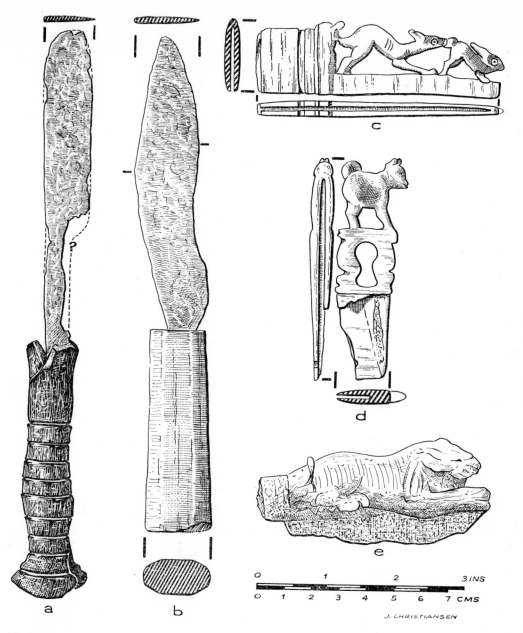

66 Knives. *a* Wood handle and iron blade, Great Chesterford, Essex.
b Bone handle with iron blade, Wendens Ambo villa, Essex. *c, d* Bone
handles, Great Chesterford. *e* Bone, in form of a tiger, Wroxeter

the dog chasing a hare or rabbit (fig. 66*c*) and a bone handle from Wroxeter
is carved in the shape of a tiger (fig. 66*e*). Bronze and silver spoons were used
for liquids and there was also a special little spoon with a pointed handle for

157

eating eggs and shellfish (fig. 67). Small bowls, really handleless cups, were used for drinking, and other food was served in larger bowls, or on plates or dishes made of pottery or glass, or sometimes even of silver. Pottery was made in quantity in Britain, but all households of any standing at all possessed at least one table service of the bright red gloss samian imported from Gaul. The custom began in pre-Roman times when the Belgic chieftains bought the Arretine ware made in Italy or the earliest samian from La Graufesenque and other potteries in the south of France. By the second century, potteries at Lezoux in central Gaul were the chief suppliers for both the army and the private customer until unrest and invasions on the continent interrupted the trade in the second half of the third century. Samian ware is sturdy hard-wearing pottery not easily broken, and complete vessels which later objects found with them show to be heirlooms, often turn up in graves. If they were accidentally dropped, the bowls could be carefully riveted. The large bowls with various complicated figure scenes or foliate ornament on their sides in relief, were modelled in decorated moulds before baking. A typical late first-century bowl (fig. 68*b*) from London has a form of scroll decoration and a deeper bowl from Sandy, Bedfordshire, now in the British Museum, shows a design of leaves with an occasional bird (fig. 68*g*). The most popular type of all is a larger bowl sometimes decorated with hunting scenes (fig. 68 *f*). The small cups and dishes (fig. 68*a, c, d, e*) are usually undecorated. They frequently have the name of the potter stamped on the inside of the base and the excavation of the potteries in France has made it possible to give a date to many of these names.[1]

Salads, vegetables and fruit must have looked particularly appetising in the big red decorated bowls and Pompeian paintings of still life show us piles of fruit in bowls of glass. Such delicate vessels were probably never made in Britain but a surprising number survive, mostly from grave groups. They had to be brought from overseas, a few from the east Mediterranean, and a number from northern Gaul and the Rhineland, particularly from Cologne. Colours vary from white to deep green or amber, and polychrome bowls also occur. Decoration includes cut glass from the end of the first century onwards, ribbing, and the application of threads of glass of a contrasting colour.[2] Small perfume flasks, wine-cups, jugs and bowls are the most common forms, large jugs and urns with handles were mostly used for burials. Some glass must have been

[1] Detailed studies of samian ware include F. Oswald and T. D. Pryce, *An Introduction to the Study of Terra Sigillata* (1920); J. Stanfield and G. Simpson, *Central Gaulish Potters* (1958).
[2] W. A. Thorpe, *English Glass* (1949); D. Charlesworth, 'Roman Glass in Northern Britain', *Arch. Ael.* (4) XXXVII (1959) 32–58; C. Isings, *Roman Glass* (Groningen, 1959); *L.R.T.* fig. 52.

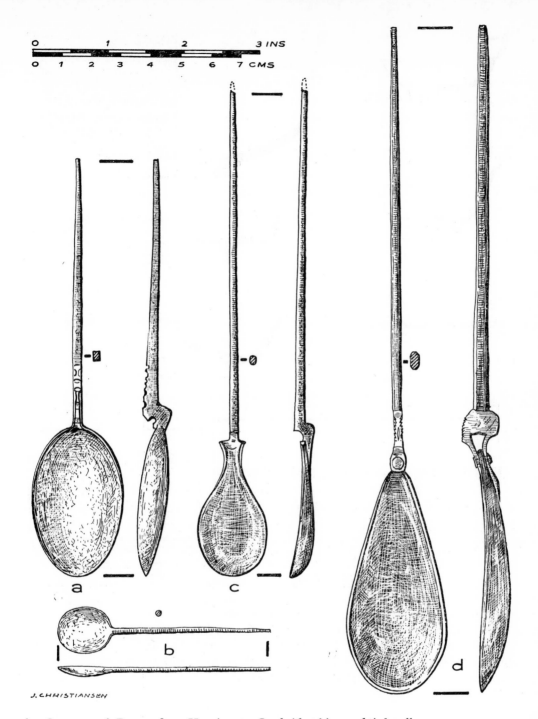

67 Spoons. *a, b* Bronze from Horningsea, Cambridgeshire, and Ashwell, Hertfordshire. *c, d* Silver from Richborough, Kent, and Icklingham, Suffolk

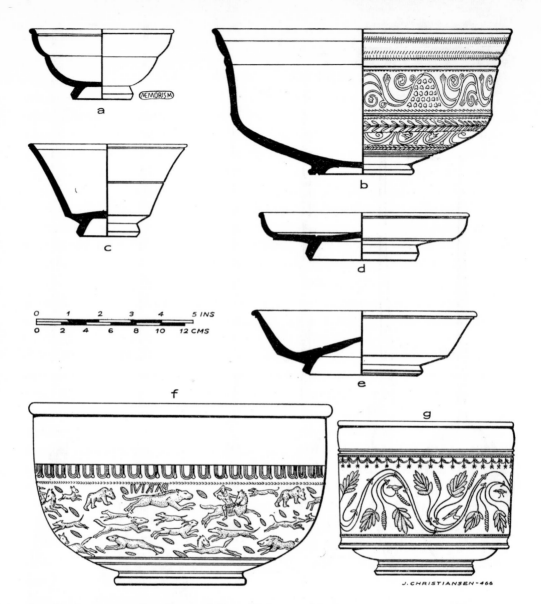

68　Samian ware. *a* Cup (form 27) from Silchester with stamp
MEMORIS. *b* Bowl (form 29), London. *c* Cup (form 33) from
Silchester with stamp QVINTI.M. *d* Dish (form 18), London. *e* Dish
(form 31), London. *f* Bowl (form 37) from Wingham, Kent, with stamp
PATERNVS. *g* Bowl (form 30), Sandy, Bedfordshire

bought purely for ornaments like the vase found in a grave at Hauxton, Cambridgeshire, a very rare find (Pl. 34).[1]

Pewter dinner services sometimes survive (Pl. 35),[2] and also silver such as the famous Mildenhall treasure, probably buried for safe keeping by some fourth-century owner and now in the British Museum. It includes a great dish nearly two feet in diameter, decorated with a central mask of Oceanus surrounded by a double border of figure scenes, the inner one showing Nereids and sea creatures, and the outer a Bacchic procession. Two charming small dishes show more Bacchic figures including Pan and dancing Maenads (Pl. 36b), the treasure also included bowls of various sizes, goblets and spoons, thirty-nine pieces in all.[3] A large square dish used for serving food, found at Mileham, Norfolk is also in the British Museum. A splendid rectangular dish, found in the river North Tyne at Corbridge in the eighteenth century, is the sole survivor of another treasure. It is decorated with mythological scenes and is now in Alnwick Castle.[4] Other silver in the British Museum includes smaller finds such as spoons, and also the saucepan-like vessels called skillets which often seem to have been votive offerings to the mother goddesses or other deities (Pl. 36a). Silver hoards such as the one from Coleraine in Ireland, and also the Traprain Law treasure now in the National Museum of Antiquities in Edinburgh, may well have been loot pillaged from Roman Britain.[5]

In the kitchen heavy earthenware bowls called *mortaria* were used for pounding up foods with a pestle (fig. 65b). They seem to have been the nearest Roman equivalent to our mincers and graters, and the inside of these bowls was sprinkled with grit before baking to assist in the softening-up process. Colanders and strainers of bronze or pottery are sometimes found, and possibly muslin or some fine stuff was used in place of our hair-sieves.

Cooking, sweeping and cleaning, bathing the baby, dressing the children and assisting at the toilet of the lady of the house, what other activities went on in the Roman home? Probably a porter or butler attended to callers and opened the heavy front door with its great lock and key in the morning (fig. 29a). Beside this door a large fierce watchdog sat on guard and a small mosaic floor showing the dog with the warning *Cave canem* (Beware of the dog), was often laid by the threshold of houses in Pompeii as a warning to unwelcome guests. Then fuel had to be carried to the stoke-hole and the fires watched when the

---

[1] J. Liversidge, 'Roman Discoveries from Hauxton', Appendix I, D. Harden, 'Four Roman Glasses', C.A.S.P. LI (1958) 12–14.
[2] See below p. 207.
[3] *A.R.B.* p. 40; Toynbee (1964) p. 308.
[4] Toynbee (1964) p. 306. [5] *Ibid.* p. 312 *et seq.*

hypocaust was alight, and water must be brought from the well or public fountain. There were lamps to be cleaned and filled ready for the evening and in a large house this task must have occupied several maids, as the small lamps of pottery or bronze cannot have burnt for very long. These lamps are round or oval in shape with a projecting nozzle from which the wick protruded. The oil in a small bowl with a spout (fig. 69*a*) was poured in through a hole in the flat top or *discus* and often the lamp was provided with a handle. The *discus* was frequently decorated with figures in relief, and illustrated are a gladiator on a lamp from London, and a winged Victory holding a palm branch in one hand and a shield in the other, found near Ely, both dating from the first century A.D. (fig. 69*b*, *d*).[1] This shield bears the inscription ANNVM NOVVM FAVSTVM FELICEM MIHI, which may be translated as, '(I wish) myself a happy and prosperous New Year', and it shows that the lamp was one of a number bought at the New Year, either as gifts, or when, as in this case, the inscription is MIHI (to me) rather than TIBI (to thee), as bringers of good luck to the purchaser and his household. The objects arranged round the Victory include three coins and sweets, cakes or nuts, things which were also exchanged as New Year presents.

The more expensive bronze lamps were sometimes fashioned in strange and beautiful shapes. One found with a burial at Thornborough (Buckinghamshire) has a leaf decorating the handle (fig. 69*e*), and the little lid which covers the oil-chamber is chained to this leaf, so that it would not get lost when the lamp was filled.[2] Another lamp, from Suffolk, is made in the form of a dolphin. Larger lamps were made with several nozzles which could all be alight at the same time; the one illustrated has two (fig. 59*f*) and other pottery and bronze examples have four or more. To get the best results, the lamps were placed on various kinds of stands, and iron lamp-holders are quite common. These resemble the Scottish cruisie and usually have a pointed piece of iron fixed through a hole in the handle which could be thrust into a wattle and daub wall wherever the light was needed (fig. 70*a*). The holder itself may also have been used as a lamp, but in that case there must have been difficulty in regulating the wick, and preventing it from setting all the oil alight. Torches, like those shown on the Low Ham mosaic,[3] and candles were also used, and pottery and iron candlesticks are sometimes found (fig. 70*b*, *c*). Occasionally luxurious bronze stands or candelabra supported the lamps and candles, and a reconstruction of one of

[1] J. Liversidge, 'A New Year's Lamp from Ely', C.A.S.P. XLVII (1954) 40.
[2] Found with bronze vessels in a burial. J. Liversidge, 'The Thornborough Barrow', *Records of Bucks* XVI (1954) 29–32.
[3] See below p. 283.

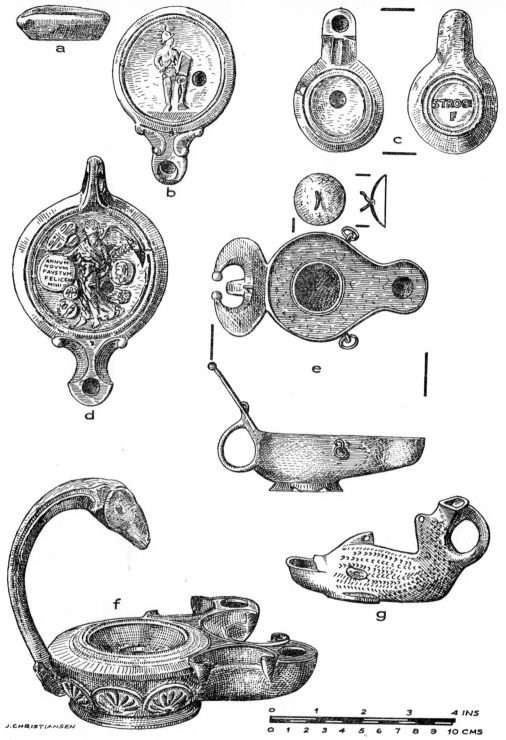

69 Lamps. *a* Pottery lamp filler, London. Pottery lamps. *b* London.
c London. *d* Ely. *e* Bronze, Thornborough, Buckinghamshire. *f* Bronze,
London

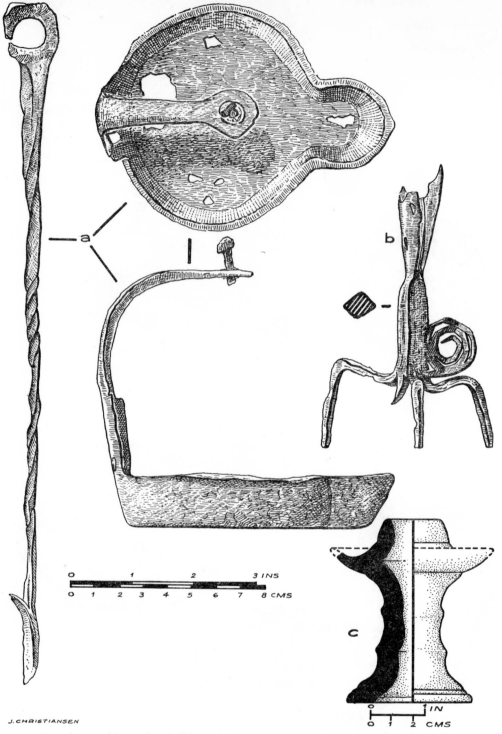

J.CHRISTIANSEN

70   *a* Iron lamp with staple, Guilden Morden, Cambridgeshire. *b* Iron candlestick, Great Chesterford. *c* Pottery candlestick, London

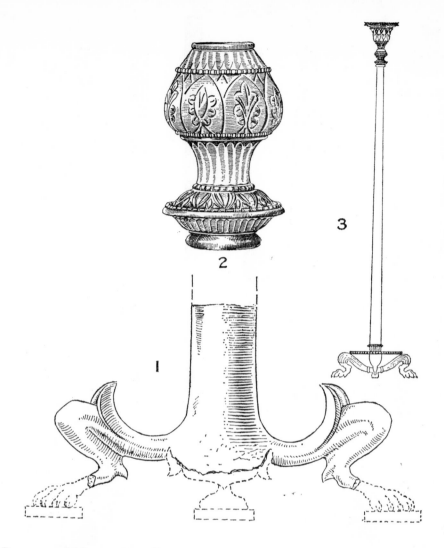

71 Bronze candelabra. 1. Base ($\frac{1}{2}$). 2. Neck (1). Both from London.
3. Complete candelabrum from Pompeii. ($c. \frac{1}{9}$)

these is made up of pieces found in London, the neck-moulding coming from King William Street, and the base from Copthall Court (fig. 71).

No good housewife allowed her maids to be idle, and when the household tasks were finished the women settled down to weave baskets, make and mend clothes, and spin. Little sewing was needed for dressmaking as pins and brooches usually replaced buttons and button-holes, and sometimes shoulder-seams, and this is fortunate as the bronze or bone needles and thread used were blunt and coarse (fig. 72c, d, f). Thimbles are found (fig. 72e) and the small iron shears took the place of scissors (fig. 48d). The fact that the household of the Empress

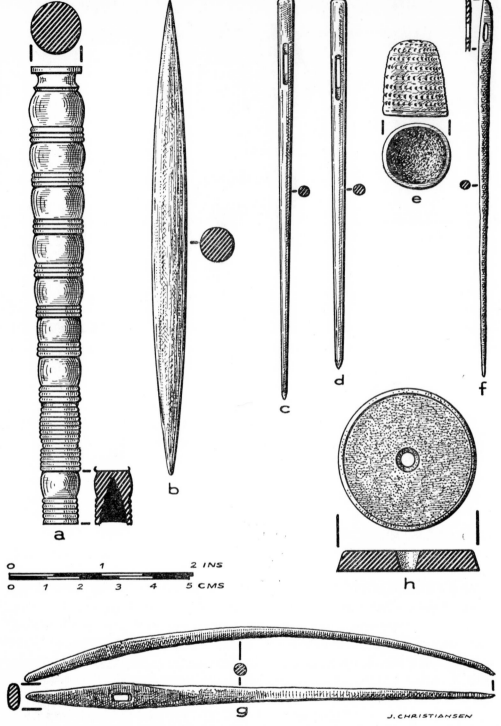

J.CHRISTIANSEN

72 *a* Bone handle with traces of iron, perhaps from a distaff, Great
Chesterford. *b, c, d, h,* Bone spindle and needles, pottery spindle whorl, Great
Chesterford. *e* Thimble *f. g* Bronze needle and netting needle, Sea Mills, Somerset

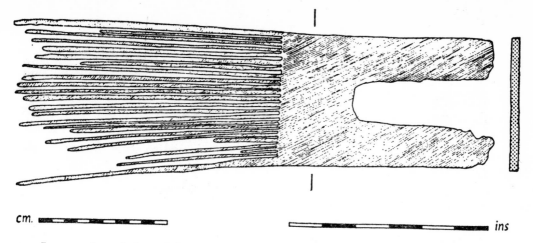

cm.

ins

73   Iron wool comb from Caistor-by-Norwich

Livia included five patchers, six women in charge of the clothing, a tailor and a cloakmaker gives some idea of the scope of the work done by the women. In spinning, the raw wool or flax was placed on a distaff, usually a wooden stick with some thickening to prevent the wool slipping down. Some distaffs have moulded ends to hold in the hand and examples of these made of amber, jet and bone survive (fig. 72a).[1] The spinner held the wool in her left hand and with her right pulled out a few strands which she twisted into a thread. The end of the thread was attached to a bone or wooden spindle (fig. 72b) weighted with a circular whorl of pottery, bone or metal; this was allowed to hang down and its weight and rotating motion helped the twisting of the thread which was wound on to the spindle as it grew long enough. The spinner had to have a good supply of spindles, consequently they turn up fairly frequently with the whorls made of any odds and ends which happened to be lying around. Regina is portrayed with her distaff and the completed balls of wool can be seen in the work basket at her feet (Pl. 2). The thread was then woven on looms either at home or in a workshop in the large villa estates or in the towns.

Comparatively little is known of the textiles produced in Britain but current research will probably soon produce fresh information about this important occupation. Implements such as the iron carding combs found at Icklingham, Caistor-by-Norwich and Worlington are now also being identified from other sites (fig. 73).[2] The actual fragments of cloth usually come from grave clothes

[1] E.g. jet from York, *Eburacum* Pl. LXIX.
[2] J. Liversidge, 'A Hoard of Romano-British Ironwork from Worlington', C.A.S.P. XLIX (1956) 89–90; W. Manning, 'Caistor-by-Norwich and the Notitia Dignitatum', *Antiquity* XL (1966) 60–2.

or were wrapped round coin hoards. Some only survive as impressions on tiles. For example a straying cow stepped on a rag lying on a tile which was drying before baking, and this tile later found its way to the Lullingstone villa bearing the imprint of the fabric. Cloth with a herring-bone weave, dating from the late fourth century, was retrieved from a well at Huntcliff, Yorkshire, and a piece of a check material woven in dark and light natural, not dyed wools was found at Falkirk.[1] While such fragments are usually presumed to come from clothes, the *tapete britannicum* mentioned in Diocletian's Edict must not be forgotten.[2] This seems to have been a saddlecloth or rug for a bed or couch, and so may also have sometimes been made at home.

[1] J. Liversidge, *Furniture in Roman Britain* (1955) p. 54; A. Henshall, 'Textiles and Weaving Appliances in Prehistoric Britain', *Proc. of the Prehistoric Society* XVI (1950) 130–62.
[2] *J.R.S.* XLV (1955) 114.

7
Industry and commercial life

While the work of the house was being done, its master, his grown-up sons, and the other male members of the family went about their business earning the money necessary for the family's wellbeing. One of them would have to go to the shops and buy food as the women rarely went to market, and before setting out he might recite his shopping list to the cook or the housewife and count up the money in his leather or metal purse (fig. 74). This might contain coins of varying value struck by the Roman mints in different parts of the Empire, including, perhaps, several *asses*, small bronze coins about the size of a farthing, a larger bronze coin like a penny or halfpenny called the *sestertius*, and one or two *denarii*, coins a little smaller than our shilling and made of silver mixed with varying amounts of copper. The *sestertius* was worth four *asses*, the value of the other coins varied from time to time. When a large and important purchase had to be made, the master of the house would probably take a small sack of *denarii* or one or more specimens of the beautiful small gold coin called the *aureus* out of his treasure chest.

Coins were circulating in Britain before the Roman conquest, struck by the kings of several tribes, so the influx of money which came in with the Roman army was welcome. Owing to various economic causes the value of the coinage varied at different times and sometimes shortages led to copying and forgeries.

74 Bronze bracelet arm purse from Barcombe Quarry, Northumberland

Normally there was no mint in Roman Britain apart from the one briefly at work in London at the end of the third and at some periods in the fourth century (fig. 75*l*, *m*).[1]

To us, however, the monetary value of Roman coins is no longer a matter for earnest calculation, and we have ceased to see in every extra *denarius* the possibility of a new cloak or an extra flask of wine at *prandium*. We are more interested in the money itself. In an age with no newspapers, radio or television, the emperors used the coins as a government news service with which they could tell the people of important events like the successful conclusion of a military campaign, show them what the reigning sovereign and his family looked like, and emphasise some of his good qualities and the blessings that his reign was bringing to the Empire. Consequently the designs on the back or reverse side of Roman coins were altered with amazing frequency, and in one year the mint at Rome alone might issue the *denarius* with over a hundred different reverse types, and the *sestertius* with over fifty. The following year some of these were discontinued and a new series was started.[2] Obviously people looked carefully at the coins; we have already seen how the empresses' heads on them were studied by hairdressers, and so expensive artists were commissioned to draw all these designs for the mints in Rome and the provinces.

Sometimes the coins are concerned with events in Britain. The conquest of A.D. 43 was commemorated by the Emperor Claudius with a coin showing his portrait on the upper or obverse side. He is wearing the triumphal laurel wreath and his abbreviated name and titles can be read among the lettering round the edge (fig. 75*e*). On the reverse side is a picture of the triumphal arch erected in Rome to mark this victory, with a statue of the emperor on horseback on top and DE BRITANN written across it. The development of Britain from a conquered land into a province proud of its Roman civilisation is reflected by

[1] Richmond (1963) p. 180 *et seq.*; G. Askew, *Coinage of Roman Britain* (1951) p. 30 *et seq.*, pp. 65, 75.
[2] M. Grant, *Roman Imperial Money* (Cambridge, 1954) p. 6.

75 Roman coins. *a* Faustina the Elder, wife of Antoninus Pius. Struck after her death. *Denarius*. *b* Faustina the Younger, wife of Marcus Aurelius. *Denarius*. *c* Julia Domna, wife of Septimius Severus. *Denarius*. *d* Helena, wife of Constantius I. *e* Claudius. Reverse showing the triumphal arch commemorating the Emperor's successes in Britain. *Denarius*. *f* Hadrian. Reverse showing Britannia, dressed as a civilian, welcoming the Emperor. *Sestertius*. *g* Hadrian. Reverse showing Britannia guarding the frontier. *Sestertius*. *h* Antoninus Pius. Reverse with Britannia seated on a globe. Below the globe, waves. *Sestertius*. *i* Caracalla. Reverse commemorating successful campaigns in north Britain. *Sestertius*. *j* Carausius. *Antoninianus*. *k* Carcausius with Diocletian and Maximian. *Antoninianus*. *l* Carausius. Reverse with the London mint mark ML. *Denarius*. *m* Constantine I. Reverse with London mint mark PLN *Follis*

another coin, dating from A.D. 134–8. This has a portrait of the Emperor Hadrian on one side and on the other *Britannia*, armed and on guard, keeping vigilant watch on the northern frontier (fig. 75*g*). No longer a conquered country, she has become a partner in her own defence as an outpost of the Empire. A variation of this design was issued by the Emperor Antoninus Pius later on in the second century after the construction of the Antonine Wall. Another of his coins shows *Britannia* afloat on the sea, seated on a globe, apparently 'ruling the waves' (fig. 75*h*), and Caracalla later commemorated successful campaigns in the north by a coin issue (fig. 75*i*). By way of contrast an issue of Hadrian dated to A.D. 134–5 has a reverse showing the Emperor being greeted by the personification of the province, depicted as a woman clad in Greek dress, holding a sacrificial *patera* in her hand. An altar stands between them (fig. 75*f*). The coin is one of a series commemorating Hadrian's visits to the provinces. *Britannia*, shown here as a civilian, welcomes him as the patron who, as we have seen, did much to encourage the growth of towns and other aspects of Roman civilisation.

Other coins reflect a romantic episode in our history in the third century, when much fighting was going on in other parts of the Empire, and the Imperial power was divided between the two Emperors, Diocletian and Maximian. Maximian, the Emperor of the West, appointed a certain Carausius as admiral of the fleet defending both sides of the Channel against the attacks of Saxon pirates. He seems to have been a born leader who soon endeared himself to the sailors, and at first he was very successful. Later he was threatened with execution for conspiring with the sea raiders and sharing their loot instead of preventing their raids. Warned in time he took the fleet to Britain, defeated an army sent against him, and had himself proclaimed Emperor in London. For six or seven years he ruled over Britain and part of Northern France, and during that time he struck coins at several mints, including London and Rouen, and probably at one or two other British sites (fig. 75*l*). On some of them he calmly hailed Diocletian and Maximian as his brothers, an impertinence which must have caused irritation, even though some kind of unofficial peace existed between them at that time (fig. 75*k*). Figure 75*j* shows another portrait of Carausius. His reign came to an abrupt end in A.D. 293, when he was murdered by Allectus, his chief minister, who was then himself proclaimed Emperor in his turn. He proved himself a hard master, and when the Roman emperors sent an expedition against him in A.D. 296 commanded by their new colleague Constantius Chlorus, Allectus was defeated and killed. The remnants of his army retreated on London and began to plunder the townsfolk, but Constantius' army pursued them and saved the city. A gold medallion struck to commemorate these events shows on one side a portrait of Constantius wearing a cuirass and a laurel wreath. On the reverse he appears on horseback approaching the city gates and being welcomed by the goddess of Londinium, the abbreviation LON being inserted so that we are left in no doubt as to her identity. In the foreground is a galley coming up the Thames with some of the troops who saved the city from destruction (fig. 40) and the whole scene has been described by a recent writer as 'The Relief of London by Combined Operations'.[1] The lettering REDDITOR LVCIS AETERNAE (Restorer of the Eternal Light) acclaims Constantius as the man who brought Britannia back into the Roman Empire.

Roman Britain possessed no banks of the type we use today, but rich men in the large towns accumulated large stocks of specie in their warehouses which they lent out at high rates of interest, and traders could obtain bills of exchange between financiers in different cities. Scenes showing such men counting out piles of money for the would-be borrowers who stand beside them, can be seen on some of the Gaulish reliefs from Igel and Neumagen.[2] The ordinary shopkeepers or farmers, however, kept their money at home in big chests or ironbound strong boxes, bolted to blocks of masonry in the living-room or hidden in a pit sunk in the floor. When the country's peace was upset by raiders from the north or from overseas this money was frequently buried for safety in sacks, large pots, or wood and metal boxes. Jewellery and other valuables were often hidden with it, and 280 *denarii* were found in a silver saucepan or *patera* at Backworth together with the jewellery described above.[3] Sometimes the owner or his heirs died or forgot where the hoard was hidden and then it is accidentally discovered hundreds of years later. Large numbers of silver and bronze coins have been found in this way. Gold coins are comparatively rare but 160 *aurei* were unearthed in a bronze jug at Corbridge (Northumberland). The coins had been struck under various first- and second-century emperors, and the latest in date belonged to the reign of Antoninus Pius, so the hoard must have been buried about A.D. 160. Two bronze coins were placed in the narrow mouth of the jug to act as stoppers, and maybe to mislead casual finders into thinking that the jug only contained *sestertii* and was not worth their stealing.[4] Children put their pocket money into savings banks consisting of pots with a slit for the coins to go in (fig. 78a), and then joyfully broke the pot when they went shopping.

[1] Richmond (1947a) p. 45.   [2] E. VI no. 5412.
[3] E. Hawkins, 'Notices of Roman Ornaments connected with the worship of the Deae Matres', *Arch. J.* VIII (1851) 35–44.
[4] H. H. E. Craster, 'Hoards of Roman gold coins found in Britain', *Numismatic Chronicle* N.S. XII (1912) 263–312.

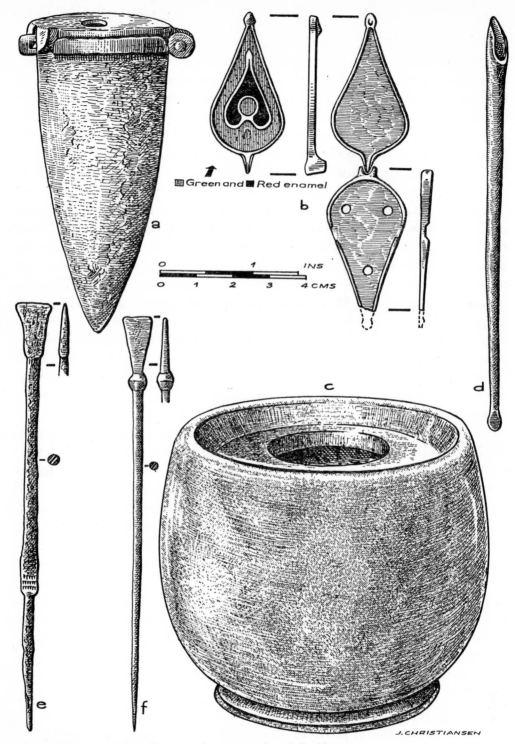

Green and ■ Red enamel

J.CHRISTIANSEN

76 Writing materials. *a* Bronze ink-pot, London. *b* Seal box,
Richborough. *c, d* Samian ink-pot and bronze pen, London. *e* Iron stilus,
Great Chesterford. *f* Bronze stilus, Cambridge

Merchants and traders in the towns kept careful note of their business affairs and occasionally we find a few traces surviving of all this commercial activity. When the clerks made out the accounts they wrote on papyrus or parchment with ink made of lamp black and reed or bronze pens. The example illustrated (fig. 76*d*) was found in London and has a cleft nib and a butt end expanded and cupped for stirring the ink. Bronze or pottery inkpots are also sometimes found (fig. 76*a, c*). Writing tablets were frequently used and these consisted of two pieces of wood, usually fir, hinged together with cords to form a little book, and recessed on the inner side to receive a coating of wax on which the message or account would be written with the *stilus*, a small pointed instrument of bone or metal with a flat butt with which the wax could be smoothed and the lettering rubbed out if mistakes occurred (figs. 76*e, f*; 120). Sometimes the clerk wrote so heavily that his point penetrated through the wax and marked the wooden tablet, and several fragments of tablets fortunately maltreated in this way have been found in London. One apparently refers to a purchase made from a shop and to the building of a ship, and another seems to be a few words from a deed of loan or purchase in which the buyer or borrower is to be paid the money due 'by Crescens or by the person concerned'.[1] Part of another tablet was found in the Walbrook mud some years ago and the word *Londinio*, and part of a name are written in pen and ink on the outside—no doubt for the address. Inside six lines of Latin are faintly visible scratched on the wood and they read in translation: 'Rufus, son of Callisunus, greeting to Epillicus and all his fellows. I believe you know I am very well. If you have made the list, please send. Do thou look after everything carefully. See that thou turnest the slave girl into cash. . . .'[2] This appears to be a letter from Rufus, the master, to Epillicus his servant—perhaps a bailiff or steward—giving instructions for the realisation of an estate. The inventory Epillicus and his fellow slaves have been making is to be forwarded to Rufus, and he is to see that the slave girl is sold and look after everything carefully; otherwise one feels there will certainly be trouble. Further discoveries of fragments of this kind are to be hoped for as they throw great light on life in Roman London. When the message had been written on the wax of the tablets, the two halves were tied together with cord and the ends of the cord were sealed in a recess provided on the outside. Sometimes the ends were threaded through a small bronze box with a hinged lid which was lifted up and the seal inserted inside (fig. 76*b*). These lids were often gaily decorated with red and green enamel.

Weights and measures were naturally important when visiting the shops and

[1] *L.R.T.* p. 55.
[2] I. A. Richmond, 'Three writing tablets from London', *Ant. J.* XXXIII (1953) 207.

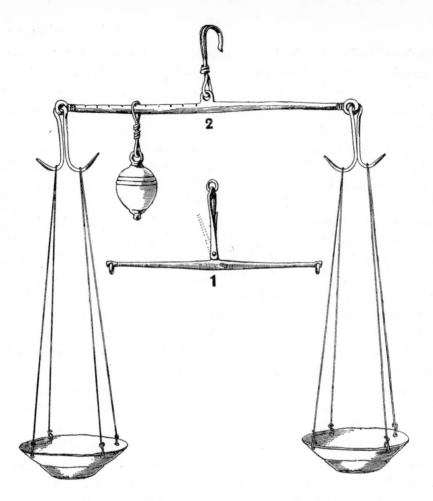

77 1 Bronze scale-beam from Finsbury Circus. 2 Bronze scale-beam (with weight restored) found near the Mansion House, with scale-pan from London Wall ($\frac{1}{3}$)

warehouses. The balance or *libra* closely resembled the scales in use today with two scale-pans, one holding the weights and the other the object being weighed. Then there was the steelyard or *statera*, an ingenious device working on the lever principle with a graduated arm or beam suspended from a hook placed at one end. Several hooks or scale-pans could be suspended from the beam at the same end and used in turn; these were for the objects being weighed and the weight moved along the beam until it balanced them (fig. 77). Sometimes there was a choice of two or three hooks with consequent changes in the relative lengths of the part of the beam acting as a lever, and this capacity for easy adjustment made it possible for the same instrument to weigh both heavy and

176

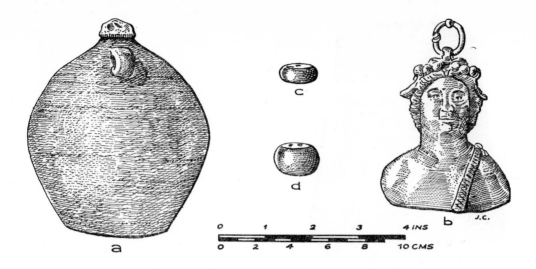

78 *a* Pottery money box, Lincoln. *b* Bronze steelyard weight. *c, d* Bronze
one and two oz. weights. *b-d* from Silchester

very light objects. It was easily portable and probably many a cautious Roman
carried his own well-tested steelyard when transacting business. The scale beam
was marked on its several faces to correspond to the use of the different hooks
and one weight could be used for all positions.[1] The Roman pound weighed
about twelve ounces avoirdupois and steelyard weights are often made in the
form of decorative bronze objects like the small bust illustrated (fig. 78*b–d*).
For measuring corn a bronze vessel shaped rather like a bucket and called a
modius was used, and one of these very rare objects was discovered outside the
fort of Carvoran on Hadrian's Wall and is now in the Chesters Museum (fig. 79).
It bears an inscription saying that it was made towards the end of the first
century during the reign of the Emperor Domitian and that it holds 17½ *sextarii*
or 16·8 pints. In actual fact it holds twenty pints and it has been suggested
that this discrepancy was a mean device to defraud the farmers when they came
to pay the corn tax (*annona*). On the other hand, Roman certified measures are
usually accurate. Traces of rivet holes show that some attachments have been
lost from the *modius* and these may have taken up the extra space.[2]

For linear measurements, folding bronze rulers were used and a fine example
found on the banks of the Walbrook near the Bank of England is now in the
London Museum (fig. 80). It is hinged in the centre and when extended is kept
steady by a clamp which fits over two studs. The upper side of the ruler is
marked off into sixteen *digiti* for measurements based upon the Greek foot or

[1] D. K. Hill, 'When Romans went shopping', *Archaeology* V (1952) 51–5.
[2] A. Berriman, 'The Carvoran modius' *Arch. Ael.* (4) XXXIV (1956) 130.

79   Bronze corn-measure (*modius*) from
Carvoran, Northumberland

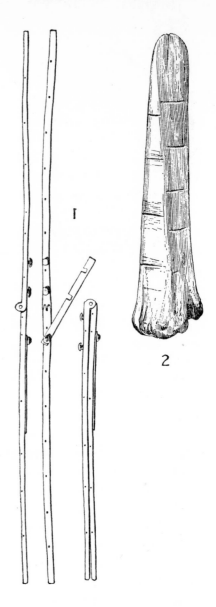

80 Bronze foot-rule and ox-bone
graduated in inches, London

pes; and one side is divided into *unciae* or inches. Twelve of these made up the
Roman foot which measured 11·6 inches, the length of this ruler. An ox-bone
marked off into a four- or five-inch scale has also been found in London (fig. 80).

It is illuminating to discover that our London traders were prepared to cut
their cloth or measure their timbers in accordance with the Greek or Roman
foot, whichever the customer preferred, and it helps us to visualise the scenes
in the Forum or along the quays by the Thames and other navigable rivers. We
can imagine the bustle in the offices of the big wholesalers when several ships

178

laden with wine and oil or fine pottery and glass were seen approaching. Customers who spoke Latin, Greek or Celtic would come to inspect the cargoes and taste the wine, and clerks, equipped with tablets and *stili* would receive them, all ready to note down their orders. Stevedores and dockers would be waiting to load and unload the vessels, and to unpack the goods, using tools like the very modern looking iron packing-case opener and big baling needles found recently in Walbrook,[1] in company with a big hook from a crane and the metal parts of small pitch-forks with hooks on the prongs. Sometimes there must have been an unnatural quiet on dockside when ships were delayed by stormy weather or even wrecked, a fate suffered by a vessel full of samian pottery which sank on the Pudding Pan Rock off Whitstable, some time in the second century. These ships sailed to Britain from ports all over Europe, bringing pottery, glass, wine and bronzes from France and the Rhineland, wine and oil from Spain, and lamps, bronze and silver ware and other luxury goods, including textiles, from Italy and other parts of the Mediterranean.

Occasionally inscriptions are found in other provinces concerned with such trade. The altar erected by M. Aurelius Lunaris at Bordeaux (see p. 421 below) was put up as a thankoffering for a safe journey and was vowed before he left York. Another Bordeaux inscription comes from a tombstone commemorating a merchant of the tribe of the Treveri who traded with Britain and died in the first century.[2] From Mainz comes the tombstone of Fufidius who may have been concerned with pottery imports from East Gaul.[3] Another thankoffering is the altar of M. Secundus Silvanus, placed in the Temple of Nehalennia at Domburg on the Isle of Walcheren. He traded in pottery with Britain across the North Sea and was grateful to Nehalennia for the preservation of his merchandise.[4]

Then there were the shops where clothes and shoes were sold. None of these have been identified but a fragment from a very large Roman shoe, found in the Walbrook mud, may have been part of a shop-sign hung out by a shoemaker, as the shoe could only have fitted a man about twelve feet tall. Shoemaker's anvils were found at Sandy (Bedfordshire),[5] and at Silchester, showing that cobblers were also busy in that town, and the wall-painting we have already discussed in the last chapter, with its cupboard full of lasts and shoes, gives us some idea of the work which went on in shops of this kind (fig. 64). Other

[1] Merrifield (1965) Pl. 126.
[2] C.I.L. XVIII 634.
[3] Frank ed. III (1935) p. 114.
[4] C.I.L. XIII 8793; A. Hondius-Crone, *The Temple of Nehalennia at Domburg* (Amsterdam, 1955) no. 23 p. 70.
[5] *A.R.B.* (1958) fig. 24 no. 9.

wall-paintings from Herculaneum give us an even clearer impression of the sale of shoes. One shows a salesman in the Forum surrounded by shoes and lasts, holding a shoe in his hand which he is exhibiting to two lady customers seated on a bench in front of him. Behind him, two more customers listen critically to his sales talk while they wait their turn. The other picture depicts an assistant on his knees measuring a man's foot or else trying on a pair of new shoes, as a gap appears in the row of shoes shown behind him.[1]

Work of another sort was done in the fulleries, where newly woven cloth was shrunk and bleached and soiled garments brought for cleaning and renovation. They were first placed in vats and washed in soda and water, treated with fuller's earth, and then, if white, they were spread out on wicker frames over a pot of burning sulphur for bleaching. Next they were washed again, hung out to dry, and then pressed in clothes presses while still slightly damp. No detailed account survives of all these processes, but sculptures and paintings from France and Italy again come to the rescue and show us slaves treading out the clothes in the vats, and workmen bringing the wicker cages and pot of sulphur for the bleaching process. New cloth was beaten with mallets to make the texture closer, combed with special combs, teazles, or brushes made of long thorns instead of bristles, to raise the nap, and then trimmed with enormous shears like the pair discovered in the Roman town at Great Chesterford. Fullers had to replace any goods which were stolen or gnawed by mice. They also had to pay up if a slave brought home the wrong laundry, and this suggests some form of delivery service. Dyeworks must also have existed in most towns and there is some evidence which may point to their presence at Silchester. There were two kinds of dyers, the *infectores* who dyed new cloth for the first time or else dyed old clothes a new colour, and the *offectores* who merely re-dipped old garments to freshen them up.[2]

The processes of spinning and weaving were so much a part of home life that they have been discussed elsewhere but the sale of the finished product by the cloth merchant must have taken place in the towns and markets. Many reliefs and wall-paintings from Italy and the Rhineland show such sales. In most cases we find salesmen exhibiting lengths of material to critical women customers, frequently with a maid in attendance. A fine relief, now in Florence, shows a shop containing both pieces of cloth and fringed cushions, and one of the reliefs from Arlon, Belgium, has a background of bales of folded material.[3]

[1] Tanzer (1939) figs. 28, 29. Also the relief showing a shoemaker at Rheims, E. V. no. 3685.
[2] Tanzer (1939) p. 8 *et seq.*
[3] E. V no. 4043, Paoli (1955) Pl. XII. For paintings from Herculaneum see Tanzer (1939) figs. 30, 31.

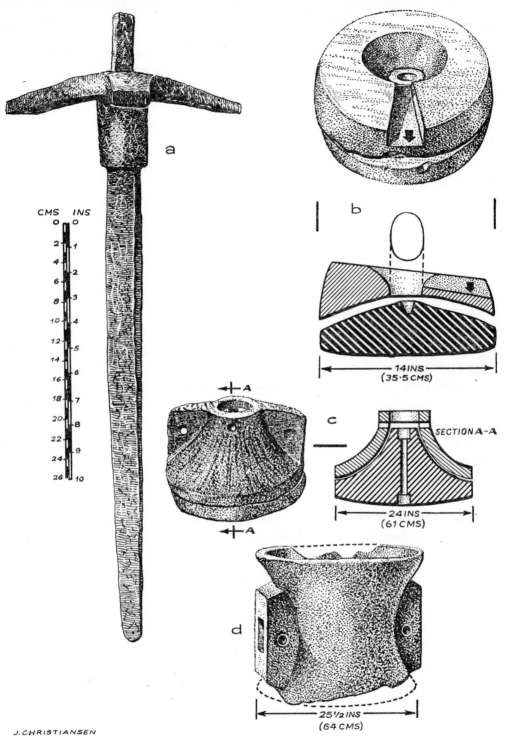

J.CHRISTIANSEN

81 Corn-mills. *a* Iron spindle from a water-mill, Great Chesterford.
b Rotary quern (and section), Iver, Buckinghamshire. *c* Local development
of upper stone of mill of Pompeian type, Ham, Poole, Dorset. *d* Upper
stone of mill of Pompeian type, London

The preparation of corn for flour occupied much time and energy in antiquity as bread was the most important item of food. Several varieties of wheat were grown and the various milling processes produced both white and wholemeal flour. The argument which crops up periodically nowadays about the palatability and food values of white versus brown bread must have first arisen in classical times, as we find Juvenal[1] and other writers describing the custom of giving dark bread to the unimportant visitor. On the other hand, one of the guests at Trimalchio's feast asks for wholemeal bread because it gives him strength and helps his digestion.[2] In the home, the corn was usually ground in a portable rotary hand-mill or quern consisting of two stones with flat or slightly curved grinding surfaces. The lower stone was bedded in earth or fixed to a bench and the upper stone rotated above it, held in position by a spindle and propelled by means of a handle (fig. 81*b*). Various coarse stones were used in manufacturing these querns and Niedermendig lava, from Andernach in the Rhineland, was often imported for this purpose.

Corn was also ground in a larger type of rotary mill turned by slaves, donkeys or blindfolded horses. The lower stone was conical and over it was fitted a hollow upper stone of hourglass shape turning on an iron spindle. The grain was poured into the widemouthed top which served as a hopper and the stone was propelled round by a beam fitted into the slots at the waist. Lava was again the favourite material for these mills and they are a noticeable feature of such Roman towns as Pompeii (fig. 82).[3] They seem to have spread westwards from Italy as several of them have been found on French sites including Rheims,[4] and an upper stone of the typical hourglass shape, made of Niedermendig lava, was found in London and is now in the Guildhall Museum (fig. 81*d*).[5] Another mill from Hamworthy in Dorset has a conical lower stone and an upper stone made like the lower half of the Guildhall specimen: this is possibly a local British development (fig. 81*c*).[6] These mills sometimes appear on reliefs and a fine representation of a horse turning one is in the Vatican Museum. A lamp appears on a shelf above, indicating that the work went on both night and day. A *graffito* from the Palatine in Rome shows a rough drawing of a similar mill turned by an ass and accompanied by the comment 'Work, little ass, as I have worked and you will profit by it'. A donkey could grind about $3\frac{1}{2}$ bushels of wheat a day

---

[1] *Satires*, V. 74–8.

[2] Petronius, *Satyricon* LXVI.

[3] For further discussion relating to mills see L. A. Moritz, *Grain-Mills and Flour in Classical Antiquity* (Oxford, 1958) and R. Forbes III (1955) p. 141 *et seq.*

[4] In Rheims Museum. One also appears on a relief from Narbonne (E. IX no. 6093).

[5] *Ant. J.* IX (1929) 221, fig. 11.

[6] H. P. Smith, 'Occupation of the Hamworthy Peninsula', D.N.H.A.S.P. LII (1930) 124.

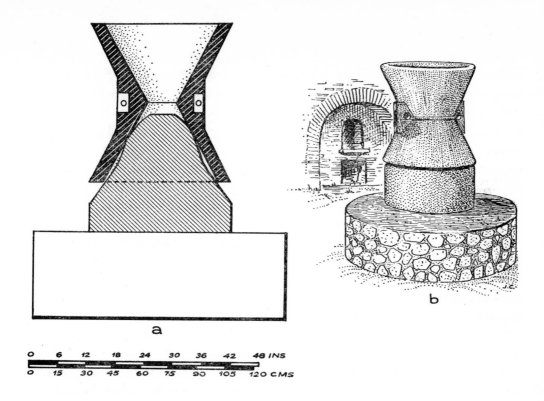

a

| 0 | 6 | 12 | 18 | 24 | 30 | 36 | 42 | 48 INS |
| 0 | 15 | 30 | 45 | 60 | 75 | 90 | 105 | 120 CMS |

82   Corn-mill at Pompeii

and his keep would cost ten pounds of it. A horse would grind five or six times this amount but would be far more expensive to buy and feed. As a contrast to the picture we receive of these patient beasts walking round and round the mills, one may recall a Pompeian wall-painting showing the feast of the *Vestalia* when the mills ceased work and the donkeys were feted and garlanded with flowers. Vesta was the goddess who watched over the millers.[1]

A pair of millstones found at the Roman villa at Woolaston, Gloucestershire, resembles those used for the portable querns but they measure $31\frac{1}{2}$ inches in diameter instead of the more normal size of around 15 inches and so are far too big and heavy for one person to turn.[2] Both stones are perforated and have dove-tailed recesses and the presence of these features provided the clues suggesting that they may come from some form of mechanical geared mill. Similar stones were found at the Saalburg, a Roman fort in the Rhineland near Bad Homburg, together with an iron spindle with dovetails at the end which fitted the recesses on the stones. Below the stones the spindle fitted into two strong

[1] Tanzer (1939) fig. 11.
[2] C. Scott Garrett, 'Chesters Roman Villa, Woolaston', *Arch. Camb.* XCIII (1938) 122.

183

oak disks bound with iron rings and held apart by six forged iron bars $6\frac{1}{4}$ inches long. A large revolving toothed wheel fitted into the drum formed by these bars, and so turned the spindle and with it, the millstones. At the Saalburg it is believed that a handle was attached to the wheel and worked by human or animal labour but at other sites, where water was more easily available, a water wheel may have provided the necessary power. Vitruvius, writing in the first century B.C., describes a water-mill of this type and an example of one has been reconstructed in the Naples Museum, based on evidence recovered from a neighbouring site at Venafro. This mill could grind 150 kilograms of flour an hour compared with the 100 kilograms (220 lbs.) ground by a mill of Saalburg type when worked by a handle turned by 4–6 men. At Barbegal near Arles in Provence, a large-scale Roman flour mill has been excavated with 16 water-mills arranged in a double row up a hillside, the water power being provided by two mill races fed by an aqueduct. This is believed to have produced flour enough to supply 80,000 people.[1]

In Britain the best evidence for water-mills comes from along Hadrian's Wall. At Haltwhistle Burn in Northumberland large millstones and part of the wooden mill-wheel were found; and at Chollerford, near the fort at Chesters, a stone axle was discovered. Hadrian's Wall crosses the river North Tyne by a bridge at this point with a tower on each abutment. On the north side is a water-channel or mill-race obviously intended to work the mill sited in the tower. Both these mills are probably of third century A.D. date and the Choller-ford example was duplicated by a similar structure further west, where the Wall crosses the river Irthing at Willowford in Cumberland. A paved mill-race was noted there and a stone spindle bearing found, belonging to either the wheel or the millstones.[2] Further south an iron spindle, closely resembling the one from the Saalburg, was found among a hoard of ironwork from the Roman town at Great Chesterford (fig. 81a). It must belong to a mill of either Saalburg type or one driven by water-power, perhaps supplied by the river Granta nearby. Evidence for two more mills, possibly sawmills, worked by water-power, has been found by the river Witham at Lincoln.[3]

Some of the flour ground by these various processes may have been made into coarse unleavened bread but methods of making lighter leavened loaves were well known. The Elder Pliny lists several, including millet or bran dipped in unfermented wine, or old dough kept until it had turned sour.[4] Yeast was

[1] Brogan (1953) p. 136; Eydoux (1962) fig. 295.
[2] Richmond ed. (1966) pp. 82, 143, 161.
[3] Richmond, 'Industry in Roman Britain' in J. Wacher ed. (1965) p. 83.
[4] *N.H.* XVIII. 102–4.

also used and Pliny tells us that the Gauls and Iberians when steeping corn to make beer collected 'the foam that forms on the surface in the process for leaven, in consequence of which those races have a lighter kind of bread than others'.[1] Probably British bakers had the same customs as the Gauls. The dough would then be kneaded, either by hand or in a kneading machine. Several of these appliances were found at Pompeii and they seem to have consisted of two or three wooden arms attached to the lower end of a vertical shaft fitted into a socket in a large basin made of lava. Holes were pierced in the sides of the basin for the insertion of wooden teeth. As the shaft turned, the dough was pushed forward by the arms and caught and held back by the teeth so that it was thoroughly kneaded.[2]

No identifiable remains of bread have survived in Roman Britain but at Pompeii actual carbonized loaves were recovered, round in shape and slashed across with eight or ten indentations. These loaves were baked in a brick oven shaped like a low beehive, heated first with wood or charcoal. When the oven was hot enough the ashes were raked out, the bread put in, and the mouth of the oven closed to retain the heat. One of the large bakeries at Pompeii had four donkey mills in one large room, and in the kneading room nearby traces of a large table and shelves survive. Through one opening the loaves went to the oven next door and through another they passed into a store-room to cool after baking. On the other side of the mill-room was a stable for the animals. In the country, bread would have to be made at home but in the towns bakers, pastry-cooks and confectioners must have done a good trade. A site which may be a bakery has been found at Springhead in Kent. In consisted of a three-roomed building with one end facing on to the street. This may have been the baker's shop. An oven was found in each of the other rooms and part of a mill-stone. The building may have had two storeys, allowing space for a grainstore above the bakery. It was occupied from about A.D. 90 to 120.[3] A set of beehive-shaped clay ovens and stone mortaria found at Holditch (Staffordshire) may also indicate the whereabouts of a baker's shop.[4] A pastry-cook's mould from Silchester shows an interesting figure-scene probably representing the Emperor Severus and his sons Caracalla and Geta in semi-military dress, with the Empress Julia Domna. They seem to be offering a sacrifice of thanksgiving, probably for some victory in Severus' British wars and the mould may have been used to decorate

---

[1] *Ibid.* 68.
[2] Mau-Kelsey (1902) p. 384.
[3] W. S. Penn, 'Romano-British Settlement at Springhead, Excavation of the Bakery', *Arch. Cant.* LXXI (1957) 56 *et seq.*; *ibid.* LXXIX (1964) 173.
[4] *J.R.S.* L (1960) 223.

cakes or sweetmeats on sale during the festival.[1] In Rome at least, some bakers delivered bread and the jurist Ulpian discusses the case of the slave employed to do this work who collected payment in advance and then ran away. As the baker was in the habit of allowing the money to be given to the slave, he was still obliged to provide the bread.[2]

Every town must have had numerous foodshops where the townsfolk bought their supplies: fruit, vegetables, grain and wine must all have been on sale. One relief in the Torlonia Museum, Rome, depicts a Roman poulterer's shop full of different kinds of game,[3] and another relief in Dresden shows us a butcher at work jointing a side of bacon on a massive block (fig. 83). Other pieces of meat are hung up on hooks around him and behind him are a spare chopper and the steelyard. His wife sits in a round-backed chair with her tablets, casting up the accounts as he sells his goods. Quantities of meat bones are found on most Romano-British sites so the meat trade must have been profitable. Flesh hooks found at Silchester probably indicate a butcher's shop and the metal spurs worn by cocks in cock-fighting may be a clue to the former whereabouts of the poultry-dealer.

Other shops sold household necessities. A heap of mortaria discovered amid the ruins of the Forum at Wroxeter reveals the site of a pottery stall, and another stall nearby must have sold samian ware, as piles of plates and dishes were uncovered by the excavators.[4] A shop at Colchester, probably burnt by Boudicca in A.D. 60, seems to have supplied glass, samian and other pottery, and also pottery lamps. The samian dishes were piled on the floor or on a low shelf, bottom upwards, with fine glass bowls and flasks on the shelf above. When the house caught fire the flames first blackened the pottery and then melted the glass until it dripped down all over them. Finally, the roof fell in on top of everything.[5] Another shop at Wroxeter made and sold wares of a different type as its stock included a series of eighty whetstones, still showing the marks of the saw, and ready for use for sharpening knives and agricultural implements. Similar stones have been found in London, Chester, and Caistor-by-Norwich so somewhere there must have been a quarry which carried on a good business providing the raw material.[6] The tinker or vendor of metal vessels must also have had his shop or market stall. A Pompeian painting shows one surrounded by cauldrons and cooking vessels with an apprentice beating out more metal on an anvil in the background,[7] and a relief from Sens shows large dishes, etc.,

[1] *Ant. J.* XXXVIII (1958) 237.
[2] Maxey (1938) p. 21.   [3] Paoli (1955) Pl. X.
[4] Atkinson (1942) p. 127 *et seq.*   [5] Hull (1958) p. 154.
[6] Atkinson (1942) p. 129.   [7] Tanzer (1939) fig. 32.

83 The butcher's shop. Roman relief in Dresden Museum

on sale in a shop.[1] Another painting from Pompeii apparently shows the guild of carpenters and metal-workers in procession, carrying a platform with a tableau of their work; wood being sawn up with a double frame-saw under a canopy borne on four pillars wreathed with strings of metal jugs and bowls.[2] The cutler also offered a variety of wares for sale as we know from the numerous knives recovered from excavations. A relief showing his shop and stock in trade can be seen in the Vatican Museum.

Many people worked as craftsmen and foremost among them was the smith, proud of his trade like the man on the York tombstone with his hammer and tongs (Pl. 25*b*). He was a very important member of the community as all depended upon his skill and industry for the tools used in many other occupations. Luckily much of his work has survived and great hoards containing numerous iron objects presumably buried in times of trouble have been found in the towns at Silchester and Great Chesterford; another hoard was discovered in a field at Worlington near Newmarket, and much ironwork was also recovered during the excavations at Caerwent. A further hoard from Newstead, the big legionary fortress in Scotland, contains ironwork which must have been made by the soldiers, and no doubt skilled veterans often ended their days as smiths in the large towns. The smith's own tools of hammer, tongs or pincers, and anvil were all found at Great Chesterford (Pl. 42*a*), and among the finest products of his craft is the great chain hanging from a swivel and ending in hooks, which may have been used for transferring sacks of grain from the wagons into the store-house loft or for suspending a cauldron over a fire

[1] G. Julliot, *Inscriptions et Monuments du Musée Gallo-Romaine de Sens* (Sens, 1898) p. 88, Pl. IX. 3.
[2] Tanzer (1939) fig. 34.

84 Frame-saw in use. From a gold-glass vessel found in the Roman Catacombs

(Pl. 42*b*).[1] The ironwork found in these hoards is naturally very rusty when unearthed, but modern methods of cleaning and preservation can perform wonders, and so good was the metal and the workmanship of these smiths that as already noted (p. 81, fig. 29*a*), one of the great locks for a heavy door found at Great Chesterford is still in working order. Handcuffs for criminals from the same hoard are also still ready for use. Two fine iron wedges used for rock-splitting were found recently embedded in Hadrian's Wall. Over ten inches long, they had obviously been left lying forgotten until wet mortar was accidentally thrown on top of them. Their state of preservation is remarkably good. Made of iron interleaved with slag, they show cut 'feathers' on the opposite edges to prevent them bouncing back when hit by a sledge-hammer.[2]

The tools used by the carpenter and largely made by the smith present a very familiar appearance and are recognised at once by the modern craftsman. Hatchets, axes and wedges for cutting down trees and trimming timber, gimlets, adzes, gouges, augers, punches and chisels have all been found (Pl. 42*a*), as well as bronze compasses and dividers. Indeed, most of the items of a modern tool kit appear, with the exception of a few things like the brace, spokeshave and fretsaw. Reliefs and wall-paintings from other parts of the Empire show us carpenters at work sawing up wood and making furniture. Saw-blades are important items among the hoards of iron work from Silchester and Great Chesterford (Pl. 42*a*) and fragments have also been found at Newstead and at the Chedworth villa. Pre-Roman saws found at Glastonbury and at Barley (Hertfordshire) have concave blades which could only be used with a pulling action but the Roman craftsmen had learnt how to set saw teeth in a straight blade which could be pushed through the wood. This is a much more efficient

[1] R. C. Neville, 'Description of a remarkable deposit of Roman antiquities of Iron at Great Chesterford', *Arch. J.* XIII (1856) 10.
[2] N. Shaw, 'Two Iron Rock Wedges from Hadrian's Wall', *Arch. Ael.* (4) XXXVI (1958) 313.

way of working in which the timber can be held by the workman's hand and knee instead of having to be fixed to a bench or post. British Iron Age and Roman blades are all comparatively small as the hammered iron used in their construction would soon buckle with too much pressure. To counteract this difficulty the Roman ones may have been used with wooden frames. The simplest type of frame-saw was a single piece of wood bent like a bow, with its two ends gripped by the two ends of the iron blade wrapped round it and fastened with rivets. Otherwise the saws, ranging in size, as we know from the various types of evidence available in the Empire, from the small hand-saw for bench work to the large two-man pit- and crosscut-saws, were either fixed in the centre of an open wooden framework and pulled to and fro by two sawyers, or used with the blade held at the ends by two uprights connected by a strut, and sometimes reinforced by a cord stretched across the top which could be tightened to maintain the tension (fig. 84). The so-called pit-saw, incidentally, does not seem to have been employed with a pit at this period, the timber being always placed across high trestles.

The plane was another important item in the carpenter's kit. In the western provinces of the Roman Empire ten sites have so far produced planes made either of wood with iron sole plates, or entirely of iron. They range in date from the middle of the second to the fourth century; apparently the form of the plane altered hardly at all during this long period. Three examples come from Britain where they have been found in the towns at Silchester (figs. 85, 86), Caerwent and Verulamium, and toothed plane-irons are also known from the fortress at Newstead. When we remember the elaborate furniture made in Roman times we realise how important this tool must have been for the cabinet-maker. In the Bristol Museum is a cupboard door, the right-hand leaf of a pair found in Egypt and of third- or fourth-century date. Its panelling and mouldings must have required, beside the jack and smoothing planes, a selection of moulding planes, ploughs, rabbit and shoulder planes. Doors of this type appear in the illustration (fig. 64) and a similar cupboard is included among the furnishings carved on the interior of the Simpelveld sarcophagus (fig. 87). Elaborate wooden doors have also been preserved in houses at Herculaneum and Pompeii and

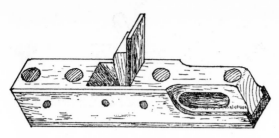

86 Reconstruction of the Silchester plane

similar ones were probably made for householders in Silchester and elsewhere in Britain.[1] The lathe was another tool which became increasingly popular at this time although its use was well understood in the Iron Age. It was extensively employed in furniture making with both wood and Kimmeridge shale. When one thinks of all the work which went on it seems surprising that even more tools have not been found, but, of course, metal was precious and the smiths' hoards usually contain scrap metal and broken handles and hinges ready for resmelting and making into new implements. Masons and stone cutters' special tools, such as mallets, hammers and trowels for spreading mortar, also turn up occasionally.

Sometimes traces of bronzesmiths' workshops can be identified. A shop in the Forum at Wroxeter contained the remains of a small furnace with signs of molten bronze and fragments of worked metal, while completed hairpins and other little objects were scattered about. On one side of the room a quantity of pulverised granite was found with pieces of fine glass, and the suggestion has been made that here we may have an enameller's workshop for the manufacture of brooches.[2] Something similar may have existed on Nornour, one of the Isles of Scilly, where over 250 brooches, some possibly Belgian imports, have been found, together with furnaces and coins of first- to fourth-century date.[3] A Latin inscription found at Malton, Yorkshire, tells us of work of a rather similar kind. It reads, 'Good luck to the Genius of this place; young slave, use to your good fortune this goldsmith's shop', and so reveals to us the existence of a North Country jeweller's establishment.[4] Tiny crucibles containing gold were also found in second-century metal workers' shops at Verulamium.[5] An anvil of a type used by gold-smiths, discovered at the village of Rushmore, Dorset, indicates that this craft was widespread. Another of the Wroxeter shops

[1] For information about Roman carpentry equipment I am indebted to W. L. Goodman, *A History of Woodworking Tools* (1964). See also Singer *et al.* (1956) II p. 228 *et seq*. For a timber merchant's tombstone from Augst see E. VI no. 5478.
[2] T. Wright, *Uriconium* (1879) p. 162.
[3] *Daily Telegraph* 4 September 1963. Excavations by Miss D. Dudley.
[4] C.I.L. VII. 265.
[5] *J.R.S.* LI (1961) 180.

87 Cupboard from the
Simpelveld sarcophagus

which was found full of animal bones and stag's horns, many of them cut and
sawn up, may have been a storehouse for the makers of pins, decorative inlays
for furniture, knife-handles and other bone objects.

The hides from these animals would be used for making leather goods or
possibly they had been sent north to the army as taxation in kind, or had been
exported. Salt was probably needed for working them; this may have been one
of the uses for the output of the British salterns. Numerous small coastal settlements connected with the production of salt by evaporation from seawater have
been found; a recent survey shows that Britain heads the list with the largest
number of sites from any European country.[1] Not all of them are of Roman
date; some are earlier and the process of saltmaking may have been introduced
about the beginning of the Early Iron Age.

Sea water can be collected in two different ways. One method depends on
finding salt crystallized by the sun on the surface of the sands at low tide. This
was placed in pots with perforated bases probably covered with straw to act as
a filter for the sand which must also have been present. The salt was washed
through with seawater into containers and then left until the water evaporated.

[1] J. Nenquin, *Salt. A Study in Economic Prehistory* (Bruges, 1961).

The result was a fairly pure salt which could be further purified in solution with fresh water and recrystallised.[1] Alternatively seawater may have been evaporated in shallow clay-lined pans. The second method required a clay hearth on which the pans were placed on cylindrical supports. They were filled with seawater and a fire was lit beneath them. The water evaporated and the salt remained on the sides of the pans. Fragments of them and also of the characteristic supports are the clues which point to a saltmaking site. Smaller vessels in which the salt may have been packed for easy transport also occur.[2] Inland salt springs like those at Droitwich, still famous for its brine baths, and Middlewich in Cheshire, were also exploited in antiquity and both are called *Salinae* by the Roman geographer Ptolemy. A clay-lined kiln site, 10 feet long and 2 feet wide, was identified at Middlewich in 1960. It may have been spanned by a number of fire bars, similar to specimens discovered elsewhere, and clay supports were also found. Similar sites are believed to have existed nearby, suggesting that this *Salinae* was indeed a thriving centre of Roman salt production.[3]

Pottery manufacture was probably Britain's most important industry and many workers must have been needed to produce all the bowls, cups and plates used in everyday life, fragments of which are now found scattered in such abundance over much of the countryside. The potter's wheel was used by some British tribes before the Roman invasion, and after the conquest it was widely adopted. An increasing number of small potteries sprang up all over the country and at first most of them either continued to make types current before the conquest or else to copy forms imported from Gaul. During the second century some of these small firms were superseded by large manufacturing centres with many kilns making different kinds of pottery which were widely distributed. The kilns usually consisted of a circular hole in the ground about 4 feet in diameter, lined with clay, tiles or stone. The furnace was constructed at one side and its heat passed through a short channel into the kiln, which had a raised floor of perforated tiles or fire-bars through which the heat could percolate. The floor was supported by a clay pedestal and the rows of unbaked pots were arranged on it in layers. Each row was separated from the one above by thin pieces of clay called kiln plates, packed round with grass, and the whole erection was finally covered over by a domed clay roof with ventilation holes. This had to be broken open to extract the pots after each firing.[4] Figure 88 shows us one of the

[1] *Ibid.* p. 123 *et seq.*
[2] *Ibid.* p. 85; S. J. Hallam, 'Romano-British Salt Industry in South Lincolnshire', *Reports & Papers, Lincs. Architectural & Arch. Soc.* N. S. VIII (1960) pp. 35–75.
[3] F. H. Thompson, *Roman Cheshire* (Chester, 1965) p. 94 *et seq.*
[4] For kilns in general see P. Corder, 'The Structure of Romano-British Pottery Kilns', *Arch. J.* XCIV (1957) 10–27.

88   Pottery kiln, Water Newton,
Northamptonshire

pottery kilns from the big manufacturing area of the Nene Valley around
Durobrivae near Castor, Northamptonshire, during excavation in 1828, and we
can see the perforated floor and the arch at the mouth of the furnace very clearly.
Probably it could take five or six hundred lots at a time. Smaller kilns would
hold two to three hundred.[1] Figure 89 is a modern reconstruction of a kiln of
Nene Valley type, showing the arrangement of the rows of pottery successfully
baked in it.[2] Sometimes a batch went wrong in the baking and then the distorted
vessels were thrown on one side by the disgruntled potter. These throw-outs
are called 'wasters' and when they are found the archaeologist begins to search
hopefully for a kiln.

The pottery produced in the Nene Valley included coarse grey and buff wares
for local markets and mortaria which were more widely distributed. The name
of one potter is known because a third-century mortarium had SENNIANVS
DVROBRIVIS VRI [T] (Sennianus fired this at Durobrivae) painted on its
rim.[3] The characteristic product, however, is the colour-coated pottery often
known as Castor ware although it was also made elsewhere. It largely consists
of beakers of various sizes, made of light coloured clay covered with a finer clay
slip rich in iron compounds and varying in colour from red or shades of brown
to black. Fingerprints still discernible on the bases show that the potters held
the beakers upside down when they plunged them into the slip. Rouletting,
applied with a toothed wheel, was one favourite form of ornament and also
barbotine decoration. This was a process in which clay was squeezed through
a nozzle to form a pattern in relief, rather as a pastrycook decorates a cake.
Simple scale patterns, intended to prevent the cup slipping out of the hand, are
frequent and leaf and scroll patterns are popular (fig. 90). Animated figure

[1] B. R. Hartley, 'Notes on the Roman Pottery Industry in the Nene Valley', *Peterborough
Museum Soc. Occasional Papers No. 2* (1960).
[2] B. R. Hartley, 'The Firing of Kilns of Romano-British type', *Archaeometry* IV (1961) 1–3.
[3] *J.R.S.* XXX (1940) p. 190 no. 30.

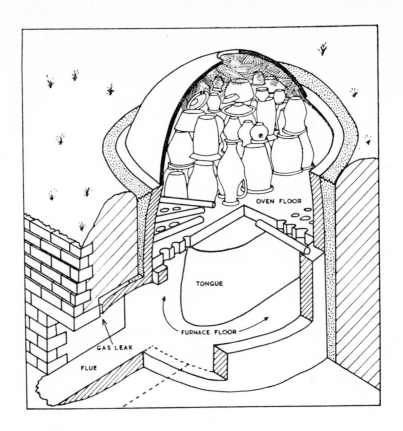

89 Romano-British pottery kiln of type used in the Nene Valley for making Castor wares

scenes showing the labours of Hercules and other mythological events (fig. 90g), or hunts and gladiatorial combats are not uncommon and were inspired by samian ware or imported glass bowls (fig. 144).[1] Other beakers have simple but effective designs of leaves and berries in white paint or painted figures (fig. 90f).[2] Boxes and lids covered with rouletting (fig. 90h), and flagons, plates and bowls decorated with circles or leaf motifs in red paint on buff slip, are other colour-coated types. Kilns for making this pottery have also been found at Colchester, and at Hartshill, Warwickshire.[3]

The New Forest potteries worked on a much smaller scale during the third and fourth centuries and their products may often represent the output of single family groups of potters; a father and son perhaps building a kiln in the Forest and continuing work until all the nearby firewood was used up, and then moving

[1] See chap. 13.
[2] G. Webster, 'Romano-British pottery with painted figures', *Ant. J.* XXXIX (1959) 91–5.
[3] *J.R.S.* LII (1962) 168.

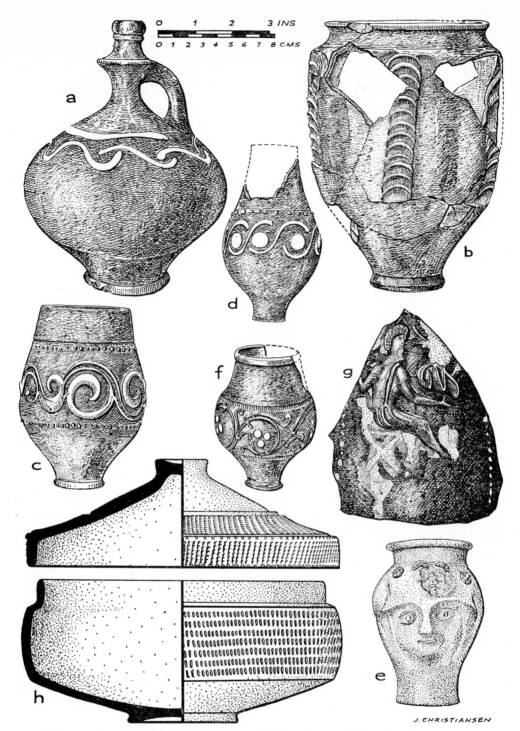

J. CHRISTIANSEN

90   Pottery. *a* Haslingfield, Cambridgeshire. *b* Great Chesterford. *c* Shefford, Bedfordshire. *d* Astwick, Bedfordshire. *e* Face-urn, Water Newton, Northamptonshire. *f* Guilden Morden, Cambridgeshire. *g* Godmanchester, Huntingdonshire, *h* Peterborough. All except *e* are colour-coated wares. *a, d, f,* are decorated with paint

on and building a fresh kiln on a new site. The finished pots were probably packed into saddle-bags and hawked round on packhorses or donkey back; they are found in Southern Britain but have not the wide distribution of Castor-ware which was sent out by the barge or wagon-load along the roads and rivers radiating out from Castor. New Forest pottery is characterised by a hard metallic surface, and the jugs and flasks are often decorated with white paint or stamped rosettes.[1] Other potteries included jars decorated with faces among their products, some of them perhaps caricatures of local worthies, and these may be the early ancestors of our Toby jugs (fig. 90*e*).

Much research is now being carried on into the manufacture of mortaria (fig. 65*b*). These bowls, so necessary in Roman kitchens, were imported in the early days of the occupation but by the mid-second century they were being extensively made in Britain. Many kilns were found at Hartshill making wares stamped with the names of eight different potters, among them MOSSIV (S) and CEVANOS.[2] From second-century kilns at Cantley (Yorkshire) come mortaria with different stamps, including SARRVS and SETIBOGIVS, and later kilns in the same district produced other examples decorated with stripes of red paint.[3] Third- and fourth-century mortaria made in the Nene Valley spread all over the eastern counties and some examples have also been found in military contexts in the north. The Colchester kilns have produced the stamps of eleven second-century potters, one of them ACCEPTVS, whose name also occurs on locally made samian ware, and even on a sherd of decorated colour-coated beaker, a unique discovery.[4] Stamps consisting of a herringbone design also occur. The mortaria with name stamps seem to have mostly sold in south-eastern England, although the products of one potter, MARTINVS, are found at York and Corbridge. The herringbone stamps, however, and a few examples of MESSOR, are largely found in Scotland and must represent an important but short-lived military contract.[5] After the end of the second century stamps were no longer applied to mortaria, so the products of the different groups of kilns can no longer be easily identified.

A little evidence is gradually coming to light that the samian ware found on so many of our Roman sites was sometimes made in Britain and not always imported. The detailed study of a samian kiln found at Colchester in 1933 sheds

[1] Heywood Sumner, *New Forest Potteries* (1927).
[2] *J.R.S.* LI (1961) 173; LII (1962) 168; K. Hartley, 'The Kilns at Hartshill', *Archaeometry* V (1962) 22.
[3] *J.R.S.* L (1960) 220.
[4] Hull (1963b) p. 91 fig. 50.
[5] *Ibid.* p. 114, K. Hartley, 'Spectographic Analysis of some Romano-British Mortaria', *Archaeometry* II (1959) 21–2.

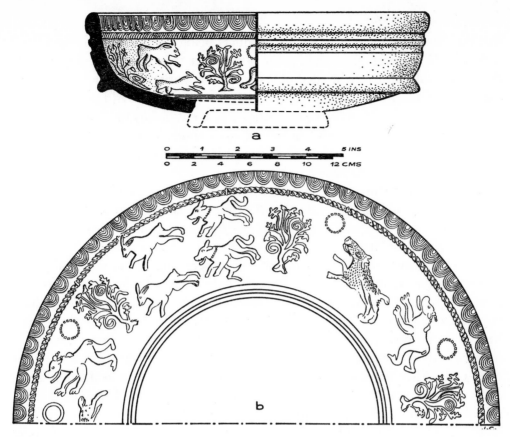

91 Mould for making samian pottery and design from Colchester

much light on the process of manufacture.[1] Plain wares stamped by more than a dozen potters have been identified, dating from the late first to the end of the second century.[2] Over 400 fragments of the moulds used for decorated wares were also collected (fig. 91).[3] They seem to have been used for bowls made by two different potters and a third potter is also suspected although his moulds still await discovery. He may have worked in Trier before he came to Britain.[4] The decorated samian dates from towards the end of the second century at a time when little continental material was being imported and that of poor quality. During the second and third centuries, many samian potters who had learnt their trade at the big manufacturing centres in central France seem to have started small factories of their own in Eastern France and Germany. Now it appears that a few of them found their way to Britain. Moulds have also been found at York and Pulborough,[5] and a waster from Aldgate, London, suggests

[1] Hull (1963b) p. 20 *et seq.*   [2] *Ibid.* p. 89.   [3] *Ibid,* p. 47 *et seq.*
[4] *Ibid.* p. 74.   [5] *Ibid.* p. 45.

that here too a kiln was at work, its products being identified at Silchester and in Sussex. The special clay used for the pottery may have had to be imported so the kilns would probably be sited near ports. The work of the Colchester crafts-men shows some originality in their choice of motifs but the Aldgate potter was more conventional. His work can sometimes be identified by the fact that having stamped the figure of Bacchus in one of his moulds he then superimposed a stamp of a girl tambourine dancer on top of it. As a result his bowls are liable to show a girl with four arms.[1]

Many labourers must have been needed to work the raw materials required for all the new buildings springing up in Britain. Most first-century houses were constructed of timber, wattle and daub, but the custom of building on founda-tion walls of stone or flint and rubble soon spread. When he visited Britain in A.D. 121 the Emperor Hadrian encouraged the erection of monumental public buildings, and as time went on the rich villa-owners built stone houses of increasing size. The quarries which provided stone for Hadrian's Wall have been identified, and inscriptions cut by some of the military units working there have been found. A quarry near Brampton in Cumberland shows several of these records on one face on what is now known as the 'Written Rock' by the river Gelt. They commemorate work done in A.D. 207 by a vexillation of the Second Legion under the *optio* Agricola in the consulates (in Rome) of the con-suls Aper and Maximus. Another stone from Coombe Crag, Cumberland, is inscribed 'Stadius did this', and underneath, 'Apollonius; I, Daminius did not |want (to do it)', while an inscription in a quarry near Chollerford (Northumberland) read PETRA FLAVI CARANTINI, 'the rock of Flavius Carantinus'.[2]

We do not know under what conditions the stone-cutters worked in the civilian areas further south, whether they were slave or free, employed by the state or by individual business men. We do find, however, extensive exploitation of local resources, and this suggests firms of builders in the towns who sent out materials and workmen wherever they were needed. Country houses also largely depended upon local resources.[3] When stone was not available close at hand it was sometimes transported from quite a distance, usually by water, and the decision to do this must have considerably increased the cost of building. Roofing materials often have quite a wide distribution, and Purbeck slate from Dorset was much used for Hampshire villas.

Ordinary earthenware tiles were also needed for new buildings and many

[1] G. Simpson, 'The Aldgate Potter', *J.R.S.* XLII (1952) 68–71.
[2] Quarry inscriptions *R.I.B.* 1008, 1009, 1951, 1952, 1442.
[3] See below p. 252.

tileries sprang up to supply them.[1] They made the curved and flanged tiles used for roofs, larger flanged tiles for drains, box-tiles which were built into the walls and up which travelled the hot air from the hypocausts, square tiles for some floors and the hypocaust pillars, and small thick tiles which were fitted together to make an attractive herringbone pattern for other floors. Many products were stamped with a recognisable mark like the capricorn, winged horse and LEG II AVG stamp which denotes the Second Legion Augusta, while the boar used by the Twentieth Legion appears on the products from the military tilery at Holt (Denbighshire).[2] An imperial tilery run by the procurators of the Emperor Nero may have existed at Silchester.[3] The *colonia* at Gloucester seems to have owned a municipal tilery which was probably in competition with a private company working somewhere nearby, possibly at Cirencester.[4] Some box-flue-tiles had their surfaces scored in various ways so that the wall-plaster would adhere to them more firmly (fig. 92*a*). In certain cases, probably dating between A.D. 90 and 150, they were decorated with a definite pattern stamped with a cylindrical die, shaped like a small roller. These come from a tilery at Ashtead (Surrey) which distributed its wares as far afield as Leicester, Kenchester and Charterhouse-on-Mendip, but the thickest concentration of them is found in South-Eastern England. Nine main types of decoration have been recognised, ranging from chevrons and rosettes to more complicated foliate designs, probably inspired by the standards carried by auxiliary regiments (fig. 92*c*). Most interesting of all, the tiles of Group Two show a lively scene of dog and stag confronting each other with the maker's initials G.I.S. or I.V.F.E. between them (fig. 92*b*).[5] Tiles for different purposes were probably made at the same tilery and one found at the Wiggonholt villa (Sussex) has a workman's tally scratched on it: 1020 tiles for hypocaust pillars, four wedge-shaped voussoirs, probably for a doorway, and 560 flue-tiles. London may have been the chief centre for the manufacture of patterned tiles but the tile-makers probably travelled to the building sites and made tiles on the spot as they were required.[6]

Other raw materials used in Roman Britain were mostly obtained by mining.

[1] F. Jenkins, 'A Roman Tilery and Two Pottery Kilns at *Durovernum* (Canterbury)', *Ant. J.* XXXVI (1956) 40–56.
[2] W. Grimes, 'A Pottery and Tilery of the Twentieth Legion at Holt', *Cymmrodorion Society Trans.* XLI (1930).
[3] Richmond (1963) p. 168.
[4] E. Clifford, 'Stamped Tiles found in Gloucestershire', *J.R.S.* XLV (1955) 68–72.
[5] A. Lowther, 'A Study of the Patterns on Roman Flue-Tiles and their Distribution', *Surrey Arch. Soc. Research Papers* (1948); and App. III to S. S. Frere, 'Excavation of a late Roman Bath-house at Chatley Farm, Cobham', *Sur.A.C.* L (1964) 94–6.
[6] S. E. Winbolt and R. G. Goodchild, 'Roman Villa at Lickfold, Wiggonholt', *Sus.A.C.* LXXXI (1940) 66.

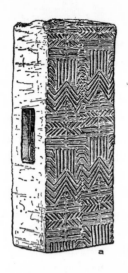
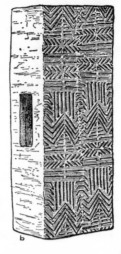

92 Flue-tiles. *a* London. *b* Reigate, Surrey. *c, d* Designs stamped on flue-tiles

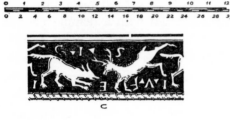

J.CHRISTIANSEN

Outcrops of coal were exploited in many parts of the country, and sometimes this coal was carried considerable distances. Recent work on farm-sites in the Fenland suggests that the barges which carried corn or Castor pottery up the rivers and canals or along the east coast to northern England returned laden with coal for the ovens which were used for drying unripe grain. Coal was systematically mined by the army and carted to some of the forts on the Antonine Wall and along Hadrian's Wall, where it was used in the baths and in the iron-smelting furnaces from the second century onwards. There is also plenty of evidence for its industrial and domestic use in the towns and villas further south.[1] Solinus, describing the Roman Spa at Bath in the third century, tells us that 'The presiding deity of these springs is Minerva, in whose temple the perpetual fire never turns into white wood-ash, but when the flame dies down, into stony masses'.[2] The 'stony masses' was cannel coal from the Somersetshire coalfield which supplied numerous sites in Somerset and Wiltshire, while Gloucestershire villas and other western sites may have drawn supplies from the Forest of Dean. This was chiefly used for domestic purposes and probably brought round

[1] G. Webster, 'A Note on the Use of Coal in Britain', *Ant. J.* XXXV (1955) 199–217.
[2] *Collectanea Rerum Memorabilium* XXII. 11.

by pedlars. Local coal was used for smelting lead at Pentre in Flintshire and for heating the baths at Wroxeter, and Flintshire coal may also have been distributed to the Anglesey village of Din Lligwy seventy or eighty miles away where it may have been needed for iron smelting. The coal was usually obtained from surface workings but occasionally traces of more elaborate mining are suspected, so far without proof.

Iron mines were numerous, the chief centres being in the Forest of Dean and on the Weald, but many smaller workings existed all over the country. A shaft of probable pre-third century date has been identified under later huts at Lydney. It is nearly two feet wide, a narrow passage which originally cut right through the hill-side with trial holes leading upwards from it at certain points (Pl. 41). Short sharp incisions are still visible on its walls, the characteristic marks of the Roman miner's pick-hammer, many examples of which have been found in mines in Spain.[1] Such shafts are exceptional, the ore being usually obtained by open cast methods from outcrops or by digging pits. Layers of slag and clinker from many sites suggest that the metal was often worked in small native mining settlements or villages. These produced low-grade smeltings which may have been sent elsewhere for resmelting in puddling furnaces and forging into tools, as Diodorus Siculus tells us was the case in Elba.[2] Blooms of iron at this stage have been found at Corbridge, and there is no doubt that they were destined for the military workshops where the smiths would make them into weapons. At Silchester iron could be obtained from iron-pan, a material occurring in the local gravels, and deposits of slag were found all over the town. A smelting furnace excavated in 1955 consisted of a clay-lined hollow filled with charcoal and iron-ore and covered with a dome of clay. The necessary draught must have been provided by bellows. The result is described as 'a spongy mass of metallic iron and slag, which needed prolonged beating at red-heat to become a consolidated 'bloom' free enough of impurities for use.'[3] Such furnaces were already known in the Iron Age but they increased in size in the Roman period and a number of examples have been found, including an interesting group of sites in Sussex which exploited the Wealden iron. In some cases, as at Tiddington, ovens for roasting the ore were also discovered. This treatment drove off water and carbon dioxide and made the ore porous and so more easily smelted.[4]

Shaft furnaces, long known in the Mediterranean, were a Roman introduction into Britain and their use must have raised production. The best examples are five found at Ashwicken in Norfolk, three miles from the villa at Gayton Thorpe.

[1] Wheeler (1932) p. 18 *et seq.*   [2] *Library of History* V. xiii, 1–2.   [3] Boon (1957) p. 182.
[4] For the treatment of iron see Tylecote (1962) and also H. H. Coghlan, 'Notes on Prehistoric & Early Iron in the Old World', *Pitt-Rivers Occ. Papers on Technology* no. 8 (Oxford, 1956).

They are all of similar construction and date from the second century, although they may not all have been in use at exactly the same time. The circular shafts may have been constructed by plastering a tree-trunk with clay and building a fire round it. When one layer was baked, more clay was plastered on, and the process was repeated about ten times until the result was a foot thick and the tree trunk was completely calcined. The shaft must have been five or six feet high, it was packed with ore and charcoal to a height of two feet and the rest acted as a chimney for an upward draught. An arched opening into the furnace was built at the base and air was blown into this through a tuyère. The slag was run off into two basins and the bloom eventually extracted. The choice of the site must have depended upon the availability locally of ore, clay and wood for the charcoal. No roasting ovens were found, possibly because this process had already been carried out at the mine workings.[1]

Rare shaft furnaces and numerous bowl furnaces are known from other sites, including three investigated near Pickworth, three miles from Great Casterton.[2] Large lumps of cinder from furnace floors, the results of repeated smeltings, are also found and one from the foundations of a barn at the Great Weldon villa weighs 80 lb. The bowl furnaces were among the types used by the smith to treat the blooms after smelting. A malleable wrought iron resulted which could be re-heated and worked into shape. At Corbridge a stone-built welding furnace of third- or fourth-century date was found. A large piece of iron made from several blooms, heated and hammered out on some form of anvil, had been placed in this furnace, surrounded by charcoal and fired. Meanwhile another bloom was also heated on a separate hearth elsewhere in the same furnace; the two were placed together and more hammering followed. As the resulting mass of iron increased in length, the furnace was built up round it. Such pieces may have been used as columns or beams for stoke-hole supports and examples known from Catterick and Chedworth measure up to sixty-eight and sixty-four feet in length respectively.[3]

Roman smiths knew that wrought iron could be converted into steel by heating with carbon (carburisation) to obtain a harder metal for cutting edges. They were also acquainted with the processes of quenching and tempering. Too little research has been done on Romano-British ironwork for it to be certain how far these techniques were employed here, and in some cases it may have been decided that it was more economic to use for rough work a softer

---

[1] Tylecote (1962) p. 220 *et seq.*

[2] *J.R.S.* LII (1962) 173.

[3] Tylecote (1962) p. 237 *et seq.*; H. R. Schubert, *Hist. of the British Iron and Steel Industry, 450 B.C.–A.D.1775*, (1957) p. 50.

tool which could be resharpened, rather than one of harder metal which might shatter on a stone.[1] A hoard of seven tons of nails of every shape and size found buried at the fortress of Inchtuthil varied in composition from high carbon steel to almost pure iron. These, no doubt, were made by military smiths, but veterans must have soon carried their army experience into civilian life after retirement. These nails were hidden at the end of the first century to prevent the Caledonians finding them in the evacuated fortress and converting them into weapons.

Iron is available over such extensive areas of Britain that it is probable that many of the workings were privately owned. Normally all metals belonged to the state and their exploitation was carried out by procurators who adapted general imperial policies to local conditions in the same way as the officials in charge of imperial estates. Some mines, however, were leased to private companies and Hadrian in particular encouraged those willing to work new or abandoned sites. Such proprietors received half their output and could even sell their holdings under certain conditions but these privileges only applied so long as the mine continued as a going concern. A second-century inscribed bronze tablet found at Vipasca near Aljustrel, Portugal, tells us that the empire's share of the profits had to be paid before the ore was smelted, and anyone reporting failure to do this to the procurator would be rewarded.[2] Regulations follow for partnership agreements among the lessees and for safety precautions in the mines. Mineworkers were mostly slaves and convicts. Some free men, however, took part and a second-century wax tablet from Dacia records the contract signed by Memmius, son of Asclepius, for six months' work in a gold mine in return for seventy *denarii* and his board. Memmius was to give healthy and vigorous work for his employer, his wages were to be paid in instalments and he was to pay five sesterces for each day he was absent while the contract was in force.[3]

Evidence for different types of administration is hinted at in the traces of copper mining found in Wales. At Great Orme's Head, near Llandudno, the miners lived in caves in the workings during the third and fourth centuries and cakes of copper (bun ingots) found in Caernarvonshire bear inscriptions which have nothing in common with imperial stamps. Possibly they belong to private companies. No traces of smelting occur. More bun ingots have been found in Anglesey but here they may be of metal obtained from the nearby Parys mines and smelted in the villages ready for collection, possibly by the firm with the stamp SOCIO ROMAE-NATSOL., found at Aberffraw in 1640 and now in the National Museum of Wales. This copper may have previously helped to finance

[1] Tylecote (1962) p. 244; Boon (1957) p. 186.
[2] Frank III (1935) p. 171.   [3] L. and R. p. 194.

the druids. Such areas would be under military control so their administration may have been complicated. The fortress at Chester and forts such as Caernarvon or Forden Gaer kept a protective watch over these and other important mining areas. Another mine, at Llanymynech, Shropshire, was entered through a cave from which radiated three galleries, one of them following the principal vein into the hillside for about 300 yards when it divided into small galleries and shafts. The other galleries were probably used for prospecting and may have proved unfruitful. Toolmarks are said to have been seen here and the blade of an iron pick was found. Again, the workmen seem to have lived in the cave at the galleries' mouth.[1]

Copper was important to the national economy because it was needed to combine with tin to make bronze, an alloy used for many purposes. Tin is mentioned by Diodorus, Caesar, Strabo, and other writers as one of the pre-Roman products of Britain, but the tin-mines of Cornwall do not seem to have developed much under Roman influence until the third century. One mining settlement of the late first and early second centuries has been identified near Bodmin, but this seems to have been a shortlived experiment. Probably it was soon realised that British tin could not complete commercially with the products of the great tin-mines of Northern Spain which were then flooding the market, and it was only after the collapse of this trade from exhaustion or local disturbances in the mid-third century that the British mines regained sufficient importance to attract official interest. This is shown by extensive work on the road system and the appearance of several milestones. A considerable increase in coin hoards also bears witness to the fact that more money was in circulation at this later period. The ore occurs in valleys in alluvial deposits one to ten feet thick, lying at varying depths underground. The prehistoric and Roman method of obtaining the metal was by placing the ore-bearing stones and sand in a sloping wooden water-channel. Surplus earth was then washed away and some of the ore already in the sand could be smelted at once. The smaller pieces of tin-stone were grouped up in hand-mills, but the larger boulders had to be smashed with hammers, and the rocks lying around a tin-mine are often pock-marked by this activity.[2]

When the bronzesmith set out to make a casting he would take one of his cakes of smelted copper and put it with a smaller quantity of tin in a small earthenware crucible, usually hemispherical in shape. In some cases zinc, in the form of powdered calamine, had already been alloyed with the copper. These additions produced a harder metal than pure copper.[3] The shape of the crucible is

[1] O. Davies, *Roman Mines in Europe* (1935) p. 160.
[2] *Ibid*, p. 147, Tylecote (1962) p. 63.   [3] Tylecote (1962) pp. 53, 135.

interesting as a similar type is still in use, the rounded base helps the ore to melt speedily and minimises the effect of heat on the vessel. It was probably covered with a loose-fitting clay lid and placed on a hearth surrounded by coal or charcoal and fired. When the metal was melted it was poured into a clay or stone mould. The settlement at Heronbridge near Chester has produced a good example of a bronze-smithy of this type. Some of the work was done in an open-fronted timber building with a clay floor but the smelting of the metal and the heating of the crucibles was probably done outside on a series of hearths on a sandstone floor. The excavator points out that this was advisable because these processes produce highly noxious fumes and there would also be the risk of the building catching fire. The fragments of moulds recovered suggest that strips of thin bronze ornamented with crescents and probably used to decorate small wooden boxes were among the objects made here.[1]

Tin was not only important for the bronze founders. By the third and fourth centuries the coastal raids of the Saxon and Irish pirates, and the barbarian disturbances on the European mainland interrupted the trade in luxury goods just when British fourth-century prosperity was increasing the demand. Instead of samian ware, fashionable hosts, if they could not obtain or afford enough silver and glass, now bought British pewter for their dinner tables. Pewter is made of tin alloyed with lead, and lead was the most important mineral produced by this country in Roman times. Most of it came from the Mendip hills in Somerset, Shropshire, Flintshire and Derbyshire, with smaller quantities in Devon, Yorkshire, Durham, Northumberland and Cumberland. The deposits were worked both opencast and by means of shafts and galleries, the ore being obtained with hammer and chisel and gathered with widemouthed oak shovels into baskets. After smelting the metal was poured into clay moulds bearing stamps in reverse, which were imprinted on the resulting lump or pig of lead. The pigs vary a little in size and weight. Four examples of Mendip lead found at Green Ore, near Wells, Somerset, in 1956, weighed between 187 and 197 lb. (260 to 274 *librae*), and may have been lost en route to the port at Bitterne (Clausentum), near Southampton. Similar hoards are known from Pulborough and Brough-on-Humber and it has been suggested that four pigs weighing *c.* 1,000 *librae* would make up a reasonable cartload.[2]

Sometimes emperors' names appear impressed on the pigs and then they can

[1] B. R. Hartley, 'A Romano-British Bronze-Worker's Hearth at Heronbridge', *J. of the Chester Arch. Soc.* XLI (1954) 1–14.

[2] L. S. Palmer and H. W. Ashworth, 'Four Roman pigs of lead from the Mendips', *Som. Arch. & N. H. Soc. Proc.* CI/CII (1956–7) 52–88; C. Whittick, 'The Casting of Lead Ingots', *J.R.S.* LI (1961) 105–11.

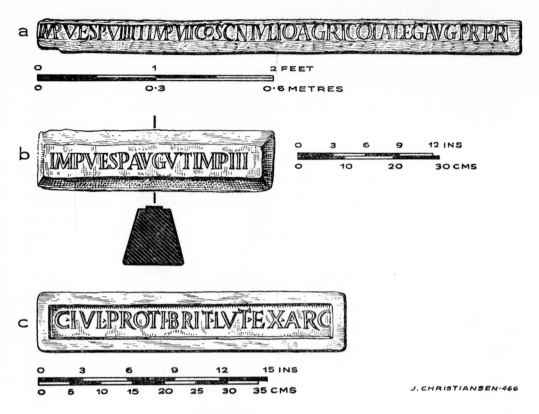

a IMP·VESP·VIIII·IMP·VII·COS·CN·IVLIO·AGRICOLA·LEG·AVG·PR·PR

b IMP·VESP·AVG·VT·IMP·III

c C·IVL·PROT·IB·RIT·LVT·EX·ARG

J. CHRISTIANSEN-466

93 *a* Fragment of a lead water-pipe with an inscription including the name of the governor, Agricola, Chester. *b* Lead pig with an inscription mentioning the Emperor Vespasian, Chester. *c* Lead pig with the inscription GAIVS IVLIVS PROTVS, lead from the Lutudarum mines, Hexgrave Park, Mansfield, Nottinghamshire

be dated (fig. 93*b*). All the Green Ore specimens must have been made beween A.D. 69–79 as they are stamped IMP. VESPASIAN AVG. On one side a smaller inscription—BRIT. EXARG VEB appears, and this probably indicates British metal which has passed through or comes from the silver-lead works at VEB, a possible contraction for the Latin or Celtic name for Charterhouse-on-Mendip. Until recently it was believed that the EX ARG stamp meant that silver had been extracted from the pigs but this now seems doubtful. The Romans obtained their silver from lead by means of the cupellation process in which the ore was smelted on a hearth lined with bone-ash. The ash absorbed the baser metal which could later be resmelted and the silver remained. Cupellation hearths have been found at Wroxeter,[1] Silchester and possibly in the Mendips. The Silchester hearths, however, were engaged in obtaining silver from argenti-

[1] Bushe-Fox (1914) p. 11.

ferous copper and possibly their raw material came from fourth-century coins being melted down for the making of forgeries.[1] Silver for the coinage was, of course, greatly needed by the Romans but analyses suggest that they soon found that the amount contained by British lead was often too small to be worth extracting.[2]

There were, however, many other uses for lead. Water supplies required miles of pipes and a stamped fragment from Chester bearing the name of Agricola shows that these were being made for the new fortress there by A.D. 79 (fig. 93*a*). Great sheets of lead were used for the Great Bath at Bath, smaller sheets for roofs, and lead cisterns were also needed. Weights and caskets occur and many containers and coffins have been found in cemeteries. The pewter industry, fed with Mendip lead and Cornish tin, seems to have flourished in Somerset from the mid-third century onwards. At Camerton,[3] and at Lansdown near Bath, stone moulds have been found for casting a small bowl, $4\frac{1}{8}$ inches in diameter, a shallow flanged dish or tray, a small skillet or saucepan, and possibly for a large plate. Such plates occur with small bowls and dishes, pedestal cups and fine flagons in table services mostly recovered from the Cambridgeshire Fens (Pl. 35). One of the largest hoards, found at the villa at Icklingham, Suffolk, and now in the British Museum, comprised forty items. Another hoard discovered in Isleham Fen, Cambridgeshire, produced eighteen. Oval dishes decorated with incised fish and of a suitable size for a fish course, have also turned up in smaller hoards from Icklingham (fig. 94) and from Appleshaw, Hampshire.[4] Silver dishes of comparable shape and decoration are known from the treasure found at Augst, Switzerland.

The distribution of pewter is interesting and surprising. Although the metals and the only known sites of manufacture are in south-west England, the bulk of the finished product comes from East Anglia. Somerset has produced only two or three hoards, one from Bath and another from the villa at Brislington. They largely consist of flagons. There are smaller finds of up to three pieces elsewhere in the county and small groups occur in Hampshire, London and Northamptonshire. Was all this pewter made in Somerset or did the lead and tin travel to some other centre nearer eastern England?

The development of these industries brings us back to the interesting question of the ownership and development of the lead mines. A pig stamped V ET P

[1] Boon (1957) p. 187 *et seq.*
[2] Tylecote (1962) p. 92.
[3] W. J. Wedlake, *Excavations at Camerton, Somerset* (Camerton, 1958) p. 82 *et seq., J.R.S.* XLIX (1959) 129; I. A. Richmond in J. Wacher ed. (1965) p. 85.
[4] J. Liversidge, 'A New Hoard of Romano-British Pewter from Icklingham', C.A.S.P. LII (1959) p. 7.

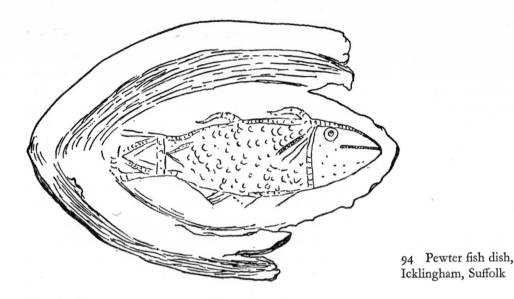

94　Pewter fish dish,
Icklingham, Suffolk

(Q. Veranius and A. Pompeius Largus Gallus, consuls under Claudius) from
Blagdon can be dated to A.D. 49 and this shows that the army soon had production under way at the Mendip mines. Two pigs from Chester bear the names
of Vespasian and his son Titus and the description, *Deceangl* (fig. 93*b*). The
Deceangli were the tribe who lived in Flintshire and these pigs can be dated to
A.D. 74. Here again rapid exploitation followed military occupation. Other pigs
with imperial stamps include one of Vespasian dated to A.D. 79, found at Syde
near Cirencester,[1] two of Domitian (A.D. 81) from Niddersdale, Yorkshire, also
marked *Brig* for *metallum Briganticum*, Hadrianic examples from most of the
mining areas, and pigs of Antoninus Pius and Marcus Aurelius from Somerset.
No imperial stamps are found after this period.

In addition to the stamps of Vespasian, the Green Ore material has letters and
numbers cold-stamped on to the pigs after they had been removed from the
moulds. The numbers may indicate their weights, the letters give the name
TI.CL.TRIFER (NA). In Derbyshire pigs marked TI.CL.TR.LVT.BR.EX.
ARG. occur, and here the inscription was cast from the mould and so replaces
an imperial stamp. Are Tiberius Claudius Trifer(na) in Somerset and TI.CL.
TR. in Derbyshire the same person, possibly a wealthy freedman who began by
operating the Mendip mines on behalf of Vespasian, and later launched out on
a larger scale as a private lessee further north? If this was the case Trifer(na) may
have had a predecessor in C. Nipius Ascanius, whose name occurs on a pig with
a stamp of Nero at Stockbridge, Hampshire, and then as the main stamp on a
pig found in Flintshire. The LVT section of the Derbyshire inscription refers

[1] *J.R.S.* LIII (1963) 162 no. 12.

208

to Lutudarum, probably Chesterfield, the centre of the Derbyshire lead industry. It occurs on other pigs and in one case the stamp mentions the *socii Lutudarenses*, the Lutudarum partners or company. At some period this firm may have included C. Iulius Protus, P. Rubrius Abascantus, and L. Ariconius Verecundus who also stamped pigs of Derbyshire lead (fig. 93*c*).[1]

The lack of late imperial stamps makes it difficult to estimate the chronology of the lead mines but they must have continued to meet the increasing demands of undertakers and town and villa builders in the fourth century. Possibly work ceased in some areas, possibly some mines were worked out. On the whole, a system increasingly organised by private lessees seems probable as time goes on. Army supervision is considered unlikely except in the less settled areas such as the north.[2] The Second Cohort of the Nervii are known to have controlled lead-workings at Alston, Northumberland, in the third century and the same situation may have existed at Machen, Glamorganshire, while lead gathered by the Britons seems to have been collected at the forts at Brough-on-Noe, Derbyshire, and Caermote, Cumberland.[3] Up to date a total of about eighty pigs has been reached, some uninscribed, and these all represent lead lost in transit, much of it probably for export. The distribution of such finds suggests that the Lutudarum partners and perhaps the Yorkshire mines sent much of their production to Brough-on-Humber where it could have been shipped to the army in the north. However, four pigs found at Pulborough may have been a load sent by TI.CL.TR, from Lutudarum to Clausentum for shipment to France. Earlier evidence for such trade is provided by a pig of the time of Nero found at St Valery sur Somme. Ascanius' pig at Stockbridge may also have been en route to Clausentum. Runcorn has been suggested as a port for lead from Flint and Shropshire, and a port on the Bristol Channel seems likely for some of the output from the Mendips and might have acted as a short cut to South Wales.[4]

Gold was also among the pre-Roman exports of Britain mentioned by Strabo, and the only gold mine so far identified in this country must have been either under direct Imperial control or leased to a very efficient private firm as it employed expensive equipment with the most advanced Roman mining techniques. The workings extend for about a mile at Dolaucothi in Carmarthenshire, and the most striking features of the area are the scattered mining dumps and the two large open cuts where the outcrops of auriferous pyrites were worked

[1] R. W. Cockerton, 'Roman Pigs of lead from Derbyshire', *Derbyshire Arch. & N. H. Soc. J.* LXXIX (1959) 88–96.
[2] G. Webster, 'The leadmining industry in North Wales in Roman times', *Flints. Hist. Soc.* XIII (1952–3) 5–53.
[3] Richmond (1963) p. 153.
[4] Tylecote (1962) p. 87.

opencast to a depth of about 30 feet. There were also underground galleries 6 feet square dug to a depth of 80 feet and their entrances are still visible on the rock face. Two crosscuts which may have been intended for drainage penetrated for over 180 feet into the sterile rock. Sledge-hammers were used for clearance and the galleries may also have been cleared by fire-setting, a process in which the rocks were first heated with fires and then soaked with cold water to crack them. This method produced much steam and smoke so it could only be employed where there was adequate ventilation. Rock pillars and heavy timbers were used as pit props. The lower galleries were drained by large waterwheels worked by men sitting above them and working a kind of treadmill on the hub of the wheel with their feet, or turning the spokes with their hands. As the wheel moved, buckets hung on its rim were filled in the galleries and emptied as they revolved and reached the higher levels. A piece of the rim of a waterwheel of this kind found at Dolaucothi shows two of the openings from which hung the bronze, wood or leather buckets. A rockcut aqueduct 7 miles long brought a water-supply from the River Cothi to the mine and this was carefully engineered with a gradient to discharge into tanks used for clearing rock debris, and a reservoir immediately above the main workings.[1] Part of one of the wooden panning cradles used in washing the ore was recovered as well as millstones, a fragment of a wooden haulage tray, part of a stone mortar, and several crucibles. Pit-head baths for the miners were among the buildings of the nearby settlement. These are an unusual luxury and support the possibility that army engineers were responsible for the work here. The fort at Llanio, 10 miles away, is known to have been garrisoned by the Second Cohort of the Asturians, soldiers who may have come from an important goldmining district of Spain and used their skill for the exploitation of British mineral wealth. Last but not least among the Dolaucothi discoveries was the hoard of jewellery already discussed.[2] This was found near the workings and it suggests that expert goldsmiths must have lived and worked near the source of their raw material.[3]

Simpler jewellery was made from Kimmeridge shale and jet. Workshops for making armlets have been found near the shale deposits in Kimmeridge Bay. Like the table legs described on p. 153 (Pl. 33) they were turned on the lathe and worked with a special form of flint chisel and are a prehistoric fashion which continued to be popular.[4] Jet, however, is shinier and altogether more

[1] G. Jones, I. Blakey, E. MacPherson, 'Dolaucothi: the Roman aqueduct', *Bull. of the Board of Celtic Studies* XIX (1962) 71–84. [2] See above p. 141.

[3] V. G. Nash-Williams, 'The Roman gold-mines at Dolaucothi (Carm.)', *Bull. of the Board of Celtic Studies* XIV (1950) 79–84.

[4] H. Davies, 'The Shale Industries at Kimmeridge', *Arch. J.* XCIII (1937) 200–19.

attractive. It occurs as underwater outcrops at Whitby and was probably collected off the beaches rather than mined. Workshops must have existed at York as blocks of jet, some partially prepared for making pins, have been found there. The Romans thought it had magical properties as, like amber, it becomes electric if rubbed. Solinus, writing in the third century, notes the good quality of British jet.[1] Hairpins with elaborately carved heads, finger-rings, bangles, bead necklaces and bracelets have survived, mostly from third- and fourth-century burials. A number of pendants shaped into animals and birds may have formed part of the necklaces and so may the medallions showing Medusa heads, probably intended to protect the wearer from ill fortune. Three pendants show portrait busts in relief, a woman (Pl. 30*a*), a man and a woman (Pl. 30*b*), and a man with a woman and child.[2] Clothes and hair styles date them all to the fourth century. Opinions differ as to whether they were commissioned as individual portraits or whether they were merely stylised representations used as gifts. Like the other jet objects they are also found in the Rhineland, and it seems more likely that most of the Rhenish material was imported from Britain in a finished state.[3] Had there been large workshops in Cologne, the distribution of their products would surely have been on a wider scale. On the other hand, the pendant (Pl. 30*a*) showing the bust of a woman with her hair bunched on either side of her head and pinned into a roll on top is hardly suitable as a gift for its beauty and charm. This does seem to be a portrait from life. Possibly small quantities of raw jet were shipped to Cologne for craftsmen specialising chiefly in these objects.

The picture revealed by the information available about the Romano-Britons' use of their natural resources is one of considerable commercial activity, sometimes inspired by state officials but usually by private individuals. Some, particularly those connected with the export trade and mining ventures, may have been freedmen from other provinces. Many must have been British born, and others, including veterans and government officials, people who had seen the world and made plans for their retirement in either their homeland or in the province where they had done most of their service. Much of this activity was based on the towns and it ranged from the many shopkeepers who made jewellery and other wares in the rooms behind their shops, to the villa owners, who may have come to town to arrange the sale of crops or building materials. Little has been found in the shape of industrial settlements of any size with the exception of the pottery centre at Durobrivae, where the small town is

[1] *Collectanea Rerum Memorabilium* XXII, 11.
[2] *Eburacum* (1962) Pl. LXVIII. For jet industry p. 141 *et seq.*
[3] Toynbee (1964) p. 363.

surrounded by groups of kilns and the opulent residences of the master potters, spreading over a large area. Elsewhere groups of kilns occur, either accompanied by few traces of settlement, or else placed near large towns, like the Colchester potteries which cover a wide area outside the *colonia*.

At Wilderspool in Cheshire a settlement which may have followed an Agricolan fort seems to have had a rather wider range of industrial occupations. Pottery was made between A.D. 90 and 160 and tiles are another possibility. Furnaces for iron smelting and smithing, traces of lead-working, and crucibles for making bronze, probably for brooches, were also found. Glass-making, for beads and possibly for window glass, is also likely, especially as suitable sand occurs nearby.[1] There is nothing in the arrangement of the simple structures discovered here to suggest military planning so it has been suggested that enterprising capitalists organised the settlement to utilise the skill of local metal-workers.[2] Another settlement at Tiddington, Warwickshire, was also engaged in tile-making, iron smithing and lead working.[3]

---

[1] D. Atkinson, 'Caistor excavations, 1929', *Norfolk Archaeology* XXIV (1932) 108–12. I. A. Richmond in J. Wacher ed. (1965) p. 78. Glass-making is also probable at Colchester and Warrington (T. May, *Warrington's Roman Remains* (1904)).

[2] F. Thompson, *op. cit.* p. 86; Tylecote (1962) pp. 235, 237.

[3] W. J. Fieldhouse, T. May and F. Wellstood, '*A Romano-British Settlement near Tiddington* (Birmingham, 1931).

8
Agriculture

As we have already noted in Chapter 1, corn, cattle and hunting dogs were among the exports of pre-Roman Britain and this suggests that in the South-East at least, agriculture was already flourishing in the first century B.C. Stock-raising and the growing of cereals in the Early Iron Age seem to have been largely carried on by families living on farmsteads of the Little Woodbury type and this practice continued into the Roman period. Before going on to consider how such farms now began to grow and develop, it may be useful to recall what is already known about agriculture in Roman Britain in general.

Apart from literary references, the evidence for cereal cultivation depends largely upon the few samples of grain recovered during excavation. In normal circumstances nothing of this nature would survive but all these specimens have been burnt, either in the drying-kiln or in an accidental conflagration. At Pompeii a number of carbonised foods can be seen, dating from the time of Vesuvius' eruption, and smaller domestic disasters in Britain have produced similar useful material. One of the most valuable examples obtained up to date is the result of a second-century fire at Verulamium. This destroyed a building in the Forum which was being used as a granary, perhaps only temporarily. All the grain found there was of unusually good quality, suggesting that it had either been grown on rich soil, particularly well-cultivated, or else selected for seed by sieving. It had been carefully threshed but some specimens showed signs of sprouting. Possibly the temperature of the granary was too warm and moist for it. The cereals identified included *Triticum compactum* and probably also *Triticum vulgare*, both naked wheats of the spelt group commonly used by the Romans for bread and called by them in Latin, *siligo*. Hulled spelt (*Triticum spelta*) was also found and rye, a few oats, and some small Celtic beans completed the list. The corn which had sprouted proved to be all rye and this may be accounted for by the fact that rye harvests earlier than other crops and may have sprouted while still standing in a wet season. Rye, however, is also a cereal which threshes easily without roasting. Spelt, on the other hand, is a hulled grain, and must be roasted before threshing and the heat would destroy the power of germination. Apparently the wheat had also been roasted, a quite unnecessary procedure suggesting that wheat and spelt were grown and reaped together as one crop and so could not be treated differently.[1]

Evidence for spelt, emmer, barley and possibly rye has been identified from North Leigh, Oxfordshire, and Caerleon. Other finds of spelt or wheat (*Triticum vulgare* or *compactum*) are known from London, Park Street (Hertfordshire), Iwerne (Dorset), Gestingthorpe, Rivenhall and Halstead (Essex), Hartlip, Otford, Lullingstone and Richborough (Kent), Wilcote (Oxfordshire) and sites in Scotland, mostly along the line of the Antonine Wall. The Romans brought spelt back to Italy from their campaigns in Germany and Switzerland and must have been pleased to discover it grown extensively in Britain. Oats and barley were also found at Park Street, and wheat and barley both occurred in rubbish pits at the legionary fortress at Newstead mixed with seeds of the corncockle, showing that this weed was already in evidence in Roman times. Gestingthorpe, Halstead, and Camp Hill near Glasgow also produced evidence of oats, and spelt; wheat and oats grew near Caistor-by-Norwich.[2] Barley was extensively grown in Britain in pre-Roman times but it only appears occasionally in the grain samples. This is probably due to the fact that it had been largely supplanted for human consumption by spelt and wheat. It makes poor bread

[1] V. Hinton, N. Kent, H. Helbaek, 'The Cereals from the Burnt Corn Level; Verulamium, 1949', St.A.A.S.T. 1953 89, 91; H. Helbaek, 'Early Crops in Southern England', *Proc. of the Prehistoric Soc.* XVIII (1953) 213.

[2] Evidence for grain crops on these and other sites as follows: M. E. S. Morrison, 'Carbonised Cereals from North Leigh', *Oxoniensia* XXIV (1959) 13–21; R. R. Clarke, *East Anglia* (1960) p. 122 (Caistor-by-Norwich); V. C. H. *Kent* III (1932) p. 118 (Hartlip; Curle (1911) p. 109; B. W. Pearce, 'Roman Site at Otford', *Arch. Cant.* XLII (1930) 158; *J.R.S.* LII (1962) 175 (Wilcote); Boon (1957) p. 176; H. Helbaek, 'The Isca Grain, a Roman plant introduction into Britain', *New Phytologist* LXII (1964) 158–64; K. Jessen and H. Helbaek, *Cereals in Great Britain and Ireland in Prehistoric and Early Historic Times* (1944) p. 14 *et seq.*

and is also a heavier crop to transport so would not be so acceptable for the *annona*. It must have been largely grown for fodder and brewing and used unthreshed. Consequently it was not exposed to carbonization in the drying kilns. Oats were also a pre-Roman crop but the Romans may have been responsible for introducing them into Scotland. On the whole, rye and Club wheat (*Triticum compactum*) seem to have been newcomers to Britain in the Roman period but a few stray grains have been found on three or four Iron Age sites. The evidence from Silchester, Caerwent and Verulamium suggests that peas, beans and flax were other field crops while fruit, vegetables and herbs were grown in orchards and gardens.

Traces of fields cultivated by the Romano-Britons can still sometimes be identified.[1] They are squarish in shape and vary from about one-third to two acres in size. The type dates back to the Late Bronze Age and is not confined to Europe. Originally it was marked out by digging and probably cultivated with a hoe before the plough was invented. Stones were collected and piled round the margins and soil blew over them forming banks of earth called lynchets. On a slope more soil would accumulate so that the lynchets are sometimes still clearly visible. The fields often occur in groups, and tracks leading to a farm or village can also occasionally be identified. Naturally they only survive on land which has escaped later cultivation, marginal land such as the Sussex Downs which was suitable for primitive agricultural methods. Fields of similar shape but outlined by drainage ditches instead of lynchets also occur in the Fens. Otherwise the evidence of the cultivation of the heavier soils appears to have all been swept away by the activities of later generations of farmers.

Finds of iron ploughshares in Britain date from the Early Iron Age onwards, and suggest that by the Roman period, ploughs of several slightly different kinds were known and used in accordance with the nature of the land under cultivation. Apart from these discoveries little is known of the ploughs. Like the Iron Age examples found in the Scandinavian peat bogs they were probably largely made of wood and have consequently failed to survive. The shares are of different types ranging from a short flanged variety which was fitted over a wooden share to economise in the use of iron, to a massive tanged example from the villa at Box. Pointed bars found in the ironwork hoards from Silchester and Great Chesterford are believed to be another special form. They are accompanied in the hoards by a corresponding number of coulters, large knife-shaped pieces of iron ending in a narrow bar or tang (Pl. 42*a*). These were thrust through the plough-beam so that the broad end would cut the soil

[1] C. Bowen, *Ancient Fields* (1963) p. 14 *et seq.*; J. Macnab, 'British Strip Lynclets', *Antiquity* XXXIX. (1965) 279-90.

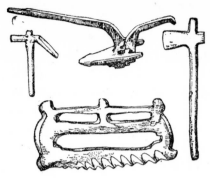

95 Bronze model tools found in Sussex

vertically in front of the ploughshare which then undercut the furrow. The coulter seems to have been a Roman introduction, specially designed for use on heavy soil and fine examples are also known from sites at Dorchester on Thames, Abington Pigotts and the villa at Witcombe. They are striking examples of good Roman craftsmanship and must have needed a stalwart plough-beam to support them.[1] A passing reference in Pliny suggests that some of these early ploughs may have been fitted with wheels but, while this is quite possible, no actual proof of it has yet been found. Also of interest are Pliny's remarks in the same paragraph about the use of coulters and different types of ploughshare for different soils.[2]

Two bronze model ploughs from Roman Britain are preserved in the British Museum. One was found with the saw mentioned on p. 189 on the Sussex Downs and it shows an arrow-shaped share and beneath this, two flat projecting wings (fig. 95). Other model ploughs found in Germany suggest that these may be ground wrests, originally used after sowing for pushing the earth into ridges over the broadcast seed and also for making furrows for drainage. If such an implement is tilted, it is also possible to turn a sod with it and the addition of a keel to the share would assist this tilting. The Sussex model has a keel and the use of mould boards to help turn the sod over may have eventually developed from ploughs of this kind. So the evidence suggests the probable existence of at least three types of plough in Roman Britain: those with and without coulters, and those with the addition of mould boards.[3] The second bronze model comes from Piercebridge and provides no information about shares etc. Instead it shows the farmer at work with a cloaked and hooded figure guiding a plough drawn by two yoked oxen (Pl. 51). Other sites, including Verulamium, have produced small iron ox-goads.

[1] W. H. Manning, 'The Plough in Roman Britain', *J.R.S.* LIV (1964) 54–65; F. G. Payne 'The Plough in Ancient Britain', *Arch. J.* CIV (1948) 82–111.
[2] *N.H.* XVII. 48.
[3] Manning, *op. cit.* pp. 57, 64.

Numerous iron implements connected with cultivation have also survived including forks, rakes, hoes (fig. 96), picks and mattocks. Shovels and spades may sometimes have had blades made entirely of wood or of iron, but the majority used both materials with an iron shoe edging the wooden blade. This was fixed on according to three different methods which are sometimes combined. In most cases the iron was grooved to fit over the blade and/or the sides, the metal was heated and then shrunk on to the wood. Sometimes iron clips at the sides also gripped the blade. With the third method, the iron was nailed to the side or even to the back of the wood. The shape of the blade varied from the more or less rectangular spades found at Verulamium, Silchester, Colchester, London, Chedworth and Bourton-on-the-Water (fig. 96*c*), to the shovels with curved ends and blades of varying length from Worlington, Caerwent, Chedworth and Woodcuts (fig. 96*d*). A large shovel from Silchester had the sidestrips of the sheath extended right round the upper edge of a blade 13 inches in length. Similar tools have been found in Belgium, Germany and other Roman provinces, and the numerous small variations of the different types bear witness to the skill and preferences of the local blacksmith and his customers.[1]

Once the fields were cleaned and dug or ploughed, other agricultural factors became important. The land had to be kept in good heart and Pliny devotes a long description to the use of different sorts of marl on both the pastures and arable lands of Gaul and Britain.[2] Chalk for this was probably obtained from the pits dug for rubbish or grain storage but marl pits, probably in use in Roman times, have been tentatively identified on Hackpen Hill, Wiltshire.[3] Animal and poultry manure may also have been spread on the fields and the importance of green manuring with such crops as lupines, beans and vetch was recognised. Cato advises the farmer to make compost from straw, chaff, lupines, bean-haulm, and ilex and oak leaves.[4] Land should also be allowed to lie fallow and the Roman farmer understood something of the principle of the rotation of crops.

When the crops were mature they were harvested, usually with sickles (Pl. 42*a*) and Columella tells us it took one man a day and a half to reap a *jugerum* of wheat. Examples of these implements have been recovered from sites such as Silchester or Traprain Law and Newstead in Scotland. One of the

---

[1] P. Corder, 'Roman Spade-Irons from Verulamium', etc., *Arch. J.* C (1945) 224–31.
[2] *N.H.* XVII. 4.
[3] O. G. S. Crawford, *Air Survey and Archaeology* (Ordnance Survey Professional Papers no. 7) (1928) p. 6, note on p. 7.
[4] *De Agricultura* XXXVII. 2.

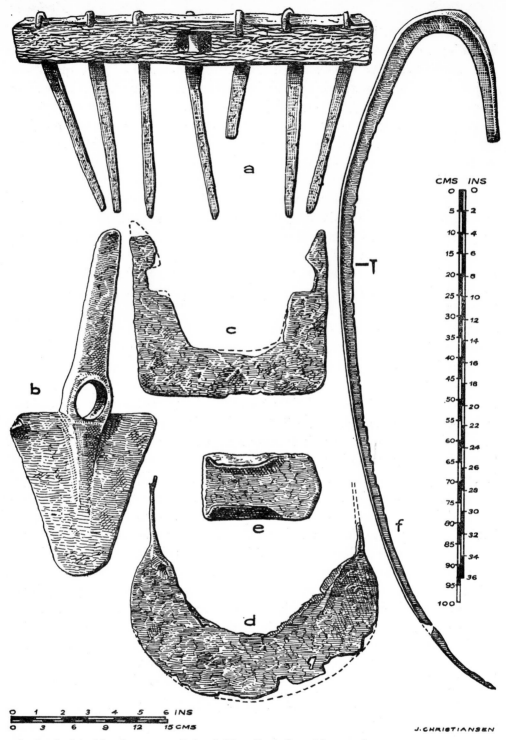

CMS INS

J. CHRISTIANSEN

96 Agricultural implements. *a* Rake. *b* Hoe. Both from Newstead.
c Spade, Verulamium. *d* Spade end, Worlington, Suffolk. *e* Ploughshare,
Silchester. *f* Outsize scythe, Great Chesterford

scenes depicted on Trajan's column shows legionaries cutting corn just below the ear with sickles of this type. The length of the straw left depended upon the purposes for which it was intended, long straws, for instance, being needed for thatching. Ancient writers on agriculture such as Varro and Pliny[1] record how methods differed—the stalk was cut either near the root or else halfway up. Diodorus Siculus notes that the Iron Age Britons only harvested the ears. The straw was also used for fodder and litter and sometimes it was burnt in the fields as a fertiliser and as a means of destroying weeds. In the same paragraph Pliny also mentions briefly the mechanical harvester or *vallus*, used on the vast estates in Gaul. A clearer description of this machine is given by Palladius. He records that on the Gallic plain one has help with the reaping as, instead of doing it by hand, one ox can clear the whole harvest. The *vallus* consists of a wagon, square in shape and with sides tilting outwards to make more room. The front has a low board with a multiple row of slightly upturned teeth set close together. There are two wheels, and two short shafts at the back are attached with ropes to the ox. He pushes the wagon along instead of pulling it so he must not be a temperamental animal but one who pays heed to the driver. As he moves, the corn ears are torn off and fall into the wagon. This machine is good in flat country for those who do not wish to keep the straw.[2] The pushing method would keep the animal from treading down the corn.

In the past these passages in Pliny and Palladius have been much discussed, but it was only in 1958 that a discovery in *Gallia Belgica* provided proof of the existence of the *vallus* and a clearer idea of its appearance (fig. 97). Excavations at Buzenol in Luxemburg uncovered part of a late second-century relief built into the dry stone walls of some later fortifications. The scene shows the wagon looking rather like a frame or a box on wheels, with the row of teeth cutting their way through the crop. A man wearing a short tunic stands by it and appears to be trying to keep the teeth clear by pushing in the corn, and the ears of corn still awaiting cutting are clearly visible. Behind the frame the head of, not an ox, but a mule or donkey is just visible; perhaps one of the Gaulish mules renowned for their docility. At this point the stone is broken but the scene is completed by another relief found some years ago, part of a funeral monument from Arlon in Belgium, only a few miles away. This shows another man, similarly dressed, resting his arms on a pair of long shafts connected behind him by a bar of wood. In front of him are the tail and hindquarters of an animal. Obviously these are the driver and those portions of the mule needed to complete the picture of the vallus.[3] A fragment from a third relief, found at Trier, also shows the

[1] *N.H.* XVIII. 72.   [2] *Agricultura* VII. 2.

[3] M. Renard, 'Technique et agriculture en pays trevire et remois', *Latomus* XVIII (1959) 77.

donkey, a wheel and part of a more capacious wagon.[1] These discoveries remind us that some of the vast Gallic estates mentioned by Pliny must have lain in the Arlon-Trier district where agriculture was flourishing in the second and third centuries. One of a series of reliefs depicting the work of the year carved on the Porte de Mars at Rheims also shows the *vallus*. It represents the work of the month of August, and this can be contrasted with Palladius' description of it as being in use in June. Obviously the agricultural calendar allowed for regional variations. The *vallus* was soon forgotten and the idea of pushing the machine through the field instead of pulling it has only recently been re-discovered. We have, of course, no proof that it was ever employed in Britain, but the big villa estates might very well have used it.

After reaping, the corn was threshed by spreading it out on a paved floor and driving horses, mules or oxen over it, or beating it out with a stick. It is possible that the jointed flail was invented in Gaul in the fourth century A.D. Another method of threshing consisted of drawing across the floor a heavy block of wood studded underneath with flints or iron nails, and weighted with heavy stones. This was known as the *tribulum*. Next, the grain was winnowed by throwing it up in the air with forks or winnowing fans so that the chaff was blown away.[2] Actual traces of these operations are not very abundant but evidence for threshing floors has been found at several Romano-British villas. At Langton in Yorkshire a roughly paved rectangular area may have been used for this purpose as no traces of walls or other structural remains were found associated with it. It was sunk nearly five feet below ground level.[3] Further south another floor, circular this time, was excavated at Ditchley. It was sur-

---

[1] K. D. White, 'The Gallo-Roman Harvesting Machine', *Antiquity* XL (1966) 49–50; *Trierer Zeitschrift* XXVII (1964) 151.

[2] Singer *et al.* (1956) p. 94 *et seq.* for this and other agricultural activities.

[3] Corder (1932) p. 48.

rounded by a low wall or curb. In the second century the floor measured 30 feet across but nearly two hundred years later it was reduced to a diameter of 25 feet.[1]

In damp climates such as Britain it was often necessary to dry the corn for storage and, as we have seen at Verulamium, crops of spelt also needed roasting before they could be satisfactorily threshed. Ovens for roasting corn and drying racks were both identified at the Iron Age site of Little Woodbury and this custom continued in an improved form in the Roman period. A small farm by the river Ouse at Wyboston, Bedfordshire, produced an unusual structure which may have been some form of corn drier. It consisted of a verandah-like building 20 feet long and 4½ feet wide, with a clay wall one foot thick on one side, and a row of postholes, presumably belonging to an open front, on the other. Traces of fire were found in a shallow trench all along the foot of the wall and the heat may have dried corn spread out on tiers of shelves.[2] The characteristic Roman corn-drier is really a variation of the hypocaust with which in the past it has often been confused. It frequently consists of a long flue, with the fire at one end, crossed at the other by shorter flues so that in plan the heat channels appear as a T. The best-preserved example so far found comes from the villa at Atworth (Wiltshire), and shows that the flues were covered by two floors six inches apart, made of stone slabs (fig. 98). The heat and smoke from the fire travelled up the leg of the T, rose up the two side channels, and then flowed back between the floors and out through a chimney cut in one wall. The heat could be regulated by adjusting flues at the stoke-hole and the cleaning outlet so that it would dry and not scorch the grain spread out on the upper floor. A wooden superstructure probably shielded it from any soot or smoke from the chimney.[3]

The T-shaped hypocausts of corn-driers have been identified on a number of sites including towns such as Silchester and Caerwent, the villas of Brading and Kingsworthy (Hampshire), and less romanised village or farm sites in Dorset or on the Yorkshire wolds. The town and villa examples are frequently of fourth-century date and are sometimes inserted into the floors of earlier buildings. A more elaborate oven known as the Double T-shaped type was found in room 5 at Park Street and dates back to the mid-second century. It had a central flue running across three-quarters of the room and two side flues

---

[1] V. C. H. *Oxfordshire* I (1939) p. 311.
[2] C. F. Tebbutt, 'A Belgic and Roman Farm at Wyboston', C.A.S.P. L (1957) 79.
[3] A. Shaw Mellor and R. G. Goodchild, 'The Roman Villa at Atworth', Appendix II, *W.A.M.* XLIX (1942) 93. For a general discussion of the corn-drying ovens, written before the Park Street excavations see R. G. Goodchild, 'T-shaped Corn-drying Ovens in Roman Britain', *Ant. J.* XXIII (1943) 148–57.

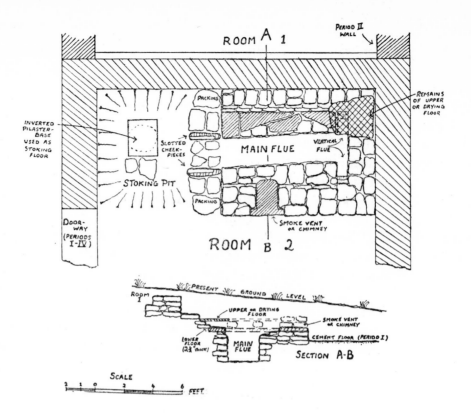

Plan of the Corn Drier, Atworth, Wiltshire

branching off it and curving back to the room corners. The furnace was out in the corridor and where the branch flues joined the main one, three shelves were found at different levels, intended to support the floors over the hypocaust. These were probably above the floor level of the room, forming a heated platform, leaving the rest of the unheated floor-space free for the labourers carrying in and out the sheaves of corn (fig. 99).[1] Another second-century furnace of the Double T-type was found at Saunderton (Buckinghamshire), and this was filled in at the end of the third century.[2] Other less elaborate types of kiln, which may have lacked the double floors, have been found in the Yorkshire villas of Langton and Rushton, and also at Norton Disney (Nottinghamshire) where they are dated to between 70 and 110 A.D.[3] A circular building with a floor heated by flues running round part of the perimeter and also radiating from the centre like the spokes of a wheel, was found at Great Casterton. It was fired from a

[1] H. O'Neil, 'The Roman Villa at Park Street', *Arch. J.* CII (1946) 46.
[2] D. Ashcroft, 'Romano-British villa at Saunderton', *Records of Bucks* XIII (1939) 401.
[3] Corder (1932) p. 56; A. Woodward, 'Roman villa at Rudston', *Y.A.J.* XXXIII (1936-8) 83 *et seq.*; A. Oswald, 'Roman fortified villa at Norton Disney', *Ant. J.* XVII (1937) 143.

99   Reconstruction of the Corn Drier at Park Street, Hertfordshire

single stoke-hole and seems, in its original form, to have provided too much heat as the main flue was later blocked. A timber building may have been erected above the heated floor (fig. 100).[1] The site which has revealed most evidence for corn-drying, however, is Hambleden (Buckinghamshire), where a variety of types including the T and Double T, and also a gridiron pattern of flues, were found. They were all built of chalk and flint and placed below ground-level. Usually they were under cover in a series of small buildings of the Great Casterton type. The presence of charred wheat first indicated their purpose, the site may have been in use for some years, and the whole complex must have belonged to a corn-drying factory used for the grain grown on the farms which existed along the banks of the Thames. A small house for the owner or factory manager was also found at Hambleden.[2]

Hay-making was another important activity which has left us a little evidence in the form of tools. Rakes and pitchforks would be needed and a wooden rake with seven iron prongs was found at Newstead. Pliny advises on the choice of the ideal position for the hayfield, well-watered and with rich soil. If infested with weeds it is best to plough and harrow it first, and then sow it with seed

[1] Corder (1954) 19. See also *J.R.S.* LI (1961) for corn driers at Old Sleaford.
[2] A. H. Cocks, 'Romano-British homestead in the Hambleden Valley', *Arch.* LXXI (1921) 151.

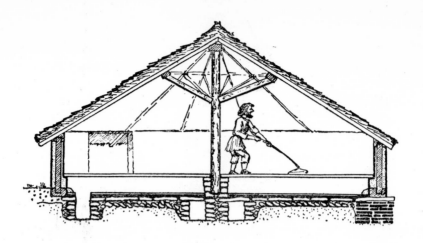

100 Drying Floor, Great Casterton, Rutland

fallen out of the hay in the hay lofts, the latter a practice which continued in England until recent times. Clover is the best crop, with grass a good second. Two kinds of scythe were known to Pliny, the short Italian one which cut both long and short grasses, and the bigger scythes used on the large Gallic farms which economise labour by cutting through the long stalks of the grass in the middle and missing the shorter ones.[1] A number of examples of large curved scythe-blades, three to four feet long, have been found in Britain at Newstead and Silchester. Provided with a stout rib as a precaution against bending, they show signs of wear, and sometimes of patching. They end in a tang bent at an acute angle where they were fitted on to the handle. They must belong to two-handed, long-handled scythes and represent a change of technique from shearing or chopping to cutting. Examples of similar blades have been found in Germany and the handle must have been long enough to allow the scythe to be swung in an even curve.[2] Remembering this, how are we to account for the thirteen great scythe blades, each about 5 feet 4 inches long, found at Great Chesterford (fig. 96f).[3] They too show signs of wear and repair. Unless they were swung by a race of giants one is forced to imagine some form of mowing machine, the haymaker's equivalent of the reaper's *vallus*. Small mower's anvils consisting of pieces of iron ending in a spike, with two or four strips of iron inserted through a hole near the top and bent up into a spiral, were also found at Silchester, Newstead and Great Chesterford (Pl. 42a). The mower sat with the anvil thrust into the ground between his legs, the spiral piece of iron being wedged with

[1] N.H. XVIII 67 67,261.
[2] A. Steenberg, *Ancient Harvesting Implements* (Copenhagen, 1943) p. 223.
[3] R. C. Neville, 'A remarkable deposit of Roman antiquities of iron', *Arch. J.* XIII (1856) 6.

224

stones to prevent it sinking in too far. The scythe blade was hammered out on the anvil and then probably given a final polish with a hone.

Winter feeding for the animals may have sometimes been a problem to the early British farmers but there is no evidence for the theory that all but the minimum number of stock needed to carry on the flocks and herds had to be slaughtered every autumn.[1] Beside the stubble left in the field after the harvest the Roman farmer regarded hay and other green field crops as most important and Cato advises that it be kept for the oxen to eat during the spring ploughing. Barley, straw, chaff and bean haulm were also used and leaves were collected in large quantities. Elm, ash and poplar seem to have been preferred, with oak and some other trees as second best. One small cow could eat about 1,600 sheaves of leaves during the winter, and a special type of large sickle or lopping knife, the *falx arboraria*, was used for cutting them.[2] A probable example of one was found at Newstead. Acorns were collected and bark was stripped from the trees in spring and dried. It could be used in pieces, ground into powder, or even boiled. According to Columella, Italian cattle were given grapeskins and the rest of the residue of the vintage and this made them sleek, plump and of good cheer.[3] British beasts were not so fortunate.

The domestic animals kept included cattle, sheep, goats, pigs and horses. Animal bones are found in large quantities on most Roman sites but research workers are only now beginning to give them the attention they deserve. At present one can only say that cattle of the breed known as *bos longifrons*, introduced into Britain in the Late Bronze Age, were still abundant in the Roman period.[4] Some sites have also produced evidence for larger animals, and these may have been strains brought over from Gaul.[5] A deposit of the jaw-bones of over 2,500 oxen was found at Silchester and a collection of 3 dozen cows' heads was excavated at Leicester.[6] These had probably accumulated as the result of some industrial process but they give us an idea of the herds which may have been built up in certain parts of the country. Horns and hides were all used as well as meat, lard, milk and cheese and some of the leather used for shoes shows that the cattle suffered from warble fly.[7] Ewes and nanny-goats were also milked

[1] E. Higgs and J. P. White, 'Autumn Killing', *Antiquity* XXXVII (1963) 282–9, H. J. M. Green, 'Romano-British farm at St. Ives', C.A.S.P. LII (1959) 28.
[2] J. G. D. Clark, *Prehistoric Europe* (1952) p. 119. [3] *De Rustica* VII. iii. 5.
[4] E.g. evidence from the first-century farm at Eastwood, Fawkham, Kent (*Arch. Cant.* LXXVIII (1963) 71).
[5] Green, *op. cit.* p. 28; S. Applebaum, 'Agriculture in Roman Britain', *Agricultural Historical Review* VI (1958) 74.
[6] Boon (1957) p. 176; *J.R.S.* XLIX (1959) 113 (Leicester).
[7] R. Chaplin, 'Animals in Archaeology', *Antiquity* XXXIX (1965) 205.

and wool and goatshair were of great importance. Swine found much of their own living in the forests and do not seem to have been quite as numerous as in the Iron Age. Geese and hens occupied the poultry yard, reminding us of Cato's direction that the farm bailiff's wife should always be well-provided with hens and eggs.[1] Villas round Pompeii also give us a little light on poultry keeping, the chickens' watering trough being found on one site, while another produced an inscription noting the date when eggs were placed under a sitting hen.[2]

Another country product of great importance was honey, but unluckily it is not one which leaves much evidence behind it. Its interest to the Greeks and Romans is shown by the amount of literature devoted to it, including Virgil's well-known fourth *Georgic*. More practical advice about bee-keeping is given by Columella and he devotes to it the greater part of one of the books of his account of Country Life. He describes the shrubs and trees preferred by bees and recommends that the apiary should be close to the farmhouse. The bark of the cork tree makes the best hives, otherwise basketwork or wood may be used in preference to brick or earthenware, as they can then be easily moved. A wall about 3 feet high is built in the apiary and the hives are stood on this in three tiers, ideally with a roughly built partition of stones between each. The swarms may be bought, in which case they must be carefully chosen, or wild bees may be caught. Directions follow for the care of the bees, the gathering of the honeycombs, and the making of honey and beeswax.[3]

Unfortunately Britain has so far produced no reliefs, paintings or mosaics showing scenes of country life. Our only illustrations are a shepherdess with sheep appearing on the handle of a silver dish (*patera*) from Capheaton (Northumberland) (Pl. 36*a*), and the bronze plough team already mentioned (Pl. 51). Reliefs like the pieces which provide the evidence for the *vallus*, from the great Gaulish funeral monuments at Arlon, Igel and Neumagen help to fill the gap a little, and a charming wall-painting of a country scene with buildings and cloaked figures was found at Trier.[4] At St Romain-en-Gal near Vienne a delightful mosaic, now in the Louvre, was found many years ago. It shows the labours of the year as a kind of rural calendar. In the centre appear the seasons shown as 4 *putti*. Spring, with a cloak over his shoulder, carries flowers and is riding on a bull; summer, with a huge sickle, rides a lion; and Autumn, with a basket full of grapes, is astride a tiger. A small, heavily cloaked Winter, looking most

---

[1] *De Agricultura* CXLIII.
[2] J. Day, 'Agriculture in the Life of Pompeii', *Yale Classical Studies* III (1932) 174.
[3] *De Rustica* IX vi, vii, R. Forbes, *Studies in Ancient Technology* V (1957) p. 94.
[4] A. Birley (1964) p. 85.

depressed and carrying a bare branch, perches precariously on the back of a boar. Each season was further illustrated by seven scenes but not all of them survive. To January may belong baking bread, sacrificing to the *Lares*, and making baskets. February has a scene of doubtful meaning which may be connected with the festival of the *Parentalia* on the thirteenth. In spring we see two men joyfully hailing the arrival of the first storks in March while two others are busy grafting trees. The scenes for April, May and June are missing but in summer, in July, there is the sacrifice to Ceres before the harvest. After another gap come harvest festival and the cutting of straw with sickles. In autumn there is the vintage and fruit-picking and then, in October, ploughing, sowing and caulking casks or storage jars. In November olives are gathered and pressed and in December beans sown, corn ground and manure carried out to the fields.[1] A villa mosaic from Zliten, Tripolitania, shows other scenes with digging, taking the flocks to pasture, picking flowers and threshing corn. Further illustrations can be found in company with the picture of the *vallus* on the Porte de Mars at Rheims.[2] The study of the Latin writers on agriculture helps to elucidate their meaning as Cato and Varro, and especially Columella, all describe the year's work on the farm.

From thoughts on Roman agriculture in general we must now turn to Britain in particular and look rather more closely at the sites where farming was carried on. So far, only country farms and villas have been briefly mentioned, but it must be remembered that townspeople also cultivated food crops and each town was surrounded by its belt of farmland, or *territorium*. How big an acreage this covered we have no way of knowing but a look at the Ordnance Survey Map of Roman Britain shows that the areas round the towns are usually almost empty of villa symbols. At Colchester, and probably at the other *coloniae*, the land would have been allocated to the citizens by the government and should have been divided up by centuriation into a regular scheme of rectangular plots. This system of Roman land division was carried out by a professional guild of surveyors, the *agrimensores*. No certain traces of it have yet been identified in Britain although it has been suspected in several areas. At Silchester the *territorium* may have extended for about two miles outside the town. This would include both light and heavy soils on which wheat, spelt, barley and oats were grown; crops similar to those still largely produced there today. An amphora cut down and re-used as a storage jar and labelled AVIIN (oats) was found during the excavations, a companion piece to a Pompeian *graffito* noting beans and barley. Some buildings and enclosures in the town may have been byres

[1] *Revue Archéologique* XIX (1892) 322.
[2] H. Stern, 'Représentations gallo-romains des mois', *Gallia* IX (1952) 21 *et seq.*

and stockyards, and woodland on the edge of the *territorium* must have provided food for swine, as well as timber and firewood. Silchester is one of the few sites where note was taken of seeds and plant remains, and these show the existence of wild flowers and trees very similar to those of modern times. Bindweed, brambles, docks and nettles inconvenienced Calleva's farmers and gardeners and a surprisingly large number of poisonous plants, such as deadly nightshade, were noted in the town rubbish-pits. Blackberries and elderberries seem to have been gathered in large quantities and also mulberries and walnuts. Seeds of various herbs including coriander, dill, fennel, chervil and parsley were found. The evidence for flowers includes dandelions, marsh marigolds, buttercups, meadowsweet, foxgloves, mallow, St John's wort and violet, and a recent writer has pictured the houses of Calleva set amid fruit-blossom, hawthorn and dog-rose, with hedges of box or laurel and surrounded by holly and other familiar trees. One surprising feature was the presence of water-loving plants, particularly a tall riverside sedge (*carex riparia*), which could not have grown in or close to the town. Possibly it was brought in for use as an inferior type of thatching for sheds and lean-to shelters, straw being kept for more important buildings.[1]

As time went on, the land outside the forts in Wales and the north of England was also cultivated by the soldiers or by the inhabitants of the extra-mural settlements which grew up outside the walls. A late first-century granary has been identified outside Caerleon and the hillside slopes outside the fort at Housesteads were used for terrace cultivation of cereals or vegetables. An inscription found at Chester-le-Street mentions the *territorium* belonging to the fort,[2] and there is also an interesting possibility that about A.D. 200 army veterans may have been given land outside the fort at Ribchester. They were Sarmatians, heavily armed cavalry whose original homes lay beyond the Danube. On the completion of their military service they may have drained the rich land of the nearby Fylde country, and settled down to grow crops and breed cattle and horses.[3]

Another form of official action connected with agriculture and land settlement was concerned with the imperial estates. These consisted of areas administered by the Emperor's procurators or else leased to private individuals. The existence of several such estates is suspected in Britain but the evidence available still requires further confirmation. For example, the Fenlands of Lincolnshire and East Anglia seem to have been largely uninhabited in the Iron Age but in the Roman period aerial photography has revealed that they were covered with

[1] Boon (1957) pp. 171, 176 *et seq.*; W. H. Hope and G. F. Fox, 'Excavations at Silchester', *Arch.* LVII (1901) 253.
[2] *J.R.S.* XXXIV (1944) 88.　[3] *J.R.S.* XXXV (1945) 22.

a patchwork of small fields surrounded by drainage ditches and approached by drove roads. The concentration is thickest in Lincolnshire, around the Wash. Further south, in parts of Norfolk and Cambridgeshire, the sites tend to lie along the edges of the banks of silt which now stand out above the peat levels of the surrounding Fens. Such banks are known as 'roddons' and they are the remains of extinct water-courses which were still flowing in the Roman period. Their water level was affected by an elaborate system of wide drains, the details of which are still not entirely worked out, but engineering work of this kind was certainly undertaken by the Romans in other provinces. One important factor was the Car Dyke, a canal probably constructed early in the second century,[1] linking the river Granta at Waterbeach near Cambridge with the Old West River and the Ouse. It may thus have formed part of a lengthy chain of water-ways leading north via another stretch of canal, the Lincolnshire Car Dyke, which joined the Nene at Peterborough with the Witham at Lincoln. At present it is surmised that by this means the Fenland produce was carried by barges to Lincoln and then, as the army moved north, the system was extended to York by means of the Fosse Dyke, Trent, Humber and Yorkshire Ouse. The dating of these waterways, however, is not entirely settled.

The Roman occupation of the Fens seems to begin in the second half of the first century with the appearance of an increasing number of small farms of about ten to fifty acres. Perhaps such sites indicate that the population of eastern Britain was recovering and increasing after the Boudiccan disaster, or possibly some of the farmers had been displaced by the laying out of *territoria* around new towns. In any case they may have attracted official attention as the stretches of long straight drove roads and the drainage ditches or waterways, which appear in the first half of the second century, appear to indicate government organisation. The farms increase in size and number and are sometimes gathered into groups but they show little signs of planning and the systems of small fields are quite chaotic. No villas are found in these areas so the farmers were probably tenants working land leased from the government, contributing a percentage of their produce as payment of rent and taxes as coins are rarely found on these sites.

The late first-century farmers may have largely depended upon fishing and fowling for their living and these continued to form an important part of the economy. Fields remain small throughout the period and the large open spaces between settlements, the drove roads and linear earthworks suggest grazing and cattle enclosures with animal husbandry possibly more important than corn-

[1] J. G. D. Clark, 'Excavations on the Cambridgeshire Car Dyke, 1947', *Ant. J.* XXIX (1949) 145–64.

growing. Leather, lard and wool may have accompanied grain up the waterways to York. The people were never very prosperous, imported samian ware was their chief luxury, and they lived in simple houses of timber or daub, often with thatched roofs. In Lincolnshire a study has been made of 300 sites of this type around the Wash and it demonstrates the complexity of the problem. One small area contained 12 sites which could represent 12 farms or 12 rebuildings of one farm. Research showed that by A.D. 100, two of the sites were occupied, and by A.D. 300 the number had risen to nine. In general, after A.D. 120, the number of isolated farms more than 500 feet apart diminishes, and is often replaced by three to seven farms loosely grouped together in a cluster. This tendency continues until about the end of the third century when the number of groups tends to diminish, with a rapid decrease after A.D. 350.[1]

South of the Wash the chronological sequence is a little different. In the first half of the second century there is the same rapid growth, and a few sites such as Hockwold-cum-Wilton (Norfolk), develop into sizeable settlements with some attempt at rectilinear planning. They have small farmyards or gardens near the centre with fields for cereal crops grouped round, and large open spaces for cattle grazing on the outskirts, sometimes marked out by boundary ditches. But about a fifth of the sites in these parts of the Fens seem to have been abandoned by the end of the century, possibly owing to freshwater flooding. Evidence for a severe inundation between A.D. 180 and 200 was found at some places including Hockwold.[2] At Welney, a band of tidal silt 6 feet thick in the bed of the Well Stream marks the end of the first period of occupation and more flooding in the third century is also suspected. The inhabitants, however, returned after the first disaster and the occupation continued on a reduced scale into the fourth century, with the fields now surrounded by protective banks and provided with new drainage channels.[3] They seem to have fought a losing battle and, on the whole, the third century in this area seems to have been a period of decline. Part of the canal system had fallen into disuse and, with the development of fresh agricultural areas further north, there may have been a reduced demand for Fen produce. Signs of increasing prosperity, however, return in certain cases in the fourth century, when the area may have been taken over by large landowners. Pottery finds show that some occupation continued well into the fifth century but by that time, increasing disorganisation and complete neglect of dredging and the drainage system, possibly complicated by

[1] S. J. Hallam, 'Villages in Roman Britain', *Ant. J.* XLIV (1964) 19–32.
[2] A detailed survey of Romano-British settlement in the Fenland-Wash area ed. by Dr P. Salway, F.S.A., for the Royal Geographical Society will be published shortly.
[3] W. Grimes ed., *Aspects of Archaeology* (1951) p. 269.

higher rainfall or a general subsidence, seem to have made the carrying on of agriculture in the Fenland increasingly difficult. By the time the Anglo-Saxons were settled in East Anglia these factors, together with the loss of the technical skill and organisation of the Roman period, had allowed the Fens to revert to a water-logged wilderness from which they were not to be rescued again for more than a thousand years.

Another imperial estate may have existed in Southern Britain, extending across Salisbury Plain in the Cranborne Chase area of northern Dorset. Unlike the Fens, this area had been much cultivated in the Iron Age, and after the conquest life continued on the farms with little change. Neither towns nor villas have been found there. This was thought to be due to the fact that the inhabitants had resisted the Roman advance and as a result, may have had to pay a heavy corn tax, probably used to feed the troops at Gloucester, and later, at Caerleon. It has been suggested that at Rotherley and Woodcuts, two of the sites excavated in the Cranborne Chase area, the number of corn storage pits containing Romano-British pottery drops sharply, in comparison with those producing pottery of pre-Roman type. On this basis the annual harvest between A.D. 10 and A.D. 45 seems to have produced about 64 bushels for store at Rotherley and 55 bushels at Woodyates. Between A.D. 45 and 175, however, the amount drops to 14 and 18 bushels respectively, exclusive of the seed corn which may have been stored in small raised granaries of Woodbury type. If the same amount of land was under cultivation, the *annona* must have taken about half or three-fifths of the harvest. Either the farmers went short, there were fewer mouths to feed, or the corn was stored in other ways. Perhaps with better tools and transport and no opportunities for the distractions of tribal warfare the standard of efficiency rose, and some of the inhabitants did leave home to work in the town or join the army. Certainly we do not seem to have here a picture of unrelieved austerity, as the excavations show that Woodcuts at least enjoyed a modest prosperity in the first two centuries A.D., and the bones and teeth of skeletons from the Cranborne Chase area show no signs of deficiency diseases.[1] Another more likely explanation is that the pre-Roman pottery types continued in use to a later date in the Roman period than was realised so their value for dating the storage pits is misleading. Such a time-lag can be paralleled in other parts of the country. In this case it would suggest that the native farms continued their way of life peacefully for a long time after the conquest and were not unduly troubled by official requisitioning.[2]

[1] C. F. C. Hawkes, S. Piggott, H. St George Gray, 'Britons, Romans and Saxons round Salisbury and in Cranborne Chase', *Arch. J.* CIV (1948) 27–81.
[2] J. Brailsford, 'The Durotrigian Culture', D.N.H.A.S.P. LXXIX (1958) 118–21.

Further west, on the edge of the Cranborne Chase area, another site was found, beside the river Stour at Iwerne. Its early history is again that of an Iron Age farm continuing into Roman times with little change until about the end of the second century. Some time in the third century, however, the thatched and wattle and daub house or houses which sheltered the earlier occupants was replaced by an oblong building with timber walls erected on flint foundations. Its roof was probably supported by two rows of posts dividing the interior in three, a 'nave' and 'aisles', in fact it seems likely that we have here one of the buildings of so-called barn or basilican plan which often occur on Roman villa sites. A reconstruction has been made of one found at Great Casterton but this seems to have been used for farming rather than for residential purposes. Much of the space at Iwerne may have sheltered the cattle but at the east end three rooms were partitioned off. Soon after A.D. 300 this house was pulled down and a longer, narrower house erected near it, with walls of flint rubble, divided into rooms by transverse partitions (fig. 101). From one of the long sides projected a tower-like structure with a raised floor; this was probably a granary. The largest room seems to have been the cattle byre or stable as it was drained by a long stone-lined drain. Querns found there suggest it may also have sheltered the women grinding corn. Next to it came a smaller room with a roughly paved floor, and beyond it a room which must have been the chief living-room as it had plastered walls with painted decoration.

Although, unlike the other Cranborne Chase sites, Iwerne seems to have developed into a simple Roman villa, it is noticeable how important a part the cattle seem to play in the economy and such a tendency has also been noted developing elsewhere in this neighbourhood. The Iron Age inhabitants already kept cattle and sheep but to the Roman period belong a series of kite-shaped enclosures, believed to be sheep-folds or cattle kraals. Examples are known further north from Yarnbury Castle hillfort and Knighton Hill. A small oblong enclosure may have been added at Rotherley but this village seems to have been deserted by A.D. 300. At Woodcuts, enclosures began to appear in Phase II, beginning at the end of the second century; and they were replaced by a new arrangement of banks and ditches in the fourth century. These developments seem to suggest that stock-farming increasingly replaced corn-growing as the chief occupation of the later Roman period. Some of the country west of Woodcuts is partly enclosed by dykes believed to be of late Roman date and these also point to cattle-ranching on an increasingly large scale. Parallels to such enclosures can be cited from Gaul and the Rhineland, notably near Trier where an area of 220 square kilometres is surrounded by a wall built by a military unit. Wool from its sheep was probably sent to Trier in the same way

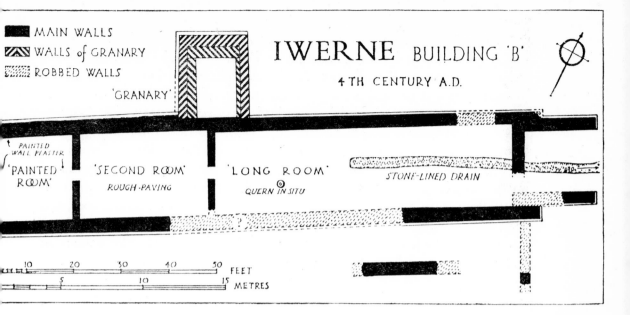

IWERNE BUILDING 'B'

4TH CENTURY A.D.

'GRANARY'

PAINTED
WALL PLASTER

'PAINTED
ROOM'

'SECOND ROOM'

ROUGH-PAVING

'LONG ROOM'

QUERN IN SITU

STONE-LINED DRAIN

10   20   30   40   50   FEET

5   10   15   METRES

101   Plan of Building B, Iwerne, Dorset

as wool from Cranborne Chase may have found its way to the Imperial weaving mills at Winchester.[1]

Other imperial estates may possibly have existed elsewhere in Britain. Evidence for the existence of the officials associated with them may come from an inscription carved on a stone re-used as the lid of a coffin, found buried near the Roman villa on Combe Down near Bath. It is dedicated for the safety of the Emperor Caracalla by one Naevius, a freedman and assistant to the procurators, on the occasion of the restoration from ground-level of the ruined *principia*.[2] A *principia* is usually a military building but a house occupied by the owner of an estate is sometimes described in this way. However, villas are so thickly concentrated in the Bath area that it seems a rather unlikely place for the residence of the administrator of an imperial estate. Presuming that the inscription was originally erected locally and not brought from somewhere else, perhaps Naevius and the procurators were connected with mines or quarries rather than with agriculture, but at present their function remains a mystery.

The type of small farm noted at Cranborne Chase and in the Fens also occurs all over the country. In many cases the sites were first occupied in the Iron Age or even earlier and life continued on them right through the Roman period. The Sussex Downs have produced numerous examples, carefully sited on sunny slopes sheltered from the prevailing winds. In the area between the rivers Adur

[1] Hawkes *et al. op. cit.* 70.   [2] R.I.B. 179.

233

and Ouse near Brighton alone, over 14 miles of lynchets have been identified
with at least 32 little farms. To the east of Brighton a settlement on Highdole
Hill probably dated from before the Roman period and continued in occupation
for many years. It is surrounded by a number of rectangular fields of varying
size defined by lynchets, and field-ways lead off in several directions. Remains
of one or two circular huts have been identified, probably built of wattle and
daub and with central post-holes. Numerous loose flint nodules were noted
and may have been piled round the foundations. Iron door fittings were also
found. A similar site in Arundel Park produced a more substantial dwelling with
a chalk floor containing a large storage pit. It probably had a thatched roof, and
daub, marked with wattle impressions, was noted, as well as a probable site for
a hearth. Flint nodules and pieces of roof tile found there may also have been
used for the walls.[1] A farm of similar type on Thundersbarrow Hill was associated
with simple corn-drying ovens.[2] At Park Brow, near Findon, an earlier prehistoric settlement was succeeded by rectangular Roman houses, one measuring
30 by 21 feet. The wattle and daub walls were plastered and colour-washed, the
roof was tiled, and some of the windows were glazed. A large lock bore witness
to a substantial front door.[3]

Many more small farms have been identified on the gravel terraces of river
valleys such as the Trent, the Nene, the Welland, or the Severn where dense
settlement is suspected in the Vale of Evesham. Along the Thames from Goring
to Lechlade, small fields and stock enclosures occur frequently, with ditches
rather than banks acting as boundaries,[4] and other evidence for simple Romano-
British farming, especially in the first and early second centuries, has been found
south of the Hog's Back near Guildford, Surrey.[5] Further north, however,
huts and fields or enclosures with dry stone walling become the rule. These
features were found at Ewe Close in Westmorland, a walled settlement of
rectangular plan.[6] It contained one large central hut with a small hut with a
furnace close by and nine other small structures, possibly cattle byres, near the
gate. Outside the walls were twelve more huts, perhaps for the adult members
of a growing family, and nearly two acres of fields. Many other sites of similar

[1] G. Holleyman, 'An Early British Agricultural Site on Highdole Hill, near Telscombe',
Sus.A.C. LXXVII (1936) 202–21; E. Hearne, 'Shepherds Garden, Arundel park', *ibid.* 222–43.
[2] E. C. Curwen, 'Excavations on Thundersbarrow Hill', *Ant. J.* XIII (1933) 109–133.
[3] V.C.H. *Sussex* III (1935) p. 62.
[4] *J.R.S.* XLVIII (1958) 99.
[5] A. Clark and J. F. Nichols, 'Romano-British Farms South of the Hog's Back', *Sur.A.C.*
LVIII (1960) 42–71.
[6] W. G. Collingwood, 'Report of the Romano-British Settlement at Ewe Close', C.W.A.S.T.
N.S. IX (1909) 295–309.

character exist in the Lake District, on the Cumberland plain,[1] and on the Yorkshire moors. In Northumberland, a recently excavated example at Huckhoe was surrounded by an inner and outer stockade constructed of timber in the first century A.D. and later replaced by dry stone walling, completed with a gateway ten feet wide. Circular huts with stone walls and floors are probably contemporary with the building of these walls. They date from the second century and may have succeeded huts of lighter construction which have only left a few postholes behind them. The interior walls of one stone hut were lined with wattle and daub. It contained a small oven, a hearth for metal working and traces of a drain. In the fourth century this hut was replaced by two semi-detached rectangular dwellings which shared a joint central wall. Two more circular huts had internal partitions and faced on to a forecourt. No fields were found associated with this settlement. The space between the enclosure walls was presumably used as a corral for animals and it seems likely that stockfarming was the chief occupation of the inhabitants, especially after the *Pax Romana*, although querns for grinding corn were also found.[2] Large areas of field systems, however, exist in Upper Wharfedale associated with farms occupied until the end of the fourth century.

Settlements of the Ewe Close and Huckhoe type occur all over the Border region into Scotland, in Wales, and in Cornwall. Like the farms of the Downs or in the river valleys they continue the pattern of pre-Roman native life. Inside the frontiers, tribal peace and the cessation of cattle raiding in Roman Britain led to an increase in the population. This resulted in a considerable expansion of the areas under cultivation or used for pasture, with the farms beginning to spread on to the fringes of the heavier soils or into more thickly wooded country. The settlements vary in size from homes for single families isolated or else spaced out along a pattern of droveways or watercourses, to those for more than one family unit with several huts clustering together which sometimes may have developed into hamlets. Certain regional differences are discernible but as the period goes on the farms tend to be more symmetrically planned and better constructed. Well-made pottery was the chief luxury, small finds of glass and metal are usually of rare occurrence.[3]

[1] Salway (1965) p. 113.
[2] G. Jobey, 'Excavations at the native settlement at Huckhoe', *Arch. Ael.* (4) XXXVII (1959) 217-78.
[3] For further discussion of these problems see C. Thomas ed. *Rural Settlements in Roman Britain.* (1966).

9
Life in the villas (1)
Buildings

While so many of the inhabitants of Roman Britain were apparently content to continue their traditional way of life, a considerable number in those parts of the country best adapted for corn-growing proved more ambitious and chose to live their lives in houses of increasing elaboration—the so-called 'Roman villas'. The problems of building on this scale in a completely new tradition must have been considerable and, for this reason, it is proposed to discuss them in some detail as their study provides one of the best ways of recapturing a picture of life at this period. Ground plans are available for probably less than half of the six or seven hundred villas so far identified and, unfortunately, many of these are too fragmentary to be very informative. However, from the small number of first-century houses excavated it is clear that several plans of different kinds already existed at this early period, one type at least probably dating from before the Roman conquest.

Two sites which have provided valuable evidence are the villas of Park Street and Lockleys in Hertfordshire.* There the earliest traces of settlement consisted of oval and circular huts of flimsy construction, dating soon after the beginning of the first century. These were probably succeeded in both cases

* To avoid constant repetition in the notes an alphabetical list of villas with select bibliography will be found at the end of this chapter.

by a rectangular hut of timber and daub, with a well-laid chalk floor, occupied during the years immediately preceding and following A.D. 43.[1] At Park Street, this single hut was replaced by two rectangular huts contemporary in date, one of which may have had its roof supported on two parallel rows of posts, so that the interior was divided into three parts, a 'nave' and two 'aisles'. Such an arrangement is variously known as the basilican plan, aisled house or barn-dwelling (e.g. fig. 103).[2] This Park Street hut came to an abrupt end, probably at the time of the Boudiccan rebellion. Another timber building, possibly of similar type and measuring 48 by 32 feet, is represented by the 17 postholes found at Ditchley (fig. 102). It is believed to have consisted of a combined dwelling-house and cattle shed, and may have been constructed about A.D. 70, together with the enclosing bank and ditch. It was occupied till the early years of the reign of Trajan.

The aisled house provides one of the most tantalising of the numerous problems which perplex those studying Romano-British villas. After the first century the posts were often partially replaced by partition walls or sometimes the whole house was built or rebuilt with the aisles divided off by continuous walls on masonry foundations. The villa at Stroud in Hampshire provides a good example of the transitional type. The plan in its final form probably dates from the fourth century when the site included baths and farm buildings arranged round a large courtyard. On the north stood the simple dwelling-house where the stone bases of two rows of columns were identified by the excavator (fig. 103a). At the west end these are overlaid by the partition walls of eight rooms, the front aisle becomes a corridor with traces of mosaic flooring, and two living-rooms, one heated, are built out at the south-east and south-west corners. At Norton Disney in Lincolnshire the same sequence of events may have occurred in a house erected about A.D. 200 (fig. 103b). This was partly divided by partition walls and the stone bases of three pillars were also discovered. Possibly a timber second-century aisled dwelling had preceded it. It was destroyed and rebuilt several times and may not have originally been the main dwelling-house, but after the latest reconstruction at the end of the third century it certainly had a luxurious series of living-rooms with painted walls and a mosaic floor. At Exning (Landwade) in Suffolk a second-century house with large timber posts underlay a villa of later date with masonry partition

---

[1] The plan of the second Belgic House at Lockleys is uncertain but a rectangular plan seems likely. See also H. O'Neil's comment in 'The Roman Villa at Park Street', *Arch. J.* CII (1945) 24.

[2] J. T. Smith, 'Romano-British Aisled Houses', *Arch. J.* CXX (1964) 1–30; Richmond (1963) p. 112.

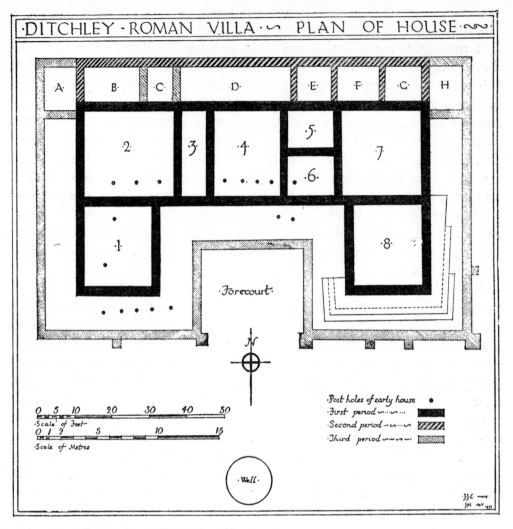

A B· ·C· ·D· ·E· F· ·G· H

·2· ·3· ·4· ·5· ·7·

·6·

·1· ·8·

·Forecourt·

N

0 5 10 20 30 40 50
·Scale of Feet·
0 1 2 5 10 15
·Scale of Metres·

·Post holes of early house ●
·First period ~~~ ...
·Second period ~~~
·Third period ~~~ ~

·Well·

102 Plan of the Ditchley villa, Oxfordshire

walls, and the same development seems to have occurred at Denton, Lincoln-shire, in the fourth century (fig. 103*d*).

In some cases where the 'aisles' are not cut off from the 'nave' by almost continuous walls, the rooms partitioned off are mostly at one end of the building. This was the case at Stroud and it occurs at other Hampshire sites such as North Warnborough and Carisbrooke, West Blatchington in Sussex or Werrington in Northamptonshire. Two aisled houses built in the late second century at Winterton (Lincolnshire) have the same tendency and these had no earlier timber phase. Such an arrangement suggests that the living accommodation in these houses may originally have been shared with livestock, produce or farming equipment. In time certain rooms were partitioned off for privacy

238

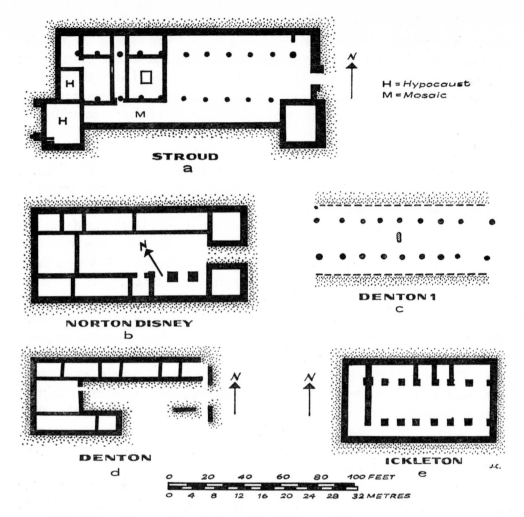

H = Hypocaust
M = Mosaic

STROUD
a

NORTON DISNEY
b

DENTON 1
c

DENTON
d

ICKLETON
e

J.C.

0   20   40   60   80   100 FEET
0 4 8 12 16 20 24 28 32 METRES

103   Aisled House Plans. *a* Stroud, Hampshire. *b* Norton Disney, Nottinghamshire. *c* Denton I, Lincolnshire. *d* Denton, II, III. *e* Ickleton, Cambridgeshire

and occupied by either the farmer or the bailiff in charge of an estate. This theory is likely because on some sites more luxurious houses were built, the aisled dwelling being retained probably as servants' quarters and workshops, as at Brading (Hampshire), and also at Llantwit Major (Glamorgan) with Building B erected about A.D. 150 (fig. 112). In some cases simple baths were added at a later date, as at Mansfield Woodhouse. Elsewhere the aisled house probably continued in use largely as a farm building and examples of this are known from Ickleton (Cambridgeshire) (fig. 103*e*), Spoonley Wood (Gloucestershire), Hartlip (Kent) and possibly Bignor (Sussex).

From the foregoing survey of dwellings of the aisled house type several outstanding points emerge. First, there now seems to be undoubted proof of their existence in the first century, and that probably at a date prior to the Roman conquest. Unfortunately, comparatively little is still known about the habitations of the later Iron Age in this country but from the evidence supplied by such sites as Park Street, it seems probable that in the Belgic areas of Britain at least, these may frequently have been of this plan.

This hypothesis, however, still awaits final confirmation. So far no exact parallels to the aisled house plan have been identified elsewhere in the Empire, unless a connection can be traced with some aisled long-houses found in Holland. Alternatively, did these buildings develop from the Italian *villa rustica*? In spite of all that has been written on the subject, it must be admitted that this problem still awaits final solution. Perhaps the use of masonry bases instead of post-holes betrays the first signs of those architectural features which we think of as typically Roman. The majority of the more elaborate examples of the use of this plan as a dwelling mostly occur in Hampshire, and it is tempting to believe that this group of sites may represent a regional peculiarity. If so, recent excavations at Winterton and neighbouring sites suggest a second regional group among the Coritani.[1] In connection with the development of the partition wall, it should also be noted that the proportions of certain buildings in other parts of the country are such as to make one wonder whether column bases or postholes may not lie beneath their foundations, and whether their narrow corridors may not have been inspired by the aisles of basilican houses. The villas at Titsey in Surrey, Whittlebury in Northamptonshire, or Grateley in Hampshire illustrate such possibilities.

The most typical form of the Roman villa in north-western Europe is the corridor house and this soon developed in Britain. At Lockleys and Park Street the early huts were completely ignored when the first house with masonry foundations was built on each site about A.D. 65. The Lockleys house consisted of a narrow oblong structure divided into four rooms, one of them subdivided into two by a cross partition wall (fig. 104). It was built of flint masonry with a timber superstructure and had a timber verandah outside the western side. The first Park Street house was of similar plan and construction and consisted of five rooms and a cellar (fig. 106*a*). From the substantial nature of its foundations it may have had an upper storey. No reference is made by the excavator to the existence of a corridor or verandah, but the plan shows a short stretch of walling belonging to this period, running parallel to part of the west side of the house and a few feet nearer it than the line of the corridor belonging to the next period. Does this represent a verandah? Alternatively, there may have

[1] Suggested by Mr Ian Stead, the excavator of Winterton.

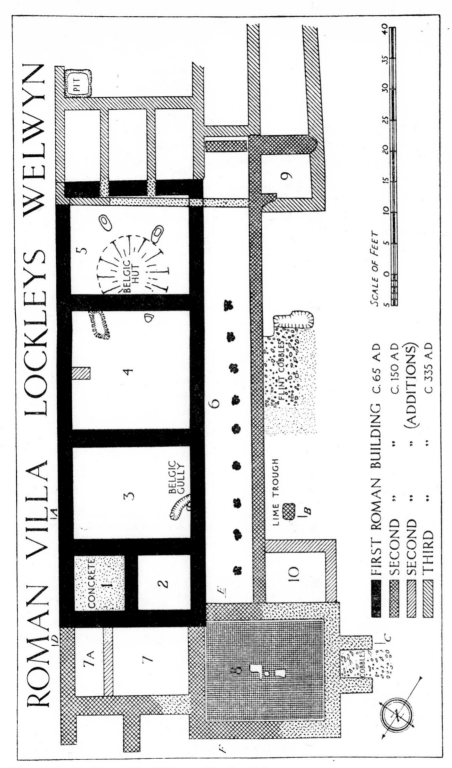

104 Plan of the Lockleys villa, Welwyn, Hertfordshire

105 Lockleys. Reconstruction

been a timber verandah, similar to the one found at Lockleys, of which no trace remained. Other probable examples of villas starting life with a single range of rooms, are known from Mansfield Woodhouse, built towards the end of the second century, and from the late third century at Frocester Court (Gloucester-shire (fig. 106*b*) where a corridor and seven more rooms were soon added. A second-century dwelling which preceded a winged corridor villa at Cox Green (Buckinghamshire) appears to have had only two rooms, while at Saunderton, in the same county, the earliest house, also built in the second century, was divided into a number of small rooms with a channelled hypocaust and a corn-drying oven. It was then replaced towards the end of the third century by three large rooms and a small room at one corner. A corridor ran in front of the house at both periods.

After the wingless corridor house, the next stage of development seems to be represented by the type consisting of a single row of rooms, a corridor, and simple wings each containing one room. At Lockleys, the first masonry house was succeeded in the middle of the second century by a house of this type, the timber verandah being replaced by a substantial stone-built corridor, the outer walls of which probably carried a dwarf colonnade (fig. 104). Owing to the character of the ground, a considerable slope had to be allowed for on the site of the north wing, and this was counteracted by the construction of a two-storied tower (room 8), a very unusual feature (fig. 105). The excavator of Lockleys, however, recalls a suggestion that the villa at Mayen in Germany may

242

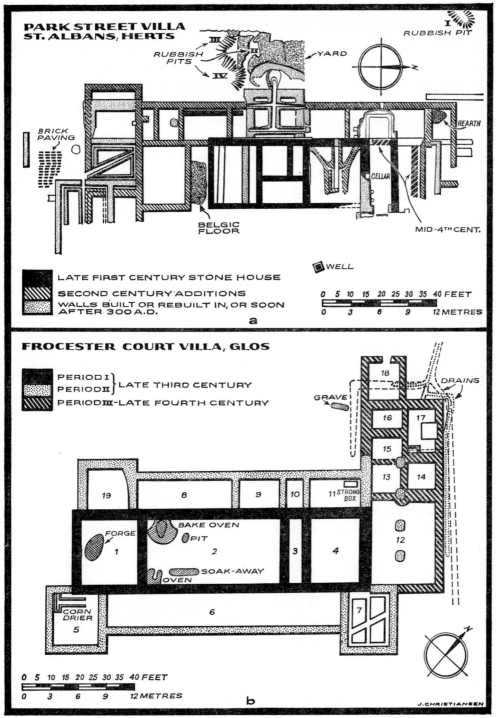

PARK STREET VILLA ST. ALBANS, HERTS

RUBBISH PIT

RUBBISH PITS

YARD

N

BRICK PAVING

HEARTH

CELLAR

MID-4TH CENT.

BELGIC FLOOR

WELL

☐ LATE FIRST CENTURY STONE HOUSE

▨ SECOND CENTURY ADDITIONS

▨ WALLS BUILT OR REBUILT IN, OR SOON AFTER 300 A.D.

0 5 10 15 20 25 30 35 40 FEET
0   3   6   9   12 METRES

a

FROCESTER COURT VILLA, GLOS

■ PERIOD I
▨ PERIOD II } LATE THIRD CENTURY
▨ PERIOD III - LATE FOURTH CENTURY

18   DRAINS

GRAVE

16   17

15

13   14

19   8   9   10   11 STRONG BOX

FORGE   BAKE OVEN   PIT

1   2   3   4   12

OVEN   SOAK-AWAY

CORN DRIER   6   7

5

0 5 10 15 20 25 30 35 40 FEET
0   3   6   9   12 METRES

b

J. CHRISTIANSEN

106 Plans of the earliest Roman houses excavated at *a* Park Street, Hertfordshire. *b* Frocester Court, Gloucestershire

243

have had something similar,[1] and also mentions the fact that towers figure in representations of country houses on some North African mosaics. Massive stone foundations discovered under the Period 5 bath building at Norton Disney and dated to the third century may also have supported some form of tower.

A clearer example of the early winged villa is that at Ditchley (fig. 102) constructed at the beginning of the second century, which probably had an entrance in the east wing, where steps led down to a verandah. This house was soon enlarged by the addition of a second corridor and five small rooms on the north side, and the whole was destroyed about A.D. 200. At Mansfield Woodhouse a corridor and wings were added to the villa sometime in the third century, and another winged corridor villa, belonging to the second half of the second century, was found at Camborne in Cornwall. A third was in existence during the third century at Newport (Isle of Wight), and probably the Period 3 house at Norton Disney, found near the aisled house and dating from about A.D. 200 to 230, was of this type. In 1958 a fourth-century example was excavated at Great Staughton (Huntingdonshire).

The addition of extra rooms and a second corridor at Ditchley and at other sites including Engleton in Staffordshire, fairly soon after the construction of the original winged corridor villa, constitutes one of the typical ways in which a house could be enlarged. Such a division of the space enclosed by the exterior walls into three longitudinal strips, which Collingwood terms tripartite, in contrast to the villa with a single corridor and one row of rooms, which he calls bipartite, was a favourite one, capable of certain variations. Buildings with this threefold division, are also known at Rodmarton (fig. 107*a*) and Cherington in Gloucestershire and at Frilford in Berkshire. Originally these probably consisted of a corridor with two rows of rooms behind it, but in the surviving plans, partition walls divide up what may once have been the corridors. In all cases one or more rooms extend slightly beyond the parallelogram represented by the main part of the plan, suggesting a rudimentary form of wing. The dating of these sites is uncertain, but, with the possible exception of Frilford which may be earlier, they probably belong to the third and fourth centuries. More orthodox wings consisting of single rooms projecting beyond the line of the corridor which connects them are illustrated by the plan of the dwelling-house at Brading, where a single room was also built out from the centre of the back of the house.

Another method of extending the villa was to develop wings at the rear of the building. The simple stages of this, as found at Engleton or at Walton-on-the-Hill (Surrey), can also be seen at such bipartite villas as Brislington in

[1] *Bonner Jahrbücher* CXXXIII (1928) 51 *et seq.*

244

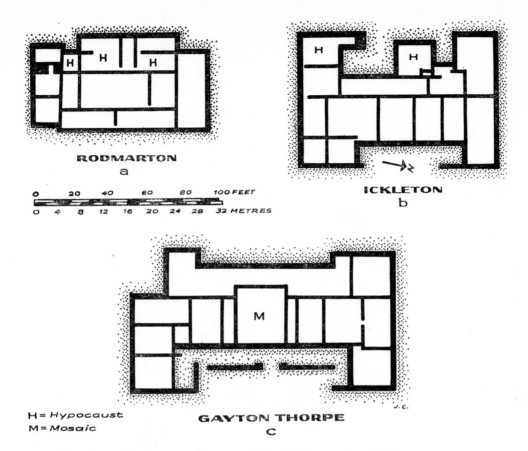

RODMARTON
a

ICKLETON
b

H = Hypocaust
M = Mosaic

GAYTON THORPE
c

J.C.

107 Villa plans. *a* Rodmarton, Gloucestershire. *b* Ickleton, Cambridge-shire. *c* Gayton Thorpe, Norfolk

Somerset or Hadstock in Essex. A more regular plan, however, with two small wings on both sides of the house connected by corridors, as well as a room projecting from the centre of the rear corridor as at Brading, was uncovered at Hambleden, a site with a long life probably extending from the mid-first to well into the fourth century. The dwelling-house at Ickleton closely resembles it in plan, but here the chronology is very uncertain (fig. 107*b*).

Elsewhere there is a tendency in both bipartite and tripartite villas for the dwelling-house to increase in length, and also to develop deeper front wings. For instance the house at Gayton Thorpe (Norfolk) (fig. 107*c*), probably dating from the late second century, may be contrasted with the more compact villas already noted at Hambleden and Ickleton. Other examples of this elongation include the early villa at Folkestone, probably dating from the first century; North Wraxall in Wiltshire, where there is some second-century material; or Dry Hill near Cheltenham, which seems to be a late site. Slightly developed front wings can be seen at Compton in Surrey, a second-century villa with just one

245

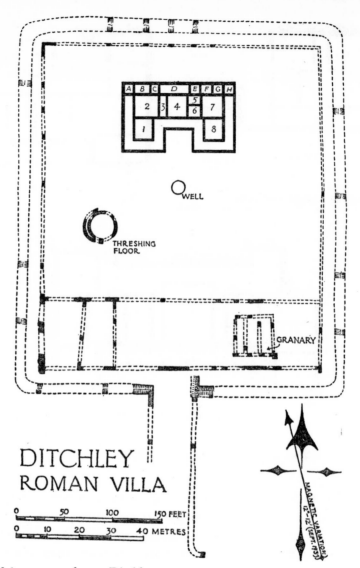

DITCHLEY
ROMAN VILLA

0   50   100   150 FEET
0   10   20   30   40 METRES

108 Plan of the excavated area, Ditchley

room added at the south-western end of the corridor. But the later villa at Folkestone which is dated from the late-first or early-second century till about 370, had two wings, each containing several rooms, and at Box or Spoonley Wood, the wings are still larger and more elaborate. The chronological evidence from the last two sites is unhappily inconclusive.

We have yet to consider whether all the houses of the type so far described were isolated or whether they are found in association with other buildings. In many cases where a dwelling-house apparently stands alone, timber buildings or even more substantial structures may have escaped discovery. Time and

246

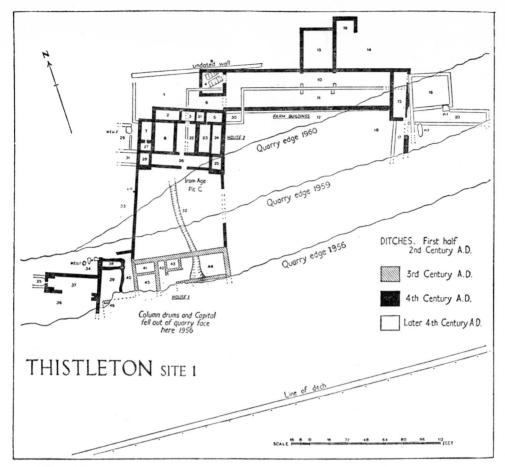

money often prevent the thorough investigation of a site and the earlier excavators, lacking the help of air-photographs, usually rested content with the uncovering of a single edifice. Some villas seem to have consisted of two major buildings, a dwelling-house and a separate structure containing servants' quarters or baths, or both. At Gayton Thorpe the main dwelling-house is believed to be older than the small house erected near it, and at a later date the two buildings were joined together. Again, the aisled dwelling at Mansfield Woodhouse appears on the site later than the corridor house, and the first stone buildings at Norton Disney (Period 3) comprised the dwelling-house and the aisled house of the third century. Ickleton and the second Folkestone villa also comprised two major buildings.

Some villas had ground plans of much larger size and greater complexity. It was formerly believed that British villas tended to be smaller in extent than those found on the Continent, but recent discoveries are beginning to suggest

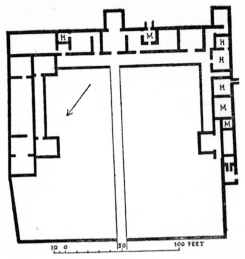

110 Plan of the villa at Spoonley Wood, Gloucestershire

that on many of our villa-sites the area occupied by buildings was far larger than that which has actually been investigated. Pioneer work in this direction was done at Ditchley where air photography led to the discovery of a well, threshing floor, granary and other subsidiary buildings (fig. 108), and also revealed what may have been an orchard and a field system nearby. A whole series of buildings intended for various purposes was found at Langton and sites which were probably far more extensive than the portions hitherto excavated include West Dean, Hartlip, North Wraxall (Wiltshire) and also Low Ham in Somerset. Part of the plan of a big villa including a large tripartite house has been recovered in a race with ironstone quarrying at Thistleton (Rutland) (fig. 109).

The buildings of the richer and more extensive villas were usually grouped round one or more courtyards, really farmyards which increased in size until a portion near the main dwelling-house may have been turned into a court or garden. Brading, Stroud and Clanville are all examples of the simple single courtyard type. On other sites corridor houses with fully developed front wings of the type already discussed at Folkestone, etc., were transformed into villas with enclosed courtyards by the simple method of adding an enclosing wall on the open side facing the house, linking the outer extremities of the two wings. Spoonley Wood is the classic example of this transformation (fig. 110). The site at North Leigh in Oxfordshire may already have developed wings of this kind at one of the earlier periods of its history. In its latest and more familiar form, which may date from the third century, the two wings with their corridors were still further lengthened, and various other alterations and improvements were made, including the construction of a new corridor in front of the main block of the house and of another corridor with a porter's lodge on the south-east (open) side, which finally enclosed the courtyard (fig. 111). Air photographs

248

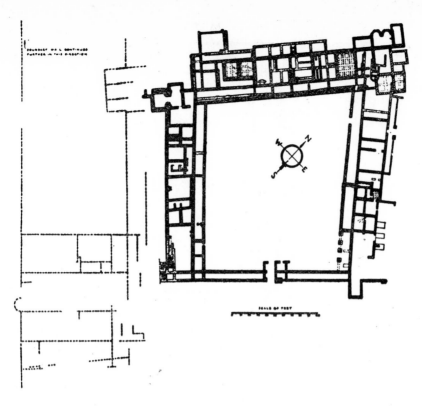

111 Plan of the villa at North Leigh, Oxfordshire, including unexcavated S.W. wing as seen from the air (1943)

show that much of this villa still awaits exploration, it must indeed have been
a very large site.

A few of the largest villas show extensive remains of buildings arranged so
as to form a second courtyard. A transitional stage of this development seems
to have existed at Llantwit Major (fig. 112), where, on the west, a deep winged
corridor house surrounded the greater part of three sides of a courtyard. On the
farther side the court expands into an outer yard, with the aisled house already
mentioned on the south side, and other buildings on the east. Other structures,
probably workshops, occur round the yard on the west and north. In this form
the villa largely dates from the mid-second century although some stretches of
enclosure wall and part of Building C, with a few other alterations, may be
third century. Recent excavations at the well-known site at Chedworth show
that the villa started with three separate buildings and a detached bath-house
in the early second century. In the third century these were all linked together
with corridors and verandahs producing a further development of the villa
type with deep wings like Folkestone, with the dwelling-house and part of the

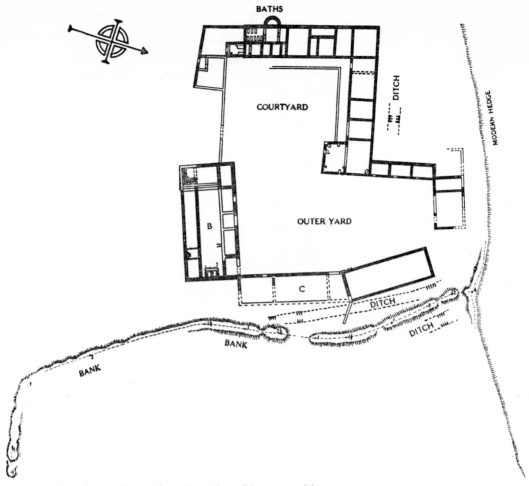

BATHS

COURTYARD

DITCH

MODERN HEDGE

OUTER YARD

B

C

DITCH

DITCH

BANK

BANK

112   Plan of the villa at Llantwit Major, Glamorganshire

wings now cut off by a colonnade from the rest of the courtyard, while further buildings continue the line of the wings. Fresh investigations at Bignor in Sussex are also revealing signs of alteration and reconstruction. The plan uncovered some years ago showed a large courtyard villa sometimes compared with North Leigh, but with rooms built out at each of the four corners. Other buildings continue into what appears to be a second courtyard to the east, the walls of which seem to have extended westwards to enclose the whole of the house proper with its central court. This second courtyard also contains the large aisled house already mentioned in one corner, and a second smaller building in another. There are indications of a large entrance gateway in the centre of the east wall. The new discoveries suggest that the west range of the villa was the earliest, being timber built in Period 1, possibly in the second century. It was then rebuilt in flint and chalk masonry in the first half of the third

250

century. In the fourth century, it was reconstructed in green sandstone and the north and south ranges added, but some earlier building may also lie beneath the south range. The five mosaics date from still later in the fourth century.[1] Other large villas of double courtyard plan include Darenth (Kent), North Wraxall, Scampton (Lincolnshire) and Woodchester (Gloucestershire).

An examination of the plans of British courtyard villas at once demonstrates that their development is quite different from that of the houses of the Italian countryside. There the arrangement round atrium and peristyle was designed for comfort in a warm climate; our houses needed to make better use of day-light and any available sunshine. Courtyard villas of the British type also occur in northern Gaul and Germany, Mienne (Eure-et-Loire) being one such ex-ample.[2] We see in their plans the same general development of the winged corridor villas as in Britain. Somewhere, perhaps in southern or central Gaul, it should be possible to find the Italian type of villa being modified into the north-western country-house or farm, possibly with a whole series of transi-tional forms.

Meanwhile in Britain it becomes apparent that probably both the aisled house and the wingless corridor house were in existence by the end of the first century A.D. In the second century the bipartite house developed simple wings, and during the later years of the century it may in some cases have been converted into a tripartite house by the addition of extra rooms, or a second corridor at the rear as at Ditchley (fig. 102). The more compact type of tripartite villa may have developed rudimentary wings, as at Cherington, or wings consisting of a single room, as at Compton, during the second century if not before. But the type of villa which inclined to length rather than breadth seems to have acquired wings at a somewhat earlier date, possibly by the end of the first century, as we have seen to be the case at Folkestone, and other examples probably include Boxted and Ridgewell. The chronology of later developments remains rather obscure. Wings of increased size and enclosed courtyards probably date from the late second and third centuries or later, but until more sites with this type of plan are completely excavated, and the phases of their development chrono-logically established, it is impossible to reach any final conclusions about them. Obviously the simpler types of plan continued in use right through the Roman period, and a villa might sometimes have its accommodation reduced or be replaced by a smaller house instead of increasing in size. Old and new fashions must have been in existence together and the variety found reflects very clearly how human prejudices and affections, as well as economic conditions, influenced a man in choosing the size and plan of his dwelling.

[1] See below p. 281.   [2] Grenier, II (2) (1934) p. 839, fig. 307.

This individual approach to the problem of villa building is brought home to us even more clearly when we consider the actual methods of construction. For Park Street, Lockleys and other early sites, perishable materials such as timber, wattle and daub, and thatch were used. These leave little evidence behind them, consequently the traces of early occupation must often have been destroyed by villa-excavators in the past. The growth of Roman influence, however, is reflected in the increasing use of masonry from the second half of the first century onwards, as well as in the gradual elaboration of the plans already discussed.

From the information available it becomes apparent that the Romano-Britons depended very largely upon local resources for their building materials. A comparison of the Geological Map of Britain with the lists of villas reveals several features of interest in this connection. On many sites the foundations and lower parts of the walls were built wholly, or largely, of flint and chalk, and their distribution corresponds closely with the chalk areas shown on the map. In the south of England, they run right across the country from Norfolk to Dorset, with such stray examples on outlying small patches of chalk as the sites at Seaton in Devon, Frampton in Dorset, Clatterford and Carisbrooke on the Isle of Wight, and Margate in the Isle of Thanet. Less is known of the villas of the chalk areas north of the Wash. Since flint is absent from the chalk in Yorkshire, the houses at Rudston and Harpham were largely built of chalk supplemented by sandstone, which may have come from as far away as the West Riding.

The use of stone mixed with flint and chalk is not uncommon, especially on the edge of the chalk zones, as might indeed be expected. At Compton in Surrey, flint was used in conjunction with the Bargate stone still quarried near Godalming. Sandstone, probably from Limpsfield Common, was used with flint at Titsey. Likewise flint is used with local ragstone and sometimes with chalk in Kent, and with chalk or various local stones at sites in Sussex, Hampshire and Dorset, such as Clanville, West Dean, Carisbrooke, Newport or Angmering.

Outside the chalk areas local stone was exploited to a large extent for villa construction. In Kent the limestone from the Lower Greensand known as Kentish Ragstone was used at several sites, including some near Maidstone. At Little Chart it is known to have been quarried on the spot, and quarries at Allington may also have been drawn upon. In Sussex, Pulborough sandstone and ferruginous limestone were frequently employed, for Bignor and Wiggonholt among other sites. Green sandstone from the quarry at Eastbourne which provided the building materials for the Saxon Shore Fort at Pevensey, was probably also used for the Eastbourne villa, and the same material, found locally, was employed for the villa at Stroud in Hampshire. In the south-west, the Cornish site of Camborne was built of local slate of Devonian age and granite.

From Dorset and the borders of Devonshire the great Jurassic zone of Lias and oolite stretches across the middle of England as far north as Yorkshire and these formations supplied the materials for sites which include many of our finest villas. Lias is reported from Somerset sites including Newton St Loe and Keynsham. Quarries round Street and Somerton, King's Weston and Queen's Camel were among the most probable sources of supply. At other sites use was made of oolites such as the shelly limestone from Ham Hill recorded at Low Ham and Lufton.

Another area in which oolites seem to have been extensively employed was Wiltshire. The excavators of the Atworth villa considered that the building stone used was probably quarried on the site, and the materials found included thin-bedded limestone, Forest Marble, Bath oolite and freestone. Freestone and other stones of oolitic age are largely quarried in the Cotswolds and were the most popular building materials in Gloucestershire, being found at Whittington Court, Dry Hill, Hucclecote and Spoonley Wood. Oxfordshire is traversed by both oolitic and Liassic belts and the oolite used at Ditchley may have come from less than a quarter of a mile away. Stone for some sites in this county may have been obtained from quarries at Headington and Shotover.

Continuing farther north, the Jurassic zone passes through Northamptonshire and Rutland, counties which still provide famous building stones already known to the Romano-Britons. These include Ketton stone, a yellowish oolite particularly favoured in Roman times, and Lincolnshire limestone, probably coming from quarries at Barnack and Ancaster. Ironstone was also probably employed for building, as well as for the extraction of iron ore, and the villa at Greetwell, near Lincoln, described as being built of local stone, is on the site of an ironstone quarry. In Yorkshire, freestone was used at Langton, Magnesian limestone at Castle-Dykes and sandstone for sites in Shropshire and Staffordshire.

A few types of stone travelled farther afield from their quarries. Oolites such as Bath stone and freestone were very popular materials for decorative features in both towns and villas and were obviously felt to be worth the cost of their transport. Ketton stone was another favourite material and appears, for example, in Cambridgeshire at Comberton and Ickleton in an area where local stone is absent. And hearthstone, a sandstone indurated with iron from the Tertiary Beds of the New Forest, was used on various sites in Hampshire, Wiltshire and Dorset for hypocaust walls, for which it was particularly suitable.

Among those materials which had a more than local distribution, materials for roof construction held an important place. Slabs of stone, usually of hexagonal form and held in place with nails, were often used, instead of the more normal earthenware roof-tiles (fig. 27*b*). Sometimes, as at Ely and Norton Disney, both occur together, or tiles replace stone at a later date or *vice versa*. When several buildings of contemporary date are found on the same site some, including the dwelling-house itself, may have a stone roof, while barns, workshops, etc., are roofed with tile or thatch.

A good idea of the distribution of building materials can indeed be gained from a brief survey of the various types, provenances and find-spots of villa roofing-stones, beginning with those areas in which stone was accessible reasonably near at hand. Slates from the Charnwood Forest rocks, for example, were discovered at Norton Disney, and also much further away at Great Staughton, Huntingdonshire. Devonian slate from Wiveliscombe was employed for the roof at Pitney (Somerset), as well as slabs of Lias limestone, and a slate roof was found at Camborne. Slabs from the Pennant Grit of the Carboniferous were much in vogue in the Bath and Bristol area and chunks of Pennant stone ready for splitting into roof slabs were discovered at the villa at Ely. This material was also noted at Llanwit Major (fig. 27*b*). Stonesfield slates were used for villas in the Cotswolds and Oxfordshire, and also at Tingewick in Buckinghamshire, and Colleyweston slates are found on Midland sites. Either Stonesfield or Colleyweston slates were brought quite a distance for the roof at Ickleton.

In those parts of Britain where builders had to be content with flint, chalk, or timber owing to the shortage of stone, roofs were usually constructed of tiles. It is, however, a fact that the discovery on a site of stone foreign to the district is often a clue to the presence of a Roman building there, and such imported stone is especially noticeable in the chalk and flint areas. A striking instance of this is the Basingstoke district of Hampshire, where a whole series of villas has been largely identified through the discovery of roof slate obtained from an outcrop of Purbeck stone from an unidentified source. The group of villas near Andover, as well as Clanville and Thruxton, have also yielded evidence of stone roofs, again from an unknown locality.

In most parts of the country, apart from those where stone is abundant, houses continued to be largely constructed of timber, wattle and daub, but now the walls were erected on masonry foundations to a height of several feet above ground level, built of whatever materials were available. The first Roman house at Lockleys, erected between A.D. 60 and 70, seems to have been of this type, and the charred remains of an oak beam 10 by 4 inches thick from one of the outer walls, were found among the debris from the fire which destroyed the building. The foundations consisted of layers of flint and chalk rubble laid alternately in a slightly V-shaped trench. Above them, came walls 2 feet 4 inches in width of dressed flint laid in carefully pointed courses. Some tile may also have been used, certainly when the house was re-built in the mid-second century, tile courses occurred in flint and mortar walls constructed less carefully than their predecessors. After this house was destroyed by fire early in the fourth century, another house was erected on a slightly different site. Little is known of it but it seems to have had foundations of unmortared flint, thin walls and small rooms, and been altogether a much simpler structure than its predecessor. The successive periods at Lockleys thus reveal a steady deterioration in construction. A similar course of events was revealed at Park Street.

So much for building in flint and chalk. In areas where stone was more abundant we find sites like Keynsham with walls of Pennant stone 18 to 30 inches thick built on wider foundations; they were preserved in some parts to a height of 4 feet 3 inches. The lower parts of the foundations were made of three courses of large rough unworked blocks of stone, set up on edge with a slight tilt. At one point they were found to be built without mortar, and they reached a depth of up to 7 feet 9 inches below ground level. The walls of the Ham Hill villa were about 2 feet wide, substantially built of faced Ham Hill stone and well laid on a set-off course. In Gloucestershire, small, roughly squared blocks of oolite were found at Spoonley Wood and the neighbouring villa of Wadfield, used with poor quality mortar made of lime burnt from the same stone and very subject to decay. The method of construction with stone courses laid slanting in opposite directions (herringbone work) was also not uncommonly used for foundations, for walls, or even as a base for floors. Examples include East Coker and Lufton in Somerset and Apethorpe and Borough Hill in Northamptonshire.

In the case of stone-built houses, evidence for alteration and reconstruction is often provided by changes in the type of building material or by the methods used. Camborne, Ely, Atworth and Ditchley are sites where this has been detected. At Box, where the local freestone was employed, the earlier walls were constructed of a rubble composed of unsquared stones with no bonding courses and plastered, inside and out. Similar rubble was used for the later walls, but instead of the exterior plastering, they were faced with squared stones 4 to 6 inches in size. Owing to the abundance of local building stone, and in view of the thickness of the foundations, it was believed that the walls of this villa were completely built of stone, used with a rather poor yellow mortar which showed no signs of any admixture of brick. Evidence for buildings entirely constructed of masonry is, however, more often provided by villa baths. The bath-house on Highdown Hill, dating from the later-first or early-second century to the end of the third, had walls of flint and mortar 1½ feet wide. Small squared blocks of chalk were probably used for building their upper courses with the addition of courses of double layers of tiles in the hot room. Tile quoins and bonding courses are, of course, frequently found incorporated with flint masonry.

On sites with a long history, it is, indeed, the bath buildings which generally reflect most closely the various vicissitudes through which a villa passed. Such changes are often marked by the enlargement of the original baths, by the construction of new ones, or by the blocking up of hypocausts when they fell into disuse. The essential elements of every Roman bath, the *frigidarium, tepidarium* and *caldarium*, can usually be identified, with the hot- and cold-water plunges or basins. The *sudatorium* is also found on some sites, including Wiggonholt. The purpose of each of these apartments was so clearly defined that it is not surprising that all Roman baths seem to bear a close resemblance to each other on superficial examination, but on closer inspection it appears possible to distinguish several different types among the British examples. One of these, probably the earliest, is characterised by rooms which tend to be rectangular with square or oblong plunges. The baths of Periods I and II at Wiggonholt provide a good example of it and also an illustration of villa bath construction in general (fig. 113). They were erected about A.D. 125 with four rooms, *apodyterium* (1), *frigidarium* (2) with cold plunge, *tepidarium* (3) and *caldarium* (4) with hot plunge. In Period II, dating from about 175, the hot-water plunge was replaced by a *sudatorium*. The excavators remarked on the similarity of this plan to others found elsewhere, and compared certain features of it with those of the baths from the villas at Wingham in Kent, Castle-Dykes and Compton, probably in use at the same period. Other sites where it occurs include Wheatley and Worsham Bottom in Oxfordshire, Hambleden, Rodmarton, Spoonley Wood, Dry Hill, West Dean and Mansfield Woodhouse.

The majority of villa bath suites, however, contain at least one apsidal room, and sometimes up to three rooms with apses are found, as at Newport or North Wraxall. Usually such rooms are heated but cold plunges in apses do occur at Witcombe and Highdown Hill. Some villas developed elaborate bath suites. One was built at Eccles in the last quarter of the first century with several heated rooms, including a circular *laconicum*, a feature usually found in military baths or in public baths in towns such as Bath or Wroxeter. A parallel to it, however, exists at the Ashtead villa. In Period II (A.D. 100–150) the Eccles

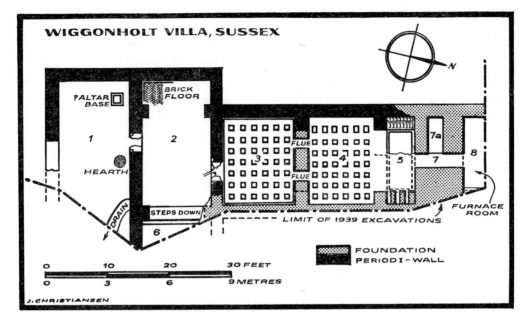

WIGGONHOLT VILLA, SUSSEX

?ALTAR BASE

BRICK FLOOR

1

2

HEARTH

3

FLUE

4

FLUE

5

7a

7

8

DRAIN

STEPS DOWN

6

LIMIT OF 1939 EXCAVATIONS

FURNACE ROOM

0   10   20   30 FEET

0   3   6   9 METRES

FOUNDATION PERIOD I - WALL

J. CHRISTIANSEN

113   Plan of the bath-house at Wiggonholt, Sussex

baths were altered and considerably extended, and in Period III (*c.* 150–290) a large cold plunge measuring 44 by 11 feet, large enough for a swimming-pool, was added. Another cold bath of swimming-pool dimensions has been found at Gadebridge Park, Hemel Hempstead, Hertfordshire, and is dated to the early fourth century.

The location of villa baths also varies. They are often built at the end of a wing, as at Box, or they occupy the whole of a small wing by themselves, as at Colerne. Again, they may form part of the main building, as in Block A at Folkestone or at Chedworth. But at certain sites, including Chipping Warden in Northamptonshire, Cobham in Surrey, Boughton Monchelsea in Kent or Old Durham, the baths form a completely separate building, probably as a precaution against fire, an ever present risk for villas with timber-built superstructures or partition walls. As a result several such isolated bath-houses with their substantial masonry have been found and excavated, while the villas associated with them have either disappeared or prove less easy to discover. Detached bath-houses seem to have been built at all periods, and in Surrey we find them in the late first century at Ashtead or belonging to the fourth century as at Farnham. They are of all types and sometimes occur in villas which also have baths as part of the dwelling-house. Ashtead provides one example of this while at Stanton Chair (Suffolk) the second set of baths is only joined to the house by a corridor. Some detached baths, including those at Wiggonholt and Worsham, were converted into dwelling-houses in the later years of the Roman period. It

257

may be that they alone survived, after the villas themselves became ruinous. But at North Warnborough events took another turn and what had been originally a house was converted into baths, which either remained detached, or were eventually attached as a wing to the fourth-century aisled house.

Like the public bathing establishments, villa baths must have played an important part in the lives of the inhabitants, providing them with much needed relaxation and recreation. It is not impossible that some of the isolated bath-houses which seem to be unassociated with a villa, may have been a centre for local people farming in a small way and unable to afford their own baths. They might have paid a small fee in money or partly in firewood. In a letter written in the fifth century, a much more primitive type of bath is described by Sidonius Apollinaris.[1] This consisted of a trench dug near a river, covered with a roof of twigs and rugs, and filled with heated stones on which water was poured for the hot bath. This was followed by a cold plunge in the river. Arrangements of this type may have been in use at some of those early British villas which have produced no traces of the more usual hypocausts.

By way of contrast, the same author also describes some villa baths in Gaul which obtained their water-supply from a channel directly connected with the river. In stormy weather the water rose until, finally, the boats were liable to come up the channel and be left stranded, much to the inconvenience of the bathers.[2] Ausonius, too, a little over a hundred years earlier, described the fine country mansions on the banks of the Moselle, some with bath-houses, probably detached, 'which smoke when Vulcan, drawn by the glowing flue, pants forth his flames, and whirls them up through the channelled walls, rolling in masses the imprisoned smoke before the scorching blast'.[3]

The remaining features of structural interest connected with villas may be briefly summarised. On account of the width and strength of the exterior walls the possibility of an upper storey, already mentioned at Box, was also suspected at Atworth (Period III), Ely, East Grimstead, Stroud and Titsey. Small rooms suitable for staircases have been noted on other sites, one at Yatton even possessing an opening believed to belong to a cupboard under the stairs. A cellar, similar to those discovered under some of the houses at Verulamium, was found at Park Street, with the slots for holding the beams of the steps leading down to it still visible, and also part of the small window lighting it. Other cellars may have existed at Hartlip, Otford and Stroud. Further evidence for windows was found in the *frigidarium* of the baths at Low Ham. Here the dis-

[1] *Epistulae* II. 9. 8. Trans. W. B. Anderson.
[2] *Carmina* XXII. 128 *et seq.* Trans. W. B. Anderson.
[3] *Mosella* 337 *et seq.* Trans. H. G. Evelyn White.

covery of numerous voussoirs indicated the existence of at least three arched windows, the one lighting the cold plunge bath being supported by columns five feet tall. Indirect evidence for the presence of windows is also sometimes provided by pieces of painted plaster shaped to fit the jamb of a splay and window glass is of frequent occurrence. Brading and Wiggonholt produced an abundance of it, including a fragment still in its wooden frame from the latter site. An iron window-frame is said to have been found on the site at Margate and window-latches at Park Street.

In discussing the development of the courtyard villa the stretches of wall which sometimes link the buildings together have been briefly mentioned. In this connection it may also be recalled that some less elaborate sites, often of early date, were surrounded by banks and ditches. Air photography has revealed a number of examples, particularly in Oxfordshire, but with the exception of Ditchley and Callow Hill little excavation has been done on them. It has been suggested that where the ditches are of later date they may sometimes have had a defensive character but this seems doubtful. Norton Disney, which may have had some form of boundary ditch at an earlier period, was surrounded in the third century by a system of ditches used for either drainage or defence, and during the fourth century three more ditches, open for only a short time, seem to have been hastily dug outside the others. Similar structures may have existed at Castle-Dykes. At Ely, a site admittedly exposed to Irish raids up the Bristol Channel, the dwelling-house was enclosed by a bank and ditch in the early years of the fourth century and a further ditch gave some protection to the baths and a subsidiary building.

The erection of the masonry walls which enclose some of the large villas must have been quite an undertaking. At High Wycombe they were traced by the excavators on either side of the main gate, 106 feet in one direction and for at least 70 feet in the other, where they probably continued down to the river. Presumably this was just one side of the villa enclosure. Over 2 feet wide, with foundations 3 feet thick, they were built of flint. Opposite the centre of the dwelling-house and 160 feet away from it, was a gateway flanked by two small rooms believed to be porter's lodges. These were built on soft sub-soil with the result that in time cracks developed in their walls and they had to be buttressed. The passage-way between them was about 10 feet wide, closed by a wooden gate consisting of two leaves which folded back. Enclosure walls and gatehouse probably date from the second half of the second century. When the baths were extended in the fourth century, they were partly demolished and the gateway was blocked up. At Woolaston, Gloucestershire, stretches of enclosure walls of fourth-century date were found, 2½ feet wide and built of coarse sandstone. The discovery of large voussoirs suggests that the main gateway may have consisted of two stone arches with a central pier. On the west, another entrance, 14 feet 9 inches wide, probably had wooden gates similar to those at High Wycombe and the stop stone against which they closed was found, still in position, in the centre of the gateway. Another possible porter's lodge is believed to exist at North Leigh and other sites with gateways possessing arches or other ornamental features include Darenth, Norton Disney, Apethorpe and North Wraxall.

One aspect of the study of Roman villas which soon impresses the student is the care shown in selecting the sites. The visitor to Woodchester, Witcombe, Bignor or Lullingstone cannot fail to enjoy the beauty of his surroundings. A sunlit slope, sheltered from the prevailing winds and with a convenient water-supply, was naturally preferred and a glance at the Ordnance Survey map of Roman Britain shows how the potentialities of the best farm lands were appreciated. The letters of the younger Pliny tell us how the cultivated, well-to-do Roman planned his house so as to take advantage of sunshine and fine views of the surrounding countryside, placing it among a series of gardens.[1] One may imagine the larger British villas in the same type of setting. Gardens, unfortunately, leave few traces for the archaeologist.

The natural features of the site selected for the villa often influenced its construction in various ways. When a sheltered position on a hillside was chosen the builders frequently had to devise ways of counteracting the slope. Hence several sites such as Witcombe, Seaton, Ditchley, Ickleton and Hartlip were built on terraces, or on ground artificially levelled. Mention has already been made of the tower added to the second century house at Lockleys, an ingenious way of disguising a sudden drop in the ground level of an awkward site. Elsewhere we find walls which have been buttressed against the slope. An outer wall at Woodchester 3 feet wide, and built of roughly hewn stones, had six such buttresses of ashlar stone, placed at irregular distances. Extra courses were added to some walls at Ham Hill to solve the problem of the slope, adjustments had also to be made at Atworth, and at Camborne the depth and width of the foundations vary with the depth of sub-soil. At Worsham Bottom (Asthall), deep and wide foundations may have been constructed because of the danger of floods. But space for a hypocaust at Little Chart was dug out of the rock on which the bath-house is built, and walls were built up inside this. A similar method may have been adopted at Hanwell, Brading and Combe Down, where some of the rock was left *in situ* and used as *pilae*. The effect of a slope is also reflected in the existence of steps between rooms as at Newport, Woodchester,

[1] *Epistulae* II. 17; V. 6.

or Wadfield, while at Witcombe the slope is also skilfully utilised to form the 'grand staircase' leading down from room 11.

The presence of water was an obvious attraction to Romano-British builders, but the sites which they chose occasionally proved embarrassingly damp. Measures had sometimes to be taken against flooding as at Hadstock, where it is clear that alterations raising the level of the bath had to be made before the house was even completed. Parts at least of the site at Frampton were also probably raised for the same reason. The first building at North Warnborough is only 200 yards from the river's bank and since the lowest courses of its foundations were below water-level, it seems likely that here, too, damp provided a problem. At Ely a site on an island formed by the river Ely and the Caerau brook was selected, perhaps for security reasons, and the bed of the stream was deepened to a depth of 5 feet and straightened so as to afford better drainage.

The need for water for domestic purposes, however, and the convenience of having it near at hand, obviously outweighed the disadvantages of flooding, and the neighbourhood of rivers continued to be a favourite haunt of the Romano-British builders. Baths in particular were frequently placed not far from the water's edge. Other sites are known to have obtained their water supplies from springs. Knowle Hill was built on a slope just above the line where springs break out and so was Saunderton; and springs exist near such sites as Seaton, East Coker, Alresford and Scampton, while Fifehead Neville actually possessed a hot spring. Cold springs have even been found under the floors of some buildings and at Southwick the cold bath was excavated to a depth of over 8 feet to make use of such a convenient natural water-supply.

Wells have been found on many villa sites, including Park Street, Langton, Brislington, Rothley, Little Chart and Boxted. At Ditchley the well was 12 feet in diameter and more than 8 feet deep, and contained debris suggesting that it had a timber lining and a small wooden well-house with a thatched roof. The well at North Wraxall was sunk to a depth of more than 68 feet, lined with masonry and enclosed in a hexagonal building. The villa well excavated at Chew Stoke in 1954 was 30 feet deep and 33 inches wide, stone-lined within a larger shaft packed with clay. Postholes of the uprights supporting the windlass were identified and out of the depths came many unusually well preserved objects. They included about 135 pots and 14 coins, mostly of third-century date, and pieces of wood, leaves, fruit and seeds. One wooden fragment bore an inscription in ink.[1] Leather sandals, pewter and copper jugs, and bronze jewellery were also found.

Vitruvius mentions three ways of conducting water in channels, through

[1] See below p. 303.

masonry conduits, through lead pipes or through pipes of baked clay.[1] In Romano-British villas, although our knowledge of how precisely water was brought from a source more distant than a well and what eventually happened to the waste water remains incomplete, all these methods were employed. We have some evidence for the existence of aqueducts. One built of stone with a concrete channel ran along one end of the building at Linley Hall (Shropshire) and was then traced to a pond, supposed to be a Roman reservoir, situated 880 feet to the north-east. At Llanfrynach (Brecon) an old water-course bringing water from a spring a mile away to the baths was found, and another is reported at Tracy Park (Gloucestershire). A small stream was diverted into a channel cut in the slope behind the baths at Low Ham. At Farnham (Surrey) an open ditch 630 feet long, 6 feet wide, and 4½ feet deep connected the site with the point at which the Bourn stream goes underground, while a tiled drain was traced at Alresford to the edge of an ancient ditch which received water from a spring in the corner of the field. It is of course possible that some of these channels were for drainage rather than for water-supply, and some of them may have contained pipes. Traces of a drain of tiles and semi-circular pieces of oolitic stone led from the house to the river at Thornford (Dorset) and drain-pipes, presumably of earthenware, are mentioned among the finds at Folkestone, Tarrant Hinton (Dorset), and Ridgewell (Essex). At Foscott (Buckinghamshire), pipes made of tree-trunks conveyed water between two tanks, and something similar seems to have existed at Cotterstock (Northamptonshire). Probably these wooden pipes had iron ring joints of the type which have been found at Silchester or Caerwent.[2] A little evidence for a fountain comes from Nuthills Farm, Calne (Wiltshire) and either fountains or shower baths may have existed in the baths at Stroud, Box and Folkestone. A *nymphaeum* or ornamental fountain-house of a quasi-religious character was discovered at Chedworth, close to the villa, and rather similar features occur at Witcombe and Brading. Rain-water from the roof and waste water from the baths was collected to flush the latrines, which have been identified in several villas, usually in the vicinity of the baths. They are mostly of the type found at Woolaston, where traces were discovered of a flagged gutter and supports for a heavy tank, probably of lead, for flushing. The seats were presumably of wood.

From water-supplies we turn to methods of heating. Wood was the most common fuel and wood-charcoal is frequently referred to in excavation reports. A few samples of it have been analysed. The wood used in the stoking pit of the hypocaust of room 11 at Park Street was oak and hazel, oak also being used

[1] *De Architectura* VIII. 6.
[2] J. Ward, *Romano-British Buildings and Earthworks* (1911) p. 280; Boon (1957) p. 161.

for some structural features on the site such as beams and stakes. Alder, oak, willow and perhaps poplar and beech, were found among the burnt debris at Ely and, as traces of ash and alder were discovered in one of the ditches here, the site may have been surrounded by woods of oak, alder and willow, which provided the necessary fuel supply. Traces of ash, alder, walnut, willow, sycamore, elder and cherry were found in the well at Langton and also stems of heather, larger pieces of oak and sweet chestnut, and hazelnuts, suggesting that there was quite a varied vegetation in the neighbourhood of this villa. Some of the wood no doubt was already converted into charcoal before it was used for fuel. Coal is also recorded from about twenty sites. Outcrops of coal in the Forest of Dean supplied villas such as Ely and Woolaston, and the Somerset coalfield others, including Stanton St Quintin, and even perhaps Foscott, 80 miles away. At Brading cannel coal and anthracite from Kidwell or the Amroth district of Cwybrywn have been noted. Methods of heating comprise the use of braziers, fireplaces, and hypocausts. No actual braziers have yet been recovered from any villa site, but sites which show evidence for no other form of heating presumably depended upon them, and it was noted at North Warnborough that the rammed chalk floor of room B was much burnt in places, as though embers had dropped on it from a brazier. Tiled open hearths are quite common, usually placed towards the centre of the room. In room 3 at the Star villa, Shipham, Somerset, however, a hearth was inserted by removing the facing stones from one wall and lining it with re-used Pennant roof slates in a semicircle with a kerb of fragments of rotary querns. Later a shallow pit was dug in front of the hearth to hold the ashes. An unusually elaborate tiled hearth was found against a wall at Newport, Isle of Wight (fig. 114). It had tiled wings enclosing it on either side and a slightly concave back. Remains of a tiled corble and possibly a plaster hood, blackened with smoke, were found in the vicinity. Originally this may have been used for heating and it recalls Sidonius Apollinaris' description of the home of a friend in winter time where 'a goodly fire crackles, which devours the great logs that are piled near at hand; the glowing cloud that comes forth in billows, curls upwards from the stove, then fades away, and with its blast now broken it spreads a mitigated heat all over the roof'.[1] Living-rooms as well as baths, were sometimes heated by a hypocaust, the raised floors being either supported by *pilae* or else resting on solid masonry cut through by heating channels. The stoke-hole was usually approached from outside the buildings where sheds for fuel storage could be conveniently provided. At Park Street an iron scoop or soot rake was found, probably used for cleaning the hypocaust flues.

[1] *Carmina* XXII. 188 *et seq.*

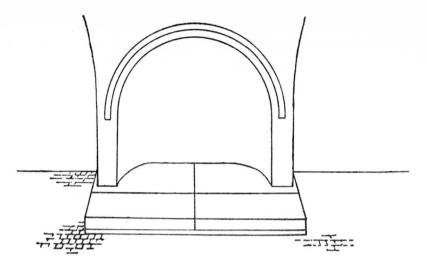

114 Reconstruction of a Roman hearth, Newport villa, Isle of Wight

Apart from the baths and heated living-rooms, it is usually impossible to determine the use of individual rooms in our Roman dwellings. Bedrooms, nurseries, offices and store rooms must all have existed but it is rarely feasible to determine which was which. However, we have a little more evidence for kitchens as the tiled hearths already mentioned must often have been used for cooking.[1] Four examples occurred in the barn dwelling at Castlefield, Hampshire, one consisting of a large tile measuring 2 by 1½ feet, bedded in a thick layer of clay. A pile of ashes was found close by. Another hearth, 17 by 13 inches, was made of ridge tiles laid on their backs and sloping slightly inwards. A nearby house of simple plan at Holbury had a larger hearth measuring 3 by 2 feet, of hard cement laid on a clay foundation 1½ feet thick. Against one wall of the same building was a smaller fireplace with hearth and back of flint pitching. Such fireplaces are very typical and many continue older traditions in which the hearth was the centre of the home, suggesting that on the farms and the smaller villas there was something corresponding to a kitchen-living-room. The German site at Mayen, so often quoted in connection with villa development, had the hearth in the central room throughout most of its history,[2] and the excavation of the villa at Boscoreale showed a similar state of things in the villa *rustica* there.[3] The plan of this Campanian villa gives us a very complete picture of the large living-room with a central hearth, together with the lead cistern holding the bath water supported on masonry foundations in one corner.

[1] J. Liversidge, 'Kitchens in Roman Britain', *Arch. N.L.* VI (1957) 82–5.
[2] *Bonner Jahrbücher* CXXXIII (1928) 51 *et seq.*
[3] Mau-Kelsey (1902) p. 361.

115   The kitchen, the House of the Vettii, Pompeii

This was fed by a reservoir in the court outside. Stairs lead to an upper storey
and a door opens into the stables next door. At the back of the room is a niche,
designed to resemble the façade of a small temple, the home of the household
gods, the *Lares* and *Penates*. Horace enjoyed dining in a room of this type when
visiting his Sabine farm, talking to his friends as he ate while his slaves sat
round another table and enjoyed their meal at the same time.

In most Italian houses by this period, however, the hearth had been moved
from the *atrium* to a separate kitchen nearby. A number of examples have been
identified at Pompeii. In many of them work was probably largely carried on
in the open air with only the shelter of a canvas awning. Their most recognisable feature is the raised platform of masonry, faced on top with tiles and often
fitted with a curb, and with a coat of *opus signinum* applied over the front. This
was the hearth. In the House of the Vettii, the bronze vessels were found lying
on it, the kettle still standing on its tripod over the charcoal and, perhaps, just
coming to the boil when the house collapsed during the eruption of Vesuvius
(fig. 115).[1] In one of the two kitchens identified in the House of the Dioscuri,
openings at floor-level in front of the hearth were used for fuel storage, a drain
led out of the room near one wall, and at one end of the hearth stood a small
rectangular oven built of rubble with a coating of mortar. This may have been
used for baking pastry as a bronze pastry mould was found nearby. In the other
kitchen, a cistern next door was presumably fed with rain-water by a pipe from
the roof, and this may have been used for washing up at the sink, a basin made
of small stones covered with mortar inside and out. A base found near a small
shelf may have supported one end of a wooden kitchen table, the other end

[1] J. Liversidge, *op. cit.* p. 85.

resting on the hearth itself.[1] In the villa of Diomedes a stone table was placed against one wall and another small oven was found standing on the hearth.[2]

In the larger British villas the kitchen was also placed in a separate room. So far the hearth on top of a raised platform of masonry has not been found, but the existence of at least one probable example in a town house at Silchester suggests that in some cases it may have been overlooked.[3] The Newport fireplace ended its life as a cooking hearth and the excavators found it still covered in ashes, with the shoulder-blade of an ox dropped nearby. Burnt material and three small cooking-pots, one containing animal bones, occurred in a small kitchen at Stroud, and potsherds and food debris with slightly raised hearths in kitchens at Folkstone, one hearth having a rubbish pit behind it. Rubbish pits may indicate the whereabouts of kitchens at Lullingstone and the contents included charcoal, animal bones with knife cuts showing where the meat had been sliced off them, and iron knives. A more substantial thatched structure 20 feet square was found in 1957 west of the house. It contained three ovens cut into the floor. A similar hut was reported from North Cray, and a kitchen identified at Frocester Court had a baking oven in one corner and a cooking oven and a soakaway partitioned off in another. Other evidence for villa culinary activities include a three-legged iron tripod found at Brading and a copper jug or kettle with an iron handle from the well at Chew Stoke. Proof that this had been used for boiling water was provided by the deposit of kettle 'fur' on the inside. It had come apart at the seams and been clumsily resoldered with tin. And a stone-paved room at Spoonley Wood contained a well and two stone uprights believed to be the supports for a table. No hearth was found, possibly one on a masonry foundation passed unnoticed, as this too was probably the kitchen. A lively picture of the kitchen staff in action is provided by one of the scenes from the Igel monument which shows one man putting the kettle on top of a raised hearth while another uses the bellows to revive the fire (Pl. 31). Nearby the bakers are at work, measuring flour out of a sack and kneading dough.[4]

Another feature of importance to the cook is the oven and some examples of this have already been mentioned from Britain and Pompeii. Ovens for baking and roasting were usually small domed constructions resembling a low beehive in shape, and built of rubble and tiles or stone. One found sunk into the *opus*

[1] L. Richardson, 'Pompeii: The Casa Dioscuri and its Painters', *Memoirs of the American Academy in Rome* XXIII (1955) 71.
[2] Mau-Kelsey (1902) p. 357.
[3] G. E. Fox, 'Excavations on the site of the Roman city at Silchester', *Arch.* LIII (1892) 278.
[4] E. VI p. 442 no. 5268.

signinum floor at the Ashtead villa was lined with tiles, sloping inwards towards its cement floor, and contained an 8-inch deposit of charcoal. Nearby was a hearth made of four large tiles with a shallow rubbish pit behind it. The floor of the room was covered with charcoal, potsherds and food debris so here we probably have an example of yet another kitchen. A small oven, oval in shape, found at Atworth, had a central flue 3 feet 8 inches long and 8 inches in width; it closely resembled two ovens found on the site of a possible bakery at Topsham, near Exeter.[1] Another example from the dwelling or *mansio* site at Leadenwell, Bourton-on-the-Water, was 3 feet long and 2 feet broad at its widest point, narrowing to 10 inches at the mouth of the flue. It was built of layers of small stones, the local oolite, which were found reddened with heat. Larger stones were used to line the flue and the clay floor of the oven sloped gradually downwards from the back to the mouth, giving a total drop of about 14 inches. The cook lit a fire of wood or charcoal inside, helped by the draught from the flue. When the required temperature was reached the ashes were raked out and the food was put in, the oven mouth being covered over to retain the heat.[2] In the towns bread and pastry may sometimes have been obtainable from the bakers but in the country all cooking would have to be done at home. The small portable oven or *clibanus*, of earthenware, iron, bronze or even of more precious metals, may also have been used for baking in small quantities or for keeping food hot, as it could be stood on the table in the dining-room. It also had a domed ceiling and double walls and floors. A charcoal fire was lit between the floors and the heat percolated between the walls. Apicius gives a recipe for meat, cooked in a *clibanus*. Neck of beef or mutton should first be boiled and then put in the oven in a pan with herbs, honey and pepper, and roasted until cooked. Stuffed dormice were among other items cooked in much the same way or they could be placed on a tile and baked in the big oven.[3]

[1] *Reports and Transactions of the Devon Association* LXXI (1939) 194.
[2] B. and G.T. LVII (1935) 260.
[3] E. Rosenbaum and B. Flower, *Apicius: the Roman Cookery Book* (1958) pp. 161, 205.

Chapter 9
Select bibliography of villas mentioned in the text

Alresford, Essex: R.C.H.M. *Essex* III (1922) p. 5.

Angmering, Sussex: *Sus.A.C.* LXXIX (1938) 3–44; LXXX (1939) 88–92; LXXXIV (1945) 82–107; LXXXVI (1947) 1–21.

Apethorpe, Northamptonshire: V.C.H. *Northamptonshire* I (1902) p. 191.

Ashtead, Surrey: *Sur.A.C.* XXXVII (1927) 144–63; XXXVIII (1929) 1–17, 132–48.

Atworth, Wiltshire: *W.A.M.* XLIX (1940–2) 46–95.

Barton Farm, Gloucestershire: B. and G.T. XXXIII (1910) 69.

Bathford, Somerset: V.C.H. *Somerset* I (1906) p. 300.

Bawdrip, Somerset: *J.R.S.* XLVII (1957) 221 fig. 28, Pl. VII. 4.

Bibury, Gloucestershire: Witts (1883) p. 55.

Bignor, Sussex: Lysons, III: V.C.H. *Sussex* III (1935) p. 20. A detailed account of the earlier excavations by G. Herbert and S. Winbolt is kept in the Brighton and Worthing Public Reference Libraries. *J.R.S.* XLIX (1959) 131; L. (1960) 234; LII (1962) 189; LIII (1963) 155.

Borough Hill, Northamptonshire: V.C.H. *Northamptonshire* I (1902) p. 191.

Boughton Monchelsea, Kent: V.C.H. *Kent* III (1932) p. 105.

Box, Wiltshire: *W.A.M.* XXXIII (1904) 236–69.

Boxmoor, Hertfordshire: V.C.H. *Hertfordshire* IV (1914) p. 154.

Boxted, Kent: V.C.H. *Kent* III (1932) p. 106.

Brading, Isle of Wight: V.C.H. *Hampshire* I (1900) p. 313; J. and F. G. Price: *A Description of the Remains of Roman Buildings at Morton, near Brading* (1881); Hinks (1933) p. 55 fig. 62.

Bramdean, Hampshire: V.C.H. *Hampshire* I (1900) p. 307.

Brantingham, Yorkshire: *J.R.S.* LIII (1963) 131, Pls. XI, XII; Toynbee (1964) p. 286.

Brislington, Somerset: V.C.H. *Somerset* I (1906) p. 303.

Broadwell, Gloucestershire: *J.R.S.* XII (1922) 262.

Burham, Kent: V.C.H. *Kent* III (1932) p. 109.

Callow Hill, Oxfordshire: N. Thomas, 'Excavations at Callow Hill,' *Oxoniensia* XXII (1957) 11–53: V.C.H. *Oxfordshire* I (1939) p. 313.

Calne (Nuthills), Wiltshire: *W.A.M.* XLIV (1929) 49–59; *J.R.S.* XIV (1924) 237.

Camborne, Cornwall: *Ant. J.* XII (1932) 71–2; *J.R.S.* XXII (1932) 216.

Carisbrooke, Isle of Wight: V.C.H. *Hampshire* I (1900) p. 316; C. R. Smith *Collectanea Antiqua* VI (1868) p. 126.

Castle-Dykes (North Stainley), Yorkshire: *Arch. J.* XXXII (1875) 135–54; *Y.A.J.* XXVII (1924) p. 212.

Castlefield, Hampshire: V.C.H. *Hampshire* I (1900) p. 302.

Chedworth, Gloucestershire: B. and G.T. LXXVIII (1958) 5–23; *Arch. J.* XLIV (1887) 322–36; Richmond (1960).

Cherington, Gloucestershire: *Arch.* XVIII (1817) 112–25.

Chew Stoke, Somerset: *Archaeology* IX (1956) 110; *J.R.S.* XLV (1955) 139.

Chipping Warden, Northamptonshire: V.C.H. *Northamptonshire* I (1902) p. 200.

Clanville, Hampshire: V.C.H. *Hampshire* I (1900) p. 295; *Arch.* LVI (1898) 1–20.

Clatterford, Hampshire: V.C.H. *Hampshire* I (1900) p. 317.

Cobham, Surrey: *J.R.S.* XXXV (1945) 88; *Sur.A.C.* L (1947) 73–98.

Colerne, Wiltshire: *W.A.M.* XLV (1932) 184.

Comb End, Gloucestershire: *Arch.* IX (1789) 319–22; XVIII (1817) 112–13.

Combe Down, Somerset: V.C.H. *Somerset* I (1906) p. 309.

Compton, Surrey: *Sur.A.C.* XXVIII (1915) 41–50.

Compton Abdale, Gloucestershire: *J.R.S.* XXII (1932) 214. Finds and report in Cheltenham Museum.

Cotterstock, Northamptonshire: V.C.H. *Northamptonshire* I (1902) p. 192.

Cox Green, Buckinghamshire: *J.R.S.* L (1960) 233.

Darenth, Kent: V.C.H. *Kent* III (1932) p. 111; *Arch. Cant.* XXII (1897) 49–84.

Denton, Lincolnshire: *J.R.S.* L (1960) 222. *Reports and Papers of the Lincolnshire Architectural & Arch. Soc.* X (1964) 75–100.

Ditchley, Oxfordshire: V.C.H. *Oxfordshire* I (1939) p. 311; *Oxoniensia* I (1936) 24.

Dry Hill, Gloucestershire: W. H. Gomonde, *Notes on Cheltenham* (1849) p. 8.

Eastbourne, Sussex: V.C.H. *Sussex* III (1935) p. 24.

East Coker, Somerset: V.C.H. *Somerset* I (1906) p. 329.

East Grimstead, Wiltshire: H. Sumner, *Excavations at East Grimstead* (1924).

East Malling, Kent: *Arch. Cant.* LXXI (1957) 228–9.

Eccles, Kent: *Arch. Cant.* LXXVIII (1964) 125–41; LXXIX (1965) 121–35.

Ely, Glamorganshire: *J.R.S.* XI (1921) 67–85; *Cardiff Naturalists' Society Transactions* XXVI (1895) 125–8; L (1920) 24–44; LV (1925) 19–45.

Engleton, Staffordshire: *Staffordshire Records Society* (1938) p. 267.

Exning (Landwade), Suffolk: *J.R.S.* L (1960) 228.

Farnham, Surrey: *J.R.S.* XXXVII (1947) 175; *Sur.A.C.* LIV (1955) 47–57.

Farningham, Kent: V.C.H. *Kent* III (1932) p. 113; *J.R.S.* XXXIX (1949) 110. Information from Lt.-Col. Meates.

Fifehead Neville, Dorset: D.N.H.A.S.P. XXIV (1903) 172–7; L (1929) 92–6.

Folkestone, Kent: S. Winbolt, *Roman Folkestone* (1925); V.C.H. *Kent* III (1932) p. 114.

Foscott, Buckinghamshire: *G.M.* (1838 i) 302; (1841 i) 81; (1843 i) 303; R.C.H.M. *Buckinghamshire* II (1913) pp. 115, 286.

Frampton (Maiden Newton), Dorset: R.C.H.M. *Dorset* (1952) p. 152, Lysons, I; D.N.H.A.S.P. LXXVIII (1957) 81–3.

Frilford, Berkshire: V.C.H. *Berkshire* I (1906) p. 207; *Arch. J.* LIV (1897) 340–54; *The Times*, 1 December 1883.

Frocester Court, Gloucestershire: *J.R.S.* LII (1962) 182; LIV (1964) 171; LV (1965) 216. Information from Capt. H. S. Gracie, R.N.

Fullerton, Gloucestershire: *Athenaeum*, 23 February 1905, 250; *J.R.S.* XXI (1931) 242; LIV (1964) 174; LV (1965) 217.

Gadebridge Park, Hemel Hempstead, Hertfordshire: *J.R.S.* LV (1965) 211.

Gayton Thorpe, Norfolk: *Norfolk Archaeology* XXIII (1927) 166.

Grateley, Hampshire: H.F.C. VI (1910) 341–2; VIII (1919) 107–8; XVII (1952) 58–9.

Great Barrington, Gloucestershire: Notes and letter from W. H. Knowles in Haverfield Library, Oxford, mentions mosaics etc.

Great Staughton, Huntingdonshire: *J.R.S.* XLIX (1959) 118; L (1960) 225.

Great Weldon, Northamptonshire: *J.R.S.* XLVI (1956) 133; XLVII (1957) 213; V.C.H. *Northamptonshire* I (1902) p. 193.

Greetwell, Lincolnshire: *Arch. J.* XLI (1884) 321; XLIX (1892) 258–62; A.A.S.R. XXI (1891) 48–52.

Hadstock, Essex: *Arch. J.* VIII (1851) 27–35; R. Neville, *Antiqua Explorata* (1851) p. 37; R.C.H.M. *Essex* I (1916) pp. xxiv, 143; C.A.S.P. XLIV (1951) 13, Pls. I, II.

Hambleden, Buckinghamshire: *Arch.* LXXI (1921) 141–98.

Ham Hill, Somerset: *J.R.S.* III (1913) 127–33; *Som.A.P.* LII (1907) 160–1; LIII (1908) 179–82.

Hanwell, Oxfordshire: V.C.H. *Oxfordshire* I (1939) pp. 308, 327.

Haresfield, Gloucestershire: Witts (1883) p. 62.

Harpham, Yorkshire: *Hull Museum Publications*, 25 January 1905; further excavations in 1949.

Hartlip, Kent: V.C.H. *Kent* III (1932) p. 117.

Highdown Hill, Sussex: *Sus, A.C.* LXXX (1939) 63–88; LXXXI (1940) 173–203.

High Wycombe, Buckinghamshire: *Records of Bucks*, XVI (1959) 227–57.

Hinton St Mary, Dorset: J. Toynbee, 'A New Roman Mosaic found in Dorset', *J.R.S.* LIV (1964) 7–14.

Holbury, Hampshire: V.C.H. *Hampshire* I (1900) p. 312; *W.A.M.* XIII (1872) 33–41, 276–9.

Horkstow, Lincolnshire: E. Trollope, *Sleaford and the Wapentakes of Flaxwell and Ashwardhurn* (1872) p. 61; H. E. Dudley, *Early Days in North-West Lincolnshire* (Scunthorpe 1949) p. 164; Hinks, p. 102, figs. 112–24.

Hucclecote, Gloucestershire: B. and G.T. LV (1933) 323–76.

Ickleton, Cambridgeshire: *Arch. J.* VI (1849) 14–26; *J.B.A.A.* IV (1849) 356–78; C.A.S.P. XLIV (1951) 14, Pls. III, IV.

Iwerne Minster, Dorset: *Arch. J.* CIV (1948) 48–62.

Kemsing, Kent: *Arch. Cant.* LXIII (1950) xliv.

Keynsham, Somerset: *Arch.* LXXV (1926) 109–38.

Kingsworthy, Hampshire: *J.R.S.* XV (1925) 243; XXIV (1944) 83.

Knowl Hill, Berkshire: *Berkshire Arch. J.* XXVI (1932) 28–36; XXXVIII (1934) 75–84.

Langton, Yorkshire: Corder, (1932).

Linley Hall, Shropshire: V.C.H. *Shropshire* I (1908) p. 257.

Little Chart, Kent: *Arch. Cant.* LXXI (1957) 130–46.

Littlecote Park, Ramsbury, Wiltshire: Mosaic illustrated in I.A. Richmond (1947a) opp. p. 33.

Llanfrynach (Brecknockshire): *Bulletin of the Board of Celtic Studies* XIII (1949) 105–8.

Llantwit Major, Glamorganshire: *Arch. Camb.* CII (1953) 89–163.

Lockleys, Hertfordshire: *Ant. J.* XVIII (1938) 339–76. For a possible bath-house see A. G. Rook, 'The Dicket Mead site', *Ant. J.* XLIV (1964) 143.

Low Ham, Somerset: *Som.A.P.* XCII (1947) 25–8; *Somerset and Dorset Notes and Queries* XXV (1950) 1–6; 61–4; 141–3; XXVII (1961) 58–61; *J.R.S.* XXXVI (1946) 142, Pl. II; XXXVII (1947) 173.

Low Leyton, Essex: R.C.H.M. *Essex* II (1921) p. 166.

Lufton, Somerset: *Som.A.P.* XCVII (1953) 91–112.

Lullingstone, Kent: *J.R.S.* L (1960) 234; XLVIII (1958) 149; G. W. Meates *Lullingstone Roman Villa* (1955); Toynbee (1964) p. 220 *et seq.*

Mansfield Woodhouse, Nottinghamshire: *Transactions of the Thoroton Society* LIII (1950) 1–14.

Margate, Kent: *J.R.S.* XIV (1924) 240.

Milhampost, Gloucestershire: Letter from Mr St Clair Baddeley to Professor Haverfield in Haverfield Library, Oxford; B. and G.T. LII (1931) 165.

Newport, Hampshire: *Ant. J.* IV (1929) 141–51; *J.B.A.A.* N.S. XXXVI (1931) 81–3.

Newton St Loe, Somerset: *J.R.S.* XXVI (1936) 43; V.C.H. *Somerset* I (1906) p. 302.

North Cray: *J.R.S.* XLVII (1958) 149.

North Leigh, Oxfordshire: V.C.H. *Oxfordshire* I (1939) p. 317; *J.R.S.* XXXIV (1944) 81; Skelton, *Antiquities of Oxfordshire*, Wootton Hundred (1823) p. 10.

North Warnborough, Hampshire: H.F.C.X. (1931) 225–36; *J.R.S.* XIX (1929) 205; XXI (1931) 242–5.

North Wraxall, Wiltshire: *W.A.M.* VII (1862) 59–75.

Norton Disney, Lincolnshire: *Ant. J.* XVII (1937) 138–78.

Old Durham, Durham: *Arch. Ael.* (4) XXII (1944) 1–21; XXIX (1951) 203–12; XXXI (1953) 116; Salway (1965) p. 153.

Orpington, Kent: V.C.H. *Kent* III (1932) p. 122.

Otford, Kent: V.C.H. *Kent* III (1932) p. 122; *Arch. Cant.* XXXIX (1927) 153–8 XLII (1930) 157–71; Hinks p. 56 fig. 64 (upper half upside down).

Painswick, Gloucestershire: B. and G.T. XXVII (1904) 156–71.

Park Street, Hertfordshire: *Arch. J.* CII (1946) 21–110; *Arch. J.* CXVIII (1963) 100–35.

Pitney, Somerset: V.C.H. *Somerset* I (1906) p. 326.

Ridgewell, Essex: *Arch.* XIV (1803) 61–74; R.C.H.M. *Essex* I (1916) p. xxiv.

Rodmarton, Gloucestershire: *Arch.* XVIII (1817) 112–25.

Rothley, Leicestershire: V.C.H. *Leicestershire* I (1907) p. 217; *Leic. Arch. Soc. Trans.* IX (1904) 157–8; A.A.S.R. XXVI (1902) 485–9.

Rudston, Yorkshire: *Y.A.J.* XXXI (1934) 366–76; XXXII (1934–6) 214–20; XXXIII (1936–8) 81–6, 321–34; I. A. Richmond, *The Roman Pavements at Rudston* (Leeds, 1935).

Saunderton, Buckinghamshire: *Records of Bucks.* XIII (1939) 398–426.

Scampton, Lincolnshire: C. Illingworth, *Account of Scampton* (1810).

Seaton, Devonshire: *Reports and Transactions of the Devon Association* II (1868) 379–81; LIV (1923) 66–8; *Ant. J.* I (1921) 237–8; *J.R.S.* XII (1922) 268.

Shoreham, Kent: *Arch. Cant.* LXI (1948) 181.

Southwick, Sussex: V.C.H. *Sussex* III (1935) pp. 25, 70; *Sus.A.C.* LXXIII (1932) 12–32; *Sussex Notes and Queries* V (1935) 52, 90–1.

Spoonley Wood, Gloucestershire: *Arch.* LII (1890) 651–68.

Stanton Chair, Suffolk: *J.R.S.* XXIX (1939) 214; *Proceedings of the Suffolk Archaeological Institute* XXV (1951) 214.

Stanton St Quintin, Wiltshire: *W.A.M.* XXXVIII (1914) 322.

Star villa, Shipham, Somerset: *Som.A.P.* CVIII (1964) 45–93.

Stonesfield, Oxfordshire: V.C.H. *Oxfordshire* I (1939) p. 315.

Stroud, Hampshire: *Arch. J.* LXV (1908) 57–60; LXVI (1909) 33–52.

Tarrant Hinton, Dorset: J. Hutchins, *History of Dorset* I (1861) p. 318.

Thistleton, Rutland: *J.R.S.* LI (1961) 175 fig. 22.

Thornford, Dorset: D.F.C.I. (1877) 41–9; R.C.H.M. *Dorset* (1952) p. 249.

Thruxton, Hampshire: V.C.H. *Hampshire* I (1900) p. 299; Hinks, p. 101.

Tingewick, Buckinghamshire: R.C.H.M. *Buckinghamshire* II (1913) p. 299; *Records of Bucks.* IV (1869) 36.

Titsey, Surrey: *Sur.A.C.* IV (1869) 214–37.

Tockington, Gloucestershire: B. and G.T. XII (1887) 159–69; XIII (1888–9) 196–202.

Tracy Park, Gloucestershire: *J.B.A.A.* XXXIV (1878) 248–9.

Wadfield, Gloucestershire: B. and G.T. LV (1933) 336; *J.B.A.A.* I (1895) 242–50.

Walton-on-the-Hill, Surrey: *Sur.A.C.* LI (1950) 65–81; V.C.H. *Surrey* IV (1912) p. 369.

Werrington, Northamptonshire: *J.R.S.* LIII (1963) 135.

West Blatchington, Sussex: *Sus.A.C.* LXXXIX (1950) 35–41.

West Dean, Hampshire: *W.A.M.* XXII (1885) 243–50.

West Meon, Hampshire: *Arch. J.* LXIV (1907) 1–14.

Whatley, Somerset: V.C.H. *Somerset* I (1906) p. 317.

Wheatley, Oxfordshire: V.C.H *Oxfordshire* I (1939) p. 322; *Arch. J.* II (1846) 350–6.

Whittington Court, Gloucestershire: B. and G.T. LXXI (1952) 13–87.

Whittlebury, Northamptonshire: V.C.H. *Northamptonshire* I (1902) p. 199.

Wiggonholt, Sussex: *Sus.A.C.* LXXVIII (1937) 13–36; LXXX (1940) 54–67.

Wincanton, Somerset. *Som.A.P.* XVI (1871) 14–16.

Wingham, Kent: V.C.H. *Kent* III (1932) p. 125; *Antiquity* XVIII (1944) 52.

Winterton, Lincolnshire: H. E. Dudley, *Early Days in North-West Lincolnshire* (Scunthorpe, 1949) p. 131; J.R.S.L. (1960) 221; LIV (1964) 159 fig. 10; *Ant.J.* XLVI (1966) 72–84.

Witcombe, Gloucestershire: B. and G.T. LXXIII (1954) 5–69.

Withington, Gloucestershire: *Arch.* XVIII (1817) 118; Hinks, p. 113 figs. 125–8.

Woodchester, Gloucestershire: S. Lysons, *Account of Woodchester* (1797); Hinks, p. 96 fig. 107; B. and G.T. LXXIV (1956) 172–5.

Woolaston, Gloucestershire: *Arch. Camb.* XCIII (1938) 93–125.

Worsham Bottom, Oxfordshire: V.C.H. *Oxfordshire* I (1939) p. 319.

Yatton, Somerset: V.C.H. *Somerset* III (1906) p. 306.

10
Life in the villas (2)
Interior decoration

As in the case of the town houses, the interior decorators were hard at work in country dwellings which were gay with painted walls and mosaic floors. One of the best examples of wall decoration yet found is the 'Painted Room' from the Iwerne villa excavated by General Pitt-Rivers and H. St George Gray in 1897. Several photographs recording it survive and these show a scheme of panels outlined by a framework of stripes and lines, described in the excavator's notes as painted red, yellow and green. Below them came a white dado stippled with small flecks of pink. Traces of a green leaf design were distinguishable between the panels. Records also survive of part of a painted wall from some other nineteenth-century excavations, those at Carisbrooke, Isle of Wight (fig. 116). The drawings show a dado *in situ* with alternate rectangles painted red or green and outlined in white, in a room with a mosaic floor.

Collections of painted fragments survive from many villa sites, silent witnesses to lost glories. The variety of designs found at Box, intended to imitate the marbles and other decorative stones used for wall-veneers, has already been mentioned (page 87). Such imitation marbling occurs at numerous other villas including Bignor, Ely, Hadstock, Llantwit Major or Great Weldon. Traces of the frameworks of stripes and lines belonging to panel decoration are also common at Box, Woodchester, Brading or Boxmoor among other sites. Purple

116 View of a room in the Carisbrooke villa, Isle of Wight

was the predominant colour chosen for the fourth-century bath-house excavated at Great Staughton in 1958 with red, blue, yellow, black and white. Evidence was found there for white panels delineated by narrow purple lines. These panels were probably decorated with geometric designs such as the multi-coloured circles surrounding the central quatrefoil found at Hadstock, with the mark of the Roman compass point still clearly visible. A graceful arabesque is among unpublished material from Witcombe and fleurs-de-lys have been found at Ickleton and Lullingstone. Floral motifs included fragments with large flowers recorded from the villa at Greetwell on the outskirts of Lincoln and from Castle-Dykes, Yorkshire. One room at North Leigh had both walls and ceiling adorned with olive foliage and fillets of red, green and yellow, above **a dado** of brown and yellow. According to the excavator, birds, flowers, stars and other fanciful objects decorated the walls at Ickleton. The birds unfortunately have failed to survive although they are known from other villas, including a possible parrot from Brading. The flowers certainly included some roses, carefully painted in varying shades of red with green leaves, which are still in existence. For other fanciful objects, Ickleton has produced the gable end of a building

275

117 Wall-painting, Comb End villa, Gloucestershire

which it is tempting to imagine belonged to a painting of the villa itself, and the
life-size foot of a dancing girl, perhaps a nymph or Maenad, from some Dionysiac scene. Obviously, this small country villa possessed very impressive wall-
paintings, the only evidence for life-size figure scenes so far found in this
country. Other sites, however, have produced evidence for figures on a smaller
scale, one example being the Winged Cupid from Winterton (Pl. 17*a*). Also
impressive is a painting recorded by Lysons in a drawing after he saw it **in** 1779
in situ on a wall from the villa at Comb End (Gloucestershire). It showed the
lower part of a large scene, 135 feet in length, with the feet and part of the
draperies of human figures, together with portions of several pillars (fig. 117).
Apparently two personages on the left are about to receive two running figures
who come from the right but their identity remains a mystery. Beyond them a
design of squares, etc., may indicate masonry, perhaps a building. The pillars
are outlined in black on a white ground and so are the figures but they are also
shaded in red. Below the scene is a red horizontal stripe edged with fine black
and white lines and an orange-coloured dado. Part of the dado is covered by a
later redecoration of white rectangles outlined in black.[1]

The most important villa of all, however, for the study of wall-painting is
Lullingstone. Excavations began there in 1949 and have so far revealed a
dwelling-house with many remarkable features, a barn and some interesting
burials. The site is beside the river Darent, near Eynsford in Kent, at the foot of a
steep slope. Since Roman times a considerable quantity of silt has been washed
down this slope until the villa became deeply buried. To this circumstance it owes
its preservation, and the fact that some of the wall-painting survived *in situ* on
walls still standing in some cases to quite a considerable height. In the second-
century baths the exterior of the walls was cream-washed and stippled in red,
yellow and blue and the fragments from the interior include realistic looking
fish, possibly trout, swimming in blue water. They probably adorned the cold-
plunge bath. At the other end of the house a tiled staircase led down to a lower
level, between walls painted to about shoulder height with a red trellis work and

---

[1] For a detailed and more fully illustrated account of villa wall-painting see J. Liversidge,
'Furniture and Interior Decoration', in A. L. F. Rivet ed. *The Roman Villa in Britain* Chap. V
(forthcoming).

a balustrade. Turning right, more steps led down into a basement room which was probably a *nymphaeum*, a shrine of the water nymphs. The white walls were decorated with panels lightly outlined in yellow, green and red with broader yellow stripes, above a dado of rectangles and lozenges with 'fried egg' marbling in the same colours. At intervals yellow trees, probably date-palms hung with bunches of scarlet fruit, separated the panels. In the south wall, nearly opposite the staircase, was a niche about 3 feet high, filled in at a later period. When the excavators removed this filling they found a charming painting of the presiding deities: three water nymphs. The best preserved nymph appears as a standing figure in the centre. She wears a yellow cloak and necklace and bracelets, and on her head is an aureole of green leaves and a diadem. In one hand she holds a green fern frond. Her companions are seated and were badly damaged when later occupants of the villa fixed up a shelf in the niche. They too have leafy aureoles and similar jewellery and also necklaces of blue beads. One nymph wore a red cloak, the other a blue, and the blue-clad damsel rests her hand upon an overturned urn from which flows down a stream of blue water. When complete this composition must have been of outstanding beauty. The wistful appeal of the face which has survived shows that this work may be compared with the finest examples of Roman art. Later, this part of the villa may have fallen into disuse. When the house was rebuilt towards the end of the third century, the *nymphaeum* was re-decorated with a simple scheme of red and yellow horizontal stripes running round the lower parts of the cream-painted walls. Red vertical stripes occur at each corner of the room; these are a regular feature of the Roman wall-paintings found in Italy and elsewhere. Two busts portraying two men, possibly father and son and probably belonging to the owner of the second-century house, were placed on the steps with two pots probably containing offerings.[1] The spirits of the earlier inhabitants having been thus propitiated, the room was then sealed up. By about the middle of the fourth century, rooms had been built above the *nymphaeum* and these were decorated with the elaborate series of wall-paintings discussed below.[2] Elsewhere in the villa the fourth-century corridor walls were painted a subdued reddish-brown enlivened with groups of thin orange stripes. In the south corridor, on the wall next to the reception room with its fine mosaic floors, was a scheme of white panels divided by deep red and purple pillars and covered with purple curvilinear motifs, probably representing the veining of marble, still a favourite type of decoration.

Romano-British villas have produced a rich harvest of mosaic floors, in fact a list of them would include several hundred items. In some cases *tesserae* of one

[1] See below pp. 284, 292.　[2] Page 459.

colour and material were used, usually red tile, to make a durable floor without a pattern. Even on sites with figured mosaics, the plain tessellation is often found, either as a surround intended to show up the designs and enable the passer-by to avoid walking on them, or else used alone in corridors and unimportant rooms. Many villas produce nothing but loose polychrome *tesserae*, a sad commentary on the amount of material which existed and has been destroyed. Plain tessellation, loose *tesserae* and geometric mosaics are found scattered all over the civilian areas of the province as far north as northern Yorkshire. The figured mosaics, however, tend to occur in the south, south-west and north-east and they form a fascinating study.[1] Like those found in town houses they illustrate Roman mythology by means of representations of deities, or of scenes from well-known myths; in many cases they must have been chosen for their religious and symbolic interest as well as designed as a pleasant decoration. This is clearly shown by a group of pavements depicting the god Orpheus with his zoological following, arranged in a manner which seems to be peculiar to Roman Britain.

Gloucestershire is a county rich in villas and also in figured mosaics, three of which are concerned with Orpheus. They come from Woodchester, Withington, and Barton Farm on the outskirts of the town of Corinium (Cirencester). A fourth example was also found in Corinium, in a town house. In all of them Orpheus appeared in the centre, sitting on a rock and playing his lyre, with his dog beside him. At Woodchester and Barton Farm (Pl. 37*a*) he is surrounded by processions of birds and animals arranged in two concentric friezes. At Withington the birds are relegated from this central position to two oblong borders running outside the circular animal frieze. Probably 11 animals are portrayed at Woodchester, 8 at Withington and 6 at Barton Farm. They are divided from one another by conventionalised trees or branches, and small twigs separate the birds at Woodchester and Barton Farm. The treatment of the subject in the mosaics of these two sites is so similar (note also the circular wreath of shaded leaves which occurs in both) that it seems very probable that they are the work of the same artist, who had adapted his design to fit rooms of varying size. The animals from the Woodchester mosaic are particularly well done and a circular band, filled with a fine acanthus-scroll sprouting from the ears of a mask of Pan or Oceanus, encloses the Orpheus scene. In the corners of the square frame of geometric motifs in which the great medallion is inscribed are pairs of graceful reclining females, possibly water nymphs. Wide borders of fine geometric work fill up the rest of the room. The pavement is uncovered

[1] For a more detailed discussion of villa mosaics see D. Smith, 'Mosaic Pavements' in Rivet ed. *op. cit.* Chap. IV; and Toynbee (1964) Chap. VI.

every few years and, while part of it, including Orpheus, has been destroyed, it is still a magnificent sight. The villa possessed at least one other figured mosaic, showing Satyrs and Maenads. One complete panel contained two boys with a basket of fruit and foliage and the words *bonum eventum* ([we wish] you happiness) inscribed beneath them and another panel had simply the words *bene c[olite]* (enjoy yourselves!). These subjects were presumably intended to represent joy and prosperity in this world and the next. The Orpheus scene at Withington occupies only one third of the pavement and the remainder comprises hunting and sea scenes, both fragmentary. A complete panel, now in the British Museum, shows Oceanus armed with a trident and with lobster claws growing out of his hair. He is surrounded by dolphins and sea beasts. Pavements from Comb End, near Colesbourne, are said to have portrayed scenes with animals and fish which may have belonged to another Orpheus mosaic, but unfortunately no pictures of these scenes survive. The pavement from the Corinium town-house seems to have had much in common with the one from Barton Farm.

In Somerset, mosaics of rather inferior workmanship decorated with friezes of animals are recorded at Newton St Loe and Whatley. Orpheus himself survived at the first site but can only be suspected at the second. Further east he appears at Brading in a circular medallion set in a corridor floor, playing his lyre to a fox, some birds and a charming monkey wearing a red cap, a smaller audience than usual. Travelling inland to Wiltshire, Orpheus reappears on a pavement found in 1730 at Littlecote Park, Ramsbury. Here he has lost all his usual companions. He stands alone with his lyre in the central medallion surrounded by a circular border divided into four panels. On these appeared the Seasons riding on a hind, a panther, a bull, and probably an antelope, respectively.

In the north-east, two Lincolnshire villas have produced figured pavements on which appeared, among other subjects, the favourite Orpheus scene. At Winterton, a frieze of animals encircles the musician, while other pavements from this site show two female heads, one with a large horn of plenty, in two medallions. On the Orpheus pavement at Horkstow the surrounding circle is divided into eight panels, which each probably contained animals or birds. Another section of the same pavement shows a circle divided into four compartments containing mythological scenes, including Cupids, a Triton and a Nereid. The arrangement of these circular designs recalls those of elaborately decorated domed ceilings reflected, so to speak, on the floor. At Horkstow an oblong panel placed at one end of the Orpheus mosaic shows a lively chariot race in progress. Further north, across the Humber, the Yorkshire villa of Brantingham has recently produced a remarkable floor. In the centre is the bust of the Goddess of a City wearing on her curly hair a crown with turrets denoting town walls. Eight tall two-handled vases surrounded her and more female busts, arranged in two rows of four, might be lesser goddesses or even portraits (Pl. 38c). They have curly top-knots but no crowns. Round the edges of the pavement come a series of reclining water nymphs. Wall-paintings from this room probably depicted similar designs. Subjects chosen for several mosaics in the villa at Rudston (Yorkshire) include a central medallion portraying Venus in her bath, a bust of Mercury, and lunettes containing wild beasts pursued by hunters. They share certain characteristics in common with the pavements from Horkstow and Winterton and, with the mosaics from Brantingham, Aldborough and Malton, may all have been the products of a single northern school, centred perhaps at York. Its craftsmen were quite capable of producing good geometric work, as these mosaics and those found on other Yorkshire and Lincolnshire sites show, and they could also depict fish and birds with some success. The animals and human figures, however, they found difficult and apparently uncongenial themes. The Rudston Venus is a grotesque object, and so are the animals and figures which surround her. The Horkstow animals are also strange creatures and the Triton and Nereid and other figures in the same pavement have some of the awkwardness of the Rudston hunters. The Horkstow chariot race, as well as the animals from the frieze at Winterton and the Brantingham ladies, are on a higher level, and must have been done by artists more talented than those who worked on the rest of the pavements. The same situation may have arisen over the wall decorations with rather crude figure painting at Brantingham, but much finer work, including the Cupid (Pl. 17a) and another figure, fish and water plants, was recently found in a room at Winterton.

If the animals stealing round Orpheus in a bemused way symbolised to Romano-Britons the soul's enchantment by a mystic saviour, a whole series of eschatological pictures was assembled by the occupier of the Brading villa. For a single site their range is almost unparalleled throughout the Empire. In one room there survives a central bust, probably depicting Bacchus, and three oblong panels. One shows a gladiatorial combat, another a fox under a tree and part of a domed building, and a third a man with the head and legs of a cock, standing by a small hut entered by a ladder, while two winged griffins occupy the right hand of the picture. These scenes seem to have some Gnostic significance concerned with the initiation of the soul with the ladder symbolising its ascent to Heaven. The gladiators' battle may indicate the ordeals of this life, the domed building may be a shrine and the griffins the guardians of the dead. Another room has an equally elaborate floor. An oblong panel showing sea gods runs along one side of the main design which is made up of four square and four

280

triangular panels arranged round a central medallion all containing figures. The medallion is occupied by a Medusa-head and the four triangular panels by busts of the Winds blowing on conch shells. The subjects depicted in the square panels are possibly all of mythological character. We may recognise Lycurgus with his double axe, attacking the nymph Ambrosia who is changing into a vine, and Triptolemus receiving corn ears and a plough-share from Ceres. The third panel, partly destroyed, shows a Maenad fleeing from a Satyr, while in the fourth are a youth wearing a Phrygian cap and carrying a shepherd's crook and panpipes, and a Maenad who seems to be playing on a tambourine. A small oblong panel depicting an astronomer, accompanied by a globe standing on a three-legged stool and a sundial, covers the threshold leading up to the next room. Here, although much of the mosaic has perished, enough remains to show that the semicircles in the corners contain heads of the Seasons, three of which survive, and birds. The square panels in the centre of the floor portrayed more mythological themes: Perseus rescuing Andromeda is the only picture which remains.

Other villas which also possessed pavements showing a variety of scenes include Bramdean, Frampton, Pitney and Keynsham, but of these only parts of the Keynsham floor survive. Fine examples of the mosaicist's art, however, can still be seen at Chedworth (Pl. 39), a site remarkable for three beautiful figures of the Seasons and some panels showing gods and water nymphs. These may have been designed by the same firm who worked at Woodchester. Busts in mosaic inserted into pavements at Bramdean, Lufton (Pl. 38*b*), Fullerton and Horkstow may be family portraits. And at Bignor we may still see some of the most beautiful mosaics yet found in Roman Britain. In one room the apse-mosaic shows a head of Venus, dark-haired, surrounded by a nimbus and wearing a diadem, in a central medallion, on either side of which is a *cornucopia* and a pheasant standing on a festoon, the whole design being enclosed in a scroll-border springing out of a vase. A long frieze of cupids playing at gladiators, recalling vividly the famous painted frieze from the walls of the House of the Vettii at Pompeii, links the apse with the rest of the room. There the pavement, although largely destroyed, still retains some of the dancing cupids who occupied panels set octagonally about the (now vanished) centre of the main design. The medallion in room 7 presents Ganymede being carried off by the eagle, a favourite subject on the Continent, where it occurs at St Colombe, and on other sites.[1] Another part of the same floor shows dancing Maenads of a type which can also be paralleled elsewhere, arranged in six hexagonal panels

[1] A. Blanchet, Inventaire des mosaiques de la Gaule et de l'Afrique I (Paris 1909) no. 209; II (Paris, 1910) no. 136.

round a shallow piscina. In room 26 only fragments survive of a large pavement which once included heads of the Seasons, cupids, birds, dolphins, and fruit among its subjects. Of the Seasons, Winter, an impressive individual muffled up in a hooded cloak, alone remains. The *apodyterium* of the baths shows a head of Medusa placed in a central medallion within a geometric surround. The excavators found this very popular and ubiquitous design in another room at Bignor but there it formed part of a pavement belonging to a later period.

The Bignor mosaics were found over a hundred years ago but the important new finds made comparatively recently at Lullingstone and Low Ham show that many similar treasures may still await discovery. The Lullingstone mosaics come from the central reception rooms of the fourth-century house. They include a large square apartment with a floor mostly covered with rather amateurish geometric mosaics but with a well-worked figure scene in the centre. Its subject is the slaying of the two-headed Chimaera by the hero, Bellerophon. He flies to the attack on the winged horse Pegasus, and despatches his victim with a thin red-coloured spear. The Chimaera is shown as a small, rather pathetic, whiskered animal, an excrescence on its back denotes its second goat-like head. The rest of the scene consists of sea beasts including very prosperous looking dolphins. Apparently these were a British favourite as dolphins also appear at other sites including Witcombe, Lydney and Hemsworth, with whole borders of them at Frampton and Fifehead Neville. The Lullingstone Bellerophon mosaic seems to be a conflation of two incidents. In one, Bellerophon crosses the sea on Pegasus and in the other, he slays the Chimaera when he reaches Lycia. This theme occurs again on the mosaic from the villa at Hinton St Mary.[1] In the corners of the same pavement at Lullingstone three of the seasons survive, shown as women: a muffled-up Winter, a charming Spring with a swallow on her shoulder (Pl. 38*a*), and Summer with flowers or corn-ears in her hair.

Continuing through this room we go up a step into an apse and find a semicircular mosaic set in a border of plain *tesserae*. This was the *triclinium* or dining-room, and the diners reclining on their couches round its edge would look at a second figure-scene spread out before them. This shows a delightful figure of Europa being carried off by Jupiter, disguised as a fine white bull with a beaming smile. He is beckoned on by a winged Cupid, while a second more cautious Cupid catches hold of his tail. The figures are shown in outline on a white ground with a deep blue sea. Europa's transparent robe floats out behind her and the Cupids have dark blue wings with red stripes. The picture is full of movement, and like its companion piece with Bellerophon, the work of a skilled hand; a different hand, presumably, to that of the individual responsible for the

[1] See below p. 460.

geometric designs. Above it comes a Latin couplet reading: 'If jealous Juno had seen the swimming of the bull, she would with greater justice on her side have repaired to the halls of Aeolus'. This is an oblique allusion to Book I of Virgil's *Aeneid* where Juno persuades Aeolus, the God of the winds, to let loose a storm to sink the ship of Aeneas, then on his way to Italy. At Lullingstone the diners were entertained by the suggestion that Juno's action would have been even more appropriate when Jupiter was making off with Europa.

In south-west Britain, the Low Ham figured mosaic must have been constructed at about the same time as the one from Lullingstone. It was found in the *frigidarium* of a luxurious suite of baths which formed part of a large villa $2\frac{1}{2}$ miles east of Langport, and it may now be seen in the Castle Museum at Taunton. The *frigidarium* was a large room measuring 38 by 17 feet, with a plunge bath 11 feet square and 4 feet deep at one end. A great pillared window is believed to have existed on one side and a wooden canopy covered the bath. In front of it was a pavement which illustrates the love story of Dido and Aeneas as told by Virgil in Books I and IV of the *Aeneid*. Scene I is the long panel to the left and it can be viewed in two ways. We see three ships of the Trojan fleet and in the centre one a head with a high-crested helmet is visible. This belongs to the *Palladion*, the ancient Trojan head of Athena which Aeneas eventually took to Italy. In the third ship a man is handing out a fine jewelled collar to a figure who stands in the same plane as scene I. This is Achates, who went back to the ship to find the gifts for Aeneas to bestow upon Dido. Scene II, in the centre of the short side, shows the meeting of Dido and Aeneas, brought together by Venus who stands in the middle. Her arm is round the shoulders of Cupid, who appears in the guise of Aeneas' son Ascanius. She wears little apart from a diadem and the omission of the black *tessera* from the pupil of her right eye gives her the appearance of winking violently at Aeneas. Aeneas is shown as a bearded figure holding a spear and clad in a cuirass and a gay striped tunic and cloak, a scarlet Phrygian cap and high boots. Dido on the other side wears a red scarf and a transparent skirt and her hair is dressed in a bun or thick curl on top of her head. Overcome by the sudden appearance of the handsome Aeneas she has her finger to her lips in a gesture of astonishment which is often seen in Roman wall-paintings. Scene III is the long strip on the other side. It shows the hunt, a very lively scene with Ascanius well in the lead while Aeneas looks back to see if Dido is following. At the top, in the small scene IV, the pair have been overtaken by a storm and Dido seeks refuge in Aeneas' arms (Pl. 37*b*). As he is wearing full armour and she only a small amount of drapery, having discarded her cloak and riding boots, this cannot have been a very comfortable embrace. By rights this scene should take place in a cave, but the artist has

283

avoided the awkward problem of depicting one by providing two storm-tossed trees in its place. In the central square, scene V, Venus sums up the end of the story. On her left is a Cupid with torch upraised representing Aeneas, alive and now again on his travels. On her right another Cupid with closed eyes and torch held down denotes the deserted Dido, fated to take her own life. Apart from its artistic merits, the pavement is of particular interest as being the only British mosaic so far known in which we find a series of successive scenes illustrating different stages in the same story. The lateral scenes face outward as if intended to be viewed from outside the limits of the picture; and in this respect they recall the arrangement of some of the figured panels in the Brading mosaics. But the closest parallels to such a scheme of composition are to be found in Gaul and Africa, as, for instance, in the villa of the Liberii at Oudna, in Tunisia. At Low Ham, however, no margin was left round the walls, as in the Gaulish and African examples, to allow room for onlookers to stand and admire the scenes; and it has been suggested that a foreign, perhaps African artist, or at least an imported pattern book, may have been behind the whole design. In support of this theory an interesting comparison may be made between some details in the scenes at Low Ham, and those in a mosaic showing the Three Graces from Sabratha in Tripolitania. In the first rectangular panel at Low Ham, Venus wears a special kind of fourfold breast-and-back-chain, while Dido is distinguished by the large round curl of her hair style. In the Sabratha mosaic the Three Graces all wear the same type of decorative chain and the central member of the trio has a coiffure similar to Dido's.

Little survives of the other decorative features which once adorned the villas. Traces are occasionally found of wall mosaic but this has only been found *in situ* at Wingham (Kent). It probably existed at some other sites including Greetwell, near Lincoln, and East Malling near Maidstone. Rare examples of statuary or figured reliefs are also sometimes recorded, among them the remains of two marble sculptures from Woodchester, which are now in the British Museum. One represents a figure of Luna with a bull at her feet and a torch in her right hand, the other, part of a group showing Cupid and Psyche. The feet of another statue resting on a pedestal were also found. Other finds now in the British Museum include a small figure of Venus from the site at Froxfield (Wiltshire), and a statue of Bacchus from a grave found near the villa-site at Spoonley Wood. Fragments of statuary were also discovered at other Gloucestershire sites including Wadfield, Hucclecote and Tracy Park near Bath. The head of Ceres found in the baths at Bignor was unfortunately stolen. The outstanding examples of the sculptor's art, however, found in a British villa, are the busts from the Lullingstone *nymphaeum*. They are both of Greek, probably Pentelic marble and over life size, designed to stand in recesses or niches. Considering the vicissitudes they suffered they are surprisingly well preserved, although as is so often the case with ancient statuary, both needed new noses. Bust I in particular is remarkably complete. Bust II was more weathered. At some period before he reached the *nymphaeum* his shoulders had been shaved away and the head had been separated from the rest of the bust which was found near it. Bust I is the earlier, probably dating between A.D. 125–35 (Pl. 57). It depicts a bearded man of about 45 to 50 with thick curly hair growing low on the brow and a serene and kindly expression. He wears a tunic and a cloak with a fringed border (visible on the left shoulder), fastened on the right shoulder with a large brooch. Bust II appears to be a less serene individual of 50 to 55. His head was the first piece of sculpture discovered at Lullingstone and photographs show him regarding the twentieth century very disapprovingly as he gradually appeared in the excavation trench. When restored to his base he proved to have straighter and less thick hair and beard than his companion. He is dressed in tunic and toga. Looking at both busts one is conscious that they represent very definite personalities. Bust I was, perhaps, the more cultured man of the world, while bust II surely took a more uncompromising view of life; a strong reliable character but probably not a very happy one. His expression, however, is partly due to the deep-drilled holes which indicate the pupils of the eyes; this is one of the technical details which date bust II to between A.D. 155–65 or even later.

When the busts were first found unsuccessful attempts were made to identify them with various emperors. As there seems to be a certain likeness between them they are now believed to be family portraits, probably of father and son or uncle and nephew. Their craftsmanship suggests that they are the work of an East Mediterranean sculptor so the question arises: were they carved in Britain from imported marble by a visiting sculptor or did they arrive with some second-century official who was posted to the province of *Britannia*? It is impossible to answer this but it is permissible to recall that imported marble has been used for other sculptures found in Britain, notably those from the London Mithraeum, and the grave stones of Regina and Victor at South Shields are believed to be the work of a Palmyrene sculptor from Syria. Presumably they stood in the Phase II house of *c.* 180–200 so they may be the father and grandfather of the owner of the villa, possibly a decurion or an official of even higher rank residing in Londinium.

Among more purely architectural features from villas are the fragments of a curved parapet or balcony, carved with an open-work S design found at Chedworth and Witcombe. At Ditchley fragments of columns were discovered which must originally have been at least 12 feet tall. These are believed to belong to a

fourth-century façade on either side of an elaborate doorway, perhaps supporting a cornice. Pillars were used to support an archway in a room at North Leigh
and probably also at Keynsham, while a fine column with a carved composite
capital was found at Bathford (Somerset). Dwarf pillars from exterior corridors
or verandahs are often discovered—six examples may be seen at Chedworth
alone, and others of varying sizes were noted at Spoonley Wood.

After this rather detailed survey of the planning, construction and decoration
of the villa, the question of its place in the life of the province requires further
consideration.[1] There seems to be no doubt about the contribution it made to
agriculture; however simple or elaborate it became, the Romano-British villa
always continued its existence as a farm. One question is whether we must
always regard it as a single farm? Here the answer must sometimes have been,
no. Small independent farms probably continued to exist throughout the period
but in many cases, as time went on, some farms grew at the expense of others.
In Gaul we know there were estates with tenant farmers. We see these portrayed
on the Igel reliefs coming to pay their rent in cash or in kind to their landlord.
One such procession of tenants is headed by a man carrying a hare, behind him
come others carrying fish, eels, a cock and a basket of fruit. The master comes
out from a curtained doorway to greet them and the tenants are turning round
to talk to each other as they walk along.[2] Another scene shows a man, probably
the steward, seated at a table or counter on to which he is emptying coins out of
a sack while another man is looking on and apparently protesting.[3] A similar
scene from one of the Neumagen reliefs also shows a pile of tablets, probably
accounts, lying on the table. One man has picked up a coin from the pile and
is showing it to another who regards it with open-mouthed astonishment.[4]
Perhaps someone was trying to pay with a forgery. We can imagine such scenes
taking place in a small room projecting into a courtyard at Chedworth. Because
it contained so many lost coins it is believed to be the steward's room where the
tenants' rents were paid and also the purchase price for wool or grain bought
from the estate. The majority of the Gloucestershire sites lie on the good sheep
pastures of the Cotswolds within an area enclosed by a line drawn from the villa
at Milhampost (north of Winchcomb), to Broadwell (north of Stow on the
Wold), then south to Great Barrington (where sites also continued east into
Oxfordshire along the valley of the Windrush), by Bibury south of Cirencester
to Rodmarton and Cherington, and back by Woodchester and Haresfield to
Stanway. Some of the smaller villas such as Compton Abdale or Withington
might well have been occupied by Chedworth tenants or younger sons.

[1] Also discussed in detail by A. L. F. Rivet in Rivet ed. *op. cit.* Chap. **VI.**
[2] E. VI. no. 5268 p. 442.   [3] E. V. no. 4037.   [4] E. VI. no. 5148 p. 343.

In the south-east, Lieutenant-Colonel Meates, the excavator of Lullingstone, has already pointed out how villa sites occur at regular intervals along the Darenth valley at Orpington, Otford, Kemsing, Shoreham, Farningham, etc. Possibly these were connected with Lullingstone or even with the very large house excavated at Darenth in the last century. Another group in Oxfordshire varies in size from small ditch-enclosed farms to large houses like Stonesfield and North Leigh, and here prosperity may partly have been the result of the exploitation of the nearby quarries for roof slates. Similarly, the riches of some houses in Somerset, for example Keynsham, may be partly due to quarrying. There are also numerous small dwellings which may be subsidiaries of Low Ham and other large villas, some perhaps the houses of bailiffs or overseers. Other suggested groupings occur near Calne in Wiltshire, near East Grimstead and West Dean on the Wiltshire–Hampshire border, and between North Warn-borough and Farnham on the borders of Hampshire and Surrey. Too little information is available for any conclusions to be drawn as to whether any of these are British versions of the Gaulish *fundus* but it does seem certain that in the fourth century, and possibly also in the second, there were some important landowners. Some of them may have possessed more than one estate. Pliny discourses on the advantages of buying a second estate adjoining the first, pointing out that it can be inspected on the same visit, and one bailiff and nearly the same number of assistants can supervise both. Only one villa need be luxuriously kept up, the other being merely kept in repair, and savings can be made in the cost of furniture, housekeepers and gardeners. On the other hand there are risks as all the crops may be lost, and it is more entertaining to have a change and travel from one estate to another.[1] In a second letter, Pliny describes another aspect of landowning. People applied to him to act as their judge or their arbitrator, the tenants grumbled and brought him many complaints, some of the farms must be re-let and it is very difficult to find new tenants.[2]

Villas naturally occur thickly in such good agricultural and stock-raising country as Kent, Gloucestershire or Hampshire. Lack of research in some areas and also of chronological material still affects our knowledge of the pattern of their distribution although increased photographic cover from the air is beginning to fill the gaps. Formerly East Anglia and the Midlands were believed to have lacked attraction for villa dwellers, but it may be that the dearth was in antiquarians rather than in sites. Now with increased local interest and air photographs the villas are beginning to appear in these areas and in others such as Berkshire or the Vale of Glamorgan where they were scarce.[3]

[1] *Letters* III. 19. [2] *Ibid.* VII. 30.
[3] E.g. *J.R.S.* XLIX (1959) 102; LI (1961) 134.

How do the villas compare with houses in the towns? The technique of erecting a rectangular building on masonry foundations with a tiled or slated roof and such amenities as tessellated floors, baths and drains, may have been learnt by countrymen on army service, from watching the erection of public buildings in towns, or from immigrants from more advanced provinces. In some cases they seem to have been apt pupils. Park Street and Lockleys were erected with masonry footings about A.D. 65 and *tesserae* and fragments of wall-painting survive from several first-century sites such as Eccles and Farningham. The presence of baths is often regarded as a definite proof of Romanisation and these are already known from Eccles, Ashstead, Angmering and probably Highdown Hill in the last quarter of the first century. Second-century examples include Chedworth, Wiggonholt, Park Street, High Wycombe, Lullingstone and possibly Witcombe. Space was often limited in towns and the need for farm buildings affected the villas so that the factors governing the planning and increasing size of houses vary too much for comparisons to be feasible. One can perhaps visualise some of the prosperous Romano-Britons of the late first and second centuries, among them probably descendants of the old tribal aristocracy, embellishing their towns with public buildings and their town houses with mosaics and wall-paintings while also rebuilding and improving the family's simple country farm, or else erecting new ones. Other people stayed at home on the farm and prospered as a result of peace, better markets and more efficient agricultural methods.

Ideas of the scale which domestic life might attain at this early period have been revolutionised by the recent discoveries at Fishbourne, near Chichester, Sussex. The site, beside an inlet from the sea, was first occupied by the army for a few years after the invasion of A.D. 43. Its civilian life appears to have started by *c.* A.D. 50/55 when a bath-house with a spacious *palaestra* surrounded by corridors was built and at least one other masonry building was begun but possibly not finished. About A.D. 75 a building which can only be called a palace was erected, corresponding in size to a small Oxford or Cambridge college. It covered over six acres and was built round a great central court surrounded by a colonnade on three sides and probably on a fourth. Suites of rooms were arranged round smaller courtyards in the northern range and a large apsed reception room with a polychrome mosaic floor was placed in the middle of the west wing. A number of mosaics, mostly patterned in black and white but some polychrome, come from other rooms, amazing discoveries in Britain at this early date. Other floors were constructed of pieces of Purbeck marble, Wealden slate and imported marbles arranged in decorative designs (*opus sectile*) and these materials were also used for wall-veneers. Fragments of wall-painting

288

were also discovered. At the moment of writing the south side of the great courtyard is being excavated where it is accessible. Beyond it gardens may have led down to the sea and an ornamental lake may have existed beyond the building on the north. After A.D. 100 the palace seems to have gradually come down in the world although new mosaics and wall-paintings were added at several different periods and new baths were also built. The ranges of rooms may have been split up among different families. The occupation ended about A.D. 270.[1]

The Fishbourne Palace seems to owe its inspiration directly to Italy rather than to any provincial dwelling. It must have been built for either a Roman official or for a very wealthy and important Briton, perhaps for the family of Cogidubnus, the pro-Roman king of the Regnenses to whom Claudius gave the title of *rex et legatus Augusti in Britannia*. While it has as yet no British parallels, its existence must have had its effect as a model to both town and country dwellers, it has provided a chronological series of mosaics beginning at an astonishingly early date and its full importance has not yet been completely evaluated.

Meanwhile, it seems possible that some late first- and second-century villas may yet turn out to be larger and more luxurious than was thought to be the case, one example being Eccles with its early baths and traces of interior decoration. Unfortunately, the dating evidence for all but the most recently excavated sites is very scanty and a conservative estimate would only ascribe about a hundred sites to the second century. What happened next in the third century is still uncertain; possibly the change from grain-growing to sheep-farming was taking place at this time. Lists of finds commence at just over fifty villas at this period, not many of them recent discoveries. This contrasts with about two hundred for the fourth century. On the other hand, more second- and third-century material must lie under some fourth-century sites and a well-built second-century house would not need rebuilding for some years.

In the fourth century there were certainly a number of large landowners with fine luxurious country mansions. They used to be suspected of doing their best to avoid urban commitments which were now hereditary but the appearance of fresh evidence for the erection of new houses decorated with mosaics and wall-paintings at Verulamium and other sites is rather upsetting the theory of the decline of town life. The lack of dating evidence is felt acutely when an attempt is made to determine the speed at which the villas spread into the Midlands and further north. Agriculture was carried on in the areas bordering these under purely military control, but how soon did it turn into villa farming? The sites with baths and mosaics so far excavated in Yorkshire and Durham flourished

[1] B. Cunliffe, 'Excavations at Fishbourne', *Ant. J.* XLV (1965) 1–11.

during this period of fourth-century prosperity. Some of them lie above farms which seem to have been of a very simple type, but here again there is room for more investigation. There is also the mysterious site at Well, near Ripon, Yorkshire, with a small house, suite of baths and separate large plunge bath, comparable to the pools found at Eccles and Gadebridge Park, dating from the second half of the second century and terminating in the fourth.[1] It has been suggested that this may be a religious site rather than a villa but even so, like Fishbourne in the south, it could have been a model of the amenities of civilised life to some of the local farmers.

At the end of the fourth century the residential quarters of some villas fell into disuse, suggesting that their owners then sought the protection of town walls and left their estates to be run by bailiffs. Llantwit Major is a recently excavated example of this phenomenon. However, our knowledge of these problems is probably best summarised by the late Professor Sir Ian Richmond when he says, 'It might be guessed that what caused the ultimate collapse of the villa system was not the insecurity of the countryside so much as the collapse of the world upon whose markets they had depended.[2] Before this the food grown in the various cultivated areas of Britain: villas and smaller agricultural settlements, *territoria* outside the towns, and the fields of the civil settlements outside the forts, had been sufficient to feed the province profitably. There may also have been some produce available for export, at any rate in times of emergency such as occurred in the fourth century when supplies were hastily sent to the army in the Rhineland.

In conclusion, what do we know of the villa dwellers themselves, the people who inhabited the small farms and fine houses? We seem to get a glimpse of them on sites like Lockleys where a villa develops from humble beginnings into a comfortable home. It is easy to imagine this being the work of different generations of the same family. We see it, too, as the villas increase in size, with the appearance of dining-rooms and domestic quarters separating the family from the servants or slaves, and then the provision of a courtyard or garden cut off from the farmyard. And the methods already discussed of solving constructional problems, awkward slopes, too much or too little water in inconvenient places, lack of building stone and the great variety of plan all reflect the human element. Two fragments from the Arlon reliefs may illustrate scenes which might take place at any villa. One shows a room, indicated by the curtains tied back at each end, with two ladies comfortably seated in chairs, holding a conversation. Another figure, probably a maid, is moving about between them.[3] The other

[1] R. Gilyard-Beer, *Romano-British Baths at Well* (Leeds, 1951).
[2] Richmond (1963) p. 120. [3] E. V. no. 4102 p. 273.

scene shows husband and wife sitting at a table and eating a meal. Several servants wait on them and above their heads is a shelf with glass vessels, possibly for wine. Below this, either as a separate scene or else a picture of what was going on elsewhere in the same room, are five children clustered round a big cauldron, some of them sitting on the floor. One child hastily restrains a pet dog who is about to thrust his nose into the cauldron. Another stands behind playing a tune on double pipes (Pl. 45).

The daily life of the Roman country house has been described by various classical authors, and although no accounts survive which relate specifically to British villas, it is illuminating to find in these sources descriptions of buildings which obviously possessed features similar to those just examined. The labours and delights of rural existence were a constant theme with writers from the late Republic onwards. Horace writes affectionately of his Sabine farm,[1] the site of which has been preserved and excavated, and can be visited today.[2] In his letters, Seneca described the farm which belonged to Scipio Africanus at Liternum. 'It is built of squared stone; there are trees round it, and a wall round them; at either end rises a tower, flanking the homestead as an outwork; below the buildings and their clump of greenery lies a reservoir large enough to water an army,'[3] a description which must have fitted many of our villa sites. Cicero makes frequent brief allusions to his country houses, although he does not unfortunately describe them with much detail. In one letter, however, he discusses improvements which are being made to his brother's house at Arcanum, including the provision of new ceilings for the colonnade, and the rearrangement of the rooms of the baths.[4] Other letters refer to the constructions of new sitting-rooms and a colonnade for his own Tuscalan villa,[5] and to the purchase of statues and furniture for it,[6] as well as to the possibility that a new basin might be needed for its bath.[7] A letter to Atticus describes preparations for his visit. Literary topics will be discussed on walks, 'I will have the bath-water heated and Terentia is inviting Pomponia; we will get your mother to come too.' The letter ends with a request to Atticus to bring him a book from his brother Quintus' library.[8] Pliny the younger is more lavish with details about his country houses. As we have seen, he discusses the administration of the estates, and describes the buildings and their surrounding scenery. Of particular interest for comparative purposes are his references to baths and central heating, folding-

[1] *Carmina* III. 4, 21.
[2] *Memoirs of the American Academy in Rome* X (1932) 135; *Parthenon* September 1933.
[3] *Epistulae* 86. Trans. E. P. Barker.   [4] *Ad Quintum* III. 1.
[5] *Ad Familiares* VII. 23.   [6] *Ibid.*   [7] *Ibid.* XIV. 20.
[8] *Ad. Atticum* II. 3; 2, 3. Trans. L. P. Wilkinson, *Letters of Cicero* (1959) 50.

doors, glazed windows and towers, and wall-paintings.[1] He also describes the daily life in the country of an elderly friend for whom he obviously has much affection. When he gets up he calls for his shoes and takes a three-mile walk. Some time is spent in reading or talk and then he goes out for a drive of about seven miles in his carriage with his wife or a friend. Another short walk and a rest, and then a visit to the baths and some form of ball-game. Later comes dinner, and more talk over the wine until a late hour.[2] Pliny himself followed much the same programme with rather more time taken up for business affairs and writing.

From later writers we can learn more of villas in the provinces. Ausonius in his description of the Moselle region refers to the country mansions to be seen along its banks, with 'their courts set beside verdant meadows, . . . their trim roofs resting upon countless pillars'.[3] They were accompanied by baths placed at the river's edge, probably detached bath-houses. During the fifth century, Sidonius Apollinaris included among his writings several descriptions of villas in Southern France. His letters are believed to have been modelled on those of Pliny the younger, and although he wrote some years after the end of the Roman period in Britain, the houses which he describes are obviously still Roman villas. For example, in the poem describing the castle of Pontius Leontius, he mentions the use of imported marbles as a decoration for the interior walls of the villa and for pillars in the baths, as well as wall-paintings, colonnades and granaries.[4] At his house at Avitacum the fuel supply consists of wood cut close at hand, the heated water reaches the apsidal hot room through lead pipes, and the *frigidarium* has a vaulted roof constructed with hollow tiles and a coffered ceiling. There follows a description of the other rooms of the villa, storerooms and corridors, etc., leading to the winter dining-room which is heated by a fire in a vaulted fireplace.[5] In another letter Sidonius describes a visit he paid to two friends who lived in the south of France on adjoining estates. Their houses were quite close together, the distance being just too far to walk but far enough to make the ride worth while.[6] Here perhaps is a picture which we might venture to ascribe to such neighbouring sites as North Leigh and Stonesfield.

A last glimpse of the villa dwellers at home is surely provided by the treatment of the Lullingstone busts. We do not know when bust II suffered the rough treatment which partly removed his shoulders and later severed his head from his body, but presumably both busts were found by the new inhabitants

---

[1] *Epistulae* I. 3; II. 8; III. 19; V. 6. [2] *Epistulae* III. 1.
[3] *Mosella* 283 ff. Trans. H. H. Evelyn White.
[4] *Carmina* XXII. 128 ff. Trans. W. B. Anderson.
[5] *Epistulae* II. 2. [6] *Epistulae* II. 9.

amid the ruins of the second-century villa when the house was rebuilt about 280. They probably felt these ancestral portraits were not comfortable company to have in the home, but, on the other hand, they must be treated with respect. So the *nymphaeum* was tidied up and simply re-decorated. Then the busts were placed down there, carefully propped up on steps and the doorway blocked up behind them. They were accompanied by two pots containing votive offerings. One was an ordinary cooking pot, the other a charming little colour-coated beaker made in the Rhineland and decorated with the word SVAVIS (Sweetness), painted on it in graceful lettering. It contained the rib-bone of a sheep. Later these pots were concealed below a fourth-century clay floor in which two more vessels were inserted between A.D. 345 and 361. Possibly libations continued to be poured to the departed spirits of the earlier inhabitants of this long-lived site, even if Christian worship was later in full swing in the house-church above.

11
The professions (1)
Law and education

Agriculture, trade and industry were not the only occupations carried on by the inhabitants of Roman Britain. Some individuals must have belonged to what would nowadays be called the professional classes, although at this time professions, such as that of the schoolmaster, were not as highly regarded as they are today. The British evidence for them, however, is still rather meagre, but it can be supplemented from the abundant material available concerning lawyers, teachers and doctors in Italy and other parts of the Empire.

The development of law at this period is perhaps the greatest of Roman achievements and the one which has probably best survived into modern times. Roman justice was available for citizens all over the Empire and although our knowledge of its processes in Britain is slight, its existence must have formed the background to Romano-British life. Under it a defendant must know the nature of the charges against him, be confronted by his accusers and given a chance to defend himself. Non-citizens were also affected by it, so a brief account of some of the more important aspects of Roman law may not be out of place. It must be emphasised, however, that much of importance is bound to be omitted from such a summary, and more detailed information will be found in the various authorities cited.[1]

[1] E.g. J. P. V. D. Balsdon ed., *The Romans* (1965) Chap. VI 'Roman Law' by F. H. Lawson, pp. 102–28.

According to tradition, the legal affairs of ancient Rome were in the hands of patrician magistrates who had succeeded the earlier kings. In the fifth century B.C. the people demanded the publication of the laws and the abolition of patrician privileges, and a delegation is rumoured to have been sent to Greece to study the legislation of Solon. A committee of ten then compiled a code based on Roman customs, and this was set up on ten bronze or wooden tablets in the Forum about 451 B.C. Two more tablets were added a year later. These Twelve Tables formed the basis of Roman civil law. They were probably destroyed by the Gauls about 387 B.C. but fragments of the text as it was known from the time of the late Republic survive, and more was preserved in citations by later authors. Children were made to study the Twelve Tables, at least up to the time of Cicero, as he recalls learning the opening passage. 'If a man is summoned to court and does not go, let witnesses be called and then let the plaintiff seize him. If he resists or runs away, let the plaintiff lay hands on him. If he is ill or aged, let the plaintiff provide an animal to carry him.'[1]

During the Empire the sources of law developed and changed in various ways. Gaius, a well-known jurist writing in the second century A.D., lists the most important enactments as *leges*, which, strictly speaking, were passed by the assembly or *comitia* although the word was later used loosely of rulings laid down by the Emperor; and *senatus consulta*, decrees passed by a majority vote of the whole senate on specific issues brought up for debate.[2] It was also customary for both the praetors, the magistrates next in rank to the consuls, and the governors to issue edicts on taking up office, giving their interpretation of the law and the actions they would take or permit in various circumstances. The praetorian edicts were exhibited in the Forum, and although each one only affected the magistrate issuing it, it became usual for a praetor to adopt most of his predecessor's edicts with his own modifications, thus ensuring some continuity, and for governors to draw not only on the edicts of their predecessors in the provinces but also on those of the praetors in Rome. In 130, Hadrian instructed the jurist Salvius Iulianus to codify this praetorian law into a permanent law under the title *Edictum perpetuum*, and this was duly confirmed by a *senatus consultum*. After this no new material seems to have been included in the praetorian edicts.

As a magistrate the Emperor possessed the power to issue edicts on any matters of state, one important example being the *constitutio Antoniniana* of A.D. 212 in which Caracalla extended the Roman citizenship to most of the free people of the Empire. Other *constitutiones* listed by Gaius which the Emperor eventually enacted by reason of his *imperium* (sovereign power), included *decreta*, the

[1] B. Nicholas, *An Introduction to Roman Law* (Oxford, 1962) p. 16.   [2] *Institutes* I. 2.

decisions in the trials where he acted as judge, and *rescripta*, often embodied in *epistulae* (letters), the written answers to legal queries or petitions (*libelli*).[1] The letters which passed between the younger Pliny, when governor of Bithynia, and the Emperor Trajan, are well-known examples of such correspondence from officials or from municipal bodies, dealt with in Rome by the secretaries in the department *ab epistulis* under imperial supervision. Petitions from private individuals had to be brought to the Emperor either in person or through an intermediary, and possibly this was the service rendered by Tiberius Claudius Paulinus to the Silures which caused them to erect a statue in his honour.[2] The department *a libellis* prepared an answer written below the petition and both were kept in the imperial archives, a copy being given to the petitioner. Many of these rescripts have survived in the *Codices* gathered together in the reigns of Theodosius and Justinian, and some of them are surprisingly trivial. One petitioner asks the permission of Antoninus Pius to make a copy of a judgement of Hadrian which interests him, and in another case the Emperors Diocletian and Maximian tell Aurelius in A.D. 293, that a partnership is valid in which one partner contributes the money and the other the labour.[3] *Mandata*, mostly special instructions to provincial officials, were also issued by the Emperors. Well-known examples include one allowing soldiers on active service to make informal wills, sometimes even without witnesses.[4]

The law resulting from the edicts of the magistrates was called *ius honorarium* to distinguish it from *ius civile*, the law arising from statutes and other sources. Both applied to Roman citizens and actually existed side by side, but in practice *ius honorarium* gradually prevailed because of its more simplified forms and flexibility. As Rome grew, it became also necessary to have a legal system which could be used for relations with other nations, international trade, and individuals in provinces either allied to Rome by treaty or conquered by her. From this developed the *ius gentium*, the law which applied to both *peregrini* (foreigners or non-citizens) and to Roman citizens alike. Presumably it developed gradually as need arose. In the early days of the Roman Republic a single praetor sufficed to carry on the legal work in Rome originally undertaken by the two consuls, but about 242 B.C. a second one was appointed. This was the *praetor peregrinus* who took over the jurisdiction between foreigners, or citizens and foreigners, leaving his colleague, the *praetor urbanus*, to devote his attention to citizens alone. As the number of praetors increased, these two posts remained, while the major function of the other magistrates came to be to act as presidents of the criminal courts.

[1] *Ibid.* I. 5.; A. H. M. Jones, *The Later Roman Empire* I (Oxford, 1964) p. 471.
[2] See above p. 31. [3] B. Nicholas, *op. cit.* p. 18. [4] H. F. Jolowicz (1965) p. 380.

The edicts of the peregrine praetors must have been of considerable importance in the development of *ius gentium*. Owing to the widespread grant of citizenship in A.D. 212, however, the compilers of *Codices* were naturally not interested in a law designed for dealing with non-citizens, so little knowledge of these edicts has survived. Possibly Iulianus codified them into a separate *Edictum perpetuum*. They may well have influenced the procedures of the urban praetors and been heavily influenced by those of the urban praetors in their turn. Cicero, in fact, tells us that in his edict as governor of Cilicia he announced that he would accommodate his decrees to the urban edict on certain matters on which, therefore, he felt it unnecessary to issue further full-scale decrees.[1] It seems that for non-citizens the Roman law was largely stripped of its formal elements and qualified by ideas from other sources, at first mostly Greek.[2] The same, no doubt, largely applies to the edicts of the provincial governors, but they would also normally permit the use of local law in the provincial courts in cases between non-citizens.

Litigation for a suit in Roman private law had to pass through two main stages. First the plaintiff summoned the defendant and both made their way to the magistrate's court. Under the Twelve Tables the plaintiff then stated his case orally, using a prescribed form of words. There were five types of these *legis actiones* dealing with disputed ownership, the division of property and the repayment of debts, and any deviation from the correct form of words was sufficient to invalidate the plaintiff's case. During the late Republic and especially from the time of Augustus, this rigidity came to be largely replaced by the formulary system in which the particulars of the dispute were written down according to *formulae* which could be varied as required. Model *formulae* were published as part of the praetorian edicts and the praetors could permit new forms when necessary. The case having been stated, in one way or another, the magistrate had to decide whether the plaintiff had sufficient grounds for taking proceedings. If he approved, he could help to settle on the best *formula*, and this could occasion some argument as the plaintiff tried to obtain the form most advantageous to his case or asked for a new one. Finally, the *formula* was settled and agreed before witnesses, and after this the plaintiff lost his right to ask for another trial on the same grounds.

The next step was the appointment of a judge to try the case, and he was chosen from a panel of citizens, originally of senatorial rank but later also drawn from the *equites*. The plaintiff nominated the judge but the defendant had the right to object if he doubted his impartiality. Once a name was agreed on and approved by the magistrate, the judge was obliged to officiate unless he could

[1] *Ad Atticum* VI. 1. 15.   [2] Jolowicz (1965) p. 102.

plead serious illness. He did not usually possess special qualifications but both he and the magistrate were assisted by a council of advisers, and in cases requiring expert knowledge a special judge, called an *arbiter*, was appointed. The case began with the consideration of the *formula*, then the evidence of witnesses and documents was considered and both sides of the dispute were presented by the litigants or their legal representatives. The judge then retired to discuss the case with his advisers. If he felt unable to reach a decision he could say so under oath, and the litigants were then obliged to return to the magistrate and ask for the appointment of another judge. If a verdict was reached the judge announced it to both the parties orally, either discharging the defendant or declaring that the plaintiff had proved his case and the defendant must repay the money, or restore the property or do whatever else was necessary to meet the plaintiff's claim. If the luckless defendant was unable to meet his debts, his treatment was severe as he either became the plaintiff's prisoner, and presumably had to work for him, or else all his property had to be sold to the highest bidder and the money divided among his creditors. This was really a form of compulsory bankruptcy, clumsy because all the property had to be sold however large or small the debt. The creditor had to obtain an order from the magistrate to enforce it, possibly with the aid of a further judgment. A debtor could escape the risk of imprisonment and disgrace by handing over his property to his creditors without waiting for this, going, in fact, into voluntary liquidation. By the late second century the harshness of this procedure was realised and a rescript from the Emperor directed that only enough property to satisfy the creditors need be seized and sold, if the debt was still owing after two months.[1]

There is some evidence that these elaborate procedures also took place in the provinces but to what extent is uncertain. Law there depended on the provincial governors who possessed powers which in Rome were divided between several magistrates.[2] The governors, however, must have been influenced by their knowledge of the Roman legal background, much of which would be incorporated in their edicts, especially when Roman citizens were concerned, the number of whom was steadily increasing. In the provinces the lack of suitable judges must sometimes have made it necessary for members of the governor's staff to be appointed, not only for the trial but also to issue the summons when the plaintiff requested it. By about the time of Augustus a new procedure called *cognitio extraordinaria* appears in Rome, side by side with the older usages which it eventually replaced. In this the magistrate, in person or through an official, also acts as judge and enforces the decision. This system may be the result of legal practices which had developed in the provinces, coupled with the needs of

[1] *Ibid.* pp. 223–6, 411.   [2] *Ibid.* p. 408.

a growing bureaucracy. It meant that cases heard in this way were no longer voluntarily submitted for arbitration. Instead, justice consisted of the enforcement of rules laid down by public authority.[1] There was, of course, the possibility of an appeal (*appellatio*) to the Emperor and this could soften for the citizen the authoritarian administration of justice involved in *cognitio*. When the passing of the *constitutio Antoniniana* produced a rapid growth in the numbers of Roman citizens, greatly increased use had to be made of the *cognitio* procedure, and the procedure for handling many more appeals had also probably to be developed. Appeals could now be referred to higher magistrates stage by stage until at last they reached the Emperor himself. Those who appealed on insufficient grounds, however, were liable for heavy costs and other penalties.

This is the complex background of the law which governors had to administer in Roman Britain, further complicated by the Celtic usages which they may have found there, and the need to deal with both citizen and non-citizen. Municipal magistrates had very limited powers, and cases of any importance had to be referred to the assizes (*conventus*) which the governor or his delegates held in the chief towns. These probably included the *coloniae*, Londinium, Verulamium and the larger cantonal capitals. Tacitus relates how Agricola encouraged the Britons to build courts of justice and how he presided over the assizes with great dignity and penetration, sometimes severe, but often more inclined to mercy.[2] There may also have been courts in almost permanent session in the governor's palace.[3]

By the time of Diocletian, legal distinctions between Rome and the rest of the Empire had largely vanished, apart from the possible survival of some local laws. Britain, now part of the prefecture of Gaul, was a diocese split into four, and later, five, provinces with governors solely concerned with civil administration who spent most of their time in their capitals, acting as judges. Appeals from their judgments were made to either the praetorian prefect or to the *vicarius* of the diocese and sometimes, ultimately, to the Emperor. With the spread of Christianity the clergy also began to arbitrate in disputes among Christians, and from the fourth century onwards the influence of the bishops' courts grew steadily in importance and popularity.[4]

An important part of the interpretation and formulation of Roman law was played by the jurists. These were men learned in the law who increasingly acted as legal advisers to the magistrates, judges and, later, the Emperors. After the earliest period they did not usually appear as advocates in court and they were paid no fees for their consultations, but their profession was one of great honour and frequently led to important official appointments. Private individuals as well as officials could consult them about the drawing up of documents or the clauses

[1] *Ibid.* p. 406. [2] *Agricola* XXI. 9. [3] Jolowicz (1965) p. 417. [4] *Ibid.* pp. 465, 468.

of *formulae* for a magistrate, sometimes obtaining the opinions of several before starting a suit. From the time of the Republic, young men were admitted to the consultations as pupils, and the jurists produced an extensive literature of commentaries on the laws and their interpretation, and also handbooks for students. Their opinions on points of law were known as *responsa*. In the time of Augustus a certain number of eminent jurists were given the *ius respondendi*, permission to give *responsa* on the personal authority of the Emperor. Rulings sent to officials with such backing were normally accepted by them. Later Emperors abandoned this system but meanwhile the custom of making the leading jurists members of the Emperor's *consilium* of legal advisers had already arisen. Their *responsa* were binding unless they disagreed, when the judge could decide between them.

Not all the jurists were of Roman or even Italian birth. Like most important professional groups they included increasing numbers of provincials from the first century onwards. The surviving records suggest that these men came mostly from North Africa or the Near East, but as time went on there may well have been some ambitious Gauls or Britons among them, students perhaps, who followed visiting jurists back to Rome. Several eminent jurists are known to have been in Britain, the first of them being Salvius Liberalis who came as a *legatus iuridicus*, a law-officer with the rank of praetor, appointed to assist the governor, Agricola, with his legal duties. He was succeeded *c.* A.D. 84–6 by Javolenus Priscus, later to become a famous teacher and the head of one of the two great schools of Roman jurisprudence to which jurists attached themselves. It has been suggested that both these *legati* may have spent some of their time comparing British and Roman law and working out a code which the governors could embody in their edicts. A fragment of an inscribed slate panel found in London mentions an imperial juridical legate of the province of Britain in the early second century but the name is lost.[1] Another *legatus iuridicus* was Crescens Calpurnianus who took charge of the province in the governor's absence at the beginning of the third century. Before this, Ulpius Marcellus, governor of Britain under Commodus, may just possibly be the same individual as the jurist who was a member of the *consilium* of Antoninus Pius and Marcus Aurelius.[2] Papinian, possibly the most renowned figure of all and the author and compiler of many books of *responsa*, accompanied the Emperor Septimius Severus to Britain in 208. He held the post of praetorian prefect, a title which originally simply denoted the commander of the praetorian guard but which by now meant the officer with general jurisdiction over all civil and criminal cases in the Empire, apart from the territory of Rome itself.[3] While Severus and Caracalla fought the

[1] *R.I.B.* 8. [2] E. Birley, *Roman Britain and the Roman Army* (Kendal, 1953) p. 56.
[3] An area of 100 miles round Rome came under the authority of the *praefectus urbi*.

Caledonii and Maeatae from their headquarters at York, Papinian administered justice and the place-name *Eburaci* survives on a rescript issued in the Emperor's name on 5 May 210.[1]

Roman criminal law did not attract the attention of the jurists to the same extent as civil law and it is only in the time of Justinian that it was properly codified. By the end of the Republic criminal courts (*quaestiones perpetuae*) had been set up where cases were tried by a magistrate, usually a praetor, and a number of jurors who decided the verdict.[2] Anyone could lodge an accusation and if the grounds seemed sufficient, a trial followed in which accuser and accused disputed the evidence. Both could challenge the choice of jurymen. The magistrate merely presided and had no vote and no powers of summing up. He accepted the verdict and imposed the sentence. Lesser crimes like theft and fraud were still regarded as personal matters actionable under civil law, unless they in any way endangered the safety of the state. The various *quaestiones* dealt with such offences as murder, sacrilege, serious injury or violence, bribery of candidates at elections, adultery and the falsification of currency, weights, and wills or other documents. Punishments for the upper classes, known as *honestiores*, from the end of the second century rarely included the death penalty. This was usually replaced by loss of citizenship and property, sometimes with confinement to an island. The poorer citizens (*humiliores*), who had less to lose, were less protected and might be crucified or condemned to the beasts in the ampitheatre. Or they were apt to lose their freedom as well as their citizenship and could be sent to forced labour, often in the mines. Prison sentences were not imposed as a penalty, as Roman punishments were designed as retribution rather than for rehabilitation. Magistrates, however, could imprison recalcitrant individuals for short periods or detain accused or condemned persons, and accused persons might spend long periods in custody, waiting for a trial. Serious crimes against the state, such as treason or accusations brought against provincial governors, might be judged in the Senate, by the Emperor, or by special *quaestiones*.[3]

The *quaestiones* only operated in Rome. In the provinces criminal law was the governor's responsibility and a governor might be given the *ius gladii* or right to put citizens to death. His powers of punishment could also include condemnation to work in the mines. *Honestiores*, however, apparently retained the right of appeal to the Emperor for certain offences, being either sent to Rome or else held in custody while imperial confirmation of the death sentence was obtained. Procedure in the provinces in fact was now more that of *cognitio extraordinaria*.[4]

[1] E. Birley, *op. cit.* p. 52.   [2] Jolowicz (1965) pp. 330–1.   [3] *Ibid.* p. 412 *et seq.*
[4] *Ibid.* p. 412. These complicated problems are further discussed by A. H. M. Jones, *Studies in Roman Government and Law* (Oxford, 1960) Chaps. iv, viii.

Under Roman criminal law slaves could be questioned under torture when evidence was being collected for serious crimes. Normally a citizen was protected from this and from castigation without trial, but the torture of witnesses among the *humiliores* did occur. As we have already seen, the consternation caused at Philippi by St Paul's complaint that he, a Roman citizen, had been publicly beaten and imprisoned without a trial, illustrates the value of the citizenship in the provinces.[1]

Literature has preserved for us a picture of a Rome humming with legal activity as the courts of the Emperor, the Senate and the magistrates and judges all went about their work.[2] The surviving speeches of distinguished orators like Cicero show us Roman advocacy at its highest, while Pliny, describing cases in his letters, mentions the fatigue of speaking for a long time. The length of an advocate's speech apparently depended upon the number of water-clocks (*clepsydrae*) allowed by the judge. Water placed in a container with a small hole in it dripped through into a larger bowl. Legal *clepsydrae* normally lasted twenty minutes so when Pliny recounts that in addition to twelve of the largest he could get, he obtained leave to use four more in an important trial in the Senate at which the Emperor (as consul) was presiding, it is not surprising that Trajan showed concern in case he overtaxed his strength. Pliny also records that his wife Calpurnia was overcome with nerves on such occasions and very happy when he spoke successfully.[3]

Jurists in the time of Cicero presented their clients' case in person as well as advising on it, but as they grew more occupied with the interpretation of law, advocacy passed into the hands of men who were mainly trained orators. With some distinguished exceptions, the advocates of the early empire often knew only enough law to make the most of the jurists' instructions. They were such an essential part of Roman litigation, however, that the praetorian edict contained a promise to supply them for clients lacking representation. In theory they were unpaid but in fact they received some reward, sometimes depending upon success in their cases. By the time of Diocletian's Price Edict, an advocate or jurist could be paid 250 *denarii* for preparing a complaint and 1,000 *denarii* for pleading in court. By now, with a growing bureaucracy, the status of advocates was rising and they were becoming much better trained in law. Ausonius mentions professors of grammar and rhetoric who were advocates,

---

[1] *Acts* xvi. 37. An interesting discussion of Roman citizenship and the powers of provincial governors and other officials will be found in A. N. Sherwin-White, *Roman Society and Roman Law in the New Testament* (1963).

[2] E.g. J. Carcopino (1956) p. 188.

[3] *Epistulae* II. 11; IV. 19.

appearing, no doubt, in the courts of Bordeaux and training pupils to succeed them.[1]

From all the mass of legal material preserved in the Roman *Codices*, little has survived of proceedings concerned with Britain. One knotty problem preserved in Justinian's *Digest*[2] concerns the case of a woman slave condemned for some crime to look after the convicts at a saltworks. There she was kidnapped by bandits, later sold and repurchased by her original owner. Presumably when her sentence was completed she would normally have been returned to her owner and as she was kidnapped while in official keeping, her owner sued the state for the repurchase money. The case is quoted by a second-century jurist and there is some evidence to suggest that the owner was Cocceius Firmus, a centurion of the Second Legion serving in Scotland, where bandits must have abounded at this period.[3] Another case occurs in the Theodosian Code as a rescript of Constantine I.[4] Dated 20 November 310, it is directed to the *vicarius* of Britain, Pacatianus, and is concerned with the taxation due to the treasury from decurions on behalf of their tenants. The exact point at issue is obscure, it may show some conflict between Roman law and British custom, but apparently it was important enough to be referred to Rome beyond the praetorian prefect to the higher authority of the Emperor himself.[5] There is also a wooden tablet found in the villa well at Chew Park, Somerset, on which part of a record relating to the sale of some real estate was written in ink. It seems to use Roman legal phraseology, but its exact interpretation is a difficult problem.[6]

Further examples of British litigation which survive are concerned with wills. The *legatus iuridicus*, Javolenus Priscus, has a case recorded about a chief pilot in the British fleet who included in his will a request to a ship's captain to hold his property in trust for his infant son. However, the boy died before he came of age so Javolenus was asked to decide who should inherit, the captain or the pilot's brother-in-law as the next of kin?[7] Unhappily his answer is not recorded. A rescript of Hadrian of about 118 A.D., directed to Pompeius Falco at a time when he may have been governor of Britain, concerns the estate of a legionary who committed suicide.[8] The Emperor directs that unless the suicide took place to avoid punishment, any will which exists is valid. If there is no will, the property is to go to the next of kin or, failing them, to the legion. An inheritance

[1] *Commemoratio Professorum Burdigalensium* II, XXIII, XXVI.
[2] 49. 15. 6.   [3] Birley, *op. cit.* pp. 51, 87–103.   [4] 11. 7. 2.
[5] C. E. Stevens, 'A Possible Conflict of Laws in Roman Britain', *J.R.S.* XXXVII (1947) pp. 132–4.
[6] E. Turner, 'A Roman Writing Tablet from Somerset', *J.R.S.* XLVI (1956) 114–18.
[7] *Digest* 36. 1. 48; Birley, *op. cit.* p. 51.
[8] *Digest* 28. 3. 6, 7.

problem also occurs in a rescript of Severus dated 19 February 197, and sent to the British governor, Virius Lupus.[1]

Allusions to inheritance occur on tombstones not infrequently. Longinus and Rufus Sita, first-century auxiliaries belonging to the Thracian cohorts and commemorated at Colchester and Gloucester respectively, both have inscriptions ending 'His heirs had this erected according to the terms of his will'.[2] At York, the legionary Lucius Crescens, was remembered by his heir who 'had this set up for his friend',[3] and Classicius Aprilis, another heir, ordered the tombstone for Flavius Flavinus before that centurion died.[4] Such thought for the future was not unusual and does not indicate any ulterior motive on the part of Aprilis. At Chester a man who had been centurion in four different legions was commemorated by his freedman and heir Aristio,[5] and altogether nearly twenty Chester military tombstones carefully record that they were put up by heirs. There are also examples from Caerleon,[6] Lincoln[7] and London.[8] One Chester inscription, relating to the legionary Titinius Felix, was put up by his wife and heiress Julia Similina.[9] This probably belongs to the third century when the Emperor Septimius Severus gave permission for soldiers to marry.

Civilian testators are less commonly recorded. Aulus Alfidius Olussa, commemorated by his heir in accordance with his will in London, may have been a merchant, as the inscription says he was born at Athens (fig. 118).[10] At Lincoln, Claudia Chrysis lived to be ninety and so kept her heirs waiting,[11] while at Chester, Curatia Dinysia succumbed at only forty.[12] The best example of all is Julia Velva at York, portrayed with her heir Aurelius Mercurialis and all his family shown around her (Pl. 26c).[13]

The ability to make a will valid in a Roman court was one of the privileges of a Roman citizen and there was much legislation concerning it as the disposition of property and legacies were matters of great interest to the Romans. Latin citizens might also possess the *testamenti factio*. Usually the will was written out on tablets by someone with legal training and then witnessed with various formalities. Codicils could be added later. The heirs in due course had to prove their rights before the praetor. Soldiers and sailors on active service could make wills with much less formality. Other special provisions included the need for fewer witnesses in remote country areas where the witnesses' signatures could also be omitted if they were unable to write. Witnesses need

[1] *Ibid.* 28. 6. 2, 4.   [2] *R.I.B.* 201, 121.
[3] *R.I.B.* 671. Whether the abbreviation A means friend is a little doubtful.
[4] *R.I.B.* 675.   [5] *R.I.B.* 509.   [6] *R.I.B.* 365.
[7] *R.I.B.* 258.   [8] *R.I.B.* 13.   [9] *R.I.B.* 505.
[10] *R.I.B.* 9.   [11] *R.I.B.* 263.   [12] *R.I.B.* 562.
[13] *R.I.B.* 688, see also *R.I.B.* 163.

A·ALFID·POMP
OLVSSA·EXTES·
TAMENTO·HER
P·S·ANNOR·LXX
H^{NA}·S^{AFI·ENT}·E ST

118   Tombstone of Aulus Alfidius Olussa, found on
Tower Hill, London

not be actually present if the testator had some contagious disease. Intestacy
was regarded as a disgrace.[1]

All this background of legal achievement shows highly educated Roman
citizens at work and so arouses curiosity about education in general. Here again
it is difficult to do more than give a description of the pattern prevailing in Italy.
This pattern seems to have been copied and adapted around the Western
Mediterranean, especially in southern Gaul, but little is known about the educational standards reached by the north-western provinces. However, one of the
best pictures depicting a Roman school appears on a relief from Trier, and
another fragment of sculpture found at Arlon shows an unpleasant-looking
schoolmaster brandishing a cane.

The importance of family life to the Romans is well illustrated by their concern for their children's upbringing, and various references to the educational
responsibilities of parents survive in literature. The earlier years of infancy were
supervised by the mother, often with the assistance of some worthy female
relative who could be relied on to act as a good influence. At the age of seven

[1] For a full discussion of inheritance and will-making see Leage (1961) p. 233 *et seq.*

the father took charge of his son. This might only mean that the boy now helped on the land or with his father's trade, especially in Rome's early days, but the more well-to-do children accompanied their fathers to the Forum and Senate, and served them at feasts. Girls stayed at home sharing their mother's occupations and both boys and girls assisted at the family sacrifices.

More formal education began at the age of seven.[1] This might consist of study at home with a tutor or attendance at school. Quintilian, who wrote a valuable account of children's education in the first century A.D., discusses the problem of the choice between the two. At home the pupil could be shielded from bad influences and would be sure of receiving individual attention. On the other hand, individual instruction should really take up very little of the school day. The child must work on his own when he is writing, thinking or learning by heart, and 'the mind is as easily tired as the eye if given no relaxation'.[2] The schoolmaster should be able to manage a number of pupils and a good schoolmaster, moreover, is unlikely to be content with a single child as audience. Parents tend to spoil children, so a school of reasonable size with a master of good character is better for them. 'The voice of a lecturer is not like a dinner which will only suffice for a limited number; it is like the sun which distributes the same quality of light and heat to all of us',[3] says Quintilian of the teacher of literature whose explanations of style and disputed passages, stories and paraphrases benefit all who hear him. Lifelong friendships were made at school and much could be learnt from the good or bad work of others. There also seems to have been competition to be first in class. The ideal pupil had a good memory, learnt with care and asked questions but was not precocious. He could be encouraged by praise, delighted by success and ready to weep at failure. Some children needed to be constantly spurred on to study, some restrained, some frightened into working, while others would be paralysed by fear.

These reflections from Quintilian have a very familiar sound, especially when he goes on to express his disapproval of corporal punishment. Unluckily for Roman children his views were not generally shared: a wall-painting from Herculaneum shows a schoolmaster flogging a boy and there are many allusions to such punishment. While a tendency to a kinder discipline does appear from Quintilian onwards, Ausonius could still write to his grandson in the fourth century about the sour schoolmaster's domineering voice and admonish him

---

[1] This account of Roman education is largely based on H. I. Marrou, *A History of Education in Antiquity* (1956); W. Barclay, *Educational Ideals in the Ancient World* (1959); and J. P. V. D. Balsdon, ed. *The Romans* (1965) Chap. XI, 'Education and Oratory' by M. L. Clarke, pp. 211–25.
[2] Quintilian, *Institutio oratoria* I. 1. 2; I. 2. 11. [3] *Ibid.* I 2. 14.

119 The lesson. Sarcophagus of Cornelius Statius

not to be afraid, even though the school resounded with many a stroke and the
master kept a cane, a full outfit of birches and a tawse. 'Your mother and father
went through all this in their day,' adds Ausonius, 'and have lived to soothe my
old age.'[1]

Not all teachers came up to Quintilian's educational standards. The primary
schoolmasters (*litteratores* or *magistri ludi*) were poorly paid, fifty *denarii* a month
according to Diocletian's Edict, and little respected. Fees might be eked out by
gifts on feast days or by part-time work drawing up wills. Schools were often
carried on in small rooms, shops or corners of the Forum, equipped with nothing
but a chair for the master and stools or benches for the pupils. Work began
before dawn and lasted all day with a break for lunch. There were summer
holidays lasting from the end of July to mid-October and probably some days
off for festivals. The pupils, both boys and girls, came to school attended by
their pedagogues, slaves who combined the functions of personal servant and
governess. Sometimes these slaves had also received some education, a large
house having its own servants' schoolroom or *pedagogium* for them so that they
could hear their charges say their lessons and sometimes help them. An account
of a day in the life of an early third-century schoolboy describes the pedagogue

[1] *Epistulae* XXII.

307

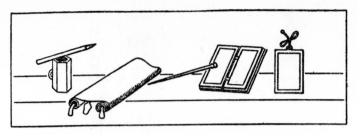

120. Pen and inkpot, parchment roll and writing tablets. From a
Pompeian wall-painting

assisting the child to get ready for school and carrying his inkpot, writing boards
and ruler, and later escorting him to the baths.[1]

The subjects learnt during the five years of primary school were chiefly the
three R's. Quintilian recommends that the names and appearance of the letters
of the alphabet should be learnt together, and as soon as they became familiar
they should be pricked out for the stylus to trace on a wax tablet, or incised on
a board so that the child's pen could be guided along the grooves. The alphabet
was practised in reverse or in various combinations, and sometimes ivory
letters were cut out and given to children to play with. Syllables and word-
building followed and then short sentences, usually moral sayings. These were
learnt by heart, recited, then written down (fig. 119). Quintilian considered
good writing important, 'a sluggish pen delays our thoughts',[2] and an illegible
hand meant the wearisome task of dictating to a copyist. Writing was practised
on wax tablets and scrap pieces of parchment and papyrus (fig. 120). Copies of
books which failed to sell were remaindered and used, as Martial points out,
as wrappers for salt fish and ploughed by schoolboys' pens.[3] Potsherds were
also handy and a second-century Egyptian schoolmaster made good use of a
nearby rubbish dump to supply material for pupils working on the Greek
alphabet. An Egyptian papyrus shows a phrase copied out seven times.[4] A
wooden writing board, whitened and ruled in columns, one of several Egyptian
examples now in the British Museum, was used for exercises in Greek grammar
and a scribbling block of small waxed tablets includes a probable portrait of the
schoolmaster.[5] Reading included lists of words difficult to pronounce, and then
selected passages of prose and poetry would be dictated, learnt by heart and
recited. Speaking correctly was important and Quintilian is anxious that even
the child's nurse should have no unpleasant accent.

The cumbersome nature of Roman numerals and the lack of a sign for zero
prevented studies in arithmetic progressing very far. A system of duodecimal

[1] Marrou (1956) p. 268. [2] I. 1. 28. [3] IV. 86. 11.
[4] J. G. Milne, 'Relics from Graeco-Egyptian Schools', *J.H.S.* XXVIII (1909) 121, 123.
[5] F. Kenyon, 'Two Greek School Tablets', *J.H.S.* XXIX (1909) 29–40.

fractions in which each fraction was referred to by name and not by number made matters worse. In Horace a child is asked: 'If we take an *uncia* ($\frac{1}{12}$) from a *quincunx* ($\frac{5}{12}$), what remains? A *triens* ($\frac{1}{3}$). And if instead an *uncia* is added, a *semis* ($\frac{1}{2}$) results.'[1] Multiplication tables of the one-and-one-is-two and two-and-two-are-four variety seem to have been recited and St Augustine recalls them as a hateful song. Counting was done on the fingers. The most useful form of arithmetic, and the one best appreciated by shopkeepers and clerks whose children would not progress beyond primary school, was done with the *abacus*, a predecessor of the calculating machine which is still in use in some parts of the world today. In Roman times it consisted of a grooved board used with beads or a marked table for counters. These were divided in columns, each identified by the Roman letter which stood for the number, i.e. units (I), fives (V), tens (X), fifties (L), hundreds (C), five hundreds (D), and thousands (M). Symbols for fractions were also sometimes used. The counters (*calculi*) were originally pebbles, and later of glass, bone or ivory.

At 11 or 12 years old until the age of 15, some children would go on to the form of secondary schooling provided by the *grammaticus*. He was a rather better educated schoolmaster paid, according to Diocletian's Edict, 200 *denarii* monthly per pupil. His class-room was still only a room off the Forum, with a few busts of authors decorating the walls, but usually he had an assistant. Some of the more important Roman grammarians are known from a treatise written by Suetonius in the early second century, and from this it appears that while a few made a good living, others could barely afford the cost of a garret. Often they were men who had been unsuccessful in other careers and they came from Gaul, Spain and other provinces as well as Italy. Most of them produced literary works of their own and several obtained posts as librarians. Lucius Orbilius Pupillus, a famous teacher in the time of Cicero, was commemorated by a statue in his native Beneventum. He seems to have had a most unpleasant temper which he vented on his pupils and he wrote a book on the wrongs inflicted on teachers by parents. M. Verrius Flaccus, on the other hand, encouraged competition in his classes, rewarding the best students with a book. He was chosen by Augustus to instruct his grandsons.[2]

Quintilian summarises the curriculum of the *grammaticus* under two headings: the art of speaking and writing Greek and Latin correctly, and the reading and interpretation of literature, especially poetry, with some reference to history, philosophy and other subjects, partly because these were necessary to understand poets' allusions. Much of the grammatical teaching was on lines already

[1] Marrou (1956) p. 271, also Ausonius, *Eclogues* 6.
[2] Suetonius, *De Grammaticis et Rhetoribus* IX, XVII.

developed in Greek schools with stress placed on parts of speech and the con-
jugation of verbs, and Quintilian provides some paragraphs on the philology and
etymology of Latin compared with Greek. Speech, Greek or Latin, should be
that of the educated man, avoiding colloquialisms or antiquated phraseology.
Diction should be clear, accurate and elegant. Pronunciation and expression
were carefully checked in reading. Once the passage had been satisfactorily
read, the teacher interpreted it, summarising the story or plot of poem or play,
describing what was known of the author and criticising his style.[1] While the
pupil must not be confused by too much detail, it is clear that Quintilian's ideal
teacher was a well-read man with much general knowledge. Quintilian, however,
also has some caustic things to say about pedantic and inaccurate scholarship.[2]

At this stage of his or her education the pupil began to paraphrase orally or
in simple compositions some of the stories he was learning. Aesop's fables, the
natural successors of the nursery fairy stories, were used for this by beginners
who then went on to more difficult themes expanded according to strict rules.
Originality was not desired, the object was to make the student fluent and well
informed. Other subjects studied at this stage included music as an aid to producing a pleasant speaking voice, and gymnastics for relaxation and deportment.
Geometry was also learnt by those who might have to deal with questions of
property or land boundaries in the law-courts.

A small number of students went on from the grammarian's classes to the
university level of the teacher of rhetoric. Most of their earlier education had
been designed to prepare them for public speaking in municipal assemblies or
law-courts or on public occasions, and now they had to learn to hold forth
according to a complicated system of rules and customs developed from Greek
precedents. According to Cicero and Quintilian an orator should have the
widest possible background of law, history and philosophy. His natural gifts
of intellect, voice and good health must be cultivated by continual practice in
writing, reading and speaking under the guidance of a skilful teacher. Tacitus,
however, believed that a student did better to work with a successful orator in
the Forum rather than attend the rhetorician's classes where he would only
debate with boys as inexperienced as himself.[3] The rhetor's pupils worked
through a preliminary course of rules and regulations and were then set to
compose and deliver speeches on various subjects, some on historical themes,
others on *controversiae*, cases, usually petitions, which they argued as if in court.
Many of the subjects were first considered in Hellenistic times and were still
popular six centuries later. They were often somewhat far-fetched. Those

[1] I. 4 and 6; Barclay, (1959) p. 185; Marrou, (1956) p. 275. [2] I. 8. 18.
[3] D. L. Clark, *Rhetoric in Graeco-Roman Education* (New York, 1957) pp. 16, 64.

collected by the elder Seneca, for example, include the following: 'Two brothers, one of whom had a son, disagreed. When the uncle became needy the nephew against the prohibition of his father supported him. Being disinherited by his father for this, he was silent. He was adopted by the uncle who by receiving an inheritance became rich. Then the young man's father began to suffer want and was supported by his son against the prohibition of the uncle, who thereupon disinherited the young man.' A variation of this problem is possibly of Greek origin: 'A man disinherited his son. The latter studied medicine, and when his father fell ill and was given up by other physicians, restored him to health. He was thereupon restored to his father's favour. His stepmother having fallen ill was also despaired of by the physicians. The father asked the son to cure her and upon his refusal disinherited him.'[1] Quintilian, in appealing for themes closer to real life, enquires where in law could cases dealing with such magicians, plagues, oracles and stepmothers more cruel than any in tragedy be found? Kidnapping, imaginary laws, and, as we have seen, disinheritance, were all debated. Some of this training must have been of more value to the future poet and author. Quintilian himself, in one of his formal declamations, raises a more original problem concerned with a poor man living on a small farm in an area being gradually engulfed by a large estate. He kept bees and the owner of the estate complained that these insects spoilt his flowers and demanded their removal. When the poor man failed to do this, the estate owner poisoned his flowers and the bees died. The poor man brought an action for damages saying that his bees were all he had, flowers inevitably fade quickly, and in any case he gave the rich man honey annually. Also he loved his bees and it was cruelty to bees to poison them. The plea is worked up to include a consideration of the value and virtues of bees with some moral asides on the shortcomings of man, and it concludes with the observation that the poison which killed the bees also killed the flowers![2]

The teachers of rhetoric were usually better paid than their junior colleagues and under the Empire some of them attained high office. Sometimes keen rivalry arose between them and then each was supported by his own pupils and followers. Quintilian received an annual payment of 2,000 sesterces for each pupil.[3] When the Emperor Vespasian created two official posts of teachers of Greek and Latin rhetoric, virtually professorships, with an annual salary of 1,000 gold pieces, Quintilian was the first of the professors of Latin and his pupils included Domitian's nephews and the younger Pliny. Marcus Aurelius

[1] *Controversiae* I. 1; IV. 5 trans. T. S. Simonds.
[2] D. L. Clark, *op. cit.* p. 247.
[3] Juvenal, *Satires* VII. 186–7.

later established another chair of rhetoric at Athens as well as four professorships for the various kinds of philosophy, but these all carried a lower salary. Vespasian also initiated the custom of exempting rhetors and *grammatici* from certain municipal taxes. From this time onward an increasing number of state schools were endowed by emperors and private persons, and money was also invested for the support and education of needy boys and girls. Eventually the majority of towns in the Empire are believed to have had schools financed either out of municipal funds or from benefactions.[1]

At its best, Roman education produced an individual with high moral and intellectual standards, speaking and writing both Greek and Latin fluently, holding Greek civilisation in high esteem and with an outlook on life broadened by encounters with influences and people from other parts of the Empire. This way of life formed part of the *Pax Romana* and its development in the provinces was given every encouragement by imaginative governors. The sons of the native nobility were gathered together and educated as Roman citizens, and eventually local initiative may have carried on the good work. The process is well known from Spain where it started early in the first century B.C. until by the end of the first century A.D. even small mining centres had elementary schools, and *grammatici* and rhetors were at work in most towns. Their efforts may have helped to produce such writers as Seneca, Martial and Quintilian himself. Similar developments seem to have taken place in Africa from the time of Caesar.

Gaul is educationally in a class by itself among the western provinces, as Greek civilisation was established along the Mediterranean coast in pre-Roman times in such Greek colonial settlements as Marseilles, and these continued as centres of learning. Autun was an early Roman centre and in A.D. 21 the Aeduan chief, Julius Sacrovir, is recorded as seizing it and gaining useful hostages from the young Gallic aristocracy gathered in the schools there. Indeed this city, built in the heart of Gaul to replace the old Aeduan capital of Bibracte, seems to have been specially suited for such educational purposes. Its schools became famous, with splendid buildings named after Maenius, a benefactor of whom nothing else is known. In 269 the town was destroyed and British masons later helped to rebuild it. In 298 the professors teaching in the *Scholae Maenianae* included the Emperor Constantius Chlorus' secretary Eumenius, and he composed a panegyric which he declaimed when the governor of the province came to see the new buildings. In this he mentions that his grandfather also taught as a Greek rhetorician in Autun. Two of Eumenius' fellow teachers were also officials at the imperial palace.[2]

[1] Marrou (1956) p. 305.
[2] P-M. Duval, *La Vie Quotidienne en Gaule* (Paris, 1952) p. 198; Chadwick (1955) p. 27.

The love which the Gauls had always had for eloquence developed well under Roman rule. In Lyons Romanisation increased from the time of the foundation of the altar of Rome and Augustus by Drusus in 12 B.C. and Suetonius recounts how Caligula introduced contests in Greek and Latin oratory there. The losers had to provide the prizes and make speeches in honour of the winners.[1] Petilius Cerealis addressing the Treveri and Lingones in A.D. 70, after the rebellion of Civilis, remarks on their regard for eloquence as a superior gift able to change good and evil. They had listened to seditious speeches but now he proposed to offer them a few plain words.[2] In the second century Lucian gives a fascinating account of the Gaulish god of poetry and eloquence, Ogmios, depicted in a picture as an old man drawing men to him by fine gold chains attached from his tongue to their ears. A Celt who spoke Greek told the author that in this connection Ogmios was equated with Heracles.[3] This is evidence for Greek spoken somewhere along the Atlantic coast, and further south it also flourished in big cities until its study began to decline in the fourth century. *Grammatici* and rhetors working in Vienne, Limoges, Toulouse, Arles and Narbonne are known from documents and inscriptions and while some of their graduates stayed at home, many others were well known as teachers and advocates in Rome.[4] A badly damaged relief built into the walls at Narbonne apparently shows about a dozen scholars seated on benches facing two seated figures, probably schoolmasters, in a room lit by two windows. Two more children are just coming in through the open door and one seems to be trying to hide behind the master's chair.[5] From Limoges comes a tombstone with the bust of the grammarian Blaesianus, 'always a lover of the muses'.[6]

The best picture of school and university life in Gaul, however, is given by Ausonius. Born at Bordeaux *c.* A.D. 310 of a father who was a doctor more at home in Greek than in Latin,[7] Ausonius himself was educated under the supervision of his uncle Arborius, a professor at Toulouse who also appeared in court at Narbonne, Vienne and in Spain. In 328 Ausonius returned to Bordeaux first as a *grammaticus*, and later as a rhetor. About 364 he was made tutor to Gratian, son of the Emperor Valentinian I, and he later became prefect of the Gauls and a consul. He retired to his estate near Bordeaux at the age of seventy. Among his poems are some commemorating the professors of Bordeaux which have been described as 'a kind of residents' list of the university staff, with testimonials appended to each entry.'[8] They include orators, Greek and Latin

---

[1] *Caligula*, 20. [2] Tacitus, *Histories* IV. 73. [3] Chadwick (1955) p. 26.
[4] Marrou (1956) p. 297; M. L. Clarke, *Rhetoric at Rome* (1953) p. 143.
[5] E. I no. 619. [6] *Ibid.* II no. 1584.
[7] *Domestica* IV. 8. [8] Chadwick (1955) p. 50.

121. Woman with two children. The boy probably
carries a pen and a school satchel

rhetoricians and many grammarians, and the author pays tribute to their learning, prodigious memories and gifts of clear expression. A note of criticism,
however, creeps in occasionally as with Delphidius, whose 'lack of diligence in
teaching disappointed the hopes of your pupils' fathers',[1] his nephew Herculanus
whom 'the swerving steps of slippery youth caused to fall headlong',[2] or the
once popular teacher Marcellus 'given a place amongst grammarians of scant
deserving'.[3]

North of Autun the evidence for education has survived less well, although
literature and inscriptions testify to the existence of centres at Avenches,
Besançon and Cologne.[4] A Strasburg tombstone shows a seated figure writing
on a partly unrolled manuscript, probably with a reed pen. Beside him stands
a child holding an inkpot and a case containing four more pens. This may be
a schoolmaster or the child's pedagogue.[5] A relief at Sens depicts a mother
accompanied by a girl and also by a boy carrying a reed pen, a school satchel
and probably an inkpot (fig. 121).[6] In the late second century Fronto, tutor to
the Emperor Marcus Aurelius, speaks of Rheims as another Athens.[7] As the
residence of the governor of Gallia Belgica, it must have been a seat of Romanisation and it has also produced a tombstone showing a child probably carrying

[1] *Commemoratio Professorum Burdigalensium* V. 32.   [2] *Ibid.* XI. 4.   [3] *Ibid.* XVIII. 13.
[4] Marrou (1956) p. 297   [5] E. VII no. 5503.   [6] E. IV no. 2796.
[7] C. Fronto, *Reliquiae* ed. Niebuhr 271.

his school satchel.[1] Trier was also a centre of intellectual life. The school scene relief from Neumagen near there, already mentioned, dates from about the end of the second century and Ausonius speaks of 'eloquence which vies with the tongues of Rome' found by the Moselle.[2] One of his letters is addressed to Ursulus, a grammarian at Trier. It suggests that teachers then worked a six-hour day and concluded with a reference to Ursulus' colleague Harmonius, the glory of the Greek and Latin muse alike.[3]

With so much evidence for a lively intellectual life in Gaul it is difficult to believe that some of this activity did not cross the Channel and the North Sea. There were strong ties of kinship between the inhabitants of northern Gaul and Southern Britain and a steady stream of officials, traders and other travellers came and went between the north-western provinces. Schools, however, leave no recognisable traces for the archaeologist and Britain had no Ausonius to celebrate the professors of Verulamium, Londinium or Camulodunum. What facts has the province produced in support of the statement that the Empire as a whole 'was covered with a fairly dense network of academic institutions: elementary school teachers were to be found more or less everywhere, grammarians and rhetors in places of importance'?[4]

The first problem is that of language. Celtic was presumably the mother tongue of the majority of the Romano-Britons and there is no clear evidence as to what proportion of the population were bi-lingual or mainly Latin speaking. Latin must have been the language of the army, of officials and of traders, and it must have been used in the courts and for religious ceremonies connected with Roman cults. The increasingly large numbers of Roman citizens probably learnt it willingly and a large number of words in the modern Celtic languages are known to have found their way there from spoken Latin.[5] Nothing has been found to suggest that the Celtic of this period was a written language and Gaulish parallels suggest that if native proper names or Celtic words were used, they could only be written down by means of the Latin or, occasionally, the Greek alphabets.[6] For commercial life it was necessary to know enough Latin words and numbers to record any kind of transaction, and to be able to read and write them. A large number of *graffiti* written on tiles before firing or scratched on pottery or wall plaster have survived and many more written on wood must have perished. Silchester has produced over fifty names on potsherds and thirteen

---

[1] E. V no. 3736. [2] *Mosella* 383.
[3] *Epistulae* XIII. The Roman hour varied in length according to the time of year.
[4] Marrou (1956) p. 296.
[5] K. Jackson, *Language and History in Early Britain* (Edinburgh, 1953) p. 76.
[6] T. G. E. Powell, *The Celts* (1963) p. 19, Pl. LXIX.

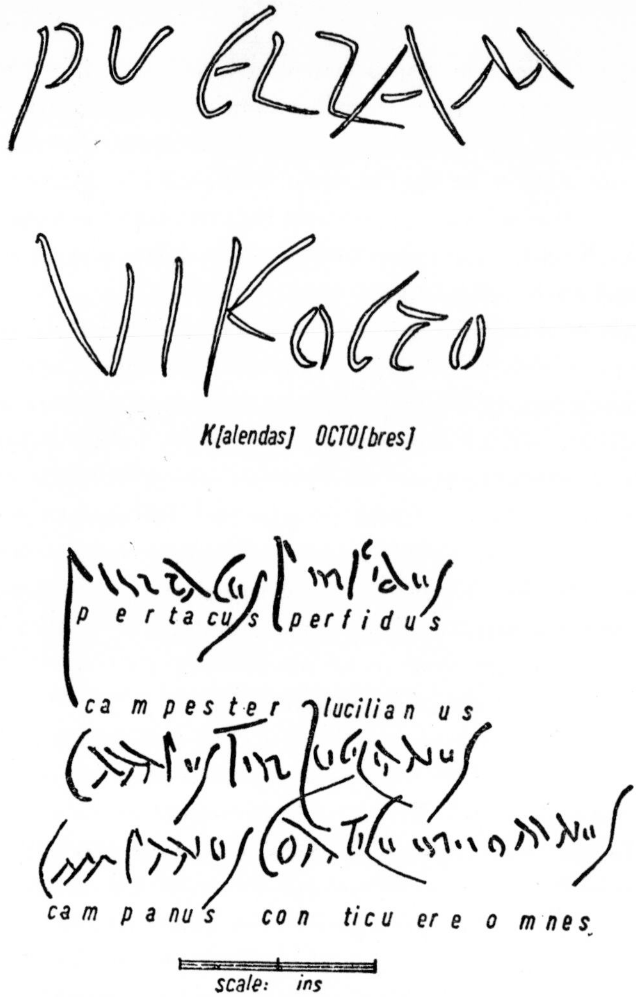

K[alendas] OCTO[bres]

p e r t a cu s   perfidus

ca m pes t e r   lucilian u s

cam p a nu s   con ticu ere o mnes

scale: ins

122   *Graffiti* found at Silchester

comments on tiles including a date, VI K[*alendas*]*Octo*[*bres*], and 'puellam'
meaning a girl! (fig. 122).[1] Another 'girl' is known from Caerleon.[2] One Silchester brickmaker wrote *Fecit tubul*(*um*) *Clementinus* (Clementinus made this box
tile), and another, possibly less enthusiastic, *satis* (enough)! York and London
have also produced numerous names scratched on pottery, usually samian. London provides another date, V[A]PRILIS (V *Kalendas Apriles*) on an *amphora* and
also M VIIS VINI for seven and a half measures of wine, although these need
not have been written in Britain. The best known *graffito* of all; AVSTALIS
DIBVS XIII VAGATVR SIB[I] COTIDIM (Austalis has been going off on his
own every day for thirteen days), comes from a tile found in Newgate. The

[1] G. Boon (1957) pp. 65, 221 n. 4.
[2] *J.R.S.* LIV (1964) 183 no. 30.

illegible scribble on wall plaster at Caerwent which may have been purposely
rubbed out as underneath it someone wrote *Puniamini'* (For shame!), has already
been mentioned.[1] Still more illuminating is a tile from Caerwent now in the
Caerleon Museum which shows the name Bellicanus written in four different
hands, possibly a writing lesson. A tombstone erected by a Julius Belicianus to
his mother, Julia Veneria, is in the same museum.[2] The first three letters of the
alphabet were found cut on a column shaft at Caerwent, coming, perhaps, from
some building partly used as a school. A 'D' was also lightly traced, possibly at
the moment when someone came and caught the culprit. Scribblings on wall
plaster include *Paternus scripsit*, written twice in a house at Dorchester (Dorset),[3]
and an incomplete comment which probably means 'Civilis is in confinement',
from a room in a recently excavated house at Leicester.[4] Remains of wooden
tablets from the Chew Park villa[5] and from London[6] are also reminders of all the
accounts and business transactions in Latin which have failed to survive.

If these *graffiti*, together with the numerous simple votive tablets and rough
little altars to native gods, testify to some knowledge of reading and writing
and so to the labours of the *litterator*, what part was played by the *grammaticus*?
Tacitus records that Agricola introduced into Britain the policy of establishing
a plan of education for the sons of the tribal aristocracy, and that as a result of
his encouragement of Roman amenities, a distaste for Latin was replaced by
an enthusiastic desire to learn it.[7] Archaeology has produced one fragment of
evidence which may support this. Two silvered bronze votive tablets found
near the possible site of Agricola's palace when he was in York, bear Greek
inscriptions dedicating them to (*a*) Ocean and Tethys, and (*b*) the gods of the
governor's residence.[8] Both were vowed by someone called Demetrius and it is
not impossible that this is the same individual whom Plutarch met at Delphi
c. A.D. 83–4. Plutarch describes him as a *grammaticus* who had travelled to the
furthest limits of the Empire.[9]

Another scrap of a writing lesson scratched on a tile from Silchester includes
the words *pertacus, perfidus, campester, lucilianus, campanus*, some of which may be
names, and two words: *conticuere omnes*, a quotation from Virgil (fig. 122). The
complete tag is '*Conticuere omnes (intentique ora tenebant)*' or 'All fell silent and
steadfast held their gaze.'[10] References to the *Aeneid* are also known from other
sites. The arm and side of a figure holding a spear survives from the plastered
wall of a room in a small villa at Otford, Kent, and is accompanied by the

---

[1] See above p. 41. [2] *R.I.B.* 375. [3] *J.R.S.* XXVIII (1938) 206 no. 20.
[4] *J.R.S.* LIV (1964) 182 no. 22 (b). [5] See above p. 303. [6] See above p. 175.
[7] *Agricola* XXI. [8] *Eboracum* p. 133 no. 142.
[9] Plutarch, *de defectu oraculorum*, 2. [10] *Aeneid* II, 1; Boon (1957) *op. cit.* p. 265.

painted inscription BINA MANV. This was probably a picture of Aeneas or Achates with the comment '*Bina manu lato crispans hastilia ferro*' (brandishing in his hand two broad-bladed spears).[1] The nearby Lullingstone villa has produced an original elegiac couplet composed in passable Latin, worked into the mosaic of Europa and the bull already described.[2] This alludes to the *Aeneid* Book I and its meaning would only be appreciated by diners acquainted with Latin literature. And in Somerset there is the quite exceptional series of scenes from Virgil illustrating the story of Dido and Aeneas from Low Ham.[3] In the north the Wolf and Twins appear not only on the mosaic found at Aldborough (Pl. 83)[4] but also on fragmentary reliefs which probably come from the interior of the Temple of Jupiter Dolichenus at Corbridge. The Corbridge representation is part of a more elaborate scene which has various allusions which could only be understood by those conversant with Virgil.[5] Here, of course, the worshippers would usually be soldiers.

Scraps of painted inscriptions, also probably quotations, have been recovered from other villas including Woodchester, and one of the fine mosaics from Frampton (Dorset) contains a reference to 'The head of Neptune, to whose lot fell the kingdom (of the sea) scoured by the winds, figured here, his deep-blue brow girt by a pair of dolphins'.[6] Neptune's head is duly portrayed in a border of dolphins. Many of the Latin words which passed into the Celtic tongues were rather archaic in form and this artistic evidence supports the suggestion that they were spread by the country landowners.[7] These would be the families whose children passed through the schools started under Agricola where the schoolmasters would insist on correct and conservative speech, unlike the Vulgar Latin spoken by traders and lower class townsfolk. The same families must also have provided many of the decurions who would have to speak in the *ordo*, on public affairs. Some of them probably completed their studies with professors of rhetoric who may well have been Gauls. After all, Juvenal remarks that 'Today the whole world has its Greek and Roman Athens, eloquent Gaul has trained the pleaders of Britain and distant Thule talks of hiring a rhetorician'.[8] A little evidence for the study of Greek has also survived; a few inscriptions including those of Demetrius described above, and a mosaic at Aldborough (Yorks.) which depicted the Muses identified by their Greek names.[9]

[1] *Aeneid* I. 313, Hinks (1933) no. 84, p. 56.
[2] See above p. 282. [3] See above p. 283.
[4] See above p. 101. Toynbee (1963) no. 184 p. 198. [5] Toynbee (1964) p. 141.
[6] Toynbee (1963) no. 199, p. 203.
[7] K. Jackson, *op. cit.* p. 109.
[8] *Satires* XV. 112. Trans. G. G. Ramsay.
[9] R. Collingwood, *Archaeology in Roman Britain* (1930) p. 177.

The predominance of Virgil in British literary allusions is reasonable as his work was of such importance in the literature of the period. According to Suetonius, the *grammatici* began to read it in school sometime in the late first century B.C.[1] Other poets such as Horace, Ovid and Lucian were also studied, but the four corner posts of the Roman secondary school curriculum were Virgil, Terence, Sallust and Cicero, and numerous commentaries were made on their works.[2] For Greek studies Homer and Menander were of particular importance. There was no lack of reading matter and there are many allusions to the dedication of books and the public readings of new works by their authors. Cicero talks of dedicating new works to Brutus, Varro and others and adds that Varro is dedicating one to him but 'Two years have passed and the old tortoise, going hard all the time, has scarcely progressed an inch'.[3] This remark is in a letter to his publisher Atticus in which he also says 'You have given my speech for Ligarius a splendid puff'. The work for Varro was re-written, the first version apparently being written out by Atticus' staff to no purpose. Numbers of slaves copied these manuscripts from dictation with varying degrees of accuracy so that a complete edition of Martial's epigrams would be ready in seventeen hours. A publisher employing fifty slaves could bring out an edition of a thousand copies in a month varying in price from half a *denarius* upwards for a cheap copy. A luxurious copy of Martial's first book of epigrams cost five *denarii*.[4] From Augustus onwards in Rome, and, no doubt, in other towns, there were a number of bookshops, their columns covered with advertisements. Authors realised they had a public spread all over the Empire. As Martial remarked, 'Nor do I give these epigrams to vacant ears but my book, amid Getic frosts, besides martial standards, is thumbed by the hardy centurion and Britain is said to hum my verses.'[5] When bishop Paulinus brought the manuscript of Sulpicius Severus' life of St Martin of Tours to Rome at the beginning of the fifth century, the booksellers were delighted with their sales and it was soon being read in Carthage, Alexandria and the Egyptian desert.

The books were written on papyrus mounted on rollers with projecting knobs, sometimes of ivory or ebony. They were stored in coloured vellum covers with scarlet strings and labels, and kept in round boxes or in rectangular bookcases set in niches. The shelves were often divided into pigeonholes, the cases had wooden doors and their exteriors might be decorated with inlays

[1] *De grammaticis et rhetoribus* XVI.
[2] For evidence for other authors see Marrou (1959) p. 279, Barclay, (1959) p. 182.
[3] *Ad Atticum* XIII. 12. Trans. L. P. Wilkinson.
[4] L. Friedlaender, *Roman Life and Manners under the Early Empire* III (1910) p. 37.
[5] XI. 3. Trans. W. Ker.

or bronze medallions. By the fourth century, vellum, previously used for small notebooks, was beginning to supplant papyrus.

The first public libraries built in Rome date from the first century B.C. Such great collections of books were already known from the eastern Mediterranean with noted examples at Alexandria and Pergamum, and now Augustus founded one connected with the Temple of Apollo on the Palatine and another in the Campus Martius. They comprised separate rooms for Greek and Latin books and a reading-room. Later emperors continued to build libraries and nearly thirty of them have been identified in Rome. Two of particular interest have also been found in Athens. An inscription records that one was built soon after A.D. 100 by Titus Flavius Pantainos, his son and daughter, and they gave the courtyard, peristyle, library with its books and all the decorations. The latter probably included a sculptural group showing Homer seated between figures representing the Iliad and the Odyssey. Another inscription provides a fragment of the library regulations: 'No book shall be removed since we have taken an oath to that effect. Open from the first hour to the sixth.'[1] The Emperor Hadrian built a larger library in Athens later in the second century.

Like baths and other amenities it became usual for decurions and other rich men to give public libraries to their towns. Pliny gave one to Como and wrote asking a friend to read the speech he made in the *curia* at its dedication, before it was published.[2] In the middle of the third century another wealthy man gave a library to the *colonia* at Timgad in North Africa at a cost of 400,000 sesterces. It included a large reading-room where teachers may have brought classes to see books and perhaps check their own copies, and several stackrooms. It faces north in accordance with Vitruvius' advice that libraries should have this aspect for the light and because in rooms facing south, books were ruined by damp winds and worms.[3] Copies of the city's laws and other legal documents were probably deposited in such libraries, with manuscripts of plays, poetry and scientific literature by local authors, and as many other books as could be collected.

Private libraries also flourished and more Roman books seem to have survived from them than from the public collections. Seneca remarks that libraries have become as necessary as baths, with numbers of books accumulated as a form of ostentation to show off the ornamented ends and labels of the rolls. A small room about 12 feet square was excavated over a hundred years ago in a villa probably belonging to L. Calpurnius Piso, just outside Herculaneum. Hundreds

---

[1] *The Athenian Agora: A Guide* (Athens, 1962) pp. 85, 162. [2] *Epistulae* I. 8. 2.
[3] H. Pfeffer, 'Roman Library at Timgad', *Memoirs of the American School in Rome* XI (1931) p. 159.

of rolls of charred papyrus were found in the bookcases round the walls and on both sides of a bookstand in the centre of the room. The books are mostly philosophical works probably written, annotated or collected by Piso's friend, Philodemus, a minor philosopher who lived in the first century B.C.[1] Pliny remarks that he had shelves placed in a sunny room in his Laurentine villa for the books he reads over and over again,[2] and Sidonius Apollinaris, nearly four hundred years later, describes a room in a friend's villa with books in abundance like the shelves of a grammarian or a bookseller's towering bookcases. They were arranged so that the books of devotions were placed near the ladies and the works of Roman eloquence near the master; Augustine and Prudentius on one side, and Horace and Varro on the other.[3]

With the knowledge that both public and private libraries existed elsewhere in the Empire, can we believe that they were also built in Britain? It seems probable, but like schoolrooms they would leave little trace. The only evidence would be an inscription or a room with niches for bookshelves. A recent writer who believes in their existence draws attention to one scrap of possible evidence in a passage written by Matthew Paris, in which he describes the Abbots of St Albans pillaging Verulamium for building materials for their new abbey. It seems that in a palace in the middle of the old city they found a recess in a wall containing books and rolls including one fine old book roll on oak rollers with silk cords. Some of the books were in a Latin recognisable to the monks, but the best roll they could not understand at first. It was said to contain a history of St Alban and after copying, the roll crumbled into dust. Such a contribution to the importance of the local shrine may be viewed with some suspicion, but it does seem possible that some actual discovery of Roman books may lie behind this story.[4]

Early British Christianity provides better evidence for British education. Besides the travels of bishops to the Councils of Arles (A.D. 314) and Rimini (A.D. 359), there is an itinerary written for nuns in southern Gaul by an anonymous lady who may have been British. Possibly she was Etheria, 'from the farthest shore of the western sea', who visited the holy places of Palestine and Egypt to pray and to learn, and the range of her knowledge is amazing.[5] Pelagius at the end of the fourth century developed a heresy of a philosophical and highly intellectual nature, suggesting that he was the product of flourishing British schools still teaching good Latin. He arrived in Rome soon after A.D. 400 and his heresy spread and caused trouble in many parts of the Empire until Celestine,

[1] A. Maiuri, *Herculaneum* (Rome, 1956) p. 74.   [2] *Epistulae* II. 17. 8.   [3] *Epistulae* II. 9.
[4] R. Irwin, *Origins of the English Library* (1958) p. 60. Wheeler (1936) p. 36.
[5] N. K. Chadwick, ed. *Studies in Early British History* (1954) p. 207.

bishop of Rome (A.D. 422–32) declared his intention of freeing Britain from this plague. He sent St Germanus, bishop of Auxerre, overseas for this purpose and St Germanus found the people of Verulamium ready to welcome him and enjoy a theological discussion in A.D. 429. A series of letters also written in the fifth century include two from a man, travelling abroad with his little daughter, to his father, probably a bishop, in Britain. He tells him he has left the little girl with a lady of austere and holy life in Sicily, and says that she must be thought of as a boy who must be sent away from home for his education. This custom of sending youths to continue their education in the homes of influential friends was not unusual among the Romans, but it is noteworthy to find it still continuing among Britons as late as this period.[1] Lastly, there is the Confession of St Patrick, also written about this time, in which he describes himself as illiterate, ignorant and rustic, blaming himself for not paying more heed to his education during childhood. Such modesty is a convention of this period, but in chapter 13 he mentions certain rhetoricians. It has been suggested that in the fourth century barbarian invasions caused Gaulish scholars to emigrate to Britain so perhaps they, or the products of their schools, were the authorities whose possible criticisms were worrying St Patrick.[2]

[1] *Ibid.* p. 211.
[2] *Ibid.* p. 218.

12
The professions (2)
Medicine

Another profession which must have been known in Roman Britain is that of the physician. An altar with a Greek inscription found at Chester and erected to the mighty Saviour Gods by Hermogenes, a doctor, is a reminder that many of the doctors at this period were of Greek origin (fig. 123).[1] The medicine they practised was also largely based on earlier Greek studies. As at all periods, sick people also turned to religion for healing, particularly to deities such as Apollo, while the Romans also invoked various minor deities for ailments affecting the different parts of the body. The most important god of healing, however, was the Greek Asclepius whom the Romans called Aesculapius. He appears in the *Iliad* as a mortal, the 'blameless physician', who was instructed by the wise centaur Chiron. Other sources describe him as Apollo's son by a human mother. His daughter Hygieia personified Health and was sometimes equated with the Roman goddess Salus. The cult seems to have been well established in Greece by the fourth century B.C. and there it was carried on by priests at temples at various sites, including Cos and Epidaurus.[2] After some preliminary rites and offerings, the sick person slept for a night in the temple precincts, relating his dreams to a priest the following morning. The priest, presumably inspired by the god, then interpreted the dreams and suggested remedies. In time other

[1] R.I.B. 461.   [2] Singer *et al.* (1956) p. 24.

123 Greek inscription of the doctor, Hermogenes, Chester

types of treatment including drugs, diet, massage, baths and various forms of exercise were also administered at these cult centres by doctors who were not priests.

Temples of healing of this type with patients sleeping within the precincts continued in use into the Roman period. In Britain the large fourth-century temple at Lydney where Nodens, a native god of healing, is known to have been worshipped, may have been used in this way (fig. 13). It stands alone in the midst of a site with large baths and a possible guesthouse. Another building with single rooms ranged along a portico may be the place where the patients slept as it resembles structures found at Epidaurus and other sites, and fits in with Pausanias' statement that beyond the temple is the place where the suppliants sleep.[1] Another temple of unusual type found in the Roman city at Augst in Switzerland may also have been a centre for medical treatment with religious supervision. Aesculapius, Apollo and Sucellus were among the deities worshipped there and a small spa existed nearby. In Britain, Bath with its medicinal waters and its temple dedicated to Sulis Minerva must also have been a place of pilgrimage for the sick. Buxton is another spa in use in Roman times.

The god Aesculapius was worshipped all over the Roman Empire and an altar dedicated to him with the Latin inscription repeated in Greek has been discovered at Lanchester (Durham), presumably as a thank-offering.[2] Another altar comes from Chester and is dedicated to Fortuna the Home-bringer, Aesculapius and Salus by the freedmen and slave household of T. Pomponius Mamilianus Rufus Antistianus Funisulanus Vettonianus.[3] Aesculapius' staff with a snake twined round it appears on the side of the altar. Other dedications were found at South Shields and Maryport, and an altar found at Overborough

[1] Wheeler (1932) p. 51.
[2] R.I.B. 1072. [3] R.I.B. 445.

324

(Lancashire) was put up to Asclepius and to Hygieia, for the welfare of himself and his own by Julius Saturninus.[1]

Hippocrates, the famous 'Father of Medicine', still remembered in connection with doctors and the Hippocratic oath, is a historical figure mentioned by Plato. He is believed to have been born at Cos *c.* 460 B.C. where he practised and taught. He also travelled to other parts of Greece and eventually died at Larissa at an advanced age. The collection of medical treatises known as the Hippocratic Corpus may have been gathered together in the course of several centuries in the library of the medical school at Cos. Some may come from a rival school at Cnidos, and the Corpus may have been edited in the third or second centuries B.C. by scholars of the flourishing school at Alexandria. It is doubtful whether Hippocrates himself wrote any of it, but it is certain that the conception of the ideal physician, wise, observant, humane and incorruptible dates from his period and has been an inspiration to good doctors ever since. The Hippocratic Corpus comprises sections dealing with all branches of medicine such as surgery, dietetics and epidemics, and including ideas of philosophy and natural science which make strange reading today. These treatises did initiate, however, the method of carefully recording facts and making inferences from them and, to quote a modern authority: 'We may even see in full force the actual process of case-taking, bedside instruction and the clinical lecture.'[2]

Greek theories on medicine probably first spread to Italy during the second and first centuries B.C. Before this the Romans seem to have treated illness with simple herbal remedies aided by the propitiation of various deities and the recitation of magical formulae and the wearing of amulets. These measures were usually carried out by the head of the house and they continued in use among the poorer or less educated members of the population, although richer families sometimes invested in slaves or freedmen with a little medical knowledge. In the beginning Greek physicians were viewed with great suspicion and Cato warned his son against them. In his household, cabbage, used both internally and externally, seems to have been the favourite prescription. The first doctors to achieve any standing in Rome seem to have been Archagathus from the Peloponnese in 219 B.C. and Asclepiades of Bithynia, *c.* 124–40 B.C. Asclepiades, previously a student in Athens and Alexandria, was the friend of Cicero and Mark Antony. He was later followed by Antonius Musa, Augustus' physician, Scribonius Largus, who accompanied Claudius to Britain and whose treatise

---

[1] *R.I.B.* 1052, 808, 609.
[2] Singer *et al.* p. 28 *et seq.* See also J. Chadwick and W. N. Mann, *The Medical Work of Hippocrates* (Oxford, 1950); and W. H. S. Jones' Introduction to his translation of *Hippocrates* in the Loeb Edition.

on Prescriptions still survives, and a whole series of court physicians of whom the most famous is probably Galen who attended the Emperor Marcus Aurelius. The status of physicians in Rome gradually improved from *c.* 46 B.C. when Julius Caesar granted the citizenship to doctors practising there, but they continued to be largely of Greek origin.

At first the only form of medical training available to a student in Rome was to attach himself to a physician like Asclepiades, and follow him on his round and examine his patients. Martial has left us a rueful account of such a visitation. 'I was sickening; but you at once attended me, Symmachus, with a train of a hundred apprentices. A hundred hands frosted by the north wind have pawed me. I had no fever before, Symmachus, now I have!'[1] Promising pupils were called on to assist the doctor more and more; they might be left to watch over his patients and report progress, and they eventually became his deputies until they set up on their own. Soon the students and doctors combined together to form societies where medical problems were discussed at a meeting place on the Esquiline Hill. Eventually the emperors built halls for their studies. Well-known doctors could command good fees from patients as well as fees from their students, and from the time of Vespasian onwards they also received state salaries as teachers.[2] A relief in the Capitoline Museum may depict one of these doctors teaching. He is reading from a scroll and more scrolls are visible in a cabinet beside him. On top of the cabinet is depicted a case of surgical instruments.

Some doctors were employed by towns to look after the poor or by guilds to attend their members. A form of state medical service had existed in Greece from about the sixth or fifth centuries B.C. This spread to the Greek colonies including Marseilles and the physicians who took part in it were sometimes highly honoured. Elections to these posts in Ephesus seem to have been competitive. During the Roman Empire the employment of doctors in the public service soon spread through Italy into Gaul and other provinces. A statute of Antoninus Pius of about A.D. 160 lays down regulations for their appointment. Small towns could employ five physicians, more important towns up to seven, and capital cities ten. These numbers were not to be exceeded. Their salaries were fixed by the *ordo* and they were encouraged to teach.[3] In time the service may have developed grades, with the court physicians gaining high rank and sometimes being appointed to important non-medical posts. Below them came the public doctors of Rome, positions which were also much sought

[1] *Epigrams* V. 9. Trans. W. Ker.
[2] Singer *et al.* p. 53; Marrou (1956) p. 192.
[3] C. Bailey, ed. *The Legacy of Rome* (Oxford, 1923) p. 292.

after, and then the doctors in other towns. All were allowed to accept any fees their patients offered them, but they were not to demand anything from those who could not pay. The doctors in private practice may have often earned more money but their position would be more precarious and dependent on fashion.

The works studied by medical students during the Empire included the *De medicina* of Celsus, Pliny's *Natural History*, the numerous writings of Galen and the *De materia medica* of Dioscorides. Celsus' work probably dated from *c*. A.D. 30 and it is believed to be all that survives of a large book which also dealt with Agriculture, Philosophy, Rhetoric and Jurisprudence. On the whole he is not believed to have been a practising physician but rather an interested and intelligent compiler who used Greek sources and translated them into Latin. The *De medicina* includes a short history of medicine, and discussions of diet, pathology, internal and external diseases and surgery.

Like Cato, the elder Pliny had a poor opinion of doctors and he devotes some chapters to Roman gossip about them, the fortunes they sometimes made and the rivalry between the different schools. 'Hence those wretched quarrelsome consultations at the bedside of the patient, no consultant agreeing with another. . . . Hence too that gloomy inscription on monuments: It is the crowd of physicians that killed me!'[1] Pliny intended his writings to replace those of the Greeks, but he actually produced only a random collection of observations and remedies, many of which are quite useless and some most obnoxious. Some of his work, however, does preserve useful material from sources now lost.

Galen started his career as physician to gladiators in Asia Minor, a post which must have provided him with much valuable experience. A well-educated man, he had studied in Greece and Alexandria and in A.D. 157 he went into practice at Pergamum. In A.D. 162 he moved to Rome, went back to Pergamum in 166, and returned to Rome in 169, remaining there until his death about thirty years later. He wrote extensively, trying to give an account of all that was known of medicine, and his treatises continued in use by both the Christian and Muslim civilisations throughout the Middle Ages. He seems to have been an excellent teacher, he made many new discoveries in connection with anatomy and physiology and he yet remained aware of the need to regard patients as individuals.

Dioscorides' *De materia medica* was written about the middle of the first century A.D. and is a collection of drugs used as remedies. The author served in the army under Nero and so travelled extensively, one of the large number of army doctors who must have spread some knowledge of Graeco-Roman medicine in the frontier districts. One of the reliefs on Trajan's column probably shows one of them at work during a battle with the Dacians, bandaging

[1] *N.H.* XXII. V. Trans. W. H. S. Jones.

124 Tombstone of Anicius Ingenuus, *medicus ordinarius* of the First Tungrian Cohort. Found near Corbridge

a wound in the thigh of a cavalry man. From the victim's expression, the wound was painful and his breeches have been cut away so that it can be dressed. Nearby, orderlies help a legionary with a damaged arm or shoulder to a seat. All wear normal military dress, and this illustrates the inscriptions which show that at best the doctors only ranked as non-commissioned officers on a level with clerks and similar administrative staff. They were exempt from the normal military fatigues and in camp they came under the orders of the *praefectus castrorum*. An inscription from the fortress at Windisch (Switzerland) gives the name of Claudius Hymnus, one of the doctors attached to the Twenty-First Legion, and Hermogenes at Chester, no doubt, cared for the sick in the legionary fortress there. At Housesteads the tombstone of Anicius Ingenuus was found, a *medicus ordinarius* aged 25, serving in the ranks of the first Tungrian cohort (fig. 124), and another inscription, now in the National Museum of Antiquities at Edinburgh, was erected by his colleagues to Gaius Acilius Bassus who had at least attained the rank of doctor with double a private's pay. At Binchester (Durham) M. Aurelius Abrocomas, doctor to a troop of cavalry, dedicated an altar to Aesculapius and Salus, probably during the third century (fig. 125).[1] Inscriptions of similar type are known from most Roman provinces.[2] Army regulations laid down the number of doctors assigned to the legions, auxiliaries and to the fleet; these varied at different periods. Medical orderlies and dressers were also on the pay-roll.

Forts and legionary fortresses were provided with hospitals where the doctors

[1] I. A. Richmond, 'The Roman Army Medical Service', *University of Durham Medical Gazette*, June, 1952.
[2] Many of them are listed by A. Casarini, *La Medicina Militare nella Leggenda e nella Storia* (Rome, 1929) p. 124 *et seq.*

125 Altar erected by a doctor to Aesculapius and Salus, for the welfare of the Cavalry Regiment of Vettonians, Binchester

could superintend the treatment of the sick and wounded. These hospitals are found in the quietest and most sheltered positions, usually near the head-quarters building. In plan they consist of two ranges of small rooms separated by a wide corridor and constructed round the four sides of a large courtyard which may have been laid out as a garden. The rooms were probably small wards holding up to three beds. They are grouped in pairs with entrances leading out on to short corridors, set at right angles to the main corridor for further peace and privacy. This arrangement must also have helped to prevent the spread of infection. At Windisch a small store or treatment room is placed between wards which must have held up to eight patients, but this is an unusual addition. Windisch and the other legionary fortresses on the Rhine frontier at Neuss and Xanten were entered through larger rooms used for reception and as operating theatres, and traces of the hearths used for heating and cleaning the surgeon's instruments, as recommended by Galen, were found there. Some of the instruments were also found, particularly at Neuss, as well as rooms for the administrative staff and for the preparation of medicines. Good water supplies were available and the Xanten hospital had its own suite of baths. All these buildings were built in stone during the reign of Claudius but they had been preceded by earlier wooden structures.[1]

In Britain a timber-built hospital dating between A.D. 83 and 90 has been found at the legionary fortress at Inchtuthil, Perthshire, with sixty small wards grouped in the usual fashion round an oblong courtyard (fig. 126). Usually the wards have sloping roofs and the corridor rose above them lit by clerestory

[1] R. Schulze, 'Die römischen Legionslazarette und andern Legionslagern', *B.J.* CXXXIX (1934) 54–63; O. Brogan, (1953). p. 41.

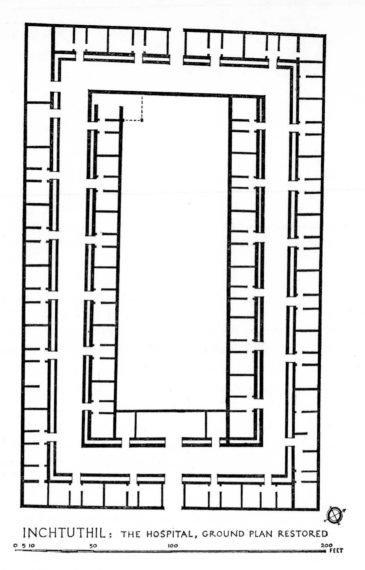

INCHTUTHIL: THE HOSPITAL, GROUND PLAN RESTORED

0 5 10   50   100   200
                                                  FEET

126   Plan of the hospital at Inchtuthil

windows. Here, however, to avoid the need for very long timbers to support
the corridor, wards and corridor were built as separate units with gabled roofs
connected by narrow covered gangways (fig. 127). A large room, probably the
operating theatre, was found opposite the entrance and other rooms at the
corners of the outer range would be used for administration or accommodation
for the staff.[1] A smaller hospital of the same period at the fort of Fendoch
roughly corresponds to one of the shorter sides of the hospital at Inchtuthil.
It comprises a row of small wards divided by the usual central corridor from

[1] *J.R.S.* XLVII (1957) 198.

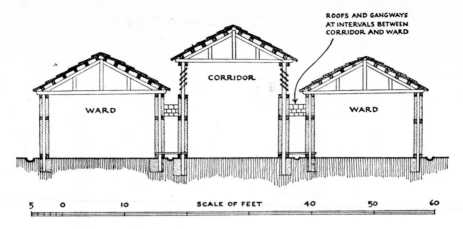

ROOFS AND GANGWAYS
AT INTERVALS BETWEEN
CORRIDOR AND WARD

CORRIDOR

WARD

WARD

SCALE OF FEET

127   Section. The hospital at Inchtuthil

a large ward or operating theatre with a room on either side (fig. 128).[1] Another hospital, on Hadrian's Wall at Housesteads, stone-built and of later date, returns to a simplified form of courtyard plan. The legionary hospital at Caerleon was identified in 1964 and seems to have been largely rebuilt or refurbished in the early second and third centuries.[2]

Hospitals also had a place in civilian life but the evidence for them is not so clear as for the military *valetudinaria*. They developed from the temples of healing, and the earliest in Rome grew up round the shrine of Aesculapius established on an island in the Tiber in the republican period. Here hardhearted masters used to leave sick or aged slaves to avoid the expense of caring for them. Later the Emperor Claudius enacted that slaves abandoned in this way who recovered were to be considered as free men.[3] From such beginnings arose a public hospital for the poor which lasted until the pagan shrines were destroyed in the fourth century. After this its history is uncertain, but the tradition was continued by the Christian hospital which stands on the site today and which goes back at least to the sixteenth century and possibly earlier.[4] Columella and Seneca mention *valetudinaria* and Celsus, discussing the practice of medicine in the early days of the Empire, mentions doctors in charge of large hospitals.[5] The earliest Christian hospitals date back to the fourth century. There were also nursing homes and clinics run by doctors in private practice. One may have been in a large house on the Via Consolare at Pompeii where the excavators found a number of surgical instruments. Passages in Galen suggest that hospitals in the provinces also date back to Roman times. Presumably they were

[1] I. A. Richmond, 'Agricolan Fort at Fendoch', P.S.A.S. LXXIII (1939) 132.
[2] *J.R.S.* LV (1965) 199.   [3] Suetonius, *Claudius* 25.
[4] C. Bailey, *op. cit.* p. 294.   [5] *De Medicina*, Prooemium 65.

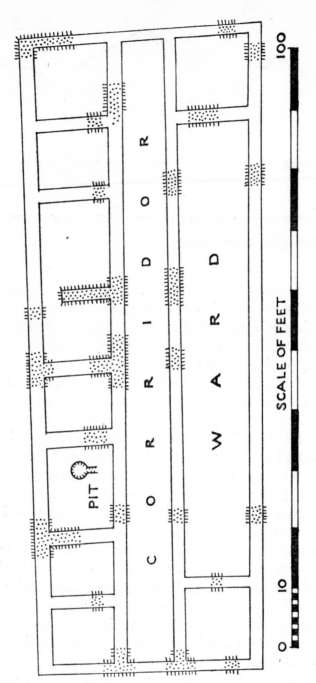

CORRIDOR

PIT

WARD

SCALE OF FEET

100

10

0

128　Plan of the hospital at Fendoch

staffed largely by veteran army doctors, with many old soldiers and their families among their patients, seeking for the same standards of medical care as they had had in the forces. Such doctors, together with good water-supplies, must have played an important part in gradually improving the health of the people.

What was the form taken by this medical care? The doctors of the Hippocratic school believed that diseases had a natural course which it was necessary to know thoroughly. Great stress was laid on the art of prognosis or predicting the course of an illness as a means of gaining the patient's confidence, and so the Hippocratic Collection includes detailed case-histories, most of them, alas, with a fatal conclusion. The physicians felt the best they could do was to assist the healing power of Nature by means of diet, exercise or rest. The few drugs available, they wisely used with caution. In Rome, Asclepiades considered these to be rather negative procedures and adopted more active measures and Celsus later on recorded ideas developed from both schools of thought. Celsus' healthy man is 'both vigorous and his own master' with no need of the doctor. His life varies between town and country with plenty of exercise, farming, hunting, or sailing, and some rest, but not too much. He goes to the baths, sometimes taking a cold one, he eats what he likes and as much, although two meals a day are better than one. The excess eating and exercise of the athlete are dangerous. Less robust individuals, however, who often include townsfolk and those fond of literary pursuits, may need more rest and should live in light and airy houses, sunny in the winter and away from damp which is conducive to colds and catarrh. Some part of the day should be used for exercise with a short rest afterwards. Overeating or excessive abstinence should be avoided and if there must be indulgence, too much drink is better than too much food.[1]

As for the doctor, who had to be called in when illness attacked even the most moderate and careful men, he should be a man of few words who learns by practice to discern well. An altogether better practitioner than he who, unpractised, over-cultivates his tongue.[2] Celsus is against too much theorising about the causes of illness and believes that it is not by eloquence but by remedies that disease is treated. The experienced practitioner does not grab his patient's arm to take his pulse on arrival. He sits down, asks how the sufferer is, and talks to calm and cheer him up before starting his examination (fig. 129).[3] If the complaint cannot be diagnosed, it should be decided what illness it most resembles and suitable measures tried. Individual traits should also be remembered, whether a patient is normally delicate or healthy and lives a strenuous or a quiet life with a high or low standard of living. The same remedies do not suit all patients, but generally rest and abstinence are advised at the outset of an illness while the symptoms are being studied. Exercise or hot or cold baths are suggested in some cases, forbidden in others. Blood-letting, emetics,

[1] *Ibid.* I. 1. 2. Trans. W. G. Spencer. [2] *Ibid.* Prooemium 39. [3] *Ibid.* III. 6.

129 Roman doctor examining a patient

clysters and, less frequently, purges are sometimes prescribed. Castor oil seems to have been known to the Romans,[1] although it is not mentioned by Celsus. Feverish patients should lie in a room with plenty of fresh air, lightly covered and not weighed down with bedclothes.[2] The need to counteract the depression caused by jaundice, known as the royal or rainbow-hued disease, was noted. The sufferer should have a specially good bed and room and be kept amused by play-acting, gaming and general jollification.[3] Convalescence after any illness should be gradual with rest, gentle exercise, sometimes a change of air and a very gradual return to normal activity.[4]

Doctors at work are shown not infrequently on Greek vase paintings, usually bleeding patients, and the same subject appears on a terracotta relief from L'Isola Sacra, the cemetery at Ostia. Blood from a man's leg has been flowing into a bowl on the ground and the physician appears to be checking the flow with a sponge or bandage. Or there may be hot water in the bowl to encourage the bleeding, in which case the doctor is holding a lancet in his other hand. A case of surgical instruments appears on the same relief. Another relief shows a doctor assisting at a birth. The patient is seated and a woman attendant is also

[1] Pliny, *N.H.* XXIII. 41.   [2] Celsus, *De Medicina* III. 7. 2.
[3] *Ibid.* III. 24. 5.   [4] *Ibid.* IV. 32 1.

334

helping her.[1] A tombstone at Metz depicts a cloaked figure of dignified appearance carrying a box. Her name is lost but enough survives of the inscription to identify her as a woman doctor.[2] And at Lyons, Phlegon, another doctor, dedicated an altar to three buxom mother goddesses.[3]

Too little research has been done on Roman skeletons to determine the most prevalent forms of illness. The custom of cremating the dead destroys most of the evidence until the rite changes to inhumation in the second century. A recent study of over 300 skeletons from a large Roman cemetery at York showed no signs of diseases due to faulty nutrition such as rickets, and traces of tuberculosis were also lacking. Osteo-arthritis, particularly of the spine, was common, and some rheumatoid arthritis. Two bone tumours, one probably associated with a brain tumour, were noted but seem to have been non-malignant. Fractures, particularly of the limbs and collar bone, were quite common and had usually healed well. Teeth were very worn but mostly free from decay. Some examples of impacted wisdom teeth were noted. In general the people were strong and muscular with an average height of five feet seven inches for the men and five feet one inch for the women. The varying shapes of skull suggest that the population included foreign elements as is only to be expected in a Roman fortress and *colonia*. The general expectation of life seems to have been between forty and fifty.[4] The presence of arthritis is supported by evidence from other Romano-British skeletons, but elsewhere the condition of the teeth is not usually so good.

Thank-offerings at shrines associated with healing cults often took the form of models of the parts of the body cured of disease by the deity. Typical of such cults was that of the Dea Sequana, practised from the first to the fourth century at a temple at the sources of the Seine. Discoveries made here include the stone head of a man, partly covered by a compress which may have been dipped in the healing water to cure neuralgia. Other busts show mental illness, goitre and eye troubles. Small strips of bronze are also decorated with various representations of eyes. Hernia and cancer of the breast are among the bodily afflictions modelled and single hands or feet show the distortions of rheumatism. In one case some trouble with the Achilles tendon is depicted being treated with a sponge which may have been dipped in the spring at frequent intervals.[5] Votive offerings of this type were also found at Lydney.

[1] G. Calza, *La necropoli del Porto di Roma nell'isola Sacra* (Rome, 1940), pp. 248, 250.
[2] E. IV no. 4363.   [3] E. III no. 1741.
[4] *Eburacum* p. 109. Report by Professor R. Warwick.
[5] R. Bernard and P. Vassal, 'Étude médicale des *ex-voto* des sources de la Seine', *Revue archéologique de l'est et du centre-est* IX (1958) 328–37; R. Martin, 'Wooden Figures from the Source of the Seine', *Antiquity* XXXIX (1965) 247–52.

Literary sources considerably increase the number of the recognisable ills known to antiquity. Malaria and chest troubles, including colds, catarrh, pleurisy and pneumonia, were the commonest complaints in ancient Greece and Rome.[1] Celsus' references to pains in the joints is supported by the skeletal evidence and his descriptions of diseases include tuberculosis, epilepsy and various forms of insanity and depression. Cancer, gallstones, colitis, dysentery, dropsy, heart disease, skin troubles, scurf or chilblains also appear in his pages or in those of Pliny.[2] Perhaps they had been read by the aggrieved individual who put up the lead tablet in London cursing Tretia Maria.[3]

The remedies for all these ills were mostly made from herbs, roots, spices and a few mineral products such as zinc and copper, used with water, wine or honey. In some cases their use must date back to pre-Roman times, and in Gaul and Britain some of them may have been known to the druids. Many drugs still in use in the early twentieth century were listed by Dioscorides in the first, including belladonna, cinnamon, colchicum, crocus, galls, gentian, henbane, lavender, linseed, mallow, mustard, poppy and wormwood. Extracts were made from these plants and stored, and the *ceratum humidum* or cold cream described still appears in many pharmacopoeias.[4] Pharmacists were apt to be quacks, selling cures in the markets or from door to door, so good doctors made up their own prescriptions. The emperors sent herb-gatherers to Crete, Sicily and Africa to seek for certain plants and Galen was so fearful of alteration or adulteration that he undertook laborious journeys to collect his own materials. Thanks to the good roads and the organisation of the *cursus publicus*,[5] supplies from Gaul, Spain, Egypt, Syria and other provinces came regularly to Rome.[6]

Pliny gives a list of medicines of human or animal origin which, with the exception of milk, are not to be recommended, but his lists of plants and their uses do include small items of interest. A hot application of turnips, for example, is said to cure chilblains and alleviate gout; garlic has many uses, cooked or pounded in milk it was given to asthmatics; and sprays of mint and pennyroyal placed in glass bottles full of vinegar, or mustard and vinegar, were used to revive people who had fainted. Mustard was also used as a gargle and for stomach troubles and mustard plasters are advised for a variety of pains.[7] A

[1] W. H. S. Jones, *Hippocrates* I pp. xlviii, lv *et seq.*
[2] *De Medicina* III. 18, 22, 23; *Natural History* VIII (1963) List of Diseases, pp. 577–83, trans. W. H. S. Jones.
[3] See above p. 113.   [4] J. A. Grier, *History of Pharmacy* (1937) p. 27 *et seq.*
[5] See below p. 390.
[6] B. Wells, 'Trade and Travel in the Roman Empire', *Classical J.* XIX (1923–4) 15, 74.
[7] *N.H.* XX. 9, 23, 54, 87; XXV. 20.

decoction from a form of dock known as *radix Britannica* was used against scurvy and is said to have been recommended to the army by tribesmen living along the Dutch and north German coasts. The lid of a small box inscribed *e radice britannica* actually turned up in the fortress at Haltern.[1] Celsus lists many remedies in Book II of the *De medicina* dividing them into substances to clean, heal and sooth wounds, and prescriptions for making poultices, plasters, dusting powders, ointments, gargles, antidotes, anodynes, pills, etc. Quantities are given but not strength so that comparisons with modern equivalents are impossible.

Eye troubles seem to have been very prevalent in the Roman period and Celsus devotes a long chapter to their treatment.[2] *Lippitudo*, variously translated as inflamed, running or bleary eyes; blepharitis, conjunctivitis or even ophthalmia; *caligo*, *nubecula*, and *caligatio*, all various forms of mistiness or dimness, including cataract; glaucoma, and various swellings and ulcers were all known to him and to Pliny.[3] They were treated with salves and poultices, and frequent fomentations with hot water when at the baths. *Carbunculus oculi*, which seems to have often been a bad stye, should be poulticed with linseed boiled in honey-wine, or flour if no linseed was available. Nileus' salve, a preparation made from Indian nard, poppy-tears, gum, saffron and fresh rose-leaves mixed up in rain-water or mild wine, was also applied.[4] Pliny recommends an infusion of myrrh, violets and saffron for conjunctivitis.[5]

Such prescriptions were used by the numerous opticians whose existence is known from the frequent occurrence of small square stone slabs with stamps cut on each of the four sides. The *collyria* or eye-salves were sometimes liquid, but more often they were made up as small solid sticks which the patient dissolved in white of egg, sweet wine or water. Instructions for use and the name of the inventor of the prescription, whether a doctor in Rome or a quack from any-where, were stamped on the sticks of ointment. More than twenty of these so-called oculists' stamps have been found in Britain, at least thirty in Germany and over one hundred and fifty in Gaul, chiefly in the north-east. Only a few are known from other parts of the Empire although eye troubles must have been prevalent in Italy and round the Mediterranean. It has been suggested that the presence of the stamps in the West, like the use of potters' stamps on mortaria and samian pottery, may be due to a Romano-Celtic liking for trade-marks when shopping![6]

[1] F. Drexel, 'Radix Britannica'; *Germania* XII (1928) 172–3.
[2] VI. 6.
[3] W. H. S. Jones, *N.H.* List of Diseases.
[4] Celsus, *De Medicina* VI. 6. 10.   [5] *N.H.* XXI. 76.
[6] R. Birley, 'An Oculist's Stamp from the Roman Cemetery in the Mount, York', *Y.A.J.* XXXIX (1958) Appendix II 303.

Typical of the inscriptions cut in reverse on the oculists' stamps is one found at Sandy, Bedfordshire, by Gaius Valerius Amandus for (*a*) a vinegar lotion for running eyes, (*b*) drops for dim sight, (*c*) poppy ointment for an attack of inflammation of the eyes (*lippitudo*), and (*d*) a mixture for clearing the sight.[1] A stamp of T. Vindacus Ariovistus from Kenchester, Herefordshire, now in the British Museum, was for an unbeatable preparation (of aniseed or dill) nard (or spikenard) and 'the green salve' (fig. 130). A stamp found in London was used for more sophisticated preparations as it includes (*a*) a scented ointment for granulations, (*b*) a salve applied with a swab for *lippitudo*, (*c*) a special salve probably intended for scars on the eyes, all made by C. Silvius Tetricus. The fourth side is illegible.[2] London has also produced an inscription on the base of a samian jar, 'Lucius Julius Senex' ointment for roughness' [of the eyes].[3] Instead of marking different preparations Julius Jucundus' stamp, found at Lydney, is for a salve to be used in three different ways: (*a*) in drops, (*b*) as an ointment mixed with honey, (*c*) applied as a tincture with a swab or brush.[4] A stamp in the British Museum found outside Britain is for either saffron ointment for scars or discharges prepared by Junius Taurus according to the prescription of Paccius, or for the anodyne of J. Taurus.[5] So here the optician was probably dispensing a remedy invented by himself as well as one learnt from others. The discoveries of British stamps show a widespread distribution of opticians throughout the country from both civil and military sites as, in addition to those already mentioned, examples are known from York, Wroxeter, Littleborough, Gloucester, Cirencester, Verulamium and Bath. A salve prescribed by a Briton named Stolus is mentioned by Galen.

On the whole the surgeon was more highly regarded by the Romans than the physician. One of the books in the Hippocratic collection is entitled 'In the Surgery' and it discusses such considerations as the positioning of the patient and the surgeon and his assistants, the use of the best available lighting, and the training of the assistants to be silent and obedient. The surgeon should practise his operations with either hand or both together, so as to attain dexterity, speed, painlessness and elegance. Celsus' surgeon should be a young or fairly young man, ambidextrous with a strong and steady hand, anxious to cure but able to ignore his patient's cries if necessary.[6] In his account of fractures in the *De medicina*, partly based on Hippocrates and other earlier sources, Celsus includes treatment for broken noses and collar-bones, and describes the setting of arms, legs and fingers and their immobilisation with six bandages and a splint.[7] For fractures of ribs, bones of the spine, palm of the hand, etc., little

[1] Burn (1932) no. 66.   [2] G. Home, *Roman London* (1948) p. 267.   [3] *Ibid.* p. 268.
[4] Wheeler (1932) p. 102.   [5] *B.M.G.R.L.* p. 183.   [6] VII. Prooemium 4.   [7] VIII. 5, 8, 10.

130 Oculist's stamp from Kenchester

could be done apart from rest and a light bandage. Dislocations are next considered, starting with the treatment of a displaced lower jaw. In some cases special apparatus was needed and this included a padded board over which a dislocated upper arm was manipulated back into place.[1] Many of these methods were learnt from the earlier Hippocratic books, including the use of the so-called 'bench of Hippocrates' in which straps and a windlass were used to help to replace a dislocated hip.[2]

The Roman surgeon gained plenty of practical experience in the treatment of wounds, Celsus directs that haemorrhage is to be checked with a pad of lint, dry or soaked in vinegar, and pressure applied by a sponge soaked in cold water. If necessary the severed blood vessels must be re-united.[3] On the other hand, the importance of allowing sufficient bleeding to cleanse a wound was appreciated. Large wounds were stitched with sutures of flax or wool or held together by pins passed through the edges and fixed by thread twisted round them. Simple dressings of plain water, vinegar and water, wine and oil or honey were used, sometimes with other cleansing agents such as thymol or yellow trisulphide of arsenic. In cases of mild infection, hot fomentations were applied and other measures were tried, often no doubt in vain, for gangrene. The amputation of limbs was sometimes necessary. This operation seems to have been greatly developed and improved by the Roman surgeons of the first two centuries A.D.[4] Artificial limbs were known from an earlier date and a bronze leg fitted over a wooden core, probably attached with iron bars to some form of belt, was found with a burial of *c.* 300 B.C. at Capua and is now in the Wellcome Historical Museum.

According to Celsus, Galen, and other authorities, surgeons in the first and second centuries removed tonsils or a polypus by surprisingly modern methods

[1] VIII. 15.   [2] VIII. 20; W. H. S. Jones, *Hippocrates* III pp. 373, 453.
[3] *De Medicina* V. 26. 21 *et seq.*   [4] W. J. Bishop, '*The Early History of Surgery*' (1960) p. 52.

and operated on goitres and hernias. Trephination, known since prehistoric times, was sometimes used for injuries and pains in the head, attempts were made to repair abdominal injuries, dropsy was relieved by drainage, and tumours were destroyed with a cautery. Antyllus in the second century performed the first operations for aneurysms. Cataracts were also moved out of the way ('couched'),[1] and by the time of Galen they were being extracted. Cosmetic surgery was not unknown and Martial mentions a surgeon who specialised in removing marks branded on slaves.[2]

Knowledge of anaesthetics and measures for the relief of pain were very limited at this period and largely consisted of preparations made from the poppy, henbane and mandrake. Dioscorides directs that the root of the mandrake should be boiled in wine and a small glassful prescribed for sleeplessness, severe pain, or before operations with the knife or cautery so that the pain may not be felt. Mandrake root yields hyoscine and atropine and Celsus also mentions its use in pills, but he may possibly be referring to *atropa belladonna*, the deadly nightshade.[3] Henbane or *hyoscyamus* is a mild narcotic also of the belladonna family and the seeds were prescribed for pain and sleeplessness, the bark as a poultice for the joints, the juice for earache, and the root for toothache.[4] Poppy juice obtained from slits cut just below the capsules, called by Celsus 'poppy-tears', is recommended by him for pills to relieve pain.[5] The plant seems to have been the wild poppy but Dioscorides mentions the cultivated variety (*papaver somniferum*).

Under the Romans, surgery developed as a science based on the study of anatomy and physiology with an increasingly detailed observation of the effects of disease or wounds on the human body.[6] As the surgeon's technique improved, so his need grew for more specialised equipment and consequently numbers of surgical instruments have survived. These were made of bronze or iron, the best iron, approximating to steel, coming from Noricum and making a knife which Galen notes would neither bend, chip nor blunt easily. On account of its flexibility, tin was also employed for certain probes and other instruments used for internal examinations, and bone ointment spoons and knife handles are common. A favourite device was the combination of two instruments in one with a probe at one end and a scoop, spatula or hook at the other.[7]

The surgical knife or scalpel generally had a straight sharp-pointed blade but there were also forms with straight or curved blades cutting on one or both

---

[1] *Ibid.* p. 55, Celsus, *op. cit.* V. 25.
[2] *Epigrams* X. 56.   [3] Celsus, *op. cit.* VII. 17.   [4] *Ibid.* III. 18. 12; V. 18. 29; VI. 7. 2, 9. 2.
[5] *Ibid.* V. 25. 4.   [6] Bishop. *op. cit.* p. 57.   [7] L.R.T. Pl. XXXVII.

sides and blunt or sharp-pointed. A Greek relief found in Athens shows a surgeon's case with scalpels of several different kinds. Individual discoveries have also been made at Silchester and Richborough. A scalpel found in London had a bronze handle ending in a leaf-shaped spatula for blunt dissection and an iron blade of unusual type, and another iron instrument has a spoon at one end and at the other a blade on one side and with a saw edge on the other (fig. 131*a*, *b*). A special form of lancet with a pointed leaf-shaped blade called a phlebotome was used for opening veins for blood-letting and examples of these are known from the Surgeon's House at Pompeii and from a grave at Cologne. A smaller form of this was used for cutting away a nasal polypus, care being taken not to injure the cartilage which is difficult to treat. The polypus was then removed with the scoop at the other end of the same instrument, the nostril gently plugged with lint soaked in something to stop bleeding, and a healing salve was later applied on the end of a quill.[1]

Probes occur not infrequently, their tips swollen into various sizes. British examples are known from London and Silchester. Ear probes show little thickening, probes for applying ointment have small olive-shaped ends and sharp ended probes were sometimes thrust into balls of wool dipped in liquid. The wool was squeezed and the ear or eyedrops ran down the probe to the point and so into the ear or eye.[2] The *spathomele*, an instrument used more for dispensing than for surgery, had a shaft of unusual length with an olive-shaped probe for mixing up preparations at one end. At the other was a spatula for spreading the result on lint. Painters also employed it for mixing colours. The surgeons used it mostly as a tongue depressor when investigating throat troubles. An instrument from Finsbury Circus, now in the London Museum, may be a *spathomele* and with it in the same Museum is another form of tongue depressor with a flat pierced blade bent at an angle to the stem (fig. 131*g*). Another tongue depressor of this type was found at Richborough with a *ligula* or small flattened spoon-like terminal at the other end.[3] These *ligulae* are very common both as toilet and surgical implements. Needles, which may also have been used for stitching bandages in position, are of frequent occurrence. For stitching wounds, however, these round needles are of no use and so curved triangular needles with cutting edges were employed for this purpose from very early times.[4] One example has turned up at the Lullingstone villa. Small metal clasps in the Guildhall Museum, London, may be the *fibulae* used to secure large wounds.[5]

[1] Celsus VII. 10.
[2] J. S. Milne, *Surgical Instruments in Greek and Roman Times* (Oxford, 1907) p. 55.
[3] J. P. Bushe-Fox (1949) Pl. XXXIX no. 142. [4] Milne, *op. cit.* p. 75. [5] *Ibid.* p. 163.

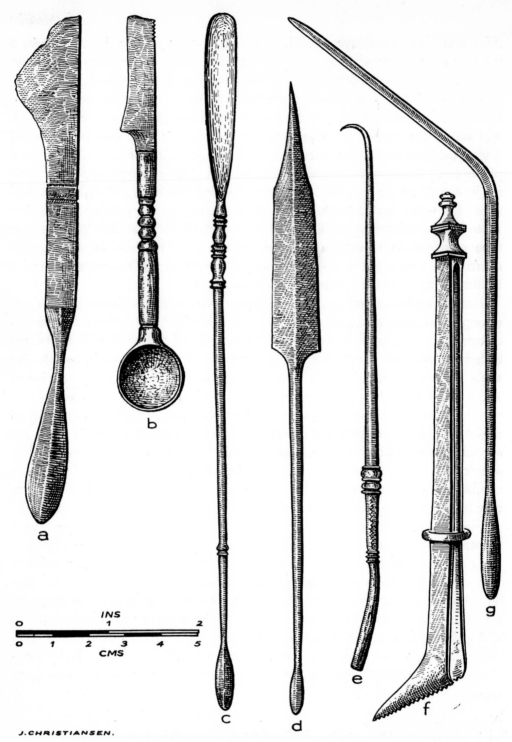

J.CHRISTIANSEN.

131 Surgical instruments, bronze unless otherwise stated. *a* Scalpel with iron blade and bronze spatula. *b* Iron scalpel with spoon at one end, sharp edge on one side of the blade and saw edge on the other. *c* Spatula with probe. *d* Flat-bladed and pointed spatula. *e* Hook. *f* Probably artery forceps. *g* Tongue depressor. *a-e* London. *f* Silchester. *g* London

The spatula is another implement of many uses and a selection now in the London Museum includes flat-bladed examples which may have been heated and used for cauterisation, and another flat-bladed type with a pointed end which would be well suited for dissection (fig. 131*d*). From Silchester comes a retractor for pulling back the edges of a wound for inspection,[1] and an artery forceps with serrated jaws at an angle to the blades and a sliding ring to keep them in position (fig. 131*f*).

Surgical instruments were carried about in containers, cylindrical for the probes, spatulae, etc., and oblong and opening in two halves for the scalpels which fitted in head to tail.[2] Sometimes the remains of these containers are found with burials and a surgeon's grave of the end of the third century, found in Paris, produced forceps, a cup for bleeding, probes, spatulae and scalpels. Fragments of a wooden chest discovered at Rheims included two small iron ointment jars, handles for scalpels and needles, five hooks, seven forceps, probes, spatulae, a small drill, a mortar, and a stamp showing that these things belonged to the oculist G. Firmus Severus who died towards the end of the second century. His practice seems to have flourished as the instruments are a fine collection, several of them being inlaid with silver.[3]

[1] Boon (1957) p. 104.
[2] Milne, *op. cit.* p. 168.
[3] *Ibid.* p. 20 *et seq.*; also M. A. Dollfuss, 'L'exercice de l'ophtalmologie à l'époque gallo-romaine', *Bull. de la Soc. Nationale des Antiquaires de France*, 1963, 116 *et seq.*, for details of this and other collections of oculists' equipment.

13
Recreations

Life was not all work in Roman Britain and some evidence survives of games and playthings, convivial evenings and outings to the theatre and ampitheatre. The baby in his basketwork or wooden cradle could play with hinged pieces of wood or clappers, and rattles with bells or jangling metal rings. A slightly older child would enjoy the noise produced by shaking terracotta animals with pebbles inside them—pigs seem to have been particular favourites for this form of activity (fig. 132e). Dolls were the favourite playthings of little girls from very early times and Roman dolls were made of wood, bone or baked clay. Small rag dolls from this period, found in Egypt, are preserved in the British Museum and the Royal Ontario Museum of Archaeology, and jointed dolls also sometimes survive. One in the coffin of a 14-year-old girl in Rome was thirty centimetres high and made of oak, with joints at shoulders and hips, elbows and knees. The face and body are carefully modelled and the hair style resembles that of the Empress Faustina, wife of Antoninus Pius (fig. 132c).[1] Crudely shaped dolls of bone or ivory have been found in the Roman catacombs and some effort is usually made to indicate the current fashions in hairdressing (fig. 132d). The jointed limbs are often missing and may sometimes have been of cloth or leather. Small pegs secured the limbs of another, more complete, ivory doll from the

[1] K. Elderkin, 'Jointed Dolls in Antiquity', *A.J.A.* XXXIV (1930) 471, fig. 23.

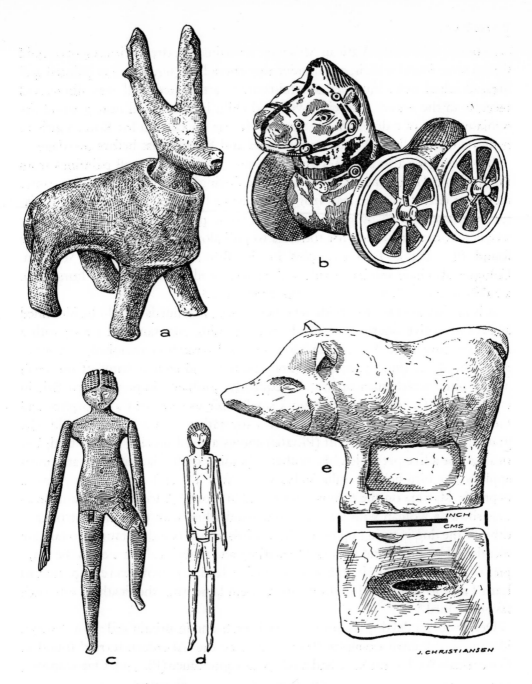

132 Toys. *a* Pottery stag, Mainz. *b* Pottery model horse on wheels,
Athens. *c* Doll of oak, 30 cm. high, Rome. *d* Doll of bone, Rome. *e* Pottery
pig-rattle, Pompeii

catacombs, now in the Vatican Museum. Remains of a dress with traces of gold thread were found with it, a reminder that these little figures were painted and dressed when new. Another second-century articulated doll was discovered recently in the grave of an eight-year-old child in Rome and near it stood the miniature pots of a doll's dinner service.[1] It was the custom for Roman girls to dedicate their dolls to Venus or the Lares and Penates just before marriage.

Boys and girls also played with hoops and tops, and the wall-paintings from Pompeii and Herculaneum show Cupids enjoying a number of familiar games including dart-throwing, leap-frog, blind man's buff and hide and seek. Miniature carriages drawn by goats appear on some paintings, and baked clay or wooden horses on wheels for toddlers to pull along on a string are sometimes found (fig. 132*b*). Two examples in the Römisch-Germanisches Museum, Cologne, also have miniature riders. A broken model of a white clay horse with a halter found at Wroxeter may have been a toy.[2]

It is not always easy to decide whether miniature animals should be identified as toys or votive offerings. A crude but appealing clay ram and a stag with a movable head from Kreuznach, now in the Römisch-Germanisches Zentralmuseum, Mainz (fig. 132*a*), must surely be toys and so may some of the small model birds which turn up not infrequently, probably imported into Britain from Gaul.[3] The one appearing on a small table in front of Callimorphus and the child Serapion at Chester is surely a toy rather than a funeral meal.[4] The grave relief from Murrell Hill (Pl. 26*a*) shows a child playing with a bird, but this may be a live pet which his mother is holding on her lap and the same must apply to the bird held by Julia Velva's daughter (Pl. 26*c*) and the six-year-old Sepronia Martina on the tombstones found at York.[5] A tombstone from Bowness shows a woman with a dove in one hand while with the other she offers a titbit to the dog jumping up beside her.[6] Birds which could be taught to talk are mentioned by Pliny, and include the starling and nightingale as well as the magpie, who could also imitate notes of music.[7] Indian parrots were imported to learn Latin in Rome and Ovid wrote a poem lamenting the death of one such favourite bird.[8]

Delightful model dogs of bronze have been found in Britain and most of them, like the well-known examples from Lydney or the 'Aberdeen terrier' found in Coventina's Well, must have had a religious significance (Pl. 44*b*). One wonders,

[1] *I.L.N.* 22 February 1964, 269.   [2] Bushe-Fox (1916) p. 34, Pl. XXIII. 2.
[3] *L.R.T.* Pl. XXI no. 7.   [4] *R.I.B.* 558.
[5] *R.I.B.* 688, 686. See also Wright (1955) no. 118.
[6] F. Haverfield, *Catalogue of the Roman inscribed and sculptured stones, Tullie House, Carlisle* (Carlisle, 1922) no. 145.
[7] *N.H.* X. 59.   [8] *Amor.* II. 6.

however, about the lively mongrel found at Aldborough (Yorkshire), running along with its bushy tail curved over its back, or the smooth-coated 'hound' from Kirkby Thore, looking up with a pleading expression and apparently offering to shake a paw (Pl. 44c).[1] Dogs' paw marks occur impressed on Roman tiles and they certainly had a recognised place in Roman households, ranging from the fierce watchdogs to the household pets.[2] A pet dog lies beside his young master on a sarcophagus lid in the Capitoline Museum in Rome, and a fat little dog with a collar from which dangles a bell or a pendant is perched on his mistress's knee on a first-century tombstone at Mainz.[3] Dogs accompany their masters on other German tombstones,[4] and the children at Arlon have to restrain their pet from poking his nose into the cauldron containing their dinner (Pl. 45). A small dog, probably trotting about with the workmen, has left his paw marks on the cement of a low wall in the barn at Lullingstone, and a kitten's footprint appears on a tile from the same villa. Lullingstone also produced the bones of a cat and similar finds occurred at the villa at Montmaurin in France.[5] 'How silently and with what a light tread do cats creep up on birds! How stealthily they watch their chance to leap out on tiny mice,' remarks Pliny.[6] A fragment of a statue of a seated and watchful cat, wearing a collar, has been found at Auxerre.[7] Aurelia Satyra, aged six, is shown sitting and playing with the cat in her lap on one Bordeaux tombstone.[8] On another a little girl appears clutching a kitten, which she is trying to rescue from a cock which is grabbing its tail.[9] A grave relief at Dijon also shows a child, in this case a boy, holding a whip (for a top?) in one hand and watching his cat walk along his other arm.[10] Part of a Lincoln grave-relief depicts a boy holding his pet hare (Pl. 43d) and a hare also appears on the tombstone of the doctor, Amicius Ingenuus at Housesteads (fig. 124). The small bronze mouse found in a child's grave at York may again have some religious significance connected with the underworld, but it would also be a very consoling toy for a child to hold in its hand (Pl. 44d).

The four-year-old Sudrenus at Corbridge,[11] and the two little Augustini at York (Pl. 25c) are portrayed on their tombstones holding balls, and ball games are known to have been favourites with young and old. They were often played in the colonnades and *palaestra* at the baths, or on special ball courts in villa gardens, and included *trigon*, where three players form a triangle and probably throw a succession of balls to each other as quickly as possible; a fast game for

---

[1] Toynbee (1964) p. 126.   [2] E.g. Publius' lapdog, Issa. Martial, *Epigrams*, I. 109.
[3] E. VI no. 5815.   [4] E. Germanie, nos. 6440, 6478.
[5] H. P. Eydoux, *Monuments et Trésors de la Gaule* (Paris, 1958) p. 239.   [6] *N.H.* X. 94.
[7] E. IV no. 2906.   [8] E. III no. 1783.   [9] E. II no. 1193.   [10] E. IV no. 3560.
[11] *R.I.B.* 1181.

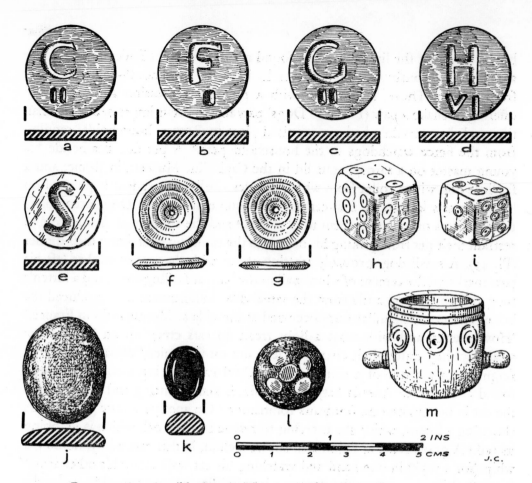

133   *a-g* Bone counters, possible theatre tickets or gaming pieces, Great
Chesterford. *h, i* Dice, possibly from Pompeii. *j-k* Glass counters, Sea
Mills, Somerset. *l* Glass counter, Lullingstone. *m* ?Dice-box, London

several players with a light ball which was struck with the palm of the hand; and
harpastum, a much rougher game which some think may be an ancestor of
hurling or Rugby.[1] It is not clear, however, whether this was a team game.

   Marbles and nuts were used for other games and knuckle bones may have been
a particular favourite with the women. To play it the bones were thrown up in
the air and as many as possible were caught on the back of the hand. Those
which were missed had to be picked up without dropping the remainder. These
bones were also used in dicing, but the familiar six-sided cubes used for gambling are also found quite frequently. The points are marked by small incised
circles, and examples made of bone are known from sites including Silchester,
London, Richborough, Wroxeter, Newstead and Great Chesterford (fig. 133*h, i*),

[1] M. Marples, *A History of Football* (1954) p. 2.

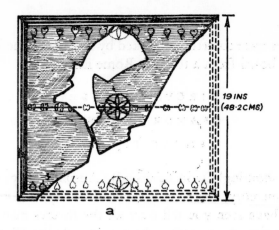

a

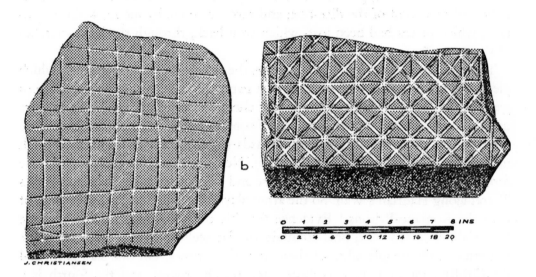

b

J. CHRISTIANSEN

134 Games boards. *a* Holt, Denbighshire. *b* Richborough, Kent

while a jet dice has turned up at York. They were thrown from a dice-box (fig. 133*m*). Gambling and dicing became so popular in Rome that legislation was passed against them and dice from some parts of the Empire have been found to be loaded.

Evidence for the two favourite Roman board games is also present in Britain. Parts of a pottery games board consisting of two rows of roughly incised ivy-leaves divided by a geometric pattern down the middle, were found at the pottery manufacturing site of the Twentieth Legion at Holt (fig. 134*a*). This must have been used for *duodecim scripta* (twelve lines), an early form of backgammon played with dice and so possibly affected by official disapproval. Nevertheless, enough boards have survived to show that it was popular. The

349

points for the pieces were sometimes marked by letters and the British Museum possesses a marble board from a tomb in Rome inscribed

CIRCVS PLENVS

CLAMOR INGENS

IANVAE TE(*nsae?*)

('Circus full! Great shouting! Doors bursting!').[1] Ausonius, in praising the orator Minervius for his memory, describes a game of this type: 'Once, after a long contested game, I have seen you tell over all the throws made by either side when the dice were tipped out with a sharp spin over the fillets cut out in the hollowed boxwood of the dice-box; and recount move by move, without mistake, which pieces had been lost, which won back, through the long stretches of the game.'[2]

The other game was *ludus latrunculorum*, the 'soldiers', a battle game in which pieces could be moved like the rook in a game of chess. Nevertheless, it is not generally believed to be an early form of chess. Pieces of different colours were used on boards with varying numbers of squares but 8 × 8 seems to have been the most common. In Britain these boards survive, cut on stone, from such military sites as Richborough (fig. 134*b*), Newstead and Corbridge, from the fortress at Chester, and from High House and Winshields milecastles and Banks Turret along Hadrian's Wall. So the army played the game and probably taught it to the Romano-Britons.[3] Evidence for this comes from Chedworth where four slabs from an octagonal fountain or flat well-head bear witness to the activities of the people who sat there at various times. On one slab is incised the Chi-Rho monogram, two more have rough crosses, and the fourth is a games board with sixty-four squares which has obviously seen much use. Evidence for a wooden games board was found placed on the lid of one of the two lead coffins in the fourth-century underground mausoleum at Lullingstone.[4] With it were two complete sets of gaming pieces, thirty small glass counters, fifteen white and fifteen brown, decorated with small coloured spots (fig. 133*l*). Such counters made of glass or of bone decorated with incised circles are known from many other sites including Sea Mills, Silchester, London, Great Chesterford, York, Chester, Brecon and Newstead (fig. 133*a–k*). The edges of bone

[1] R. G. Austin, 'Roman Board Games', *Greece and Rome* IV (1935) 30.
[2] *Professorium Burdigalensium* I 25. Trans H. Evelyn White.
[3] Austin, *op. cit.*; H. J. R. Murray, *History of Board Games other than Chess* (1952) p. 33; H. P. Eydoux, *La France Antique* (Paris, 1962) fig. 199.
[4] See below p. 480.

counters found at Leicester were so worn that there is a suggestion they might also have been used for tiddleywinks.[1]

Cicero, Ausonius and Sidonius Apollinaris give us some idea of how leisure time might be spent in the homes of educated people in conversation, reading or writing. Pliny, with a letter to his friend Paternus, encloses some verses composed when driving, in the baths or at dinner, describing his jokes, witticisms, loves, sorrows, complaints and annoyances.[2] Sometimes he would gather a few chosen friends together in his dining-room for readings of some of his lesser works, and when he was preparing the speech he made accepting the consulship for publication, an informal invitation to his friends to come and hear it if they really had the time, brought them flocking for three days, in spite of bad weather.[3] Pliny was also assiduous in both attending and performing at the many public readings of history, poetry or comedy given in Rome and these must have taken place in other cities. At Colchester the grave of a child, buried about the time of the foundation of the *colonia* in A.D. 49, produced a number of clay figurines, mostly of elderly men. Four of them are standing, leaning forward and gleefully reading from scrolls they hold in their hands, the others mostly represent guests reclining at a dinner party, listening attentively, or sometimes firmly clutching a wine-cup or scratching a bald head (Pl. 44*a*).

Dinner at the end of the day was the special time for recreation. Relaxed after a visit to the baths, the toga discarded and wearing tunics or a light robe (the *synthesis*), the family and its guests reclined on couches in the *triclinium*. The couches held three people side by side, and were arranged in groups of three round a small table, the chief guest being placed in the seat of honour at the head of the couch adjoining that of his host. Questions of precedence were important at formal dinner parties. The meal began with a libation and then *mulsum*, wine sweetened with honey, was served with the *gustatio*, hors-d'œuvres such as eggs, salad or shellfish. Next came the *fercula* or chief dishes, varying in number and elaboration. Apicius, whose first-century recipe book survives in a fourth or fifth-century compilation, used herbs and sauces extensively in cooking and he often directs that the ingredients are to be pounded in a mortar, a wearisome task for some unfortunate kitchenmaid. His dishes include birds ranging in size from thrushes to partridges, peacocks, pheasants, geese and even ostrich, mostly boiled or roast, and about fifteen recipes for cooking chickens. Ham boiled, slashed with incisions filled with honey and baked in a pastry case, roast boar, venison and a variety of methods of cooking sucking pig, all these were

[1] Kenyon (1948) p. 266. [2] *Epistulae* IV. 14.
[3] *Epistulae* III. 18.

favourite dishes for the *fercula*.[1] It was followed by dessert consisting of pastries, sweetmeats and fresh or dried fruit.

It is possible to imagine this food being brought to British diners on large polished silver, bronze or pewter dishes. The servants would keep the guests supplied with small hot rolls, the wine-jugs would be brought in or the *amphorae* uncorked, and the wine poured through a strainer into a large bowl already containing water, and mixed to the strength preferred. Sometimes the water was hot or else the wine was cooled with snow. Bronze wine-strainers, pierced with holes in decorative patterns, have been found at Great Chesterford and other British sites. The wine was then ladled out into small cups of glass, samian pottery or pewter. After they had finished eating, the guests continued to recline, look round at the painted walls and mosaic floors and drink toasts. In his store their host may have had choice Italian wines which took many years to mature like the famous Falernian, a red wine grown on the slopes of Mount Falernius in Campania, Surrentine from near Sorrento, Caecuban from vines found along the coast from Terracina to Formia, or Alban, grown in the hills round Rome. Or the wine may have come from Gaul, *picatum* grown near Vienne, the products of the vines growing round Bordeaux or on the banks of the Moselle, mentioned by Ausonius, or wine from Beaune, known in the time of Constantine.[2] Home-grown wine is unlikely to have been drunk in Britain although beer and mead are very probable. A number of small beakers, some British made, others imported from the Rhineland, may have been used to drink some of these toasts as they have remarks of a convivial nature painted on them. Besides SVAVIS (Sweet!) at Lullingstone, [B]IBE (? Drink!) was found at Verulamium, while York has produced examples with DA MI (*da mihi*, 'Give me'), MISCE MI[HI] (Mix for me!), NOLITE SITIRE (Don't be thirsty!), and VIVATIS (Long life to you!).[3] The evening's pleasures might include gambling, entertainers or a little light music.

While the Romans did not regard music as highly as the Greeks, it played a part in their way of life and a certain amount is known about it. Much of it was vocal and it seems to have been a mixture of Greek and Etruscan elements with some influences coming in from further east. Greek melody was based on the tetrachord, a group of three or four notes fitted into the interval of a fourth. The last note of one tetrachord could be repeated as the first note of another to give a succession of seven notes, or the second tetrachord could follow on at the interval of a tone giving eight notes to form the octave. The intervals of the

[1] B. Flower and E. Rosenbaum, *Apicius: the Roman Cookery Book* (1958).
[2] H. Warner Allen, *A History of Wine* (1961) p. 111 *et seq.*
[3] *Eburacum* nos. 151 a-f.

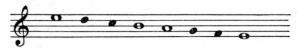

135 The Dorian mode, shown built up from the notes of two tetrachords. The black notes could be varied in pitch to produce different shades of expression

136 Notes playable on the Alesia syrinx

notes within the tetrachord originally varied, these different variations being known as modes. Melodies built round them are described by Greek authors as producing certain states of mind, sad, serene or joyful, etc., and they may have had much in common with music such as the Indian *ragas*, complex patterns of traditional sounds and rhythms. By the time of Ptolemy in the second century A.D., the Dorian mode (fig. 135) may have become a central, recognisable landmark, rather like the scale of C major to a modern music student.[1]

The total written evidence for music surviving from the Graeco-Roman period consists of allusions in about twenty literary sources, largely concerned with philosophy, mathematics or acoustics, and perhaps a dozen pieces of music, and with so little material it is impossible to bring forward any very clear conclusions about its tonality. The music was written on papyrus or parchment or incised on stone in a notation which used the letters of the Greek alphabet.[2] It included two very incomplete hymns to Apollo found carved on the treasury of the Athenians at Delphi, dating from the middle of the second century B.C., and some hymns to the Muse, to Nemesis, and to the Sun by Mesomedes, written in the time of the Emperor Hadrian and surviving in ancient manuscripts. While harmony and counterpoint had not yet been much developed, the growth of instrumental playing may have led to something more than the unison or parallel octaves which came naturally to the singers, and accompaniments at intervals of a fourth or fifth, for example, may have been permitted. Symbols indicated the lengths of notes and, as in poetry, various metrical rhythms were used, several of which could be combined in a single piece.

One of the less well rendered British mosaics, presumably the product of a native artist working from a Graeco-Roman copybook, survives at Sherborne and shows the musical contest between the god Apollo and Marsyas.[3] Apollo

[1] D. J. Grout, *A History of Western Music* (1962) p. 17; C. Sachs, *A History of Musical Instruments* (1942) pp. 35–40.
[2] Sachs, *op. cit.* p. 44. [3] Toynbee (1964) p. 252.

sits there, holding a large concert lyre or *cithara*, and Marsyas stands facing him, playing the double pipes. Apollo won the contest, and the mosaic illustrates for us two of the most important classical instruments. On Greek vase paintings the lyre appears with a tortoiseshell or a skin stretched over a wooden bowl for a sound box. Two slender, slightly curved arms springing from this were joined at the top by a cross-bar. The strings were stretched from the cross-bar under the sound box, from which they were kept away by a bridge, and the instrument was held slanting or even horizontally away from the player. It was largely used by amateurs or for accompanying singing, and by the Roman period it was beginning to die out. The *cithara* and lyre had five or seven strings and with the *cithara* the number eventually rose to nine or even eleven. The *cithara* had a broader wooden sound box extending up into the two side-pieces and this helped to amplify its sound (fig. 137*a*). By Roman times both these instruments had their strings looped round bone pegs which could be turned for tuning. Virtuosi performed elaborate pieces on the *cithara*, plucking the strings with both hands, but most reliefs and wall-paintings show the performers using a plectrum.[1]

It is difficult to identify the instruments played by Orpheus on the mosaics from Dyer Court and Barton Farm, Cirencester (Pl. 37*a*), Littlecote,[2] Withington or Brading, but the player's upright position and the shape and size of the instruments on the whole suggest the *cithara*. A thin piece of ivory in the Corinium Museum at Cirencester may have come from one of these instruments. In the north of England Maponus, a native God of youth and music, with a probable sanctuary at Clochmabonstane on the north side of the Solway Firth, and dedications at Corbridge, Whitley Castle and Ribchester, seems to have been identified with Apollo *citharoedus*, or Apollo the bard.[3]

Other Roman stringed instruments included the small harp, mainly played by women, often Oriental slave girls. One appears on a painting from Stabiae beside a woman who also holds a *cithara* while a girl stands looking at her in surprise and admiration.[4] The lute was also known. It had a small body, three or more strings and a long neck with frets. Both lute and *cithara* appear clearly on the sarcophagus of Julia Tyrrania at Arles.

Even a superficial acquaintance with Roman art probably brings to mind the panpipe or syrinx as an essential element of pictures of country life or Dionysiac revelry. The simplest type consisted or seven or eight reeds of varying length tied together, but the number could increase to thirteen and the instrument is

---

[1] Behn (1954) p. 87 *et seq.*; Sachs, *op. cit.* p. 132. [2] Richmond (1947) Pl. opp. p. 33.
[3] Toynbee (1964) p. 153; R.I.B. 1120, 583, 1198.
[4] M. Brion, *Pompeii and Herculaneum* (1960) fig. 122.

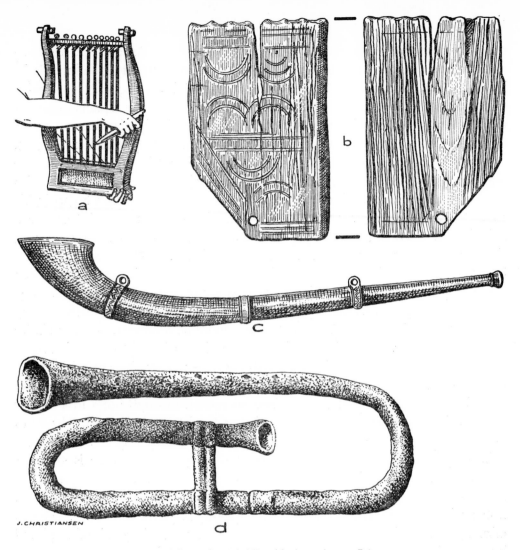

137 Musical instruments. *a* The *cithara*. *b* The Alesia syrinx. *c Lituus*
found at the Saalburg. *d* Instrument from Andes' tombstone, Mainz

sometimes portrayed in a cover with a carrying strap. It was played like a
vertical flute or flageolet. Sometimes the pipes may have been stopped at the
bottom and this would cause them to sound an octave lower. Actual examples
made of wood, bronze or pottery survive in Gaul and Germany and clay moulds
for the pottery variety with the stamp POTTALVS have been found in the
potteries at Rheinzabern near Spire.[1] Panpipes of boxwood found in wells at
the Gallo-Roman town of Alesia (fig. 137*b*) and near a Roman building at
Barbing-Kreuzhof, Regensburg, in Bavaria, originally had eight holes and

[1] Behn (1954) p. 110 *et seq.*

355

probably date to the late second or early third century. An attempt has been made to identify the notes produced by the Alesia syrinx (fig. 136) and the Barbing-Kreuzhof instrument may have sounded a semitone higher.[1] No British examples have been found as yet but the syrinx does occur on a panel of one of the Brading mosaics, with a figure of Attis on a recently discovered altar at Gloucester,[2] and on several silver dishes from the Mildenhall treasure (Pl. 36*b*).

Simple bone whistles and fifes have also been found in the Rhineland, one whistle found at Mainz taking the form of a small cloaked and hooded man with a tube inserted at the back of his head, the air escaping through a gap in his cloak.[3] The most important wind instrument, however, was the *tibia* (the Greek *aulos*), really a whole family of pipes with a cylindrical bore, reed blown with single or double reeds, rather resembling the clarinet and oboe. Actual examples of wood, bronze or ivory have been found at Pompeii and in Egypt. The pitch could be altered by means of holes covered by the player's fingers, and the range was increased by the practice of varying the air-pressure known as overblowing. A device consisting of a rotary sleeve which could be rotated to block the holes and change the mode was invented when the players found they needed more holes than they had fingers. These seem to have been moved by a primitive form of key. The instruments were often played in pairs, and then the musician kept them in position by inserting them into his mouth through holes in a leather band—this went over his mouth and tied at the back of his head. The band helped to maintain regular air pressure with the cheeks acting as bellows, and paintings frequently show musicians puffing away. Indeed there is a Greek description of double pipes as 'one wind, two ships, ten sailors rowing and one steersman directs both'.[4] One pipe may have supplied a single sustained pedal note or drone as an accompaniment to the melody played on the other. The end of one pipe sometimes turns up like a shepherd's crook, this type is often played by Maenads and Satyrs. It appears on a fine mosaic from Cologne, showing Dionysiac scenes, and here the keying arrangement for altering the pitch seems also to be indicated by the mosaicist.[5] Simpler *tibiae* are used in pairs for religious ceremonies; they appear on the distance slab from Bridgeness playing the accompaniment to the *suovetaurilia*, the sacrifice of the pig, sheep and bull, which probably marked the building of the Antonine Wall. Double pipes also occur played by a Maenad on a mosaic from the Frampton villa, on one of the Milden-

---

[1] G. Ulbert, 'Ein römischer Brunnenfund von Barbing-Kreuzhof' *Bayerische Vorgeschichtsblätter* XXIV (1961) 56.

[2] *J.R.S.* LII (1962) Pl. XXXIV.   [3] Behn (1954) fig. 144.

[4] J. Scott in *The New Oxford History of Music* I (1959) p. 410.

[5] F. Fremersdorf, *Das römischen Haus mit dem Dionysos Mosaik* (Berlin, 1956) figs. 9, 10.

hall silver dishes (Pl. 36*b*) and a little bronze statuette from Silchester shows a girl carrying a single *tibia* (Pl. 53*b*).

For the bass part a special form of *tibia* was used, blown by means of a reed inserted into a mouthpiece placed at the side. This was more in the nature of a bassoon and may have been a Roman invention. It appears on a sarcophagus in the Vatican, two bronze instruments of this type have been found at Pompeii, and two wooden examples with bronze rings are in the British Museum. So the *tibiae* may have included soprano and alto types, a tenor instrument an octave lower, and a bass, the whole family having a total range of at least three octaves. The tenor was probably the chief concert instrument.[1]

Sometimes the bulging cheeks of the musicians playing the *tibiae* seem to have been replaced by a windbag, resulting in a primitive form of bagpipe.[2] The Emperor Nero, according to Suetonius[3] and Dio Chrysostom,[4] is the most distinguished performer on this instrument known from this period, and generally it seems to have been played by low-class musicians, and probably also by country folk. 'Do you believe,' asks Martial, 'That a parrot speaks with the voice of a quail and Canis longs to be a bagpiper?'[5] Canis was a famous *tibia* player.

An invention of a Greek engineer, Ctesibios of Alexandria, about the end of the third century B.C., led to the development of the *hydraulis*, a form of organ described by Vitruvius and other writers. One or two attendants pumped air for the *hydraulis* into a chamber which contained an inverted metal bell immersed in water. The balance between the water pressure and the incoming air forced air up to the wind chest which was connected with rows of pipes. Under each pipe was a box with a sliding top with a hole. A keyboard was provided and each key pushed in a slide so that the hole lay beneath the pipe and allowed air to pass into it.[6] Many representations of this organ survive and some actual fragments. The most illuminating example is a terracotta model from Carthage, dating from the beginning of the second century A.D. It shows that the air and water apparatus was hidden in a large central box flanked by two containers, presumably of metal, for the air pumps. The lower half of the organist survives and shows him standing on a pedestal with the keyboard in front and three rows of eighteen or nineteen pipes of varying length.[7] Using the organist's legs as a scale, the size of the instrument is estimated as 12 feet high and 6 feet wide.[8] A picture of the *hydraulis* on a mosaic from the Nennig villa near Trier shows the organ from the other side with the head and shoulders of the organist appearing

---

[1] Behn (1954) p. 105 *et seq.*, figs. 135, 140.   [2] A. Baines, *Bagpipes* (1960) p. 63 *et seq.*
[3] *Nero*, 54.   [4] *Orationes* lxxi. 9.   [5] *Epigrams* X. 3.
[6] W. Apel, 'The Early History of the Organ', *Speculum* XXIII (1948) 191–216.
[7] *Ibid.* fig. 6.   [8] *Ibid.* 196.

above the pipes. The figures blowing the instrument are usually omitted but they do appear on a gem.[1] Other features on the Carthage model probably indicate stops used to alter the mode by shutting off certain pipes or rows of pipes. Another form of organ in which bellows replaced the hydraulic mechanism was a rather later development, and the earliest reference dates it to *c.* 120. A poetic account exists of such an organ, probably heard in a church in Istanbul by the Emperor Julian in his youth before his apostasy, and one is actually shown on a fourth-century obelisk in the same city.[2] Another appears on a sherd of pottery made at Rheinzabern.[3]

Actual remains of Roman organs have been found at Pompeii and pipes which may belong to one are in the Saalburg Museum. In 1931 many fragments were found in the cellar of a Roman house in the *colonia* of Aquincum (Old Buda, Hungary). They must have fallen from an upper room after a fire and they include fifty-two pipes, four stops, the keyboard and the top of the wind chest, all made of bronze. An inscription on a bronze plate relates that Julius Victorinus, a decurion and former aedile of Aquincum and president of the guild of wool-weavers, gave the organ to the guild in A.D. 228.[4]

Other musical instruments were chiefly used by Roman military bandsmen. The straight trumpet, known as the *tuba*,[5] may have been an Etruscan invention. The Roman examples so far found consist of a conical tube of iron or bronze gradually widening to a slightly expanded bell, with mouth-pieces of horn or bronze.[6] They were up to four feet in length and needed vigorous blowing (fig. 138). Fragments with mouth-pieces believed to come from such instruments had been found at Great Chesterford, Water Newton, Colchester,[7] and in the fort at Castle Cary on the Antonine Wall; and an altar, once in the Blackgate Museum at Newcastle-upon-Tyne, is believed to show one in relief on one of its sides.[8] The Great Chesterford example may be a relic of an early military occupation, a votive offering like the pieces of the earlier Irish trumpets recovered from the hoard at Llyn Cerrig Bach, or an instrument used in some entertainment, religious ceremony or funeral rites, as another mouthpiece is

[1] *Ibid.* fig. 5.

[2] *Ibid.* 200, fig. 7.   [3] Behn (1954) fig. 149.

[4] W. W. Hyde, 'The Recent Discovery of an Inscribed Water-Organ at Budapest', *Trans. & Proc. of the American Philological Ass.* LXIX (1938) 392–411; M. E. Klar, 'Musikinstrumente der Römerzeit in Trier', *Kurtrierisches Jahrbuch* VI (1966) 105 *et seq.*

[5] Quite unlike the modern tuba.

[6] Sachs, *op. cit.* p. 145.

[7] G. Webster, 'The Roman Military Advance under Ostorius Scapula', *Arch. J.* CXV (1960) 75 no. 43; 80 no. 104; 94 no. 230.

[8] *Catalogue of the Inscribed and Sculptured Stones of the Roman Period preserved in the Blackgate Museum, Newcastle-upon-Tyne* (1922) no. 5 (Lost).

138   Reconstruction of a Roman _Tuba_

also known from the excavations at Lydney.[1] A _tuba_ found in the Temple of
Mars in Klein Winternheim, near Mainz, seems to have been a votive offering
and a reconstruction suggests that it was a C trumpet with a compass of six
notes, like a modern bugle.[2] Mosaics and reliefs give the impression that a
chain or cord sling was attached near the bell, and the trumpeter pulled on this
with one hand to press the instrument more firmly against his lips.

In addition to the straight trumpet, examples also occur of a hooked variety,
the _lituus_, which probably originated as a cane or wooden tube stuck into a
cow-horn. The Roman variety was a bronze tube about 79 cm. long, curving
gracefully upward at the end into a bell (fig. 137c). Literary sources mention it
and several examples have been found in the Rhine and the Main in Germany.
The best example was discovered near Dusseldorf and is now in the Saalburg
Museum. It is in A with a range of six notes and a modern trumpeter can produce
a powerful, but also a light and pleasant sound from it. It may have been used
for signalling by the auxiliaries, a purpose for which the legions used the _tuba_.
An instrument, possibly a _lituus_, was found at Caprington in Scotland.[3] Fragments of another were dredged out of the Witham at Tattershall Ferry in 1762.
Alternatively these discoveries may belong to a Celtic form of this trumpet
which developed in the late Iron Age, known as the _carnyx_. Such instruments
appear on the Roman arch at Orange, easily identified because the bell-shaped
end is replaced by a fierce dragon's head with open mouth. The Tattershall
example is believed to date from the first half of the first century A.D. A boar's
head from Deskford, Banffshire, may also belong to a _carnyx_.[4]

Another development of the trumpet, the _cornu_, took the form of a tube with
an even conical bore curved into the shape of the letter G. A wooden cross-bar

[1] Wheeler (1932) p. 81 no. 47, fig. 16.   [2] Behn (1912) 37.   [3] Behn (1954) p. 137.
[4] S. Piggott, 'The Carnyx in Early Iron Age Britain', _Ant. J._ XXXIX (1959) 19-32.

359

joined the two sections of the curve and was held by the player's left hand against his left shoulder, and the rest of the tube with its bell-shaped end, curved above his head (fig. 139). Actual instruments found at Pompeii had tubes 11 feet long and others are depicted, played by soldiers, on a relief dated to A.D. 109 in the National Museum, Budapest,[1] and also accompanying the standards on Trajan's column. A small model in the form of a brooch comes from Mainz,[2] and mosaics from Nennig and Zliten show the *cornu* being played in the amphitheatre.[3] The Pompeian *cornu* was tuned in G and it would be possible to produce a range of seventeen notes from it, with a tone rather like that of a French horn.

A small curved trumpet appears on the tombstone of the cavalryman, Andes, at Mainz, with a small double cross-piece joining one section to a point just below the mouth-piece (fig. 137*d*). This may possibly be the *bucina*, an instrument used for giving non-tactical signals in the army and a favourite with countryfolk.[4] Not all authorities, however, agree with this identification and some would see in Andes' instrument a form of trombone, with a slide rather than a cross-piece.[5] Unfortunately no relief survives of Longinus, *bucinator* of the First Cohort of the Batavians, whose tombstone was found at Carrawburgh.[6]

To complete the list of instruments, the cymbals, the tambourine, and various forms of castanets and wooden clappers used for beating time, may be mentioned. The first two frequently figure in scenes of Dionysiac revelry, and tambourines played by maenads duly appear on one of the Mildenhall platters (Pl. 36*b*) and on mosaics from Fullerton, Keynsham and Brading. Bells were also used, singly or in strings. The *sistrum*, a kind of rattle consisting of an oval or horseshoe shaped frame with thin bars of metal strung with jangling discs fixed across it, is chiefly associated with the worship of Isis. A complete example was found at Vidy in Switzerland,[7] and one appears on a mosaic from Carthage in the British Museum.[8] Discs of metal with a hole for suspension were also struck, sometimes as signals by drivers approaching narrow streets.[9] Some form of drum is also probable.[10] A tombstone from Cologne shows a portrait of a soldier, Caius Vetienius, described as a *tubicen* of the First Legion. *Tubicen* normally means a trumpeter but Vetienius proudly holds in front of him not a *tuba* but the staff of a drum major, its oval-shaped end surrounded by a circlet

[1] A. Buchner, *Musical Instruments through the Ages* (1961) fig. 83.
[2] Behn (1954) fig. 143.
[3] Behn (1912) 41 *et seq.* for further examples.
[4] J. Scott, *op. cit.* p. 406.   [5] Behn (1954) p. 140.   [6] R.I.B. 1559.
[7] *Die Schweiz zur Römerzeit. Austellung zur Feier von 2000 Jahren vollzogenen Gründung der Colonia Raurica* (Basel, 1957) fig. 32.
[8] Hinks (1933) p. 93 fig. 101.
[9] Sachs, *op. cit.* p. 149.   [10] Behn (1954) p. 118.

139   Reconstruction of a Roman *Cornu*

of small studs or bells.[1] Another *tubicen* on a tombstone from Carnuntum, however, has both *tuba* and staff of office carved on his tombstone.[2]

When were these wind instruments played? In the army the *tuba* was used to signal attack and retreat, spur on an advance or call a halt. It marked the times for changing the guard in camp, so its sound must have been a familiar one in

[1] E. VIII no. 6446.   [2] Behn (1954) p. 141.

the forts along Hadrian's Wall and it was also played at the emperors' triumphs. With so many important tasks it seems reasonable that the drum major should be a *tubicen*. The *bucina* or the *cornu* sounded the watches and the *bucina* had the privilege of playing the *classicum*, the salute for the commander-in-chief or other persons of importance. The *cornu* is often shown on reliefs as advancing with the standards, and the *cornicines* sounded the order to march and joined with the *tubicines* in encouraging the army in battle.[1] Parties of either or both must occasionally have been detached, with orders to deceive the enemy with misleading calls.

Four musicians playing the double *tibiae*, two with *cornua* and one possibly playing a *lituus* accompany a funeral procession on a sarcophagus in the Museo Aquilano, Abruzzi,[2] and the *cornu* and *hydraulis* formed part of the orchestra which accompanied the gladiatorial games. The *hydraulis* is sometimes described as being a noisy instrument, and no doubt it did its best to give an adequate performance in the amphitheatre. Athenaeus, however, writing in the third century, mentions the sweet and joyous sound of a *hydraulis* heard in the distance from a neighbouring house, which charmed him with its tunefulness.[3]

The *tibia* and the *cithara* must have been the most popular instruments in everyday life and they occur frequently on mosaics and wall-paintings. As already noted, a soloist on the *tibiae* played at religious rites, partly to obliterate any other noises which might interrupt the ceremony. The pipers also accompanied dancers and singers, often enlivened dinner parties, and held positions of honour with the various guilds.[4] Accomplished concert soloists playing either the *tibiae*, or still more, the *cithara*, had successful and profitable careers, being mobbed by crowds of fans, exhibiting artistic temperament and travelling from city to city. Wall-paintings depict musicians playing these instruments and one example from *Herculaneum* shows a duet between a pipe and *cithara*. Solo singing was popular at home, at concerts or in the theatre, and choirs performed presumably mostly in unison, at big religious festivals and occasions of national rejoicing or at the theatre or games.

The Greek influence on Roman music was strong but the Romans did not have the same high regard for music as did the Greeks. Quintilian praises it chiefly as a means for the orator to improve his rhythm and the quality of his speech, and on the whole it seems to have been an accomplishment to listen to rather than one for amateurs to attempt. Several of the emperors, however,

[1] J. Scott, *op. cit.* p. 410.
[2] A. Birley (1964) p. 119. The Twelve Tables forbade the employment of more than ten *tibia* players at a funeral.
[3] W. Apel, *op. cit.* 197. [4] J. Scott, *op. cit.* p. 413.

besides Nero, are known to have been musical. Hadrian played the *cithara*, Severus Alexander the lyre, *tibia*, *tuba* and organ, and Verus travelled round Greece with a train of singers and instrumentalists.[1] Pagan music was so firmly suppressed by the church that it is not surprising that little evidence survives. The part eventually played by music, especially vocal music, in the ensuing centuries, however, suggests that its importance in the Roman world may easily be underestimated.

Fishing and hunting were favourite Roman sports, in addition to supplementing food supplies. Rod and line or nets were the usual means of catching fish, but the trident or fish spear and traps were also employed, chiefly in Mediterranean waters. A winged *amorino* hauls in a fish on a Chester relief,[2] and Pompeian paintings show fishing being carried on from boats and on land. A late second-century poem by Oppian discusses the subject in some detail and tells us that fishing lines were made of flax or twisted horsehair with rods long enough to keep the lines clear of boat or rocks.[3] Hooks were of various types and barbed hooks have been found at the Keynsham villa and at the settlement at Stockton. Hand lines with several hooks attached were trailed behind boats, and the nets were of all sizes. Bait included earthworms, ants, pork fat and shellfish.[4] Aelian, another late second-century writer, describes fly-fishing for trout in Greece,[5] and Martial mentions the greedy sea-bream deceived by the fly he has gorged.[6]

Salmon may only have been known to the Romans after their campaigns in Gaul. Pliny the Elder mentions that river salmon is the favourite fish in Aquitania,[7] and Ausonius alludes to it as well as to trout and other fish.[8] He also describes a throng of fisherman along the river bank, some busy with rod and line leaning over the rocks, and others in mid-stream casting nets buoyed up with cork floats.[9] One of his friends living by the seaside in the Médoc has his house overflowing with sturgeon, stingray, plaice and tunny fish caught with casting nets, drag nets and various types of lines.[10] A fisherman with a trident appears on one side of a sarcophagus in the Museum at Metz,[11] and fishermen with rod and line are shown, catching large fish, on a bronze fragment, probably enamelled, from Lydney.[12] Perhaps Flavius Senilis, the officer in charge of a supply depot of the fleet, whose name occurs on a mosaic showing fish at Lydney, sometimes spent his leave salmon-fishing in the Severn. In any case, many Romano-Britons must have taken advantage of the sporting opportunities offered by sea and rivers.

---

[1] *Ibid.* p. 416.   [2] Wright (1955) no. 143.
[3] A. J. Butler, *Sport in Classic Times* (1930) p. 118 *et seq.*   [4] *Ibid.* p. 170.   [5] *Ibid.* p. 163.
[6] *Epigrams* V. 18.   [7] *N.H.* IX. 32.   [8] *Mosella* 97.   [9] *Ibid.* 240 *et seq.*
[10] *Epistulae* XIV. 54 *et seq.*   [11] E. V no. 4306.   [12] Wheeler (1932) p. 42, no. 113, fig. 21.

'Are you reading, fishing, hunting or doing all three?' Pliny asks his friend Caninius Rufus. 'You can do all three together on the shores of Como.'[1] The hunting of various game for food or sport was a favourite recreation. Fowling was carried on with a variety of methods involving nets, jointed rods daubed with bird-lime used for knocking birds out of trees, traps, bows and arrows, the use of decoys or of hawks.[2] Pliny describes how tame hen partridges were used to attract cocks at mating time and ducks in some parts of the Empire were enticed with wooden decoys.[3] A mosaic from Bosceaz (Switzerland) shows birds being taken with bird-lime, probably made from mistletoe berries or sap from the oak. Not only man was dangerous to birds, however, as a Pompeian mosaic shows a cat catching a partridge.[4]

Celtic enthusiasm for the chase on horseback dates from pre-Roman times and was noted by Caesar,[5] while Arrian writing in the mid-second century A.D. observes that the Celts hunted with the help of good dogs without using nets or beaters. Various writers mention numerous breeds of dogs from Britain, Gaul, Iberia, Italy or the Near East and the possibilities of breeding and cross breeding were realised.[6] Certain dogs were trained to follow the quarry at all costs, day or night, while others learnt to keep beside the huntsman and guide him to the quarry. The Gallic hound was rough-coated with long or short fur, rather noisy but fast and pertinacious. The *vertragus*, a particularly fast dog, more like a greyhound, was used for hunting hares,[7] and frequently appears in action on Castor ware beakers (fig. 140). An altar from Bisley probably shows one standing on its hind legs to reach a dead hare in the hand of the god Silvanus,[8] and another is depicted on an altar from Nettleton, Wiltshire.[9] The British hunting dogs mentioned by Strabo were probably of several breeds, including a larger beast able to tackle boar or stag, perhaps resembling a mastiff.[10] One is probably portrayed on a grave relief from Chester (Pl. 43*a*)[11] and another is carrying off a deer on a relief found near Bath.[12] Others confront a boar in the forest on a slab from Cologne,[13] and appear on a relief at Trier.[14]

Chasing the hare is vividly shown on an incised glass bowl found at Banwell (Somerset), and made at Cologne. The hunter is mounted and flourishes his

---

[1] *Epistulae* II. 8.   [2] A. J. Butler, *op. cit.* p. 181.   [3] *N.H.* X. 51.
[4] M. Brion, *Pompeii and Herculaneum* (1960) Pl. LXXVIII.   [5] *B.G.* VI. 21.
[6] A. J. Butler, *op. cit.* p. 45 *et seq*. See also Richmond (1963) p. 162.
[7] Martial, *Epigrams* XIV. 200.
[8] E. Clifford, 'Roman Altars in Gloucestershire', B. and G.T. LX (1939) Pl. LV no. 7.
[9] Toynbee (1964) Pl. XLVa.
[10] M. Aymard, *Les Chasses romaines* (Paris, 1961) p. 268 *et seq*.; Duval (1952) p. 253 *et seq*.
[11] Wright (1955) no. 142a.   [12] Toynbee (1964) Pl. XXXVIIIa.
[13] E. X no. 6530.   [14] E. VI no. 5064.

140   Hunt scene from a Castor ware beaker, Hauxton, Cambridgeshire

whip while two hounds drive the hare into a net.[1] One relief from Bath shows a hare escaping from a dog held by a hunter on a leash (Pl. 43c), and another from Piercebridge shows a victim held by its hindlegs in the hunter's hand, with the horse in the background.[2] A boar and another hare are shown being brought home on a fragmentary relief from the villa at Box,[3] and Winter from a Chedworth mosaic carries a hare in his hand (Pl. 39). A hunting scene on a mosaic from Oudna, Tunisia, shows the hounds *Ederatus* (Ivy-crowned) and *Mustela* (Weasel) chasing a hare and a fox,[4] and a fragment of a statue of a beater in the Châtillon Museum has a game bag, probably of leather, out of which pop the heads of two hares.[5]

The stag hunt is well illustrated on a mosaic from Lillebonne.[6] The hounds, beaters and hunters on horseback are shown assembling to offer a sacrifice to Diana; among them is an attendant leading a stag to be used as a decoy. Another scene shows the hunt setting out through the forest and this rather recalls the lively figures of Dido, Aeneas and Ascanius riding to the hunt on the Low Ham mosaic pavement. A third scene at Lillebonne depicts the quarry, a stag and two does, with a hunter just fitting an arrow to his bow. Hunting scenes also appear on mosaics from the villa at Frampton and on colour-coated pottery (fig. 141),[7] and part of a weathered relief from Jarrow appears to show an archer with his bow and arrow, stalking a stag.[8] Knives and hunting spears were the other weapons used, and hunting spears appear clearly in the hands of hunters carrying a dead doe home from the hunt, hung on a pole, on a mosaic from the villa at East Coker.[9] A heavy iron spearhead found in a late third-century corn-drying oven at Huntsham (Hereford) was probably used for hunting.[10] Bears were

[1] Toynbee (1963) no. 142.
[2] F. Haverfield, *Catalogue of Sculptured and Inscribed Stones in the Cathedral Library, Durham* (Durham, 1899) no. 3. See also Duval (1952) p. 255.
[3] Toynbee (1964) p. 179.   [4] Toynbee (1948) 33, Pl. VIII, fig. 23.   [5] E. IV no. 3400.
[6] A. Blanchet, *Étude sur la Décoration des Édifices de la Gaule* (Paris, 1913) Pl. VII.
[7] Toynbee (1964) pp. 251, 410.
[8] *Catalogue, Blackgate Museum, Newcastle, op. cit.* no. 12.
[9] A. Birley (1964) p. 92.   [10] *J.R.S.* LI (1961) 171 fig. 20.

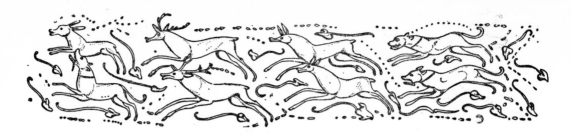

141 Hunt scene on a beaker from Benwell

another possible quarry and the statuette of Minerva in Devizes Museum is probably wearing a British bearskin.[1] No Briton, however, is likely to have rivalled the first-century officer in Germany who put up an altar to Diana commemorating a bag of fifty bears in six months.[2] Nevertheless, no one knows what degree of success was attained by the hunters from Bewcastle who put up an altar to Silvanus at Birdoswald.[3]

The boar hunt was a dangerous sport appealing to the bravest, and Ausonius warns his friend Theon against getting too close to this animal, and reminds him of his brother's scars, the result of boar-hunting.[4] Boars are among the other quarry depicted in the hunting scenes on Castor ware beakers.[5] Lances, with which the animal was attacked as in pig-sticking, or heavy hunting spears were the usual weapons, and the dogs used were protected with heavy nailed collars as they were apt to be casualties.[6] Martial tells us of the faithful hunting dog Lydia who died not of old age but slain by a huge boar,[7] dying uncomplaining as she could not meet a nobler death, and two incised bowls from the Cologne glass factories show us hunters and dogs at work.[8] On the moors at Stanhope in Weardale, miles away from any known Roman habitation, British hunting dogs may have been in action. There an altar to Silvanus erected by Gaius Tetius Veturius Micianus, cavalry commander in the Roman army, was set up gladly 'for taking a wild boar of remarkable fineness which many of his predecessors had been unable to bag'.[9] Another Martial epigram discusses the cooking of a boar slain with the spear. He remarks sadly that the kitchen fire is ablaze with timber from an entire hilltop, the cook will use a huge heap of expensive pepper and Falernian will be needed for the sauce. 'Go back to your owner, my fire is too small for you, O boar that would bankrupt me! 'Tis less

[1] Toynbee (1964) p. 133.
[2] W. Monk-Gibbon, *Western Germany* (1955) p. 126.
[3] R.I.B. 1905. [4] *Epistulae* XIV. [5] Hull (1963b) fig. 53 no. 9.
[6] Aymard, *op. cit.* p. 327. [7] *Epigrams* XI. 69.
[8] D. Harden, 'The Wint Hill Hunting Bowl', *J. of Glass Studies* II (1960) 54 figs. 16, 17.
[9] R.I.B 1041.

ruinous to starve.'[1] Small bronzes from various British sites depicting boars may be hunters' votive offerings.[2]

A more sophisticated form of amusement than hunting was a visit to the theatre. Not a great deal is known about the drama during the Roman Empire. There seem to have been few new plays and those which were written were probably intended for public readings rather than for actual theatrical production. Some early plays may have been revived occasionally but more frequently the theatrical performances were made up of favourite scenes from old plays which gave good parts to popular actors. The Emperor Nero seems to have initiated a drama festival and he also acted himself, singing the part of Oedipus in Exile at his last public performance before his suicide.[3] The *Octavia*, an historical drama of uncertain, possibly late first-century, date, sometimes attributed to Seneca, probably mistakenly, may just possibly have been a new production. Otherwise there is little evidence, with one notable exception. The *Querolus*, a delightful Latin comedy by an unknown author of late fourth- or fifth-century date, was most probably written in southern Gaul as an after dinner entertainment for a cultivated audience. This suggests that some interest in a good play still survived at this time. A modern production of this play is sadly overdue.[4]

The pantomime had greater popular appeal and for this themes taken from mythology were danced by actors wearing masks, while a chorus chanted the story to an instrumental accompaniment which included *tibiae* and percussion. Well-known poets wrote some of the libretti because such work was well paid.[5] The actor might assume several parts, each with its own mask and costume, and different actors, usually slaves or freedmen, each had their own group of enthusiastic supporters. A mosaic from Pompeii shows a servant dressing one of these actors in the wings of a theatre. Near him two dancers are practising their steps and a musician is trying out a passage on his *tibiae*. A seated older man, perhaps the producer, is obviously issuing last-minute instructions and choosing among the masks lying round him.[6] Another Pompeian mosaic shows three masked women sitting round a table.

Pantomime seems to have been a sophisticated if not particularly elevating form of entertainment, demanding some knowledge of its themes from the audience. However, it was not coarse. Crude jokes and horseplay were the speciality of the mime whose performers enacted scenes of daily life with topical allusions in the theatres, or as bands of strolling players setting up a stage and

[1] *Epigrams* VII. 27. Trans. W. Ker.   [2] Toynbee (1964) p. 125.
[3] Suetonius, *Nero*, 10 21, 46.   [4] Chadwick (1955) p. 134.
[5] W. Beare, *The Roman Stage* (1955) p. 224.
[6] M. Brion, *Pompeii & Herculaneum* (1960) fig. 85

a curtain wherever they could attract an audience. A large part of their performances seem to have been improvised but some literary fragments survive,
mostly from prologues. Another form of popular farce was the *fabula Atellana*
in which stock characters appeared wearing masks. They included a clown,
grandpa, 'Fat cheeks', and a dog, etc., and may, perhaps, be the ancestors of the
characters of the Commedia dell'Arte or the Punch and Judy show.[1]

The theatres themselves consisted of an auditorium or *cavea* built with a curve
of rather more than a semicircle with seats rising in tiers, and an arena or
orchestra occupied not by musicians but by the most important members of the
audience. This was unroofed but might be protected from the weather by
awnings, and the *cavea* might have a covered-in passageway round the top.
Behind the raised stage (*pulpitum*) came the stage building or *scaena*, reaching to
the same height as the top of the *cavea* and provided with doorways on to the
stage, niches, columns and other architectural and decorative features. Stage
and stage building were roofed. The seats were reached through vaulted
corridors and boxes for various dignitaries, including the magistrate or other
citizen financing the performance, were sometimes built above the entrances
into the auditorium. Good examples of theatres have survived at Pompeii,
Orange and other French sites.

In Britain the inscription at Petuaria (Brough-on-Humber) records the erection of a theatre for the Parisii by the aedile M. Ulpius Ianuarius, in the second
century. The site, however, still awaits discovery.[2] Air photography revealed
the presence of a theatre with the Roman D-shaped plan in the Gosbecks area
outside Colchester. This awaits further excavation but preliminary surveys
suggest an artificial earth mound revetted by stone walls for the *cavea*, with tiers
of wooden seats and wooden stage buildings. At least one vaulted entrance
existed, placed on the north side in the middle of the semicircle. Traces of
timber buildings found below the mound suggest an earlier building entirely
constructed of wood.[3] Another theatre is suspected within the walls of the
colonia.[4] A timber-built theatre of Gosbecks type was constructed at Canterbury
towards the end of the first century, and in the second century it was enlarged
and rebuilt in stone on a monumental scale.[5]

The only British theatre so far fully excavated is the one at Verulamium. It
seems to have started life about A.D. 160, soon after the mid-second-century
fire, on a site previously unoccupied. A blank space within the city at this period
is surprising but may be explained by the existence of a large temple of Romano-

---

[1] W. Beare, *op. cit.* Chaps. XVI–XVIII. [2] *R.I.B.* 707.
[3] Hull (1958) p. 267; (1963) p. 122. [4] Hull (1958) p. 80.
[5] S. S. Frere, *Roman Canterbury* (Canterbury, 1962) pp. 11, 28.

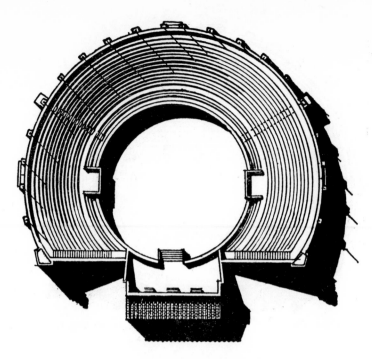

142 Reconstruction showing the original plan of the theatre at
Verulamium

Celtic type to the south-west.[1] A spacious precinct was probably attached to this
temple to accommodate big gatherings for religious festivals. Such festivals
often included dramatic performances, choral singing or gladiatorial games
dedicated to the presiding deity of the temple, and the theatre may have been
erected for ceremonies and events of increasing elaboration. A parallel is provided by the temple and the other shrines known to exist on the Gosbecks site
at Colchester. This theory is also supported by the plan of the Period One
theatre at Verulamium which included a circular orchestra surrounded for
three-quarters of its circumference by tiers of seats. These were built up on a
mound of earth excavated from the orchestra and piled up against an exterior
wall. The curve of the interior wall continued across the front of the stage
which probably had several doorways leading into a room behind. Many of the
seats look inwards into the orchestra rather than at the stage (fig. 142). Green
plaster was recovered from the orchestra wall, and a fragment of carved cornice
painted yellow, with acanthus leaves picked out in dark red and orange, came
from the stage area.

The Period One building was soon converted into a more conventional
theatre with part of the orchestra used for seating. A straight wall was built
[1] See below p. 439.

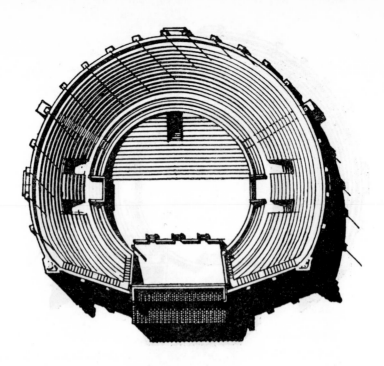

143　Verulamium theatre in the late second century

across the semicircular front of the old stage, making it larger, and a line of
columns with Corinthian capitals provided the usual Roman architectural scene
at the back (fig. 143). One of the columns has been re-erected on the site, on a
base located during the excavations. The floor of the stage was of timber at all
periods. About A.D. 200 another stone wall was built in front of the stage. This
may replace an earlier wooden wall. Behind it was a trench or slot three feet
three inches deep. Probably this was a socket into which a drop curtain could be
lowered by means of weights, and an iron counterpoise weighing 154 lbs. found
in this area is possibly a relic of this mechanism. The stage curtain is believed
to have been a Roman invention and the slots for it have been found at other
sites.[1] Wing rooms attached to the theatre to the south-east were, perhaps,
dressing-rooms for the actors.

By the end of the century the theatre needed repairs and soon after 300 it
was rebuilt and enlarged. A new outer wall was built and a vaulted corridor
probably ran between it and the old outer wall with more seats above the
corridor. Further seats were provided at the bottom of the *cavea* by flattening
the curve of the orchestra wall. The orchestra itself, however, is believed
to have been cleared of its seats and covered by a cement floor. The stage was

[1] W. Beare, *op. cit.* p. 257.

restored with the same plan as before and with the same columns.[1] The theatre continued in use at least until the end of the fourth century, possibly later, and it may have been closed down as a result of Christian disapproval. At some time it seems to have acted as the town rubbish dump and its disuse was formerly believed to be a sign of the collapse of town life. It has now been realised that the rubbish merely represents the sweepings of a market hall situated nearby. About 390–400 the temple was re-organised and its entrance moved to the opposite side. Whether this indicates its transformation into a Christian church is unknown, the change may well coincide with the closure of the theatre.[2]

Periods One and Four in the Verulamium theatre when the orchestra was kept clear of seats, probably indicate that attention was directed more towards this central area than to the stage. The ceremonies and entertainments taking place at these times may have been more suited to the amphitheatre than the true theatre and it is noteworthy that no separate amphitheatre has yet been found at Verulamium. Small theatres, sometimes called cockpit theatres, of this type are known from a number of sites in west, central and northern France, directing attention more to the stage or to the orchestra in varying degrees at different periods. Some, such as Drevant (Cher), have dens for wild beasts. At Augst (Switzerland) an early theatre was replaced by an ampitheatre *c.* A.D. 74 and turned back into a theatre *c.* 150. Paris seems to have possessed a small theatre on the site of the Lycée Saint-Louis and also a combined amphitheatre/ theatre with accommodation for animals in the Rue Monge.[3]

Games with gladiators and wild beasts took place in the amphitheatres. They were a survival of the funeral games of the Etruscans and Campanians which may have been intended to send brave companions to join deceased warriors or to satisfy the craving of the dead for blood. Entertainments such as games took place on certain dates in the Roman calendar and by the fourth century 101 days were allotted each year to the theatre, 64 to chariot racing and 10 to the amphitheatre. The emperors or other citizens also gave games to mark special occasions and Claudius celebrated his successful campaign in Britain in this way. Admission to both theatre and amphitheatre was free, and counters of pottery, bone or ivory are found with letters or numbers incised on one side and various designs, often masks, on the other (fig. 133). These were probably tickets indicating the whereabouts of seats.

Criminals, prisoners of war and slaves were trained for the amphitheatre, as

[1] K. Kenyon and S. S. Frere, *The Roman Theatre at Verulamium* (1964); K. Kenyon, 'The Roman Theatre at Verulamium', *Arch.* LXXXIV (1935) pp. 213–61.
[2] Frere (1946b) 76.
[3] P.-M. Duval, *Paris Antique* (Paris, 1961) pp. 179, 193.

well as a certain number of free men who adopted this career in a desperate attempt to redeem their fortunes and who took an oath to fight for a certain period. They lived in barracks supervised by contractors and trained by special instructors (*lanistae*). Doctors, such as Galen at one period of his life, kept an eye on their health and diet and treated their wounds. In the provinces, parties of combatants were hired out by the contractors for the highest fees they could obtain. In Rome both men and beasts were usually controlled by imperial agents who produced them as required. The men fought armed in various ways. The Samnites and the *mirmillones* were heavily protected with oblong shields, short swords and helmets with visors, the *mirmillo*'s helmet being of a Gallic type decorated with a fish. The Thracian type of gladiator had a round buckler and a curved scimitar, and the *retiarius* fought with little or no armour, with only a net and a trident. These different types appear clearly on a mosaic from Kreuznach, Germany.[1] Another mosaic, from the Bignor villa in Sussex, shows Cupids playing at gladiators, with an instructor, identifiable by his wand of office, superintending four pairs at a training session. The combats are between *mirmillones* and *retiarii*, with one fight in progress, a second fight in which a *retiarius* has been disarmed, a third incident in which the combatants are preparing for battle, and a fourth in which the *retiarius* has been hurt. A disarmed or defeated gladiator would be killed unless his opponent spared him or the crowd cried out in his favour, waved their handkerchiefs or held up their thumbs for mercy. The Emperor or whoever was presiding over the games, usually accepted the popular verdict. An epitaph from Milan belongs to a gladiator who was killed by an adversary whom he had spared at a previous encounter. Bets were placed on the results of the various combats.[2]

Gladiatorial games began with a parade of the gladiators in splendid military dress. Fine helmets belonging to them have been found at Pompeii. They were followed by attendants carrying their arms. Lots were drawn and the fighting commenced to the sound of the *tibiae, cornua* and the hydraulic organ. The winners were handsomely rewarded with money or gifts piled on silver dishes, and a frequent winner would eventually be offered his freedom. Not all accepted it, preferring to continue to take part in the excitement and the good living of the gladiatorial barracks. Successful participants became the idols of the crowd. A tombstone from Orange commemorates a *mirmillo* who won 53 fights,[3] and a Greek who fought in a chariot at Nîmes, won 20 contests before his death.[4] Inscriptions also survive mentioning retired gladiators who had accepted the

[1] K. Parlasca, *Die Römischen Mosaiken in Deustchland* (Berlin, 1959) Pl. LXXXIX.
[2] C.I.L. V. 5933.
[3] C.I.L. XII. 5837.   [4] C.I.L. XII. 3323.

SPICVLVS COLVMBVS CALAMVS HOLES PETRAITES PRVDES PROCVLVS COLVMBVS

[50]

144 Gladiators on a glass vase, Colchester

wooden sword, sign of their freedom, and who remained with the troop as instructors.[1]

British interest in gladiatorial combats may be reflected in the *graffito* of Verecunda the actress and Lucius the gladiator found at Leicester.[2] It is also probably shown by the appearance of gladiators among the subjects used to decorate imported glass and also colour-coated pottery. A shallow green glass cup from Colchester of mid-first-century date depicts eight gladiators and gives their names (fig. 144). Speculus, Petraites and Proculus appear to have defeated Columbus, Prudens and Cocumbus, Proculus indeed already holds the palm of victory. Meanwhile Calamus and Holes carry on the fight.[3] A fragment of another glass from the same mould and with some of the same names was found at Leicester, and other pieces of glass beakers with combined gladiatorial and circus scenes are known from Southwark, Hartlip and Topsham.[4] Another scene appears on one side of a colour-coated beaker, also found at Colchester, showing the 'Samnite' Memno defeating the *retiarius*, Valentinus.[5] The inscriptions add '*legionis xxx*' so these two may have been stars of a troupe attached to the Thirtieth Legion at Xanten in the Rhineland whose fame had spread to other provinces. Or they may even have come over on a visit. Part of a similar combat is incised on a fragment of a samian mortarium of *c*. A.D. 160, found at York (fig. 145),[6] and the subject occurs again on one of the Brading mosaic pavements. Here the *retiarius* seems to be having better luck. Bronze statuettes of 'Samnites' have been found in London and figurines of gladiators in ivory come from Colchester and South Shields.[7] Recently a helmet of gladiatorial type was found at Hawkedon, Suffolk. It has holes for the attachment of a visor and resembles examples found at Pompeii.[8]

Acrobats, wrestlers and boxers also contributed to the entertainments in the

[1] C.I.L. XII. 4452; XIII. 1997.   [2] Burn (1932) p. 64.
[3] Hawkes and Hull (1947) Pl. LXXVI.   [4] Toynbee (1964) p. 379.
[5] Toynbee (1963) no. 158.
[6] B. Hartley, 'A fragment of samian ware', *Ant. J.* XXIV (1954) 233.
[7] Toynbee (1964) p. 359.   [8] *I.L.N.* 12 June 1965.

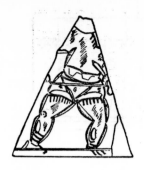

145   Gladiator incised on a samian fragment from York

amphitheatre. A colour-coated beaker found at Water Newton shows a crude but lively scene with a pair of gladiators and a female acrobat, leaping or somersaulting from the back of one animal (? horse) to another (? lion or leopard).[1] A small bronze statuette in Guildhall Museum, London, depicts another acrobat doing a backbend. Evidence for acrobats forming living pyramids, and also for jugglers, is known from other parts of the Empire.[2]

Professional wrestlers appear on a mosaic from Aquincum where one has seized the other in a body hold,[3] and a mosaic from Tusculum shows boxers, jumpers, and discus throwers also in action.[4] These athletes were probably members of one of the athletic guilds which existed in Rome. Boxing was a cruel sport as from the fourth century B.C. the hands were protected by hard leather thongs and then by elbow-length gloves with a hard leather ring encircling the knuckles. The Romans weighted these knuckledusters and added metal spikes. With such equipment, defensive fighting was important especially as the contests were not divided into rounds, neither were the boxers confined within a ring.[5]

The other form of amphitheatre sport was the *venatio*, the wild-beast hunt, in which armed gladiators fought lions, tigers, bears, panthers, bulls or the occasional rhinoceros or sometimes the animals were matched against each other. These contests were a favourite theme for mosaic pavements. The villa at Nennig near Trier, for example, shows a tiger and an antelope, a gladiator killing a leopard, an attendant leading in a triumphant lion, and gladiators beating off a bear which has killed a man.[6] Scenes of similar type survive from Bad Kreuznach.[7] Christian influence led to the amelioration of the cruel events in the amphitheatre. They were first partly replaced by turns in which skill and comedy predominated, and then finally suppressed altogether.[8]

[1] Toynbee (1963) no. 156.
[2] M. Bieber, *The History of the Greek and Roman Theater* (Princeton, 1961) pp. 249, 252.
[3] V. Kuzsinsky, *Aquincum* (Budapest, 1934) fig. 16.
[4] E. N. Gardiner, *Athletics of the Ancient World* (Oxford, 1930) fig. 70.
[5] *Ibid.*, p. 198 *et seq.*   [6] K. Parlasca, *op. cit.* Pl. XXXVII.   [7] *Ibid.*, Pls. XC, XCI.
[8] G. Jennison, *Animals for Show and Pleasure in Ancient Rome* (Manchester, 1937) p. 179.

A large trade grew up with the frontier provinces, particularly Africa, to provide the animals needed for the games, and many late mosaics show the hunters at work, collecting exhibits. An account of the preparations necessary for a performance in Rome can be found in the letters of Symmachus when he was busy arranging events to celebrate his son becoming quaestor in A.D. 393 and praetor in 401. Symmachus writes to friends who have promised to give or help him find animals, he sends agents all over collecting them, and he writes to various officials asking them to help the agents. Horses for the chariot races came mostly from studs in Spain and a few through a friend at Arles; lions seem to have been scarce, as indeed the full-maned lions always were, although the aid of two officials is asked to secure lions, leopards (? maneless lions) and antelope. Crocodiles from Egypt, bears from Italy and provinces to the north and east, and seven Irish wolfhounds completed the bill.[1] A pictorial record of the collection of such animals appears on the floors of the late fourth-century villa at Piazza Amerina in Sicily. Here the master, presumably the owner of the villa, is superintending the operations of a team of hunters, on foot or on horseback, who are protected by heavy shields.[2] Methods of trapping included pits, and the driving of animals into nets or into enclosures. The captives were placed in wooden boxes with sliding doors and the Piazza Amerina mosaics show these boxes being carried on poles by huntsmen, placed on wheels and drawn by oxen, and finally put aboard a boat.

Scenes from the *venatio* do not appear on British mosaics. Possibly they were not to British taste and in any case, transport difficulties probably prevented the appearance of many exotic animals in the arena here. Bullfights and boar hunts may have taken their place. The odd appearance of some of the animals who march around Orpheus make it doubtful if the mosaicists were very familiar with elephants, for example, and possibly they did not always quite believe what they saw in their pattern-books. Some attempt is made, however, to show men and animals fighting on a brooch found at Lakenheath (fig. 146) and on colour-coated pottery, and lions appear on two fragments from Colchester.[3] The Colchester beaker with the gladiators Memmo and Valentinus also shows the *venator* Secundus, holding a whip and contending with a bear while his companion Mario, armed only with a stick, looks on. This might be an illustration of bear-baiting. Bears were exported from Britain and Martial records the appearance of a Caledonian bear in the arena in the time of Domitian, a possible trophy from Agricola's campaigns. Bears may well have appeared in British

---

[1] *Ibid.* pp. 95, 183.
[2] G. V. Gentile, *La Villa Erculia di Piazza Amerina* (Rome, no date).
[3] Toynbee (1964) p. 412.

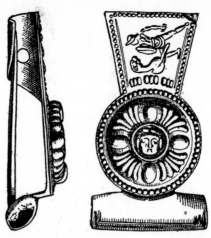

146 Brooch showing a man fighting an animal. Mid-first century. Lakenheath, Suffolk

amphitheatres as either entertainers or combatants. Circus acts with trained animals are recorded from Rome, including tame bears appearing in a farce in the third century.[1] A mosaic from Rades in Tunisia shows a team of performing bears, among them six called *Nilus*, *Fedra*, *Alecsandria*, *Simplicius* (Frank), *Gloriosus* and *Braciatus* (Brawny). Some of them are sporting with bulls and other animals and birds while *Fedra* climbs a pole.[2] British interest in bears is further shown in the form of small jet carvings found at York, Malton and Colchester. These may possibly be children's playthings.[3]

The amphitheatre where the *venatio* and the gladiatorial games took place consisted of an oval arena. Unlike the theatre, it was surrounded on all sides by tiers of seats built up on banks of earth revetted with timber, or stone walls high enough in front to keep the audience safe from the animals. In Italy and southern France these buildings developed into imposing monuments, like the Colosseum, or the amphitheatres at Arles and Nîmes, still used for bullfights. At Trier a stockade was put up in the arena, eight feet from the wall, as an additional safety precaution for the spectators, and the dens of the animals and the dungeons of the condemned prisoners still survive underground. At one point under the arena a section of the ceiling was hung on weights to make a lift on which men, animals or dramatic scenes could be hauled up to make a sudden appearance as part of the show. The Trier amphitheatre was built in stone in the early second century. It probably replaced an earlier timber structure and was then outside the town boundary, but in the fourth century it was incorporated in the town walls. It may have held about 7,000 people.

Amphitheatres occur associated with military and also with small civilian

[1] G. Jennison, *op. cit.* pp. 78, 94, 132. [2] Toynbee (1948) 36. [3] Toynbee (1964) p. 364.

sites, as well as with towns, and the military examples often start in a small way as a centre for military training besides sports and amusements. In Britain the only amphitheatre extensively explored so far is the one outside the fortress of the Second Legion at Caerleon. It was hollowed out of the hillside with an arena 184 by 136½ feet, and the earth bank for the wooden seats originally rose to a height of 28 feet. A stone wall 12 feet high, carefully covered with smooth mortar so as to provide no foothold for a wild animal, bounded the arena, and the exterior stone wall was stuccoed and painted with false joints outlined in red. The two main entrances at either end led straight into the arena through vaulted approaches. Two other entrances midway between them led up stairs into private boxes, and a small half-domed recess in front of one of these may have been a shrine to Nemesis at some period. Four more entrances led to the tiers of seats. The amphitheatre is estimated to have held 6,000 and it was probably used as a parade and exercise ground as well as for shows. It was built by the legionaries *c.* A.D. 80, and in places where the mortar coating has perished, inscriptions mark the work of various units, e.g. 'From the tenth cohort, the century of Flavius Julianus (built this)'.[1] About A.D. 125 the amphitheatre was extensively repaired and the boxes ceased to be used. Further reconstruction was done *c.* 213–22 and minor repairs up to *c.* 296.[2]

Only a few miles from Caerleon a smaller amphitheatre constructed at Caerwent in the late third or fourth century was built above earlier houses and within the circuit of the town walls. The Silchester amphitheatre seems to be slightly larger, it lies outside the town and is still unexcavated. Much larger was the structure outside Dorchester (Dorset) with an arena measuring *c.* 196 by 176 feet. This seems to have been entirely timber-built and it survives today as Maumbury Rings, its earth banks still 30 feet high. Excavations are now being carried out on the Cirencester amphitheatre which has an arena of 150 by 135 feet. Five periods have been distinguished to date, the earliest, so far undated, belonging to an earth and timber structure. Masonry retaining walls appear with Period Two in the second century. Alterations were made later in the second century—in Period Three, in Period Four, still undated, and in Period Five in the late fourth century.[3]

Another military amphitheatre, comparable to the one at Caerleon, is being uncovered outside the fortress at Chester. Its arena is rather larger, *c.* 190 by 162 feet, bordered by a wall about 12 feet high, and its outer wall may have reached a height of 35 feet. Probably it held about 8,000, room for both the

[1] *R.I.B.* 343.
[2] M. and T. V. Wheeler, *The Roman Amphitheatre at Caerleon* (1953).
[3] J. Wacher, 'Cirencester', *Ant. J.* XLIII (1963) 23; XLIV (1964) 17.

Twentieth Legion and the civilian population. Clear traces of an earlier timber structure of *c.* A.D. 78 were found underlying it, and the stone amphitheatre may have replaced this *c.* A.D. 102, or even as early as A.D. 80, contemporary with Caerleon.[1] At the other end of the scale is a smaller amphitheatre suspected in an earthwork outside the auxiliary fort at Tomen-y-Mur,[2] and one of very similar size associated with the mining settlement at Charterhouse-on-Mendip. Another small amphitheatre with an arena measuring only 50 by 70 feet exists close to the small settlement at Woodcuts. It was built in the fourth century over an earlier approach road.[3]

The third type of Roman public building designed for mass entertainment was the circus for chariot racing. This popular sport could be carried on wherever a large enough space could be cleared and levelled for a racecourse, but in Rome and other large cities, circuses with the plan of two parallel sides and a rounded end, rather like a hairpin, were laid out with tiers of seats for the spectators. The other end held twelve stables for teams who might compete together, eight at a time, or, more frequently, in groups of four. A central rib, the *spina*, ran down part of the centre of the circus with broad based pillars with pointed tops, the *metae*, at each end. Each race comprised so many laps and to save distance, the charioteer had to turn sharply round the *metae*. The presiding magistrate dropped his handkerchief to start the race and the laps were shown by various symbols including eggs, dolphins and attributes of Castor and Pollux or other deities associated with horses.

Chariot racing was a favourite subject for mosaicists, and fragments of a panel from the Horkstow Villa, now in the British Museum, portray one such event. In the upper row a chariot has met disaster, possibly through a misjudged turn round the last *meta*, as a wheel has come adrift. The charioteer is just falling out as an attendant, who has leapt from his horse, rushes to catch him. Behind them another mounted attendant comes galloping up with a lasso in his hand, ready to catch the runaway horses. Below, on the other side of the *spina*, are three chariots which have successfully negotiated the turn, the victor, in red, on the right, just reining in his horses, while the buff-clad charioteer behind him is still whipping on his team.[4]

In Rome there were four racing factions, red, white, blue and green. The successful charioteers, the popular idols of the crowd, wore their colours. The names of some of them still survive on a series of mould blown glass cups, companion pieces to the glasses depicting gladiators already described. One

[1] F. H. Thompson, *Roman Cheshire* (Chester, 1965) p. 42.
[2] V. Nash-Williams, *The Roman Frontier in Wales* (1954) p. 37.
[3] Hawkes (1948) 48.　[4] Toynbee (1963) no. 198.

found at Colchester and now in the British Museum, shows the circus with the *metae* and various shrines and other features.[1] There are four teams with the inscriptions *Cresce[n]s ave* for the victor, and *Hierax vale*, *Olympae vale*, *Antiloce vale* for the losers. Other fragments from Topsham, Hartlip and Southwark combine circus and arena scenes and give the names of the charioteers *Pyramae* and *Crescesia* and the gladiators *Petraites* and *Hermes*. More chariots occur, but with nameless protagonists, on some colour-coated beakers.[2]

Inscriptions also give the names of charioteers, notably the one on the monument erected by his admirers and stable companions to Diocles in A.D. 146, possibly the date of his retirement from the circus at the age of 42. He was a Spaniard and his career lasted twenty-four years under the red, white and green colours. He ran in 4,257 races, winning 1,462 of them, an average of 177 races a year, some with six-horse teams. He made some horses winners a hundred times, and with one of them he won two hundred races. 'The champion of all charioteers . . . he excelled the charioteers of all the stables who ever participated in the races.'[3]

Oppian gives a list of the different breeds of horse found round the Mediterranean in the second century. The Libyan breeds were renowned for their speed and staying power and some of them were crossed with Spanish and Gallic breeds.[4] Like the charioteers, the racehorses are often identified on monuments or on mosaics. Four hundred and eighty names have survived, some describing colour or markings such as *Glaucus* (Grey), *Maculosus* (Piebald) or *Murinus* (Mousy), others speed, like *Volucer* (Flyer). This was the Emperor Verus' horse, fed on grapes and given luxurious horsecloths and a tomb on the Vatican Hill. Other names included *Phosphorus* (Morning Star), *Cirratus* (Curly-Locks), *Reburrus* (Bristly), *Eustolus* and *Volens* (Ready and Willing), *Temerarius* (Hothead), *Animator* (Life and Soul of the Team), *Victor*, *Cupido*, *Adamatus* (Much-Beloved), *Puerina* (Girly), *Fastidiosus* (Choosy) and *Verbosus* (Chatterbox).[5]

Some mosaics show these animals off duty. A charming example of an anonymous second-century horse is in the Landesmuseum, Trier, another horse from Cherchel in Algeria is identified as *Muccosus* (Snuffler) of the Greens owned by Claudius Sabinus. Horses from a villa at Sousse have the name of their owner, *Sorothi*, inscribed on their flanks. On one pavement two pairs, *Campus* (Field), *Dilectus* (Pet), *Hipparchus* (Chief) and *Patricius* (Noble), are resting on either side of a palm tree, each with a Cupid holding a garland hovering above his back.[6]

Metae from circuses have been found at Arles and Vienne in France, and there

[1] Toynbee (1964) p. 378. [2] *Ibid.* p. 414. [3] L. and R. p. 230.
[4] A. J. Butler, *op. cit.* p. 41 *et seq.* [5] Toynbee (1948) p. 26 *et seq.* [6] *Ibid.* p. 31.

is literary and other evidence for others at Paris, Trier, Nîmes and Lyons. From Lyons comes a particularly vivid mosaic picture of a chariot race showing the stable entrances at the start and the magistrates' box. Britain has so far produced no evidence for circuses, but with the well-known Celtic love of horses it would be surprising if the sport did not attract supporters here. A fragment of sculpture from Lincoln actually shows a boy driving a chariot, perhaps taking part in games organised by the local youth organisation of the *colonia* (Pl. 43*b*), and a tombstone from Old Penrith possibly depicts a winner holding a whip and a palm branch.[1]

[1] R.I.B. 932.

14
Transport and communications

Other vehicles besides chariots must have existed in Roman Britain, as officials and business men seem to have travelled extensively up and down the famous roads. A casual glance at the majority of the one-inch maps of England and Wales issued by the Ordnance Survey usually reveals somewhere the words 'Roman Road'. These are placed either alongside some important modern traffic artery or else they identify the course of a dotted line which proceeds fairly directly across country, sometimes becoming a metalled by-road or elsewhere remaining a mere bridle-way or footpath. In this manner are recorded the surviving stretches of the six thousand or more miles of road which the Roman administration built in Britain. Nothing on this scale existed in the country before, and until the coming of the turnpikes in the eighteenth century, no government attempted anything similar. Stretches of Roman construction continued in use for centuries and they still underlie many of the busy roads of the present day.[1]

Travelling north from London, for example, the Roman road, later known as Ermine Street, leaves Bishopsgate and passes through what is now Shoreditch, Stoke Newington and Edmonton. It was planned to avoid low-lying

[1] The most complete account will be found in I. D. Margary, *Roman Roads in Britain* (2 vols., 1955, 1957).

marshy ground as much as possible, so at Edmonton it chose a different line to the modern road (A.10) which follows the valley of the river Lea. At Bull's Cross it is in use as a minor road, and after this its course has been identified via Ware, Godmanchester and Huntingdon. After Alconbury Hill, it joins the Great North Road (A.1) and largely follows its course. North of Chesterton the modern road turns north-west, and Ermine Street continues ahead through the pottery manufacturing town of Durobrivae, probably crossing the river Nene by a wooden bridge supported by stone piles which were destroyed in the eighteenth century. The town also seems to have been provided with a by-pass road skirting it on the east. A milestone found at Durobrivae, dated to A.D. 276, gives the distance from here to Lincoln as 50 or 51 Roman miles. The line of the road then continues north along lanes and hedgerows via Castor station, Sutton Cross, Southorpe and Burghley Park at Stamford. Other Roman roads cross it at various points. The seventeenth-century antiquary, William Stukeley, noted it as a high ridge descending from Burghley Park to the crossing of the river Welland and noted that 'the overseers of the highways had in a sacrilegious manner digged it up to mend their wicked ways withal'.[1]

Ermine Street rejoins the Great North Road beyond Stamford and continues with it to Colsterworth. Then it makes for Lincoln, where in the early days of the Roman campaigns it may have terminated for a time. From Lincoln, Ermine Street sets out for York, leaving by the north gate, now surviving as the Newport Arch. It avoids the marshy ground round the estuary of the Ouse by travelling for 32 miles along a ridge of high ground to the Humber crossing, dead straight for almost the whole distance and appearing as a broad embankment 5 to 6 feet high. Another less direct route to York turns off to the west via Bawtry, Doncaster, Castleford and Tadcaster and so avoids the Humber crossing (Map III). Travellers along Ermine Street crossed the Humber by ferry-boat from Winteringham to Brough. The Roman road then largely coincides with the main Brough to Market Weighton road and was obviously planned to escape the steep escarpment of the Wolds.

After York the Roman road to the north is now usually called Dere Street, and it pursues much the same course as the modern highway until this bears away to the west, and Dere Street continues to the Roman town of Isurium (Aldborough). Before this, however, it is joined by a Roman road from Tadcaster, a continuation of the more circuitous route from Lincoln already mentioned which, after avoiding the Humber crossing, now also bypasses York. A junction with an important road from Chester also occurs at Tadcaster. From Aldborough, Dere Street goes on to Catterick, continuing ahead through the

[1] T. Codrington, *Roman Roads in Britain* (1928) p. 122.

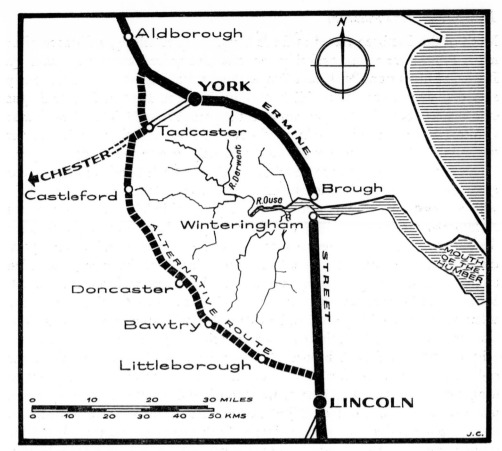

Map III. Part of the course of Ermine Street

Roman settlement of Cataractonium to a point about a mile to the north of Scotch Corner. Then it continues in a northerly direction as a minor road (B6275). At Piercebridge it passed a Roman fort and crossed the river Tees by a bridge, and then goes on to the Roman fort at Binchester. From there the route lay by the Roman sites at Lanchester, Ebchester and Apperley Dene, followed for some of its course by modern roads, but elsewhere unmetalled and sometimes unidentifiable. At last it crosses the North Tyne to the Roman supply base at Corbridge and is soon joined by the modern road to Carter Bar. It has been suggested that a change of alignment near Hadrian's Wall indicates that it was planned before the Wall was built, probably during Agricola's governorship. Continuing north, its course has been traced for more than 70 miles into Scotland. No doubt it was heading for the important port of Cramond to the west of Edinburgh. Travellers making their way deeper into Scotland must have continued up the Firth of Forth and inland to Camelon, the starting-point for the only road so far identified north of the Antonine Wall.

Much of this has been traced as far as Strageath (Perthshire), a distance of 27 miles. From there a road probably continued for at least another 40 miles via Bertha, $2\frac{1}{2}$ miles from Perth, and Coupar Angus, leaving the important military sites of Fendoch and Inchtuthil further to the west. Beyond Coupar Angus evidence has been found suggesting that it passed near Meigle to the fort at Cardean, and on to Kirriemuir, north-west of Forfar. Probably this was not the end of it, in any case it is the most northerly road in the Roman Empire.

Our survey of the 450 or more miles of this road from London to Kirriemuir gives us a picture of the Roman army gradually advancing through Britain with a network of communications developing behind it. Road-making was an important legionary activity and the army must have been responsible for the earliest roads. The routes were worked out by parties of trained surveyors, the *agrimensores* or *gromatici*, so-called from their use of the *groma*, a wooden staff with its pointed end shod with iron where it was inserted into the ground. Some form of curved wooden bracket with iron supports fitted into a bronze collar at the top of the staff, and this bracket supported a cross with four wooden arms of equal length, covered in iron sheeting. The cross was fixed with a bronze pivot and four bronze plummets hung on plumb-lines from the ends of the cross-bars. The provision of the bracket enabled the plummets to hang clear of the staff as the cross was turned, and to assist the surveyor, the plummets are in pairs of two different types.[1] This contrivance was used with ranging poles and smoke or fire signals. Such means are best employed for straight stretches of road, which can make use of high ground where sighting could be done most easily, especially when it was necessary to change direction. The changes of direction are often angular, reminding us that the Roman surveyors had little to avoid apart from natural obstacles. Occasionally a road skirts a group of prehistoric burial mounds or a hill fort, but otherwise the human problems which beset later road-builders do not arise at this period. The Roman surveyor often had no maps to help him, so the surveys must have required careful exploration to discover the best points for crossing rivers and the whereabouts of marshy ground, usually carefully avoided. Detours had sometimes to be made along the sides of steep-sided valleys until it was possible to continue ahead, and hills were sometimes ascended by means of zigzag terraceways. Often the work must have been carried on under the threat of enemy attack.

Some ideas about road-making, including the occasional construction of paved streets, were inherited by the Romans from their forerunners, including

[1] O. A. W. Dilke, 'The Roman Surveyors', *Greece and Rome* (1962) 176 *et seq.* Remains of a *groma* were found at Pompeii with ferrules from surveyors' poles and other equipment.

the Greeks, the Carthaginians and the Etruscans, and they soon developed them further. Little practical information about road-building survives in their literature but Statius, writing about A.D. 90, says that furrows should first be dug and then the soil excavated between them. This excavation was filled in with a foundation layer and above it came a layer on which the road surface could be laid, 'lest the soil give way and a treacherous bed provide a doubtful resting-place for the o'erburdened stones, then to bind it with blocks set close on either side, and frequent wedges'.[1] Meanwhile, those not working on the road itself were cutting down trees and clearing the way for it, or collecting building materials, usually local stone or gravel. Statius' furrows may have been the marking-out ditches which seem to have defined the area occupied by a road. These are still occasionally distinguishable in Britain; they survive, for example, beside Stane Street not far from the Bignor Roman villa. There they are 86 feet apart; the average is 84 feet, with a distance of approximately 62 feet for secondary roads. In this area an embankment was constructed, often incorporating large stones and intended to provide the road with a well-drained foundation. The embankment, which the Romans called the *agger*, can be up to 45 to 50 feet wide and 4 to 5 feet high, and this substantial construction is the reason why these roads survive so well today. The stretch of Stane Street just mentioned shows up clearly on the Sussex Downs. Its 30-feet wide *agger* was constructed of layers of rammed chalk and flint, topped with gravel and flint to a depth of nearly 2 feet in the centre, the whole embankment being about 4 feet high. Ermine Street, north of Durobrivae, had an *agger* 36 feet wide and 2 to 5 feet high and for the particularly fine stretches near Ancaster, it increases to 42 feet in width and 6 feet thick. Another road which also attains considerable dimensions runs from Badbury Rings in Dorset, an important road junction, to Old Sarum (Wiltshire). Like Stane Street it crosses downland, sometimes with side ditches 84 feet apart, and an *agger* up to 50 feet wide and 6 feet high. No marshy ground or other natural features requiring such elaboration exist in this area so it has been suggested that some of these great embankments were constructed to impress the local population. The Britons would be obliged to provide parties of labourers to work on the roads, so the scale of the result may also have depended upon the amount of labour available.

The *agger* of the minor roads is usually not so thick but in some places it still had a considerable width. The Fen Road running from Denver in Norfolk to the potteries at Durobrivae, via March and Whittlesey, crosses country which is apt to be marshy in places, and there it was laid on a foundation of tree branches resting on the peat. Clay and gravel have blended into concrete

[1] *Silvae* IV. iii. 40–55, trans. J. Mozley, Loeb Ed. (1928) p. 220.

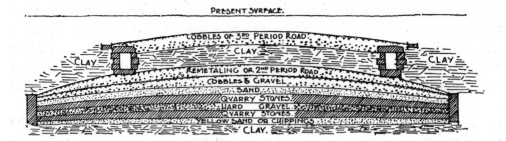

PRESENT SURFACE.

COBBLES OF 3RD PERIOD ROAD.

CLAY

CLAY

CLAY

REMETALING OR 2ND PERIOD ROAD

COBBLES & GRAVEL

SAND

QUARRY STONES

HARD GRAVEL

QUARRY STONES

YELLOW SAND OR CHIPPINGS

CLAY.

147 Roman road repairs near the bridge at Corbridge. Shown in section

in the upper layers and the low *agger*, usually about 20 feet wide, expands to 40 feet at some points and even to 50 near Durobrivae. The actual road surface was probably gravel and this is typical of most roads, the metalling consisting of layers of gravel, crushed stones, or flint rammed down hard, to a depth which varies from 2 to 3 inches to 2 feet. Paved roads are occasionally found, and stretches of one only 8 feet wide are well preserved in the Forest of Dean. The most impressive example known in Britain, however, occurs along the route across the Yorkshire moors from Rochdale to Ilkley, where it climbs a steep hill at Blackstone Edge (Pl. 40). The road is 16 feet wide and paved with stone setts laid in sand and rubble. Ditches exist on either side, stone curbs border the paving and it has a middle rib of large flat slabs of millstone grit. This exhibits a deeply worn central groove at the steepest part of the hill where there is a gradient of 1 in $4\frac{1}{3}$. This may have been caused by the friction of the brake-poles of carts descending the slope, as it is missing when flatter ground is reached. In later Roman times this steep climb was by-passed by an unpaved road, terraced in zigzags. Another fine moorland road has been preserved by the Ministry of Public Building and Works at Goathland, between Malton and Whitby, Yorkshire, and here small culverts passed under the road for drainage. In Sussex a road at Holtye, near East Grinstead, had been paved with slag from nearby iron-workings.

All these roads needed to be maintained and re-surfaced from time to time, and surface layers of unusual thickness are often due to road repairs. A good example of this occurs on Dere Street soon after it crosses the North Tyne at Corbridge (fig. 147). The original road was nearly 36 feet wide from curb to curb, with a cambered gravel surface above a foundation of quarry stones, laid on sand on the clay of the original ground surface. Possibly this gravel surface did not prove strong enough as it was later repaired with another layer of stones. Next, the road was remade more thoroughly, with a layer of sand and a surface of gravel and cobbles. More repairs followed and then, in the fourth century, a further reconstruction took place. The road now became narrower and it was provided with culverts and new curbs, as well as a fresh surfacing of cobbles laid over a thick layer of clay.

The fords used for crossing rivers must frequently have been of pre-Roman date, but a ford with a paving of rough stone blocks, found in a stream at Iden Green near Benenden, Kent, on the line of the Rochester to Hastings Roman road, may belong to the Roman period. Another example is known from the river Yeo at Ilchester in Somerset, and the paved area of the ford across the Trent at Littleborough (Nottinghamshire), was defined by a timber curb kept in place by piles.[1] Fords of a similar type have also been found in Roman Gaul.[2] Vegetius, writing in the fourth century, pointed out the hazards of fording broad or rapid rivers, when baggage, servants and the most indolent soldiers were in particular danger. He advises army commanders to first discover the depth of the water, and then to station two lines of mounted cavalry across the stream, one above the ford to break the violence of the flow, the other below, ready to rescue anyone who was swept away.[3]

Bridges must have been constructed at important river crossings, but few traces of them survive in Britain. The army practised building bridges based on boats or pontoons as a regular exercise, and one of the scenes on Trajan's column shows the light canoes with their turned over prows being hollowed out of tree-trunks by legionaries. On another scene, the bridge of boats appears at its most successful, used for the Emperor's crossing of the Danube. Boats and pontoons carry a plank roadway with railings, and a second bridge is visible in the same scene. Dio Cassius gives instructions for building a bridge of this type, and a mosaic found at Ostia suggests that one was used as a permanent structure at Arles.[4]

Caesar describes the building of a simple wooden bridge over the Rhine, laid across two rows of piles. Timber buttresses broke the force of the water, and more piles were placed upstream to prevent enemy attempts to destroy the structure, by floating down boats or tree-trunks. A detailed study of the remains of the the later Rhine bridge from Mainz to Castel has revealed the pointed stakes used for the piles, their tips protected with iron shoes. They were grouped to act as foundations for the piers and held in place by a frame-work

[1] D. P. Dymond, 'Roman Bridges on Dere Street, Co. Durham', *Arch. J.* CXVIII (1963) 149.
[2] A. Grenier, *Manuel d'archéologie gallo-romaine* II. i (Paris, 1934) p. 185 *et seq.*
[3] *Epitoma Rei Militaris* III. 7.
[4] I. A. Richmond, 'Trajan's Army on Trajan's Column', *Papers of the British School in Rome* XIII (1935) 7 n. 3.

of stout beams. On one side the pier was built out in a triangle to break the force of the water, and each one took up to 200 piles.[1] On this foundation the rest of the pier was built of stone, held in place with iron cramps. In Italy and in some provinces, the superstructure was also of stone and concrete, and notable examples still survive in Spain at Alcantara and Merida. The upper parts of the Rhine bridges at Mainz, Trier and Cologne, however, seem to have been of timber, and their probable appearance is well illustrated by another scene from Trajan's column, the Danube bridge built by Apollodorus. This was famous for the unusual height of its 20 piers, and on them clearly rests a timber bridge with a balustrade.

All these varieties of bridge may have existed in Britain, as it has been suggested that a coin of Caracalla may possibly commemorate the construction of a bridge of boats over the river Forth.[2] Recent research along Dere Street north of Binchester has shown how the road was built up on a ramp, which formed an abutment on either side of streams which could not be easily forded. Wooden bridges are presumed to have existed at these points. Bridges of a similar type at Denver in Norfolk and Asthally in Oxfordshire, seem to have replaced earlier fords. Wooden roadways carried on stone piers are suspected from sites including Castor and also from Newcastle, where the piers of the bridge built by Hadrian rested upon timber rafts and iron-shod piles. Its construction resembled that of the Rhine bridge at Mainz, and it seems to have been kept in repair and used until 1248, when much of its material was incorporated into a new mediaeval structure. Altars dedicated to Neptune and to Oceanus have been dredged out of the Tyne at this point and may well have stood in a shrine on the Roman bridge (fig. 148).

Dere Street crossed the river Tees on a stone and timber bridge at Piercebridge, and at Corbridge ten stone piers and two solid stone abutments indicate the crossing of the North Tyne. These piers had upstream cut-waters and, as they partly blocked the river, they may have been pierced by flood arches. Such methods of construction are still familiar to modern architects, and the piers and their foundations must have been built up inside wooden caissons. A recent writer suggests that the piles were driven into the river-bed by metal weights, 'travelling between guide-rails, falling by gravity and raised by pulleys and winches'.[3] Remains of bridges of two periods survive at Chesters and Willowford, carrying Hadrian's Wall across the rivers North Tyne and Irthing. The earliest structures are Hadrianic and a complete pier from Chesters survives with double cut-waters. The Willowford bridge had stone arches and a defensive tower. The post-Hadrianic bridges are wider; in addition to the Wall and its

[1] Grenier, *op. cit.* II. i. 196 *et seq.*   [2] Dymond, *op. cit.* p. 145.   [3] Dymond, *op. cit.* p. 147.

148 Altars dedicated to Neptune and Oceanus. These probably stood in
a shrine on the bridge over the river Tyne

rampart walk, they also carried the Military Way. At Chesters the piers of this
period only have upstream cut-waters. Iron cramps and tie-rods held the stones
in place. Stone bases for the posts of a timber bridge have been found in the
Severn near Wroxeter.[1]

As time went on, road maintenance away from the military areas presumably
became the responsibility of the *civitates*, while landowners would have to look
after the roads and bridges adjoining their estates. The work may have been
done through contractors, and in the towns the junior magistrates may have
had gangs of slaves to keep the streets in order. For towns which were important
road junctions, this must have been quite an undertaking. Seven important
roads, for instance, have been identified at Silchester, and the diagram, worked
out with the help of air photographs, shows how they radiated out of the town
(fig. 149). The main road to London led out of the east gate, and in a little over
3 miles, another road forks off to the left to St Albans. The roads from Winchester and Chichester meet outside the town and approach the south gate at
an angle to avoid marshy ground, while another road to Old Sarum leads out
of the south-west gate. On the west is the road leading to Caerleon either by
Cirencester and Gloucester, or else via Bath and the Severn ferry at Sea Mills.
The seventh road sets out from the north gate for the midlands through
Dorchester (Oxon.), Alchester and Towcester.

[1] *J.R.S.* LIV (1964) 165.

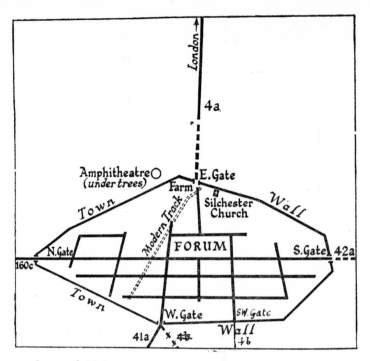

149 Roman roads round Silchester

The courses of certain roads tended to change as time went on. Originally they were designed to cover the country in the shortest possible distance. Later roads, however, were planned to fit in with the transport needs of the civilian population and some earlier roads probably fell into disuse. Private roads must also have existed leading from the main routes to villas, or from villa to villa. The pre-Roman trackways across open country must also have continued in use.

Traffic along the roads may be described as private or official. In the second category must be included the army and the government officials and also the *cursus publicus*. This was the imperial posting service invented by the Emperor Augustus. The administration of the Empire depended very largely upon the rapid interchange of dispatches, so relays of horses were stationed at intervals of 6 to 16 miles along the main roads, with an inn or *mansio* for an overnight stop every 20 to 30 miles. The cost of this service was largely borne by the communities along the route and was the cause of bitter complaint. Besides the imperial messengers, high officials and their families could use the service, but they needed special permits to do so, and Pliny's letters to Trajan describe how he issued such a permit to his wife in an emergency. Apparently a stock of dated permits was sent to the provincial governors, none of which could be used when once they had expired. Sometimes private individuals seem to have

390

secured them by dubious means, and then laws were enacted tightening up the organisation. The permits also covered ships and ferries, and there was a slower service of ox wagons used for the transport of less important officials, invalids, or army equipment and other forms of government property.[1] The tombstone of a *strator*, the official in charge of the governor's establishment of horses, has been found at Irchester.[2]

To assist travellers to find their way, under the earlier emperors milestones were erected along the roads at intervals of a thousand Roman paces (1,620 yards or 1,480 metres), although in Gaul the league of 2,430 yards was used. These gave the distances from the road head or the nearest town either incised as part of an inscription, or else added in paint when the stone was erected. One of the reliefs from the Igel monument shows a milestone just appearing in the background of a scene showing a two-wheeled cart, and this tells us that it was four leagues to Trier.[3] Sixty-three milestones have so far been found in Roman Britain. When the inscription survives, it gives the name and titles of one of the emperors and may indicate that road repairs were undertaken in his reign, or it may merely have been set up in his honour. The earliest belong to the reign of Hadrian, and the best example is the one found near Llanfairfechan (Caernarvonshire) (fig. 150). The inscription dates it to A.D. 120-1 and shows that it marks a spot 8 Roman miles from *Canovium* (Caerhun), known to be the site of a Roman fort.[4] Other milestones give distances of 2 miles from Ratae (Leicester), 22 miles from Eboracum, and 11 miles from Navio (Brough, Derbyshire).[5]

The early milestones are cylindrical in shape, and a Gaulish stone of this type appears on one of the Arlon reliefs, together with a pair of prancing steeds presumably drawing a carriage.[6] Later on, any large piece of stone was used and two milestones of this type were found beside the Roman road at Girton, two miles from Cambridge. Both were inscribed with the name of the Emperor Constantine, but one has its inscription recut on top of an earlier version, presumably because the original quickly weathered, or else it was incorrect and had to be emended. No clue as to the mileage survives as the relevant portions of the stone are missing.[7] In any case, it may only have been painted on. In other provinces, inscriptions erected beside the highways are sometimes more informative. One found in Serbia beside the Danube, dating to A.D. 100, announces that Trajan built this road by cutting through mountains and eliminating curves.[8] In A.D. 123 Hadrian reconstructed $15\frac{3}{4}$ miles of the Appian

---

[1] Details and bibliography in R. J. Forbes, *Studies in Ancient Technology* II (Leiden, 1955) 153.
[2] *R.I.B.* 233. [3] E. VI p. 451 no. 5268. [4] *R.I.B.* 2265. [5] *R.I.B.* 2244, 2274, 2243.
[6] E. VI no. 5268. [7] *R.I.B.* 2237. [8] C.I.L. III no. 8267.

150 Milestone from Llanfairfechan, Caernarvonshire

Way by adding 1,147,000 to the local landowners' contributions of 569,100 sesterces, and he also had the road from Carthage to Theveste in North Africa re-paved by the Third Legion Augusta.[1] In A.D. 152, also in North Africa, Antoninus Pius repaired a road in mountainous country, rebuilding bridges, draining marshes and replacing stretches lost through subsidence. In fact, the Romans knew most of the troubles which beset the modern road-builder.[2]

Stones bearing inscriptions which give more information about mileage than the normal milestones, have also been recorded. One, the *milliarium aurum*, stood in the Forum in Rome and gave the distances to all the important cities of the Empire. Fragments from a six- or eight-sided column found at Tongres give lists of towns belonging to routes in Northern Gaul and Germany, with the distances between them in leagues. On one side, place-names along the road beside the Rhine from Bonn to Worms can be identified, and the complete inscription may have given an itinerary starting at Tongres and proceeding via Cologne. Details of the road from Rheims to Amiens survive on the adjacent side, and on the third side Arras and Bavai are mentioned.[3] Evidence for stones inscribed with itineraries has also been found at Autun and Jünglister (Luxemburg) and one can easily imagine town councils in Britain erecting them at such important road junctions as London or Silchester. In Spain, baked clay tablets with lists of place-names scratched on them seem to have been nailed to walls. Portable itineraries were also used in the form of inscribed goblets imitating the road-stones, and four of these have been found in Italy, by a medicinal spring at Vicarello. They may date from the beginning of the second century A.D. and

[1] C.I.L. LX no. 6075; VIII no. 10,048.
[2] An American scholar, Mr R. Jones, has estimated that it would cost over £100,000 to construct one mile of the Appian Way (*Daily Telegraph*, London, 3 May 1962).
[3] Grenier, *op. cit.* II. i. 108.

give a route from Spain, starting at Cadiz, to Rome. The small enamelled bronze bowl found at Rudge in Wiltshire seems to have been inspired by the same idea, as it has the names of five of the forts on or near Hadrian's Wall incorporated in the decoration. They read A MAIS ABALLAVA VXEL(L)OD(VN)VM CAMBOGLAN(NI)S BANNA and have been identified as Bowness on Solway, Burgh by Sands, (?) Castlesteads, Birdoswald and (?) Bewcastle or Carvoran. A very similar bowl, turned into a *patera* by the addition of a handle, was found more recently at Amiens, and this adds the fort at Aesica (Greatchesters) to the list.[1]

The same method of giving the names of towns and the distances between them was used in the Antonine Itinerary. This was a collection of routes from all over the Empire probably compiled for travelling officials in the late second or early third century, with possible fourth-century revisions. Fifteen routes survive from the British section, extending up to Birrens (Dumfriesshire) and High Rochester (Northumberland), a little north of Hadrian's Wall. Research has enabled many of the roads and places to be identified, although some gaps and problems remain. Usually the distances between the places prove reasonably accurate, allowing for the shorter Roman mile. One surprise that emerges from it is the fact that the official traveller did not necessarily choose the most direct route (fig. 151). To go from London to Chichester, for example, the main road via Pulborough, Alfoldean and Hardham is ignored, although it is known to have been supplied with posting stations, and a much longer journey is made through Staines (Pontes), Silchester (Calleva), Winchester (Venta Belgarum), and Bitterne (Clausentum). Lincoln is reached from London by way of Leicester, instead of straight up Ermine Street, and the journey to York continues the long way round by Tadcaster. The explanation probably lies in the fact that these routes take in important towns where officials in the third century would be more likely to have business. The direct routes cross less thickly inhabited country.[2]

The Ravenna Cosmography, a seventh-century list which seems to have been largely based upon a third- or fourth-century road-map, confirms many of the place-names of the Antonine Itinerary and adds new ones, some of them in Scotland. Further supporting evidence for south and east Britain is also provided by the Peutinger Table, a road-map based on ancient sources. Ptolemy's Geography is another important source, but one full of problems. It was compiled in Alexandria towards the end of the second century A.D., and consists

[1] J. Heurgon, 'The Amiens Patera', *J.R.S.* XLI (1951) 22, Pl. III. 1, fig. 4; J. D. Cowen and I. A. Richmond, 'The Rudge cup', *Arch. Ael.* (4) XII (1935) 310–42.
[2] All the routes are given in Margary, *op. cit.* II. 250 *et seq.*

REFERENCE

Places named in Itinerary............ PONTES	Actual distances (in Roman miles) 16
Unidentified places ....[AD ANSAM]	Roads, known. ....
Conventional numbers of Itinera VII	Roads, unknown ....-------
Itinerary distances....................xvii	Through measurements................ˣˣᵛⁱⁱ...

151   The British Section of the Antonine Itinerary

of a list of points fixed by latitude and longitude, from which maps could be drawn.[1] Errors have produced a somewhat distorted picture of Britain in which the island north of Hadrian's Wall is swung over to the east. Other maps and itineraries available to the Romans included a map of the Roman world, which Agrippa planned to have painted on the walls of a portico. After his death Augustus completed it with a written commentary, scraps of which survive. According to Vegetius, a general should obtain a full description of an area where he intended to campaign, specifying the distances between places, the shortest routes and the state of the roads, and the presence of mountains and rivers. Some of this information might be gathered from local people who might also be employed as guides, but care had to be taken to obtain guides who really knew the way as well as they promised.[2] Sometimes actual maps and plans seem to have been made. A fragment copied from such a map was unearthed at Dura Europos, drawn on a soldier's leather shield. It shows ships on the Black Sea and also gives details of the coast road beside it from the mouth of the Danube to Artaxata in Armenia.[3]

What evidence survives of the traffic which once travelled these roads? Pack animals there must have been, but these would leave no trace and we must depend upon relief sculpture for proof of their existence (Pl. 21). In Britain, apart from the wheel-ruts which have been noted at the entrances to such sites as the forts at Housesteads or Mumrills, three wheels and various fragments were recovered from rubbish-pits at Newstead. The best preserved example has a wooden rim or felloe of a single piece of ash, bent into a circle with the ends secured with an iron plate. An iron tyre was fitted on to this while red-hot. As it cooled, the shrinking iron gripped the wood so that no nails or other fastenings were necessary. The eleven spokes of willow, and the elm hub, were all turned on the lathe. Iron rims strengthened the ends of the hub, and on the inside it was protected from wear by a smaller, wider iron ring. An iron linch pin kept the wheel from slipping off the axle. A wheel of similar type was found in the Antonine Wall fort at Bar Hill, and others have turned up at pre-Roman sites such as Glastonbury. Tyres and other iron fittings were found in the Early Iron Age hoard from Llyn Cerrig Bach, Anglesey. There is no doubt that these are wheels of Celtic type, and the Bar Hill and Newstead examples have been described as chariot wheels captured from the Caledonians. Curle, however, wisely points out that many Roman vehicles seem to have had a Celtic origin, and the wheels probably belonged to more prosaic carts.[4] The third example

[1] Richmond (1958) p. 131 *et seq.* [2] *Epitoma Rei Militaris* III. 6.
[3] F. Cumont, 'Fragment de Bouclier portant une liste à Etapes', *Syria* VI (1927) 1–15.
[4] Curle (1911) p. 293 *et seq.*

from Newstead was a rather heavier specimen with twelve squared spokes, the ends of which probably projected beyond a felloe made, in this case, of six separate sections fixed together with wooden dowels. Bar Hill also produced fragments of this variety made of oak,[1] and both types have been found in Germany at Zugmantel and the Saalburg.[2] The projecting spokes may have protected the felloe and taken the place of the iron tyre. Four iron tyres, 3 feet 7 inches in diameter, turned up in the smith's hoard at Great Chesterford, together with nave-hoops of two different sizes, very like those used for the hub of the Newstead wheel. Linch pins of a more decorative type than the simple Newstead variety are also known from Great Chesterford, Silchester and other sites.

Unhappily no vehicles appear on any of the British reliefs yet found, although single wheels of purely religious significance are occasionally depicted on votive slabs or tombstones.[3] We have to rely on literature or on occasional illustrations from Italy and Gaul to recreate the busy scenes round the big towns. Traffic jams in the narrow streets of Rome had obliged the Senate in the time of Julius Caesar to forbid the entry of wheeled vehicles into the city during the daytime, with the exception of certain ceremonial occasions. Only the carts used in building and demolition work were permitted, otherwise people walked or rode, or were carried in litters or sedan chairs. Juvenal records how he was swept along by the jostling crowds, banged on the head by the wine-cask on the shoulder of a passer-by, while another man tramped on his foot with a heavy military boot and his newly mended tunic got torn again. And by night the incessant rumbling of the wagons bringing in supplies for the city made it impossible to sleep. As they met and blocked each other's way at cross-roads 'the swearing of the drovers brought to a standstill would snatch sleep from a sea-calf or the Emperor Claudius himself'.[4] Claudius extended the traffic laws to other Italian cities, and Marcus Aurelius to all the towns of the Empire, so that we may suspect that the transport problems of London, for example, are not a phenomenon of recent growth. Accidents, too, cannot have been unknown, and a pathetic epitaph at Ostia records the death of a small child run over by a cart.[5]

For fast journeys the light two-wheeled *cisium* or *essedum* was used. A *cisium* appears passing a milestone on the relief from the Igel monument mentioned

[1] G. Macdonald and A. Park, *The Roman Forts on the Bar Hill* (Glasgow, 1906) p. 99.
[2] 'Kastel Zugmantel. Die Ausgrabungen', *Saalburg Jahrbuch* III (1912) 68 Pl. XVI.
[3] E.g. F. Haverfield, *Catalogue of the Roman Inscribed and Sculptured Stones, Tullie House, Carlisle* (Carlisle, 1922) no. 128; *R.I.B.* 549.
[4] Juvenal, *Satires* III. 236–59.
[5] C.I.L. (Ostia) no. 1806 or R. Meiggs, *Roman Ostia* (1960) p. 463.

152　Roman *cisium* on the Igel column, Trier

above, with the passenger and driver perched up high and two mules between the shafts (fig. 152). Pieces of such a vehicle were found in the House of Menander at Pompeii. Then there were the four-wheeled *rheda* and the *carruca*, more substantial vehicles probably of Gaulish origin, employed for both freight and passenger traffic. A relief from Langres shows one of them drawn by four horses, with a driver and two or three passengers.[1] A tombstone in Belgrade depicts a similar type of carriage in use by the *cursus publicus*.[2] It is drawn by three horses and carries the driver on the box, an official on a bench behind him, and a servant sitting on the luggage at the back. Other examples appear on a mosaic in a building just inside the Porta Romana at Ostia, including one with passengers drawn by two mules, and another with only one.[3] Awnings or more elaborate coach-like bodies protected some travellers and a carriage of this type, depicted on a relief found near Klangenfurt, may have been a *carruca dormitoria* in which travellers could sleep, eat or write.[4] A small sarcophagus in the Museo Nazionale in Rome shows two views of a covered carriage occupied by a family, and a relief from the Roman town at Vaison in Southern France depicts a driver, cracking his three-thonged whip at his team of two horses

[1] E. IV no. 3245.
[2] M. Rostovtzeff, *Social and Economic History of the Roman Empire* (1957) Pl. 74. 1.
[3] G. Calza and G. Becatti, *Ostia* (Rome, 1958) fig. 5.　[4] Singer *et al.* (1956) II, fig. 494.

or mules, as they haul along a coach. On top sits an official attended by a *lictor* carrying his ceremonial axe. Inside, two heads appear in profile, variously described as passengers or as busts carried to some ceremonial or in a funeral procession.[1] Some of these carriages were elaborately decorated with bronze or silver fittings.

The four-wheeled cart frequently appears in military contexts on the columns of Trajan and Marcus Aurelius, and a lively example drawn by two mules can be seen on a soldier's tombstone at Strasburg.[2] Bodies vary from box or trolley shapes—sometimes with open rails—to platforms with loads tied to them. Another relief from Langres depicts this platform variety with a load of wine lashed to it, and another scene on the same block shows the mules being led away to their stable.[3] Wickerwork structures were also used and a two-wheeled cart with a deep container of this type appears on a relief from Arlon.[4] It is supposed to be taking clay to a brickworks and may well have also been used for spreading manure on the fields. Heavier wagons were drawn by oxen. A soldier leads a team of two of them on a Carnuntum tombstone, with a peasant driving and his dog following behind.[5] Another example appears on a mosaic from Bosceaz (Switzerland).

Carriages and wagons could be hired from private companies, but large contracts may have had to be fitted in at periods when work was slack on the estates and oxen were available. The Theodosian Code gives up to 1,500 *librae* (1,100 lb. or 492 kg.) as the maximum weight for the baggage-carts of the *cursus publicus*. Possibly this was on the light side to safeguard public vehicles and roads, as Cato records the removal of an oil mill of 3,560 *librae*, the load being divided between three yoke of oxen who took it 25 miles in two days. The types of harness in use at this time were more suited to the ox than the horse. Rudimentary horse-collars have been noted on Trajan's Column and their development, and that of shafts and traces, may begin in the Roman period. The types of harness usually depicted by the sculptor, however, would tend to partly throttle the horse pulling a load of any great weight. A recent writer has suggested that in any case the horses were largely kept for riding or pulling light carriages, and a mettlesome beast rearing or straining at the reins was viewed with approval.[6] Certainly much money was spent on colourful horse-trappings. One of the Chester tombstones shows an attendant sadly leading along a horse with the dead man in a saddle which may possibly be padded, and has been strapped on over a saddle-cloth. Nearby stands another memorial with a cavalry-

[1] *Ibid.* fig. 506.   [2] E. VII no. 5499.   [3] *Ibid.* IV p. 276 no. 3232.   [4] *Ibid.* V no. 4031.
[5] Rostovtzeff, *op. cit.* Pl. LXXIV. 2.
[6] A. Burford, 'Heavy Transport in Classical Antiquity', *Economic History Review* XIII (1961) 9.

man galloping along and riding down a foe.[1] The horse's headstall and the saddle-cloth are plainly visible, and the carefully arranged mane and tail are features found on three other cavalry tombstones which portray similar scenes. Sextus Genialis at Cirencester also appears at the gallop, in the act of spearing his unfortunate enemy whose whiskery face has been turned by the artist into a splendid hairy mask. Traces of an elaborate saddle-cloth survive, as well as details of bands and straps decorated with metal roundels or *phalerae*. At Gloucester the memorial to Rufus Sita, like Genialis a member of the Sixth Thracian Cohort, shows less evidence for harness and no saddle-cloth, but these features appear with increased elaboration on Longinus' tombstone at Colchester.[2] Long saddle-cloths are also shown as part of statuettes of soldiers on horseback, and a clear example appears on one found at Westwood Bridge, near Peterborough.[3] Traces of paint surviving on a cavalryman's tombstone at Mainz show how colourful such equipment could be, and include a yellow saddle, green saddle-cloth with red streamers, brown fringe and red straps. In addition to *phalerae*, other small metal ornaments sometimes occur, and from his tombstone at Hexham Abbey we learn that the standard-bearer Flavinus hung a strap with a crescent-shaped pendant from his horse's martingale.[4]

Actual fragments of harness in Britain come mostly from military sites, particularly from Newstead. Both snaffle and curb-bits were in use (fig. 153*a*), and snaffles of bronze, or iron covered with bronze, have been found in native first-century contexts, among them the hoard from Llyn Cerrig Bach. Iron curb-bits turned up at Newstead and this would be the type used by the Roman cavalry. Longinus and Rufus Sita appear to ride with a single rein, but double reins are clearly shown on the tombstone of Genialis. An iron headstall decorated with a medallion of millefiori enamelling was also found at Newstead. The rings through which the reins passed, called terrets, were also used in Iron Age Britain and are often decorated. Newstead produced iron examples with traces of bronze or brass plating, and also brass loops, pendants and *phalerae*. One *phalera* has a central boss of silver surrounded by mouldings of silver and brass. Two more bronze examples are decorated in relief with a lion's mask and the face of a boy wearing a Phrygian cap. Three silver plated bronze pendants, tooled with a leaf and berry design possibly filled in with niello, may also come from *phalerae*, and can be paralleled by a find from Xanten in Germany.[5]

Iron horseshoes were known in pre-Roman times, and their use may have

---

[1] *R.I.B.* 538, 550. [2] *R.I.B.* 109, 121, 201.
[3] M. V. Taylor, 'Statuettes of Horsemen and Horses and other Votive Objects from Brigstock', *Ant. J.* XLIII (1963) 265, Pl. XLI.
[4] *R.I.B.* 1172. [5] Curle (1911) p. 299.

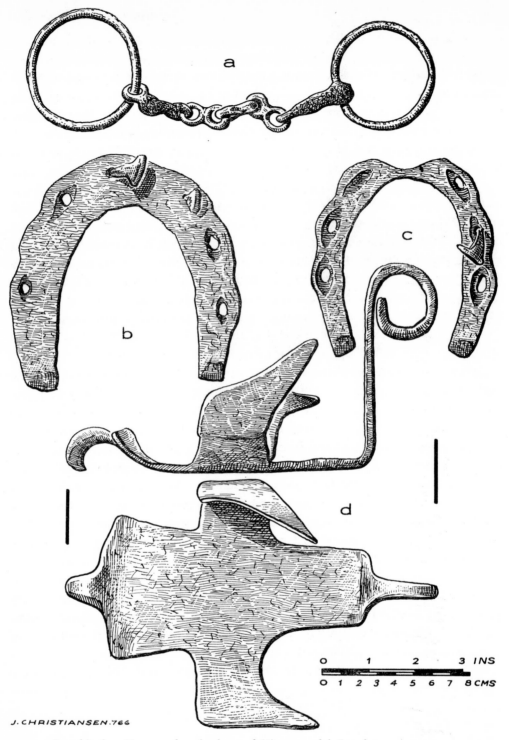

J. CHRISTIANSEN. 766

153   *a* Iron bit. *b, c* Horse and mule shoes. *d* Hippo-sandal, London

increased with the need to protect horses' feet on paved or cobbled roads. Shoes for both horses and mules have been found in London, one with some of the T-headed nails still in position (fig. 153*b*, *c*). So-called 'hippo-sandals', iron plates with raised side pieces, a hook in front, and then a piece of iron ending in another hook standing up at the back (fig. 153*d*), are of fairly frequent occurrence, probably because they are of good quality iron which survives well. Their exact purpose is still in doubt but they have been discovered fixed on to horses' hooves. They may have been tied on as hobbles, to protect a sore foot, or as a safeguard on slippery surfaces as they are sometimes channelled on the underside. Two were found lying on the fourth- or fifth-century road surface of Watling Street at Verulamium and one London example had an ordinary horse-shoe fixed to its sole.[1] Iron or bronze prick spurs are found occasionally, mostly on military sites, but specimens are also recorded from Colchester and other towns, Woodeaton, and the villa at Chedworth.[2] Stirrups were not used, but a riderless horse on a tombstone at Cologne shows a saddle with high padded bows in front and behind, which would help to keep the rider in position.[3]

Good land communications were essential for the Roman civilisation, but waterways were even more important for the transport of loads of any size. Animals must either be allowed time to graze or food must be provided for them, but wind and water are free for all so water transport was much cheaper. Imperial enterprise improved thousands of miles of navigable rivers in Italy,[4] and research work has shown how valuable the rivers of Gaul were to the country's economy. Cargoes could travel up the Rhône to Lyons and then either continue up the Saône with a land link with the Moselle and Rhine, or reach the Seine or the Loire by various other streams. These routes had been used in pre-Roman times, the Romans improved them and in some cases built artificial links, usually to increase transport facilities for army supplies. The earliest was a canal, the *Fossa Maxima*, which made easier the navigation of the mouth of the Rhône, but this was allowed to silt up during the first century A.D. The junction of the Rhône and Saône was also improved at Lyons when an inconvenient spur of rock was bypassed. Dams were made in some stretches to raise the water level and check the current. In A.D. 58, during the reign of Nero, one of the legionary commanders in Germany advocated the construction of a canal between the Arar and the Moselle, which would make it possible to

---

[1] L.R.T. p. 150; Wheeler (1936) p. 220.
[2] H. de S. Shortt, 'A Provincial Roman Spur from Longstock, Hants and other spurs from Roman Britain', *Ant. J.* XXXIX (1959) 61–76.
[3] E. VIII no. 6463.
[4] B. W. Wells, 'Trade and Travel in the Roman Empire', *Classical Journal* XIX (Iowa, 1924) 7–16.

travel entirely by water from the Rhône to the Rhine and the North Sea, but this plan was not adopted. Other works, however, had already been carried out round the mouth of the Rhine. Augustus' adopted son, Drusus, explored the North Sea in 12 B.C. and cut a canal which connected it with the Rhine by way of the Zuiderzee, a short cut for ships travelling to the Ems and Elbe. He also constructed a mole to protect the area between the rivers Rhine and Waal from flooding, and this work was improved on in the reign of Nero.[1] During the reign of Claudius, another canal 23 miles in length was dug, joining the Rhine and the Meuse. This also assisted drainage and enabled ships to avoid some miles of open sea. It was used by both the army on the Rhine and by troops travelling to Britain.[2]

The building of these Rhenish canals is of interest, because work of the same character was probably organised by the army in Britain to enable the corn grown in the Fens to be easily transported to the troops at Lincoln, York and further north. The work may have begun in the Cambridgeshire Fens and the first section takes the form of an artificial link, 8 miles in length, joining the Cam at Waterbeach with the branch of the Ouse known as the Old West River, about 2 miles south-east of Aldreth. This is known as the Car Dyke, and excavations carried out in 1949 showed it to be about 28 feet wide and flat-bottomed. The sides sloped outwards to give a width of about 45 feet at ground level and it was about 7 feet deep. These measurements compare well with those of modern barge canals. Severe fen flooding in 1947 brought water back to the Car Dyke and gave some idea of its appearance in the Roman period (Pl. 47). How river traffic made its way from the Ouse into the Nene is still uncertain.[3]

At Peterborough the Car Dyke strikes out for the north and after 56 miles it enters the river Witham near Lincoln. Another artificial cut forms a link with the Trent at Torksey, and the route continues up the Ouse to York. The barges carrying grain to the north may have come back laden with coal and building materials, and the pottery made in the Castor area must have been distributed in both directions. A branch road south of Castor leads to a bend in the Nene where a dock or one of the loading points for the boats may have existed.[4]

This must have been the pattern all over the country wherever the waterways were deep enough to allow the passage of barges. Other canals of varying size probably await discovery, especially in the Fenland. A short one, for example,

[1] Tacitus, *Annals* XIII. 53.   [2] *Ibid.* XI. 20.
[3] J. G. D. Clark, 'Report on Excavations on the Cambridgeshire Car Dyke,' *Ant. J.* XXIX (1949) 145–63.
[4] Margary, *op. cit.* I. p. 202.

at Swaffham Prior, might have been used to bring clunch from the quarries at Reach down the river Cam.[1] Near Norwich, an extensive timber platform found in 1961 beside the river Yare, probably belonged to a Roman wharf.[2] Further south, Colchester probably owed some of its importance from the Iron Age onwards to its position up the river Colne and near the estuaries of the Blackwater and Stour. The exact site of the Roman harbour has not been identified but ships could certainly be rowed or sailed near the *colonia* and much trade with Gaul and Germany must have passed this way. Boats of all sizes would be able to travel up the Thames to London, and the wrecks found under County Hall and by Blackfriars bridge are believed to be those of sea-going sailing ships (see below, p. 411). Again the whereabouts of the wharves and quays are uncertain but the fine sculptures of a river god and of Bonus Eventus with the prow of a ship at his feet, emphasise the importance of the Tamesis to Londinium. The Medway from the mouth of the Thames to Rochester, and the Great Stour to Fordwich, the port for Canterbury, were other important waterways.

Every stream able to take a boat was probably used to move grain, vegetables, pottery and other manufactures as well as the vast quantities of building and other raw materials which had to be transported, but little evidence of landing-places has so far been found, probably because in the past, wharves and warehouses of timber often passed unnoticed. Other town sites besides London were certainly chosen on account of their accessibility to water, and Exeter, with the probable port settlement at Topsham at the head of the estuary of the Exe, is one such example. Caerwent is also conveniently near the Severn, and excavations at Caerleon have uncovered a massive quay beside the river Usk. A timber stage supported by oak posts had been built in front of a revetment wall 5 feet thick, and the corner of the quay was protected by a groyne of planks. The wall had two periods, early to middle and later third century, and behind it the mud-flat was metalled with ballast largely made up of Preseli Grey slate, held firm with heavy stone kerbs. The excavators calculated that ships of $5\frac{1}{2}$ foot draught could have come alongside at high tide.[3] At Gloucester the late first-century harbour grew up in a bay down a creek, just off the main stream of the Severn. Timber landing stages have been found there and a ferry probably crossed the river at this point. It has been suggested that the Severn's tidal bore which could swamp a boat caught in mid-stream, made such a haven for shipping very necessary.[4] Two wooden quays or jetties found beside the river

[1] G. Fowler, 'The Extinct Waterways of the Fens', *Geographical Journal* LXXXIII (1934) 30–9.
[2] *J.R.S.* LII (1962) 176. [3] *J.R.S.* LIV (1964) 152.
[4] *J.R.S.* XXXII (1942) 48.

Dour at Dover are also probably of Roman date.[1] Further north a substantial wall over 20 feet long was found outside the *colonia* at Lincoln near the river Witham. This could have been a quay well placed for traffic along the Car Dyke.[2]

The army were always awake to the value of sea and river communications, particularly when land routes were difficult. In Wales, where these factors apply, the auxiliary forts at Caerhun, Pennal, Carmarthen, Loughor, Neath and Cardiff are all near river estuaries while Caernarvon guards the Menai Straits. The legionary fortress at Caerleon lies beside a loop in the navigable river Usk, a tributary of the Severn, and the fortress at Chester occupies much the same position beside the tidal river Dee. It was called Deva, a Celtic word meaning goddess, presumably in this case a river deity. Silting in the Middle Ages ended Chester's importance as a port, but in Roman times the river was much wider and passed near the west side of the fortress. Substantial remains of masonry have been discovered at a point where a creek probably ran towards the south-west angle, and this may well be a revetment wall belonging to the harbour (Pl. 48). Behind it, traces of warehouses or administrative buildings have been noted, and corn brought by sea could have been carried straight into the granaries just inside the west gate. Almost opposite, and presumably on the other side of the old river channel, are traces of a timber wharf. The use of slate from North Wales at Chester, and of Chester sandstone in the fort walls at Caernarvon, shows that building materials may have been among the cargoes ferried up and down the Dee. In the opposite direction, barge-loads of pottery must have come down to Chester from the potteries and tileries of the Twentieth Legion at Holt, 12 miles upstream. Two miles from Chester the Dee becomes rocky and shallow, so it is possible that these cargoes were transferred to wagons at the small settlement at Heronbridge which has been excavated at this point. The site lies close to both the river and to Watling Street, and seems to have started life towards the end of the first century as a small collection of metal-workers' huts and workshops. In the second century some rebuilding and expansion took place, and included a small dock flanked by quays. Stone store-houses of strip plan, their narrow ends facing on to Watling Street, were also found.[3]

The problems of transport and communications had also been carefully considered at York where the waterways were of particular importance. The supply route from East Anglia via the Car Dyke, Witham, Trent and Ouse has already been discussed, and much overseas shipping also travelled up the Humber. An

[1] *J.R.S.* XLVI (1956) 146. [2] *J.R.S.* XLV (1955) 131.
[3] F. Thompson, *Deva: Roman Chester* (Chester, 1959) pp. 36, 44.

altar found in Micklegate was dedicated to the Mother Goddesses of Africa, Italy and Gaul by Marcus Minucius Mudinus, described as *gubernator* of the Sixth Legion; in fact, a river-pilot who guided army supply-boats travelling to and from York.[1] The wharves seem to have been sited beside the river Foss, a small tributary of the Ouse which ran near the south-east gate of the fortress. On the further side of this stream a timber jetty supported by a revetment wall of piles was found in 1829, and in 1938, rough stone columns, associated with Antonine pottery, which may have sustained another platform. On the fortress side of the river, a massive stone platform on the bank and a double row of piles in the river-bed are also probably concerned with shipping.[2]

The British boat which is best known from the Roman period and the one which still survives today, is the coracle, with its wicker framework constructed rather like an oval, shallow basket, covered on the outside with an ox- or horse-hide. About $4\frac{1}{2}$ by $3\frac{1}{2}$ feet in size, such one-man boats are still in use for fishing on some Welsh rivers. Their control with a single-bladed paddle is a skilled operation, and when they reach land the fisherman can carry his boat home on his back.

The curragh was a larger boat of more substantial construction. Caesar seems to have noted it on his British excursions, and either remembered it or else was reminded of it by something similar when he needed to cross a river to extricate himself from a tight corner in Spain seven years later. He directed his soldiers to make keels and ribs of light timber filled in with wickerwork, and covered with hides. These craft were carted down to the river and the troops rowed across. The size and the fact of rowing shows that the boats in question were curraghs and not coracles, as no one could start straight out in a coracle without previous experience. Large curraghs probably up to 24 feet long and using as many as eight hides, are believed to have existed. These craft were very buoyant and their descendants are still in use off the west coast of Ireland. In Romanised Britain they were probably largely supplanted by timber-built boats. On the frontiers of the province they are the prototype for a later vessel in which the planks overlap, the clinker-built boats like the one interred in the Anglo-Saxon burial mount on Snape Common, Suffolk.[3] Accounts survive of the journeys of the sixth-century Irish saints in sailing curraghs, and these speedy boats also carried the Irish raiders who attacked Britain from the fourth century onwards.

The coracle and the curragh, however, were hardly cargo boats, and something more substantial was needed to move pottery and building materials about our inland waterways. The dug-out canoe hollowed out of a large tree-

[1] *R.I.B.* 653. [2] *Eburacum* (1962) p. 64, altar, no. 32.
[3] T. C. Lethbridge, *Coastwise Craft* (1952) p. 8.

trunk was known in Britain from Neolithic times. Sometimes its stern was fashioned and fitted separately, and this type of craft can soon develop into a more elaborate boat by the addition of planks on either side. Such a boat, which may have been a river barge or ferry, was found at North Ferriby, Yorkshire. It had two central oak timbers joined end to end and more planks built on to them on either side. The lower edges of these planks were bevelled to fit into grooves cut in the upper sides of their neighbours, the joins were covered with thin oak battens and caulked with moss. Yew fibres were used to stitch all together, and the result may be described as an Early Iron Age flat-bottomed, sewn, carvel-built canoe over 51 feet long.[1]

Apart from such canoes there is a gap in our knowledge of British river craft, but this can be partly filled by our knowledge of shipping in Gaul. There the *nautae* who controlled the traffic on inland waters were organised in powerful guilds, and the names of their members appear on many tombstones. In some cases they may have been responsible for transporting goods by both land and water as several of the most powerful guilds, including those of the Rhône and Saône, had their headquarters at Lyons. One inscription records a *nauta* from the Saône guild who was also a *duumvir* at Arles and a *sevir* at Apt,[2] so presumably no one was forced to confine his operations to one particular river. Cargoes could be conducted down to the coast at Arles and vice-versa. One such cargo probably appears on a relief from Cabrières-d'Aigues in the Museum at Avignon.[3] It shows a boat, presumably flat-bottomed, with a curved bow and raised stern, being hauled along by ropes fixed to a mast or post. A pilot sits in the boat behind the cargo of two barrels, and three men (one missing), leaning on stout sticks, take the strain on the river-bank. A similar scene on the Igel monument depicts another such barge, filled with bales. Here the bow curves inwards. Reliefs found at Mainz probably show a boat being loaded as workmen roll barrels up the gangway. Another fragment depicts a grain ship being unloaded. Two sacks have come ashore across the shoulders of two of the men, and a third man is running down the gangplank. The fourth, however, has tripped and gone sprawling, and ruefully regards his sack, which seems to have burst open.[4] Also at Mainz is the tombstone of the *nauta*, Blussus, shown as a very prosperous mid-first-century personage aged 75, sitting beside his wife who is laden with jewellery. On the back of his tombstone is a boat with a small mast for the tow rope, and also men with paddles or oars, a simple useful boat used as a raft, barge, or ferry.[5] A far more splendid vessel laden with wine casks appears on one of the Neumagen reliefs.[6] Its prow was probably crowned by

[1] *Ibid. Boats & Boatmen*, (1952) p. 128. [2] Grenier, *op. cit.* II. 2 (1934) p. 552.
[3] E. IX no. 6699. [4] E. VII no. 5833. [5] E. VII no. 5815. [6] E. VI no. 5193.

a figurehead, possibly a ram or sea-beast, while the high curved stern is surmounted by a fierce wolf's head. Six men are visible behind a railing which
runs along the side of the ship and they seem to control a surprisingly large
number of oars, their stroke timed by a member of the crew who sits facing
them, clapping his hands. A steersman completes the party. The keel is pointed
at one end and two eyes are carved on the front of the boat above it, giving
the appearance of a dolphin. The custom of giving a boat eyes so that it can
see where it is going, still persists in some parts of the world, and may be a
survival of early religious beliefs in which the eyes formed part of a protecting
deity painted on the prow.[1] Both the men hauling the barges and the crews
rowing them are known to have sung or shouted to maintain the rhythm of
their work, songs which must be the forerunners of many later sea shanties.
Apparently this was not always a welcome sound, as Martial points out when
he praises the peace of the Janiculum gardens at Rome, away from the noise of
traffic and boats, the bargees' cries and the shouts of the boatswain.[2] Ausonius
describing life along the river Moselle also mentions the busy husbandmen
exchanging shouts in boisterous rivalry, the wayfarer tramping along the bank,
and the bargees floating by, who 'troll their rude jests at the loitering vine-
dressers, and all the hills, and shivering woods, and channelled river, ring with
their cries'.[3] Earlier in the same poem the poet remarks on the two types of
vessel just discussed: 'when boats move down thy stream with current favouring
and their oars thrash the churned waters at full speed', while 'along the banks,
with tow-rope never slackening, the boatmen strain on their shoulders hawsers
bound to the masts'. Light skiffs with oars or paddles are also mentioned in
which the local youth have mimic battles in midstream, circling in and out or
leaping about on stern or painted prow.[4]

At the river's mouth passengers and cargoes would go aboard a seagoing
vessel, probably the property of one of the *navicularii*, business men who controlled the shipping on which so much of Rome's prosperity depended. They
were responsible for bringing the grain which fed the Roman townsfolk and
they were organised in powerful guilds. *Collegia* of *navicularii* are known from
Narbonne, Lyons and Arles, but the most striking illustration of their importance is the Piazzale delle Corporazioni at Ostia. Here a large colonnade existed
with sixty-one small rooms, and in front of most of them, black and white
mosaics showed the occupation of the owners, and the parts of the world with

---

[1] T. C. Lethbridge, *Boats & Boatmen* (1952) pp. 68, 137.   [2] IV. 64. 22.
[3] *Mosella* 165. Trans. H. G. White. Cp. Sidonius Apollinaris who, a century later, describes
the men hauling on a tow-rope and singing a hymn (*Epistulae* II. x. iv).
[4] *Mosella* 39, 200–21.

which they traded or from whence they came. Many are concerned with Africa and a fine elephant represents dealings with Sabratha. One relief showing a pontoon bridge over the meeting-point of three streams may denote the famous bridge at Arles, with the river Rhône and its tributaries, another includes the inscription 'Narbo', and depicts a ship in full sail.[1]

As well as guilds of ship-owners there were also guilds of shipwrights, with the same careful distinction between the builders of river-boats and sea-going vessels as we find between *nautae* and *navicularii*. Diocletian's Edict also discriminates between the two, paying the latter group sixty *denarii* a day, ten more than could be demanded by the builders of river craft. A tombstone from Ravenna depicts a man actually at work on a ship with the comment, 'Longidienus pushes ahead with his work.'[2] A sarcophagus now in the Camposanto, Pisa, describes Marcus Annius Proculus as patron of the shipwrights at Ostia, and an inscription from Trinquetaille, on the opposite side of the Rhône from Arles, mentions a naval architect.[3]

Nowadays underwater exploration is gradually bringing to light Roman wrecks in the Mediterranean, and the fragments of woodwork which survive bear witness to the skilled workmanship of the shipyards. A ship found off Mahdia on the Tunisian coast, early in this century, proved to be full of works of art including the drums of unfinished columns of Greek marble. Their destination is uncertain as if they were en route from Greece to Italy, the ship had been blown well off course. Another cargo of *objets d'art* of the first century B.C. is known from Anticythera, while other ships laden with amphorae have been found at Anthéor, west of Cannes, and off Albenga. Large-scale traffic in wine and oil was clearly already flourishing in the western Mediterranean by the first century B.C. The cause of the disasters remains uncertain, but overloading of the deck cargoes seems likely. The Mahdia ship had all its anchors out when it sank, and was obviously trying frantically to avoid being blown out to sea.[4]

Until the progress of underwater archaeology is further advanced it is still necessary to rely upon illustrations for information about ships. These are not always satisfactory, as artists frequently take liberties with their proportions so that the vessels can be neatly fitted into the picture. The mosaic found at Althiburus in Tunisia depicts a number of sea and river craft, many identified by name, but its accuracy has been much disputed.[5] The two chief types of

---

[1] R. Meiggs, *Roman Ostia* (1960) p. 287, Pl. XXIIId.
[2] L. Casson, *Ancient Mariners* (1959) Pl. XVa.
[3] L. Bonnard, *La Navigation Intérieure de la Gaule à l'époque gallo-romaine* (Paris, 1913) p. 160.
[4] Casson, *op. cit.* p. 193; P. Diolè, *4,000 Years Under the Sea* (1952) pp. 64, 98.
[5] E. K. Chatterton, *Sailing Ships* (1914) p. 84 *et seq.*

seagoing sailing ship, the *corbita* and the *ponto*, appear, however, and these are known from elsewhere. Several reliefs from Narbonne show the *corbita* as a vessel with a rounded hull, from which the stem and stern rise up in gracefu arcs. With the *ponto* the keel projects in front of the stem post, in a manner more like a battleship's ram. Probably this was to protect stem and keel from damage when the ship had to be beached. A *ponto* heavily laden (or overladen) with *amphorae* appears on a second- or third-century mosaic from Tebessa in Algeria, and both types of ship can be seen on a sarcophagus of *c.* A.D. 200 found at the mouth of the Tiber, and now in the Ny Carlsberg Museum, Copenhagen (Pl. 22). This coffin tells the story of an accident at sea, and it may be the last resting-place of either the victim or else one of the ships' captains involved. The man or boy fell out of the small boat which appears in the foreground, into a rough sea. The two ships on the left and in the centre went to his rescue, but just as the central ship reached him, it realised it was going to collide with the ship on the right, which was about to enter harbour. Its rescue attempt had to be abandoned as all hands rushed to trim the sails to turn the vessel back towards land. The incoming ship hastily backed its mainsails to reduce speed, but the small foresail remained to help turn the vessel outwards. In any case the hand who should be adjusting it appears overcome with shock, and is resorting to prayer. The third ship, on the left, continued the rescue attempt, but obviously without success as the drowning boy fails to see it. The people standing on the mole, shown at the end of the sarcophagus on the left, may be his sorrowing parents.

This relief illustrates many of the essential features of Roman sailing vessels. Clearly visible on the sides of all the ships are the great wales or strips of timber, which run round the hulls and protect them from rubbing against the quays. The incoming boat has the pointed forefoot of the *ponto*, and in the stern of the ship on the left can be seen the goose's head so often seen on Roman vessels, placed there because the bird was sacred to the Egyptian moon-goddess, Isis, the protecting deity of seafarers. A gallery is often built out round the stern post to shelter the little shrine of the goddess, and sometimes one was added round the forward end of the ship to protect the hands working the sails. All these craft were steered by means of two paddles or quarter-rudders, placed on either side of the stern. They appear clearly, and could be raised when necessary by means of ropes attached to the blades, and bollards on the rail of the ship. The large square mainsails are almost furled on the vessels to the right and left, and a clearer picture of them is given by fig. 154. They seem to have been made of squares of linen. One large sail, set on the main mast, hung from the yards, with one or two triangular sails above it. Such sails were only efficient

154 Roman merchantman, based on a ship on a sarcophagus from Sidon

with a following wind and without it, progress was slow. To counteract this a little, a smaller sail, known as the *artemon*, was placed further forward. This is clearly visible on the right-hand ship on the sarcophagus (Pl. 22) and on fig 154. Some authorities believe that through its use, the Romans did learn the art of sailing into the wind. The central ship on the sarcophagus may have a sprit sail, although not all are convinced of this identification. Other reliefs may show a short luffed lug, a forerunner of the lateen sail.[1]

Some of these ships were of considerable size. St Paul travelled to Rome with 275 fellow passengers, and the account of his adventurous voyage has provided valuable material for students of ancient shipping.[2] Sometimes scenes showing the arrival of a ship in harbour are found and a fine example on a tomb in Pompeii shows the bands being taken from the quarter-rudders and sails furled as the vessel glides into calm waters. This symbolises death with the soul finding rest and peace.[3] A lamp in the British Museum, however, depicts a less tranquil homecoming. Of the crew of six, three are busy with the sails, one is about to let down the anchor, a fifth is steering and the sixth is perched on the stern gaily blowing a trumpet to announce their safe arrival.[4] And the well-known relief from Portus, now in the Torlonia Collection in Rome, shows the docking of a splendid ship with many details of the tackle and sails.[5] The main-sail is still up and is decorated with a scene showing the wolf feeding Romulus and Remus, but the *artemon* is down, and a man stands by its mast ready to lower the gangplank. The stern is also decorated, a reminder that all these vessels were

[1] Casson, *op. cit.* p. 219.
[2] *Acts* XXVII, Casson, *op. cit.* p. 238; Chatterton, *op. cit.* p. 79.
[3] Mau-Kelsey (1902) p. 415, fig. 243.   [4] Chatterton, *op. cit.* p. 83.
[5] Casson, *op. cit.* Pl. XII.

gaily painted. The ship's boat, which the Althiburus mosaic shows was towed astern at the end of a long line, is being hauled up near the quarter-rudder. The deck-house, which the Mahdia wreck proved was sometimes roofed with tiles, appears clearly behind the goose's head, and on its roof the skipper is conducting a sacrifice in gratitude for a successful voyage. On the right, another ship, its sails already furled, is tied to a ring in the harbour wall. Its small boat is also securely moored and stevedores trudge across the gang-plank, unloading *amphorae*.

No anchors are visible on any of these reliefs but enough actual specimens have been found to leave us in no doubt as to the appearance of this very vital piece of equipment. One found with the two great barges built for the Emperor Nero and sunk in lake Nemi had a wooden shank 16½ feet long and a lead stock. More stocks of lead have been recovered from the Mediterranean, including four from the Mahdia wreck. A fifth, between 11 and 15 feet in length was so heavy, it could not be lifted. An anchor from Sardinia, in the Römisch-Getmanisches Zentral Museum, Mainz, has iron fittings instead of lead, and iron examples have also been found at Cherchel in Africa and Étaples in France.[1] An anchor appears on the altar dedicated to Oceanus found in the Tyne at Newcastle (fig. 148).[2]

A little more evidence for Roman seafaring is available from Britain. In 1910 part of a vessel was found on the banks of the Thames near the east end of Westminster Bridge, on the site of the present County Hall. It was carvel-built of oak, and probably originally 60 feet long and 16 feet wide, but only 38 feet of it survived. The thick protective wales so prominent in the reliefs were found in place, and several of the ribs and other timbers had been repaired in Roman times. A fragment of the mast was found nearby, and a block for two pulleys and a belaying pin lay in the boat. Coins of the late third century were also found among the woodwork, dating the boat to A.D. 290 at the earliest. It may have run aground on a sandbank, and broken up there. The fragments are preserved at Lancaster House. No clues survive as to its cargo or ownership.[3] A fragment of a writing tablet found in Lothbury makes some reference to the building of a ship and the granting of permission for some purpose, including the making of a rudder (. . . *navem faciendam et permissionem dedisse . . . clavi faciendi*.[4] This, a bronze goose-head from the stern of a model Roman ship found at Richborough, and a little model of a galley prow, also of bronze and found in London,[5] suggest that such ships may have been British built.

In 1959 the upward curving keel and part of the fender of another Roman

[1] Diolè, *op. cit.* p. 293 *et seq.*   [2] *R.I.B.* 1320.   [3] *L.R.T.* p. 151.   [4] *Ibid.* p. 54.
[5] *A.R.B.* (1964) p. 78, fig. 42; p. 71, fig. 37 no. 1.

boat were found in a silted up channel of the Thames, during the rebuilding of Guy's Hospital, Southwark, but this had to be re-buried. It had a beam of at least 12 feet and a probable length of 60 feet, and was probably associated with late second-century potsherds.[1] In 1962 a third ship was discovered at Blackfriars Bridge, a hundred yards out from the Roman embankment and near the mouth of the river Fleet (fig. 155). It was a carvel-built, flat-bottomed, barge-like craft without a keel, about 55 feet long with a beam of 22 feet and a depth of more than seven. The skeleton of the bottom ribs had survived in the Thames mud with some of the planking of the sides. The starboard side had collapsed at some period after the wreck and so sealed layers of Roman material, including a worn copper coin of Domitian dating to A.D. 88–9. The reverse showed Fortuna holding a ship's rudder, and the coin had been placed in the mast-step beneath the fixed mast, probably as an offering for good winds. A piece of leather with pierced decoration outlining a dolphin was in the bottom of the boat, and an unfinished millstone lay in the bows. The vessel had been caulked with hazel twigs, and the eight timbers recovered had been held in position with great iron bolts with cone-shaped heads, placed in drilled holes. The woodwork was riddled with holes by the *teredo*, a salt-water worm, and this may have been the cause of the wreck. Its presence shows that the ship went to sea, and its final cargo was a pile of Kentish ragstone found at one end, probably brought from the Medway for some building in Londinium.[2] It was a clumsy craft, possibly a local type, and was probably afloat during the second century. Trojan warships appear on the Low Ham mosaics, and another warship is clearly shown on the medallion of Constantius I which depicts the relief of London (fig. 40).

We have already seen that seagoing ships could sail up some of the larger British rivers and join the river craft at cities like London, York or Colchester. Comparatively little attention has been directed to port installations at such sites and, indeed, in many cases, little evidence can survive. Chester, perhaps, where the old harbour has not been built over, may eventually produce some. Still less is known about harbours along the coast and fresh discoveries in this field are not impossible. The coastline, however, has changed since Roman times, so many sites may now lie under water. Recent excavations have revealed the existence of an unsuspected harbour town at Caister-on-Sea (Norfolk), not far from Yarmouth. Its life began about A.D. 125, and the reason for its existence was probably the short sea-crossing to the mouth of the Rhine and the growing trade in Rhenish glass, pottery, and also millstones of Niedermendig lava. By the mid-second century the town had a stout flint enclosure wall, and a building

[1] *J.R.S.* L (1960) 230.   [2] *J.R.S.* LIV (1964) 168.

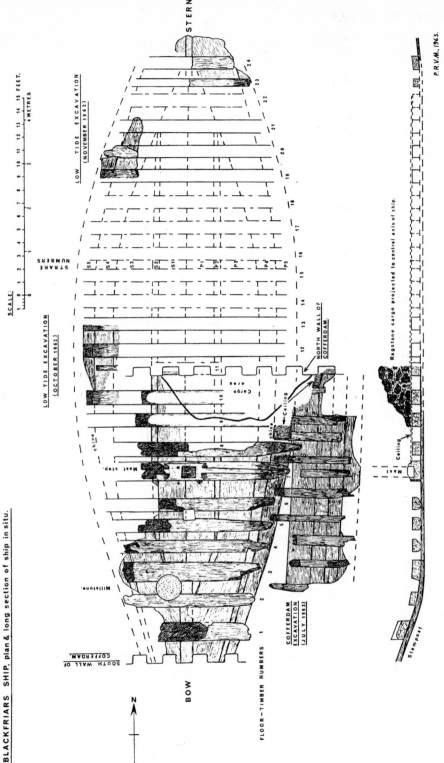

155 The Blackfriars boat

413

was later constructed just inside the south gate as a *mansio* or boarding-house for seamen. Parts of this continued in use until the end of the fourth century. A road led out of the south gate down to the harbour and of this, alas, little is known.[1]

Numerous other harbours of this type may be suspected, especially where roads make for the coast for no apparent reason. One Yorkshire example passes several villas and then ends among a few scattered finds in Bridlington Bay, and another may have had some better reason than the signal station for ending at Scarborough. The site at Meols, Cheshire, with its sheltered anchorage and nearby markets, may have been a port of call for trade with Ireland.[2] Many havens must have been in use along the south coast and one can suggest at random, Hastings, round Selsey Bill and the Isle of Wight, Poole Bay, Weymouth, Lyme Regis or Seaton, all in areas with abundant Roman occupation. Such a hypothetical survey can be continued all round the English coast. Recent excavations at Bitterne support the theory that a Roman port existed here from the first century onwards, a forerunner of Southampton,[3] and an outlet for the export of lead.

We know a little more about the sites of ports under military control. Boulogne, where the naval squadron concerned with Britain had its headquarters from the time of the invasion until the fourth century, was ideally placed at the end of the big main road to Cologne via Bavai. Speedy communications could be maintained with the German armies and naval squadron, and with the whole system of Rhine–Rhône waterways. Many tiles stamped CL BR (*Classis Britannica*) have been found here, as in Britain. The ships in use were probably triremes, and one called *Radians* appears on a relief at Boulogne. There were also the faster Liburnian galleys which the Romans had adapted from craft used by Jugoslav pirates. All could be sailed but when a skirmish was expected, the mast was lowered and the vessels depended upon the oars. The naval ratings seem mostly to have been Syrians, Egyptians, Phoenicians, Greeks, Slavs, or Gauls. As in the army, a man could work his way up and the chief posts, including those of the prefects of the fleets, were only open to Roman citizens.

Briefly summarised, our knowledge of the *Classis Britannica* begins about the time of the invasion. Loss of some ships was the reason given for the recall of Suetonius Paulinus, and in A.D. 70, when assisting in the reduction of Civilis' rebellion in Germany, the fleet was defeated off the Dutch coast. Agricola pre-

[1] R. R. Clarke, *East Anglia* (1960) pp. 119, 128; *J.R.S.* LIII (1963) 137.
[2] F. H. Thompson, *Roman Cheshire* (Chester, 1965) p. 98.
[3] M. A. Cotton and P. Gathercole, *Excavations at Clausentum, Southampton, 1951–1954* (1958).

sumably brought it up to strength and made great use of it, on both the east and west coasts. By the end of his campaigns the fleet had reconnoitred Ireland and explored much of the coast round Scotland, including the Orkneys and probably the Shetlands. Tacitus describes how the army and the navy were sometimes encamped together, and rivalled each other in relating stirring tales of their adventures. The soldiers told of barbarians conquered and of marches through forests and over mountains, and the sailors retaliated with accounts of storms at sea and the wonders of the deep. The Britons in the north were accustomed to rely on the sea as a means of escape, and Tacitus tells us that they viewed the arrival of the fleet with consternation.[1]

After Agricola, little is known about naval affairs for some time. Presumably the fleet was occupied patrolling, transporting troops, or convoying supplies as the armies consolidated their hold in the north. An inscription on a building slab from Benwell shows that detachments of sailors were helping to construct Hadrian's Wall.[2] There is also a Chester tombstone which records the fate of an *optio* who, while waiting for his commission as a centurion, the next rung in the ladder of promotion, died in a shipwreck, probably in the course of duty.[3] Apparently his body was never recovered. In A.D. 286 came the revolt of Carausius and in A.D. 296, with the aid of the fleet, Constantius Chlorus restored the province to the Empire. Soon after the middle of the fourth century the raids of the Picts, Scots, Attacotti and Saxons became increasingly violent, until they resulted in the disastrous attacks of A.D. 367 when Nectarides, the commander of the coastal defences, was killed. Sometime during the fourth century the area between the Wash and the Solent which was most exposed to the Saxons received the name of the Saxon Shore, and the officer in charge of its defence had the title of *Comes Litoris Saxonici*. Whether Nectarides held this post or not is uncertain, it may belong to a later date.

The invading troops of A.D. 43 are believed to have landed in Kent at Richborough near Sandwich, Lympne, which was then by the sea, and Dover— Portus Ritupis, Portus Lemanis and Portus Dubris according to the Antonine Itinerary. Of these, Richborough became a great supply base. It provided good shelter for ships, and was well placed for travellers and goods arriving from Gaul. The site now stands high above a marsh away from the sea, and the area presumably occupied by the harbour has been heavily eroded since Roman times. So once again this valuable evidence has been lost. Damage was also done when the cutting was made for the railway. The invading forces protected themselves from surprise attacks by a bank and two ditches, but as the campaign prospered, these were replaced by the storehouses and other buildings of the

[1] *Agricola* 25.　[2] *R.I.B.* 1340.　[3] *R.I.B.* 544.

military depot, which must have been very active during the conquest of Wales and Agricola's forays into Scotland. About the end of the first century a large triumphal monument was erected, possibly a tetrapylon or four-way arch. It was covered with imported Carrara marble and had columns at least 50 feet high. Fragments have been found of the large bronze statues which surmounted it. As the armies moved further north the military value of Richborough seems to have declined, but it remained an important commercial port. In the mid-third century pirate raids led to part of it being re-fortified. The monument was either demolished or used as a look-out post. Later in the century the massive walls visible today were constructed, and the current theory is that Carausius built the fort and some of the others along the so-called Saxon Shore to resist the armies of the legitimate Roman rulers. After his death and that of Allectus,[1] Richborough fort became the chief base for the *Classis Britannica*. Its history from the beginning of the fifth century is obscure, but the harbour continued in use, and it is the traditional landing place of St Augustine in 597.[2]

The site of the Roman harbour at Dover lies beneath the modern town, probably stretching eastwards from the Market Square, and the Roman town of Dubris seems to have developed in the late first century.[3] Lympne now lies inland and landslides have scattered the walls of the fort and probably confused the *strata*. It has been little investigated and might yield some evidence of the port. An altar dedicated to Neptune by Gaius Aufidius Pantera, Admiral of the *Classis Britannica*, was built into the foundations of the main gate, and may date back to the first part of the second century.[4] On the other side of Richborough is Reculver, in the Thames estuary at the northern end of the Wantsum channel. The Roman site originally stood on a peninsula, which would give a sheltered anchorage to shipping travelling down the Thames and into the Wantsum and vice-versa. One ship, at least, probably failed to reach it in time, as Roman pottery found hereabouts and covered with salt-water deposits, is believed to come from a vessel wrecked on the Pudding Pan rock near Whitstable. Recent excavations in the fort have produced an inscription dating to the early third century, but the history of the site is still being worked out and it has unfortunately suffered much erosion from the sea. The fort seems too large for a cohort so it has been suggested that accommodation was provided there for other troops, probably including naval units.[5] Possibly Reculver and

[1] See above p. 172.
[2] D. White, *Litus Saxonicum* (Madison, 1961) p. 36; Bushe-Fox (1949) p. 6.
[3] L. Murray Threipland, 'Excavations in Dover', *Arch. Cant.* LXXI (1958) 14–37.
[4] R. Jessup, *Archaeology of Kent* (1930) p. 194; *R.I.B.* 68.
[5] I. A. Richmond, 'A new Building Inscription from the Saxon Shore Fort at Reculver, *Ant. J.* XLI (1961) 227.

Brancaster in Norfolk were early Saxon Shore forts contemporary with the third-century earth fort at Richborough, but the discovery of a defensive ditch of mid-first-century date at Reculver also hints at a Claudian occupation.

The complete series of Saxon Shore forts extends from Norfolk to the Solent. How many of them were built under Carausius remains uncertain until further excavation is carried out, but in the fourth century they all belonged to a series of coastal defences maintained against the Saxon raiders, and they were interspersed by a series of signal stations and minor forts which are gradually being recovered.[1] Their significance here lies in the fact that they probably indicate the sites of earlier harbours and anchorages. Burgh Castle, for example, overlooks Caister-on-Sea; Walton Castle, near Felixstowe, is near the estuaries of the Deben, Stour and Orwell, and Bradwell guards the mouth of the Blackwater. Of the remaining sites, Portchester on the Solent is perhaps the most spectacular of all, as at high tide the sea still comes up to its walls, and it is easy to look out to sea and imagine a Roman ship rowing up to the water gate. The walls, strengthened by bastions, are substantially Roman, although the site as it survives today is largely that of a mediaeval castle. Other late fortifications for the protection of Britain from raiders were built in Wales at Cardiff, Caernarvon and Holyhead. The late fourth-century temple at Lydney has produced a mosaic incorporating a dedication to Nodens by Flavius Senilis, officer in charge of the supply-depot of the fleet, the work being supervised by Victorinus, interpreter on the governor's staff. Where this supply-depot was located is a mystery but it does illustrate the continuing importance of the fleet at this late date.[2] And what languages, we may wonder, was Victorinus required to interpret into Latin!

Further north there are a few more possible harbours and naval bases. Recent excavations have shown that from the second century onwards, a fort existed for the protection of shipping at South Shields, at the mouth of the Tyne opposite the end of Hadrian's Wall. In the time of the Emperor Severus it grew into a great supply-base for his Scottish campaign. Storehouses and granaries were built, and cargoes were probably collected and reorganised here before sailing off north to the harbour at Cramond on the Forth. In the early fourth century these supplies were no longer needed, and some of the granaries were turned into dwellings.[3] The *Notitia Dignitatum* tells us that at some period the garrison included the *Barcarii Tigrisiensis*, a naval unit sometimes visualised as skilled in transhipping cargoes from seagoing ships into the barges which

[1] For a full account see D. White, *op. cit.* [2] Wheeler (1932) p. 102.
[3] I. A. Richmond, 'The Roman Fort at South Shields', *Arch. Ael.* (4) XI (1934) 81–102; *The Roman Fort at South Shields* a guide (South Shields, 1953).

would convey them up the Tyne. Further north still, Agricola's naval base is believed to have been on the Firth of Forth, or possibly the Firth of Tay, where Bertha seems a likely site. On the west coast there may have been a harbour on the Clyde, probably in the vicinity of Dumbarton, for supplies for the Antonine Wall.

Discoveries at Portus, the port of Rome at the mouth of the Tiber, give us excellent illustrations in sculpture or mosaic of the busy scenes which may well have taken place at Richborough or other British ports.[1] The harbour of over 170 acres was artificially dredged out of the river bank and a large ship, which had brought an obelisk from Egypt, was sunk at the mouth to make a breakwater. Claudius started the project in A.D. 42 and sailed out of Ostia on his way to Britain, but the work was still going on in Nero's reign until A.D. 54, and considerable extensions were added about fifty years later during the reign of Trajan. The relief already mentioned (p. 410) shows ships in the Claudian harbour with a triumphal arch in the background. A funerary relief from the nearby cemetery of Isola Sacra shows another scene with a ship with furled sails being towed into position by its small boat, and on the right, sailors celebrating at an inn. On both these reliefs, and on several of the ship mosaics in the Piazzale delle Corporazioni, appears the famous Claudian lighthouse, a tower built in four stepped storeys of decreasing height, the lowest three squared, and the top with the beacon, cylindrical.[2] It was built on the breakwater formed by the sunken ship. The idea of the lighthouse may have arisen in the Mediterranean as a result of the value of the volcanoes Vesuvius, Etna and Stromboli as beacons, and the first important example was the famous Pharos at Alexandria, built in the third century B.C. By A.D. 400, over thirty lighthouses are known, marking the entrance to harbours between the Black Sea and the Atlantic. They include examples at Capri, Fréjus in Southern France, and Caepio and Corunna in Spain.[3] In A.D. 40 the Emperor Gaius visited Boulogne to consider an expedition against Britain. Although he gave up the idea he ordered 'a tall lighthouse to be built, not unlike the one at Pharos, in which fires were to be kept going all night to guide ships'.[4] The site of this lighthouse is known and it was only destroyed in the sixteenth century. On clear days its signals could be seen by the people of Roman Dover who could reply from two lighthouses, one on each side of the harbour. Only a mass of fallen masonry remains from the one on the western hill, but the other one partly survives in the precincts of

[1] L. Casson, 'Harbour and River Boats of Ancient Rome', *J.R.S.* LV (1965) 31–39.
[2] Meiggs, *op. cit.* p. 158 gives an account of the lighthouse and harbour.
[3] D. A. Stevenson, *The World's Lighthouses before 1820* (1952) p. 19, map on p. 2.
[4] Suetonius, *Caligula* XLVI. Trans R. Graves.

Dover Castle (Pl. 46). Originally it may have been about 80 feet high with an octagonal plan, and walls 12 feet thick which could be stepped back on each storey. Inside there was a space nearly 14 feet square. The walls were of rubble faced with stone with tile bonding courses. The lighthouse was probably built soon after the invasion, and it was altered and added to in mediaeval times. The top 19 feet belong to this later period and so does the large west door, but the windows and much of the remaining walls are of Roman date.[1]

[1] R. E. M. Wheeler, 'The Roman Light-houses at Dover', *Arch. J.* LXXXVI (1930) 29–46.

15
Religion

When we come to consider the ideas of the Romano-Britons about religion, death and the after-life, we are brought into the most intimate contact with our ancestors that the passage of time allows us. Occasionally we can identify in the town or country house the possible site of the household shrine or *lararium*, where the father of the family poured his libations in honour of the gods of hearth and home. A shrine of this kind found against the wall of a house in Silchester consisted of a platform over 6 feet square approached by a step on one side and with a panel of mosaic in front of it.[1] On the platform there probably stood a model of a classical temple, the home of the household gods or *lares*. From *lararia* found in Pompeii we know that the contents of this shrine should include a figure of the *Genius Paterfamilias* or *Genius Familiaris*, clad in a toga which was drawn up over his head to keep out sounds of ill omen during the sacrifice and holding a *patera*, or sacrificial dish, and a napkin. On either side of him there would have stood the *Lares*—dancing figures each holding either a *patera* or a horn of plenty (Pl. 53*d*). Statuettes depicting both a *genius* and a *lar* have actually been discovered at Silchester. Small bronze figures of other deities are also sometimes found. They include Mars, the god of war and of agriculture; Mercury, the messenger of the gods, who also watched over commerce (Pls. 50,

[1] Boon (1957) p. 124.

53*a*); Bacchus, the jolly god of wine; and Venus, whose activities hardly, perhaps, require explanation (Pl. 49). Small white pipeclay statuettes of Venus or of Juno Lucina, the goddess of childbirth, shown nursing a baby and sitting in a wicker chair, may also have been placed in the *lararium*. These were imported from Gaul and there seems to have been quite an extensive trade in them. All these deities, of course, are well known all over the Roman world; and references to them on inscriptions show that they found in Britain worshippers as fervent as in the other provinces. They were revered both as part of the official state religion and also in the unofficial cults of everyday life.

The official state-religion was concerned with the worship of the *numen*, or spiritual power, of the reigning Emperor, and with that of his predecessors who were usually deified after death. Often the cult of imperial persons was associated with that of important Roman gods such as Jupiter, Juno and Minerva. One of the first acts of the Romans in Britain was to build the great Temple of Claudius at Colchester[1] and to organise a priesthood of important Britons to serve in it; Claudius was, in this instance, worshipped as a god even while still alive. A priest's term normally lasted a year, during which time he was expected to live near the temple and to pay for various festivals and games associated with its cult. This was an expensive honour, probably esteemed during the prosperous years of the second century, but not always appreciated by the mid-first-century priests, who speedily got into debt. Whether Colchester always remained the chief centre for the Imperial cult we do not know for certain. But the temple destroyed by Boudicca was rebuilt and maintained and there is no definite evidence that any cult centre in other towns was ever important enough to supplant it.

From the *coloniae* of York and Lincoln we also have evidence of temples in honour of the Emperor and his relations. The priests serving this cult were known as the *Seviri Augustales* and were always elected from among the wealthy freedmen. Inscriptions tell us of their existence. One, commemorating a *sevir* called Diogenes, occurs on a coffin found in York in the reign of Elizabeth I, the first Roman discovery ever recorded in that city.[2] Another comes from an altar found at Bordeaux in 1921. It reads in translation: 'In honour of the protecting goddess Boudiga, Marcus Aurelius Lunaris, *Sevir Augustalis* of the *coloniae* of York and Lincoln, in the province of Lower Britain dedicates the altar which he had vowed on leaving York. He pays his vow willingly and duly.' *Votum solvit libens merito*, the words of the last sentence, give the formula customarily

---

[1] See above p. 21. See also D. Fishwick, 'The Imperial Cult in Roman Britain', *Phoenix* XV (1961) 159–73, 213–20

[2] *R.I.B.* 678.

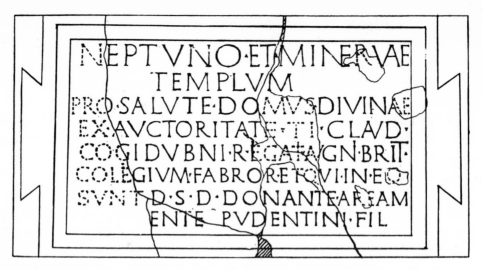

156 Dedication slab to Neptune and Minerva and the welfare of the
Imperial House. Erected by the guild of smiths with the authority of
Cogidubnus, king of the Regnenses, Chichester

used in dedicating such altars; and Lunaris then adds that this altar was erected
in the Consulship of Perpetuas and Cornelius. When such information is given
it is usually possible to get an exact date and here it seems that this vow was
fulfilled in A.D. 237. Lunaris seems to have been a prominent business man
trading, probably in wine, from Bordeaux. His altar may have been erected
solely as a thankoffering for a good journey from Britain. It has been pointed
out, however, that in 237 the Emperor Maximian won a great victory in
Germany, driving back the barbarian tribes and penetrating as far as the Elbe.
What would be more likely then that a priest of the Imperial Cult should celebrate an important public event by dedicating an altar at the first opportunity.[1]

The Imperial Cult is also associated with honours offered to other gods of
Roman origin. There is the well-known inscription preserved at Chichester
dedicating a temple to the sea-god Neptune and to Minerva, by the smith's
guild, made . . . 'for the welfare of the Divine House by the authority of
Tiberius Claudius Cogidubnus, king and Imperial legate in Britain . . . the site
being presented by Clemens, son of Pudentinus' (fig. 156).[2] Cogidubnus,
Claudius' staunch supporter, we have already met in Chapter 10! For an example
of a dedication of a less official nature there is the altar at Chester 'For the welfare
of our lords, the most invincible Emperors, to the Genius of the place Flavius
Longus, military tribune of the Twentieth Legion Valeria Victrix, and Longinus,
his son, from Samosata, fulfilled their vow'.[3] To the Romans, and those influ-

[1] Paul Courteault, 'An Inscription recently found at Bordeaux', *J.R.S.* XI (1921) 101–7.
[2] *R.I.B.* 91.   [3] *R.I.B.* 450.

157 Altar erected to Jupiter, Best and Greatest, by the First Cohort of Spaniards, commanded by M. Maenius Agrippa, Maryport

enced by them, every place had its Genius, or guardian spirit, who must not be offended, and we would very much like to know what particular good offices this one had performed for Flavius and Longinus, making them feel that it deserved the expense of an altar.

The most important gods, however, associated with the Emperor in the official cult were Jupiter, Juno and Minerva, often called the Capitoline Triad, because the great temple that stood on the Capitoline Hill at Rome contained shrines dedicated to them. This was the temple to which the new consuls came to make their vows and offer sacrifice and to which the victorious generals rode in triumphal procession to give thanks for their victories. To Jupiter Optimus Maximus, Jupiter the Best and Greatest, the most powerful of the gods and lord of rain, storms, thunder and lightning, the legions dedicated fresh altars every year, burying the old ones, so that they should not fall into sacrilegious hands. A number of these altars have been excavated from pits outside the fort at Maryport, Cumberland, and a typical inscription reads (in translation): 'To Jupiter Optimus Maximus the First Cohort of Spaniards, which is commanded by Marcus Maenius Agrippa, tribune, set this up' (fig. 157).[1] This dedication ceremony probably took place on New Year's Day, or January 3, when the vows for the safety and welfare of the Roman state, the Emperor and his family

[1] *R.I.B.* 823.

and the Empire were all renewed.[1] Jupiter's attributes included the thunderbolt and the eagle; and a fine example of the latter was found carved on an altar discovered at Piercebridge, Durham. Here a centurion, Julius Valentinus, erects the altar to Jupiter Dolichenus, that is to a Near-Eastern god identified with Jupiter, a god who specialised in answering the questions of the worried and perplexed.[2]

Most of the dedications to these important Roman gods come from military sites where their worship formed part of army routine. Less evidence survives from the civilian parts of Britain, partly because suitable material for making altars was often lacking there, and any stone used was apt to be stolen by post-Roman builders. The Romano-Britons themselves in times of emergency were not above hastily collecting old altars and tombstones for building purposes, and the Grosvenor Museum, Chester, owes its fine collection of sculptures and inscriptions to the re-used material from the north city wall, built in the late third century. For Juno, wife of Jupiter and Queen of Heaven, the goddess who looks after women from the moment of their birth until death, and especially on such important occasions as marriage and childbirth, we seem to have no dedication at all, although a statue found at the military base at Corbridge may be a representation of her.[3] Minerva, the third member of the Triad, was the daughter of Jupiter. As patroness of arts and crafts and of all forms of wisdom, she was invoked by all who wished to do well in teaching, painting, dyeing, potting, spinning, weaving, etc.; she guided men wisely in the strategy of war and she was believed to have been the inventor of musical instruments. Besides the Chichester inscription already mentioned, an altar to her survives from the Roman fort at Ebchester, Durham, dedicated by a clerk in the army accounts department,[4] and another dedication was found at Chester.[5] More impressive evidence for her worship is the beautiful head in Italian marble found in the temple of Mithras in London in 1954.[6] Another allusion to Minerva in stone may be seen in part of a frieze also found at Chester. This is decorated with an acanthus scroll in relief, the spaces between the loops of the scroll being occupied by birds, apparently the peacock, the dove and the owl, companions of Juno, Venus and Minerva respectively.[7]

Various other Roman deities also found worshippers in Britain. Apart from

---

[1] Evidence for such ceremonies is preserved in a third-century papyrus from Dura Europos. This includes part of a calendar of official festivals observed by the Roman army. R. Fink, A. Hoey and W. Snyder, 'The Feriale Duranum', *Yale Classical Studies* VII (1940) 1–222.
[2] *R.I.B.* 1022.   [3] Richmond (1943) 156–8.   [4] *R.I.B.* 1101.
[5] *R.I.B.* 457. See also *R.I.B.* 2104 from Birrens.
[6] See below p. 450.
[7] Wright (1955) p. 15 no. 9.

those who appear on the mosaic pavements already discussed, we may mention the altar to Diana found on the site of the Goldsmiths' Hall, Foster Lane, London, with its charming relief of the goddess clad in a short tunic, bow in hand and with her dog at her side.[1] Representations of Apollo with his lyre and Hercules with his club both occur at Bath,[2] and an inscription addressed to Hercules Saegon came to light in the Forum at Silchester.[3] Such a list could be continued indefinitely, but it may be more profitable to turn our thoughts from the worship of these gods in their purely Roman form to something more intimately connected with the pre-Roman religious ideas of Gaul and Britain.

Both Romans and natives in Britain gradually adopted the custom of linking the names of gods of similar function, the name of the native god being added as an epithet to the name of the Roman deity. Two dedications which may serve as illustrations of this habit, come from the Roman town at Caerwent. One is an altar dedicated to Mars Ocelus by Aelius Augustinus;[4] the other is an inscription on a carved pedestal for a statue reading (in translation), 'To the God Mars Lenus or Ocelus Vellaunus, and to the deity of the Emperor, Marcus Nonius Romanus, in return for freedom from liability of the college, gave this gift from his own resources on 23 August in the consulship of Glabrio and Homulus.'[5] Mars, the god of war, is mentioned in inscriptions elsewhere in Britain, but at Caerwent he is identified with Ocelus, probably a native British god, and also with Lenus, a Celtic god of healing worshipped in the Moselle area around Trier. He is thanked for bringing Romanus and his other worshippers some benefit, probably tax relief, so he appears here as the protector of townsfolk. What kind of college this was is not stated, but Romanus may have been its master or one of its patrons; perhaps a native of Trier who settled at Caerwent but did not entirely forget Lenus, the god of his homeland. The Emperor whose Divinity is mentioned may be Antoninus Pius and the consuls' names show that the inscription was set up in A.D. 152. On top of the pedestal the remains of a pair of sculptured human feet, the webbed feet of a bird, and a socket sunk in the stone are all that survives of the statue. Probably a conventional figure of Mars in full armour originally stood there with a goose beside him. The bird is a rather unusual companion for Mars, but it has been found accompanying Mars Lenus in the Trier area. Another dedication to Mars Ocelus, found in the Roman cemetery on Harraby Hill, Carlisle, couples the god with the Deity of the Emperor Alexander Severus and his mother Julia Mamaea. This slab can be dated between A.D. 222 and 235.[6]

[1] Toynbee (1963) p. 152 no. 64.
[2] H. M. Scarth, *Aquae Solis* (1864) p. 41.
[3] Boon (1957) 125.   [4] R.I.B. 310.   [5] R.I.B. 309.   [6] R.I.B. 949.

Further north we have evidence which may show the effects of Roman influence on a cult which probably goes back to pre-Roman times: the worship of Brigantia.[1] She was the tutelary goddess of the Brigantes, a large tribe who seem to have occupied much of Yorkshire and the country to the north and west. The river names Braint (Anglesey) and Brent (Middlesex) are believed to be derived from her name, encouraging us to see her as a River-goddess, whose power originally extended over a much wider area. But it must be remembered that the tribal name and these place-names are all the evidence we have to support this theory. Her earlier worshippers were not in the habit of putting up inscriptions to their deities and all those that we possess date from the second or third centuries, when Roman influence had become established. One group found in Yorkshire includes a simple dedication by a woman reading '*Deae Brigan(tiae) d(onum) Cingetissa p(osuit)*, 'To the goddess Brigantia Cingetissa set up this offering'.[2] This was discovered at Adel, near Leeds. Another altar, found at Greetland, hails the goddess as Victoria Brigantia in company with the Imperial Divinities, and this was the gift of T. Aurelius Aurelianus on behalf of himself and his family.[3] Aurelianus may have been an army veteran who received the citizenship when he retired. He obligingly added the names of Antoninus and Geta as the consuls then holding office in Rome, so the altar was dedicated in A.D. 208.

Further north Brigantia was also worshipped in the vicinity of Hadrian's Wall, either alone or coupled with vows for the Emperor's well-being. At Corbridge she is mentioned on an altar in an interesting dedication that we may consider in some detail. It reads (in translation): 'To eternal Jupiter of Doliche and to Caelestis Brigantia and to Salus Gaius Julius Apolinaris, centurion of the Sixth Legion, by order of the gods (set this up)' (fig. 158). We have already encountered Jupiter Dolichenus, and here Brigantia seems to be allied with Dea Caelestis and Juno Caelestis, a romanised version of Tanit, Goddess of the Heavens and also the chief goddess of North Africa. Salus is the Roman goddess of health and personal well-being, and as both Jupiter Dolichenus and Caelestis had healing powers, it may be that Apolinaris dedicated his altar for health reasons. The altar is decorated with figures in relief showing a Genius with a horn of plenty pouring a libation over an altar and a Cupid, carrying a bunch of grapes and a sickle, who may personify autumn, a suitable season for invoking the powers of heaven against the winter's ills. Professor Sir Ian Richmond pointed out that the worship of Jupiter Dolichenus was not an official cult subsidised by the state, so that its priests would be

[1] N. Joliffe, 'Brigantia', *Arch. J.* XCVIII (1942) 36–61.
[2] R.I.B. 630. [3] R.I.B. 627.

158 Altar dedicated to Jupiter Dolichenus, Caelestis Brigantia, and Salus, by G. Julius Apolinaris, centurion of the Sixth Legion, Corbridge

dependant upon the offerings of the faithful and quite willing to widen their appeal by including other deities in his cult. They may have advised Apolinaris, who, as a centurion of the Sixth Legion, presumably came from York, to dedicate his altar to the familiar Brigantia and the purely Roman Salus, as well as to the more exotic Caelestis and Jupiter Dolichenus. This idea is confirmed by the phrase IVS DE, *iussu dei*, by order of the god, with which the dedication ends. If the unfortunate centurion was already feeling ill and dedicated his altar, not as a precaution, but as a result of consulting Jupiter Dolichenus and these priests professionally, as healers, the god may have directed that Brigantia and Salus should undertake his case and he may have been advised to visit other shrines of Brigantia, as part of his treatment. It has also been noted that the last three lines of the inscription have been cut over some erased letters, but we must hope that Julius Apolinaris was not fobbed off with the altar originally belonging to a patient who had succumbed before he had time to carry out his treatment. At any rate, this inscription serves to illustrate the all-embracing nature of the religion of the period with its wide choice of gods.[1]

Before we leave Brigantia we must remember the fine relief portraying her which was found at Birrens. It was dedicated by Amandus, an architect or engineer, and one scholar has suggested that he was the Valerius Amandus mentioned on an inscription from Iversheim (Germany) dated to the year A.D. 209.[2] He may have been transferred from the First Legion at Bonn to the

[1] Richmond (1943) 43; *R.I.B.* 1131.
[2] S. N. Miller, 'Note on an inscription from Birrens', *J.R.S.* XXVII (1937) 208–9; *R.I.B.* 2091.

Sixth Legion at York to help in the urgent reconstruction work which went on in Britain under the Emperor Septimius Severus. This may have included some rebuilding of the fort at Birrens. The relief shows the goddess standing in a gabled shrine holding a spear and a globe. She wears a tunic and cloak, the folds of which partly hide a round shield leaning against the wall of the shrine. This shield, together with the medallion of the Gorgon's head on her breast, her crested helmet and her spear, mark her out as Minerva. She also has wings, which identify her as Victoria Brigantia, while the mural crown on her helmet proclaims her as protectress of the land, whose full extent is suggested by the globe. The conical stone at her side is a symbol of Caelestis.

Brigantia, it has been noted, was probably revered before the Roman conquest and at this point it is interesting to pause for a while and consider what we know of other deities who were not usually allied with any of the Roman gods and so may be of pre-Roman origin. No doubt at the beginning of the first century A.D. every tribe had its own particular favourites, but the successes of the Legions must have seriously affected their credit with their worshippers, while encouraging the spread of the Roman cults. Almost the only literary references that we have to non-Roman religion in Britain are concerned with the druids and of these perhaps the most interesting is Caesar's comment that 'The druidic doctrine is believed to have been found existing in Britain and thence imported into Gaul; even today, those who want to make a profound study of it generally go to Britain for this purpose.' Whether Caesar was right in his belief that druidism was of British origin seems doubtful, as most of our knowledge of it comes from Gaul, where it may date back to the fourth century B.C., its fame being spread abroad by Greek traders. Caesar, in a very interesting passage in his Commentaries on the Gallic War, describes them as one of the two important social classes among the Gauls, the other class being that of the knights. They officiate at sacrifices, public and private, and the interpretation of ritual questions; they decide most disputes and the punishment of criminals; and they elect one of their number as their leader. This election took place after the death of a chief druid at one of the annual meetings of all the druids held somewhere in central Gaul. Young Gauls, wishing to become druids, spent many years in study learning all the druidical lore. Caesar also records that the druids believed in the immortality of the soul and its rebirth, although whether in this world or the next is not really clear. They also held many discussions about the stars and their movements, the size of the universe and of the earth, the order of nature, and the powers of the immortal gods.[1] These aspects of the druids' beliefs and activities may have been derived from Greece via the

[1] N. K. Chadwick, *The Druids* (Cardiff, 1966) pp. 44, 60.

428

Greek colony at Marseilles founded *c.* 600 B.C. and writers of the Alexandrian school seem to hold the druids in high regard as philosophers in the Pythagorean tradition.[1] Other writers, notably Strabo, suggest that there were also two lesser grades of druid, the bards, who were singers and poets and whose songs and incantations in front of two contending armies sometimes prevented battles; and the vates, natural philosophers, skilled in the art of divination. Unfortunately most of these writers, including Caesar, appear to blame the druids for an aspect of life in Gaul which aroused the Romans' hostility: their practice of human sacrifice. The vates, in addition to studying the flight of birds and the entrails of the sacrificial animals, the usual way of obtaining auguries at that period, were said upon important occasions, to stab a man in the back and then foretell the future from the form taken by his death struggle. More serious still, individuals in time of war or sickness would also engage a druid to perform a human sacrifice on their behalf, while numbers of victims were burnt alive at public ceremonies in cages made of twigs in the shape of human figures. Many of these people may have been criminals or prisoners of war, but when the supply of these was exhausted, the innocent took their place. A recent writer has pointed out, however, that while human sacrifice, like head-hunting and the preservation of the heads of enemies, is known to have been a Gallic practice, it is not clear that the druids were responsible for the existence of this custom. The strongest accusation which can be levelled against them is that they condoned it by their presence, probably to see that the rites were correctly carried out.[2]

In any case, the Roman conquest of Gaul broke the druids' power because it divided the tribes into pro- and anti-Roman factions, and the opening of the Roman schools at Augustodunum and elsewhere[3] must have destroyed their influence by providing the young with an alternative means of education.[4]

Soon the Emperors were passing laws of increasing severity against druidism, until Claudius is recorded by Suetonius as thoroughly suppressing this barbarous and inhuman religion in Gaul, probably because it was a subversive political element.[5] Meanwhile, many druids had made good their escape to Britain and we can imagine that their arrival stirred up a wave of anti-Roman feeling in some quiet philosophical circles. Owing to the frequent strife among the British tribes it seems unlikely that the druids in this island were ever as well-organised as those in Gaul. But we do possess two other possible sources

---

[1] *Ibid.* p. 58.   [2] *Ibid.* pp. 28, 45 *et seq.*   [3] See above p. 312.
[4] For some survivals of druidic traditions, however, see Chadwick, *op. cit.* p. 82, and N. K. Chadwick (1955) p. 31 *et seq.*
[5] Chadwick, *The Druids,* p. 73.

of evidence concerned with their existence in this country: the great hoard of objects found at Llyn Cerrig Bach, Anglesey, and Tacitus' account of Suetonius Paulinus and the Fourteenth and Twentieth Legions attacking the Isle of Mona (Anglesey), the last stronghold of the Welsh tribes and a great centre, possibly *the* great centre, of druidism, in A.D. 60.

Llyn Cerrig Bach is a lake surrounded by ancient peat bogs in the south-east corner of Anglesey; and in 1942 work was carried out there in preparation for a new Royal Air Force landing-ground. The teeth of a harrow turned up a stout iron chain and the discovery proved very useful when a tractor was needed to haul the lorries out of the surrounding bog. This chain was nearly two thousand years old and eventually, as other metal objects and animal bones were dug up, its existence was reported to the National Museum of Wales, which then investigated the matter. The whole hoard comprises 138 objects of bronze and iron including slave-chains, metal fittings from chariots and horse harness, weapons, a trumpet, and thin bronze ribbon from ceremonial staves, one piece still coiled round a fragment of wood, later identified as ash. Obviously the material chiefly consists of the spoils of war, the things coming mostly from south-west Britain and northern Ireland, with the exception of the slave-chains, believed to hail from eastern Britain, as similar examples occur there. Considered as a whole, the discoveries are believed to be the votive offerings of a Celtic tribe or tribes to the god of the lake over a period lasting from *c.* 150 B.C. to A.D. 60. Not all the objects are of the same period, but none of them seem to be of any later date. Such deposits are not uncommon and other examples are known from France and Switzerland. The dedicated objects from them were usually rendered unserviceable before they were offered, and this applies at Llyn Cerrig Bach, where many of the things seem to have been damaged deliberately. Possibly this is not the only hoard there; there may have been other pools and sacred groves in the vicinity which still await discovery.[1]

The latest objects in the hoard from Llyn Cerrig date from *c.* A.D. 60 and about this time Suetonius Paulinus resolved to crush the rebellious tribes of North Wales by attacking their Anglesey refuge, which he knew to be a violently anti-Roman stronghold. Tacitus describes how the general ferried his army over the Menai Straits in specially built flat-bottomed boats while the cavalry swam their horses over. On the beaches stood the British army in dense array and among them appeared black-robed women with dishevelled hair like the Furies, brandishing torches. Nearby a crowd of druids lifted up their hands to heaven and poured forth a flood of curses. For a time the Roman soldiers stood petrified with horror as spells and curses had only too real a meaning to

[1] C. Fox, *A Find of the Early Iron Age from Llyn Cerrig Bach* (Cardiff, 1946).

them. Then, realising their danger and urged forward by their officers, they told each other not to be afraid of a crowd of frenzied women, and charged with the standards. The British were overwhelmed among the flames of their own torches.[1] Suetonius garrisoned Anglesey, the sacred groves were destroyed and this seems to have been the end of druidism as a factor of any importance in Roman Britain.

Few other traces of pre-Roman worship survive from the civilian areas of Britain, as they soon passed under Roman rule, but Dio Cassius does mention that the Iceni at the time of the Boudiccan rebellion worshipped a goddess called Andate. Ancasta is a deity known from Bitterne, and a water-goddess, Arnemetia, presided over the Buxton hot springs. A curious bronze group consisting of a three-horned bull carrying three figures on his back, one the bust of a draped bare-headed female, one a now headless bust and one a human-headed bird, was found in a Romano-Celtic temple of fourth-century date in the middle of the imposing Iron Age hill fort at Maiden Castle, Dorset.[2] This bull, associated with various figures, also occurs on the continent, where its name is known from inscriptions to be *Tarvos Trigaranus*. It may represent yet another Celtic god associated with water.

In the north a number of inscriptions mentioning local deities survive. Perhaps the most attractive of them is the water nymph Coventina, guardian of a sacred spring which still bubbles up into its stone tank at Brocolitia (Carrawburgh).[3] This tank was once the central feature of a stone temple and coins dating from almost the whole of the Roman period have been found in it as well as pottery and incense-burners, brooches and pearls, suitable offerings to a young nymph who might like pretty things. Altars and sculptured tablets were also thrown into the water, possibly by fifth-century Christians. This spirit of the spring was also adopted and worshipped by the soldiers in the nearby fort. A relief, now in Chesters Museum, Northumberland, of three classical water-nymphs, all with slightly different hair styles, may all be representations of her shown in triplicate to express the 'intensification' of her power. Reclining comfortably, they pour water from overturned urns, and each flourishes a cup in one hand (fig. 159). Another relief shows Coventina, so labelled in the inscription put up by the prefect of the first Batavian Cohort, holding a branch and floating gently along on a water-lily leaf.[4] Along Hadrian's

---

[1] Tacitus, *Annals* XIV. 29, 30.

[2] Toynbee (1964) p. 103.

[3] Until recently she was believed to be a purely local British goddess but now several inscriptions dedicated to her have been found in Galicia. *L'Année Epigraphique* 1950, 24; 1954, 251; 1957, 322.

[4] Toynbee (1963) p. 155 no. 75.

159　Relief showing the water nymph, Coventina, Carrawburgh

Wall, at Benwell, we find the remains of a temple still surviving among the traces of the village which grew up at the gates of the Roman fort at Condercum. A small oblong building, for most of its life it was entered by a door in one of the long sides and there, on the left, the worshipper saw a statue of the god standing in an apse (fig. 160).[1] Two altars, both dating from the middle of the second century, give the name of the god as Antenociticus or Anociticus; and his portrait in stone is now in the Museum of Antiquities, Newcastle-upon-Tyne.[2] Other gods worshipped in the north, particularly in the vicinity of Hadrian's Wall, include Maponus, sometimes associated with Apollo, Belatucadrus, and Cocidius, also equated with Mars.[3]

Next we come to those fascinating little deities, the *Genii Cucullati*. They are depicted as small male figures clad in the hooded cloak or *cucullus* already described above,[4] and were worshipped over a large area of the Graeco-Roman world, chiefly in the north-west. As Professor Toynbee has pointed out in a recent article,[5] they seem to have attracted worshippers in two particular areas of Roman Britain: the region of Hadrian's Wall and what is now Gloucestershire. Seventeen representations of them are known and all but two appear to have been made in Britain for local devotional purposes. In some cases only

[1] M. J. T. Lewis, *Temples in Roman Britain* (Cambridge, 1966) p. 72.
[2] Toynbee (1963) p. 146 no. 41.
[3] See also Toynbee (1964) p. 178 for examples of Celtic and British gods whose names are unknown.
[4] P. 124.
[5] J. M. C. Toynbee, 'Genii Cucullati in Roman Britain', *Collection Latomus* XXVII (1957) 456–69.

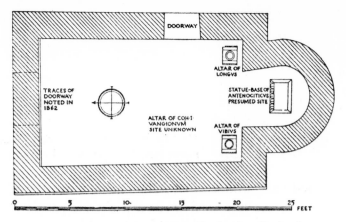

DOORWAY

ALTAR OF
LONGVS

TRACES OF
DOORWAY
NOTED IN
1862

STATUE-BASE OF
ANTENOCITICVS
PRESUMED SITE

ALTAR OF COH·I·
VANGIONVM
SITE UNKNOWN

ALTAR OF
VIBIVS

0   5   10·   15   20   25
FEET

160   Plan of the Temple of Antenociticus, Benwell, Northumberland

one *Genius* appears, but no less than eight of the reliefs show a trio of *Genii Cucullati*, and their worship in triads seems to have been a peculiarly British aspect of the cult. One relief, from Housesteads, depicts a frontal view of the three heavily draped figures, with cloaks reaching almost to their feet and wearing soft leather shoes. In another example, from Netherby, much shorter cloaks appear and each figure holds an object, apparently an egg, in his right hand. The egg was a favourite symbol of fertility and immortality at this period. Three *Genii Cucullati* in knee-length cloaks appear on a relief found at Ciren-cester, trotting to the right instead of standing still and facing to the front in the more customary and certainly more dignified manner. Another Gloucester-shire relief found at Daglingworth, two miles from Cirencester, is the most interesting of all. This shows a group of three muffled-up male figures, one of whom is giving something, possibly a bunch of grapes, to a female figure on the right-hand side of the relief. She is seated in a high-backed chair and has a large egg or oval object of some kind on her lap. It is suggested that here we have a triad of *Genii Cucullati* making an offering to a Mother-goddess, their superior in the Romano-Celtic hierarchy of deities.

Other reliefs in the Corinium Museum at Cirencester show that the local population also revered the Mother-goddesses whether represented singly or as a triad. Like the *Genii Cucullati*, their worship was widespread, and probably continental in origin, and their cult must go far back into the mists of time. Sometimes we have a single statuette sitting in a high or round-backed chair, but at Cirencester the Mothers are depicted on two reliefs as a triad of deter-mined looking matrons, seated and looking straight ahead, while a third relief shows them much more freely rendered and playing with children. Reliefs from London and Ancaster (Lincolnshire) show that they were sometimes seated on a straight, high-backed wooden bench. Other more comfortable-looking ladies

433

161 Dedication to the Mother Goddesses of his native land from overseas, by Aurelius Juvenalis

worked in the round have wooden or wicker chairs; a number of examples of these were found at Housesteads and are now in the Newcastle Museum.[1]

In the north the army remembered the Mother-goddesses of their homelands and one relief in the Newcastle Museum bears the inscription 'To the Mother-goddesses of his native land Aurelius Juvenalis made this offering'.[2] And there they are, three goddesses sitting on chairs, each in her own niche (fig. 161). Another inscription, found at Benwell, is dedicated to the three Campestrian Mothers and to the Genius of the First Ala of Spanish Asturians by Terentius Agrippa, the prefect, who 'restored this temple from ground-level' (fig. 162).[3] Presumably this slab originally adorned the interior of a temple of the Mother-goddesses and another temple 'fallen in through age' was repaired by a centurion, Gaius Julius Cupitianus, at the fort of Castlesteads, Cumberland, and dedicated 'to the Mother Goddesses of all nations'.[4] Further inscriptions mentioning the same deities have been found at Chester, Binchester, London and other places.

Before turning our attention to certain other religious cults which seem to have been imported from the Near East, it might be interesting to consider the way in which the gods whom we have already considered were worshipped. What do we know of their temples and shrines, festivals and ritual?

Reference has already been made to the Imperial Cult and to the deities associated with it in connection with the temple at Colchester. Presumably there were also temples of classical plan in Lincoln and York in which the *Seviri Augustales* performed their duties, although their relics still elude us.[5] Otherwise the closest approach to a temple of classical pattern with its pediment supported on a row of columns and standing on a *podium* or raised platform is one found at Wroxeter in 1913.[6] It stood in an enclosed space or *temenos* and occupied one side of an open courtyard which was surrounded on the other three sides by an open colonnade (fig. 163). The rectangular temple building or *cella* was based on a substantial well-built *podium* in which blocks of stone measuring 4 by 3 feet were used. When it was constructed in the second half of the second

[1] Toynbee (1964) pp. 101, 171 *et seq.*   [2] *R.I.B.* 1318.   [3] *R.I.B.* 1334.
[4] *R.I.B.* 1988.   [5] Lewis, *op. cit.* p. 71.   [6] *Ibid.* p. 69.

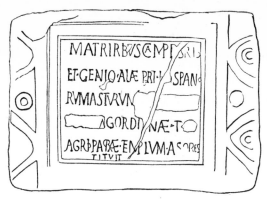

162 Inscription dedicated to the Mother Goddesses of the Parade Ground by the First Cavalry Regiment of the Asturians, Benwell

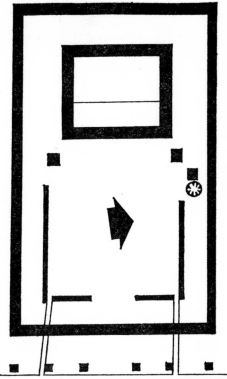

163 Plan of the Temple, Wroxeter, Shropshire

century it was reached up a flight of steps. It was decorated with wall-paintings not only on the inside, but also on the outside, which means that the outer walls were protected by a verandah with a roof supported by columns, although no columns were retrieved *in situ*. However, the top part of a Corinthian capital from a column is among the numerous fragments of sculptured stone recovered from the site, some of which seem to belong to a cornice. We must then imagine a fine stone temple standing here, the sunlight emphasising the light and shadow in the foliage of the column capitals, some of which may have supported a pediment adorned with figure scenes (fig. 164). The sculptures from this temple include the lifesize head of a horse wearing a bridle, and parts of several human figures, one the small head of a woman. Two gaily-painted bases placed on the *podium* in front of the *cella* are probably pedestals for statues. From outside, the temple courtyard was reached by an important looking entrance under a portico of six columns, probably part of a continuous colonnade, along one side of Watling Street. A temple of similar plan but standing on a raised *podium* was found at the big military base at Corbridge, Northumberland, one of a Roman type of which temples such as that of Mars Ultor in Rome or Jupiter Heliopolitanus at Baalbek (Syria) represent the richest development. The Wroxeter temple is also frequently compared with one found at Timgad

435

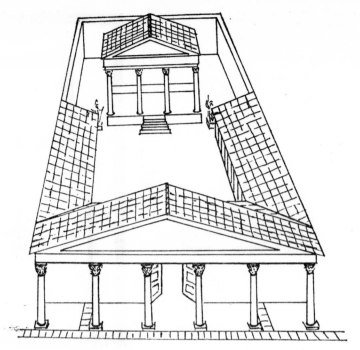

164   Reconstruction of the Wroxeter Temple

in Algeria. Another temple found at Corbridge consisted of a *cella* with a portico of five columns extending across the front and an elaborate doorway. Altogether five temples were discovered in this area at Corbridge, placed close together on what was obviously hallowed ground carefully avoided by later Roman builders and lining part of one side of the main street. Another temple area proved to be less crowded, with smaller shrines probably standing in gardens or sacred groves. Both areas seem to have been carefully planned as part of the rebuilding which went on at Corbridge in the third century.[1]

Our last example of a classical temple comes from Bath and is included not for the details of its structure—about which regrettably little is known—but on account of its dedication and the sculptures which adorned it.[2] It was sacred to Sulis, the Celtic deity presiding over the healing hot springs here, conflated with the great Roman goddess Minerva. The sculptures come from the pediment over the façade and Minerva's shield supported by winged Victories, whose feet rest on globes, forms the centre piece (fig. 165).

The shield is decorated with two concentric wreaths of oak leaves surrounding a mask, the famous Bath Gorgon, a motif most appropriate to Minerva's

[1] *Ibid.* p. 64; Richmond (1943) 136 *et seq.*
[2] For a preliminary account, however, of fresh discoveries see B. Cunliffe, 'The Temple of Sulis-Minerva at Bath', *Antiquity* XL (1966) 199 *et seq.*

436

165   OPPOSITE   Sculptured decoration from the pediment of the
Temple of Sulis Minerva, Bath

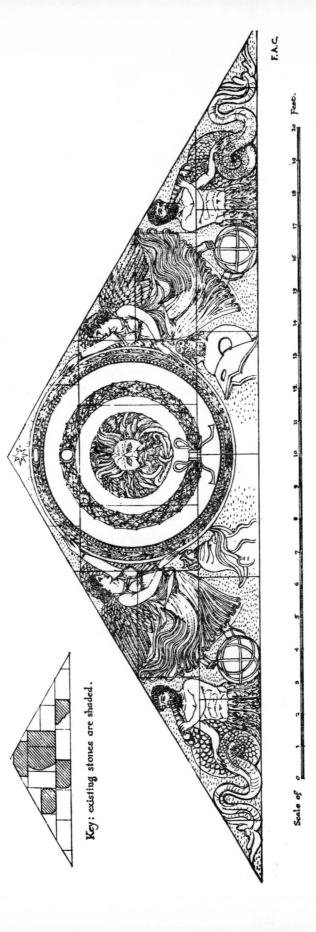

Key: existing stones are shaded.

Scale of 0 1 2 3 4 5 6 7 8 9 10 11 12 13 14 15 16 17 18 19 20 Feet.

F.A.G.

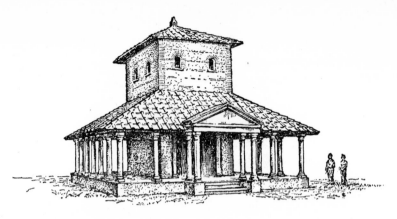

166 Reconstruction of the Temple, Insula xxxv, Silchester

shield. But this is no conventional female Gorgon, but a fierce male mask whose trap-like mouth, lined scowling brows, and huge, deeply-drilled out, penetrating eyes grip and shatter the beholder'.[1] It has two elephantine ears, wings sprout from the top of the head, and a luxuriant moustache flows into the halo of hair and snakes which forms a back-ground for the head. This is, in fact, part of a Water-deity, possibly the old god of the springs absorbed by the healing powers of Sulis or else the god of the nearby river Avon. Or Sulis-Minerva may have been believed to be the daughter of a Water-god. There are various possibilities of this nature.

The winged Victories with their feet resting on globes symbolise Sulis-Minerva's conquest of sickness, and Minerva's helmet appears, suitably enough, just below the right hand of the Victory on the left. It is a rather unusual type of helmet, however, combining the cheek pieces and false ears, which sometimes appear on the magnificent sports helmets kept for special occasions, with a bonnet or crown in the shape of an animal's head with snub nose and fins or whiskers, perhaps a seal or an otter. This type of helmet is unparalleled, but a small bronze plaque found at Lavington, Wiltshire, shows Minerva wearing a beast's pelt in place of a helmet, the animal's head being clearly visible and probably representing a British bear. This discovery has led to the tentative suggestion that behind the fantastic creature on the Bath helmet there may have lurked some idea of Minerva as a local Mistress of Wild Animals. This helmet was most probably balanced by a second helmet of similar design. Below the left hand of the Victory on the right there is a human hand apparently clutching the underpart of the outspread wing of a small rotund owl, Minerva's bird, and it is possible that these two details belong to the crest of the missing helmet. From the rest of the design only one slab survives, showing part of a seaweed

[1] I. A. Richmond and J. M. C. Toynbee, 'The Temple of Sulis Minerva at Bath', *J.R.S.* XLV (1955) 97–105.

438

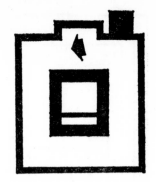

167 Plan of the Temple, Insula xxxv, Silchester

skirted torso, possibly a Triton, perhaps blowing on a conch-shell and balanced by a similar figure on the other side; suitable personages to appear in connection with sacred waters. It is virtually certain that originally the whole pediment was brilliantly painted.

Less grandiose but more plentiful in Britain were the smaller buildings usually described as Romano-Celtic temples. Each normally comprised a small box-like *cella* of varying height lit by windows placed high up in the walls; the sanctuary of a god and not intended to hold a congregation. Inside there was a tiled or mosaic floor and the walls were decorated with wall-paintings. The outside walls were also plastered and painted and they were protected by a verandah surrounding the *cella* on all four sides, and consisting of a low sloping roof sometimes supported by dwarf stone or wooden pillars standing on a low wall or platform. The illustration (fig. 166) shows the reconstruction of an example of this type found at Silchester; even when no traces remain above ground, the foundations of the *cella* and the verandah wall provide a characteristic plan of two concentric rectangles (fig. 167) which is easily recognisable to the archaeologist in air photographs or in an excavation. The foundations of another of these temples may be seen at Caerwent and other examples are known from Harlow, Essex, and Richborough, Kent.[1]

Temples of Romano-Celtic type are found in Britain in both town and country. Sometimes they seem to be isolated shrines, elsewhere they occur in groups of two or more. The majority are built with the simple plan of two concentric rectangles but some elaboration or variation is not uncommon. The temple near the theatre at Verulamium, for example, started in an orthodox fashion in the second half of the first century but later two annexes were built on to it, while internal and external colonnades and an imposing gateway were added to the precinct wall (fig. 168). The settlement at Springhead (Kent) has produced five temples with rectangular plans and one of these was of the typical pattern with the addition of a small extra room at the back. Small wings and a

[1] For a detailed study of these temples with a discussion of some variations of this type of superstructure see Lewis, *op. cit.* p. 1 *et seq.*

439

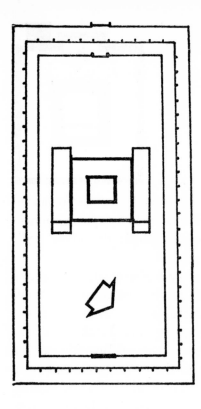

168 Plan of a Temple with *temenos* at Verulamium

porch were built on in front at a later period. Other temples are polygonal or possibly circular in plan. Octagonal examples have long been known from Weycock (Berkshire) and Caerwent, and another with a wall with sixteen buttresses instead of a colonnade has recently been excavated at Pagans Hill, Chew Stoke, Somerset (fig. 169). This seems to have been in use from the late third until well into the fifth century.

A small circular temple or shrine dating from the second century was found at Lullingstone, and two more at Collyweston (Northamptonshire) form part of a group of small buildings which also includes an octagon and a hexagon, all presumably shrines. A circular and a polygonal shrine, both dating from the second half of the third century and forming part of a larger group, were excavated at Brigstock (Northamptonshire) in 1961. A much robbed shrine found on a hilltop at Bruton (Somerset) included a small cellar cut in the rock and nearby a hoard of six bronze statuettes of Hercules, Minerva, Mercury (Pl. 53*a*) and a priest was unearthed with late third- and fourth-century coins. An open-air shrine at Carrawburgh, not far from Coventina's well, may be typical of other structures near water which may still await discovery (fig. 170).[1]

[1] D. J. Smith, 'The Shrine of the Nymphs and the Genius Loci at Carrawburgh', *Arch. Ael.* (4) XL (1962) 59–81.

169   Reconstruction of the Temple on Pagans Hill, Somerset

It consisted of a paved area, open to the sky but bounded on the south side by a lightly built apsidal wall with a low bench on the inside, and on the north by a curb or low wall and a well. An altar dated to the beginning of the third century and probably earlier than the structural remains, was found standing on a pedestal within the paved area. It is dedicated to the Nymphs and the Genius of the Place by Marcus Hispanius Modestinus, Prefect of the Fourth Batavian Cohort, the garrison of the nearby fort. A bronze statuette of a *genius* was found during the excavation so this dedication was probably maintained until the shrine was demolished by worshippers restoring the Carrawburgh mithraeum at the beginning of the fourth century.[1] Open-air shrines of this kind may have existed at many places.

Little is known about the interior arrangements of the temples, but at Great Chesterford a panel of mosaic near the entrance seems to have been intended to support a cylindrical object, possibly an altar, a column or the pedestal for a statue. At Worth in Kent two sculptured fragments were found which may belong to a statue of Mars or Minerva, as they show one hand grasping a spear

[1] See below p. 452.

441

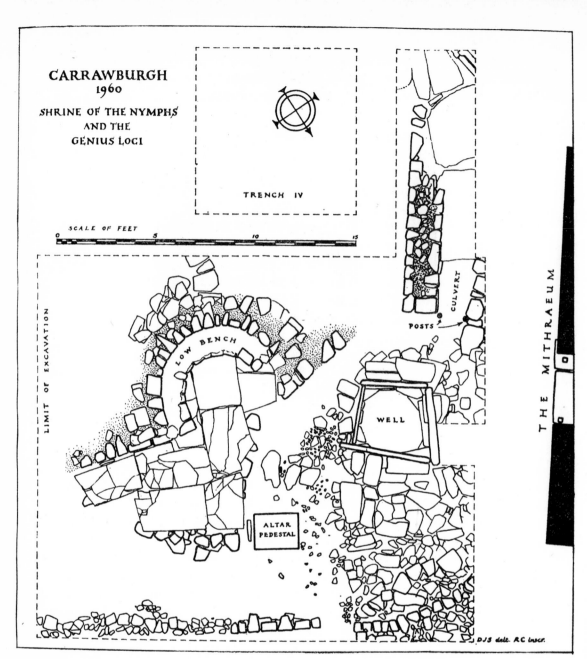

CARRAWBURGH
1960

SHRINE OF THE NYMPHS
AND THE
GENIUS LOCI

TRENCH IV

SCALE OF FEET
0   5   10   15

LIMIT OF EXCAVATION

LOW BENCH

CULVERT

POSTS

WELL

ALTAR
PEDESTAL

THE MITHRAEUM

DJS delt. R.C inscr.

170   Plan of the Shrine of the Nymphs, Carrawburgh, Northumberland

and part of another holding the edge of a shield.[1] The temple at Silchester contained a platform three feet high at one end of the *cella* and on this may have
stood two or more of the statues found in pieces on the floor. Three fragments

[1] W. Klein, 'The Roman Temple at Worth', *Ant. J.* VIII (1928) 76–81.

442

belong to legs wearing greaves decorated with lion-masks, another shows a hand holding part of a horn of plenty, and a third is a portion of the shoulder of a statue larger than life-size. Fragments of three votive inscriptions of third-century date, dedicated by the 'Strangers' Association' (*peregrini*) of the town were also found, but the name of the god they wished to honour has unfortunately failed to survive.[1] Probably here again it was Mars, shown in both his warlike and his more peaceful aspects.

This brings us to the vexed question of the dedications of these temples. An altar dedicated to Apollo Cunomageus was found in one of the sites at Nettleton (Wiltshire).[2] As we have seen, Mars seems to be a likely owner of the temples at Worth, Caerwent, and Silchester, and this suggestion is supported by the fact that two Romano-Celtic temples on the continent are known to have been dedicated to him. Outside Britain, many temples of this type are known, mostly found in France, north of Lyons, in Switzerland, and in the Rhineland, and the known dedications from these sites also include Mercury, Apollo and the Mother-goddesses. In Britain there is another site where Mercury was probably worshipped, at Gosbecks Farm, $3\frac{1}{2}$ miles from Colchester.[3] Here air photographs and preliminary excavations have revealed a sacred area with a temple enclosed by a boundary wall, dating from the second century, standing in the corner of a precinct approximately 300 feet square. This was surrounded by a colonnade with a double portico. A continuation of the north boundary to the east showed it included five shallow bays, or *exedrae*, perhaps used as shrines. The theatre stood nearby.[4] Further excavations on this site will also probably reveal more temples, sacred groves and open-air shrines, and a fairground. The area has already produced an exceptionally large bronze statuette of Mercury 21 inches high, a nude figure wearing neither cloak, cap nor sandals but identifiable by the two small wings which here sprout from the hair instead of from the cap and from the ankles as in the majority of statuettes of Mercury (Pl. 50). The arms are missing, but may have held the purse and *caduceus*, or herald's snake-entwined staff. From the position of the feet, the god must have been shown just alighting on a rock, and large triangular holes in the soles of the feet show how the statuette was secured by studs to a pedestal, while the position of the head suggests that it was talking to someone. The figure is hollow-cast and in a number of places faults in the casting had been repaired by inserting squares of new metal. While hardly large enough to be the cult figure from a temple, it may have been a votive gift. As the messenger of the gods and the patron of merchants, fluent of speech and resourceful in

[1] Boon (1957) p. 121, *R.I.B.* 69–71.   [2] Lewis, *op. cit.* p. 45.
[3] Hull (1958) p. 259; (1963) p. 121.   [4] See above p. 368.

intrigue, Mercury would be a very suitable divine patron for the visitors to the temples and fairground, and the discovery of this statuette gives us another glimpse of life at Colchester, less ceremonious than that suggested by the temple of Claudius. Beneath the temple at Gosbecks Farm lie traces of a shrine of pre-Roman date, possibly in the form of a simple rectangular hut, and similar traces have been found at Worth, under a crude circular temple at Frilford, and on the Iron Age Site at Heath Row.[1] Other temples were also found in and around Colchester and two inscribed bronze tablets suggest that one of them may have been dedicated to Silvanus.[2]

The temples have fortunately left us some concrete evidence for their existence but of the rites and ceremonies associated with them we have hardly any knowledge. The distance slab from Bridgeness is the only relief which shows such typically Roman religious processions as the *suovetaurilia*.[3] Our imaginations have only a few small clues, and knowledge of the customs current in other provinces, to inspire them. Of the literary evidence perhaps the most useful is the well-known passage from Pliny's *Natural History* describing the importance of the mistletoe and the oak to the druids. This was written in A.D. 77 so it may show us the rather milder practices still carried on by the more peaceful druids who survived the earlier repressive measures. It may also reflect earlier traditions. Pliny says that the druids find groves of oak and never perform any of their rites except in the presence of an oak branch; anything which grows on this tree has been sent from heaven and is a proof that the tree has been chosen by the god. The mistletoe is found but rarely upon the oak; and when found is ceremoniously gathered on the sixth day of the moon. It is called 'all-heal'. Preparations having been made for a sacrifice and for a banquet beneath the trees, they bring in two white bulls.

Clad in a white robe, the priest ascends the tree and cuts the mistletoe with a golden sickle, and it is received by others in a white cloak. Then they kill the victims. . . . They believe that the mistletoe, taken in drink, imparts fecundity to barren animals and that it is an antidote to all poisons.[4]

Several interesting facts are learnt from this passage: the use of groves, often holy places in the various religions of this period, the description of the sacrificial animals and the white robes. Another passage, describing the gathering of a sacred clan, also mentions the preliminary purifications: the clothing must be white, the feet washed and bare, and an offering of wine and bread made before the gathering. The identity of the god worshipped with all these rites is quite

[1] Lewis, *op. cit.* pp. 10, 49, 81, 84.   [2] Hull (1958) p. 239.   [3] Toynbee (1964) p. 148.
[4] Pliny, *N.H.* XVI. 249. Trans T. Kendrick, *The Druids* (1927) p. 89.

unknown. Bronze coins of Cunobelinus dating from the early first century A.D. depict a Celtic priest who has just completed a human sacrifice. He is walking away from an altar on which a fire is still burning. He wears some form of drapery, possibly including an apron hanging from his shoulders, and a belt, and his long hair is sometimes worn rolled up round his head. In his left hand he holds a sceptre of the type discussed on p. 446 and in his right is a severed head held by the hair.[1]

For other priestly duties and festivals we have little evidence, but the druidical custom of taking auguries may have been carried on by the priests of other cults in Britain.[2] In Rome the Augurs officiated in a special area known as the *templum* divided into squares, left and right, front and back, so that the significance of the signs observed depended upon where they appeared. Auguries were taken from the cries and flight of the birds and the word for the taking of omens is *auspicium* (lit. bird-watching). Other omens were discovered from studying the entrails of the sacrificial animals.

But if we lack evidence for the form of the ritual, we do possess a few things which were probably used or worn by the officiating priests. At Hockwold-cum-Wilton in Norfolk five diadems and a crown made of sheet bronze were ploughed up from a hole in the chalk floor of a Roman building in 1957, together with a brooch, pottery and coins of the second and third centuries. Each diadem had an adjustable headband suggesting that these things were not personal property bought to fit a single owner but were rather used by different members of a community. They were decorated with thin silver plaques, show-ing among other subjects, a male figure, a vase and two birds *en repoussé* (Pl. 58*a, b*). The more elaborate crown had cross-pieces meeting in a roundel with a spike on top of the head and was ornamented with medallions showing a male face where the cross-pieces joined the head-band (Pl. 55).[3] Two diadems of similar type were found some years ago on Cavenham Heath, Suffolk, and one of these seems to have had a now vanished jewel or glass ornament set in front. Peculiar imprints on the sides suggest that silver plaques may also have been soldered on to it. These diadems were accompanied by a headdress con-sisting of five bronze discs joined together by chains; this may have been worn over a cap.[4]

The type of plaques which may have adorned the Cavenham crowns

[1] D. Allen, 'Belgic Coins in the Late Pre-Roman Iron Age of Britain', *Proc. of the Prehistoric Soc.* XXIV (1958) 61, Pl. VIII no. 68.

[2] For an altar erected to Sulis Minerva by Lucius Marcius Memor, an augurer at Bath, see B. Cunliffe, *op. cit.*

[3] Toynbee (1964) p. 339; *J.R.S.* XLVII (1957) 211. [4] Toynbee (1964) p. 338.

remained a mystery until it was remembered that some silver plaques of similar dimensions had been found at Barkway, Hertfordshire, and Stony Stratford, Buckinghamshire. The Barkway examples were found in 1743 and one shows a war-god with spear and shield standing in a shrine above an inscription telling us that it was dedicated to Mars Alator by Dum (? nonius) Censorinus, son of Gemellus, in payment of a vow (fig. 171). Another plaque depicts the god Vulcan with hammer and tongs. Both show the shrine on a background of slanting lines and the tops of the plaques curve over as if they were intended to resemble feathers. This is another interesting feature, as such bronze feathers were also used to decorate the Cavenham crowns. The Stony Stratford hoard includes more plaques showing deities in shrines and feather decoration. One bears an inscription telling us that Vassinus promises Jupiter and Vulcan six *denarii* as a thank-offering for restored health, as long as they preserve his life.[1] A silver plaque of similar type found in London shows us three Mother-goddesses seated on a bench, again in a shrine.[2]

Also associated with religious practices must have been the remains of bronze sceptres and a miniature club from a hoard found some years ago in Willingham Fen, Cambs. The club is a unique discovery and it consists of two fragments of the bronze sheathing of a wooden staff. The lower piece expands into a swollen base ornamented with small clawlike excrescences. The other fragment from midway up the club is decorated in high relief with a bull's head with three horns, rather reminiscent of the figurine from Maiden Castle; the god Taranis trampling on a victim and accompanied by his usual symbol of a wheel, a dolphin, a globe and an eagle (Pl. 52). The top of the club is missing and the purpose of this object was for many years a complete mystery, as the reliefs and heavy base make it an awkward object to hold. Then in 1949 Professor Alfoldi pointed out its likeness to a club depicted in one of the wall-paintings in Livia's House on the Palatine in Rome. This shows a rustic scene with an open-air shrine surrounded by a curved wall or niche on which stand statuettes of the goddess Hecate. In the centre, in the place where the cult image would usually be placed, is a huge bronze club standing on a stone pedestal. The sides are ornamented with the heads of a stag, a boar and an antelope and on top is a large flat bronze disc decorated with hooks (possibly degenerate representations of griffins' heads) and hanging metal pendants, rattles to frighten away evil spirits. A golden crown set with gems is lying by the club and the shrine is believed to be dedicated to the goddess Diana. The resemblance of the club to the Willingham example suggests that this may have been set up in a shrine in the same way, but the identity of the deities worshipped there still

[1] *A.R.B.* (1922) p. 35 *et seq.* [2] *L.R.T.* Pl. 22.

171 Inscribed bronze plaque, Barkway, Hertfordshire

remains uncertain.[1] Remains of four sceptres were found with the same hoard, some of them probably ornamented with a small model owl and another three-horned bull as well as the bust of a bearded man who bears some resemblance to the Emperor Antoninus Pius.[2] A large hollow-cast helmeted bust, believed to represent the Emperor Commodus, and found at Cottenham a few miles away, may also have adorned a sceptre,[3] as may the fine head (Pl. 54) which was found with a hoard of Roman ironwork at Worlington, Suffolk. Originally this may also have been supplied with a helmet as the hair on top of the head is left smooth and unfinished and traces of iron suggest the existence of rivets. Or he may have worn some kind of horned head-dress. Simpler versions of the Willingham sceptres were found with a burial at Brough, Yorkshire, surmounted by bronze busts wearing helmets, but here the artists seem to have been inspired to depict not emperors but typical soldiers, influenced by the memory of the type of Celtic head which appears on such pre-Roman objects as the famous Aylesford bucket. Interest in this comparison grows when it is realised that the remains of a wooden bucket accompanied the sceptres in the Brough burial and that it was decorated with a very fine human bust, a man's head with slightly wavy hair combed on to the forehead, a moustache, small pointed beard, thick lips and a grim, but rather humorous, expression.[4] This small object, only three-quarters of an inch in size, is of much better workmanship than the stiff and rather inhuman heads which surmounted the sceptres; it may even have been a portrait of a Romano-Briton.

During the first three centuries of our era various exotic cults from Egypt and the Eastern provinces found their way to Rome and in time some of them

[1] A. Alfoldi, 'The Bronze Mace from Willingham Fen', *J.R.S.* XXXIX (1949) 19–22.
[2] Toynbee (1964) p. 53.
[3] *Ibid.* p. 54. [4] *Ibid.* p. 120.

were carried to the West by the army or by travelling merchants.[1] Surely the most tantalising discovery we have in this connection is an earthenware jug found in Southwark and dating from the second half of the second century A.D. This bears the inscription LONDINI AD FANVM ISIDIS, 'London, at the temple of Isis', suggesting that somewhere in London, perhaps in the bridge-head settlement itself, there was a temple dedicated to the great Egyptian goddess with all that continual round of ceremonies developed through the centuries which made its daily ritual far more elaborate in character than the observances kept in honour of any Greek or Roman god.[2]

The worship of Isis had an especial appeal to women, so it is rather a strange coincidence that, besides her shrine, the only other temple of an oriental cult so far identified in Londinium is the one dedicated to Mithras, a god whose cult was confined to men only. He originated in Persia, a deity of the Zoroasterian religion, and seems to have found his way to Italy in the first century B.C. probably brought there by soldiers returning home from campaigns in the Near East. There is one entertaining theory that the Mediterranean pirates defeated by Pompey, who were all known to have been among his worshippers, brought their god to the West with them when Pompey showed mercy to those who survived and later settled them in Italy. Virgil knew one of these pirates, a reformed character who developed into an enthusiastic and successful market gardener. To the Zoroasterians the world was the battlefield for a long drawn out war between good and evil. Mithras was miraculously born from a rock and after various adventures he caught and sacrificed a huge bull. This sacrificial act, the means by which he won 'salvation' for the human race, forms the culminating point of his legend and it is frequently depicted in the reliefs, sculptures in the round, and paintings from his temples. From the mystic blood of the bull sprang life-giving forces useful to mankind. Mithras was also closely connected with the Sun God and is sometimes addressed as *Sol Invictus*, the Unconquered Sun. A high standard of physical and moral courage was expected of his worshippers, who gradually worked their way through seven grades of initiation, each with its own revelations, ceremonies, and ordeals.[3] St Jerome has preserved for us the names of some of these grades: they were the Raven, the Bride (male), the Lion, the Soldier, the Persian and the Father. With such searching requirements the number of worshippers can never have been very large. They seem mostly to have been soldiers, with the addition of some

---

[1] For cults not mentioned here see E. and J. R. Harris, *The Oriental Cults in Roman Britain* (Leiden, 1965); Lewis, *op. cit.* pp. 115, 117 *et seq.*
[2] Harris, *op. cit.* p. 79.
[3] For a detailed study of the cult see M. J. Vermaseren, *Mithras, the Secret God* (1963).

448

merchants and higher officials in the big towns, and in this country actual Mithraea have so far been found only in London, at Caernarvon, and along Hadrian's Wall, although they must, judging from the finds, have existed at York, Chester and Caerleon. More sites will probably be discovered; there seems a strong probability that temples existed at Verulamium, Colchester and Gloucester, for example.[1]

The existence of the London Mithraeum had been suspected for many years before its discovery, because a fine stone relief showing the god stabbing the sacred bull was found near the small stream called the Walbrook in 1880 and is now in the London Museum. On either side of the god stand two torch-bearers, Cautes with his uplifted torch, which symbolises Light and Life, and Cautopates with his torch lowered, standing for Death and Darkness. The scene is set in a circular frame carved with the signs of the Zodiac and outside this are the chariot of the rising sun drawn by four horses; another chariot, of the setting moon, drawn by two oxen; and the busts of an old and a young man with wings in their hair, probably Wind-gods. An inscription on the stone tells us that it was the votive offering of Ulpius Silvanus, a veteran of the Second Augustan Legion, which was stationed at Caerleon. Among other sculptures in the same Museum are a splendid marble bust of a River god, and the marble figure of a Genius found at the same time and on the same site as the relief. These, too, would not be out of place in a Mithraeum.

These three sculptures assumed a new significance when traces of a rect-angular temple with an apse at the west end began to come to light near the Walbrook in 1954 (fig. 172). For a Mithraeum, it is on the large side, 60 feet long and 25 feet wide without the apse and the narthex, with stone walls strengthened by tile courses. It was built on marshy ground which appears to have been previously used as a rubbish dump. Consequently, some anxiety seems to have been felt about the stability of the apse and massive buttresses were built to support it. The temple was entered at the east end through a narthex or vesti-bule, the worn stone threshold still surviving, with the iron collars for the pivots of the double doors still in place. Inside, a few small windows, probably placed high up below the eaves of the tiled roof, admitted a little dim light and the worshipper, as he went down the wood-faced steps, saw an interior divided into a nave and two aisles, an arrangement which would remind us of a Christian church. When the temple was built in the second half of the second century A.D., the floor of the nave, 11 feet wide, was sunk below the level of the aisles from which it was divided by a colonnade with seven pillars on each side,

[1] Harris *op. cit.* p. 42 *et seq.*

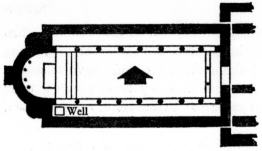

172 Plan of the London Mithraeum

possibly to symbolise the seven grades of Mithraism. The aisles at first had timber floors and probably timber benches on which the worshippers reclined. In the apse the sanctuary took the form of a raised platform and here would have stood a representation of Mithras slaying the bull. In front of it there may have been columns or some form of support for a beam to carry a curtain hiding the god, except at the culminating moments of the ritual. Altars were set up at the sanctuary entrance and a timber-lined well supplied water for the priests.

During the third century damp from the marshy ground underlying the temple caused the floor of the nave to be raised and stone benches were constructed in the aisles, largely concealing the column bases. In the final phase of the temple's history, in the early fourth century, the floor of nave, aisles, and sanctuary were all more or less at the same level and a new stone altar was installed. But before this period was reached some emergency seems to have arisen; the stone colonnade appears to have been deliberately dismantled; and from holes dug below the temple's floor, and sealed over by the fourth-century levels, the excavators recovered an amazing collection of religious sculptures, apparently purposely concealed there at the beginning of the fourth century. First and foremost was the beautiful head of Mithras himself, wearing a Phrygian cap and looking upwards as he fought his battle with the bull. This showed signs of intense heat, probably from the altar fires, so possibly it formed part of the cult-image from the sanctuary. Buried with him was a head representing Minerva, originally wearing a metal helmet which she has lost in her misadventures. From another cache in the nave came the head of the god Serapis, the curls of his hair and beard surviving in wonderfully good condition, wearing a *modius* or corn measure on his head, the symbol of fertility. Similar heads have been found in Mithraea at S. Prisca in Rome,[1] and at Merida. All these heads were, to judge by the tenons below their necks, carved separately from their bodies and had been removed from the latter for burial. From the same hole

[1] Vermaseren, *op. cit.* pp. 49, 56.

450

as the Serapis came a colossal marble hand holding the pommel of a dagger, in the attitude of Mithras the bull-slayer, but probably attached to an isolated now vanished arm of stone or stucco rather than to an enormous group. A stone bowl, and a seated statuette of the god Mercury wearing wings in his hair, carrying a purse, and accompanied by a ram and a tortoise, were unearthed along with the Serapis and the hand. All these sculptures are believed to be of late second-century date. It would seem that the concealment of these precious marble carvings was carried out by early fourth-century Mithraists anticipating an attack on the temple by Christian iconoclasts. The bodies belonging to the three heads, probably of stucco or other inferior material, were abandoned to their fate. At any rate no traces of them came to light.[1]

Another little sculptured group found among the ruins of the temple is of a less high standard of workmanship and may be of mid-third-century date. It was not buried but found above the level of the latest floors of the shrine. It shows Bacchus obviously in a happy frame of mind and rather unsteady on his feet, supported by a Satyr and accompanied by Pan, a Maenad and a panther. A smiling Silenus, bearded and clutching a wine-cup, rides beside him on a donkey. The scene denotes bliss in paradise and below the figures runs an inscription HOMINIBVSBAGISBITAM, that is, since *b* and *v* were interchangeable at that period, *hominibus vagis vitam*, probably meaning 'Life to wandering men!' A circular marble plaque showing the Thracian counterpart of Castor and Pollux on horseback, flanking a goddess who stands with a small three-legged table in front of her with an object representing a fish lying on it, was also found and dates from the third century. There were also two broken fragments of marble statues and three of British stone sculpture. Finally, a beautiful little silver casket decorated on lid and sides with hunting scenes and containing a strainer, was discovered as the excavations came to an end.[2]

The London mithraeum was unusually large and well-furnished and no doubt its second-century worshippers included wealthy merchants, officials and other well-to-do citizens. It is interesting to compare it with one of the simpler examples built by the soldiers along Hadrian's Wall in the third century, the temple excavated in 1949 just outside the fort at Carrawburgh (Brocolitia), near the shrine of the Nymphs and not far from Coventina's well. As in London, it was not a cave or underground room but a long low building with nave, aisles and sanctuary, entered through an anteroom (fig. 173). Inside it must have been in almost total darkness, air for ventilation rather than light being admitted

---

[1] Harris *op. cit.* p. 3 *et seq.*; Lewis *op. cit.* p. 100 *et seq.*
[2] Toynbee (1964) p. 315.

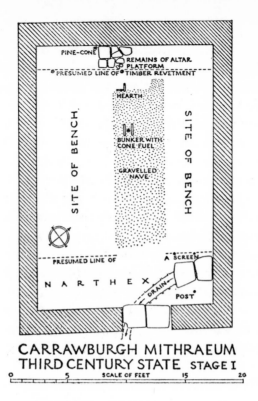

CARRAWBURGH MITHRAEUM
THIRD CENTURY STATE STAGE I

173 Plan of the Carrawburgh Mithraeum. Stage 1

through the clerestory windows. The anteroom was cut off from the shrine proper by a wooden screen, and, as in London, curtains may have veiled the sanctuary, except at the appointed moments of the ceremony. A small stone container or bunker in the nave held the remains of hazel and pine-cone charcoal and nearby a cone from the Mediterranean stone pine was found. Such cones are known to have cost a *denarius* apiece in Egypt in the third century and must have been expensive fuel to use on Hadrian's Wall. Apparently they were first roasted and then they would burn on the altars with a clear red glow and a bracing pungent odour of pine, which must have been one of the predominant impressions of the ceremonies left on the minds of the worshippers.

The history of the Carrawburgh Mithraeum can probably be divided into three phases.[1] At first it was so small (26 feet in length) that it can only have held about a dozen worshippers. The excavator, Professor Sir Ian Richmond, remarks that there would only be room for complete sets of initiates from two of the grades and possibly the cult was introduced by the commandant of the regi-

[1] Harris *op. cit.* p. 17 *et seq.*; I. A. Richmond and J. Gillam, 'The Temple of Mithras at Carrawburgh', *Arch. Ael.* (4) XXIX (1951) 1–92.

ment who only expected it to appeal to certain senior officers. But it must have prospered, as the building was extended until it measured 36 by 15 feet without the apse, and the remains of a stone shelf have been found in the sanctuary which may have supported the usual bull-slaying scene. On either side the aisles have raised boarded floors which acted as benches on which the worshippers reclined. Pedestals near the entrance from the ante-room may have supported statues of Cautes and Cautopates, the torch-bearers. Later in the period proof was found that a thick layer of heather covered the floors. Bones and other food remains from the ritual banquets were discovered on the anteroom floor and a hearth was found just inside the door, with a large stone bollard by the entrance to prevent anyone accidentally falling into the fire on entering (fig. 174). Near this hearth an oblong stone-lined hollow was cut in the floor 7 feet long and 19 inches wide, reminiscent of a coffin. This discovery reminds us that the aspiring initiate of Mithras could only rise from grade to grade by passing certain tests and there seems little doubt that here was one of the places where the ordeals of hunger allied with extremes of heat and cold were carried out, probably with the added horrors of darkness and the feeling of being practically buried alive.

After undergoing much refurnishing and reconstruction the Mithraeum seems to have been largely destroyed about A.D. 296–7. It was soon rebuilt with a larger anteroom and a sanctuary which had been reduced in size from an apse to a mere niche. In the anteroom there now appeared a small pedestal originally surmounted by the statue of a very depressed looking Mother-goddess with a jar of offerings placed in front of her. She must have been brought in from outside. An altar dedicated to the Mother-goddesses was also found placed unobtrusively in the nave. These seem unexpected deities to find in a temple intended for men only, but the Mother-goddess could be associated with Mithras as a god of fertility and the after-life. The body of a statue of Cautes and the remains of one of Cautopates were found in the nave and in the sanctuary in front of the niche were three altars. They must have been preserved from the earlier temple and were now re-erected over a votive deposit containing a Castor-ware beaker, pine-cone fuel, and a small tin cup full of chicken bones. One altar was dedicated to the Unconquered God Mithras by Aulus Clementinus Habitus, prefect of the First Cohort of Batavians whose home was at Larinum in Eastern Italy: this dedication dates the altar between A.D. 205 and 211 so it must belong to the First phase of the Mithraeum. Another prefect, Lucius Antonius Proculus, dedicated the second altar probably between A.D. 213 and 222 and he may have later continued his career as one of the governors of Egypt. His altar presumably belongs to Phase II. The third altar is believed to be still

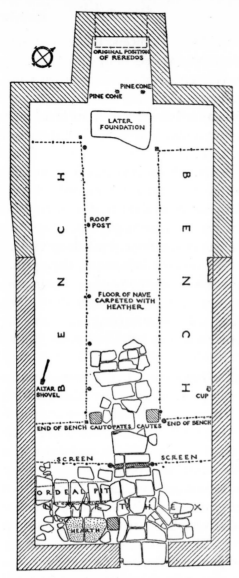

CARRAWBURGH MITHRAEUM
THIRD CENTURY STATE STAGE IIB
SCALE OF FEET
0   5   15   20

174 Plan of the Carrawburgh Mithraeum. Stage iib

later in date and the prefect who dedicated it was named Marcus Simplicius Simplex and was probably born in the Rhineland. He was not content with a mere inscription; his altar shows a relief of the head and torso of Mithras depicted as a powerfully built young man, naked except for a cloak fastened on the shoulder with a penannular brooch (Pl. 29). Originally his face was plastered and painted white and the cloak was coloured scarlet. His curly hair

454

has a halo of rays, which were pierced so that the head might be illuminated by a lamp placed behind it, giving the impression of the shining rays of the sun god whose emblem, a whip, he carries in his right hand. Mithras' appearance here is in striking agreement with the picture suggested in the opening prayer to Mithras preserved in a Greek papyrus of the fourth century A.D. 'Thou shalt see a young god, fair of aspect with flaming locks, clad in a white robe and scarlet cloak and having a crown of fire.'

These three altars remain, yet of the Mithraic relief from the sanctuary nothing survives but the tip of the bull's horn; the statue of Cautopates had been practically destroyed and Cautes had been beheaded. Who was responsible for this destruction? The answer can probably be supplied by considering what was the emergency which caused the burial of the sculptures from the London Mithraeum—violent action, or the threat of it, by the early Christians! The rites of Mithras were particularly hated by the Christians as having to their minds a devilish similarity to certain features of their own faith, and many Mithraea were destroyed in the fourth century when Christianity became the official religion of the Roman state. The prefect who was such an earnest follower of Mithras that he initiated his worship at Carrawburgh may have had as a fourth-century successor an equally fervent Christian who destroyed it. Other cults, such as those of the Sun-god and the Mother-goddess, did not arouse such disapprobation and, as also occurred at similar shrines in Germany, Mithras was destroyed while the associated cults were respected or ignored. It seems that in London enough warning was given to allow the burial of some of the sacred images.

These events then remind us that in A.D. 312 the Emperor Constantine made Christianity the official religion of the Roman Empire. The first Christians, however, must have reached Britain long before that date and we can imagine them practising their religion with many of the same hopes and aspirations that we now cherish, but in the midst of all the pagan cults described above. Literary references suggest that by the end of the second century the faith was fairly widespread, the Gospel is said to have been preached in some of the unromanised parts of the island, and the existence of the Church in Britain was known to the Christians in Rome.[1] So far the archaeological material in support of this evidence for pre-Constantinian Christianity in Britain is slight; and the most illuminating clue provided is the word square found in 1818 scratched on the painted wall of one of the houses in Corinium (Cirencester). This reads ROTAS/OPERA/TENET/AREPO/SATOR, and is usually translated as 'the sower Arepo holds the wheels carefully' a somewhat meaningless

[1] J. M. C. Toynbee, 'Christianity in Roman Britain', *J.B.A.A.* XVI (1953) 1–24; J. Wall, 'Christian Evidence in the Roman Period', *Arch. Ael.* (4) XLIII (1965) 200–25.

phrase. But later scholars have realised that the letters of the square can be re-arranged to form a cross composed of the words PATER NOSTER with the letters A and O (alpha and omega) before and after them and that here we probably have a Christian cryptogram. The same word square appears twice at Dura Europos on the Euphrates where it must have been inscribed before A.D. 256 and it has also been twice found at Pompeii, presumably dating before the eruption of A.D. 79. The Corinium house is unfortunately not dated, but obviously it is possible that our British cryptogram may be of third- or even second-century date and could have been inscribed by one of a small group of Christians who may have been living in fear of persecution.

```
            A
            _
            P
            A
            T
            E
            R
A|PATERNOSTER|O
            O
            S
            T
            E
            R
            _
            O
```

We also find Christian inscriptions appearing on a variety of portable objects. The Chi-Rho monogram (the first two letters of the name of Christ in Greek) is engraved on several gold rings from places as far apart as Fifehead Neville in Dorset and Brentwood, Essex. Another ring, discovered in the Roman fort at Brancaster, Norfolk, shows on the bezel two crude human heads face to face, in intaglio, with the words VIVAS IN DEO (Live in God) scratched beneath, added, perhaps when the ring was given to a Christian. And the inscription on a fourth ring suggests that it may have had a very eventful history. For the first chapter of it we must look among the objects recovered in excavations at the pagan temple of Nodens at Lydney, Gloucestershire, and here we find a small lead plate with the following Latin inscription reading (in translation) 'To the god Nodens, Silvianus has lost a ring, he hereby gives half of it (i.e. half its value) to Nodens. Among those who are called Senicianus do not allow health until he brings it to the temple of Nodens.[1] Whether Senicianus suffered in health or spirits as the result of this curse is unrecorded but we have reason to believe that Silvianus did not get his ring back. For near Silchester a fine Roman gold ring has been found, its bezel decorated with an engraved female head clearly labelled VENVS while round the loop some later hand has engraved the words SENICIANA VIVAS IIN DE. Mistakenly the engraver incised IIN for IN and so left himself no room for

---

[1] Wheeler (1932) p. 100.

175 Lead tank with Chi-Rho and Alpha/Omega symbols. Found near the Icklingham villa, Suffolk

the O of DEO. The meaning is clear enough but the question remains: Is this the same Senicianus, and is this Silvianus' lost ring? As a recent writer has remarked, 'Did some Christian, more zealous than strictly conscientious, steal it from Silvianus to save it from being devoted to a pagan purpose? Did he cause a Christian inscription to be engraved upon it, and did he then present it to a Christian friend, Senicianus: And did Silvianus know that Senicianus had got it?'[1]

Silver spoons inscribed with a proper name and the aspiration VIVAS are sometimes found and may well be christening presents for children or adult converts at baptism. PAPITTEDO VIVAS and PASCENTIA VIVAS may be seen on spoons from the Mildenhall treasure and AVGVSTINE VIVAS was noted on a spoon now in the Dorchester Museum. The Chi-Rho not only occurs on small objects; it is also found occasionally as part of the geometric decoration ornamenting large round lead tanks which may hold anything up to 65 gallons (fig. 175). Their use is unknown but it is possible that they may have been intended for purposes connected with religious purifications, sometimes pagan, or when bearing the sacred monogram, for baptism. Several pewter bowls adorned with Christian emblems have also been found and one from the Isle of Ely, now in the Cambridge University Museum of Archaelogy and Ethnology, has an unusually ornamental setting. It is on a shallow heavy bowl with a pedestal foot and an octagonal flange below the rim cut into points like the rays of a star (Pl. 56). These rays are decorated with incised decoration. At the top we see the Chi-Rho flanked by the alpha and omega, and on either side are crudely drawn Nereids representing baptismal regeneration; peacocks and peahens, the symbols of immortality; and an owl, denoting divine wisdom (fig. 176). Such elaborate symbolism would seem to indicate that this bowl must

[1] Toynbee, op. cit. 20.

457

176 Drawing from the flange of a pewter tazza incised with the Chi-Rho and other Christian symbols. Found near Ely

have been used for religious purposes, it has even been suggested that it may have been a portable font. On the underside of the base is an inscription, so worn that its meaning is obscure; suggested readings have varied from 'Through patience we conquer', a very proper Christian sentiment, to 'This is the property of the bishops and clergy'![1]

After discussing some possible examples of church plate, it is appropriate to consider where these early Christians held their services. Literary evidence tells us that in A.D. 314 three British bishops attended the Council of Arles from York, London and probably Colchester, or Lincoln, but their cathedrals still await discovery. Bede mentions 'a church of wondrous workmanship' built on the site of St Alban's martyrdom, a centre of miraculous cures, and this was restored and used by the converted English in the eighth century. Canterbury is another town where two churches mentioned by Bede seem to have survived from the Roman period. Excavation has revealed buildings at Silchester and Caerwent which could be churches, but no actual proof in the form of altars or objects marked with Christian symbols were found there. Recent research at Silchester, however, encourages the idea that this was indeed a church, possibly

[1] L. C. G. Clarke, 'A Roman pewter bowl from the Isle of Ely', C.A.S.P. XXXI (1931) 66–75.

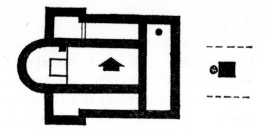

177 Plan of the church at Silchester

with a baptistery outside it (fig. 177).[1] More tangible evidence for a place of worship comes from the country and it is of a very striking nature. Reference has already been made in earlier chapters to the Lullingstone villa with its amusing mosaics and fine marble busts reverently shut away in the Basement Room or nymphaeum. Towards the end of the fourth or early in the fifth century the house was destroyed by fire. Before this catastrophe occurred a room had been built above the Basement Room and at some time in the middle of the fourth century its walls were covered with paintings. As a result of the fire, the floor of this upper room, together with some pottery and painted wall-plaster, crashed into the room below and these were later followed by the roof, more wall-plaster and part of the walls. The fragments of wall-paintings were carefully collected and cleaned and the task of piecing them together was undertaken by Mr C. D. P. Nicholson, F.S.A., one of the archaeologists working on the site. After several years his patient work met with astonishing success. The west wall of the upper room, 14 feet in length, was found to have been completely covered by a series of six human figures depicted between the pillars of a portico which rose above a dado several feet deep and covered with a design of flowers outlined in pink, red and purple on a white background. Three of these figures are standing, one figure is missing, another is standing in front of a curtain, an indication in fourth-century symbolism that this person was dead, and the last figure on the right may have been seated. They are all richly dressed and three of them stand with outstretched arms as if at prayer, the *orante* attitude so familiar from the Roman catacombs (Pl. 16a). This factor immediately aroused hopes that the paintings might be connected with Christianity and further research dramatically confirmed them. Pieces showing leaves and berries were gradually fitted together until they were seen to be part of a great gaily-coloured wreath three feet in diameter and surrounding a representation of the Chi-Rho painted in red on a shining white background. The wreath is tied with a bow of orange ribbons, scarlet seeds fall from it, and two birds, perched on the ribbons, eye the seeds. The whole scene bears an astonishingly close resemblance to the reliefs on a mid-fourth-century sarcophagus found in Rome which shows a similarly

[1] *J.R.S.* LII (1962) 185; Lewis *op. cit.* p. 108 *et seq.*

bewreathed Chi-Rho surmounting a cross. There two birds standing on the crossbars peck at the wreath, and at the foot of the cross sit two Roman soldiers. The scene obviously depicts the Resurrection, with the monogram representing Christ.[1] At Lullingstone this Chi-Rho was probably originally placed at the west end of the south wall of the upper room A, opposite the point at which a doorway almost certainly connected it with an anteroom, B, and in the anteroom another Chi-Rho enclosed in a wreath was found, with portions of an omega to the right of it.

While it is impossible to prove that rooms A and B were anything more than living rooms with Christian wall-paintings, it is much easier to believe that the owners of the villa had decided to create a domestic oratory or house-church, of a type known to exist on the continent, in this part of their house. Room A would have been the chapel with room B as an ante-chapel or narthex. Between room B and a small room, C, there was a door. C, which had once been a kitchen was cut off by a blocked door from the triclinium-corridor and had a new door leading into the outside world. It would seem, then, that steps were taken to isolate this group of rooms from the rest of the house and to give them a separate entrance. Whether the painted figures in room A depict members of the family, some already dead when the work was done, or whether they illustrate some religious theme, there is no way of telling, but work on the paintings is not yet completed and pieces of a third Chi-Rho, which probably fell from the east wall of room A, were found in 1956.

Further evidence which may also bear witness to Christian worship in villas comes in the form of mosaic floors from Hinton St Mary and Frampton in Dorset. The Hinton St Mary floor was found in 1963 and occupied a large rectangular room divided into two unequal parts by short cross-walls and a strip of geometric mosaic.[2] The smaller half of the room contained a roundel showing Bellerophon attacking the Chimaera, a scene rather reminiscent of the one at Lullingstone but here the Chimaera is more substantial. The larger half has a design set in a square consisting of a central roundel, four semi-circular panels each placed along one of the straight outer edges of the floor, and four quarter circles, one in each corner. Busts in the quarter circles may denote wind gods. One semi-circle is filled by a large tree and the other three, and also two panels bordering the Bellerophon design, show dogs chasing deer. In the central roundel is the carefully worked bust of a man, clean-shaven and with fair hair falling in curls on either side of his neck, and wearing a tunic and cloak

[1] Toynbee (1964) p. 225.
[2] J. M. C. Toynbee, 'A New Roman Mosaic Pavement found in Dorset', *J.R.S.* LIV (1964) 1–14.

or *pallium* (*Frontispiece*). Behind the head is the Chi-Rho monogram and a pomegranate appears to the left and right. The identity of this personage has been much discussed and the current view is that the bust is most likely to be a representation of Christ. To find such a rare and exciting discovery of great importance to the history of early Christian art, in the middle of a floor seems surprising. Three examples of Christ in the symbolic guise of the Good Shepherd, are known, however, from mosaics at Aquileia, and an imperial decree of A.D. 427 forbids the representation of the Cross on mosaic floors. So it seems possible that the Hinton St Mary interpretation may be correct. The mosaic dates from the fourth century, some years before the imperial decree.

If the roundel is accepted as a bust of Christ, then the other motifs of the mosaic fall into place. The tree in the semi-circle immediately beneath may be the Tree of Life and the hunting scenes in which no hunters appear and in which the dogs do no more than chase the deer, may allude to the natural world or to the abundant life of Paradise. Pomegranates often denote immortality. The symbolism of the Wind-gods is more difficult to explain but pomegranates also appear with two of them and rosettes with their companions. Bellerophon may be defeating death and evil in the shape of the Chimaera and it is interesting to recall that at Lullingstone this subject occurs on a fourth-century mosaic near the room with the Christian wall-paintings. At Hinton St Mary four chalices appear filling in the corners and so complete the floor with the Bellerophon mosaic and this is the motif which is of importance at the other Dorset villa, Frampton. Here a large country house with a fine series of mosaics depicting mythological scenes was excavated some years ago. The largest and most magnificent room includes representations of Cupid, opposite the doorway, and of a fine blue-bearded Neptune, opposite an apse built out from the square room. The apse mosaic depicts the two-handled chalice and it is divided from Neptune by a border of leaf scroll, in the centre of which is a large Chi-Rho.[1] This part of the room could have been shut off by a curtain and, if the mosaic floors of apse and square room are all of the same period, as appears to be the case, possibly we have here another Christian oratory. On the whole, this seems unlikely, but it does suggest that at some period the villa may also have had a Christian owner especially as both the Frampton and Hinton St Mary mosaics may have been designed by the same firm. It is true that at this early period in Christian art, pagan motifs continued in use and developed an increasingly Christian symbolism, the conversion of Orpheus playing to the animals into the Good Shepherd being one outstanding example; so that it is sometimes difficult to

[1] Toynbee (1963) p. 202 no. 199.

decide with what religious persuasion we are dealing. But the Christian monogram would have no artistic appeal to a pagan.

This juxtaposition of pagan and Christian motifs reminds us that even when
Christianity had become the official religion, the old pagan gods were far from
being forgotten; indeed, in the later years of the fourth century we even find
them gaining ground afresh. Several typical Romano-Celtic temples, including
the one built in the centre of the great Maiden Castle Iron Age hill-fort, date
from this period and so does the restoration by a governor of part of Britain
(Britannia Prima) of an earlier cult column erected in honour of Jupiter at
Cirencester.[1] The prosperity of the times and the experience gained from generations of building in stone is shown in the erection in the second half of the fourth
century of the great temple at Lydney, a temple dedicated to Nodens, a native
and quite un-Roman god (fig. 13). The arrangement of his temple and its associated structures as a sanctuary of healing has already been discussed; it only
remains to remark that the temple plan with its nave, ambulatory, and the side-
chapels added at a slightly later period, is unusual and original; and while it has
some features in common with contemporary buildings in other provinces, it
may also reflect the influence of the new Christian churches. Wheeler, in discussing the side-chapels, points out that their nearest parallel occurs in St
Paulinus' description of the new church he was building at Nola *c*. A.D. 400, but
Lewis considers Lydney to be a combination of the Graeco-Roman basilical type
with the Romano-Celtic temple.[2]

Other discoveries at Lydney shed further light upon the activities of Nodens.
He seems to have shared some of the character of the Roman Silvanus as a god
of hunting, and a fragment from a bronze ritual crown decorated in repoussé
may portray him as a sun-god carrying a whip and driving a chariot. Other
scraps of bronze show a sea-deity with tritons and fishermen. A mosaic in the
temple decorated with sea-monsters and fish further suggests an association with
water or the sea, and in this connection the closeness of Lydney to the tidal
phenomenon of the Severn Bore may be significant.

These reflections on the temple at Lydney make a fitting conclusion to a
survey of religion in Roman Britain. As the victories of the Roman armies in
the first century may have discredited the earlier native cults and attracted
worshippers to the conquering gods of Rome, so now the successes of the
barbarian raiders may have shaken the faith of some of the weaker brethren
among the Christian converts. Others may have turned back repentantly to try
and re-establish themselves in the good graces of Jupiter and other Roman
deities, and in this they were doubtless encouraged by the reign of the Emperor

[1] Toynbee (1964) p. 145. [2] Wheeler (1932) p. 38; Lewis *op. cit.* p. 90.

Julian the Apostate. Still others may have begun to pay attention to the gods of the invaders, and it is interesting to remember that there are those who believe Nodens to have been a god with Irish connections, or even of Irish origin. Religious problems must have provoked considerable thought among our ancestors in the fourth century and even the Christians appear to have produced a heretic. Pelagius, whose denial of the doctrines of Original Sin and the necessity for Divine Grace led to prolonged controversy throughout the Empire, seems to have been a gentle and much loved Briton who travelled through Italy, Africa and the east, accompanied by an Irish monk called Caelestius; but his views were firmly refuted by St Augustine and other authorities. In A.D. 429, they were still being discussed in Britain so vigorously that literary sources suggest that the more orthodox Britons appealed for help to the bishops of Gaul. St Germanus of Auxerre was sent to their aid and preached in several places both in churches and in the country, defending the faith against the Pelagians at a big open-air discussion. He is also said to have visited the tomb of St Alban at Verulamium. When the Picts and Saxons attacked during his visitation, the good bishop led the Britons into a battle of a different nature to that which he probably anticipated. St Germanus had been a noted soldier before he became a bishop, and giving his followers 'Alleluia' as their war-cry, he won a resounding victory.[1] At the end of the fourth or the beginning of the fifth century St Patrick must also have been carrying on his work, and, as a last glimpse of religious life in Roman Britain, we find Fastidius, a British bishop, writing a book 'On the Christian Life' for a devout British widow named Fatalis.

[1] But see N. K. Chadwick (1955) p. 253 for a critical discussion of these events.

16
Burial and the after-life

The Romano-Britons who participated in the various forms of religion just described were also very much concerned with ideas of the after-life and the burial of the dead in a seemly and proper manner.[1] They lived at a time when such topics were arousing much speculation and the ideas which we find recorded by writers in Rome and illustrated by Italian graves and inscriptions seem also to have been widespread in the provinces. At the beginning of our period Roman theories regarding the after-life were still largely influenced by earlier sources, particularly by those inherited from Greece. Some of these suggested that the spirits of the dead were either re-absorbed as part of a universal life-force, or continued to lead a dim and shadowy existence which sometimes culminated in their return to life on earth in another body, or, in the case of outstanding personalities, travelled up through the heavens and shone out among the stars. So we find Ovid describing how the soul of the murdered Julius Caesar passed into a comet which was noted at the time of his death,[2] while Hadrian's favourite, Antinous, was identified with a new star.[3] In this

[1] For a fuller discussion of these ideas see I. A. Richmond, *Archaeology and the After-Life in Pagan and Christian Imagery* (1950); F. Cumont, *The After-Life in Roman Paganism* (New York, 1959), and the references contained therein.
[2] Ovid, *Metamorphoses* XV. 840.   [3] Dio Cassius, *Roman History* LXIX. 11. 4.

464

connection several writers have pointed out the importance of Cicero's *Somnium Scipionis*, an imaginary dialogue between the two great Roman statesmen Scipio Aemilianus and his ancestor Scipio Africanus whom he sees in a dream. 'All who have saved, succoured, or glorified their country have a sure allotted place in heaven, where these blessed souls will enjoy everlasting life,'[1] says Cicero, and Scipio Africanus is described as taking his place as a bright star in the Milky Way. Here we seem to find the idea that good conduct in this world might be rewarded in the after-life and, while according to one interpretation this might be only a rather unattractive form of rarefied and shadowy existence, Cicero does show us an Africanus who is a recognisable and inspiring personality, ready to prophesy the future to Aemilianus and urge him on to great deeds.

The idea of the survival of individual personalities recurs in the sixth book of the *Aeneid* where Virgil describes Aeneas journeying through an underworld which largely follows an earlier Greek pattern although its topography is a little different. It is entered through a cave near Lake Avernus in Campania, and peopled by souls who are not dim shades but individuals who still recall their past lives. The gates of Hades are guarded by the Furies, Discord, Sickness and other evils, and also by supernatural beings such as the Centaurs, Gorgons and Harpies. Further on, the grim old ferryman, Charon, waits with his boat to transport the souls over the great rivers and marshes of the underworld. A crowd of souls, whose bodies lie unburied, wander there for a hundred years before he will carry them across. On the other side, Aeneas sees the two heroes, Minos and Rhadamanthus, judging the dead, many of whom are found suffering fearful dooms as a result of their evil doing during life, while others simply wander aimlessly through the marshes and forests. He recognises there many who were known to him on earth, among them Dido. Further on, however, are the Elysian fields where the blessed spirits live in sunshine, dancing, listening to music or enjoying various sports. Here Aeneas finds the object of his journey, his father, Anchises. Beyond lies the river of Lethe, the waters of which bring forgetfulness of their past lives to souls who are about to be reborn. Proserpine and Hecate are the chief deities who preside over this underworld and Aeneas offered sacrifices to them before he dared to descend into their realm.

From the beginning of the Empire such theories of personal survival gradually developed, and with them grew the idea of trial and judgement after death and the belief that a well-spent life would be rewarded in the hereafter. Even so, many individuals were still not satisfied, and so the various mystery religions which offered their initiates knowledge to guide them on the way to paradise,

[1] Richmond, *op. cit.* p. 9.

became widespread. Some reference has already been made to the worship of Mithras and another important cult of this type was centred round Dionysus, a god of Thraco-Phrygian origin. Fortunately scenes connected with it formed a favourite subject for the sculptor and much has been learnt from a series of sarcophagi found in two underground vaults belonging to the Roman family of the *Calpurnii Pisones*. These are now in the Baltimore Museum and date from the mid-second to the beginning of the third century.[1] They show the great ecstatic processions of Dionysus and other deities with their faithful followers, dancing and carrying torches, cymbals and tambourines. Initiates of various grades are also represented and a medley of Satyrs and Maenads with various sacred animals, depicted with a wealth of symbolism. Through initiation the worshipper could attain mystical union with Dionysus and a place in the Bacchic paradise, the Isles of the Blest, which lie beyond the furthest waters of the ocean. Religious feasts on earth symbolised the eternal banquets of which his soul would partake in heaven if it proved worthy, and wine the intoxicating ecstasy he hoped to attain in the hereafter.

Scenes of this type occur on the great silver dish from Mildenhall, with its central mask of Oceanus surrounded by a band showing the souls of the dead as Nereids, carried over the waters on the backs of gambolling denizens of the deep. The outer zone depicts their arrival in a paradise represented by the myth of the drinking contest between Hercules and Bacchus (Dionysus). At the top of the dish at this point is the handsome Bacchus, his long hair crowned by a diadem and with one foot resting on the back of a panther which looks thirstily and adoringly up at him. In his right hand he holds a bunch of grapes and in his left the Bacchic staff or *thyrsus*. A bent figure of Silenus holds out to him an empty cup. Further along is Hercules, full of wine and supported by two Satyrs and with his club and lionskin lying on the ground in front of him. On the opposite side of the dish is the god Pan, his horns and cloven hoofs clearly depicted. Flourishing his reed pipes he leaps over a pile of fruit and appears to beckon on the wildly dancing Maenads and Satyrs who fill in the rest of the space. Some play cymbals, tambourines or double pipes and another panther gallops along, joining in the fun. More of these dancers appear on the two small platters from the same treasure (Pl. 36*b*) and a lid from a covered bowl is surmounted by a small triton or sea-centaur blowing a conch-shell. This small figure, which bears traces of gilding, may be a later addition to the lid. Scenes concerned with Tritons frequently symbolise journeys to the Isles of the Blest and sometimes occur on tombstones. A fragment from a small archway or window opening found at Chester shows two tail to tail, one holding a palm

[1] K. Lehmann-Hartleben and E. C. Olsen, *Dionysiac Sarcophagi in Baltimore* (Baltimore, 1942).

and with a dolphin swimming underneath, the other holding a palm and a wreath. The left-hand half of a similar fragment shows the Triton with his seashell trumpet and a *cornucopia*.[1] Both these pieces probably decorated funeral monuments and we meet the Tritons again at Chester on the tombstone of Curatia Dinysia, where two of them blow their trumpets above the niche which contains the relief of the dead woman.[2]

But although the spirits of the dead might be visualised as living on in another world, the belief still persisted that they also regarded the grave as their home, either returning to it for certain festivals or always inhabiting it with some element of their being. The fear of failing to achieve burial after death was a very real anxiety to the living—we have already noted Virgil's reference to the unburied souls waiting beside the Styx, and the need to bury their dead was well understood by the survivors. The dead, after all, were not necessarily well disposed towards the living, especially if they had died sudden or unnatural deaths. So where affection alone might not have provided burial with all the traditional ritual, fear would ensure it. Immediately after death the dead person was laid on the ground and loudly mourned by all present, so that he would be satisfied that no one had wished to get rid of him. In the case of an important person the undertaker's staff then laid him out on a couch, dressed in a toga or other everyday dress, not a shroud. There he lay in state until the day of the burial when he was carried to his grave. Musicians and professional mourners provided by the undertaker preceded him and the family followed behind. A halt might be made in the Forum for a funeral oration to be delivered. This kind of scene appears on several Roman reliefs, such as the well-known example from Amiternum.[3]

In Roman Britain in the first and second centuries the dead were usually cremated, so on arrival at the burial place the body would be placed on the funeral pyre or *ustrinum*. In the fire the body was burnt away like so much dross, leaving the soul free and purified. Virgil describes how the pyre was built of oak and pine logs cut from a nearby forest, interwoven with cypress.[4] The ashes were collected, washed with wine and placed in an urn or other container in the grave. A funeral feast followed, and a ceremony which purified the survivors from the contamination of their contact with death. Because the ashes of the dead had now been laid in the earth a sow was offered for the appeasement of the earth goddess, Ceres. Sacrifices were also made to the Lares and the

---

[1] Wright (1955) p. 54 nos. 161, 162.
[2] *R.I.B.* 562.
[3] H. Stuart-Jones, *Companion to Roman History* (1912) p. 274, Pl. XLV.
[4] *Aeneid* VI. 176 *et seq.*

members of the household were sprinkled with water and had to step over fire.
The period of mourning lasted nine days and ended with a sacrifice to the spirit
or Manes of the dead and a solemn feast. Other feasts followed on the anniver-
saries of the death or on the dead man's birthday. During the festival of the
Parentalia, which lasted from the 13th to the 21st of February of each year, there
was also worship at the family tombs with offerings of wreaths, corn, salt and
bread, or violets. At the *Rosalia*, in May, the graves were decked with roses.

As the tomb was regarded as in some sense the home of the dead, it must
be made a suitable residence. Sometimes the dead are visualised as lying there
hungry and lonely. In some mysterious way they could partake of offerings of
food and drink left for them and they enjoyed being summoned by name.
Burial in some peaceful spot remote from the bustle of everyday life did not
appeal to the Romans. For reasons of hygiene and the price of land in towns it
was against the law for anyone to be buried in a settlement so the roads just
outside the gates of Roman towns are usually lined with tombs or cemeteries.
The Appian Way near Rome and the streets of tombs outside Ostia, Pompeii
and Herculaneum provide well-known examples of this practice and occasionally
seats or fountains encourage the passer-by to linger and read the inscriptions,
or look at the reliefs which decorate the tombs. The burial laws were occasionally broken, but in general the discovery of the graves of an ancient site may
help to indicate the whereabouts of roads, walls or gates, while an illegal burial
within a settlement arouses suspicions of foul play. A discovery of this kind was
made during the excavation of a shop or tavern in the civil settlement which
lies just outside the fort at Housesteads. At the end of one room the skeletons
of a man and a woman were found, lying on the original floor, covered by a
thick layer of clean clay. The man still had a sword-point remaining in his ribs.
Presumably the people who lived here found it difficult to carry the bodies out
unobserved so they disposed of them under the pretext of laying down a new
floor.[1] It is a pity that history does not relate whether this inn was later believed
to be haunted. Infant burials are found in settlements not infrequently, they do
not seem to have been affected by the laws.

Cremation burials are often accompanied by some material objects for the use
of the dead while others, including clothes, were burnt with him on the pyre.
Such deposits are of great value to the archaeologist as he knows that the grave
goods must all have been buried at the same time and fragile things, such as
glass vessels, frequently survive intact. Their age may differ, however, as the
objects may not be new ones and some may even be family heirlooms. Their
number naturally varies according to the importance of the person and the

[1] E. Birley, 'Excavations at Housesteads in 1932', *Arch. Ael.* (4) X (1933) 88 *et seq.*

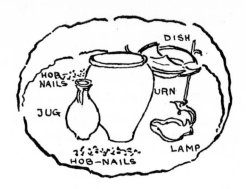

178 Cremation group, cemetery at Guilden
Morden, Cambridgeshire

wealth or poverty of the family. Consideration of some typical Romano-British
burials will illustrate all these factors.

On the Hertfordshire border of Cambridgeshire a large ancient cemetery has
been partially excavated at Guilden Morden. It seems to have continued in use
for several hundred years from the beginning of the first century A.D. until well
into the fourth or even into the fifth. Both cremation and inhumation burials
were found, with the skeletons of the inhumations lying in all directions, earlier
burials being disturbed by later. They also disturbed the still earlier cremations
so that it is impossible to be certain whether these were arranged in rows or not.
Stone is scarce in this area so presumably no tombstones were erected, unless
the burials were marked by some wooden memorial which eventually decayed.
Nothing may have remained on the surface to indicate to future generations that
they were committing the serious offence of disturbing a grave. On the other
hand, there were cases when the excavator felt that the later Romano-British
grave-diggers had deliberately chosen a site for a new burial which risked destroying an earlier interment, probably because it is much easier to dig into soil
which has been previously disturbed than into hard fresh chalk. For a typical
cremation a round pit had been dug and in it was placed a tall jar of coarse red
ware containing the ashes (fig. 178). This was accompanied by a small jug, probably originally full of wine, and a fine samian dish with the stamp of BRICCVS,
a Lezoux potter of mid-second-century date. These things date the burial to the
second half of the second century. Besides the pottery there was a thin piece of
iron, pointed at one end so that it could be stuck into a daub or plastered wall.
From the other end hung the small iron lamp which lay with it (fig. 70a). The
blackened greasy earth around it was probably caused by the wick and oil which
was spilled when this lamp was buried. Two clusters of hob-nails from the soles
of a pair of boots or shoes were also found, one cluster indicating a sole about
10 inches long.[1] Such nails were found with other burials. At Litlington, a few

[1] T. C. Lethbridge, 'Further Excavations in the Early Iron Age and Romano-British Cemetery
at Guilden Morden', C.A.S.P. XXXVI (1936) 112.

469

miles away from Guilden Morden, is another cemetery in use over much the same period, but excavated in the nineteenth century so the grave groups are not so well recorded. It consists of an enclosure measuring 114 by 81 feet surrounded by a wall of flint and Roman tile, traces of which survive. The land still bears the name of Heaven's Walls and the excavator noted that local traditions declared that it was peopled by supernatural beings. Roman cremations from Verulamium found at Everlasting Lane, St Albans, may provide another example of the survival or revival of a dim memory of burial rites in the area. The cremations at Litlington lay 3 feet apart, in rows parallel to the early, possibly Roman, road known as Ashwell Street which passes by outside the boundary wall. At the south-east and south-west corners of the enclosure heaps of wood ash, each sufficient to fill at least five carts, are recorded and these are believed to have been the sites of the funeral pyres. The cinerary urns and accompanying grave goods at Litlington were sometimes covered with a single large roof tile (fig. 179) or by several overlapping tiles. Others were surrounded by little walls of flints or placed in wooden chests, the nails and bronze fittings of which sometimes survived. On the whole the graves seem to have belonged to simple people, probably the estate workers from the big courtyard villa which is known to exist nearby, but several rare objects were also discovered. A beautiful jug of pale blue glass with a long narrow neck and a medallion showing Medusa on the base of the handle (Pl. 34), is among the surviving Litlington material now in the Cambridge University Museum of Archaeology and Ethnology. Other burials produced a small clear glass bowl and part of a barrel-shaped vessel of white glass, the latter decorated with a yellow spiral trail. A rare type of incense burner in the form of a bowl with the top perforated to form the name INDV(L)CIVS was probably imported from the Rhineland and was made of the same cream ware as a small cup of eggshell delicacy found with another burial. Metal objects were scarce but they did include iron pincers and a small shovel used for sprinkling incense.[1]

Elsewhere in Cambridgeshire cremation burials with more elaborate furnishings were found, all of second-century date and sited near a Roman road just outside the Roman town at Cambridge. During the erection of houses along Arbury Road in 1953 one example turned up with no fewer than seven samian cups and dishes piled up in tiers, the smaller vessels being placed in the larger. Near them were four square blue glass jugs, two of which at least contained calcined bones. These survived intact but a fine big green jug was only recovered in fragments. An iron lamp like the one found at Guilden Morden, and a small

[1] A. J. Kemp, 'Account of Sepulchral Vessels found in 1821 at Litlington', *Arch.* XXXVI (1836) 368–76.

179 Cremation group, cemetery at Litlington, Cambridgeshire

pottery flagon completed the group.[1] Two or three cremations were also found
at Girton College beside another Roman road and on the site of a later Anglo-
Saxon cemetery. They seem to have been buried in wooden boxes. In one case
the ashes survived in a large hexagonal green glass jug. They were accompanied
by two dishes and a samian cup, an imported pottery bowl with an unusual
brown glaze, and a lovely bowl of pale green glass decorated on its base with an
incised design showing a duck flying, or about to land, on a waterlily leaf.
Bronze bosses moulded to represent boars' heads, and bronze rings with traces
of iron attachments probably belonged to the fittings of a wooden casket or
jewel-box. A nearby rubbish pit produced fragments of worked stone, one piece
apparently belonging to a human torso, part of a statue. This was two-thirds
life-size and wearing a garment, probably a tunic, with a belt. Other pieces came
from a sculpture representing a lion. They include a very fine head, paws and a
tail. All this stone work may have come from some kind of elaborate funeral
monument.[2]

Some form of villa or suburban settlement certainly existed near the Arbury
Road burials and there may have been something of this nature at Girton. For
cemeteries on a really elaborate scale, however, we have to turn to such cities

[1] W. Frend, 'Further Romano-British Burials at Arbury Road in 1953', C.A.S.P. XLIX (1956)
25–37.
[2] E. Hollingworth and M. O'Reilly, *Anglo-Saxon Cemetery at Girton College* (1925) p. 32 *et seq.*

as Colchester and York. At Colchester many burials have been found in cemeteries lying on the south, north and especially the west side of the *colonia*, along the Roman road to London. Several hundred graves have been recorded, mostly in the nineteenth century, with the result that although many interesting objects were added to the museum collections, much valuable information was missed. On the south-western outskirts, graves of the Belgic period including the Lexden tumulus, sometimes described as the tomb of King Cunobeline, were succeeded by Roman graves dating from the first to the third century. On the north side of the Roman road as it leaves the Balkerne gate, a large cemetery lies near St Mary's Hospital. It contains both cremation and inhumation burials found during operations connected with the general rubbish tip of later Colchester and so particularly ill-recorded. The situation was further complicated by the fact that part of it may also have been used as a rubbish dump in Roman times. The most interesting facts discovered concerned the inhumations. The natural soil is sandy and on it a sheet of clay brought from elsewhere was spread to a depth of two feet. The body was placed on this and the side of the sheet was then turned over to cover it and the ends tucked in. The clay left clear traces on the sand wherever it had lain.

Burials continue along the Roman road leading to London and most of the stone sculptures in the Castle Museum, Colchester, come from this area. They include the famous Sphinx (Pl. 58) which must have decorated a tomb of some pretensions, and a small bronze sphinx and part of a military tombstone were found lying near it. In the grounds of the Royal Grammar School a walled cemetery measuring 38 by 27 feet was found, with a large internal bay along one side which probably held an important monument. Like the walls, this had been extensively robbed for building materials but a carved finial and a scrap of painted plaster give us a hint of its probable magnificence. The enclosure walls may have been built soon after A.D. 100 and, as they were 2–5 feet thick, they may have had niches for cremations. At least nine cremations and five inhumations were placed inside the enclosure, probably marked by tombstones, while sockets with traces of decaying woodwork may have held wooden memorials. The burials were made during most of the Roman period and the whole site may have belonged to one family, or to a guild or burial club. Nearby three furnaces of unusual type were found; these may have been used for the cremations.

Further along the road and so farther away from the town are some of the earliest and most important burials. The famous tombstone[1] erected by the freedmen Verecundus and Novicus for Marcus Favonius Facilis was found here

[1] See above p. 18.

with the cylindrical lead box which probably held his ashes, a glass phial and some delicate pottery. The relief gives us a fine portrait of a Roman centurion wearing a metal breastplate and shoulder plates over a tunic with short sleeves and a double kilt (Pl. 7). A cloak is draped over one shoulder and an elaborate belt is visible round his waist. Armed with the typical legionary short sword and dagger, Favonius holds his vine stick, the swagger cane which was the centurion's badge of office, in his left hand. Near him was found the tombstone of the auxiliary officer, Longinus, a native of Bulgaria who served in the Thracian Cavalry. He was aged 40 when he died after fifteen years' service, and his tombstone was erected by his heirs. He appears on horseback, wearing scale armour and riding down an enemy. A sphinx between two lions surmounts his monument. Made of oolite brought from the Bath area, the relief is unweathered and may well have been uprooted and left lying face downwards during the Boudiccan rebellion.[1]

The first-century child's grave with the twenty-one toy figurines (Pl. 44a) also comes from this area.[2] They were accompanied by 13 glass and pottery vessels, coins, bone combs and the remains of caskets damaged during cremation. They were found in the nineteenth century by George Joslin who excavated many burials and amassed a large collection including some unusual finds. Another mid-first-century grave group included a small pottery jug, beaker and oil lamp, and the bronze lock-plate and nails from a box which had contained a blue inlaid bead, rings and a circular mirror. In the second century the ashes of a woman were buried in an urn accompanied by a pottery beaker and a samian dish, ten dark blue and two purple beads, probably the remains of a necklace, an enamelled silver pendant, silver armlets and a bunch of toilet implements on a ring, including tweezers, ear and nail cleaners. A third-century grave also produced a necklace of green beads strung on a chain of bronze rings together with single faience and amber beads, a jet bead armlet, and a finger-ring and hairpins, also of jet. Spearheads are occasionally recovered from other graves, presumably those of men, and children were buried with small pots and occasionally with toys. Some of the cremations were deposited in a small tomb with walls, roof and floor each made of a single large tile.

Another cemetery lay more to the south of the town, on the site of the later St John's Abbey and the Artillery Barracks. Slightly further west many cremations and inhumations were found in 1839. The antiquarian Wild was of the opinion that some of the skeletons were buried in coffins hollowed out of tree-trunks and covered with a thick slab of wood as the nails which survived were very large, some of them a foot in length. In some cases wood still adhered to

[1] Toynbee (1964) p. 190.   [2] See above p. 351.

them. Lead coffins, one at least with scallop-shell decoration, were also found. Other cemeteries existed on the north of the town and one of them, near the railway station, produced gold ear-rings, a silver spoon and another jet necklace, as well as grave groups with one or more pots, and in one case, six glass vessels.[1]

Some variations in the methods of cremation or of interring the ashes are known from other towns. At Wroxeter several sites were found where the dead had certainly been burnt on the spot where they were buried. A square pit was made and the pyre was erected on its floor. Fragments of unburnt wood were found sunk into the floor and the ground beneath was reddened with heat. One of the excavators remarked that one side of the pit was more burnt than the other, suggesting that the flames were fanned by a westerly wind. Possibly the burial was in autumn. Another pit had to be dug in sandy soil so it was provided with a clay lining more than a foot thick which was well baked by the fire. The ashes had been collected and put in a large urn under which lay a coin of Trajan.[2] Such pits were also identified in the cemetery of the Roman fort at Beckfoot, Cumberland, and here the deceased seems to have been laid out on an oak bedstead with a feather mattress, and pinewood was used for the fire.[3] A similar type of burial in which the skeleton and coffin were apparently burnt *in situ* is recorded from Guilden Morden, but here the heat proved insufficient and charred wood and bones remained.

Some cremations were provided with unusually rich grave goods and notable discoveries of this nature have been made in Kent and Sussex. A few miles from Chichester burials were found at Avisford, Aldingbourne, Densworth and Westergate. They were mostly placed in a grave or cist lined with sandstone slabs and at Avisford brackets were made in the stonework at each corner and lamps placed on them. Shoe soles, studded with bronze nails, were found and pottery in great variety.[4] At Bayford, near Rochester (Kent), more rich burials occurred. In one the ashes in a green glass jug had been accompanied by more glass and by a bronze jug and *patera* of the type used for libations, the jug-handle being decorated with a siren in relief. There were also a bronze lamp, another jug, and an iron strigil attached to a small bronze vessel decorated with three negroid masks. This probably held oil for the bath. Six dishes, three cups of samian ware and some brown pottery complete the inventory, dating the burial to the late second or early third century. Twenty yards away another grave of similar date contained more fine glass, fifteen samian cups and dishes as well

---

[1] Hull (1958) p. 250 *et seq.*   [2] T. Wright, *Uriconium* (1872) p. 346.
[3] R. Bellhouse, 'Roman Sites on the Cumberland Coast, 1954', C.W.A.S.T. LIV (1955) 51 *et seq.*
[4] V. C. H. *Sussex* III (1935) pp. 49, 54, 67.

180 Detail from the handle of a bronze jug
found with a burial at Bayford, Kent

as other pottery, an iron lamp, three bronze strigils and a bronze *patera*. There
was also a fine bronze jug, its handle decorated at the base with a relief of a naked
man brandishing a sword (fig. 180). A cloak is wound round his other arm and
a bull reclines at his feet. The severed head and body of a goat or sheep and the
head of a boar appear on either side. Further up the handle are other animals
including a happily prancing goat and near the top sits a man holding a crook.
A thin band of silver surrounds the handle at the top and the rim of the jug is
encircled by the heads of two birds with inlaid silver eyes.[1]

   Two other cremation burials are of particular interest. They were found close
together in Warwick Square, London, within the limits of the Roman walls
built long after their interment. The ashes from one of them were discovered
in a fine two-handled urn of green porphyry or serpentine, $2\frac{1}{4}$ feet high and
turned on the lathe. It was covered by a lid with a peaked top and also contained
a coin of Claudius I, suggesting a first-century date. Near it was the second
burial with the ashes in a glass urn of rather similar shape, even to the lid. This
had been placed in a cylindrical container made of lead and decorated in relief
with a horizontal band and several St Andrew's crosses in reel pattern. Between

[1] G. Payne, *Collectanea Cantiana* (1893) p. 48.

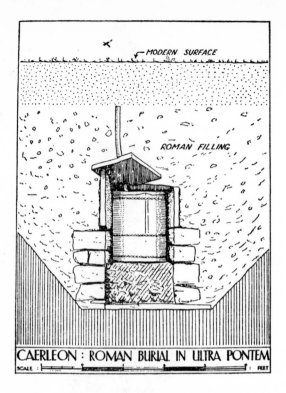

CAERLEON : ROMAN BURIAL IN ULTRA PONTEM

181   Pipe-burial, Caerleon

the crosses appears the sun, driving his chariot with its four horses. Three more lead containers were also found nearby, with simple geometric decoration. Outside Caerleon a cremation also occurred buried in a lead container, but this time it was undecorated. It was placed in a stone cist and the ashes had been wrapped in a cloth made of flax. Between one of the walling slabs and the cover slab, which had been roughly shaped to accommodate it, appeared a lead pipe leading upwards from the container above the level of the old ground surface (fig. 181). Through this, libations may have been poured. Graves of this type are known in Italy and France, some with the pipe inserted into an altar. Nothing of this nature survived at Caerleon.[1]

The change from cremation to inhumation was probably made gradually during the second half of the second century. As time went on, the change may have been encouraged by the spread of Christian ideas, but unexpectedly early or late examples of each rite occasionally occur. A cremation found at Guilden Morden was accompanied by pottery of late third- or fourth-century types and an inhumation dated to the first century was also found there. With it was a fine cream pottery jug, a small black beaker and a plate of *terra nigra* ware imported from Gaul. On the plate lay the bones from four mutton cutlets, food for

[1] R. Wheeler, 'Roman Pipe-Burial from Caerleon', *Ant. J.* IX (1929) 1; G. Boon, 'Cloth from the Caerleon Pipe-Burial', *ibid.* XXXIX (1959) 288.

476

the after-life. The fragments of a grey bowl, apparently deliberately broken as it was possible to reconstruct it, lay round the skull of another inhumation found nearby. The example of the skeleton only partially burnt in its grave, already mentioned, may represent some form of transition between the two rites.

Like most burials of this type the Guilden Morden inhumations were poorly provided with grave goods. Bronze brooches and bracelets are sometimes found in addition to the usual pottery, and a child's skeleton had a tiny bell hung on its wrist with two bronze beads. Another child had been buried with a coin of Vespasian in its mouth, ready to pay Charon's fee when it came to his ferry. This custom was fairly widespread but, even so, such coins are not found as frquently as one would expect. This may be due to accidental loss or theft, but it is also possible that the custom was only adopted by people with some sympathy with Roman views of the after-life. Even then it may only have continued in use among the more cautious or superstitious, especially as the influence of Christianity became more widespread. Superstition or old-fashioned ideas may also account for cremations of late date.

Another curious feature noted at Guilden Morden was the discovery of two female skeletons which had been beheaded after death. One woman was carefully buried lying on her back with straightened legs and arms folded on her breast. Her skull and several vertebrae, however, had been placed on her ankles. The excavator considered that her head had been severed by a sideways cut. Further examination showed that the head of one femur was badly distorted by arthritis, no doubt making its owner lame and in pain with possible bad effects on her temper. Perhaps she was suspected of being a witch so no chances were taken by her relatives in case she rose again and haunted them. This method of laying a witch is well known from other periods. The other woman was found with her skull in her lap.[1] Four examples of a similar type of burial rite are known from the Dorset area, all probably women as they were buried with little apart from spindle whorls of Kimmeridge shale. They lay in cists lined with slabs of Purbeck marble, and one had been placed in a decorated lead coffin originally enclosed in a wooden one. Again, one skeleton at least showed signs of arthritis. She was found at Kimmeridge and the formation of some of her bones and the discovery of sling stones suggested that this lady may have been an active rider and slinger in youth. Perhaps she was a keen huntress grown cross-grained with age when she was obliged to stay at home with her distaff.[2] A third beheaded skeleton found at Guilden Morden may have belonged

[1] T. C. Lethbridge, *op. cit.* p. 116.
[2] J. Calkin, 'Some Archaeological Discoveries in Purbeck', D.N.H.A.S.P. LXXIV (1953) 51; *ibid.*, 'Two Roman Burials at Kimmeridge', D.N.H.A.S.P. LXIX (1948) 33–41.

to a man. He lay face downwards with his arms crossed as if they had been bound and his severed head lay in its correct position. He may have been a criminal!

Another interesting feature occurred with a skeleton found in the ditch of an earlier Romano-British enclosure at Rams Hill, Uffington (Berks). In its mouth were two coins wrapped in a bit of thin silver foil, a silver *siliqua* and a bronze imitation. Seven more silver *siliquiae* were found further down, suggesting that they had been buried in a bag or purse hung round their owner's neck. All these coins were probably struck between A.D. 400–10 but they had been so ruthlessly clipped that the details which would date them more closely are mostly lost. The edges are so sharp that the clipping must have been done just before burial and it must have removed up to 50 per cent of the value of the coins. Apparently it was considered easy to fool the dead for the profit of the living. A similar lack of observation or business acumen seems to have been attributed by their worshippers to the tutelary deities of some wells or other sacred sites, and the excavator at Rams Hill refers to the well at Bar Hill which contained ten forged *denarii*.[1]

The lead and wooden coffins in which some inhumations were buried have already been mentioned; the most impressive and expensive coffins, however, were of stone. A short distance from the Arbury Road cremations described above (p. 470), six skeletons were found by the mechanical digger preparing the building site.[2] Four of them (nos. 2, 3, 5, 6) were presumably buried at various times in wooden coffins which had perished, and at some period after their interment two further burials were made. The first (no. 4) was that of a woman between 40 and 55 years of age, just over 5 feet in height. She lay in an undecorated coffin with its base and long sides cast as a single sheet of lead. Two separate pieces formed the ends, which were soldered in place on the inside and another sheet was used for the lid. This lining was lying in a stone coffin about 7 feet long, cut from a single block of Barnack ragstone and varying in width from 2 feet 5 inches at the head end to 1 foot 10½ inches at the foot. It was covered by a slightly keeled or coped lid which was found broken in half. After the stone coffin was deposited in the burial place it must have been discovered that it was wrongly orientated. The funeral party apparently felt it was too late to try to move it so the burial in the lead lining was placed in it reversed, with the head lying at the narrower end really intended for the feet. About 5 feet away a similar burial (no. 1) in a stone coffin was discovered. This time the skeleton was that of a man 5 feet 9 inches tall. Care had been taken with the positioning of his coffin as he lay in it correctly orientated, with the lead lining

[1] S. and C. Piggott, 'Excavations at Ram's Hill, Uffington', *Ant. J.* XX (1940) 465–80.
[2] C. Fell, 'Roman Burials found at Arbury Road', C.A.S.P. XLIX (1956) 13–23.

in its proper position. The stone coffin was found broken and lifted in two pieces, and it was only when it was being reassembled and the lead lining replaced that it was realised that this particular funeral had met with an even worse setback than incorrect orientation. The stone coffin was not big enough. Its length is only 6 feet 8 inches, giving an internal length of 5 feet 11 inches owing to the thickness of the stone, and the lead lining is 6 feet 4 inches long. One can imagine the consternation when this was discovered and the trouble there was afterwards when the time came to settle the undertaker's bill. Here was this fine coffin brought all the way from Northamptonshire with no expense spared, and now the only solution was to break it in half and pull the two ends apart to make room for the lead lining. Or perhaps the coffin had been bought in readiness for someone else and its occupant, who was aged between 30 and 45 and tall for a Romano-Briton, died unexpectedly. Fragments of a thin glass bowl lay on top of the lead lining, possibly from some offering made just before the stone lid was put in position.

These Arbury Road burials provided some other useful information. The anatomical report on the five skeletons whose skulls and/or lower jaws had survived points out that their teeth were in a shocking state, worn, encrusted with tartar, full of caries and sometimes showing traces of abscesses. The front teeth were also markedly overcrowded, so strikingly so that a family relationship between the various individuals is not impossible. In this case they must represent several generations.

Stone coffins of similar type are known from other sites in the Cambridge area and they must have been transported there by water, probably from North-amptonshire. Over the coffin which contained the man's skeleton at Arbury Road was a rectangular masonry tomb, built of chalk blocks and covered by a tiled roof. One of its foundation walls rested on the lid of the woman's coffin showing that she must have been buried first, although not necessarily long before. The tomb chamber had a floor of rammed chalk 6 inches thick and the man lay below this, a very unusual discovery as normally sarcophagi are placed in the tomb and not under it. Possibly the mausoleum was used for funeral banquets and rites connected with the cult of the dead. The closest parallel to these Arbury Road finds seems to be one of the discoveries made at the Lulling-stone villa. In 1958 a small building was found there which was at first believed to be a temple of normal Romano-Celtic type with a rectangular *cella* approached through a columned doorway with a wooden door.[1] Fragments of wall-painting, some of them showing the legs and feet of figures on a green background, occurred in the *cella* with voussoirs of tufa covered with *opus signinum*. The

[1] *J.R.S.* XLIX (1959) 132, Pl. XVIII nos. 1–3.

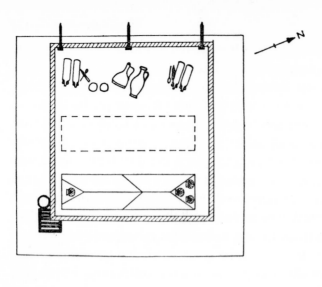

SCALE OF FEET

182 Plan of the tomb,
Lullingstone villa, Kent

ambulatory outside had a floor and walls of pink cement and a recess for an altar or possibly a funerary relief; for underneath the building the excavators found a burial vault 10 feet square cut into the chalk (fig. 182). It had contained two adult inhumations in lead coffins but one lead coffin had been removed in the late fourth century; presumably without its grave goods, as the vault still contained two identical groups, each with a glass flask with dolphin-shaped handles, a knife and a spoon. The bases of two glass bowls were also recovered and two flagons, one of bronze, the other of colour-coated pottery. The surviving coffin was decorated in relief with scallop shells and cable pattern and on its lid, near the head, lay the games board and thirty gaming pieces already discussed.[1] The skeleton inside the coffin had been buried wearing some form of leather clothing and pieces of linen were also identified. A pebble with a hole in it lay by its left hand. Originally the two burials had been enclosed in a wooden cist 7 feet square and 4 feet high which had been bolted into the clay with eight heavy 9-inch bolts and angle irons, one of which was used as a wedge for levelling one corner. Above this came layers of puddled chalk and gravel, the top layer forming the *cella* floor. As the wood of the cist decayed, the weight of these upper layers crushed the burials beneath.

One continental site has features in common with the discoveries from Lullingstone and Arbury Road: the mausoleum excavated at Weiden near Cologne. It consisted of an underground vault built of tufa and reached down a flight of 27 steps. Its walls were lined with niches for small cremation urns.

[1] See above p. 350.

480

Three arched recesses each containing a representation of a couch were found and in each of them stood a fine carved bust of Italian marble portraying a man, a woman and a girl, portraits perhaps of some of the inmates of the tomb. Two life-size models of wicker chairs were also discovered there. All these objects seem to have been of second-century date but they were accompanied by a sculptured sarcophagus which can hardly have been interred before the late third century. This remained a problem until it was realised that the sarcophagus was associated with much loose stonework and plaster, some of it apparently the remains of a barrel vault. Obviously it had originally been placed in a tomb chamber at ground level, above the earlier burials. In time this became ruinous, the floor and the ceiling beneath collapsed, and the heavy sarcophagus fell into the vault below.[1]

The Arbury Road stone coffins had no decorative features and plain un-decorated sarcophagi of their type are known from other parts of the country, especially where stone was more readily available. They are usually either rec-tangular in shape inside and out or the head end may be rounded internally. Others, specially common in the Bath area, had the head end rounded both inside and out and the sides narrowing to a squared-off foot, a plan which has been described as resembling a bath.[2] A coffin of this type containing a woman's skeleton was found near the Keynsham villa in 1922 and a rectangular coffin containing a man's skeleton lay nearby.[3] For sarcophagi with more decorative features we have to turn to town sites such as York and London.

A variety of inhumation burials interred in various ways has been found at York where the extensive cemeteries of the soldiers and civilians of the fortress and *colonia* have produced much information of interest. The road to Tadcaster in particular was lined with monuments and cemeteries and the discovery of altars suggests that there may have been shrines as well. About half a mile from Micklegate Bar in this direction is Trentholme Drive where excavations carried out between 1951 and 1959 showed that the site was in use during the mid-second, third and fourth centuries. There seems to have been an overlap of some years between the two forms of rite, as evidence was found for funeral pyres continuing in use into the third century, while the inhumations start in the second.[4] Remains of about 250 skeletons were found as well as a number of

[1] F. Fremersdorf, *Das Römergrab in Weiden bei Köln* (Cologne, 1957).
[2] H. H. Williams, 'Stone Coffins in Gloucestershire', B. and G.T. LXI (1940) 140; F. Jefferies, 'Roman Burial at Wickhouse Farm, Saltford', *Som.A.P.* XCV (1951) 106–11.
[3] Dom E. Horne, 'The Roman House at Keynsham', *Arch.* LXXV (1926) 109–38; H. St George Gray, 'Roman Coffins discovered at Keynsham, 1922', *Ant. J.* II (1922) 371–5.
[4] P. Wenham, 'Trentholme Drive Excavations', *Yorks. Architectural Soc. Annual Report* (1951–2) 20–5; *Eburacum* p. 101.

cremations. Two cremations found together may have belonged to members of a family who died at the same time. Their ashes were placed in identical urns of coarse red pottery, obviously newly purchased and fresh from the kiln, unlike the rather battered domestic vessels which are often used for this purpose.

The Trentholme Drive cemetery seems to have mostly been used by the poorer inhabitants of York. Over 5,000 nails belonging to the wooden coffins in which they were interred have been found, with only one or two pots accompanying each burial. Two stone coffins were also discovered and a bronze coin of Domitian lay on the lid of one of them. Its stonework was roughly tooled in a crude chevron pattern and it contained the skeleton of a boy of about fourteen. In shape and dimensions both coffin and lid resemble the woman's burial from Arbury Road, Cambridge, but there was no lead lining. Instead the body had been covered by a thin layer of gypsum. This custom is one of the most unusual features of the York burials and gives us a final illustration of the initiative shown by the Romano-Britons in making use of local materials. Gypsum comes from a rare mineral, hydrous calcium sulphate, which is found abundantly at Hillam, near Monk Fryston, about 15 miles from York. It was poured into the coffin as a liquid. As it set, as well as helping to preserve the inmate and any accompanying grave goods, it also made a cast of them and these casts show such details as textiles which would otherwise fail to survive. The hair, still secured with the jet hairpins mentioned on p. 134, was preserved in this way. Another coffin was found in 1932 a short distance from the Trentholme Drive excavations, on the opposite side of the road nearer York. Both coffin and lid had each been hewn out of a single piece of red gritstone and the interior of the coffin was roughly hollowed out to the shape of the body. The head and feet were encased in gypsum but the rest of the body lay on and was covered by gravel, over which came a layer of fine sand. Presumably the supply of gypsum ran out. A slight slope leading down to the level of the lid was observed by the excavators and it is believed that this may have been the ramp made when the coffin was interred.[1] Other burials, both cremations and inhumations, occurred near this area, one of them probably a child's grave as the bronze mouse (Pl. 44*d*) was found here.

Along the same road, called here the Mount, and nearer to Roman York are the sites of some important tombstones and sarcophagi. Several more stone coffins were found not far from Trentholme Drive and the inscription on one of them shows that it was bought by a certain Theodora for her son Theodorianus, an Italian who died aged thirty-five. The skull discovered inside was described

[1] C. Dickinson and P. Wenham, 'Roman Cemetery on the Mount', *Y.A.J.* XXXIX (1958) 283–323.

as being of noble proportions.[1] Near it came the coffin dedicated to the baby Simplicia Florentina.[2] It contained the skeleton of a 12-year-old child so must have been re-used. Several more coffins and a lead container came from close by. Continuing towards York the discoveries include the tombstone set up by his friend and heir to Babius Crescens, a soldier of the Sixth Legion, and further stone coffins, one of them erected to Aelia Severa, widow of Caecilius Rufus, by the freedman Caecilius Musicus. The skeleton found inside, however, was male and its cover consisted of the tombstone of Flavia Augustina. On the other side of the road lay Julia Velva and Corellia Optata, whose tombstone was erected by her father, Q. Corellius Fortis. Only the feet survive of a sculptured figure which surmounted it but the ashes of the 13-year-old girl were discovered, sealed with lead into a glass urn and accompanied by pottery.[3]

At No. 104 The Mount a funeral vault still survives in the cellar. The stone walls enclose an area approximately 8 by 5 feet and are surmounted by a tiled barrel vault about 6 feet high. The construction of this on a centering of overlapping timbers is shown by the imprint of the grain of the wood on the cement. In the vault is a stone coffin containing a woman's skeleton accompanied by two glass perfume bottles.[4] Near the coffin was a pottery jar containing a cremation. Other cremations occurred near the vault and an almost life-size stone head of a woman, probably from a funeral monument, was built on to the house at No. 86 The Mount. Still nearer the town centre and just outside Micklegate part of a tombstone was found in the cellar of St Mary's Convent, Blossom Street. It probably commemorates a young girl, Decimina, and was decorated with a small bust, with a basket of fruit on one side and a chaplet of laurel on the other.

During the building of York Railway Station more burials of all kinds were found and with them numerous grave goods. The trinkets included a variety of bronze bracelets and armlets and the ivory fragments of the fan and parasol mentioned on p.148 come from this area. Burials in other parts of York include three coffins from near the Scarborough Railway Bridge. They belonged to the *decurion* Flavius Bellator and to the *sevir* Verecundius Diogenes and his wife Julia Fortunata, described by him as his most faithful spouse. Although her husband was a Gaul she seems to have been a native of Sardinia. Discoveries in a small cemetery in Castle Yard produced a coffin commemorating Julia Victorina and her 4-year-old son Constantius. It was dedicated to her by her husband Septimius Lupianus, a soldier who had served in the praetorian guard and then been promoted centurion. Presumably he was attached to the Sixth Legion. On each side of the panel with the inscription is a charming

[1] *York Museum Handbook* (1891) p. 50.   [2] See above p. 120.
[3] *Eburacum* p. 122.   [4] *Ibid.* p. 95.

183 Roman coffin, Westminster Abbey

winged Cupid, supporting the panel with one hand and holding a torch aloft with the other. A sarcophagus decorated in this way must have been designed to stand in a funeral vault and the fact that it was found buried suggested to the excavators that it must have been re-used. Sure enough it was found to contain not Julia and Constantius but the skeleton of a man lying on gravel and covered with gypsum. Other burials in stone or wood coffins had been discovered in the vicinity and one child's skeleton found in a lead coffin had been covered with gypsum before being wrapped in a shroud, another example of economy with gypsum. Mr Ramm, in his report on the Castle Yard Burials, comments on the re-use of some of the stone coffins and suggests that the fine funeral monuments belonging to the families of the centurions, decurions and rich business men must have become ruinous and then been robbed before the end of the Roman period.[1]

One other York burial must not be forgotten; that of the woman whose stone coffin was found in 1901 in Sycamore Terrace, Bootham Bar. Her skeleton was accompanied by a small glass jug, a number of jet, bone and bead bracelets and armlets, two glass ear-drops and a mirror. With these was a small strip of bone which may have ornamented a jewel box. On it letters appear in openwork spelling out the words S[OR]O[R]AVE/VIVAS/IN DEO, 'Hail, sister, may you live in God.'[2] There seems no doubt that here we have a Christian burial and we are reminded that one of the bishops who travelled from Britain to the Council of Arles came from York.

Apart from the York discoveries, few burials have survived in decorated or inscribed stone sarcophagi. There are, however, three examples from the Lon-

[1] H. Ramm, 'Roman Burials from Castle Yard', *Y.A.J.* XXXIX (1958) 400–18, especially 408.
[2] *Eburacum* p. 73.

484

184   Roman coffin, the Minories, London

don area, one of them found on the site of Westminster Abbey (fig. 183). This is covered by a lid bearing a cross in relief, probably a later addition, suggesting that the coffin may have been brought there and re-used, possibly in Saxon times. It bears an inscription incised between two Amazon shields and this tells us that it was erected by Valerius Superventor and Valerius Marcellus for their father Valerius Amandus. A more ornamental white marble sarcophagus, found at Clapton in 1867, is now in Guildhall Museum. Most of the front is decorated with fluting and in the centre is a portrait bust in a medallion above an inscribed altar, both shown in relief. The inscription is too weathered to be legible but it may say that the coffin contained the remains of a very dear daughter.

The third sarcophagus is made of Barnack ragstone and was found in 1854 in Haydon Square, Minories (fig. 184). A portrait bust again appears in the centre of one long side and in addition, baskets of fruit decorate each end. No room has been left for an inscription. The ridged lid was held in place by iron clamps and a band of acanthus ornament decorates the front, showing that the sarcophagus was designed to stand against the wall. Inside it was the skeleton of a boy of ten or twelve years old, in a lead coffin. Unlike the linings from York and other sites discussed above, this one had its lid decorated in relief, with crossed diagonals and groups of short lines of bead and reel work. Three scallop shells are placed in the spaces between the diagonals (fig. 185c). Lead coffins decorated in this way have been found elsewhere in London, notably at Battersea and Old Ford. Like the Minories example, all are in the British Museum.

These lead coffins seem to have been particularly popular in North Kent which has produced nearly 20 examples, more than half of them decorated. The most ornamental is a cover from Milton-next-Sittingbourne showing a series of Medusa masks between two St Andrew's crosses of bead and reel motif (fig. 185b). One group is divided from the next by lions placed on either side of a vase containing torches. Another coffin from Chalkwell, Sittingbourne, had a scheme of circles, crosses and diamonds in cable pattern containing a curious

485

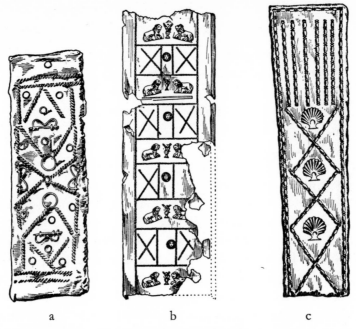

a   b   c

185 Decorated lead coffins. *a* Near Sittingbourne. *b* Milton-next-Sittingbourne. *c* The Minories, London. Found inside fig. 184

design described as an ox's yoke (fig. 185*a*). This decoration continued from the lid on to the sides and ends. Inside was the skeleton of a 6-year-old child buried with armlets of jet and twisted gold wire, and a small ring of solid gold. These suggest a third-century date for the burial which had originally been placed in a wooden coffin fastened by iron bolts. A secondary burial in a lead coffin was found in the Roman barrow at Holborough[1] and it belonged to a baby of about a year old (Pl. 60). The lid is outlined in bead and reel work and two rods of it placed end to end occupy two-thirds of the centre, forming the stem of a Y with scallop shells on either side. The two arms of the Y divide the remaining space, each arm stretching to a corner. Three figures appear in the centre of the resulting triangle. They include a naked man dancing towards the right and leading a young child by the hand, probably a satyr and a baby satyr. Above them is a half-draped Maenad with her *thyrsus*. These are all characters connected with the Dionysiac mysteries and their appearance on a lead coffin is so far unique in Roman Britain. Only three other lead coffins in this country have produced human figures as part of their decorative scheme. One from Colchester shows two individuals apparently offering a sacrifice; a lost fragment from London had two small figures of Minerva; and an interesting piece from Cefn On, Glamorgan, found in 1951, has a man driving a two-horse chariot,

[1] See below p. 494.

486

a soldier with shield and plumed helmet on horseback, and traces of a lion and a sphinx.[1] The decorative scheme of most of these coffins indicates that they were designed to be looked at from the foot or lower end. As all were intended for burial, one must presume that the spirits of the dead also inspected them from this angle.

The numerous references made to the tombstones which marked many Roman graves have already shown their value as a source of evidence for the archaeologist. With the exception of London and Colchester their erection was largely confined to those parts of the country where stone is readily available for them; elsewhere they may have been replaced by memorials of wood. Like other Roman inscriptions their wording normally follows a well-known formula which sometimes allows the restoration of missing words. They commence with the letters D.M.; an abbreviated form of the phrase *Dis Manibus* usually translated as 'To the spirits of the departed'. Then follows the name of the dead person, various information about his or her nationality, rank or occupation, and age; and finally the name of whoever erected the memorial, probably husband, wife, child, heir or freedman. First-century tombstones like those of Facilis and Longinus often end with H.S.E. for *Hic situs est*, 'He lies buried here.' H.F.C., or *Heres faciendum curavit*, 'His heir had this set up' is another common formula. Age is given most punctiliously in years, months and days. On some late tombstones, however, the formula changes to *Vixit annos plus minus*, 'Lived about . . . years', an approximate number only being given. This may indicate a Christian tombstone where earthly life was felt to be less important compared with eternity.

Up to the present York, Chester and Caerleon have produced the largest selection of tombstones, but others have been found along Hadrian's Wall and further examples, some of them already mentioned, are known from Lincoln, London, Colchester, Gloucester, Cirencester, Bath and other sites. At Chester more than sixty tombstones were found, built into the defensive wall surrounding the fortress which was probably erected at the end of the third century. They have been successfully extricated but other examples exist which it has not yet been possible to remove. Twenty-six of the tombstones now in the Museum commemorate members of the Twentieth Legion which was stationed at Chester. Ten examples erected to both men and women bear sculptured representations of funeral banquet scenes, with the dead reclining on couches with short legs decorated with mouldings and with small tables placed in front of them. Some of

---

[1] A discussion of the manufacture and symbolism of all these lead coffins will be found in J. M. C. Toynbee, 'The Lead Sarcophagus at Holborough', *Arch. Cant.* LXVIII (1954) 34, and Toynbee (1964) p. 345 *et seq.*

these couches are so alike they must surely have all been made by the same firm of monumental masons. One of them is the memorial to Callimorphus and his little son Serapion mentioned on p. 120 and this was found outside the Roman fortress and not built into the wall. With it were discovered two skeletons, one much bigger than the other and a coin of Domitian. A massive gold ring found at the same time was 'appropriated by one of the workmen, who left Chester with it in his possession next day'.[1]

Reliefs showing the dead reclining and feasting in this way are of very ancient origin, examples being known from Assyrian, Greek and Etruscan sites. As the idea of the dead enjoying life in the Elysian Fields or the Isle of the Blest became increasingly important to the Romans the upper parts of the tombstones might be occupied by the 'heavenly' banquet, while scenes of everyday life on earth occur beneath. British reliefs, however, have usually only an inscription on the lower part of the stones. They are most closely akin to the tombstones found in the military areas of the Rhineland. Like most Roman sculpture they must have originally been painted in gay colours.

Fragments of nearly thirty tombstones have been found in cemeteries outside the fortress and settlement at Caerleon. On the whole they are less decorative than the Chester examples, the majority being rectangular slabs, flat-topped or gabled. Some are simply decorated with rosettes, crescents, dolphins, etc., incised or in low relief, but two almost identical memorials show a human bust framed in a laurel wreath, a man in one case, a woman in the other. Many of the inscriptions are of great interest and four or five of them have already been mentioned. Occasionally a slab was obviously designed for two epitaphs, appearing side by side. The lower half of one such stone had lettering in both panels, unluckily too incomplete to be intelligible,[2] but the left-hand half of another example shows that it was erected to the 32-year-old Julia Veneria by her husband, Julius Alesander and her son, Julius Belicianus. Possibly J. Alesander was eventually commemorated on the right. This slab was found with others in 1815 in a large tomb about 22 feet long and 15 feet broad.[3] They were accompanied by scattered ashes, burnt bones, potsherds and a coin of Trajan, so probably the burial place had been rifled. The tombstones also included the inscriptions of Julia Iberna, Julia Secundina and Julius Valens discussed on p. 121. The remaining four were dedicated to Julia Nundina by her husband Agrius Cimarus; Julia Senica aged sixty; G. Julius Decuminus, another

[1] W. T. Watkin, *Roman Cheshire* (1886) 215.
[2] *R.I.B.* 367. A second epitaph on the right of the Lincoln tombstone (Pl. 4), *R.I.B.* 250, seems to be intrusive.
[3] *R.I.B.* 375.

veteran of the Second Legion, by his wife; and Caesoria Coroca by her husband Rentius and her sons Munatius, Lestinus and Leontius. Some letters of the last stone are barely legible so these names may not be quite correct. It is interesting to note that two of the people commemorated here are veterans and the others are all women. Their discovery together suggests either a family tomb or a plot owned by a burial club.

Burial societies were one of the few types of association allowed during the Roman period and a good deal is known about them in various parts of the Empire. They were groups of people, slave or free, who were not rich enough to be sure of being able to afford an adequate burial when the time came. They banded together to assure their future in the next world by meeting in this at monthly intervals and at festivals, and paying subscriptions, performing sacrifices and eating a meal. A favourite deity would be chosen as patron, and human patrons were often invited to honour the society as well. A new member wishing to join a society had to be prepared to pay an entrance fee and contribute an *amphora* of wine. A copy of the type of rules he would then be expected to observe has survived from second-century Lanuvium in Italy, and they make fascinating reading. No claim for burial could be allowed for a member who had failed to pay his dues for six consecutive months. If anyone died more than twenty miles from Lanuvium three members were deputed to go and arrange his burial and were allowed a travel allowance. If the society had not been notified in time the funeral expenses could still be claimed from it by whoever had attended to the burial if he sent an affidavit witnessed by seven Roman citizens. No claims could be entertained on behalf of anyone who took his own life, as even the most punctilious observance of funerary ritual could not lift the curse which rested on the suicide. Consequently his company would not be wanted by the other dead resting in the communal tomb.

The other Lanuvium burial club rules are more concerned with this life, particularly the arrangements for the dinners. Anyone causing a disturbance or quarrelling with another member on one of these occasions could be fined and—a wise precaution—'it was voted further that if any member desires to make any complaint or bring up any business, he is to bring it up at a business meeting, so that we may banquet in peace and good cheer on festive days'.[1]

Another side of this picture is provided by an inscription of A.D. 167 found in Dacia. This announces the dissolution of a burial club because the membership had fallen from 54 to 17. The master and treasurer gave notice that they had made up the accounts and returned their dues to the members. There was now no money left for burial expenses or a single coffin in store and they

[1] L. and R. p. 274.

publicly gave notice 'that no member is to think that if he dies he has a burial society, or that any request for burial will be entertained by them'.[1]

Two British tombstones were also probably erected by burial societies. One found at Bath was dedicated to Julius Vitalis, armourer of the Twentieth Legion Valeria Victrix. Of Belgic race, he was buried at the cost of the Guild of Armourers.[2] The other was found at Halton Chesters, one of the forts on Hadrian's Wall. It commemorates the slave of Hardalio and the guild of his fellow-slaves set it up to their deserving comrade.[3] There is also an altar dedicated to the *Parcae* or Fates found built into a Lincoln church in 1884 and dedicated by C. Antistius Frontinus who describes himself as *curator*. This office was that of guild treasurer and the dedication to the Fates who spun the thread of every life and decided when it should be severed, suggests that here again we may have proof of the existence of a burial society. It has even been suggested that the altar stood in club premises which were destroyed when the stone was taken to build the defences of Lincoln.[4]

By way of contrast a fragmentary inscription from a Chester tombstone, however, ends with the phrase 'He lies here buried in his own ground',[5] and this is our only British example referring to the ownership of a tomb and the land on which it was sited. A strip of land alongside the main roads often belonged to a town and the council could grant burial lots there to citizens who had rendered valuable public service. Other people could buy a plot and references to such purchases or to the construction of a grave are not uncommon in other parts of the Empire. At Ostia, Gaius Calpenius Hermes built a tomb for himself, his family, his freedmen and freedwomen, and for their descendants, with a chamber on the right of the entrance, sarcophagi on the pavement outside, and niches for urns and sarcophagi in some of the walls.[6] Such tombs were frequently planned during life, and the most detailed directions for a memorial of this kind are given by an inhabitant of the Roman town at Langres (France) during the early second century and preserved for us in a tenth-century parchment copy. He begins by saying that he wishes the mausoleum or chapel which he has already built as a memorial to himself, to be completed according to his plan. It is to be provided with an *exedra*, or broad deep recess, and in this is to be placed his seated statue at least five feet high and made of the best quality bronze or marble. A litter was to be placed at the entrance to the *exedra* and two benches of imported stone, probably marble, were to stand on either side. Two coverlets, two pairs of cushions of the type suitable for a dinner, two cloaks and a tunic were to be spread on them when the mausoleum was opened for the

[1] *Ibid.* p. 277.   [2] R.I.B. 156.   [3] R.I.B. 1436.
[4] R.I.B. 247; Richmond (1947b) 56.   [5] R.I.B. 555.   [6] C.I.L. XIV no. 4,827.

commemorative rites. The ashes of the dead man were to be placed in an altar of the best Carrara marble decorated with fine sculptures and this altar placed in front of the mausoleum. The building itself was to be closed by a slab of Carrara marble in such a way that it could easily be opened and shut. This is a rather obscure description. Perhaps it means that the stone moved on a pivot.

The tomb at Langres stood in a garden with a lake and directions are given for the freedmen Philadelphus and Verus who are to supervise the site. Money is provided for repairs or reconstruction, and three gardeners and their apprentices were to keep things in order. Each gardener is to receive 60 *modii* of wheat and 30 *denarii* for clothing every year. 'My nephew, Aquila, and his heirs must singly or together see to these things.' An inscription on the mausoleum was to give the dead man's age, and presumably his name, and also the names of the magistrates in office when the building was begun. If anyone else is ever cremated or buried in these gardens or anything occurs contrary to his directions, the dead man's heirs will be held responsible for it. The site is to be the testator's burial place for ever and if Aquila and his descendants fail in their duty they will be liable to pay a fine of 100,000 sesterces to the public treasury in Langres.

Aquila and his heirs and all freedmen and freedwomen manumitted by the dead man were to pay so much annually for the sacrificial food and drink, and four men were appointed to see that the sacrifices were performed at the altar on the first day of April, May, June, July, August and October. The nephew, Aquila, his freedman and bailiff, Priscus, and two other men were to take charge of the funeral rites. With him were to be cremated all his hunting and fowling equipment including spears, swords, knives, nets, traps and snares; tents, scarecrows, all the apparatus needed when visiting the baths including his litters and sedan chair; the Liburnian boat woven from rushes, and whatever damasks and embroideries he possessed at the time of his death as well as all the stars from the elk horns. With this last mysterious item (? hunting trophies), the list ends and the rest of the will has failed to survive.[1]

The phrase 'He lies here buried in his own ground' must surely have applied to a few tombs more elaborate than most of those we have already discussed, and some of them may have possessed features in common with the mausoleum just described. At Harpenden (Herts) a circular building 11 feet in diameter, found in 1937, contained an isolated masonry base set in front of a niche. On it may have stood a life-sized statue, some fragments of which were found lying about although the building had been heavily robbed. Outside, two cremation burials were discovered dating from the first half of the second century and the whole area, about 100 feet square, was surrounded by a wall with an entrance

[1] C.I.L. XIII no. 5,708. For a fuller translation see L. and R. p. 277.

in the centre of one side and a V-shaped exterior ditch. Indications of the probable existence of other tombs have been noted nearby.[1]

The Harpenden mausoleum may have been at least 20 feet tall but it was probably surpassed in magnificence by another tomb recently discovered at Beaufront, near Corbridge. Here again there may have been a central tower-like structure and it contained a shaft more than 4 feet deep, measuring approximately 9 by 6 feet. Nails found at the bottom suggest a burial in a wooden coffin, no trace of which survived. Higher up, a layer of soot probably connected with the funeral rites contained fragments of a pottery jar of mid-second-century date. A boundary wall surrounded the site and outside it many other burials crowded round. A pit was also found containing blocks of dressed stone, some carved, including two fragments belonging to a group of a lion devouring a stag. A fragment of another lion was found elsewhere. Possibly these groups were placed on ornamental stone pedestals at each corner of the enclosure wall. After about two hundred years the main monument seems to have been dismantled as sherds of late third- or fourth-century pottery were found in the pit with the stones. The excavator suggests that it may have been the grave of a senior officer or official.[2]

Other imposing monuments have been noted in Kent at Langley and Sutton Valence and it is possible that some of them may have been funeral pillars resembling the type of the Igel column which survives near Trier. The more elaborate tombs and the walled cemeteries are found mostly in south and east Britain near settlements or sometimes in the country near villas. At Litlington the site lay close to a large courtyard house and it included a buttressed stone tomb just outside the cemetery in addition to the grave groups, etc., already described. Other groups of burials in and near walled cemeteries have been noted in Kent at Borden and Plaxtol.[3]

One last series of burials merits consideration, those which lie beneath a large mound of earth, the barrow or tumulus. Single or multiple interments of this type in mounds of varying shapes and sizes were popular in Britain long before the Roman period, but the Romans built bigger and better ones. Whether barrow building can be regarded as a continuous tradition practised from Neolithic times right through into the Anglo-Saxon era but waxing and waning in popularity, is uncertain. Probably the story is one of periods of bare survival in remote country districts and then a revival encouraged by continental in-

---

[1] R. F. Jessup, 'Barrows and Walled Cemeteries in Roman Britain', *J.B.A.A.* XXII (1958) 22.
[2] J. P. Gillam and C. M. Daniels, 'The Roman Mausoleum at Shorden Brae, Beaufront', *Arch. Ael.* (4) XXXIX (1961) 37–61.
[3] Jessup, *op. cit.* 11 *et seq.*

fluences and fashions or even actual immigration. A mound of this kind makes a fine memorial to the dead and the Roman ones average 80 feet in diameter and survive to a height of between 18 to 45 feet. Usually they have a flat top so they may have been crowned by a statue or a tombstone. So far about one hundred Roman barrows have been found concentrated, like the walled cemeteries, in southern and eastern Britain but a few examples are known from farther afield, one being suspected as far north as Hovingham, Yorkshire, while a late first-century example was found recently at Knob's Crook, Woodlands, Dorset.[1] Occasionally inscriptions seem to allude to them. At Caerleon, Tadia Exuperata in dedicating a tombstone to her mother and brother, mentions that she has set it up near the tomb or *tumulus* of her father.[2] The same word for tomb occurs again on a stone from Colchester.[3]

Roman barrows in Britain have been very fully studied by Mr Ronald Jessup,[4] and here it is only proposed to take note of two recent excavations and the most notable of the earlier discoveries. In 1935 a man digging out a ferret from the side of a mound at Riseholme, 2½ miles north of Lincoln, found a stone slab covering a Roman cinerary urn containing a cremation. This discovery led to further investigations in 1952 which showed that this was a secondary burial in the side of a Roman barrow, in the centre of which was the burial in whose honour the barrow had been erected. This lay in a small trench and had apparently been cremated on the spot, fragments of burnt human bone being found with scraps of bronze, lumps of fumed glass, potsherds and bits of a lamp. The dead person seems to have been laid on the pyre fully dressed and wearing trinkets or jewellery and surrounded by offerings of oil, food and drink, etc. Possibly the lamp was used to light the fire and then left burning beside it. Two unidentified animal bones were also found, probably from the funeral feast. Afterwards the ashes were heaped in the trench with clay and soil and then sealed over with a layer of clay. Then the barrow was erected and sections through it showed the original turf line under the thin layers which indicate the tipping lines as the fresh stony brown earth was brought from nearby and piled up over it. The pottery suggests that this took place between A.D. 80–100 and the secondary burial may possibly be added soon after. A Lincoln grave-group of the same period may possibly come from another barrow, the most northerly so far excavated.

The custom of inserting secondary burials into the side of an already existing

[1] P. J. Fowler, 'A Roman Barrow at Knob's Crook, Woodlands, Dorset', *Ant. J.* (XLV 1965) 22–52.
[2] *R.I.B.* 369. [3] *R.I.B.* 204.
[4] *Op. cit.* 1 *et seq.*; G. C. Dunning and R. F. Jessup, 'Roman Barrows', *Antiquity* X (1936) 37–53. Refs. for all barrow sites mentioned above will be found in these articles.

barrow so that they do not disturb the original interment is one which had not previously been found in Roman Britain although post-Roman graves of this type are known to have been added. Roman interments also occur in prehistoric burial mounds. The same phenomenon was found, however, in the next barrow to be investigated, the site at Holborough, near Snodland, Kent. There the excavations of 1954 showed a mound about 100 feet in diameter, still standing to approximately 18 feet in height and surrounded by an imposing ditch up to 13 feet wide and 7 feet deep. When cleaned out, the outline of this ditch showed up so clearly in the chalk that it was possible to discern the original Roman pick marks. Some of the ditch material had been used for a low retaining wall built into the body of the mound. Fortunately earlier excavators had missed the primary burial which was now found almost in the centre. It lay in a grave cut out of the natural chalk and probably lined with branches of boxwood. The dead man and the funeral offerings must have been cremated somewhere in the vicinity and then the ashes, calcined bone, bits of fused glass, animal bones and other remains were collected. Most of them were placed in a wooden coffin 6 feet 9 inches in length but only 6 inches wide and 5 inches deep. Others were found in three small pits nearby. Post-holes showed that a flimsy hut of hazel wattles had sheltered the grave for a short time and near one end of it five imported *amphorae* had been smashed and a libation of resinated wine poured over them. When the last rites had been performed, a domed layer of chalk fourteen inches thick was piled over the grave and the hut was burnt down. Among the grave goods were a worn coin of Antoninus Pius and the iron framework and bronze mounts of the folding-stool which had probably possessed a straw-stuffed seat cushion decorated with bronze ribbon (fig. 63). Potsherds found in the Holborough primary burial date the barrow to the first quarter of the third century which is unusually late for this type of funeral rite. Other examples of it are known, however, in Roman Britain at this period. The method adopted of using a long but surprisingly narrow coffin for the ashes suggested to the excavator a cremation carried out against a background of established inhumation practice. The secondary burial found in the south part of the mound actually consisted of an inhumation, the skeleton of a small child lying in the lead coffin described on p. 486 (Pl. 60). The coffin seems to have stood on a wooden frame or bier and inside it some of the fair hair of the inmate was found with traces of a silk head-dress. At the child's feet lay a leather purse with a linen lining. As at Riseholme no great lapse of time need have passed between the primary and secondary burials. The Holborough lead coffin may date from the first half of the third century and its inmate was probably the son or grandson of the owner of the barrow.

494

The Riseholme and Holborough barrows seem to have been isolated specimens of their kind but elsewhere we find barrows occurring in groups. The Six Hills which lie beside the Roman road underlying the Great North Road at Stevenage are well-known landmarks and four barrows were found in a row near a Roman building (? villa) at Rougham, Suffolk. Three contained cremation burials, two of them in tiled cists. The grave goods included glass, pottery of early second-century date, iron lamps and traces of a wooden casket. In the fourth was a skeleton which had been wrapped in skins and laid in a lead coffin. It lay in a tomb in the shape of a miniature house with flint and tile walls 2 feet high, gabled at each end to a height of 5 feet and covered by a tiled roof. Presumably these were family graves.

Finally we come to the Bartlow Hills in north-west Essex. Nine barrows, originally arranged in two parallel rows, the western one containing five small mounds and the eastern, four large steep-sided ones. All were excavated in the nineteenth century or earlier. The majority of the objects recovered were kept at Great Easton Lodge, Dunmow, where they were unfortunately destroyed in a fire in 1847. Luckily they were well recorded and published. Nos. 1 and 2 of the western group are supposed to have contained skeletons in stone coffins and in 1832 John Gage explored the other three small barrows. In nos. 3 and 4 he found cremations in wooden chests or coffins, an iron lamp and staple and the remains of a small wooden casket or jewel-box. Barrow 3 contained a bronze trefoil mouthed jug and a *patera* with a handle decorated with a ram's head, and two glass jugs. Barrow no. 4 also produced two glass jugs, a pottery flagon and samian ware dating to the second half of the first century. Barrow no. 5 covered a cist of tiles with a cement floor (fig. 186). A coin of Hadrian lay on top of the remains of the cremation which was placed in a glass jug.

In the western group the barrows are only recorded as standing about 8 or 9 feet high; the eastern group is far more imposing (Pl. 59). No. 1 was investigated in 1815, the year of the Battle of Waterloo, and only produced an iron lamp, a bronze *patera* and a small knife, all in the Saffron Walden Museum. Nos. 2–4 all contained cremations in wooden chests with rich grave goods. No. 2, now 25 feet high, was seriously threatened when the railway line was being constructed. The remarks made at a meeting of the Essex Archaeological Society at Bartlow in 1811 have a rather familiar sound in the ears of present day archaeologists when their president lecturer says, 'The assurance of a lilliputian company setting out its nine miles of line and clearly intending to sweep away ancient memorials which belong to the nation, is only too typical of much work of this kind being done by our enlightened pioneers of progress.[1] The

[1] A. R. Goddard, 'The Bartlow Hills', *Essex Arch. Soc. Trans.* VII (1900) 349.

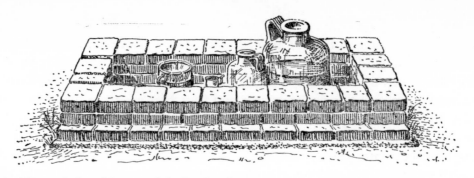

186 Tile tomb found in one of the Bartlow barrows

barrow just escaped, the railway cutting passing close beside it. It contained among other things, a glass jug too small for the ashes so some of them had to be put in a pottery jar, another iron lamp, second-century samian ware, and a fine bronze jug, its handle decorated with a female mask, with eyes inlaid with silver. Vegetable remains noted by the excavators may have been the petals of some flower, a poppy or a rose.

Barrow no. 4 is 35 feet high and its wooden chest and grave goods were found placed on a chalk floor. A similar arrangement occurred in one of the Thornborough barrows (Buckinghamshire) where the body seems to have been actually cremated on a rough limestone floor and then protected by some kind of timber construction. Very rich grave goods including two bronze jugs, a *patera*, a two-handled bowl and a lamp, two *amphorae* and glass, etc., accompanied this burial.[1] The contents of Barrow no. 4 of the eastern group at Bartlow also included a fine bronze jug ornamented with a lion's head and a claw foot, inlaid with copper and silver, and a *patera* with an elaborately decorated handle. Jug and *patera* seem to have been wrapped up in linen or some other textile and a sponge lay near them. The bones of a bird, probably a chicken, were found in a samian dish of second-century date. Traces of vegetation showed that leaves, probably of box, had been thrown into the tomb before the glass jug with the ashes was placed in it and a wreath may have been twined round an iron lamp.

Barrow no. 3 stands no less than 45 feet high. The cremation was placed on a slightly raised chalk platform and it contained the most interesting objects of all. They included two long-necked glass perfume bottles, two bronze strigils for the bath, traces of a wooden casket, three glass jugs, late first-century samian ware and a small *amphora*. A bronze *patera*, its long handle ending in a ram's head, a lamp with a lid and an acanthus leaf shielding the handle from the heat also occurred. Another bronze jug had a chased design round its neck picked out in silver, and its handle was decorated along the rim with a sphinx resting

[1] J. Liversidge, 'The Thornborough Barrow', *Records of Bucks.* XVI (1954) 29–32.

187 Bronze jug from one of the Bartlow barrows

its forefeet on two birds. A bull's head in relief appears where the handle joins the body of the jug (fig. 187). A bronze casket inlaid with red, green and blue enamel was a unique find and, finally, there was another folding stool of Holborough type with fragments of its leather seat still adhering to the seat bars.[1]

While the majority of the barrow burials in Britain are of second-century date a few may go back to the first century A.D.[2] and an occasional example, like the tomb-house at Rougham or the barrows excavated at Holborough and Richborough, may belong to the third century. Individual Bartlow Hills were probably being erected during most of this period so they may represent the last resting-places of several generations of a single rich and powerful family. Barrows 3 and 4 of the smaller western group appear to be the earliest, followed by no. 5 and the four large barrows on the east as the family grew more affluent. By the time the stone coffins were placed in nos. 1 and 2 of the western group their prosperity may have been declining. Where these people lived is a problem. A small villa found nearby seems far too small and unimportant. Possibly more of it or another house await discovery unless the Bartlow family returned to bury their dead near their original ancestral home. A larger house is known at Hadstock a few miles away, but nothing on the scale we should expect to produce burials of such magnificence. A similar problem exists in relation to a rich group of three bronze jugs and some glass found in a Romano-British cemetery at Hauxton. One glass vessel is the slender vase already described

[1] The best accounts of the Bartlow excavations are those by J. Gage in *Arch.* XXV (1834) 1–23; XXVI (1836) 300–17; XXVII (1840) 1–6; XXIX (1842) 1–4.
[2] E.g. a small barrow of Flavian date at Woodlands, Dorset. *J.R.S.* L (1960) 232.

(Pl. 34), and the whole group might very well come from an unrecorded barrow now destroyed.[1]

We have considered the possibility that a predilection for barrow building in Britain may have lingered on sporadically from prehistoric times and then been encouraged to burst forth into renewed vigour by foreign influences. When we look for the source of such influences we have not far to seek. Across the North Sea many of the great series of Roman barrows in Belgium lie along a line between Bavai and Tongres, a section of the main road from Cologne to Boulogne which was built for the invasion of Britain. Like the British examples they occur singly or in groups and they have the same form with a top like a flattened cone. When they have escaped robbery their contents are frequently spectacular. Table services of bronze and pottery, some with the remains of food offerings of meat, fish or poultry are customary, together with the bronze jug and *patera* for libations so frequently mentioned in Britain. Glass, oil and perfume bottles, and strigils for the bath also occur. The Herstal barrow, not far from Tongres, contained a bronze casket of the same shape as the one found at Bartlow, but here the decoration consists of figures of philosophers shown in relief instead of enamelling. Finds from one of a group of three barrows at Tirlemont (Brabant) included a bronze ring with the inscription *concorde commun(ioni)* which must have been given to a girl at her betrothal. Another assemblage of grave goods from two barrows at Cortil-Noirmont (Brabant) included a lizard of rock crystal, its claws and scales perfectly carved, and also a piece of amber decorated with a shell and a winged monster, carved in relief, another symbol of the journey to the Isles of the Blest.

Some Belgian barrows, however, show signs of different traditions, and outstanding among them is the magnificent tomb at Antoing near Tournai. Here the earth was piled inside a circular retaining wall of blocks of Tournai marble resting on a broader foundation, and covering a subterranean passage-way leading to two chambers with niches. Unfortunately the tomb had been robbed, but it has been dated to the early second century and a walled cemetery has been found close beside it. The existence of the important stone quarrying industry round Tournai must be one reason for stone built tombs in this area, but examples have also been found near Trier. They may have been partly inspired by the large Italian mausolea and are more the result of Roman influence than of native tradition.[2]

---

[1] J. Liversidge, 'Roman Discoveries from Hauxton', C.A.S.P. LI (1958) 7–17.

[2] Dunning and Jessup, *op. cit.* 42; De Loë, *Belgique Ancienne* III (Brussels, 1937) p. 94 (Tirlemont); p. 145 (Herstal) ; M. Amand, 'Roman Barrows in Belgium', *Analecta Archaeologica: Festschrift Fritz Fremersdorf* (1960) 70. Further references to Antoing will be found in *L'Antiquité Classique* XXIII (1954) 446, Pl. IV; *Ann. 36e Cong. Fed. Arch. et Hist. Belgique (1956), 160.*

498

In Britain there is also a little evidence for tombs with circular retaining walls of masonry. Examples have been found as far afield as Pulborough (Sussex) and High Rochester (Northumberland).[1] At Keston (Kent) the flint and tile walls had six external buttresses which may have supported statues, and an entrance 2·5 feet wide on one side. The interior may have been plastered and painted as a small fragment of wall-painting with a geometric design was discovered there.[2] And at West Mersea (Essex), the circular wall was 65 feet in diameter with twelve external buttresses and six internal walls radiating out like the spokes of a wheel from a central hexagonal chamber.[3] This has also been compared with tombs along the Appian Way and elsewhere in Rome.

So once again we find the theme which has kept recurring throughout these pages: some ideas which may have come straight from Rome and others strongly influenced by customs emanating from North-Western Europe or even farther afield. All crossed the seas to mingle with traditions inherited from prehistoric times. Together they made up the life of those who lived in that province of the Roman Empire known as *Britannia*. We know them as our ancestors, the people of Roman Britain.

[1] P. J. Martin, 'Stane Street Causeway', *Sus.A.C.* XI (1859) 127–46; R. C. Bosanquet, 'The Roman Tombs near High Rochester', *Proc. Soc. of Ant., Newcastle-on-Tyne* (4) VI (1935) 246–51.
[2] R. F. Jessup, *J.B.A.A.* XXII. 24.
[3] A. W. Clapham, 'Roman mausolea of the "cartwheel" type', *Arch. J.* LXXIX (1922) 93–100.

Bibliography and abbreviations

A.A.S.R. *Reports of the Associated Architectural Societies.*

Abbott, F., and Johnson, A. C. *Municipal Administration in the Roman Empire* (Princeton, 1926).

A.J.A. American Journal of Archaeology.

Allen, H. Warner, *A History of Wine* (1961).

Ant.J. The Antiquaries Journal.

A.R.B. (1964) *British Museum Guide to the Antiquities of Roman Britain* (1964).

Arch. Archaeologia.

Arch. Ael. Archaeologia Aeliana. Newcastle-upon-Tyne; first to fourth series.

Arch. Camb. Archaeologia Cambrensis.

Arch. Cant. Archaeologia Cantiana.

Arch. J. The Archaeological Journal.

Arch. N.L. The Archaeological News Letter.

Askew, G. *The Coinage of Roman Britain* (1951).

Atkinson, D. (1942) *Report on the Excavations at Wroxeter*, 1923–7 (Oxford, 1942).

Aymard, M. *Les Chasses romaines* (Paris, 1961).

Balsdon, J. P. V. D. *Roman Women* (1962).
                        The Romans (1965).

Barclay, W. (1959) *Educational Ideals in the Ancient World* (1959).

B.A.S.T.P. *Birmingham Archaeological Society Transactions and Proceedings.*

Beare, W. *The Roman Stage* (1955).

Behn, F. (1912) 'Die Musik im römischen Heeres', *Mainzer Zeitschrift* VII (1912) 36 *et seq.*; (1954) *Musikleben im Altertum und frühen Mittelalter* (Stuttgart, 1954).

B.G. Julius Caesar, *De Bello Gallico.*

B. and G.T. *Bristol and Gloucestershire Archaeological Society Proceedings.* Gloucester.

Bieber, M. *The History of the Greek and Roman Theater* (Princeton, 1961).

Birley, A. (1964) *Life in Roman Britain* (1964).

Birley, E. *Roman Britain and the Roman Army* (Kendal, 1961).

Bishop, W. J. *The Early History of Surgery* (1960).

B.J. Bonner Jahrbücher.

Blanchet, A. *Inventaire des mosaiques de la Gaule et de l'Afrique* (Paris 1909–10).
   Étude sur la décoration des edifices de la Gaule romaine (Paris, 1913).

B.M.G.R.L. *British Museum Guide to Greek and Roman Life* (1922).

Bogaers, J. *De Gallo-Romeinse Tempels te Elst* (The Hague, 1955).

Bonnard, L. *La Navigation intérieure de la Gaule a l'époque gallo-romaine* (Paris, 1913).

Boon, G. (1957) *Roman Silchester* (1957).

Bowen, C. *Ancient Fields* (1963).

Brion, M. *Pompeii and Herculaneum: the Glory and the Grief* (Toronto, 1960).

Brogan, O. (1953) *Roman Gaul* (1953).

Buchner, A. *Musical Instruments through the Ages* (1961).

Buckman, J., and Newmarch, C. H. *Illustrations of the Remains of Roman Art in Cirencester* (1850).

Burn, A. R. (1932) *The Romans in Britain* (Oxford, 1932)
        Agricola and Roman Britain (1953).

Bushe-Fox, J. P. (1914) *Second Report on the Excavations on the Site of the Roman Town at Wroxeter, Shropshire, 1914.* (Reports of the Research Committee of the Society of Antiquaries of London, II, Oxford, 1914.)

— (1916) *Third Report on the Excavations on the Site of the Roman Town at Wroxeter, Shropshire, 1914.* (Reports of the Research Committee of the Society of Antiquaries of London, IV, Oxford, 1916.)

— (1949) *Fourth Report on the Excavation of the Roman Fort at Richborough.* (Reports of the Research Committee of the Society of Antiquaries of London, XVI, Oxford, 1949.)

Butler, A. J. *Sport in Classic Times* (1930).

Calza, G. *La Necropoli del porto di Roma nell'Isola Sacra* (Rome, 1940).

Carcopino, J. (1956) *Daily Life in Ancient Rome* (1956).

Casarini, A. *La Medicina militare nella leggenda e nella storia* (Rome, 1929).

Casson, L. *Ancient Mariners* (1959).

C.A.S.P. *Cambridge Antiquarian Society Proceedings.*

Chadwick, J., and Mann, W. N. *The Medical Work of Hippocrates* (Oxford, 1950).

Chadwick, N. K. (1955) *Poetry and Letters in Early Christian Gaul* (1955).
        The Druids (Cardiff, 1966).

Chadwick, N. K. ed. *Studies in Early British History* (Cambridge, 1954).

C.I.L., *Corpus Inscriptionum Latinarum.*

Clark, D. L. *Rhetoric in Graeco-Roman Education* (New York, 1957).

Clark, J. G. D. *Prehistoric Europe* (1965).

Clarke, M. L. *Rhetoric at Rome* (1953).

Clarke, R. R. *East Anglia* (1960).

Collingwood, R. *Archaeology of Roman Britain* (1930). (New edition ed. I. A. Richmond forthcoming.)

Collingwood, R., and Myres, J. N. L. *Roman Britain and the English Settlements* (1956).

Corder, P. (1954) *The Roman Town and Villa at Great Casterton, Second Report* (Nottingham, 1954).

Corder, P., and Kirk, J. (1932) *The Roman Villa at Langton near Malton, Yorkshire* (Leeds, 1932).

Cumont, F. *The After-Life in Roman Paganism* (New York, 1959).

Curle, J. (1911) *A Roman Frontier Post and its People. Newstead* (Glasgow, 1911).

C.W.A.S.T. *Cumberland and Westmorland Antiquarian Society Transactions.*

Davies, O. *Roman Mines in Europe* (1935).

Dessau, H. ed. *Inscriptiones Latinae Selectae* (Berlin, 1892–1916).

Diolé, P. *4,000 Years under the Sea* (1952).

D.N.H.A.S.P. *Proceedings of the Dorset Natural History and Antiquarian Field Club* or *of the Dorset Natural History and Archaeological Society.*

Duval, P.-M. (1952) *La Vie quotidienne en Gaule pendant la paix romaine* (Paris, 1952).

Bibliography and abbreviations

E. Ésperandieu, E. *Bas-Reliefs de la Gaule romaine* (1907–38).

E. Germanie. Ésperandieu, E. *Bas-Reliefs de la Germanie romaine* (1931).

Eburacum. Roman York. An Inventory of the Historical Monuments in the City of York (Royal Commission on Historical Monuments, England, 1962).

Eydoux, H. P. (1962) *La France antique* (Paris, 1962).

Flower, B., and Rosenbaum, E. *Apicius: The Roman Cookery Book* (1958).

Forbes, R. J. *Studies in Ancient Technology* (Leiden, 1955–63).

Fox, A. *Roman Exeter* (Manchester, 1952).

Frank, T. ed. *An Economic Survey of Ancient Rome* (Baltimore, 1933–40).

Fremersdorf, F. *Das Römergrab in Weiden, bei Köln* (Cologne, 1952).

Frere S. S. (1961) 'Civitas, a Myth?' *Antiquity* XXXV (1961) 29–36.

— (1962) 'Excavations at Verulamium, 1961', *Ant.J.* XLII (1962) 148–59.

— (1964a) 'Verulamium—Then and Now', *Bull. of the Institute of Archaeology* IV (1964) 61–82.

— (1964b) 'Verulamium, Three Roman Cities', *Antiquity* XXXVIII (1964) 103–12.

Gardiner, E. N. *Athletics of the Ancient World* (Oxford, 1930).

G.M. Gentleman's Magazine.

Goodman, W. L. *A History of Woodworking Tools* (1964).

Grenier, A. *Manuel d'archéologie gallo-romaine* (Paris, 1931–1960).

Grier, J. A. *A History of Pharmacy* (1937).

Grout, D. J. *A History of Western Music* (1962).

Harris, E., and J. R. *The Oriental Cults in Roman Britain* (Leiden, 1965).

Hawkes, C. F. C. (1948) 'Britons, Romans and Saxons round Salisbury and in Cranborne Chase', *Arch. J.* CIV (1948) 27–81.

Hawkes, C. F. C., and Hull, M. R. (1947) *Camulodunum.* (Reports of the Research Committee of the Society of Antiquaries of London, XIV, Oxford, 1947.)

H.F.C. Hampshire Field Club and Archaelogical Society. Papers and Proceedings.

Hinks, R. P. (1933) *Catalogue of the Greek, Etruscan and Roman Paintings and Mosaics in the British Museum* (1933).

Hondius-Crone, A. *The Temple of Nehalennia at Domburg* (Amsterdam, 1955).

Houston, M. *Ancient Greek, Roman and Byzantine Costume* (1961).

Hull, M. R. (1958) *Roman Colchester.* (Reports of the Research Committee of the Society of Antiquaries of London, XX, Oxford, 1958).

— (1963a) V. C. H. *Essex. III. Roman Essex.* Introduction by Sir I. A. Richmond (Oxford,1963).

— (1963b) *Roman Potter's Kilns at Colchester.* (Reports of the Research Committee of the Society of Antiquaries of London, XXI, Oxford, 1963.)

I.L.N. Illustrated London News.

Isings, C. *Roman Glass* (Groningen, 1959).

Jackson, K. *Language and History in Early Britain* (Edinburgh, 1953).

J.B.A.A. Journal of the British Archaeological Association.

Jennison, G. *Animals for Show and Pleasure in Ancient Rome* (Manchester, 1937).

Jessen, J., and Helbaek, H. *Cereals in Great Britain and Ireland in Prehistoric and Early Historic Times* (1944).

Jolowicz, H. F. (1965) *An Historical Introduction to the Study of Roman Law* (Cambridge, 1965).

Jones, A. H. M. *Studies in Roman Government and Law* (Oxford, 1960).

Jope, E. ed. *Studies in Building History* (1961).

J.R.S. Journal of Roman Studies.

Kenyon, K. (1948) *Excavations at the Jewry Wall site, Leicester.* (Reports of the Research Committee of the Society of Antiquaries of London, XV, Oxford, 1948.)

Kleberg, T. *Hôtels, restaurants et cabarets dans l'antiquité romaine* (Upsala, 1957).

L. and R. Lewis, N., and Reinhold, M. *Roman Civilisation* II (New York, 1955).

L.R.T. Wheeler, R. E. M. *London in Roman Times* (London Museum Catalogue no. 3, 1930).

Leage, R. W. (1961) *Roman Private Law* (1961).

Lethaby, W. R. *Londinium. Architecture and the Crafts* (1923).

Lethbridge, T. C. *Boats and Boatmen* (1952).
                Coastwise Craft (1952).

Lewis, H. J. T. *Temples in Roman Britain* (Cambridge, 1966).

Liversidge, J. *Furniture in Roman Britain* (1955).

Lysons, S. *Reliquiae Britannico-Romanae*, I–IV (1813–17).

Margary, I. D. *Roman Roads in Britain*, I–II (1955–7).

Marrou, H. I. (1956) *A History of Education in Antiquity* (1956).

Mau-Kelsey (1902) Mau, A. trans. Kelsey, F. W. *Pompeii: its Life and Art* (1902).

Maxey, M. (1938) *Occupations of the lower classes in Roman society* (Chicago, 1938).

Meates, G. W. *Lullingstone Roman Villa* (1955).

Meiggs, R. *Roman Ostia* (1960).

Merrifield, R. (1965) *The Roman City of London* (1965).

Milne, J. S. *Surgical Instruments in Greek and Roman Times* (Oxford, 1907).

Moritz, L. A. *Grain Mills and Flour in Classical Antiquity* (Oxford, 1958).

Murray, H. J. R. *A History of Board Games other than Chess* (1952).

N.H. Pliny the Elder, *Naturalis Historia.*

Nicholas, B. *An Introduction to Roman Law* (Oxford, 1962).

Paoli, U. E. *Vita Romana: La Vie quotidienne dans la Rome antique* (Bruges, 1955).

Parlasca, K. *Die römischen Mosaiken in Deutschland* (Berlin, 1959).

Price, J., and F. G. *A Description of the Remains of Roman Buildings at Morton near Brading* (1881).

P.S.A.S. Proceedings of the Society of Antiquaries of Scotland.

R.C.H.M. Royal Commission for Historical Monuments, England.

R.I.B. Collingwood, R. G. and Wright, R. P. *The Roman Inscriptions of Britain* (Oxford, 1965).

Bibliography and abbreviations

Richmond, Professor Sir I. A. (1943) 'Roman legionaries at Corbridge, their supply-base, temples and religious cults', *Arch. Ael.* (4) XXI (1943) 127–224.

— (1947a)   *Roman Britain* (Britain in Pictures, 1947).
— (1947b)   'The Roman City of Lincoln' and 'The four *coloniae* of Roman Britain', *Arch J.* CIII (1947) 26–84.
— (1950)   *Archaeology and the After-Life in Pagan and Christian Imagery* (1950).
— (1960)   'The Roman Villa at Chedworth', B. and G.T. LXXVIII (1960) 5–23.
— (1963)   *Roman Britain* (2nd edition, 1963, or reprints, 1964 or 1966).

Richmond, Sir I. A. ed. (1966). J. Collingwood Bruce, *Handbook to the Roman Wall.* (Newcastle-upon-Tyne, 1966).
   (1958) *Roman and Native in North Britain* (1958).
Rivet, A. L. F. *Town and Country in Roman Britain* (1964).
Rostovtzeff, M. *Social and Economic History of the Roman Empire* (1957).

Sachs, C. *A History of Musical Instruments* (1942).
Salway, P. (1965) *The Frontier People of Roman Britain* (Cambridge, 1965).
Scarth, H. M. *Aquae Solis* (1864).
Singer *et al.* Singer C., Holmyard, E. J., Hall, A. R., and Williams, T. I. *A History of Technology* II (Oxford, 1956).
Smith, C. Roach, *Illustrations of Roman London* (1859).
Som.A.P. Somerset Archaeological and Natural History Society Proceedings.
Spinazzola, V. *Pompei alla luce degli scavi nuova di Via dell' Abbondanza* (Rome, 1953).
St.A.A.S.T. St Albans Architectural and Archaeological Society Transactions.
Sur.A.C. Surrey Archaeological Collections.
Sus.A.C. Sussex Archaeological Collections.

Tanzer, H. (1939) *The Common People of Pompeii; a study of the graffiti* (Baltimore, 1939).
Thomas, C. ed. *Rural Settlements in Roman Britain* (1966).
Thompson, F. H. *Roman Cheshire* (Chester, 1965).
Thorpe, W. A. *English Glass* (1949)
Toynbee, J. M. C. (1948) 'Beasts and their Names in the Roman Empire. *Papers of the British School at Rome* XVI (1948).
— (1963)   *Art in Roman Britain* (1963).
— (1964)   *Art in Britain under the Romans* (1964).
Tylecote, R. F. (1962) *Metallurgy in Archaeology* (1962).

V.C.H. Victoria County History.
Vermaseren, M. J. *Mithras, the Secret God* (1963).

Wacher, J. (1960) 'Petuaria. New evidence for the Roman town and its early fort', *Ant.J.* XL (1960) 58–64.

504

— (1961)   'Cirencester, 1960', *Ant. J.* XLI (1961) 63–71.

— (1964)   'A Survey of Romano-British Town Defences of the Early and Middle Second Century', *Arch. J.* CXIX (1964) 103–13.

Wacher, J. ed. (1966). *Civitas Capitals of Roman Britain* (Leicester, 1966).

W.A.M. Wiltshire Archaeological Magazine.

Ward, J. *The Roman Era in Britain* (1911).
  Romano-British Buildings and Earthworks (1911).

Wedlake, W. J. *Excavations at Camerton, Somerset* (Camerton, 1958).

Wheeler, R. E. M. (1932) *Report on the Excavation of the Prehistoric, Roman and Post-Roman Site at Lydney Park.* (Reports of the Research Committee of the Society of Antiquaries of London IX, Oxford, 1932.)

  (1936) *Verulamium. A Belgic and two Roman Cities.* (Reports of the Research Committee of the Society of Antiquaries of London, XI, Oxford, 1936.)

  (1943) *Maiden Castle, Dorset.* (Reports of the Research Committee of the Society of Antiquaries of London, XII, Oxford, 1943.)

White, D. *Litus Saxonicum* (Madison, 1961).

Wilson, L. M. *The Clothing of the Ancient Romans* (Baltimore, 1938).

Witts, G. B. (1883) *Archaeological Handbook of the county of Gloucestershire* (Cheltenham, 1883).

Wright (1955) Wright R. P. and Richmond, I. A. *A Catalogue of the Roman Inscribed and Sculptured Stones in the Grosvenor Museum, Chester* (Chester, 1955).

Y.A.J. Yorkshire Archaeological Journal.

Index

1 *Above* Tombstone of Facilis, Colchester
2 *Above right* Tombstone of Regina, South Shields
3 *Right* Stone tomb relief, Chester

4 *Right* Stone tomb relief, Lincoln
5 *Middle* The Roman town wall on Balkerne Hill, Colchester
6 *Below* Reconstruction of the Temple of Claudius, Colchester

IMP·TITVS·CAESAR·DIVI [VE]SASIANI[F] [VE]SPASIANVS·AVG
P·M·TR·P·VIIII·IMP·XV·COS·VII[D]ESIG·VIII·CENSOR·PATER·PATRIAE
ET·CAESAR·DIVI·VESPAS[IA]NI·F·D[O]MITIANVS·COS·VI·DESIG·VII
PRINCEPS·IVVENTV[TIS] COLLEGIORVM·OMNIVM·SACERDOS
CN·IVLIO·A[GRI]COLA·LEG·AVG·PRO[PR]

7 *Above* Fragments of the inscription from the north-east entrance
   to the Forum, c. 79 A.D., Verulamium
8 *Middle* The south-east gateway at Verulamium after excavation.
   The men are standing on the two main roadways within the gate,
   and the abutment of the city wall can be seen in the foreground
9 *Below* Reconstruction of the south-east gate, Verulamium

10 *Above* Cellar in building Insula I.1, Verulamium, showing two
doorways and blocked up window
11 *Below* View across the *frigidarium* of the public baths,
Silchester, with a hypocaust in the foreground

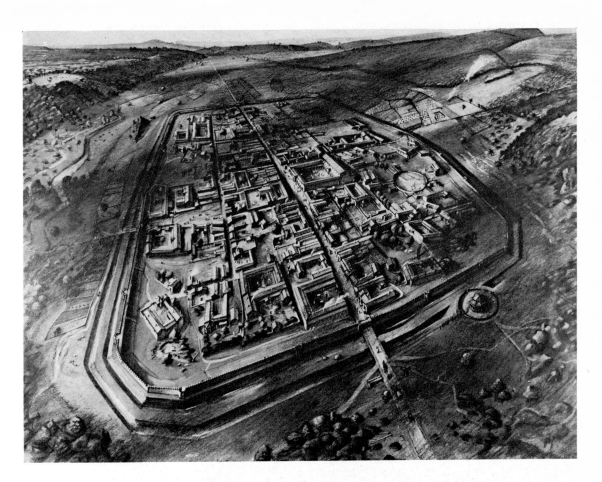

12 Reconstruction of the Roman
town, Caerwent

13 Floor-mosaic, Aldborough,
showing the Wolf and Twins

14 *Above* Reconstruction of the design from an early second
century painted wall, Cirencester
15 *Below* Scallop shell floor-mosaic, Verulamium

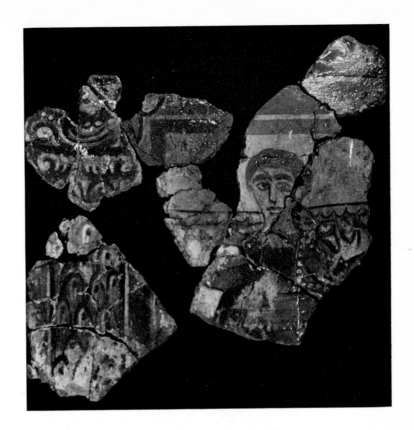

16 Wall-paintings
  a Fragment of a figure from the Lullingstone villa. Fourth
     century
  b, c Girl's face and hand holding flower. Caerwent. Second
     century

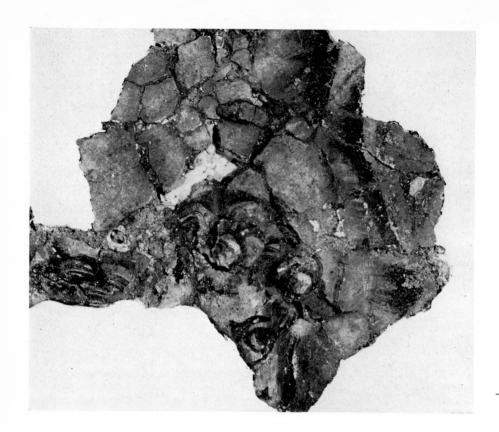

a
─────
b

17 Wall-paintings
  a Part of the head of a winged
      Cupid. Winterton Roman
      villa. Fourth century
  b Ceiling-painting from
      house, Insula XXI.2.
      Verulamium. Second
      century

18 Wall-painting showing a portico
with columns above a dado

19 Floor-mosaic depicting a fountain
Both from house, Insula XXVIII.3
Verulamium. Second century

20 *Above* London in the third century
21 *Middle* Pack mules on a hill. Stone relief from the Igel Column,
    Trier
22 *Below* Sarcophagus from Portus

23 Bronze head of Minerva, Bath

24 The great bath, Bath

25 Stone tomb reliefs from York
   a Aelia Aeliana, her husband and ?daughter
   b The smith
   c Flavia Augustina and her family

26 Stone tomb reliefs
  a Mother and child with pet bird. Murrell
       Hill, Cumberland
  b Julia Brica and her daughter. York
  c Julia Velva and her family. York

27 Stone tomb reliefs
a Lady and her maid. Chester
b York
c Philus, Cirencester

<table>
<tr><td>a</td><td>b</td></tr>
<tr><td>c</td><td></td></tr>
</table>

28 Stone heads
   a York
   b Bath
   c York

29 Altar of Mithras. Carrawburgh

30 Jewellery
  a, b Jet pendants, York
  c, d Gold necklet(?) set with carnelians or blue pastes, and
        pearls, and bracelet. Nantmel, Rhayader
  e Gold pendant set with blue-green stones and pearls.
     Southfleet
  f Jet pin. York

a	b
c	
d	f
e	

31 *Above* Scenes of cooking and bread-making. Stone relief from
the Igel Column, Trier

32 *Left* Wicker chair imitated in stone. Weiden tomb, Cologne

33 *Right* Table leg of Kimmeridge shale, Colliton Park,
Dorchester

34 Glass. Back row from Shefford, Bedfordshire, Hauxton and Litlington,
Cambridgeshire. Front row, Hauxton and Gravel Hill, Cambridge

35 Pewter. Back row from Sutton-near-Ely, Quaveney and Whittlesea
Mere. Front row from Abington Pigotts, and between Reach and
Upware, Cambridgeshire

36 Silver
  a Skillet handle. Capheaton
  b Platters from the Mildenhall
       Treasure

$\dfrac{\quad|a}{b\ |\quad}$

37 Floor-mosaics
   a Orpheus and the Beasts. Barton Farm, near Cirencester
   b Dido and Aeneas. Low Ham villa

a | b

  | c

38 Floor-mosaics
  a Spring. Lullingstone villa
  b Male bust. Lufton villa
  c Female bust. Brantingham villa

39 Floor-mosaic. Winter. Chedworth villa
40 Paved Roman road on Blackstone Edge, Yorkshire

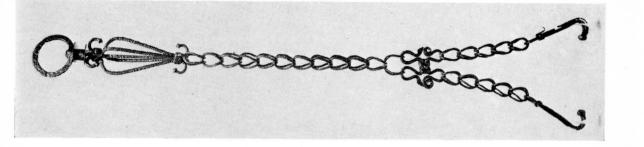

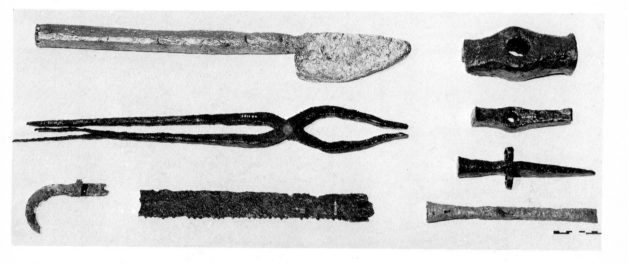

41 Entrance to a Roman iron-mine. Lydney Park

42 Iron tools, etc.

a Top left, sickle or reed-cutter from Worlington. On right, coulter from Abington Pigotts. Saw-blade, smith's pincers, socketed chisel, mower's anvil and hammers all from Great Chesterford

b Cauldron chain. Great Chesterford

$$\frac{a \mid b}{c \mid d}$$

43 Stone reliefs
   a Large dog. Chester
   b Boy charioteer. Lincoln
   c A hound hunting hares. Found near Bath
   d Boy with a hare. Lincoln

44 Toys
  a Pottery figurines from a child's
       grave. Colchester
  b Bronze dog. Carrawburgh
  c Bronze dog. Kirkby Thore
  d Bronze mouse from a grave.
       York

45 Stone tomb relief from Arlon, Belgium, depicting a family
meal. Above, the master and mistress sit at table, waited on by
servants. Below, the children gather round a cauldron, one
playing a single pipe, another holding back a pet dog

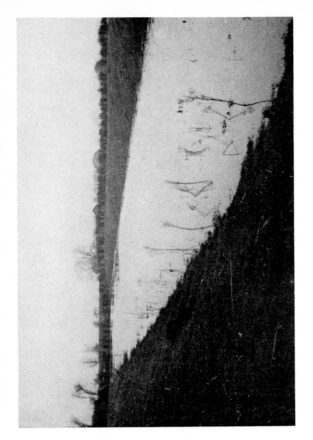

46 The Roman light-house, Dover Castle
47 The Car Dyke, a Roman canal near
    Cottenham, Cambridgeshire, when filled
    with water after the 1947 floods
48 The Roman quay wall. Roodee, Chester

49 *Above left* Bronze statuette of Venus. Verulamium
50 *Above right* Bronze statuette of Mercury. Colchester
51 *Left* Bronze statuette of a ploughman with plough and oxen.
    Piercebridge
52 Bronze fragments of a priest's or magistrate's staff of office.
    Willingham, Cambridgeshire

53 Bronze statuettes. *a*. Mercury. Bruton. *b*. Girl playing a single *tibia*. Silchester. *c*. Priest, Barham. *d*. Lar. Lakenheath. *e*. River God. Great Chesterford

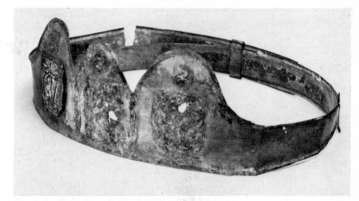

54 Bronze head, probably of a deity.
Worlington
55 *a, b* Bronze Crown and diadem.
Hockwold-cum-Wilton

56 Pewter bowl, the flange incised with Christian symbols. Isle of Ely

57 Detail of marble bust. Lullingstone
villa

58 Stone Sphinx from a funerary
monument. Colchester

59 Air photograph of four of the Bartlow barrows
60 Child's lead coffin decorated with scallop-shells and Bacchic
figures. Holborough barrow

DATE DUE

1-30-70			
AG 25 80			
GAYLORD			PRINTED IN U.S.A.